DISCARD
AUG 24 1992
I.C.S.B.

HEATH
Earth Science

Author   **Bill W. Tillery**
Professor of Science Education
Arizona State University, Tempe, Arizona
Former Junior High School Teacher
Jefferson County Public Schools
Colorado

Content Consultants   John Arthur Day   METEOROLOGIST
Emeritus Professor, Linfield College
McMinnville, Oregon

Gerald S. Hawkins   ASTRONOMER
Washington, D.C.
Former Chairperson, Department of Astronomy
Boston University, Boston, Massachusetts

Les Picker   MARINE BIOLOGIST
Professor, Department of Marine Biology
University of Delaware, Newark, Delaware
Director of Project Coast

Robert W. Ridky   GEOLOGIST
Associate Professor of Geology
University of Maryland, College Park, Maryland

D.C. Heath and Company
Lexington, Massachusetts   /   Toronto, Ontario

Series Editor: Roland E. Boucher
Project Editor: Pamela Cunningham

Series Design: Robert H. Botsford
Production Coordinator: Donna Porter

Cover Photo: Titcomb Basin, Wyoming; Sharon Gerig

Teacher Consultants

Jeffrey H. Alexander
Earth Science Instructor and Planetarium Lecturer
Charlotte-Mecklenburg Schools
Charlotte, North Carolina

Howard Arrowood
Earth Science Teacher
Meadowbrook Junior High School
Orlando, Florida

Richard E. Cooper
Director, K–12 Science and Mathematics
Danvers Public Schools
Danvers, Massachusetts

Diane P. Horn
Earth Science Teacher
Norfolk Public Schools
Norfolk, Virginia

Larry A. Irwin
Principal, Franklin Middle School
Weld County District Six
Greeley, Colorado

Paul Quay
Science Teacher
Ford Junior High School
Brook Park, Ohio

Series Consultants

Napoleon Bryant
Professor of Education
Xavier University
Cincinnati, Ohio

James H. McGill
Science Department Chairperson
Hill Country Middle School
Austin, Texas

Sister Rita Meredith, O.P.
Former Science Teacher
St. Agnes High School
Rockville Center, New York

Richard Merrill
Curriculum Specialist
Mt. Diablo Unified School District
Concord, California

William D. Thomas
Science Supervisor
Escambia County Schools
Pensacola, Florida

Reading Level Consultant

J & F
Milton D. Jacobson, Founder
Charlottesville, Virginia

Field Test Teachers

Grateful acknowledgment is given to the teachers and students who participated in field tests for this program.

ARIZONA
Harold Pruitt, Pima Middle School, Scottsdale

CALIFORNIA
L. Meyer, C. W. Tewinkle Middle School, Costa Mesa
Catherine Baird, Rancho San Joaquin Intermediate School, Irvine
Patrick Croner, Venado Middle School, Irvine
Patrick Gleason, Vista Verde School, Irvine

ILLINOIS
Kristin Ciesemier, Naperville North High School, District 203, Naperville
David Klussendorf, Michael Sommers, Jefferson Junior High School, District 203, Naperville
Jean Kriebs, Butler Junior High School, Oakbrook
Kelly Douglas, Wilson Middle School, Rockford

INDIANA
Nancy Watson, Burris Lab School, Ball State University, Muncie

MASSACHUSETTS
Brian Flaherty, Ronald Gomes, Plymouth Carver Intermediate School, Plymouth
Warren Phillips, Nathaniel Morton Elementary School, Plymouth
Paula Garten, Russell Magee, Middle School East, Salem
Alan Chasse, North Intermediate School, Wilmington
Joseph Gilligan, West Intermediate School, Wilmington
Priscilla Lockwood, Wilmington High School, Wilmington

MISSOURI
Beverly Edwards, Visual and Performing Arts Center, St. Louis
Marie Globig, Investigate Learning Center, St. Louis

NEW JERSEY
Joan Camarigg, Eisenhower School, Freehold
Susanne Flannelly, Joseph Herman, Barkalow School, Freehold

NEW YORK
John Spring, Trinity Lutheran School, Hicksville
Sam Alaimo, Hoover Middle School, Kenmore
Elain Johnson, Kenmore Middle School, Kenmore
James Morgan, Benjamin Franklin Middle School, Kenmore
Edith Newfield, Hendrick Hudson High School, Montrose
A. Charles Rossi, Blue Mountain School, Peekskill
Alan Goodman, Pamona Junior High School, Suffern

PENNSYLVANIA
Anna McCartney, Tidioute Junior/Senior High School, Tidioute

TENNESSEE
Jo Quarles, Jefferson Middle School, Jefferson City
Ted Frisby, Westwood Junior High School, Manchester
Peggy Mason, Gary Mullican, Central Middle School, Murfreesboro

TEXAS
Mary Jane Vasquez, Lake Travis Junior High School, Austin

Copyright © 1987 by D.C. Heath and Company
Copyright © 1984 by D.C. Heath and Company

Published simultaneously in Canada

Printed in the United States of America

International Standard Book Number:
0-669-11365-4

All rights reserved. No part of this publication may be reproduced or transmitted in any form or by any means, electronic or mechanical, including photocopy, recording, or any information storage or retrieval system, without permission in writing from the publishers.

TABLE OF CONTENTS

CHAPTER 1   Introduction to Earth Science   1
1.1   Why Is Earth Science Important to You?   2
1.2   Thinking like an Earth Scientist   6
1.3   The Laboratory   10
1.4   Collecting and Interpreting Data   14
Science and Technology   18
Chapter Review   19

The Universe   23   Unit One

CHAPTER 2   Outer Space   25
2.1   Looking into Space   26
2.2   How Can You Tell What's Out There?   30
2.3   Mysteries of the Universe   34
Biography   38
Chapter Review   39

CHAPTER 3   The Milky Way Galaxy   43
3.1   Your Galaxy   44
3.2   Study the Stars in Your Galaxy   46
3.3   The Search in Space   50
Science and Technology   56
Chapter Review   57

CHAPTER 4   The Solar System   61
4.1   The Sun   62
4.2   The Earth and Moon   66
4.3   Features of the Solar System   70
Biography   76
Chapter Review   77

CHAPTER 5   Space Exploration   81
5.1   History of Space Travel   82
5.2   Exploring the Planets   88
5.3   The Future in Space   92
Career   96
Chapter Review   97

iii

Unit Two The Earth's Gaseous Envelope 101

CHAPTER 6 The Atmosphere and Its Movement . 103
6.1 The Air around You................ 104
6.2 Warming the Atmosphere............ 108
6.3 Wind 112
6.4 Global Wind Patterns 116
Science and Technology 120
Chapter Review 121

CHAPTER 7 Water in the Atmosphere......... 125
7.1 Water on the Move 126
7.2 Condensation 130
7.3 Fog and Clouds................... 132
7.4 Precipitation and the Hydrologic Cycle..... 136
Career 138
Chapter Review 139

CHAPTER 8 Weather 143
8.1 Air Masses...................... 144
8.2 Weather......................... 146
8.3 Forecasting 150
8.4 Major Storms.................... 154
Science and Technology 158
Chapter Review 159

CHAPTER 9 Climate 163
9.1 Sunlight and Precipitation 164
9.2 Climate: Local Influence 168
9.3 Describing Climates 172
Career 178
Chapter Review 179

Unit Three The Waters of the Earth 183

CHAPTER 10 Fresh Water 185
10.1 Earth's Water.................... 186
10.2 Fresh Water on the Surface......... 188
10.3 Fresh Water below the Surface 192
10.4 Fresh Water as a Limited Resource ... 198
Career 202
Chapter Review 203

CHAPTER 11   Oceanography 207
11.1   Waves and Currents 208
11.2   Beaches and Shorelines 214
11.3   The Ocean Floor 218
11.4   Composition of Ocean Water 222
11.5   Life in the Ocean 224
Science and Technology 226
Chapter Review 227

The Earth's Structure 231   Unit Four

CHAPTER 12   Minerals 233
12.1   Atoms and Crystals 234
12.2   The Physical Properties of Minerals 238
12.3   Identification of Minerals 242
Science and Technology 246
Chapter Review 247

CHAPTER 13   Rocks and the Rock Cycle 251
13.1   How Rocks Form 252
13.2   Igneous Rocks 256
13.3   Sedimentary Rocks 260
13.4   Metamorphic Rocks 264
Career 268
Chapter Review 269

CHAPTER 14   Internal Structure of Earth 273
14.1   A Model of the Earth's Interior 274
14.2   Indirect Evidence from Space 276
14.3   Earthquakes and Seismic Waves 278
14.4   Evidence from within the Earth 282
Science and Technology 286
Chapter Review 287

CHAPTER 15   Plate Tectonics 291
15.1   Continental Drift 292
15.2   The Rock Record 296
15.3   Evidence for Plate Movements 300
15.4   Unanswered Questions 306
Science and Technology 308
Chapter Review 309

v

CHAPTER 16 Mountains and Crustal Movement . 313
16.1 Folding and Faulting 314
16.2 Volcanic Mountains 318
16.3 Other Mountain-Forming Processes 322
16.4 The Distribution of Mountain Ranges 326
Biography 330
Chapter Review 331

Unit Five   The Rock Story 335

CHAPTER 17 Mapping the Earth's Surface 337
17.1 Models of the Earth's Surface 338
17.2 Topographic Maps 342
17.3 The Major Landforms of the United States . . 346
Career 350
Chapter Review 351

CHAPTER 18 Weathering and Erosion 355
18.1 Weathering and Erosion of Rocks 356
18.2 Erosion by Running Waters 360
18.3 Erosion by Wind 364
18.4 Erosion by Ice 366
Career 370
Chapter Review 371

CHAPTER 19 The Rock Record 375
19.1 The Rock Record 376
19.2 Gaps in the Rock Record 378
19.3 Clues in Sedimentary Rocks 382
19.4 Interpreting What You See 386
Biography 390
Chapter Review 391

CHAPTER 20 Dating and Geologic Time 395
20.1 The Concept of Geologic Time 396
20.2 Geologic Dating 400
20.3 Dimensions of Geologic Time 404
Career 408
Chapter Review 409

CHAPTER 21   The Fossil Record **413**
21.1   Types of Fossil Preservation 414
21.2   Recognizing and Identifying Fossils 418
21.3   Dating Fossils 420
21.4   The Fossil Record at Different Times 422
Science and Technology 426
Chapter Review 427

The Earth's Bounty 431   Unit Six

CHAPTER 22   The Earth's Resources **433**
22.1   Metallic Resources of the Land 434
22.2   Nonmetallic Resources of the Land 438
22.3   Resources of the Ocean 442
22.4   Where the Resources Are Found 446
Biography 450
Chapter Review 451

CHAPTER 23   Nonrenewable Energy Resources . . **455**
23.1   Petroleum 456
23.2   Coal 460
23.3   Nuclear Fuel 464
Science and Technology 470
Chapter Review 471

CHAPTER 24   Renewable Energy Resources **475**
24.1   Solar Energy 476
24.2   Water, Wind, and Plants 482
24.3   Geothermal Energy 486
Science and Technology 490
Chapter Review 491

CHAPTER 25   Your Environment, Earth **495**
25.1   Land 496
25.2   Air 502
25.3   Water 504
24.4   Making Choices 506
Biography 510
Chapter Review 511

Appendices **514**
Glossary **516**

vii

Chapter 1
Introduction to Earth Science

Lesson Titles
1.1 Why is Earth Science Important to You?
1.2 Thinking Like an Earth Scientist
1.3 The Laboratory
1.4 Collecting and Interpreting Data

Earth is a very dynamic planet. There are many changes occurring above, on, and below the earth's surface. Scientists study these changes in order to learn about the past and to be able to predict how the earth may change in the future.

Of course, a great many scientific observations involve features of the earth's surface. Consider the example of glaciers. Many different kinds of observations are made at glaciers. Scientists consider the climate of the area where the glacier formed. They observe the changes that resulted after the glacier plowed across the landscape. They study the soil and rocks at the edge of the glacier. They even test the ice to find out how much dissolved air it contains.

What would you do if you had a chance to study a glacier? Would you sort through the boulders in front of the glacier? Would you measure the thickness of the ice? Would you check the temperature of the water in the glacial stream? Your answer probably depends on which branch of earth science interests you most.

In this chapter you will identify the branches of earth science. You will also learn a scientific model for studying objects like glaciers.

Figure 1.1 *opposite:* Deposits of rocks and soil were left behind as the glacier receded.

1.1 Why Is Earth Science Important to You?

You will find out
- what information can be learned from scientists studying the earth;
- what some of the instruments are that are used to study the earth;
- why you study the earth.

What are some of your ideas about the earth? Where can you get new information about the earth? Many scientists help you learn about the earth. **Astronomers** [uh-STRAHN-uh-muhrs] use telescopes to see and photograph objects in space. They may also listen to the sky with radio telescopes. Astronomers use what they learn from their studies to infer certain information about the earth as a body in space.

Meteorologists [mee-tee-uh-RAHL-uh-jists] study the atmosphere. Their information about the weather helps people plan trips at the right time and decide how to

Figure 1.2 *left:* An astronomer looking through a large telescope at Mauna Kea Observatory, Hawaii

Figure 1.3 *right:* A meteorologist reviewing weather charts

2   1 / Introduction to Earth Science

dress. You may have used information provided by weather forecasters to decide what to wear to school today. Meteorologists save millions of dollars when they correctly predict a big storm.

Oceanographers [oh-shuh-NAHG-ruh-fers] study the oceans. From oceanographers people learn about the nature of the oceans and the ocean floor. For example, the tallest mountains in all the world are found on the ocean floor. Oceanographers can't see them directly because these mountains are covered by water. However, instruments can show you that they are there.

Other scientists, called **geologists** [jee-AHL-uh-jists], study the solid outer and liquid inner parts of the earth. They help reconstruct the history of the earth. From studying rocks they can even learn about animals that lived long ago. Geologists also find oil, which supplies both power and chemicals. They even find the raw materials that make up the metal or plastic in the chair you are sitting in.

Figure 1.4 *left:* An oceanographer diving to examine underwater oceanography equipment

Figure 1.5 *right:* A geologist collecting rock and mineral samples in the field

1 / Introduction to Earth Science

Astronomers, geologists, meteorologists, and oceanographers are all earth scientists. How do they learn about the earth? One way is to make observations. They observe the earth by using their senses of sight, touch, hearing, taste, and smell. Sometimes they use a combination of these senses. If you think about it, you used these senses earlier today in getting to school.

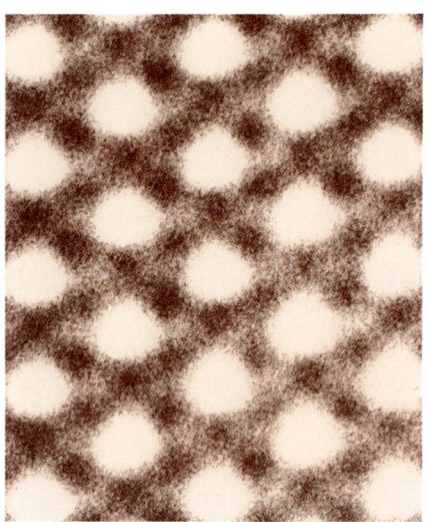

Figure 1.6 *above:* A picture of a rock magnified by an electron microscope showing the rock's internal structure

Figure 1.7 *right:* A thin section of granite magnified 20 times by a microscope shows the crystals in the rock.

Instruments can be used to extend your senses. The **optical microscope** [AHP-ti-kuhl MY-kruh-skohp] lets you look at a small piece of a rock. A microscope is an instrument for magnifying objects too small to be seen by the naked eye alone. The **electron microscope** [ee-LEK-trahn MY-kruh-skohp] magnifies objects even more. It uses a stream of electrons to magnify pieces of an object as much as 50,000 times. By using instruments like these, you can sometimes see unexpected things.

Figure 1.8 This electron microscope is nearly two stories high. It is so powerful, it can magnify as much as 300,000 times.

Earth scientists observe and explain a changing earth. That's what you'll do as you take this course. You'll use instruments and make measurements. You'll observe patterns and solve problems about the earth.

You study earth science to understand the earth and space in which you live. By knowing how the earth "works," you can enjoy living on it to the fullest.

Study Questions for 1.1

1. What information about the earth do you learn from astronomers? Geologists? Meteorologists? Oceanographers?
2. List three instruments that are used in studying earth science.
3. Why is earth science important for you to study?

1.2 Thinking like an Earth Scientist

You will find out
- what kinds of events make scientists curious;
- what the steps are in the scientific process;
- what a scientific model is.

Imagine that you are this geologist looking at some rocks high up on a mountain. As you pick away gently at the rock layers you suddenly see the clear fossil outline of a fish. But fish can't climb mountains. What would you think? Would you try to find out how the fish fossil got where it was? What questions would you ask?

Figure 1.9 *above:* Geologists sometimes find an interesting discovery that leads them to more questions about the earth.

Figure 1.10 *right:* Are you curious about how this boy rides his bicycle in the air?

Earth scientists act like that too. They make observations of the earth and sky. Suppose they find something wrong. Something they see doesn't seem right. What do they do? They ask questions. Often it's a lot of questions. Then they try to find answers to those questions.

Here is an example of how this works. Suppose workers have just finished building a road through a hill. Now imagine you are looking at the cut hillside. You are a geologist trying to understand how the rocks have made the pattern you see. What do you do?

First you back off and observe the cut from a distance to see the broad picture. This overall visual inspection of the broad details of the road cut is called **observation** [ahb-zuhr-VAY-shuhn].

Figure 1.11 What do you see in this hillside? How were these rocks formed?

Figure 1.12 A close-up shows details that can be used to answer your questions.

Next you **analyze** [AN-uh-lyz] what you are seeing by asking yourself questions. When you analyze, you separate things in order to see what is important and what is unimportant. Some things look normal and the questions are easily answered. The answers to other questions may require a closer look. You move up close so you can touch the rocks in the road cut. You look carefully at the rocks. You move from place to place until you begin to see some answers to the other questions you asked.

Then you move back and look at the road cut again. Perhaps you begin to relate the process that deposited the layers to the forces that pushed and bent those layers into the pattern you see. In this process you begin to **synthesize** [SIN-thuh-syz] your questions and answers. When you pull together ideas to make a complete picture, you are synthesizing.

1 / Introduction to Earth Science

Figure 1.13 Visual models sometimes make explanations easier to understand.

Figure 1.14 An ancient Chinese model portrayed the earth as resting on a frog.

The complete picture or pattern you construct to explain or answer your questions is also called a **scientific model.** A model may be an idea of the way something is, or it may be a physical construction that is similar in form to something. An airplane model is a physical model of the real thing. A picture, a story, or an explanation can be a model that accounts for the way something is. The early Chinese had a model to explain earthquakes. They thought the earth was supported on the back of a frog. When the frog moved, it caused earthquakes. A model is useful because it represents the best explanation based on what is known.

Once you have a model, you begin to **test** it. Testing can be done through experimentation or by direct observation. Models change as more is learned about what is being explained. Finally, you draw conclusions based on your model.

That's the way it is with models. If new information conflicts with the model, then the model is changed to fit what has been observed. Models are tested again and again by scientists. If the model continues to seem correct when tested, people begin to believe in it. If the model fails some test, it is rechecked, changed, or rejected.

Some people describe scientists as seekers. A seeker is a person who looks for something. Scientists search for new facts or for new ideas about old facts. In earth science as in any other science, this is done by observing, analyzing, synthesizing, and testing. First you get the broad picture. Then you subdivide the picture into little pieces that are easier to study. Later you pull back and put your thoughts together. You test and revise as necessary. This procedure is called the scientific process. By applying this process you can learn about the earth and the space around it.

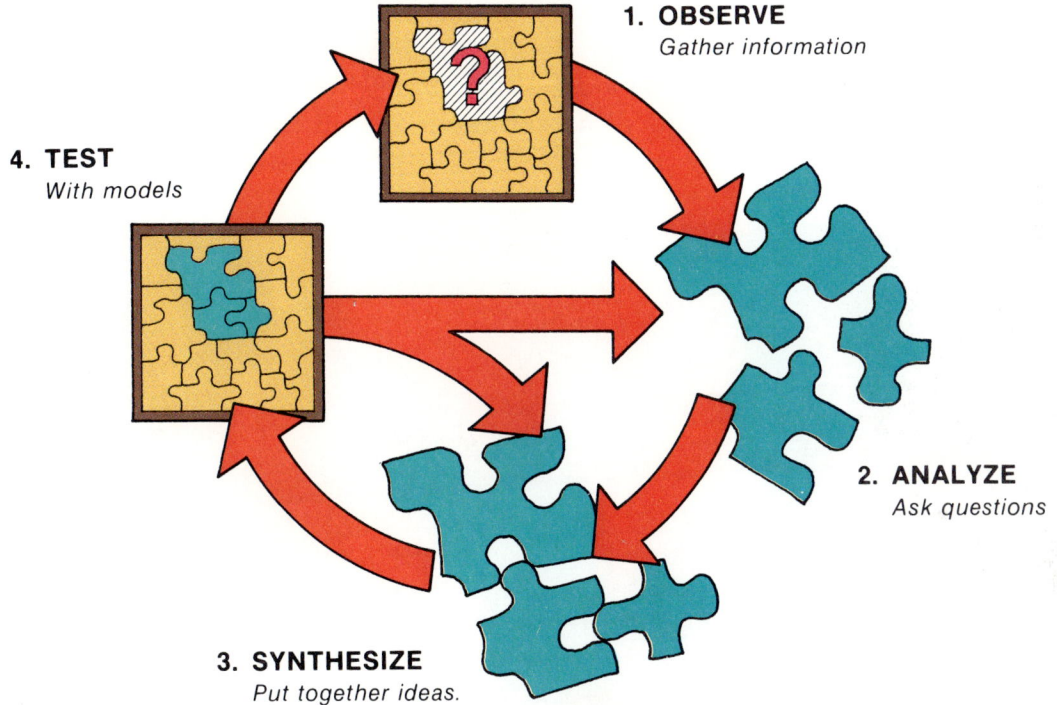

Figure 1.15 Solving a puzzle is like using the scientific process. You study the pieces, analyze how they may fit together, and try possible arrangements until the puzzle is done.

Study Questions for 1.2

1. What kinds of events will likely catch the eye of an earth scientist?
2. List the processes earth scientists use in studying the earth and space.
3. What is a scientific model?

1 / Introduction to Earth Science

1.3 The Laboratory

You will find out
- what a science laboratory is;
- the role that laboratory work plays in an earth science course;
- some basic laboratory safety procedures.

What do you think when you hear the words scientific **laboratory?** Do you picture some place with huge instruments? Maybe you think about a neat, clean place filled with animals that are fed special foods. Or perhaps you see a person carefully examining some objects that were recently collected. Just what is a laboratory?

The dictionary defines the word *laboratory* as a place equipped for scientific study and testing. Earth scientists accept that definition. But where is the earth science laboratory? All the earth and all that surrounds it are really the laboratory of earth scientists.

Figure 1.16 In the laboratory you can observe, test, and handle materials firsthand. Be sure you follow all directions carefully.

10   1 / Introduction to Earth Science

You can use laboratory work as a special way to learn something you don't already know. In the laboratory you can solve problems by searching for answers. Each laboratory activity has a question for you to answer. It is in the laboratory where you apply what you know. You think as you manipulate equipment or measure. You apply the scientific processes of observing, analyzing, synthesizing, and testing. For a moment you are an earth scientist. In the laboratory you experience science directly.

In laboratory activities you sometimes have to handle chemicals or to use things that break easily. For your own safety as well as that of others, it is important for you to follow safe laboratory practices. Here is a list of safety procedures.

Safety Procedures

Tie up long hair and tuck in loose clothing.

Wear laboratory aprons.

Wear eye protection when doing activities that may be hazardous to your eyes.

Watch for any hazards around you and report them to your teacher.

Report all accidents or injuries immediately to your teacher.

Use safety tongs or heat-insulated mittens when handling hot objects.

Do not perform unauthorized experiments.

Do not play around. Unauthorized activity is the greatest hazard in the laboratory.

Clean thoroughly all work surfaces after each use. Do not eat or drink in the laboratory.

You have been reading about the processes that earth scientists use to obtain information. Now you can apply these processes to a laboratory activity.

Here's the setting. Near the rubble of what appears to have been a city, there is a hill. The hill was made by dumping waste in a pile and covering it with dirt. Then more waste was dumped and covered. This process was repeated over and over to make a big hill filled with pockets of waste surrounded by dirt. See Figure 1.17.

1 / **Introduction to Earth Science**

It is now 10,000 years later, and holes have just been dug into the hill. You are to find out when this waste was deposited and what the people did then.

Activity

When Was This?

Materials
magnifying glass
pencil and paper

Procedure

1. Look at each waste pocket and make a list of the items it contains. Use the magnifying glass if necessary. Try to guess at what time in the past each might have been used.

2. List the waste pockets in order from oldest to youngest.

Questions

1. Which item is the oldest in each waste pocket? How do you know?

2. Which item is the youngest in each waste pocket? How do you know?

3. Explain your reasoning for listing the pockets in the order that you did.

4. Are any of the waste pockets out of order? How do you know? How can you explain any that are?

5. Make up a story that could explain all your findings. This is your model.

Figure 1.17 A 10,000 year old dump

Think about this laboratory activity. You looked at the hill and figured out the relative ages of the waste pockets. Then you made up a story describing how the hill was made. These are exactly the kinds of things earth scientists do in their laboratories. They look at the sky, the rocks, the water, or the slope of the land. They try to describe how things got to be as they are—a model. It's like putting together a giant puzzle.

Study Questions for 1.3

1. Define the word *laboratory* as an earth scientist might.
2. List four things that are done in a science laboratory.
3. List at least five important safety procedures for the laboratory.

1.4 Collecting and Interpreting Data

You will find out
- what things earth scientists measure;
- what the metric system is;
- how to make a representative measurement;
- how to graph data.

Did you ever catch a fish and then try to describe it to someone? How did you do it? You probably mentioned how long it was and how much it weighed. Before you could do this, you had to measure the fish.

Since scientists generally use the metric system for expressing measurements, you'll use that system in this course. The metric system is used by most people in the world.

The most common basic things measured in the metric system are distance, time, and mass. Distance is the interval separating two points in space. Time is the interval between two events. Mass is the amount of matter in an object. Each measurement is expressed by using a number and a unit. For example, your home may be more than 10 kilometers from school. The length of time for this class may be 45 minutes. You may have a mass greater than 40 kilograms. The units in these examples are kilometers, minutes, and kilograms. The other units of the metric system and the relationship between units are found in Figure 1.19.

Figure 1.18 *above:* What does this picture tell you about the mass of these two objects? *right:* Do you believe that each of these containers has the same amount of liquid in it?

14

Other things frequently measured in earth science are speed, area, volume, density, and temperature. A thermometer is used to measure temperature. In the metric system the units for measuring temperature are Celsius degrees (°C).

Figure 1.19 Units of the metric system

Metric Units of Measurement					
Measurement	1/1000	1/100	1/10	1	1000
Length	millimeter (mm)	centimeter (cm)	decimeter (dm)	meter (m)	kilometer (km)
Mass	milligram (mg)	centigram (cg)	decigram (dg)	gram (g)	kilogram (kg)
Volume	milliliter (mL)	centiliter (cL)	deciliter (dL)	liter (L)	kiloliter (kL)

Temperature	Degrees Celsius (°C)
Speed	Distance/Time = Meters/Hour (m/h)
Density	Mass/Volume = Grams/Liter (g/L)

Some units of measurement are combinations of the basic units. Here is a closer look at some of these. Area is expressed as square units such as square centimeters. It is found by multiplying units of length by units of width. Volume is an amount of enclosed space. Volume is determined by multiplying units of length by units of width by units of height. Volume is expressed in cubic units such as cubic meters or as a liter for liquid measurement. Speed, for example, can be expressed as meters (distance) per second (time). The density of an object is found by determining its mass and dividing that by its volume.

Sometimes there are problems in making measurements. Suppose you are trying to measure the temperature of the air. Perhaps you have noticed that sometimes it is much hotter in a parking lot than it is in the park. Which place would you use for measuring the temperature of the air?

Figure 1.20 Which thermometer should this girl believe?

1 / Introduction to Earth Science 15

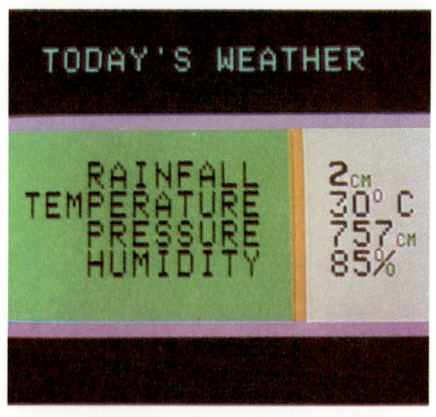

You need measurements that are comparable from place to place. To do this requires measurements made in a prescribed manner. Holding a shaded thermometer over grass is an example of a prescribed procedure. Measurements made following a prescribed procedure are called representative measurements. Temperature of air, air pressure, and speed of stream flow are examples of measurements that must be made following prescribed procedures. All the air temperature or pressure readings on a TV weather map are representative measurements. They are all comparable.

Figure 1.21 The reports from the weather bureau are representative measurements.

Activity

What Is the Temperature of the Air Today?

Materials
thermometer
pencil and paper

Procedure

1. Select a place outside to measure the temperature. Hold the thermometer in that location for at least one minute. Make a note of where the thermometer is located and record the temperature.

2. Now choose another location that you think is either cooler or hotter than the first one. Place the thermometer in that location for one minute. Again note the location and record the temperature.

3. The third measurement is to be made as follows: Hold the thermometer about 1.5 m above a grassy area and shade the thermometer from the sun. Read and record the temperature after one minute.

Questions

1. What was the highest temperature you recorded? Where was the thermometer located?

2. What was the range in temperature of your readings (lowest to highest)?

3. If you were to go outside again, where would you place the thermometer to record where it was coolest?

4. Which of your three readings do you think best represents the temperature of the air? Explain your choice.

16   1 / Introduction to Earth Science

Another class of students did the activity you just completed and recorded the **data** [DAY-tuh] shown in Table 1-1. Data are information you record from your observations.

That class then made a **graph** of its data. A graph is a picture of the data. Graphs are helpful in explaining observations because they organize the data. To make a graph like this, the horizontal scale is used to represent the temperature. Every temperature reading can be located some place on the horizontal scale. The vertical scale was used to show how many students found the same temperature reading. This kind of graph is called a **histogram** [HIS-tuh-gram]. From the histogram you can see that the temperature readings ranged from 15 to 25. The most frequent reading was 20°C.

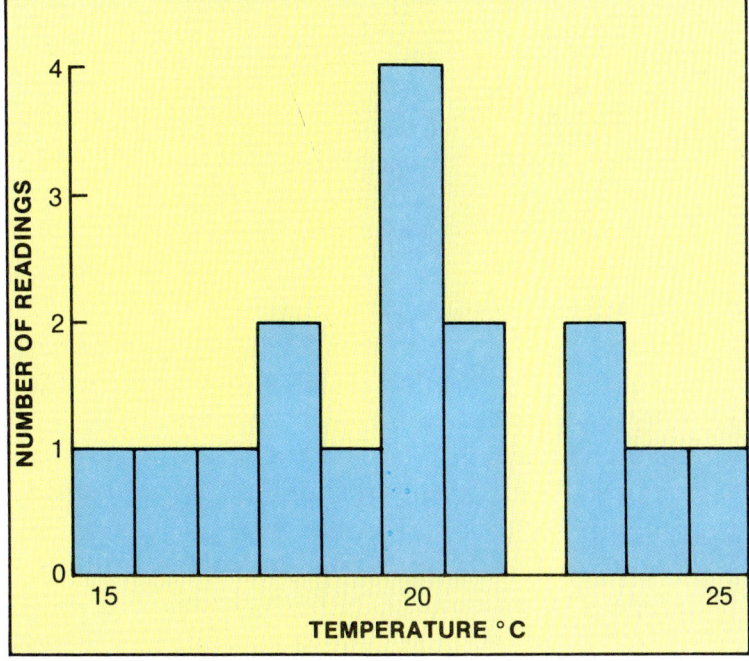

Figure 1.22 An example of a histogram made from the data found in Table 1-1

Table 1-1	
Student at 1st Location	Temperature °C
A	20
B	23
C	15
D	25
E	18
F	21
G	20
H	23
I	16
J	17
K	24
L	18
M	21
N	20
O	19
P	20

Study Questions for 1.4

1. Name three basic measurements. What is one unit for each?
2. List five things that earth scientists measure.
3. Define *representative measurement*.
4. What is a histogram?

Science and Technology

Observations and Astronomy

You learned in this chapter that the study of earth science begins with observations. You also learned that many observations require instruments that extend the senses. The science of astronomy is an excellent example. Astronomers will soon be able to make observations with an exciting new telescope. This telescope is to be built on the top of a high mountain in Hawaii. It will be the largest telescope of its kind in the world.

The Hawaiian telescope will be a reflecting telescope. For many years, the largest active reflecting telescope in the world has been the one located at Mount Palomar Observatory in California. Its mirror is over 500 cm, or more than 5 m, in diameter. The mirror of the new Hawaiian telescope will be twice as large, or about 10 m across.

Because the Hawaiian telescope is so large, new methods are being used to build it. One of the most interesting changes involves the structure of the mirror. A single mirror in the size needed for the Hawaiian telescope would weigh so much that it would sag under its own weight. The shape of the mirror would be distorted, so that the light entering the mirror could not be made to focus at a single point.

To solve this problem, the Hawaiian telescope will not use a single, large mirror. Instead, it will consist of 36 small mirrors working together as one large mirror. Each of these small mirrors will be about 1.8 m in diameter.

How can 36 individual mirrors ever be made to focus their light clearly on a single point? A computer will constantly adjust the position of each mirror so that it reflects its light accurately.

Astronomers are most excited about the fact that this telescope will be able to see into the dusty gas clouds that occur in space. These clouds are places where new stars form. By finding stars in the process of forming, astronomers hope to learn more about the history of our own solar system.

CHAPTER REVIEW

Main Ideas

- Astronomers, meteorologists, oceanographers, and geologists are scientists who study the earth.
- Astronomers study the earth as a body in space; meteorologists study the atmosphere; oceanographers study the oceans; geologists study the outer and inner parts of the earth.
- Optical microscopes and electron microscopes are two instruments used to extend your senses.
- You study earth science so that you can understand the earth and space in which you live.
- Scientists are curious about events that appear strange or unusual.
- The scientific processes are observing, analyzing, synthesizing, and testing.
- A scientific model is an idea or a physical device used to explain or depict something else.
- An earth science laboratory is any place where you apply scientific processes to answer a question.
- There are required safety procedures to be followed in laboratory work.
- Distance, mass, and time are three basic measurements in the metric system.
- Representative measurements are made by following agreed upon procedures.
- A graph is a picture record of data.

Using Vocabulary

On a separate piece of paper, write a paragraph explaining how scientists study earth science. Use and underline each of the following words used in your explanation.

astronomer	electron microscope	test
geologist	observation	laboratory
meteorologist	analyze	data
oceanographer	synthesize	graph
optical microscope	scientific model	histogram

1 / Introduction to Earth Science

Remembering Facts

Number your paper from 1 to 15. Match each term in column **A** with a phrase in column **B**.

A
1. astronomer
2. meteorologist
3. geologist
4. oceanographer
5. observation
6. analyze
7. synthesize
8. test
9. scientific model
10. laboratory
11. metric measurements
12. time
13. representative measurement
14. length
15. histogram

B
a. interval separating two points in space
b. distance, time, mass
c. one who studies solid outer and liquid inner parts of the earth
d. idea or physical device to explain or describe something
e. pull together ideas to make a complete picture
f. measurement that follows a prescribed procedure
g. visual inspection of broad details
h. interval between two events
i. separate the important from the unimportant
j. place for scientific study and testing
k. one who studies the oceans
l. one who studies objects in space
m. one who studies the atmosphere
n. a type of graph
o. evaluate a scientific model

Understanding Ideas

On your paper, answer each question in complete sentences.
1. Describe an example of something that an earth scientist could study only by using a special instrument.
2. Describe an earth science event that is related to more than one branch of earth science. Explain how the event is related to those branches.
3. Representative measurements limit the number of variables which could affect the data collected. What variables could affect coastal recordings of water temperature?
4. Modern earth scientists rely on technology to help them make observations. How has this technology changed the field of earth science?
5. Why is the study of astronomy included in earth science?

Applying What You Have Learned

1. Identify the metric unit of measurement that should be used with each of the following: (a) mass of a candy bar; (b) diameter of a pencil; (c) length or width of your classroom; (d) volume of water in a glass; (e) volume of a marble; and (f) length or width of your textbook.
2. Make a histogram of these data:

mass (kg)	36	38	40	54	40	52	40
student	A	B	C	D	E	F	G

3. Observing safety procedures in the laboratory is extremely important. When should you (a) wear goggles; (b) tuck in loose-fitting clothing; (c) wear an apron?

Challenge

Pollution is an accumulation of irritating or dirty substances in the air or water. These substances can be chemical gases, dust and waste particles, and smoke. The level of pollution in an area can vary greatly from month to month. The graph shows the pollution levels in one city over a 12-month period. Use your understanding of the scientific process to answer each of the following questions.

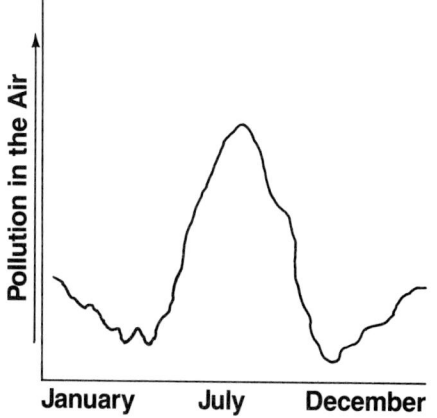

1. Analyze the graph. What questions come to mind when you observe the graph?
2. Synthesize what you know about the causes of air pollution to arrive at an answer to your questions. What is your model?
3. Describe how you could test your model.
4. What do you do if the results of the test do not agree with your model?

Research and Investigation

1. Do library research on recent discoveries in astronomy, meteorology, oceanography, or geology. Prepare a report on how a scientific model was changed because of new information.
2. New instruments are developed as scientists attempt to measure and understand things. Read about Halley's Comet in journals and magazines. Find out what new instruments were developed to study the comet. Prepare a report for your class about how these instruments led to new information about the famous comet.

UNIT ONE

The Universe

Chapter 2
Outer Space

Chapter 3
The Milky Way Galaxy

Chapter 4
The Solar System

Chapter 5
Space Exploration

Chapter 2
Outer Space

Lesson Titles
2.1   Looking into Space
2.2   How Can You Tell What's Out There?
2.3   Mysteries of the Universe

The photograph of M31 shows a fuzzy looking object, but M31 is really a group of stars. In fact it is millions to hundreds of thousands of millions of stars. This group is also called the Andromeda Galaxy. It is one of the closest of such groups to earth.

How close is this? In reality it is a long way away. Think about this. Light travels at a speed of 300,000 km per second. That's fast—seven times around the earth in one second! Your heart beats about 72 times per minute. In one minute light could travel 60 times 300,000 km or 18,000,000 km. Just think, 18,000,000 km in the time your heart makes 72 beats! In the time of about 1,200 heartbeats light can go to the sun and back. But compared to distances in space, that's not very far.

The distance to Andromeda is so far that it is measured in light-years. A light-year is the distance light can travel in one year. So a light-year then is 60 seconds times 60 minutes times 24 hours times 365 days times 300,000 km or about 9,500,000,000,000 km. Or while your heart is beating a mere 38,000,000 times during a year, light travels 9,500,000,000,000 km. Now get ready for this. Andromeda is 2,200,000 light-years away!

Figure 2.1 *opposite:* The Andromeda Galaxy, M31

2.1 Looking into Space

You will find out
- that astronomers have tried to classify the objects in space for many years;
- what the difference is between refractor and reflector telescopes;
- what some of the objects are that telescopes have helped to find.

As you gaze upward at the sky on a clear night, you get the impression that the sky is a great sphere. The center of the sphere seems to be where you are on the earth. The Greeks called this imaginary sphere to which the stars appear to be attached the **celestial sphere** [suh-LES-chuhl SFEER]. The ancients imagined that the celestial sphere slowly rotated, carrying the stars across the sky. They observed that some objects even wandered across the celestial sphere.

The Greeks, as people had before them, divided the sky into the groupings of stars that are called **constellations** [kahn-stuh-LAY-shuhns]. Certain characters in Greek mythology were honored by assigning them a position on the celestial sphere. Sections of the sky are still referred to by their constellation name.

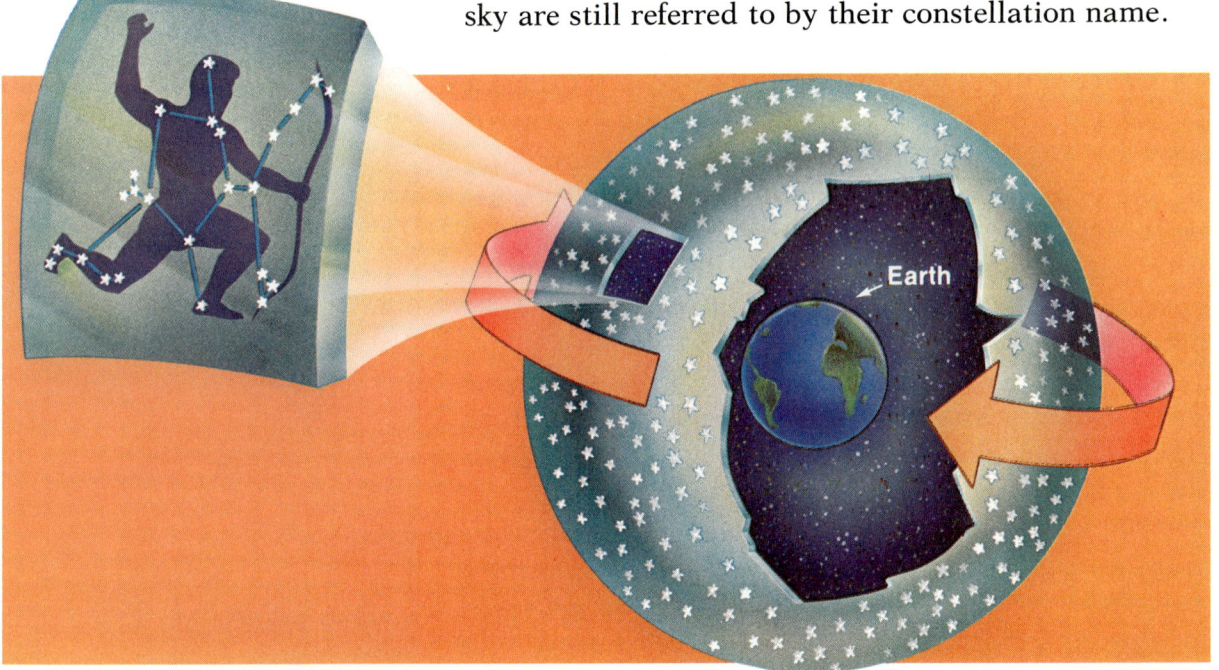

Figure 2.2 Some ancient people believed the earth was inside a large rotating sphere. Do you recognize this constellation of Hercules?

26

2 / Outer Space

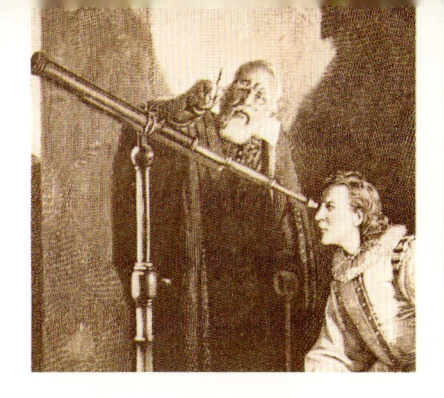

Figure 2.3 *left:* Galileo and his early telescope

Figure 2.4 *right:* Tycho Brahe's early observatory

Through time, people made better and better observations of the sky. In the 1550's Tycho Brahe constructed a superbly equipped observatory near Copenhagen. His observatory was equipped with the most accurate instruments ever designed before the time of the telescope. He planned to observe the sun, moon, planets, and stars regularly.

In 1609 the optic tube was invented by Galileo. This primitive telescope, no more powerful than field glasses of today, revolutionized the study of the sky. Galileo was the first to see Jupiter's moons and craters on the earth's moon. Astronomy has come a long way from Galileo's optic tube to the wonderful telescopes of today.

Some of the modern telescopes work the same way as Galileo's. Light coming from an object in space passes through a lens and forms an image. You look at this image with another lens. Telescopes that work in this way are called **refracting telescopes** [ree-FRAK-ting TEL-uh-skohps]. The largest existing refractor has a 102 cm lens through which the light enters.

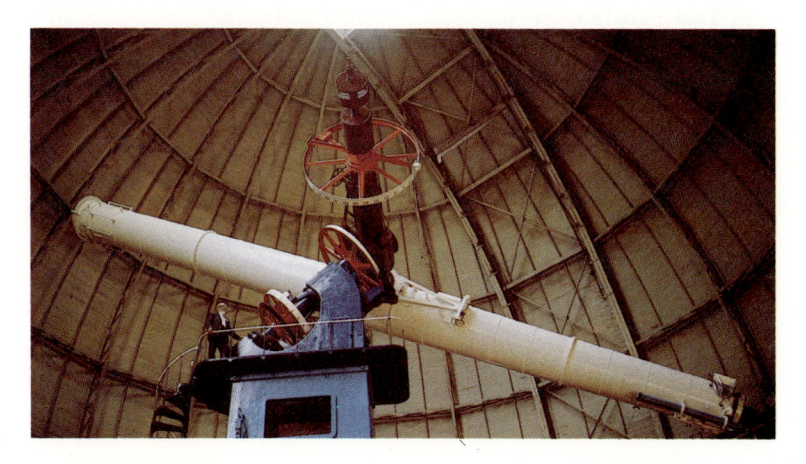

Figure 2.5 *top:* A refracting telescope; *bottom:* The diagram shows the positions of the lenses in a refracting telescope.

Figure 2.6 One-meter refractor telescope at the Yerkes Observatory, Williams Bay, Wisconsin

2 / Outer Space

Figure 2.7 Horsehead Nebulae in the constellation Orion

Figure 2.8 *left:* A reflecting telescope; *right:* Special mirrors are used with a lens in a reflecting telescope.

Figure 2.9 Star clusters

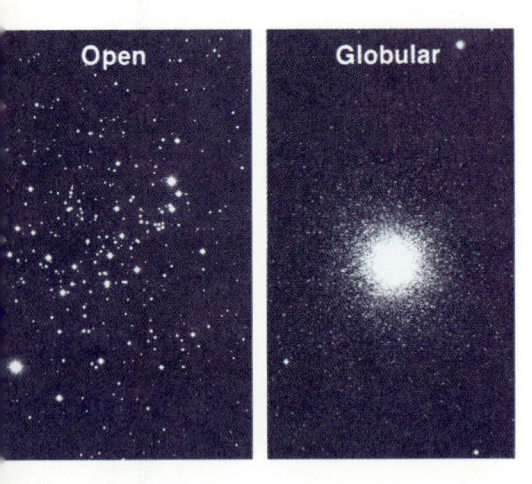

Open

Globular

Refractor telescopes are most useful for looking at objects close to earth. With refractor telescopes you can see the planets, the sun, stars, and moons. You can also see **nebulae** [NEB-yoo-lie]—thin, wispy-colored, glowing-gas clouds. Many **comets** [KAHM-its] have been discovered by observers using refracting telescopes. Comets are small bodies of icy and dusty matter that orbit about the sun.

In the year of Galileo's death a new type of telescope was created. This telescope uses a mirror to reflect light and form an image of an object. The image is seen through a lens. Telescopes that work in this way are called **reflecting telescopes** [ree-FLEK-ting TEL-uh-skops]. This was a wonderful invention because it allowed people to look farther and farther into space. Reflector telescopes have been able to see objects more than 4 billion light-years away.

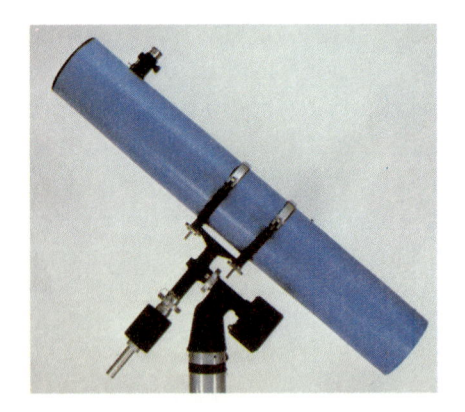

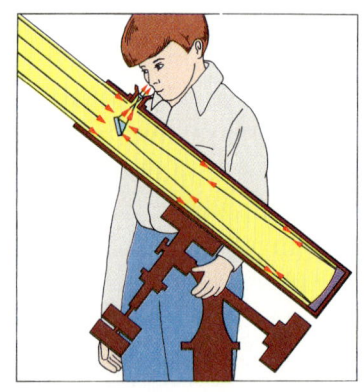

What kinds of objects are found in outer space? Glowing nebulae have already been mentioned, but not all nebulae give off light. Some gases absorb light and appear dark as in the constellation Orion. With reflector telescopes groups of stars can also be seen. Loose groupings of stars, containing from a few dozen to a few thousand, are called **open clusters. Globular clusters,** which contain thousands of stars in a close grouping, are also found. The most common objects found in far outer space are called **galaxies** [GAL-uhk-sees]. Galaxies are large assemblies of stars containing millions to billions of stars.

2 / Outer Space

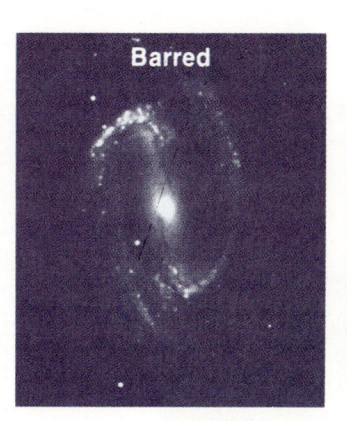

Figure 2.10 Examples of the major types of galaxies

There are four major types of galaxies—ellipticals, spirals, barred spirals, and irregulars. Look carefully for an example of each in these photographs of galaxies.

People using reflector telescopes have discovered that some stars vary in brightness at regular intervals. These stars, called **Cepheid** [SEE-fee-uhd] **variable stars,** get bright, then dim, and then bright in a period of a few days. Some take three days to go through the brightness to dimness cycle. Others take as many as 50 days. Polaris, the North Star, is a familiar example of a Cepheid variable star, but its change is so slight the human eye can't detect it.

Don't you think Galileo would have loved to be living today? He didn't know about galaxies, nebulae, open clusters, globular clusters, or Cepheid variable stars. How he would have loved to know just what you know about the sky! You really do know a lot about the sky. But you have begun to see that the more you know, the more you realize how little you really know. Every new discovery raises more questions than it answers. There are a lot of questions that haven't yet been answered by using the big telescopes.

Figure 2.11 Four-meter Mayall reflector telescope at Kitt Peak National Observatory near Tucson, Arizona

Study Questions for 2.1

1. Describe how early people classified the stars.
2. Explain how refractor and reflector telescopes work.
3. Make a list of the objects that are found in outer space.

2 / Outer Space

2.2 How Can You Tell What's Out There?

You will find out
- what electromagnetic radiation is;
- how spectroscopes and radio telescopes are used to tell us about distant objects;
- what objects are identified by radio waves.

The information astronomers receive from outer space tells them what is going on out there. It's like playing hide-and-seek. You are "it" and looking for your friend. You hear a noise, you see a shadow, or you see something move. You know what's going on by the information you receive. That's the way it is when astronomers use telescopes to look for objects in space. If an object sends out some information, you know it's there.

The information astronomers receive from objects in outer space is energy. The energy comes in the form of waves from space and is called **electromagnetic radiation** [ee-lek-troh-mag-NET-ik ray-dee-AY-shuhn]. Visible light is the most familiar form of this radiation. Other types of radiant energy are radio waves, infrared waves, ultraviolet waves, X rays, and gamma rays. Figure 2.13 shows the complete spectrum of electromagnetic radiation. All types of electromagnetic radiation travel at the speed of light, or 300,000 km per second.

It takes different kinds of instruments to detect each type of radiation. Radio receivers detect radio waves.

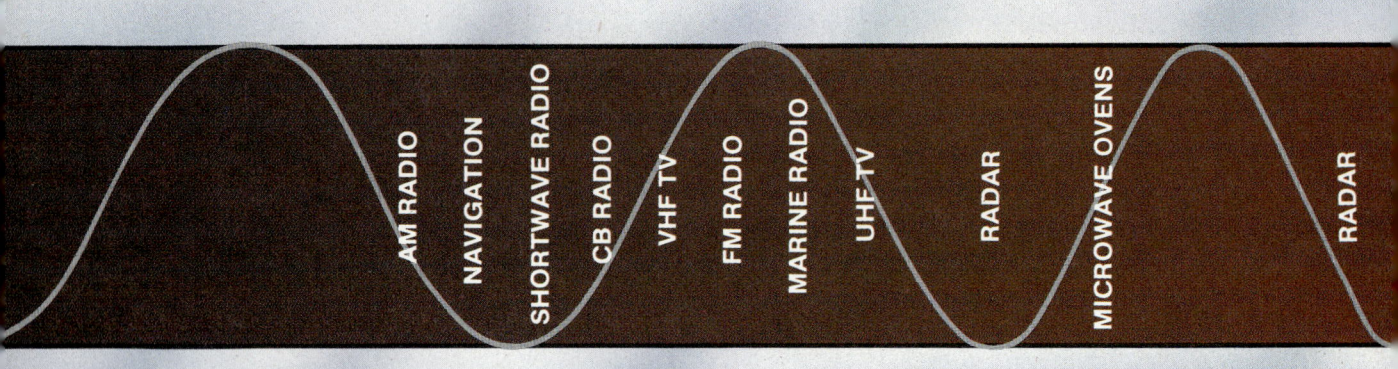

Figure 2.12 A spectrum from sunlight

Do You Know?
On a clear night the naked eye can see a candle at about 8 km.

Figure 2.13 The electromagnetic radiation spectrum. Wavelengths are longest for radio waves and shortest for cosmic rays.

AM RADIO · NAVIGATION · SHORTWAVE RADIO · CB RADIO · VHF TV · FM RADIO · MARINE RADIO · UHF TV · RADAR · MICROWAVE OVENS · RADAR

30   2 / Outer Space

Infrared, light, and ultraviolet radiation are detected by optical telescopes using film. X rays and gamma rays are detected by X-ray and gamma-ray telescopes.

Much of what is known about outer space has been built on what has been learned by studying light energy. The light energy from each star carries its own message about that star.

That message can be studied by examining the light from that star. One way of examining light is to pass it through a **prism.** If light is passed through a prism, it is separated into different colors. The prism bends the light waves passing through it. Different colors are bent in different amounts. The pattern the light makes after passing through a prism is a **spectrum** [SPEK-truhm].

You can get a spectrum of the light from each star by using a **spectroscope** [SPEK-troh-skohp]. A spectroscope is an instrument which can be attached to telescopes and is used to examine light. It uses lenses and a prism or **diffraction grating** [di-FRACK-shuhn GRAY-ting] to form a spectrum. A diffraction grating is a piece of glass or plastic that has hundreds of narrow slits per centimeter. As light passes through it, the waves interfere with each other in such a way as to make a spectrum. By studying the spectrum of each star, you can read the message that the light carries. Large telescopes use the spectroscope more than half of their observation time.

Figure 2.14 A spectrogram of a star cluster

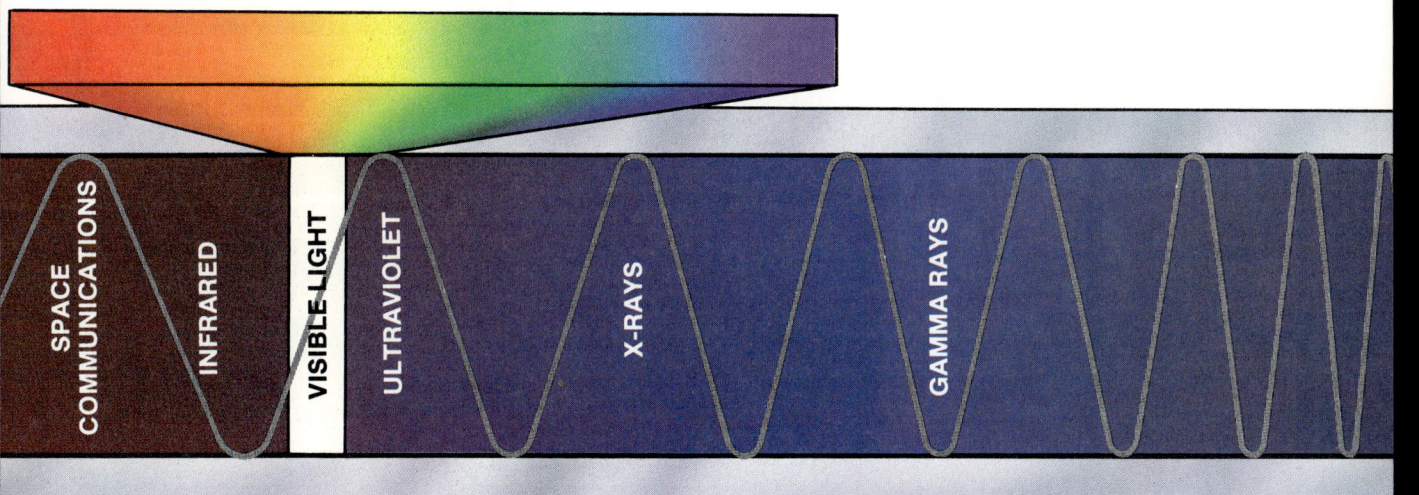

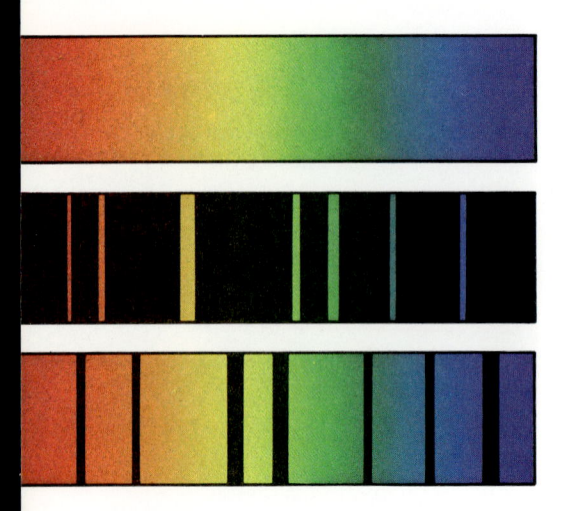

Figure 2.15 *top:* Continuous spectrum; *middle:* Bright line spectrum; *bottom:* Dark line spectrum

There are three kinds of spectra. A **continuous spectrum** is like a rainbow. A **bright line spectrum** has narrow bright lines at certain positions. A **dark line spectrum** has narrow dark lines at certain positions. A bright spectrum comes from a hot, shining object. When light is cut off or absorbed by passing through a cold gas, a dark spectrum is recorded. Much of what is known about the stars in the visible wavelengths has been learned by reading these spectra.

Each substance in a star or galaxy can give off energy. That energy is like a fingerprint, as each substance has its own color pattern. The astronomer focuses the telescope on the distant object. The light from that object passes through a spectroscope and is separated into its spectrum fingerprint. By matching the fingerprint with that produced by substances on earth, you can tell what an astronomical object is made of.

Activity

What Do the Light's Fingerprints Tell?

Materials
index card
pencil
paper

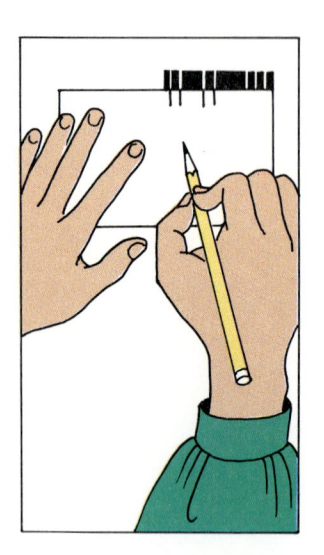

Procedure

1. Place an index card along the bottom edge of spectrum 1. Use your pencil to mark the position of the lines in spectrum 1 on your index card.

2. Compare the lines from the unknown spectrum with the lines from the known spectra.

3. List each substance(s) contained in unknown spectrum 1 that matches a known spectrum.

4. Repeat this process for the two other unknown spectra.

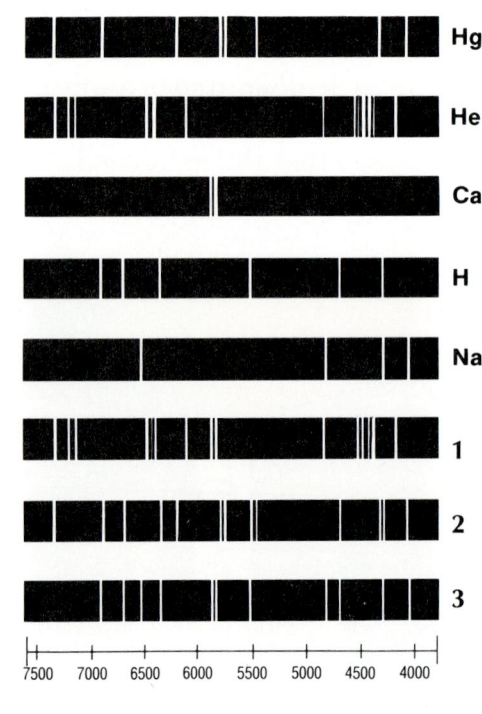

Questions

1. What substances does unknown spectrum 1 represent? Spectrum 2? Spectrum 3?

2. Explain how you might find the composition of a galaxy.

Figure 2.16 Ears on the universe. *left:* Very Large Array, radio telescopes near Socorro, New Mexico; *below:* Radio telescopes receive radio waves from stars and feed the waves to computers for reading.

Only within the last 30 years have instruments other than optical telescopes been used to study outer space. Radio telescopes have been developed to read the radio waves received from space. Astronomers use huge radio telescopes to listen to the sky. The weak radio energy from space is collected by one or more reflecting dishes. Then the energy is carried to a receiver. The receiver converts the radio energy into an electrical signal which can be recorded on a graph. In this way the radio telescope receives and records the radio signals from space. Radio maps have been drawn of the sky. Studies of these radio maps have revealed two types of radio energy sources never known to exist before radio telescopes were invented. These sources, **quasars** [KWAY-sahrs] and **pulsars** [PUHL-sahrs], were discovered in the 1960's. Quasars, radio energy stars, are objects in space that emit strong radio signals. Pulsars are radio energy stars that emit energy in sharp, intense, and regular pulses. They were discovered in 1967. In 1960 there were two known radio energy stars. By 1979 more than 20,000 quasars had been identified, and more than 600 pulsars were known.

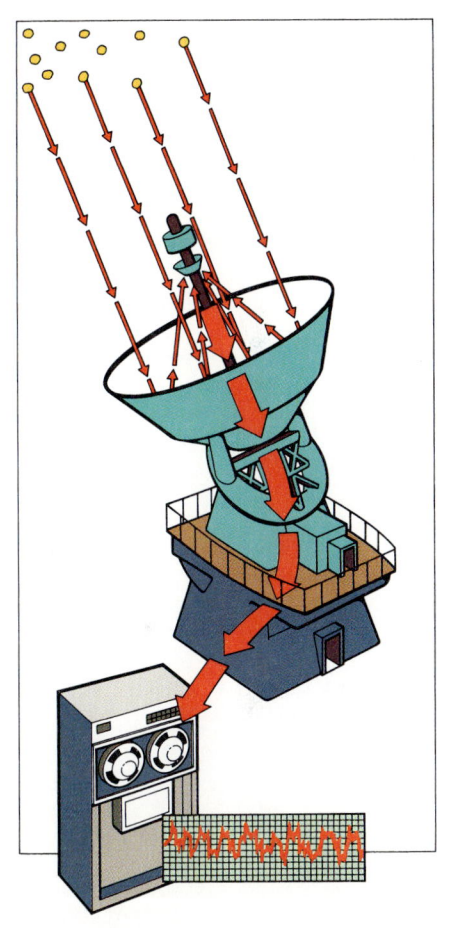

Study Questions for 2.2

1. What is electromagnetic radiation?
2. Explain how you can determine the composition of a star.
3. List two objects that are studied with radio telescopes.

2.3 Mysteries of the Universe

You will find out
- that many observations in space are unexplained;
- how the Doppler effect is used to explain the shift of spectral lines;
- why the red shift supports the big bang theory.

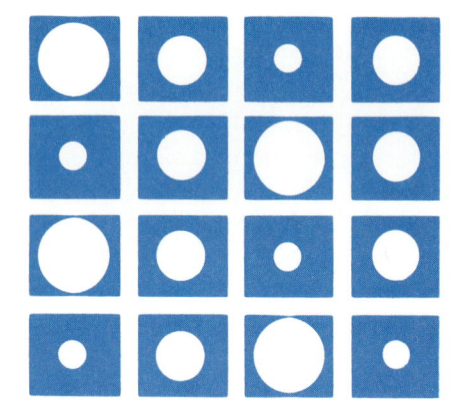

Figure 2.17 Over a period of time this could be the pulsation pattern of a Cepheid variable star.

Figure 2.18 *left:* Nova Hercules at the time of its explosion, March 10, 1935; *right:* It then rapidly faded to a low magnitude as shown in the photo taken May 6, 1935.

Have you ever been curious? Consider this example. Your teacher has given you two eggs to study. One egg is hard-boiled; the other is uncooked. You are to find out which is hard-boiled. You can't break or crack the egg. What would you do? You have a mystery to solve. That's what happens to astronomers when they find things they can't explain by what they know. These things are mysteries.

What are some of the mysteries for astronomers? One such mystery is the more than 700 Cepheid variable stars. Imagine the sun swelling in size and then shrinking back to normal every few days. That would be very strange, yet some stars do just that. How can a star do that? Present-day physics can't adequately explain how this is possible. A star's size is dependent upon balanced forces. Energy-making processes in the star's interior tend to make the star increase in size. Gravity tries to hold the material together. Yet in some stars there is a sequence of swell–shrink–swell that is repeated time and again. The star pulsates at regular intervals. Cepheids are thought to cease pulsating as they grow older. How long will a Cepheid pulsate? What might cause one to stop pulsating?

Another mystery object is a star that blows off its outer skin and just keeps getting bigger. It's an exploding star called a nova. These firecrackers in space don't happen very often, but when they do, it's a big explosion. A super giant star can also explode in a glorious burst called supernova. Which stars are next going to become a nova or supernova?

Pulsars are objects that give off lots of radio energy in brief but intense pulses. The amount of radio energy emitted during one pulse is from one million to ten billion times the energy the sun emits from a similar

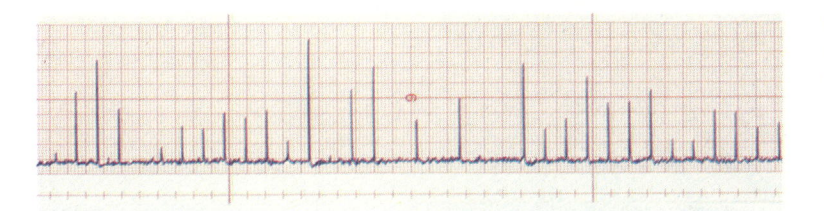

Figure 2.19 Each peak on this graph is a record of the intense pulses of radio energy received from a pulsar.

amount of surface area. These small stars may have about the same mass as the sun, but they are only 10 to 30 km in diameter. One cubic centimeter of a pulsar has a mass of about 10^{11} kg. A cubic centimeter is only about the size of a sugar cube, but there isn't a truck in your town that could haul that much of a pulsar. Pulsars rotate rapidly, and the pulses of radio energy are caused by this rotation. There is a lot yet to be learned about what makes a star so dense and spin so fast.

There are other mysteries of the heavens besides objects that give off lots of energy. For example, some of the lines in the spectra from distant objects appear to be shifted when compared to laboratory spectra.

There may be an explanation for this. You can use this example. Imagine you are watching an auto race. As a car approaches, the sound of the car gets louder and has a certain pitch. Notice how the pitch changes as the car passes by you. The pitch of the car is higher coming toward you than it was going away. Actually the sound didn't change pitch, but you hear a pitch change because the car was moving. The change in pitch is called the **Doppler** [DAHP-luhr] **effect**.

Do You Know?
$10^{11} = 100,000,000,000$

Do You Know?
When the first pulsar was discovered, astronomers thought the signals were coded and might have been sent from some place in space. They half jokingly dubbed the source LGM for "little green men."

Figure 2.20 The sound pitch of the race car is higher as it comes toward you and lower as it moves away from you.

Shorter Wavelengths
Higher Pitches

Longer Wavelengths
Lower Pitches

2 / Outer Space

Figure 2.21 In this picture, the color of the rocket ship coming toward you is blue-shifted, and the color of the rocket ship going away is red-shifted.

It is believed that the shift in the spectral lines in the spectrum of a distant object in space is also due to motion. The faster the object moves, the greater the shift. Lines shifted toward the red, longer wavelength, are caused by objects moving away. Lines shifted toward the blue, shorter wavelength, indicate that the object is moving toward us. This is called the **Doppler shift.** The far away objects of outer space all show such a red shift. Quasars are the objects showing the greatest shift and the fastest motion.

Astronomers now believe that the motion is related to how the universe began. They propose that the universe started with a big bang. From that moment on, the universe expanded. All the objects in space appear to be moving apart from each other. It's like putting spots on a balloon. As you blow it up, the spots move farther apart. All far away objects seem to be fleeing away and getting farther apart. Is this the way the universe began? Or is there some other explanation for the red shift?

The greatest mysteries of all are **black holes.** A black hole is thought to be an object in space from which no light can escape. Without any light you, of course, can't see it. If you can't see it, how do you know it even exists?

Black holes are revealed by X rays. The X rays come from the areas where black holes are suspected to be. It is believed that matter from nearby space is pulled into the black hole. As the matter approaches the black hole, it speeds up and it heats up to give off X rays. There's more to learn about black holes. One theory for black holes is that they start with the collapse of a massive star. Near the end of its life cycle, the star runs out of fuel and collapses. Black holes may grow by swallowing matter from other stars or from swallowing whole stars in a gulp. There may be huge black holes having masses equal to millions of stars. There may be black holes the size of a star. There also may be mini black holes the size of a planet or smaller.

Because black holes are so dense, they have tremendous gravitational fields. Imagine the earth shrunk to the size of a golf ball. That ball would then be about as dense as a black hole. Anything that dense has a strong enough gravitational field to prevent light from escaping. The light would try to get away, but gravity would pull it back.

Do black holes exist? Most astronomers believe they do, but some do not. How were black holes formed? How do they work? It is not known for sure. Black holes are one of the greatest mysteries in space.

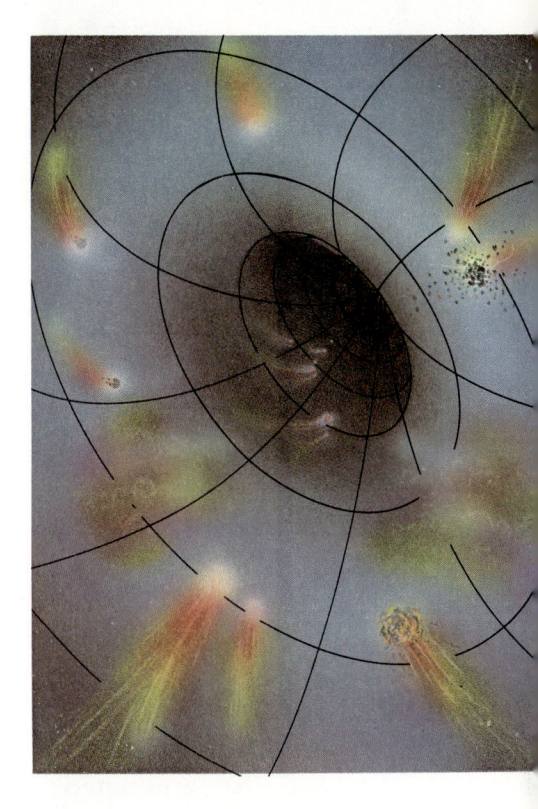

Figure 2.22 This is an artist's conception of a black hole. Why aren't there any photographs of black holes?

Study Questions for 2.3

1. Select one mystery of our universe and explain why it is a mystery.
2. What does the Doppler effect explain?
3. What does the red shift imply about how the universe was started?
4. Use the scientific processes discussed in Chapter 1 to support or reject the big-bang model of an expanding universe.

Biography

Edwin Powell Hubble (1889-1953)

Edwin Hubble was an active athlete. He took part in track, boxing, and rowing. As a boxer he was successful enough to be considered as a contender for the heavyweight championship.

Hubble graduated from the University of Chicago in 1910 with a B.S. degree in astronomy. He studied law at Oxford University, England, and practiced law for a year in Kentucky. Unsatisfied with law, Hubble entered graduate school at the University of Chicago. He graduated in 1917 and joined the army. He was wounded and left the army as a major. His career in astronomy began after World War I.

Hubble's discovery of Cepheids and other variable stars in nebulae served as the basis for investigations into the evolution of the universe. His discovery of the relationship between the shift in spectral lines and the speed of galaxies is known as Hubble's law. Hubble found that for every million light-years a galaxy is away from us, its speed increased 30 km per second. This relationship is used in determining the size of the universe. Results of Hubble's work rank as the most significant contributions to the study of the universe since the time of Copernicus. Hubble was a giant in the field of astronomy.

CHAPTER REVIEW

Main Ideas

- Early people classified the stars by grouping the stars into imaginary patterns, or constellations.
- Refracting telescopes use two lenses to magnify light from an object.
- Reflecting telescopes use a curved mirror and a lens to magnify the light from an object.
- Objects found in outer space include nebulae, stars, open clusters, globular clusters, galaxies, and Cepheid variable stars.
- Electromagnetic radiation is energy in the form of waves from space. It includes radio waves, infrared, visible light, ultraviolet, X rays, and gamma rays.
- Every substance gives off a unique spectrum of radiant energy that will identify it. A spectroscope separates this spectrum, and the composition of an object can be identified.
- Radio telescopes measure radio waves from radio energy sources such as quasars and pulsars.
- Not all that has been observed in space can be explained with current knowledge.
- The Doppler effect explains that the red shift of distant objects means the objects are moving away. This is the same effect we would suppose happened if the universe started with a big bang.

Using Vocabulary

On a separate piece of paper, use the following words to make a crossword puzzle. Exchange puzzles with a classmate.

celestial sphere	galaxy	bright-line spectrum
constellation	Cepheid variable star	dark-line spectrum
refracting telescope	electromagnetic radiation	quasar
nebula	prism	pulsar
comet	spectrum	Doppler effect
reflecting telescope	spectroscope	Doppler shift
open cluster	diffraction grating	black hole
globular cluster	continuous spectrum	

Remembering Facts

On your paper, write the word or words that best complete each sentence.
1. Imaginary groupings of stars are called _____.
2. A telescope that has two lenses is a _____ telescope.
3. Radio waves, infrared, ultraviolet, and X rays are all forms of _____ _____.
4. Thin, glowing-gas clouds in space are called _____.
5. The _____ _____ explains the changing pitch of an approaching car horn.
6. Stars that occur by the thousands in a close grouping are called a _____ _____.
7. A common grouping of millions to billions of stars is called a _____.
8. A star that varies in brightness at regular intervals is the _____ _____.
9. A telescope that has a curved mirror and a lens is a _____ telescope.
10. A _____ can be used to determine the composition of a star.
11. _____ and _____ are stars that give off radio waves.
12. An object that is so dense that light cannot escape from it is called a _____ _____.
13. Stars that occur in a loose grouping are in a(an) _____ _____.
14. A star moving away from you shows a color shift toward the color _____.
15. The Doppler shift supports the _____ _____ model of how the universe started.
16. A _____ and _____ are used in many telescopes to separate light into a spectrum.

Understanding Ideas

On your paper, answer each question in complete sentences.
1. Visible light from a star is said to carry a message about the star. What is the message and how is it read?
2. Explain the statement, "You can tell the composition of an object in space without touching it."
3. Why are black holes black? Why are they called holes? What are they?

Applying What You Have Learned

1. Explain why the early Greeks had a model of space as a huge rotating sphere with stars attached to it.
2. Describe the balanced forces that keep a star the same size.
3. You are in a moving car, and the horn is sounding. Explain why you would or would not hear a change in the pitch of the sound.
4. What information can be learned by studying the energy given off by objects in space?

Challenge

Astronomers learn a great deal about objects in outer space by studying the electromagnetic radiation given off by these objects. The form of energy which has contributed the most to our knowledge of objects in space is light. One of the messages carried by light is the relative position and direction of motion of an object. The Doppler shift is used to determine whether something is moving toward the earth (blue shift) or away from the earth (red shift). Scientists use the following formula to determine how fast an object such as a star is moving:

$$\frac{\text{amount of shift}}{\text{point of origin}} \times \text{speed of light}$$

The illustration is of an imaginary laboratory spectrum and the spectra of two imaginary stars. Consider the speed of light to be 300,000 km/s and answer the following questions:

1. Which star is approaching you?
2. Which star is moving away from you?
3. How fast are the two stars moving?

Wavelengths

← Red   Blue →

Lab Spectrum
5,010   5,000   4,990

Star Alpha
5,010   5,000   4,990

Star Beta
5,010   5,000   4,990

Research and Investigation

1. Select one of the astronomical objects mentioned in this chapter and write a paper describing that object.
2. Prepare a poster for display on one of the astronomical objects mentioned in this chapter.
3. Make a tape recording of the Doppler effect. These are suggestions for a sound source: a car horn, a trumpet player on a bicycle, a swinging tuning fork safely attached to a cord, or anything that makes a continuous sound while moving past you.

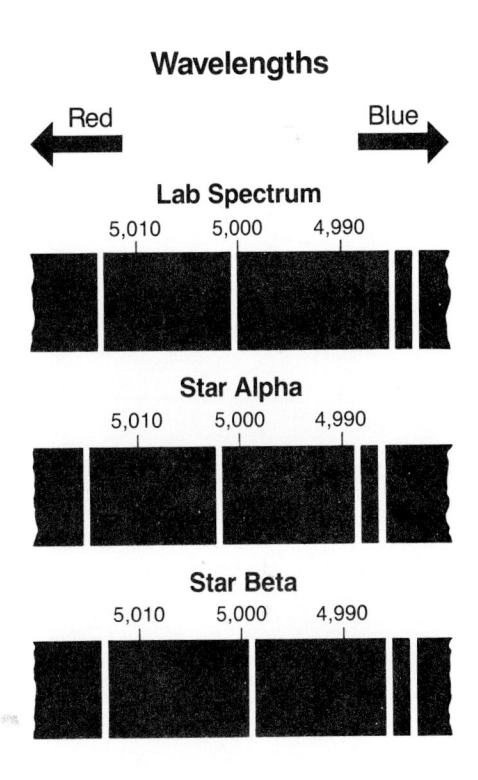

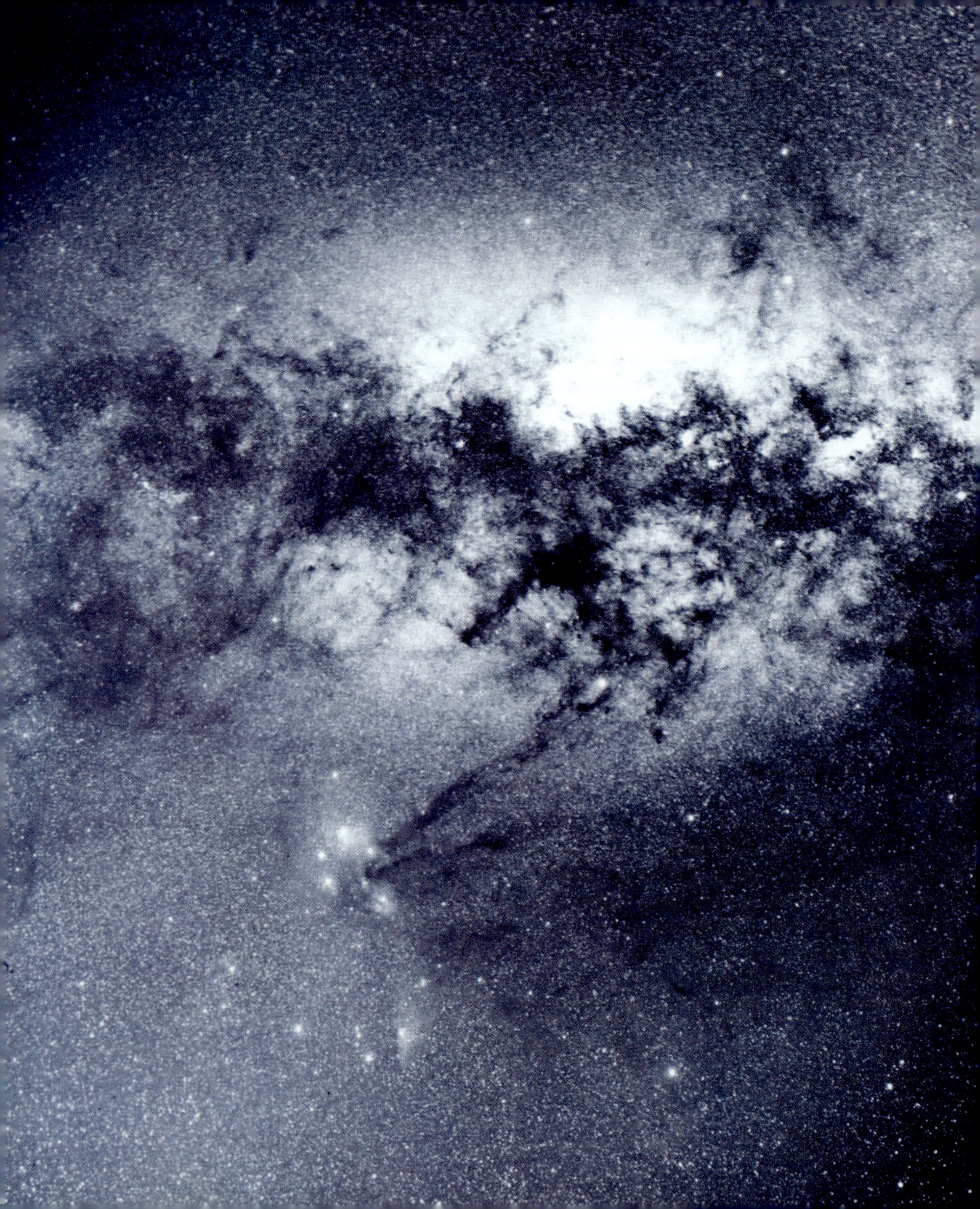

Chapter 3
The Milky Way Galaxy

Lesson Titles
3.1 Your Galaxy
3.2 Study the Stars in Your Galaxy
3.3 The Search in Space

As your journey from outer space continues, you begin to find that things are becoming more crowded. What you saw earlier looked like many other galaxies, but now it seems to be millions of stars all around you.

You wonder why it is that you see so many more stars in some directions than others. You also seem to pass through areas where there are more stars and then less stars. This begins to tell you something about the shape of this special galaxy that you are now going to study.

You can't help doing what scientists have done for a long time. You speculate about whether there is life somewhere on a planet circling one of those stars. In this chapter you will learn about some of the new tools astronomers use. What mysteries will they solve? But more exciting, what new mysteries will they turn up?

Figure 3.1 *opposite:* The Milky Way Galaxy as viewed from Earth

43

3.1 Your Galaxy

You will find out
- how your galaxy is structured;
- how your galaxy is changing;
- the galaxy you live in is called the **Milky Way Galaxy**.

Do you ever get the chance to view the sky away from city lights? You would notice a sky full of stars. On a dark, clear night you might notice a white milky band of light running the entire length of the sky. This band contains millions and millions of stars. The reason it looks this way is because you are really looking out through our galaxy toward its edge. Because this galaxy looks this way to you it is called the **Milky Way Galaxy**.

Figure 3.2 *bottom:* This drawing is an artist's idea of the Milky Way Galaxy as it would appear from space. *top:* The photograph shows another galaxy that is believed to be similar to the Milky Way.

Do You Know?
If the sun were the size of a basketball, the earth would be the size of a BB pellet located 30 meters from the basketball and the galactic disk would be 200 million km across.

If anyone outside the Milky Way Galaxy were to look at it, they would see an ordinary spiral galaxy somewhat like M-31. What is known about the Milky Way Galaxy? A lot is already known. It is lens-shaped with two or more spiral arms. It's big—about 100,000 light-years in diameter. It is about 10,000 light-years thick and is rotating. The center of the Milky Way Galaxy lies in the direction of the constellation Sagittarius. The sun and its family of planets are about 30,000 light-years from the center in one of the spiral arms. It will take the sun in its position about 225 million years to make one complete turn around the galactic center.

44

3 / The Milky Way Galaxy

The center of the galaxy shows up dark in optical telescopes because of clouds of gas and dust. Recently, radio telescopes have been used to study the region of space near the center of the galaxy. Radio energy penetrates through the light, gas, and dust. Consider, for example, a foggy or smoggy day. You may not be able to see very well, but your radio and TV set still work fine. Astronomers use radio telescopes to study the material between the stars near the center of the galaxy. The radio telescope helps them study areas where they are unable to see with optical telescopes.

From radio astronomy, astronomers learn that the galaxy has spiral arms. The spiral arms contain vast clouds of gas and dust between the stars. These clouds are not very dense, as they have only 25 or 50 very small particles per cubic km. Astronomers believe that these clouds are the birthplace of new stars. The material will someday collect together, and new stars will be born.

Measurements of different stars show that they move with respect to each other. They do not all move together. You can notice this when you compare very old star maps with new ones. The ancients saw the stars in a slightly different pattern than you see today. The next time you look at the stars, find the Big Dipper. Fifty thousands years from now the position of these stars will have changed some. They may no longer look so much like a dipper.

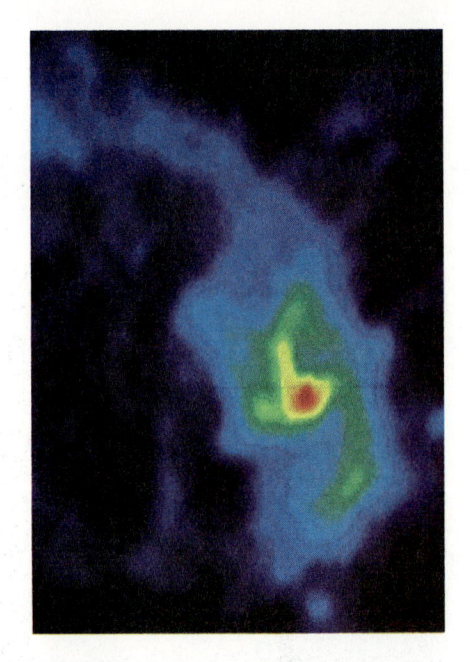

Figure 3.3 A picture of radio energy received from the nucleus of the Milky Way Galaxy

Figure 3.4 Changes in the Big Dipper over time

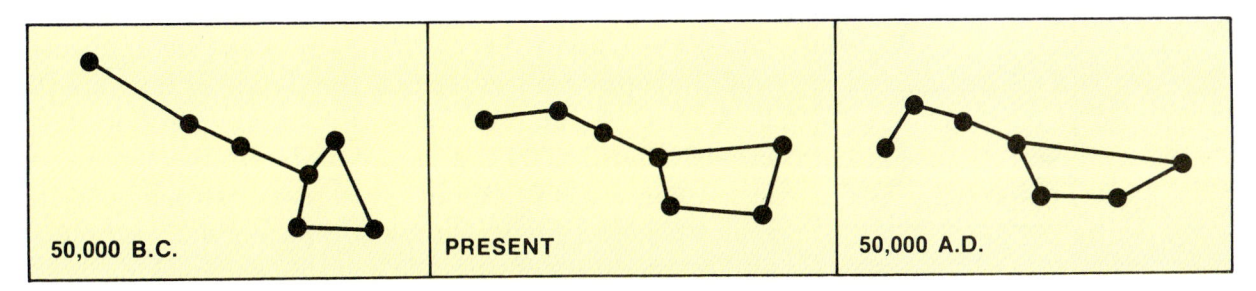

50,000 B.C.   PRESENT   50,000 A.D.

Study Questions for 3.1

1. Draw a top view of your galaxy. Label its dimensions. Locate the sun.
2. Describe two ways your galaxy is changing.

3 / The Milky Way Galaxy

3.2 Study the Stars in Your Galaxy

You will find out
- the four different types of stars;
- the life history of a star;
- the relationship between temperature and brightness of stars.

Do You Know?
The largest telescopes can see stars that are a million times fainter than those you can see with your naked eye.

Figure 3.5 Seven spectral types of stars according to their temperature

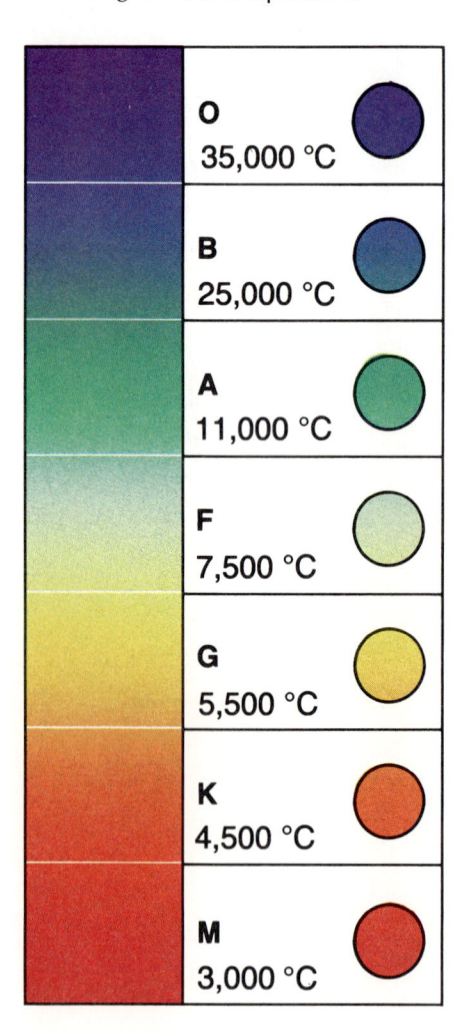

O	35,000 °C
B	25,000 °C
A	11,000 °C
F	7,500 °C
G	5,500 °C
K	4,500 °C
M	3,000 °C

The most prominent members of the Milky Way Galaxy are the stars you see. Stars are objects in space that make their own light. The best known and nearest star to you is the sun. Even as near as the sun appears to be, it takes light from the sun about eight minutes to reach you. If the sun were to suddenly stop giving off light, how long would it be before total darkness would come? The sun, even though smaller than many other stars, appears bright to you because it is close. There are many brighter stars, but they are much farther away.

One way of judging a star is by how much light it gives off. The brightness of a star can be measured by using telescopes. In most cases the brightest stars are the hottest stars. Just as astronomers analyze the light from galaxies by using spectroscopes, they can do the same thing with starlight. By examining a spectrum of a star, they know much about that star's composition. Each star has its own fingerprint, or spectrum. Astronomers can classify the stars from the spectrum information. In Figure 3.5 you see that the classes of stars are O, B, A, F, G, K, and M. Class O stars are the hottest—greater than 25,000°C. Class M stars are the coolest at less than 3,000°C. About 1910 two astronomers in separate places made a graph comparing the brightness and temperature of stars. This graph is named for those two astronomers. It's called the **Hertzsprung-Russell (H-R) diagram** [HUHRTZ-spruhng—rus-sehl]. Look at this graph closely because most stars can be shown in the H-R diagram. On the H-R diagram the sun is a class G star. It isn't very hot and it isn't very bright. The sun is a rather ordinary star.

Astronomers were surprised to learn how the stars showed up on the H-R diagram. They found that there were four types of stars. Most stars are included in the first type, and they lie on the diagonal band from upper left to lower right. Stars that fall close to this band are called **main sequence stars.** You will note that the sun is a main sequence star. The second type of star lies above and to the right of the main sequence band. These brighter stars are called **giants.** Some because of their color are called red giants. The third type includes stars that are even brighter than normal giants. These are called **supergiants,** and you find them in the upper right of the H-R diagram. Although supergiants are cooler, they give off more energy because of their enormous size. The fourth type of star, the **white dwarf,** is found to the left and below the main sequence. They are fainter and smaller than main sequence stars. Sometimes they are called faint hot objects.

Figure 3.6 A Hertzsprung-Russell (H-R) diagram is a plot of temperature versus brightness. The hottest stars are on the left side of the graph. The brightest stars are on the top of the graph. When plotted on an H-R diagram, the stars lie mainly on a diagonal band from upper left to lower right. Thus the hotter stars are brighter than the cooler stars. Stars on the main sequence are called dwarf stars. The sun is a type G dwarf.

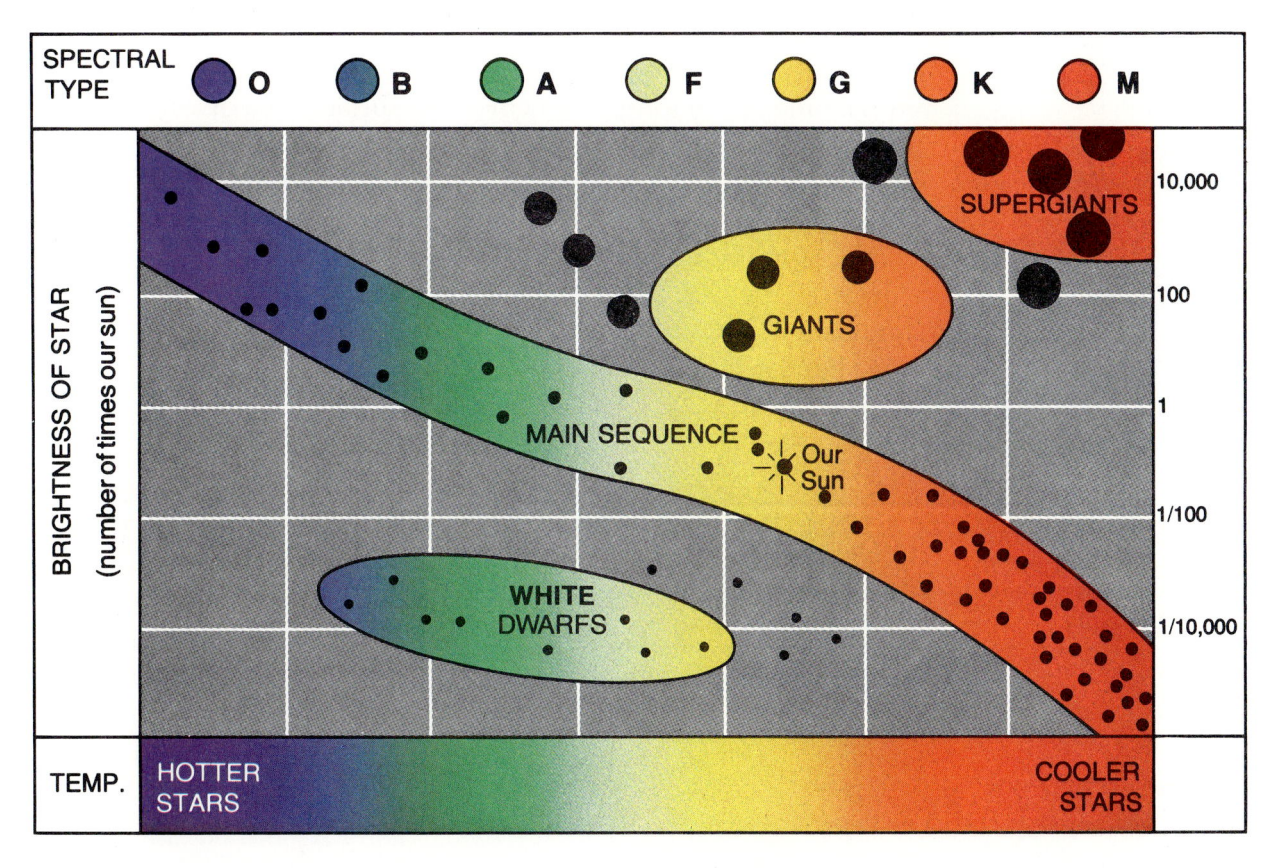

3 / The Milky Way Galaxy

Figure 3.7 A small section of the Milky Way Galaxy is the Sagittarius region.

Astronomers also make surveys of the number of stars in the Milky Way Galaxy. They find that the number of stars is not the same when they look in different directions. Earlier you saw the Milky Way Galaxy as a band of light across the sky. This is because there are so many stars in that direction. How can you count so many stars? One way is to count the stars in one small piece of the sky. Then you can determine the number in the whole sky.

Activity

How Many Stars Can You See?

Materials
pencil
tape
typing paper
paper for sky charts—
 three sheets,
 1 m × 1.6 m

Procedure

Make three sky charts as follows: Place 20 to 30 stars randomly scattered on chart 1, 10 to 25 stars on chart 2, and 30 to 50 stars on chart 3. The charts are then posted on 3 different walls of the classroom.

1. Roll a sheet of typing paper into a tube 28 cm long and 4 cm in diameter. Fasten with tape.

2. Sight through the paper tube toward sky chart 1.

3. Count the number of stars you can see. Record this number.

4. Repeat steps 2 and 3 for sky charts 2 and 3.

5. Add together the number of stars you saw in each count. Divide by three. This is your average number of stars (As) seen for each view.

6. Calculate the number of stars by answering these questions. Use the Table. What is the surface area of a sphere with a radius of 28 cm?

_____ sq. cm (Sa)

What is the area of view for tube 4 cm diameter?

_____ sq. cm (A)

Number of stars = $\dfrac{Sa}{A}$ × As

= _____ stars

Table Information for Calculations

Surface area of sphere with a radius of 28 cm (Sa)	Area of view for tube with 4 cm diameter (A)
9,847 sq. cm	12.6 sq. cm

Questions

1. What is the area of the end of your tube?

2. What was the average number of stars counted?

3. How many stars would you see in the whole sky?

Astronomers believe that stars change over a period of time. They think that a star is born out of a cloud of gas and particles of dust pulled together by gravity. With time it contracts and becomes very hot. A nuclear reaction begins. Its brightness increases, and the star becomes a main sequence star. Ninety percent of all stars are at this point in the life cycle. The mass of the star will determine its position on the main sequence.

As more and more matter is used up in making energy, the composition of the star changes. The star eventually gets larger, cooler on the outside, and brighter. It becomes a red giant star. In time the star changes further. It stays about the same brightness but becomes hotter and smaller. The star continues to get hotter and smaller finally ending up as a white dwarf. Some dwarfs flare up with a sudden burst of light that may last for years. A white dwarf that flares up this way is called a nova. Other dwarf stars simply collapse into a dark region in space called a black hole.

For the average-sized star, this entire life cycle lasts about 10 billion years. Astronomers believe that the sun is presently somewhere in the middle stages of its life cycle. They estimate the sun's age to be approximately 5 billion years.

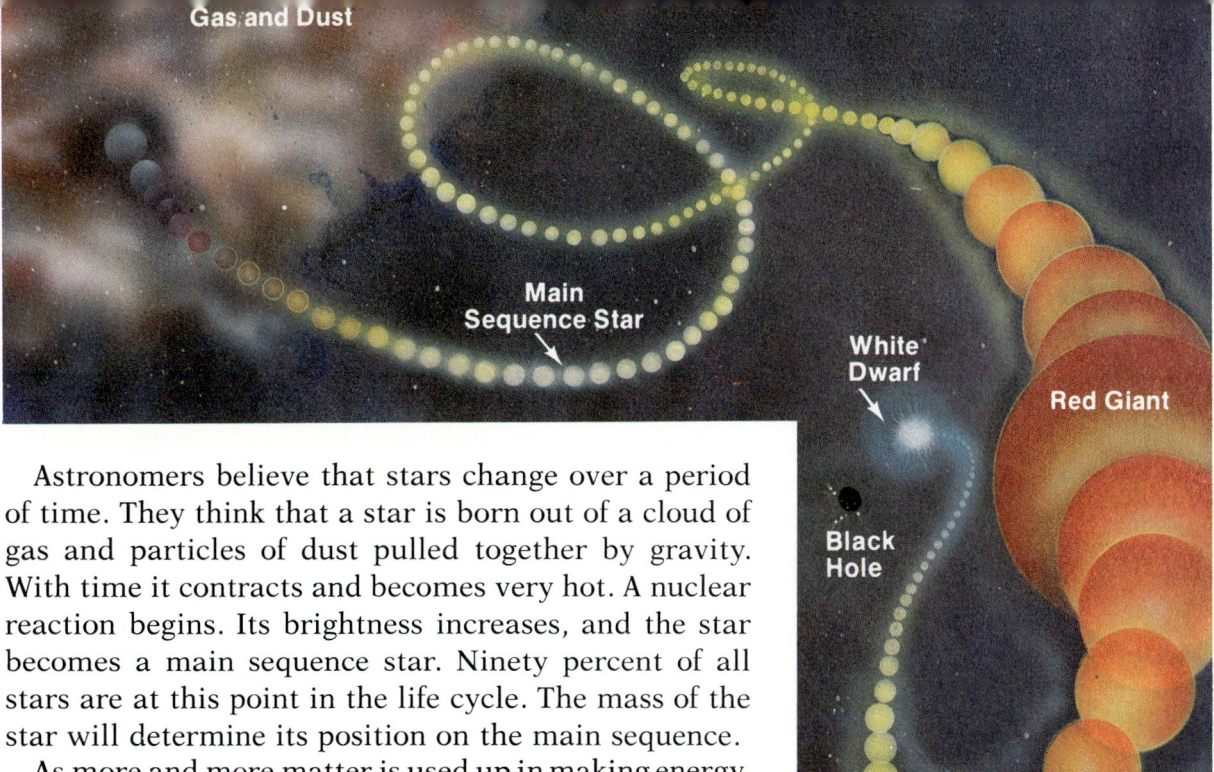

Figure 3.8 An artist's picture of the life of a star from its birth until it ends up billions of years later as a white dwarf. Some stars may also become neutron stars or even black holes.

Study Questions for 3.2

1. List the four types of stars.
2. Describe the possible life cycle of a star.
3. What is the relationship between temperature and brightness of stars?

3.3 The Search in Space

You will find out
- why space observatories are so useful;
- what the major parts of a space observatory are;
- how scientists have searched for life in space.

Why would you want to put a telescope into space? One of the best reasons is to take it out of the atmosphere. Think about the atmosphere outside your classroom right this minute. Is it clear? Foggy? Smoggy? Hazy? The atmosphere prevents a clear view of space. It absorbs some energy from space. It blocks out some energy and at times makes the images from space look strange. It is like looking through a dirty window. The atmosphere is something astronomers would like to do without.

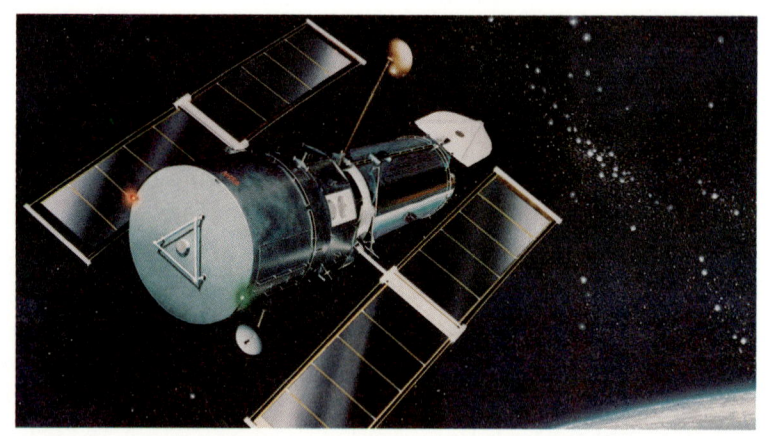

Figure 3.9 *above:* The hazy atmosphere over this observatory outside Paris, France, limits ability to peer into space.

Figure 3.10 *above right:* An artist's picture of the NASA space telescope.

Space observatories eliminate these problems. In a space observatory the telescopes are outside the earth's atmosphere. Will viewing be better? If the 5-m telescope on Palomar Mountain in Southern California were above the atmosphere, it could see 50 times better.

Another reason to take telescopes outside the atmosphere is to escape light. The atmosphere gives off scattered light from stars and from cities. The amount of darkness sets the limit on the faintest objects that can be seen. It is becoming difficult to find a location on the earth that is as dark as astronomers would like. But above the atmosphere it is completely dark.

50

3 / The Milky Way Galaxy

Telescopes have been lifted above some of the atmosphere by balloons and jet aircraft. But the most successful way to eliminate the atmospheric problems of telescopes has been to put them in a spacecraft. Spacecraft can place telescopes in orbit about the earth completely above the atmosphere.

In Figure 3.11 you see an artist's concept of a space observatory. The space observatory has one or more telescopes. The large panels convert sunlight into electrical energy that supplies power to operate the observatory. This observatory has a guidance system so that the telescopes can be pointed at any part of the sky. There is also a system to maneuver the observatory and maintain it in a specific position in space. A radio transmitter and receiver will be used to communicate with the observatory.

Do You Know?
Prior to the first orbiting solar observatory, the technique of studying the sun hadn't changed much since Galileo made his first observations some 350 years ago in 1610.

Figure 3.11 A future space observatory may look like this picture. Notice the solar cells for power and the style of construction that is used under the conditions of weightlessness.

3 / The Milky Way Galaxy

Figure 3.12 Vehicles such as these carry instruments aloft to study radiation without the interference of Earth's atmosphere.

The observatories orbiting in space make the same kinds of studies of the sky that are made with telescopes on the earth. These studies include visual observations and searching for X-ray and gamma-ray sources. Some observatories are designed to study the infrared and ultraviolet part of the electromagnetic spectrum coming from the sky.

More and more is being learned about your galaxy all the time. The main reason for this is that now all parts of the electromagnetic spectrum are studied. Galileo and all astronomers after him for the next 350 years studied only the visible part of the spectrum. Now with space observatories the entire electromagnetic spectrum is being studied from above any interfering atmosphere. There are many wonders yet to be learned about the Milky Way Galaxy.

One of the wonders that has persisted from ancient times is the question of life. In all of the Milky Way Galaxy which contains billions of stars is there only one sun with an inhabited planet orbiting around it? In every way it appears that humans on the earth are alone in this universe. Even so, the thought of other living beings persists.

One reason for thinking there might be other planets that could support life is the vast number of stars. But of all these stars which ones should you even consider? The very bright, hot stars are unlikely stars to have planets with human life. Other stars are too cool to keep a planet warm. The most likely stars are similar to our sun. But for now there is no information on how many of those stars also have planets.

Some astronomers say the highest number of such possible places for life in the Milky Way Galaxy is as high as 10 million. They also say the smallest possible number of places may be as few as 20. The only number you can be sure of is one.

Do You Know?
If the thickness of one playing card represents the distance to the moon, you would need 30 km of cards to show the distance to the nearest star.
    J. Allen Hynek, Astronomer

Figure 3.13 *left:* Do you think the moon is a good place to locate an observatory?

Figure 3.14 *below:* The Pleiades. These are new stars. Do they harbor new worlds?

3 / The Milky Way Galaxy

Figure 3.15 *right:* This astrogram was first radioed into space from the Arecibo National Radio Astronomy and Ionosphere Center in Puerto Rico in 1974. Will it be answered?

Figure 3.16 *below:* Radio telescope at Arecibo, Puerto Rico

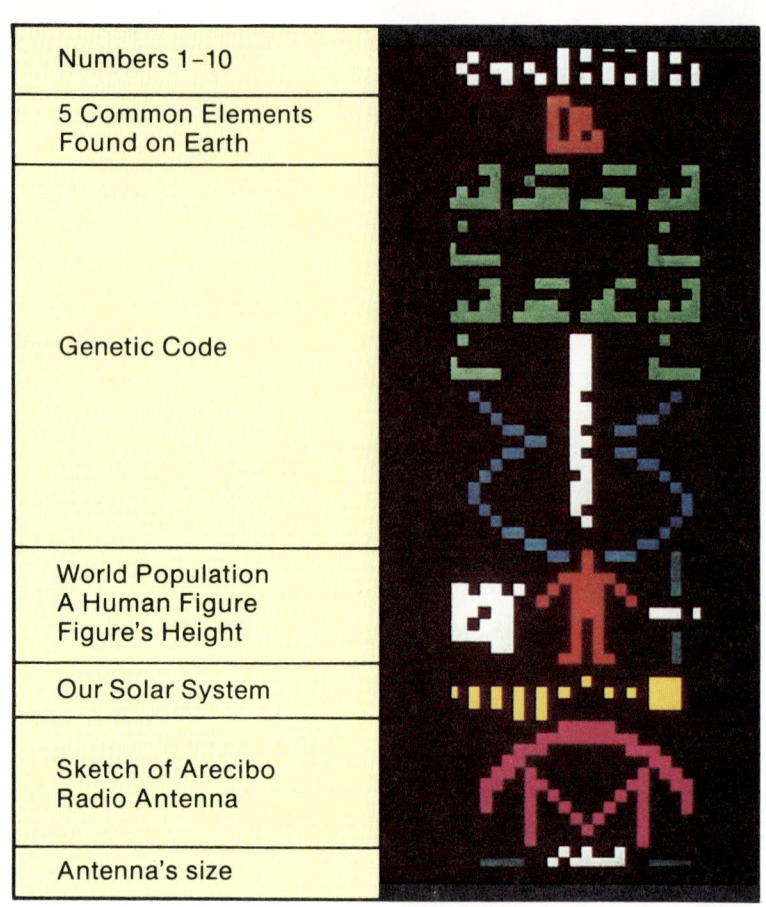

Numbers 1–10	
5 Common Elements Found on Earth	
Genetic Code	
World Population A Human Figure Figure's Height	
Our Solar System	
Sketch of Arecibo Radio Antenna	
Antenna's size	

Space travel has been eliminated in any search for other living beings because the distance to any other star is too great. Even traveling at the speed of light, your trip would take many years. If you can't search by a space voyage, what can you do? One way is to send a radio message into space and hope that another living being receives. Another way is to make radio surveys of the sky in the hope of picking up a message from somewhere else.

This is just what has been done with the radio telescope at Arecibo, Puerto Rico. It has been sending a message, called an **astrogram** [AS-troh-gram]. This message contains information about life on the earth, descriptions of the solar system, and a sketch of the radio telescope. Suppose you received a message from space like Figure 3.15. Could you interpret it?

3 / The Milky Way Galaxy

Several of the earliest space probes were programmed to leave the solar system. They carried thin metal plates with line sketches of people and other messages describing our world. Other space probes have carried phonograph recordings with descriptions of the earth. Although there is no known evidence to support the expectation of a message from space, it is not likely that people will ever stop thinking about it.

Do You Know?
In 1899, an eccentric electrical pioneer Nikola Tesla undertook to transmit a powerful electrical signal into space from his Colorado laboratory and to detect any replies.

Activity

What Does the Astrogram Say?

Materials
index card
pencil

Procedure
1. Think about the characteristics of a particular animal.
2. Make up a message that describes this animal. Write your message on the index card. Do not write the name of the animal on the card.
3. Trade your index card with someone else.

Questions
1. What was your animal?
2. What was the animal on the card you got in trade?
3. What are good clues to show an animal in a message?

Study Questions for 3.3

1. Name three advantages of a space observatory for studying the stars.
2. List the major parts of a space observatory.
3. Why are modern observations more thorough than those made by early astronomers?
4. Describe some of the messages that have been sent out beyond our solar system.

3 / The Milky Way Galaxy

Science and Technology

The VLBA

You learned in this chapter that some of the most important discoveries about the Milky Way Galaxy have been made with radio telescopes. Now astronomers are excited about a plan to build a large radio-telescope network. With this system, astronomers will be able to make much more careful studies of many objects and areas within our galaxy.

The new radio-telescope network will be called the Very Long Baseline Array, or VLBA. It will consist of 10 radio-telescope receivers. Each receiver will have a reflecting dish 25 m in diameter. But unlike the Very Large Array at Socorro, New Mexico (Figure 2.16), these receivers will not all be in the same place. Instead they are to be located throughout the United States, from Puerto Rico to Hawaii.

The distance between the receivers, called the baseline, is very important. As this distance increases, the ability of the radio telescope to detect and measure smaller and smaller objects increases also.

Now you should be able to see why the VLBA needs to be so widespread. The best radio reception comes from a large number of radio telescopes placed as far apart as possible.

How will the VLBA work? Each radio telescope will listen to the same part of the sky at the same time. The data each collects will be stored on magnetic tapes. These tapes will then be mailed to a central control station. There, a computer will change the data on the tapes into radio maps of the sky. By working together, the individual radio telescope of the VLBA will become the most powerful telescope—radio or optical—in the world.

Scientists other than astronomers are also excited about the potential work of the VLBA. Geologists, for example, can use the VLBA to detect any shifts in the positions of Earth's crustal plates. Astronomers can use the VLBA to detect tiny changes in the positions and motions of stars and in the orbits of satellites moving around Earth.

CHAPTER REVIEW

Main Ideas

- The Milky Way Galaxy is a lens-shaped, rotating galaxy having at least two spiral arms.
- The solar system is about 30,000 light-years from the center of the galaxy.
- When you look towards the edge of the galaxy from Earth, you see the Milky Way.
- Radio telescopes are used to study the region near the center of the galaxy.
- New stars develop in the gas and dust found in the spiral. Stars move with respect to each other.
- Four different types of stars are main sequence, giant, supergiant, and white dwarf.
- Stars appear to have a life cycle. In time, a main sequence star may become a red giant, then a hotter star towards the main sequence. Eventually it may become a white dwarf. A white dwarf may become a cold lump of matter or it may flare up to become a nova.
- Stars with the higher temperatures are generally the brightest.
- A space observatory would provide a clear view of space. City lights would not interfere with observations in space. All radiant wavelengths would be received.
- A space observatory would have telescopes, guidance equipment, a power supply, and radio transmitting and receiving equipment.
- Scientists listen for and send messages in the search for life outside the planet Earth.

Using Vocabulary

On a separate piece of paper, write a sentence for each of the words below. Each sentence should give a *clue* to the meaning of the word.

Hertzsprung-Russell diagram	supergiant
main sequence star	white dwarf
giant	astrogram

3 / The Milky Way Galaxy

Remembering Facts

On your paper, write the word or words that best complete each sentence.
1. The Milky Way Galaxy is (elliptical, spiral, irregular) in shape.
2. Our sun is about (10,000, 30,000, 100,000) light-years from the center of the Milky Way.
3. The Milky Way Galaxy contains (thousands, millions, billions) of stars.
4. The Milky Way Galaxy is (pulsing, not moving, rotating).
5. Our sun is a (white dwarf, main sequence, giant) star.
6. The Hertzsprung-Russell diagram compares (size and temperature, brightness and temperature, temperature and color).
7. The last stage in the life of a star is (main sequence, red giant, white dwarf).
8. In most cases the brightest stars are (hotter, middle temperature, cooler).
9. Stars form from (gas and dust, energy, a vacuum).
10. Most new stars are thought to form in the (spiral arms, center, outer part) of the Milky Way.
11. Space observatories would eliminate the problems of excessive (sunlight, city light, starlight).
12. Astronomers could make better observations without (gravity, radio waves, the atmosphere).
13. Life is known to exist on (1, 20, 10 million) planet(s).
14. Radio astronomers have heard (astrograms, messages, nothing) from other planets.
15. Life is thought to exist elsewhere because of the (number, temperature, size) of stars.

Understanding Ideas

On your paper, answer each question in complete sentences.
1. Explain why it takes eight minutes for light from the sun to reach the earth.
2. Why are observations outside the visible light spectrum important to astronomers?
3. Scientists believe that the universe is expanding. What clues would support this theory?
4. How does the sun compare to other stars in brightness and temperature?

Applying What You Have Learned

1. What type of star is 10,000 times brighter than the sun, with a temperature of 3,000°C? What type of star has the same brightness as the sun, with a temperature of 11,000°C?
2. Suppose that life on a planet on the opposite side of the Milky Way Galaxy beamed a radio message toward Earth. Radio waves travel at the speed of light. How much time would it take for the message to arrive?

Challenge

Some stars on the H-R diagram have changed in brightness because of their stage in the life cycle of stars. But what about all the stars in the main sequence? What is the difference between one main sequence star and another? The table lists the spectral type and brightness for eight imaginary stars. It also lists their mass as compared to the mass of the sun. Make an H-R diagram like the one in Figure 3.6. Write the name and the mass of the imaginary stars along the main sequence band.

1. What is the mass of faint, red stars compared to other main sequence stars?
2. What is the mass of bright, blue stars compared to other main sequence stars?
3. What seems to determine where a star is in the main sequence?

Star	Spectral Type	Brightness	Sun Masses
iota	M	1/1,000	0.1
delta	A	10	2
omicron	K	1/100	0.5
kappa	O	10,000	10
phi	G	1	1
zeta	B	100	4
epsilon	M	1/10,000	0.04
omega	O	100,000	60

Research and Investigation

1. Write a description of the work of one of these famous astronomers: Henrietta Leavitt, Galileo Galilei, Sir Isaac Newton, Maria Mitchell.
2. Write a report on the research and development of the big bang theory.

Figure 4.5 Hydrogen particles collide and fuse, producing helium particles and enormous amounts of energy.

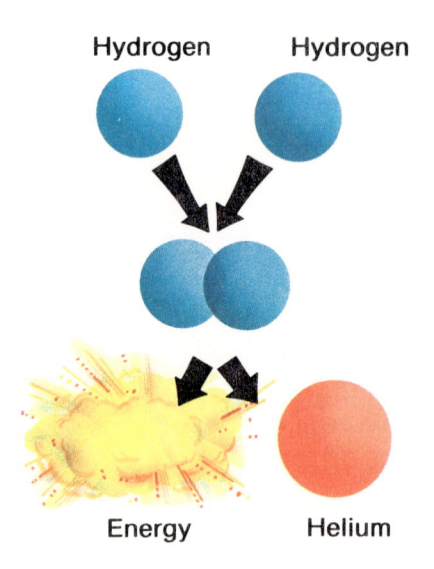

Where does the sun's enormous energy come from? The sun produces energy by converting hydrogen into helium. Every second, the sun converts 600 million metric tons of hydrogen into 596 million tons of helium. Four million metric tons of matter are converted into energy. This is a lot of hydrogen to use up in one second. Will the sun burn out soon? Not really, since it is expected to last at least another five billion years. Fortunately the sun has lots of hydrogen.

This enormous source of energy is very important to you as nearly all energy on earth comes ultimately from the sun. This includes coal, oil, gas, and even the winds and water power. Plants as well as animals use solar energy. Changes in solar activity may affect weather and climate and even radio communication.

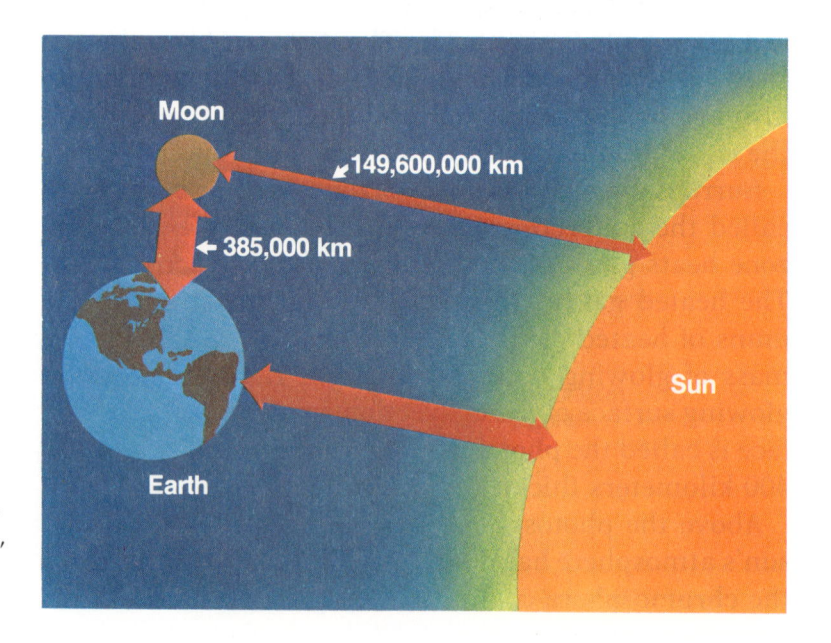

Figure 4.6 Distance also affects gravitational force. Earth, closer to the moon, exerts greater pull on the moon than the distant, but more massive, Sun.

In addition to its energy the sun has another powerful effect. As you learned earlier, every object in the universe is attracted to every other object. This force of attraction is called **gravitation.** The greater the mass of the object, the stronger the force of gravitation. With its enormous mass the sun exerts a powerful gravitational pull on all the objects around it. If it weren't for this gravitational

Do You Know?
The sun contains 99.6 percent of the solar system's mass.

4 / The Solar System

attraction, each of the planets would go zipping away into space rather than staying in orbit around the sun. There are nine planets, with their related moons, and thousands of other interesting objects all orbiting around the sun. All of these objects make up the **solar system.**

Figure 4.7 The order of the planets as they orbit the sun is shown below. Normally they do not align so perfectly, and some are spaced farther apart than can be shown. In 1979, Pluto crossed inside Neptune's orbit and will travel there until 1999.

Key:	1. Mercury	4. Mars	7. Uranus
	2. Venus	5. Jupiter	8. Neptune
	3. Earth	6. Saturn	9. Pluto

Study Questions for 4.1

1. Name two of the sun's surface features.
2. Describe the three inner layers of the sun.
3. Describe how the sun produces its energy.
4. Explain why the planets orbit around the sun.

4 / The Solar System

4.2 The Earth and the Moon

You will find out
- how the earth moves;
- why eclipses occur;
- what the phases of the moon are;
- how the sun and moon cause tides.

For thousands of years, people did not realize that the earth moves. Today we know that the earth is in constant motion. In fact, the earth is experiencing two kinds of motion at the same time. The first kind of motion follows a nearly circular pathway around the sun. This pathway is called an orbit. The motion of the earth as it orbits the sun is called **revolution.** It takes one whole year for the earth to make a single revolution.

The second kind of motion is like a spinning top. Earth spins, or turns completely around, once every 24 hours. This daily spinning of the earth is called **rotation.** The earth rotates around an imaginary line that passes through the North and South poles. This imaginary line is called the earth's **axis.** The earth appears to rotate around its axis.

There are two important characteristics of the earth's axis. First, the axis is not straight up and down as the earth revolves around the sun. It is tilted to an angle of 23.5°. Second, the direction that the axis points remains constant no matter where the earth is in its orbit. As Figure 4.8 shows, the tilt of the earth's axis causes seasonal changes in both the Northern and Southern hemispheres.

Figure 4.8 Earth's rotation results in changes between night and day. Earth's revolution results in seasonal changes.

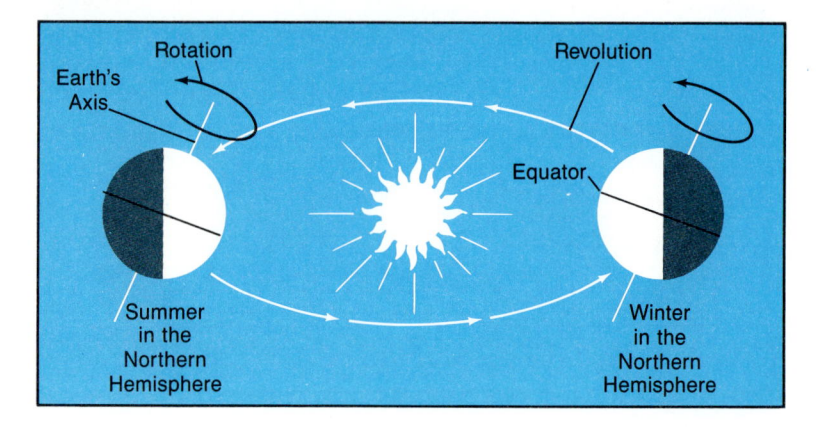

4 / The Solar System

Like the earth traveling around the sun, the moon travels around the earth. Of course that means the moon also travels around the sun as it circles the earth. This makes the moon's path quite different from the earth's path as you can see in Figure 4.10. At times the moon is between the earth and the sun. At other times it is the earth that lies between the moon and the sun. At times the moon passes directly between the sun and the earth blocking the sun's light. When this happens, there is a **solar eclipse** [ee-KLIPS]. Sometimes the earth is between the sun and the moon, and there is a **lunar eclipse**.

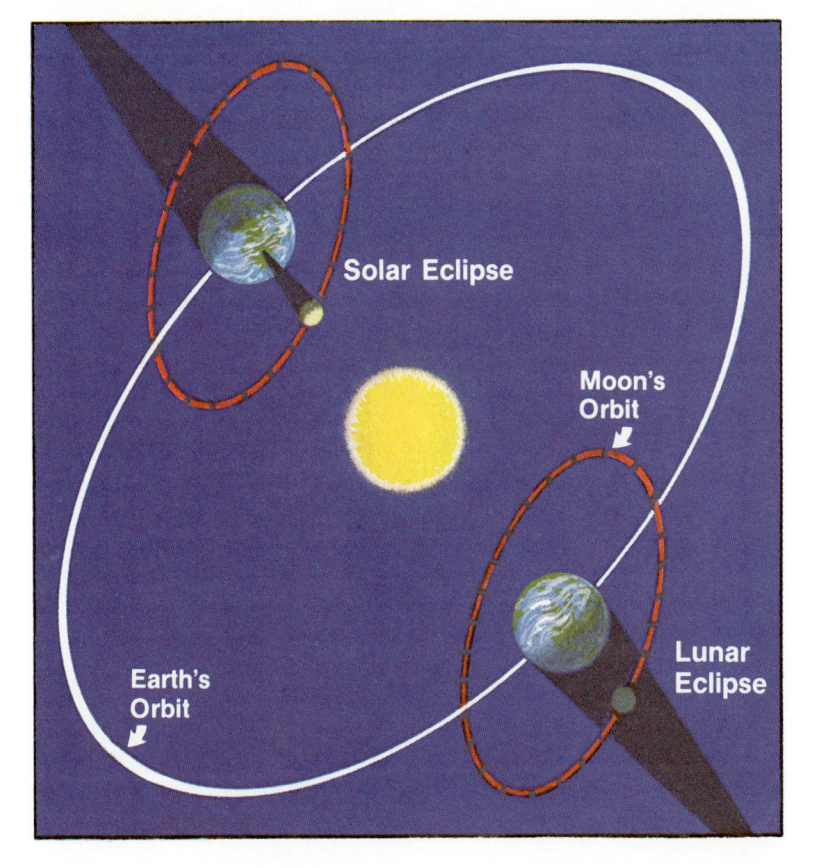

Figure 4.9 *above:* Earth is about six times larger than its moon.

Figure 4.10 *left:* Eclipses occur when the earth and the moon are directly aligned with the sun. Have you ever witnessed an eclipse?

Do You Know?
Laser measurement of the moon's distance from the earth shows that the moon is slipping away from the earth at about four centimeters a year.

The moon is much smaller than the earth. Therefore it casts a shadow only on a small part of the earth's surface during a solar eclipse. On the other hand, the entire moon is covered by the earth's shadow during a lunar eclipse.

4 / The Solar System

Figure 4.11 During a total eclipse of the sun, it is possible to view the sun's corona for a brief period.

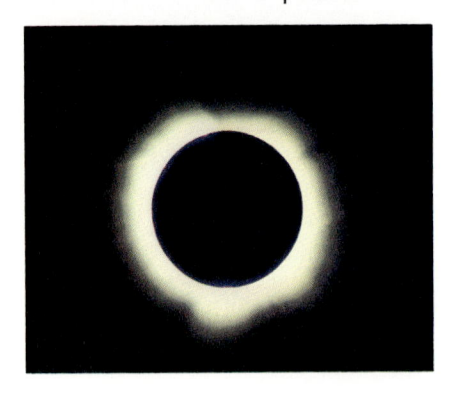

Figure 4.12 The moon goes through these phases.

You might think that there would be an eclipse of the sun and moon every time the moon passes between the earth and the sun. This doesn't happen because the moon, the earth, and the sun don't always line up in a straight line. Most often the moon's shadow is above or below the earth, or the earth's shadow is above or below the moon.

The orbiting of the moon around the earth causes something else to happen. The moon doesn't always look the same. The changes in the appearance of the moon during a month are called the **phases of the moon.** The phases are the shapes of the unlit areas as seen from the earth.

How does the moon's orbit cause the phases of the moon? Look at Figure 4.12. When the moon is in the direction of the sun, the side toward you is dark. This is called a **new moon.** When the side of the moon toward you is in sunlight, you see a **full moon.** When you see half of the moon's lighted side, it is a called a **quarter phase.** The moon goes around the earth every 27.3 days, and these phases occur over and over.

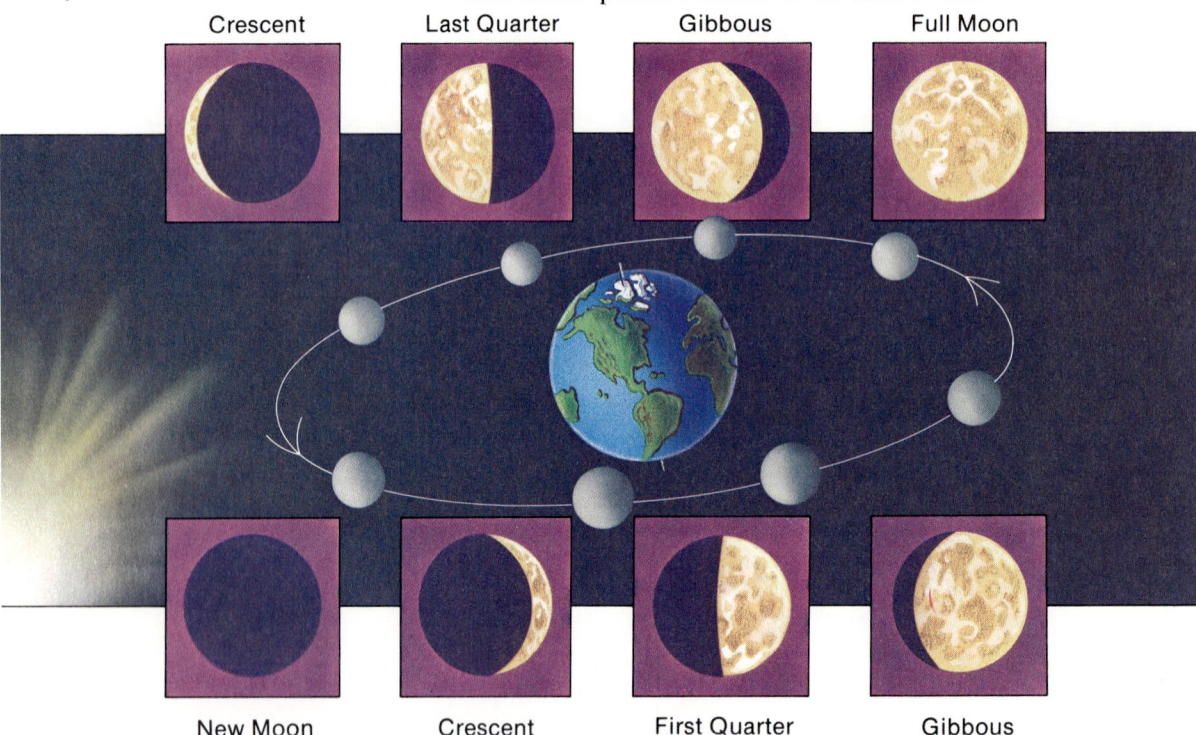

Crescent   Last Quarter   Gibbous   Full Moon

New Moon   Crescent   First Quarter   Gibbous

68

4 / The Solar System

Earlier you learned of ways the sun affected the earth. Does the moon affect the earth? Does the earth affect the moon? The answer to both questions is yes. The gravitational pull on each other changes the shape of the moon and the earth ever so little. This pull also causes the ocean water to actually move toward the area below and opposite the moon. As a result the level of the water rises and falls. This is called a **tide.** In Figure 4.13 you can see that the sun sometimes helps the moon to make larger tides than normal. At other times the sun's gravitational pull tends to offset the moon's effect.

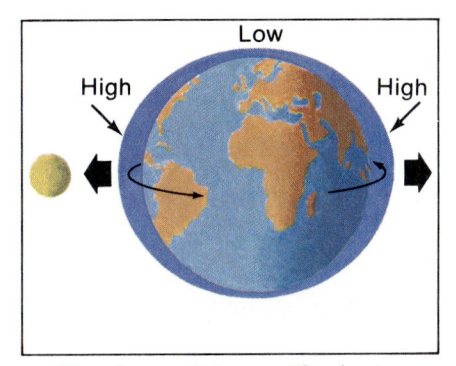

Time Lapse: 6 hours, 12 minutes

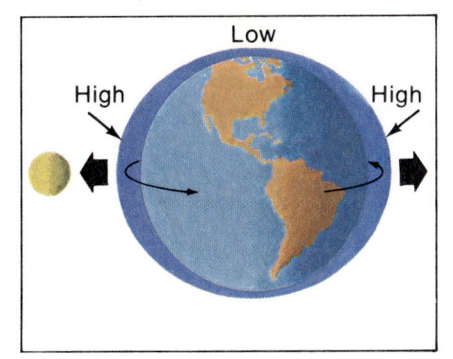

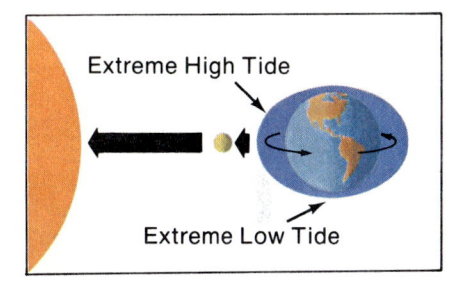

Figure 4.13 *top:* High tide on the eastern coast of North America; *middle:* As the earth rotates, North America is at low tide. *bottom:* The sun's influence can increase tidal forces.

Figure 4.14 Compare high and low tides in the pictures of the Bay of Fundy in New Brunswick, Canada.

Study Questions for 4.2

1. Explain the difference between the *rotation* and *revolution* of Earth.
2. Make a drawing that shows the positions of the earth, moon, and sun during a solar eclipse.
3. Describe the phases of the moon.
4. What is the force that causes tides?

4 / The Solar System

4.3 Features of the Solar System

You will find out
- how Kepler's laws relate to planetary movement;
- some features of the planets;
- what meteors are;
- how the solar system may have been formed.

Do You Know?
The planets have been assigned symbols. The symbols are the following:

Symbol	Planet
☿	Mercury
♀	Venus
⊕	Earth
♂	Mars
♃	Jupiter
♄	Saturn
♅	Uranus
♆	Neptune
♇	Pluto

The movement of the planets in the sky has been studied since ancient times. Many theories were proposed about their movement. In time astronomers developed better tools and made more accurate observations. In the 1600's Johannes Kepler explained the movement of the planets around the sun by using three laws. These are the following:

- Each planet moves around the sun in a closed orbit shaped like an **ellipse** [ee-LIPS]—an oval shape.
- A line joining the planet and the sun would sweep out equal areas in space in equal time. Each of the shaded portions in Figure 4.15 represents swept out areas made over equal time. The areas are equal.
- The farther the planet is from the sun, the longer it takes the planet to go around the sun. The closer the planet, the shorter is its time to go around the sun. The length of time to go around the sun is called the **period of revolution**. The earth's period of revolution is 365 1/4 days, which is also called a year.

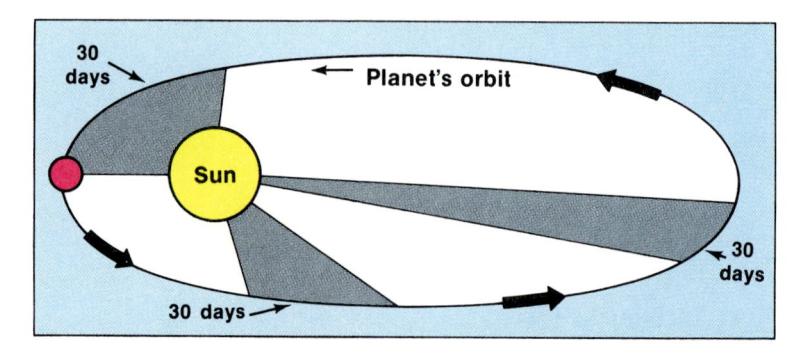

Figure 4.15 Kepler's second law of planetary motion

There is a great variation in the distance between objects in space. Do the planets vary as much in diameter? Figure 4.16 shows a comparison of the relative sizes of the planets. That important planet Earth is one of the smaller planets.

Figure 4.16 Comparing planet sizes

Activity

How Far Apart Are the Planets?

Materials
ruler or meterstick
pencil
4-m strip of adding-machine paper

Procedure

1. Near the end of the paper strip place a dot for the sun.
2. Plot the planets on your paper strip. The table gives the distances. One astronomical unit (AU) is the distance from the earth to the sun. Use 0.1 m as equal to 1 AU.

Table

Planets	Distance in AU*
Mercury	.39
Venus	.72
Earth	1.0
Mars	1.5
Jupiter	5.2
Saturn	9.2
Uranus	19.2
Neptune	30.0
Pluto	39.4

*One astronomical unit (AU) is the distance from the earth to the sun.

Questions

1. On this scale how many centimeters is it from the sun to Mars?
2. On this scale how far is it from Earth to Jupiter? To Saturn?
3. It takes eight minutes for light to travel from the sun to Earth. How long does it take for light to go from the sun to Saturn?

4 / The Solar System

Planets are not the only members of the solar system. There are other objects that move in orbits around the sun. Between the orbits of Mars and Jupiter, for example, there is a zone with thousands of small rocky objects called **asteroids**. As you saw in Figure 4.7, asteroids orbit the sun in a band called the asteroid belt. Some people think the asteroids are the remains of one or more planets that were broken apart by a collision.

Figure 4.17 Halley's Comet follows a very elliptical orbit.

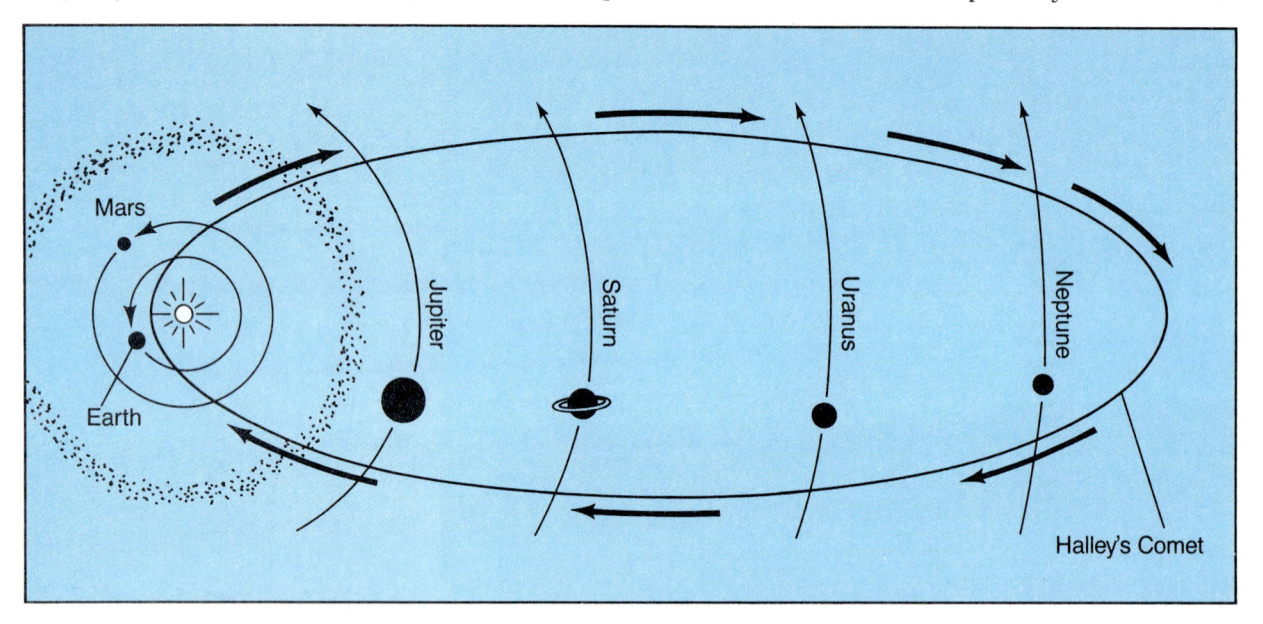

Figure 4.18 Halley's Comet as photographed in 1910.

Other familiar objects in the solar system are orbiting masses of ice and tiny dust particles called comets. A comet is like a huge snowball. It follows an elliptical orbit as it circles the sun. As the comet nears the inner region of the solar system in its journey around the sun, the ices are warmed. When close to the sun, comets develop tails that are made of dust and vapors. The tail may extend millions of kilometers from the head. The solar wind pushes the tail away from the head, so the tails of comets always point away from the sun. The gases in the head and tail appear to glow due to the reflection of sunlight.

The most famous comet is Halley's Comet. Records show that Halley's Comet passes near the earth every 75 or 76 years. You may recall that it passed near the earth early in 1986. Halley's next visit will be in 2061.

4 / The Solar System

Scientists believe that comets come from a cloud of icy fragments that surrounds the solar system somewhere outside the orbit of Pluto. The cloud contains trillions of these fragments that look like huge, dirty snowballs. Whenever the cloud is disturbed, one of these snowballs may be caught in the gravitational pull of the sun. Then the icy snowball becomes a comet trapped in orbit as part of the solar system. Each time it orbits the sun, however, a comet loses part of its mass by evaporation. Eventually, it becomes gas and dust scattered through space.

Both comets and asteroids may produce meteors. A **meteor** is a small piece of dust or rock that enters the earth's atmosphere from space. Air friction causes them to become so hot they glow. Most meteors burn up in a streak of light and smoke. Comets scatter dust particles along their orbits. When the earth encounters these particles, thousands of meteor trails are visible in one night. These glowing trails are referred to as a meteor shower. Sometimes a meteor or an asteroid is large enough to survive the trip through the atmosphere. The solid remains that reach the earth's surface are called **meteorites.** Most are small, but the one that blasted out the crater in Arizona has a calculated mass of about a million tons.

Figure 4.19 This color-enhanced photograph of Halley's Comet was taken in 1985. Notice the comet's cloudlike shape.

Figure 4.20 This huge meteorite crater is located in Arizona.

4 / The Solar System

73

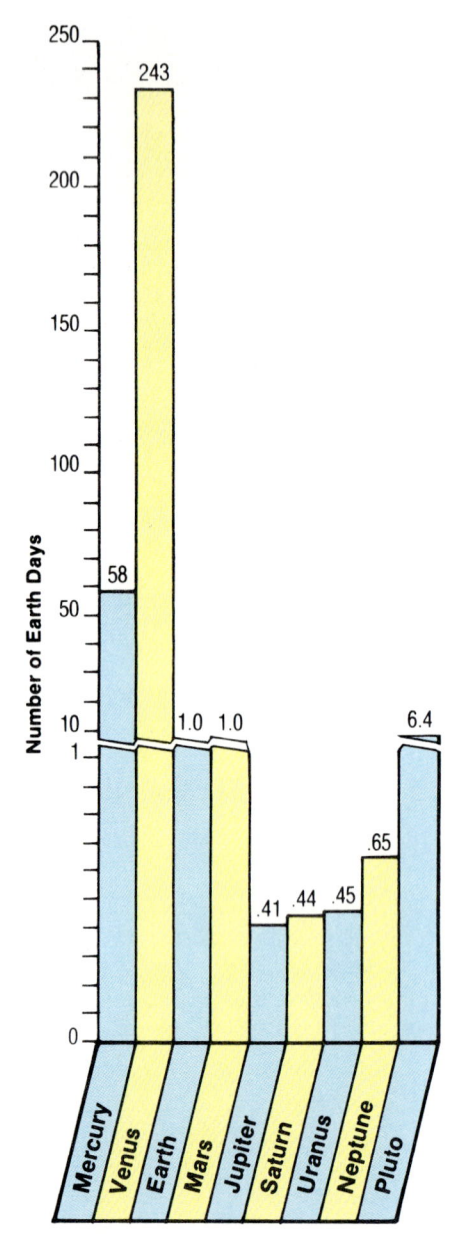

Figure 4.21 A histogram comparing rotation rates of the planets. Can you identify the slowest planet?

Table 4-1				
Planet	Mass	Volume	Revolution Period	Discovered Satellites
Mercury	0.05	0.06	0.24	0
Venus	0.81	0.88	0.62	0
Earth*	1.0	1.0	1.0	1
Mars	0.1	0.15	1.9	2
Jupiter	318	1,318	11.9	16•
Saturn	95	769	29.5	17•
Uranus	1.5	50	94	15
Neptune	17	42	165	2
Pluto	0.002	0.38	248	1

*All values are compared to the earth.   • at least

One of the most surprising comparisons of the planets is their different rates of rotation. Generally the largest planets rotate the fastest. A graph of the rotation rates is found in Figure 4.21. Notice the length of the day on Mercury. One "day" on Mercury lasts about 58 earth-days. A "day" on Jupiter lasts less than 10 earth hours.

There are other comparisons that can be made between the planets. Table 4-1 shows the major physical characteristics of each planet compared to Earth. As you look at Table 4-1, put your finger on one of the physical characteristics, for example, mass. Move your finger vertically from planet to planet. Notice which planets are more massive than Earth. Which are less massive?

How did the solar system begin? No one really knows. There are many models regarding its origin, and the popularity of different models varies from time to time. What are some of the things any theory must be able to explain? All of the planets revolve around the sun in nearly the same plane. The planets move in nearly circular orbits about the sun. All of the planets rotate and revolve in the same direction except Uranus and Venus.

Descartes in 1644 proposed that the planets formed from whirlpool-like motions in a rotating cloud of gas. Emmanuel Kant in 1755 visualized a rotating cloud in the beginning that condensed into the sun and planets. Later, Laplace suggested that the rotating cloud threw off rings that condensed to become planets.

The most widely accepted explanation of the solar system's origin is the **protoplanet** [PROH-toh-plan-iht]-**nebular model**. A protoplanet is the earliest form of a planet.

Stage A—At the most distant time you can conceive, there was a huge, slowly rotating mass of gas and dust. This blob of gas and dust, called the solar nebula, extended far past the current orbit of Pluto.

Stage B—With time the solar nebula condensed, rotated more rapidly, and flattened. The nebula had a concentrated mass of material near its center that was to become the sun. Visualize a relatively cool, huge, rotating, flat disk of gas with whirlpool-like eddies.

Stage C—The gases continue to condense, and larger solid particles form in the eddies. Solid particles in the whirlpool-like eddies collide with each other to grow larger, making protoplanets. Gravity pulls pieces of matter together. The protoplanets in this stage are made of gas and solid particles. Particles rushing together as the sun becomes denser start the sun to warm. The sun begins to produce energy.

Stage D—As the sun grows hotter, the nearby planets lose their atmosphere. The outer planets retain some of the original gases. The sun becomes a G type star, and the solar system stabilizes. Later, Earth, Venus, and Mars develop an atmosphere by holding gases that come from their interiors.

At the moment, the protoplanet-nebular model accounts for many observations better than any other. Future work perhaps will give an even better explanation.

Figure 4.22 An artist's picture of the origins of the planets. From some gas and dust that collected and began to rotate, whirlpool-like eddies, or protoplanets, formed. These protoplanets became denser and formed the planets in orbit about the sun.

Study Questions for 4.3

1. What do Kepler's laws explain?
2. What is a meteor and where do meteors come from?
3. Select one planet and compare its mass, period of revolution, and time of rotation with Earth.
4. Select one model of how the earth formed. Diagram your model and write an explanation of it.

Biography

Johannes Kepler (1571-1630)

Johannes Kepler, born to a poor family in 1571, had exceptional talents that were recognized by others at an early age. With the help of grants, Kepler was able to enroll in Tubingen University, Germany. He became a Protestant theologian. At that time the study of theology required extensive study in the liberal arts, which included mathematics and astronomy. His astronomical thesis concerned the moon and has to this day never been discovered.

Kepler taught mathematics for a time but continued his study of astronomy by trying to combine geometry and astronomy.

Kepler was a Protestant. When the Catholics came to power in his region, he was forced from his teaching position. Fortunately Tycho Brahe had a secure position and was able to invite Kepler to the observatory in Prague. Kepler's work began with an analysis of data on Mars. It was during this analysis, which involved hundreds of tedious calculations, that Kepler recognized that the planets do not move with constant velocity in orbit. The orbits of the planets were ellipses. This revolutionary idea lead him to further discovery, and he stated the first two of his three laws in 1609. Kepler's third law was published in 1618.

It is remarkable that this man was able to accomplish anything in astronomy. Wars, religious conflict, living with a family that didn't understand his work, seeing the death of loved ones, hounded by requests for unimportant data and charts of the heavens, and lack of acceptance by others were only a few of the obstacles he overcame to publish his theories of the solar system. His friend Pierre Gassendi in Paris wrote "Men like Kepler should never really die." That wish has been fulfilled.

CHAPTER REVIEW

Main Ideas

- The major regions of the sun's exterior are the photosphere, chromosphere, and corona.
- Inside the sun, hydrogen is converted into helium. This process releases enormous amounts of energy.
- Gravitational attraction between the sun and planets holds the planets in orbit around the sun.
- Earth rotates on its axis as it revolves around the sun. The seasons result from the fact that the earth remains tilted on its axis.
- Eclipses occur when the earth blocks sunlight from the moon (lunar eclipse) or the moon blocks sunlight from the earth (solar eclipse).
- The phases of the moon occur when different amounts of the moon's surface receive sunlight.
- Tides are caused by the gravitational pull of the moon and the sun.
- Kepler's laws explain the movement of planets.
- Asteroids and comets are members of the solar system.
- A comet is like a huge snowball made of ice and tiny dust particles.
- Meteorites are bits of dust or rock that enter the earth's atmosphere from space.
- The protoplanet-nebular model is one explanation for the origin of the solar system.

Using Vocabulary

Make up a matching-column quiz. On a separate piece of paper, list the words below in one column and describe each word in another. Exchange quizzes with a classmate.

prominence	corona	solar eclipse	ellipse
sunspot	solar wind	lunar eclipse	period of revolution
core	gravitation	phases of the moon	asteroids
radiation zone	solar system	new moon	meteors
convection zone	revolution	full moon	meteorites
hotspots	rotation	quarter phase	protoplanet-nebular model
photosphere	axis	tide	
chromosphere			

4 / The Solar System

Remembering Facts

On your paper, write the word or words that best complete each sentence.
1. The spinning motion of the earth is called _____ .
2. The changes in the level of ocean water due to the moon's gravitational pull are called _____ .
3. The _____ is the visible surface of the sun.
4. Earth's orbit has an _____ shape.
5. A meteor that reaches the earth's surface is called a _____ .
6. A _____ is a huge mass of ice and dust that orbits the sun.
7. When the earth is directly between the sun and the moon there is a _____ eclipse.
8. The sun's energy is produced in its _____ .
9. When the moon is in the direction of the sun, the moon is in the _____ _____ phase.
10. The stream of particles that flows from the sun is called _____ _____ .
11. Small, rocklike objects that orbit between Mars and Jupiter are called _____ .
12. _____ are dark areas on the sun's surface.
13. When the moon passes directly between the sun and the earth, there is a _____ eclipse.
14. All of the objects that orbit the sun make up the _____ _____ .
15. It takes one year for the earth to make one _____ around the sun.
16. The outermost part of the solar atmosphere is called the _____ .

Understanding Ideas

On your paper, answer each question in complete sentences.
1. Does a lunar eclipse of the moon occur during any particular phase of the moon? Explain your answer.
2. Explain why an average of a little more than 12 hours goes by between high tides.
3. How does the makeup of a comet support the protoplanet-nebular model of the solar system?
4. What is the source of the reflected light you see during different phases of the moon?

Applying What You Have Learned

1. Scientists have observed dark spots on the sun's surface. What is the probable cause of these dark spots?
2. Imagine that the moon is in the new moon phase and you were instantly transported to it. If you looked back at the earth, what phase would it be in?
3. You are an astronaut on a mission to explore the sun. Your spacecraft must travel at a speed of 40,200 km per hour to escape the earth's gravity field. How many days will it take for you to reach the sun?

Challenge

Looking into the evening sky from here on Earth, the planet Venus can often be seen as a brilliant star just after sunset. At other times, it can be seen as a brilliant morning star just before sunrise. To understand how this happens, we must consider the orbits of Venus and Earth. Venus travels between Earth and the sun. It takes 225 days for Venus to revolve around the sun. Earth, however, takes 365 days to orbit the sun. Use the diagram to answer the following questions.

1. Which position must Venus be in with respect to the sun and Earth to be seen as a morning star?
2. Which position must Venus be in to be seen as an evening star?
3. Would it be possible for Venus to be a morning star all year round?
4. Would we ever be able to see Venus in the hours close to midnight?

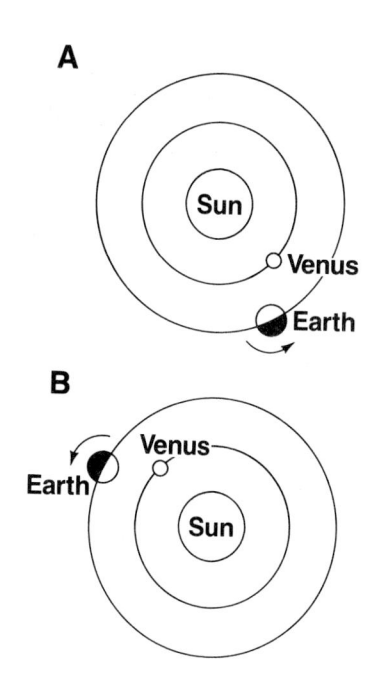

Research and Investigation

1. Use binoculars to study one of the planets. Make sure you observe the planet at the same time each day. Record the position of the planet, using nearby stars as a reference point. Prepare a poster to show the path of the planet.
2. The moon has many surface features, such as craters, "seas," and mountain ranges. Many of the features have been given names. Use an encyclopedia to identify the surface features of the moon. Use a telescope or binoculars to find these features.

4 / The Solar System

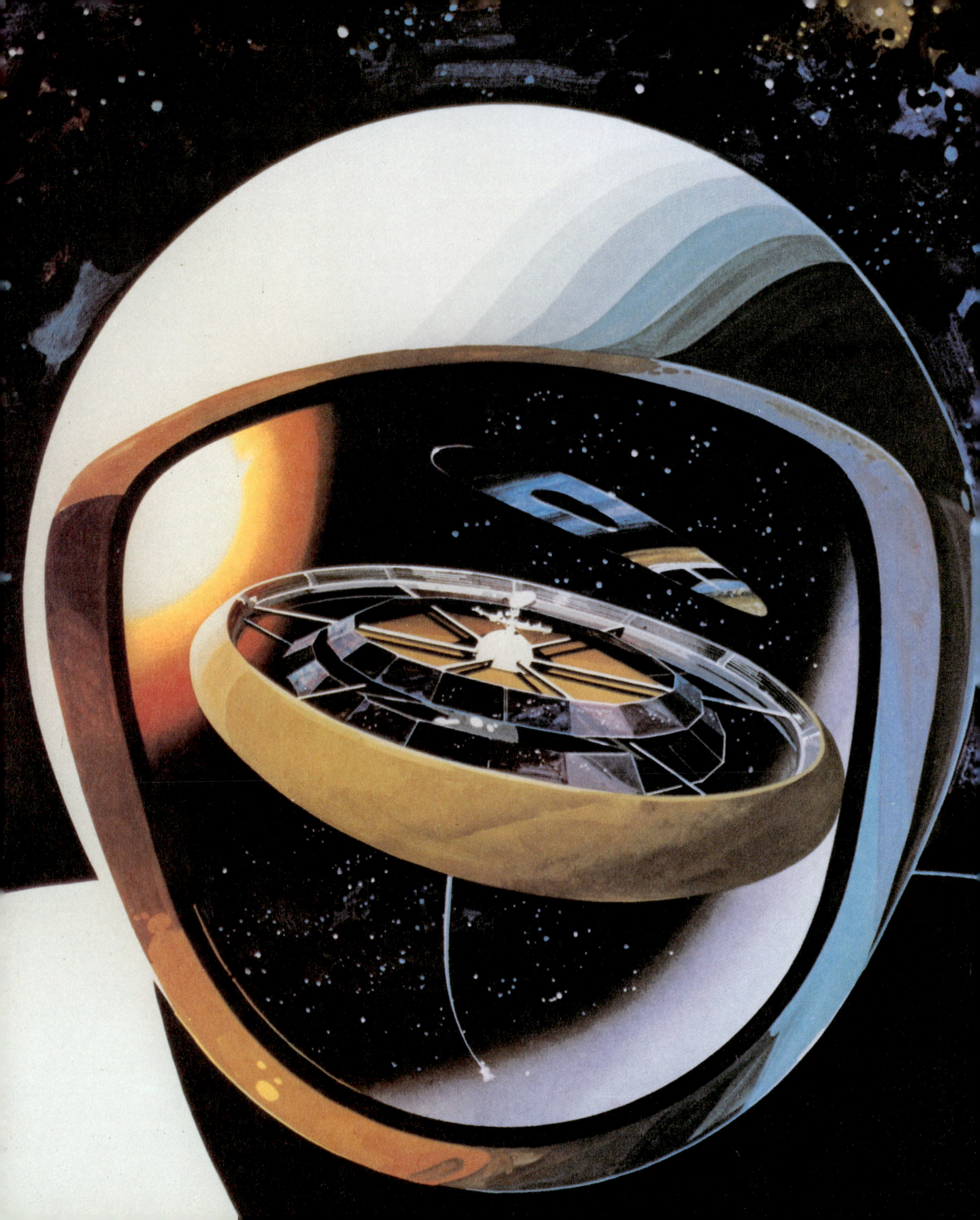

Chapter 5
Space Exploration

Lesson Titles
5.1　History of Space Travel
5.2　Exploring the Planets
5.3　The Future in Space

People have studied the planets and outer space for thousands of years. However, actual space exploration began only about 30 years ago. Many fascinating discoveries have been made in this short time. Dramatic pictures of the surface of Mercury, Venus, Mars, Jupiter, and Saturn have been received from space probes. Space probes have landed on Venus and Mars, sending pictures and information back to Earth. Astronauts have visited the moon. There they conducted experiments and collected soil and rock samples from the moon's surface. Space-shuttle crews have placed satellites in orbit and conducted experiments to provide data about living and working conditions in space. Scientists are using this information to plan future space exploration.

One of the projects currently being planned is the construction of a space colony. Shuttles will carry construction crews and materials into space, where the orbiting colony will be assembled. Many complex problems will be solved before the colony can be built. Imagine what it will be like to commute to work in a space shuttle. In this chapter, you will learn about the exciting discoveries that have occurred during space exploration. You will also learn more about what is planned for the future.

Figure 5.1 *opposite:* This artist's drawing shows some of the proposed structures and features of a space colony.

5.1 History of Space Travel

You will find out
- how artificial satellites affect our daily lives;
- why space probes were designed;
- what the early space flights accomplished;
- why the space shuttle was developed.

On October 4, 1957, the world watched with awe as the Russians launched the first artificial **satellite**, *Sputnik I*. *Sputnik I* circled the earth every 90 minutes at a height of 200 km. This aluminum ball measured 60 cm across and had a mass of about 85 kg. It contained instruments to measure the temperature and density of space. It also had a radio that could send information back to Earth. With the launching of *Sputnik I*, the space age was born.

Since 1957, many satellites have been positioned in space. A satellite is an object that orbits a larger object. Each one has been programmed to perform a specific task. Weather satellites help forecast weather. They also aid scientists in their efforts to understand how weather is made. Communications satellites make it possible to receive telephone messages, radio broadcasts, and television programming all over the world. Sailors and pilots can pinpoint their exact location in bad weather with the help of navigation satellites. Much information regarding the earth's magnetic field, radiation in space, and the upper parts of the atmosphere is provided by scientific satellites.

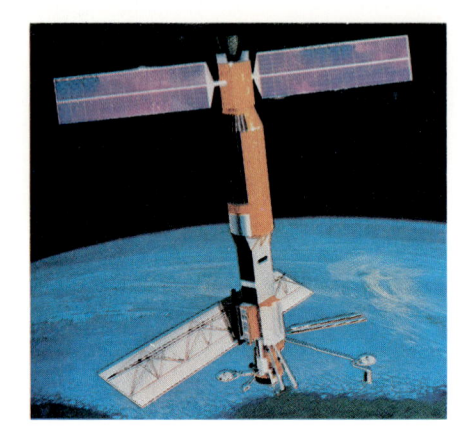

Figure 5.2 A painting of NASA's weather satellite *Seasat*

Do You Know?
If the weather could be predicted accurately five days in advance, about 15 billion dollars could be saved each year by farmers, construction workers, and industry.

Figure 5.3 Information from satellites is used in making weather forecasts.

The actual path and the speed at which a satellite should move are predetermined. Many satellites are programmed to orbit the earth at a particular speed. These are called orbital satellites. Others are programmed to travel at a speed equal to that of the earth's rotation. These satellites are referred to as **geosynchronous** [jee-oh-SIHN-kruh-nuhs] **satellites.** They move in time with the earth, remaining in a fixed position over a specific point on the earth's surface.

Today, there are almost 5,000 artificial satellites in either orbital or geosynchronous positions above the earth. These satellites are gathering information about the earth's surface, the atmosphere, and outer space, and are providing a worldwide communication network.

Figure 5.4 *above:* This communications satellite is being released from the cargo bay of the space shuttle. *left:* This communications satellite had to be captured and brought to the space shuttle's cargo bay for repairs.

In addition to satellites, **space probes** were also introduced in the late 1950's. These probes were designed to explore regions beyond the earth's atmosphere. They were operated by computers, electronic sensors, mechanical devices, and radios. Three of the probes developed at this time were the sounding rocket, lunar, and planetary probes. Each of these types of probes had a specific mission.

Sounding-rocket probes were designed to collect information about the earth's upper atmosphere. Measurements such as temperature, pressure, and levels of radiation have been recorded by these spacecraft.

Do You Know?
Special photographs taken from satellites can be designed to identify different types of rocks and soils associated with hidden mineral and petroleum deposits.

Figure 5.5 *Surveyor III* landed on the moon on April 19, 1967. Astronaut Conrad is seen here checking the camera on *Surveyor III* two years later.

Figure 5.6 An artist's picture of one of the space probes in the *Lunar Orbiter* series

The next type of probe, the lunar probe, was launched in an effort to learn more about the surface features and atmospheric conditions on the moon. Two Russian *Luna* and *Zond* lunar probes were also developed during the 1950's and 1960's. They were the first probes to take pictures, orbit, and land on the moon.

In the early 1960's, the United States launched its own lunar probes. The *Ranger* probes took over 17,000 photographs of the moon before crashing into it. The *Surveyor* landed on the moon, took pictures, and collected soil samples for analysis. The *Lunar Orbiters* circled the moon and took additional photographs of its surface. All the information gathered by these probes paved the way for astronauts to go to the moon.

The last probe, the planetary probe, was designed to observe planets at very close range. Some of these probes were programmed to fly by a planet. They recorded information about the atmospheric conditions, the magnetic fields, the temperature, and the levels of radiation near the planet. They were also equipped to take many photographs as they passed by a planet. Orbiter probes were designed to record and photograph the same kinds of information as they circled the planet. Lander probes were specifically designed to rest on the planet. These probes collected soil and rock samples, recorded climatic and atmospheric changes, and took pictures of the surface.

Most of the planetary probes built by the United States during the 1960's and 1970's were designed to fly by Mercury, Venus, and Mars. Most of the probes in the *Mariner* series collected vital information about temperature and atmospheric conditions on Mars and Venus. One of the *Viking* probes landed on Mars, while another two were placed in orbit around the planet. Two *Pioneer Venus* probes reached an orbit around Venus in 1978. They were still transmitting information back to Earth in the mid-1980's.

The Russian planetary probes *Mars* and *Venera* were also studying Mars and Venus. These probes collected a great deal of information about the surface composition and atmospheric conditions of each planet. Two *Venera* probes landed on Venus in 1982 and analyzed soil samples.

Figure 5.7 An artist's drawing of the *Voyager* space probe

Figure 5.8 A final check on *Pioneer I*

In the early 1970's, the United States sent probes to study the planets beyond the asteroid belt. Two series of probes *Pioneer* and *Voyager* were developed for this research. *Pioneer X* and the *Voyager I* and *II* probes have flown past Jupiter and Saturn. Much has been learned about these planets and about their moons. Evidence has shown that both planets have rings. *Pioneer X* traveled beyond all known planets in June of 1983. It is expected to be broadcasting data from beyond our galaxy until the 1990's.

5 / Space Exploration

Figure 5.9 *Apollo 11* Astronaut Aldrin walking on the surface of the moon

Figure 5.10 *Apollo 16* Astronaut Young working on the lunar rover vehicle

Many of these probes are still sending information back to Earth long after they were launched. *Voyager I* and *II* were launched in 1977. They are now headed for more distant planets. These two probes flew past Uranus in 1986 and are scheduled to fly by Neptune in 1989.

Spacecraft designed to carry astronauts were also developed in the 1960's. The United States *Mercury* and *Gemini* series were designed to test equipment, perform experiments, and determine human capabilities in space. These space flights orbited the earth, gathering information that would later pave the way for future space travel. The *Apollo* series was primarily designed for lunar exploration. After three years of testing, *Apollo XI* landed on the moon on July 29, 1969. Information about solar winds, meteor impacts, and moonquakes have been provided by equipment left on the moon's surface by the *Apollo* space flights. All of the photographs and rock samples that were brought back to Earth have contributed a great deal to our understanding of both the moon and the earth.

Work began in the 1970's on the **space shuttle.** This spacecraft was designed to take off like a rocket and land like an airplane. The United States developed a series of reusable space shuttles: *Challenger, Columbia,* and *Discovery.* Most of the shuttle missions were designed to launch, retrieve, and repair satellites and probes.

Many experiments have been performed in the shuttles during these space missions. Some experiments analyzed the atmosphere above the earth. Other experiments tested the reactions of plants, insects, and animals to the weightless environment. Continued research and experimentation during these shuttle missions make the shuttle an important tool for the planned space station.

Table 5-1

Spacecraft	Launch Data	Milestone
Sputnik I	October 4, 1957	First artificial satellite
Vanguard II	February 17, 1959	First weather satellite
Volstok I	April 12, 1961	First person in space
Telstar I	July 10, 1962	First communications satellite to relay television programs
Luna IX	January 31, 1966	First soft landing on moon
Apollo XI	July 16, 1969	First persons to walk on moon
Mariner IV	May 30, 1971	First probe to orbit Mars
Pioneer X	March 2, 1972	First probe to fly past Jupiter
Columbia	April 12, 1981	First flight of a reusable space shuttle
Pioneer X	June 1983	First probe to leave our solar system

Figure 5.11 Space shuttle approaching the landing strip on its return trip

Study Questions for 5.1

1. Name four types of artificial satellites and explain what each one does.
2. Why were three different probes designed?
3. What did we learn from the early space flights?
4. Why was the space shuttle developed?

5 / Space Exploration

5.2 Exploring the Planets

You will find out
- what the atmosphere of the planet Venus is like;
- what the atmosphere of the planet Mars is like;
- what has been learned about Jupiter and its moons;
- why Saturn is called the jewel of the sky.

The brightest object in the sky besides the sun and moon is planet Venus. Venus is about the same size as the earth. Some people think of it as a sister planet, but the relationship is not very close. Imagine trying to live on a planet where the atmospheric pressure is 90 times Earth's atmospheric pressure. There is no water and very little sunlight, and its atmosphere is 96 percent carbon dioxide. The upper atmosphere contains droplets of sulfuric acid. The surface temperature is between 448°C and 459°C, and it's dry and dusty.

Using radar, the *Pioneer Venus Orbiter* has mapped more than 93 percent of Venus' surface. Sixty percent of the surface is a relatively flat, rolling plain. Rising above the plain are three continent-sized plateaus. At one end of the highest landmass, Ishtar Terra, is Maxwell Montes. This is the highest point on Venus—10.8 km above the plains. This is higher than Mount Everest.

Lowlands occupy about ten percent of the surface. The lowest point on Venus lies in a great valley. This is one of the largest valleys in the solar system. It is 1,400 km long, 280 km wide, and 5 km deep. There are many large old craters in the lowland plains. When a Russian spacecraft landed on Venus, it found a very rocky surface.

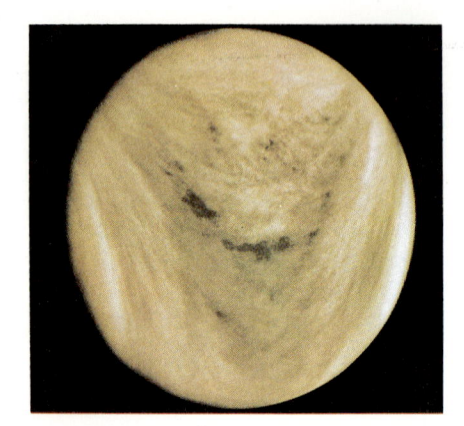

Figure 5.12 *top:* The surface of Venus is covered with dense clouds.

Figure 5.13 *lower:* An artist's drawing of canyons on Venus based on radar surveys of the surface.

Figure 5.14 *right:* A photograph of the surface of Venus taken by the Russian *Venera 13* satellite

People have dreamed for centuries about Martians and the possibility of life on Mars. These dreams ended with the *Viking* spacecraft that landed on Mars. It found no evidence of life.

Figure 5.15 A photograph of the surface of Mars taken by *Viking 1*

Mars has a thin atmosphere with a normal pressure about 1/100th of the earth's. Mars has dust storms, high level carbon dioxide clouds, and lower-level clouds that are believed to be ice crystals. The thin atmosphere is 95 percent carbon dioxide. The temperature at the equator ranges from −75°C to +30°C. Mars has two polar caps containing frozen carbon dioxide and water. These caps grow and shrink with the seasons.

Volcanic activity has taken place on a large scale. There are at least 12 volcanoes. The most spectacular is Olympus Mons. This mountain is 25 km high and 600 km wide. This is five times larger than the greatest volcano on Earth—Mauna Loa, in Hawaii— even including all that is below the surface of the ocean. Another major surface feature is a huge, narrow canyon 5,000 km long, 75 km wide (on the average), and 6 km deep. Since this canyon appears to have been shaped by running water, Mars must have had running water at one time. Ancient islands and dry streambeds are also found. Compared to Venus, Mars would be a better place to visit, but don't expect to run into any Martians.

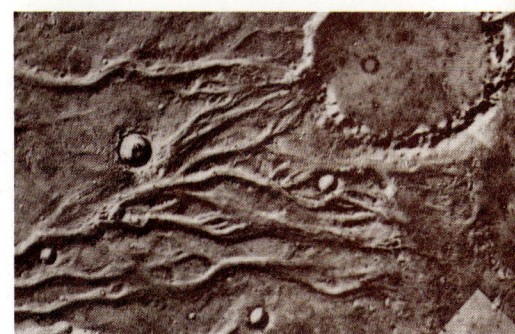

Figure 5.16 This *Viking 1* photograph of Mars' surface indicates there must have been streams and running water at one time on Mars.

5 / Space Exploration

Jupiter is the largest planet in the solar system. Two spacecraft, *Voyager I* and *II*, have taken spectacular photographs of this gigantic planet. No surface features are visible on this planet because of a thick cloud cover. Jupiter's atmosphere is primarily hydrogen and helium which show complex patterns of movement. High-speed winds of 120 km per hour have been detected. This speed is equivalent to the hurricane wind speeds recorded here on Earth.

One of the most prominent features, the Great Red Spot, is a tremendous atmospheric storm. Wind speed at its top, toward the equator, is in one direction. At its bottom, toward the polar area, winds are reversed. Above and below the Great Red Spot the clouds show as alternate light and dark bands.

Jupiter has at least 16 moons. The outer ones revolve around Jupiter backward with respect to most motions in the solar system. The size of the moons varies from Almathea, the size of California, to Ganymede, about as large as Mercury. Jupiter's moons are some of the most interesting objects in the solar system. Seven volcanoes were observed on the moon Io and more have been predicted. A surprising discovery was Jupiter's ring.

The jewel of the sky is Saturn. Showing up brilliantly through even the lowest-power telescopes, Saturn with its rings is something to see. Now imagine seeing it even closer as from *Voyager I* and *II*. From every view the dominant visual objects are the rings—not one but thousands of rings. The size of particles making up the rings ranges from dust flecks to boulders each in its own orbit around the planet.

Saturn has a banded, layered atmosphere that flows in the same direction around the planet. Wind velocities greater than 500 km per hour have been detected. This is four times the speed of Jupiter's winds. The planet rotates in 10 hours and 39.4 minutes. The atmosphere is about 90 percent hydrogen and helium and 10 percent ammonia, methane, and water vapor.

Four big mysteries surround the exploration of Saturn. Why does Saturn have rings? How is it possible for the rings to remain there? Where did its large number of

Figure 5.17 *top:* Close-ups of Jupiter show bands of colored clouds whirling across the surface. *bottom:* The Great Red Spot on Jupiter is a storm large enough to swallow several earths.

Do You Know?
The first recorded observation of one of Jupiter's moons (probably Ganymede) was in China in 364 B.C. almost 2,000 years prior to Galileo's discovery of Jupiter's moons.

moons come from? What causes the dark radial spokes in one ring? As one astronomer said, "Saturn has become more mysterious than ever before."

Beyond Saturn are two other giant planets. These large planets are Uranus and Neptune and both are apparently cloud covered. Photographs taken by *Voyager II* show that Uranus has 15 moons. Additional rings were also noticed in these photographs.

The usual outermost planet is Pluto. Pluto has an unusual orbit that at times takes it inside the orbit of Neptune. Since January 22, 1979, Pluto has been closer to the sun than Neptune, and it will remain that way until March, 1999. Pluto's orbit is also inclined with respect to the others. Another very strange feature of this outermost planet is its small size with a mass only 1/400th or so of the mass of the earth.

Figure 5.18 *above:* This photo of Uranus was taken on January 17, 1986 by *Voyager II*. *left:* The rings of Saturn have been color enhanced in this photo. *below:* Miranda, one of Uranus's moons, was photographed by *Voyager II* on January 24, 1986.

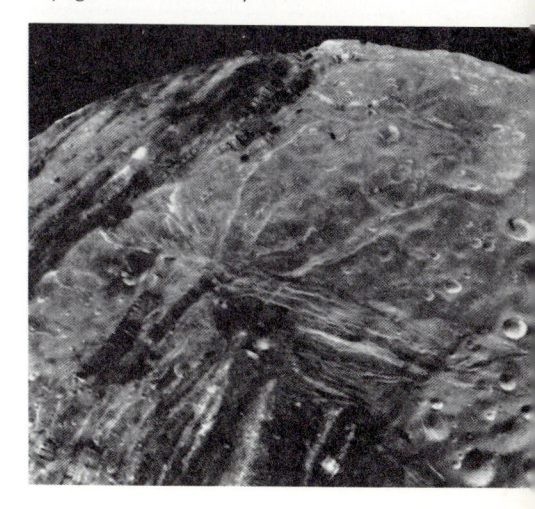

Study Questions for 5.2

1. Describe the atmosphere of Venus.
2. Describe the atmosphere of Mars.
3. List some of the information *Voyager I* and *II* collected about Jupiter.
4. Describe Saturn's rings.

5 / Space Exploration

5.3 The Future in Space

You will find out
- what possibilities exist for exploration in space;
- what space observatories and platforms are;
- what new questions astronomers are asking about the universe.

Would you like to visit the moon or live on Mars? People have dreamed about such adventures for centuries. Now, more than ever before, such dreams may be closer to coming true. People have traveled in space, walked on the moon, and photographed planets by using space probes. What possibilities are there for future space activities?

There are two ways that people on Earth can extend their world into space. One way is to send space probes like the Mariner and Voyager spacecrafts out into the solar system and beyond. These probes will radio back even more information than has already been learned. The information may unlock secrets about the birth of the solar system and the nature of other planets. By studying these things, scientists may also learn more about life on Earth. In addition, space probes may help locate mineral resources on nearby planets or on the asteroids. Someday these resources may be brought to Earth.

The second way people can reach further into space is through continuing space travel. Someday, this may lead to the establishment of a colony on the moon. Can you think of a reason why people would want to be on the moon? Space observations are easier to make outside Earth's atmosphere. The moon may be a perfect location for future astronomers, geologists, and researchers.

Figure 5.19 Traveling in space is one way people can explore space's mysteries further.

Figure 5.20 Space probes bring information back to Earth from places too far away for people to visit.

Do You Know?
The space telescope is capable of detecting a 100-watt light bulb from eight million kilometers away.

92

Some scientists believe that Mars may someday be a good place for an earth colony. Could we make Mars habitable? Why would we want to do that? Perhaps engineers will want to live on Mars to mine its mineral resources. Others may want to go there for adventure. It is possible that Mars may become a new home for people who can adapt to living there. Do you want to be a Martian?

Figure 5.21 *top:* This is an artist's idea of what another inhabitable planet may be like. Would you want to visit here?

Figure 5.22 *bottom:* A type of space platform designed for orbiting Earth

How can scientists answer the questions they ask about space? Astronomers believe they will learn more about the universe in the next ten years than has been learned throughout history. One way they will do this is by using a space telescope positioned above the atmosphere, in Earth orbit. The space telescope will be able to search the skies 24 hours a day because outer space has a night sky at all times. Actually, the space telescope will be part of a complete observatory. Astronomers hope space observatories will be like giant eyes on the universe, used to gather information and solve new mysteries.

The space telescope will be placed in orbit by the space shuttle. The shuttle is really a fancy truck that carries materials into space. Someday the shuttle will carry materials into orbit so they can be assembled into a space platform. A space platform may look like the drawing in Figure 5.22. It will contain everything that is needed for people to live and work in space.

5 / Space Exploration

Do You Know?
Some materials that cannot be mixed under surface gravity conditions can be mixed in space. This suggests that stronger, lighter, and more temperature-resistant metal alloys may be produced in space.

Figure 5.23 What questions about our galaxy and others will be answered in the future?

How would you use a space platform? Of course, a space platform can be an observatory. However, scientists also believe that space platforms will be useful as manufacturing sites. A space platform has a weightless condition. Over 150 possible products have already been identified that could be more readily manufactured while weightless. They range from perfectly round steel ball bearings to ultrapure chemicals for treating disease. Manufacturing in space will be reserved for the kind of work that cannot be done in Earth's gravitational field. Many new products will be created on space platforms in the future. Someday you will be buying products or using medicines that were made partly in space.

What questions will astronomers of the future be asking? You have already learned about some of the questions by studying this book. For example, what more can be learned about black holes? What happens to time in a black hole? Some astronomers think time slows down or stops in a black hole. Are some black holes actually giant galaxies that are disappearing? Also, the old question of whether or not life exists elsewhere remains to be answered.

The nature and shape of the universe are popular topics among astronomers. Their ideas about the nature of the universe vary. Some describe the universe as being closed. This means it will stop expanding someday and collapse into itself. Others describe the universe as being open. They believe it will continue to expand forever. Many astronomers argue that the universe has a definite limit to its size, but some believe it does not. There are even some astronomers who suggest that there may be other universes besides the one that can be seen.

Sometimes people refer to space as a frontier like the wild west used to be. This is because they are excited by the adventures and new experiences that space study promises. Can answers be found to some of the questions raised about space? No one knows for sure, but curious people will always look for answers and ask new questions.

Activity

The Magical Mobius Strip

Materials
paper
tape
scissors
wide-tipped felt marker

Procedure

1. Cut two strips of paper each about 27 cm long and 2.5 cm wide.

2. Tape the ends of one strip together to make a loop.

3. With the other strip, make a twist and then tape the ends together without untwisting it. You have made a Mobius strip.

4. Using the marker, follow along the edge of the paper loop until you return to the starting point. *Do not lift the marker from the paper's edge.*

5. Repeat step 4 on the Mobius strip.

Questions

1. How are the resulting marks you made on the two loops different?

2. Why are the results different?

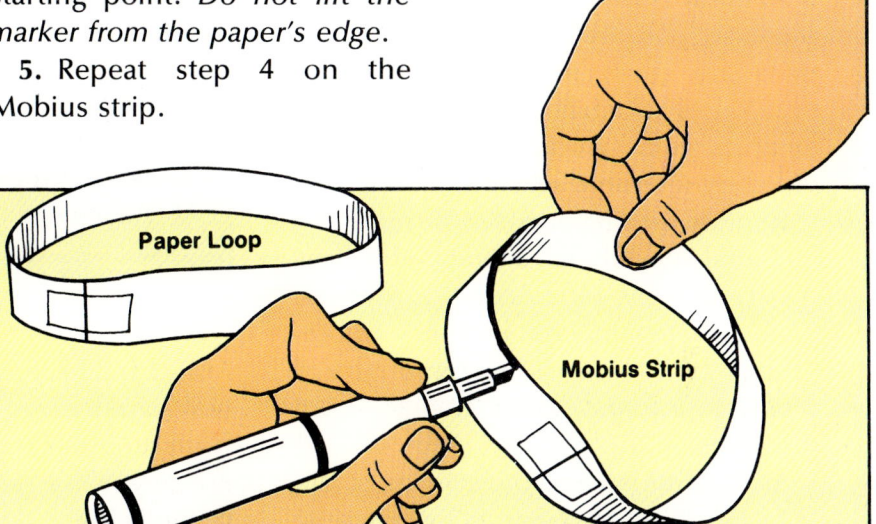

Study Questions for 5.3

1. What are two ways the solar system can be explored in the future?
2. How may space observatories and platforms be useful?
3. Name three questions that have not been solved in astronomy.

5 / Space Exploration

Career

Remote Sensing Scientist

Are you concerned about pollution? Would you like to study what an increasing population does to land and water resources? Would you like to identify natural hazards at the same time you find new mineral and fuel sources? Would you like to provide information that would help farmers increase food production? These questions are about problems that affect everyone's existence on Earth. The answers come from information provided by a remote sensing scientist.

Remote sensing involves the mapping and analysis of Earth's land and oceans using airplane and satellite images. These images include ordinary photographs as well as computer analyzed temperature and radar images from satellites.

Aulis Lind is a remote sensing scientist. She does research on remote sensing of Earth's environment. This includes studying conventional photographs taken from high-flying airplanes and satellite images. Sometimes this means just finding out what the images mean about the environment. Aulis Lind also teaches others interested in Earth's environment how to use the imaging tools of the space age.

Remote sensing is very exciting to Aulis Lind because there are constantly new challenges. There are new data from satellites that need analysis. There are new sensors being developed that provide new kinds of information. There are new resource problems that require solutions. And there are new opportunities to help others understand remote sensing. Aulis Lind says that remote sensing of the environment allows her to become involved with places all around the world—places where much remains to be discovered. Remote sensing is a new and fascinating career.

CHAPTER REVIEW

Main Ideas

- Today, weather, communication, navigation, and scientific satellites provide scientists and engineers with a great deal of information.
- Sounding rocket probes collect data about the earth's atmosphere. Lunar probes were designed to orbit and land on the moon. Planetary probes were launched to observe planets at close range.
- The *Gemini* and *Apollo* missions tested equipment, performed experiments, and determined human capabilities in space.
- Space-shuttle missions were designed to launch, retrieve, and repair satellites and probes.
- The surface of Venus is very hot and dry. The atmosphere contains carbon dioxide and sulfuric acid.
- Mars shows evidence of water erosion and volcanic activity. Mars is veiled in a thin layer of carbon dioxide gas.
- Jupiter rotates rapidly and has a turbulent atmosphere of hydrogen and helium. One of its moons has the only known active volcano in the solar system.
- Saturn shows a ring structure far more complicated than scientists can explain.
- Space can be explored through space probes, space travel, and space observatories.
- Space observatories are artificial satellites with telescopes and infrared, ultraviolet, X-ray, and other types of instruments.
- Scientists believe that space platforms will be useful as manufacturing sites.

Using Vocabulary

On a separate paper, write a sentence for each word listed below. Each sentence should give a *clue* as to the meaning of the word.

geosynchronous satellite
satellite

space probe
space shuttle

5 / Space Exploration

Remembering Facts

On your paper, write the word or words that best complete each sentence.

1. Two polar ice caps can be found on the planets Earth and _____.
2. The earth's only natural satellite is the _____.
3. The _____ spacecraft series was designed primarily for lunar exploration.
4. The first artificial satellite was named _____.
5. The Great Red Spot is located on the planet _____.
6. A _____ satellite circles the earth, yet stays in the same position above the earth's surface.
7. _____ _____ were designed to explore regions beyond the earth's atmosphere.
8. The planet _____ has thousands of rings.
9. The first space probe to leave the solar system was _____.
10. The atmosphere on the planet _____ contains sulfuric acid.
11. High-speed winds produce whirling bands of clouds on _____.
12. A smaller body that circles a larger one is called a _____.
13. The orbit of the planet _____ is inclined in comparison with other planets.
14. Satellites that circle the earth at varying speeds are called _____ satellites.
15. One of the moons of _____ has an active volcano.
16. The atmospheric pressure on Mars is much _____ than the pressure found on Earth.
17. _____ _____ were first launched in the late 1950's.
18. The _____ and _____ spacecraft series tested equipment, performed experiments, and determined human capabilities in space.
19. The first artificial satellite to record information about the temperature and density of space was _____.

Understanding Ideas

1. The *Apollo* lunar series was preceded by space probes designed to fly by, orbit, and land on the moon. Why was this particular sequence followed?
2. Describe how an empty metal can would be affected if it was lowered onto the surface of Venus.
3. Describe how an empty metal can would be affected if it was lowered onto the surface of Mars.

Applying What You Have Learned

1. What advantages would a telescope positioned in space have over a telescope found on the earth's surface?
2. What are the expected benefits of a space platform?
3. Compare and contrast the characteristics of Jupiter and Saturn.
4. What characteristic do Jupiter, Saturn, and the sun have in common?
5. Explain the statement: The moon may be a perfect location for future astronomers, geologists, and researchers.

Challenge

Command centers here on the earth monitor the path, speed, and progress of satellites, probes, and shuttles in space. These centers receive and interpret all of the information obtained from space. Instructions can be transmitted by the command centers to these objects in space by means of radio waves. Data and additional information travel back to the earth via radio waves. Radio waves, like all electromagnetic radiation, travel through space at a speed of 300,000,000 meters per second. Use the table to answer the following questions.

Distance from Earth (millions of kilometers)	
Sun	150
Mercury	92
Venus	42
Mars	78
Jupiter	629
Saturn	1,280
Uranus	2,720
Neptune	4,350
Pluto	5,750

1. How much time would it take for a command sent from Earth to reach a space probe near the planet Uranus?
2. A lander on Mars was programmed to travel over the planet's surface and record information. If a cliff was in the path of the lander, how much time would it take for a "stop" command to reach the lander?
3. Suppose the sun stopped giving off light. How much time would pass before scientists on Earth would know this?

Research and Investigation

1. Prepare a report on how the first cloud pictures from satellites changed meteorology.
2. Assemble a collection of space photographs of planets and their moons that have been enhanced. Write a description of each, explaining how enhancement has made it more useful.
3. Use your library to research the history and accomplishments of the space probe *Voyager 2*. Prepare a report on your findings.

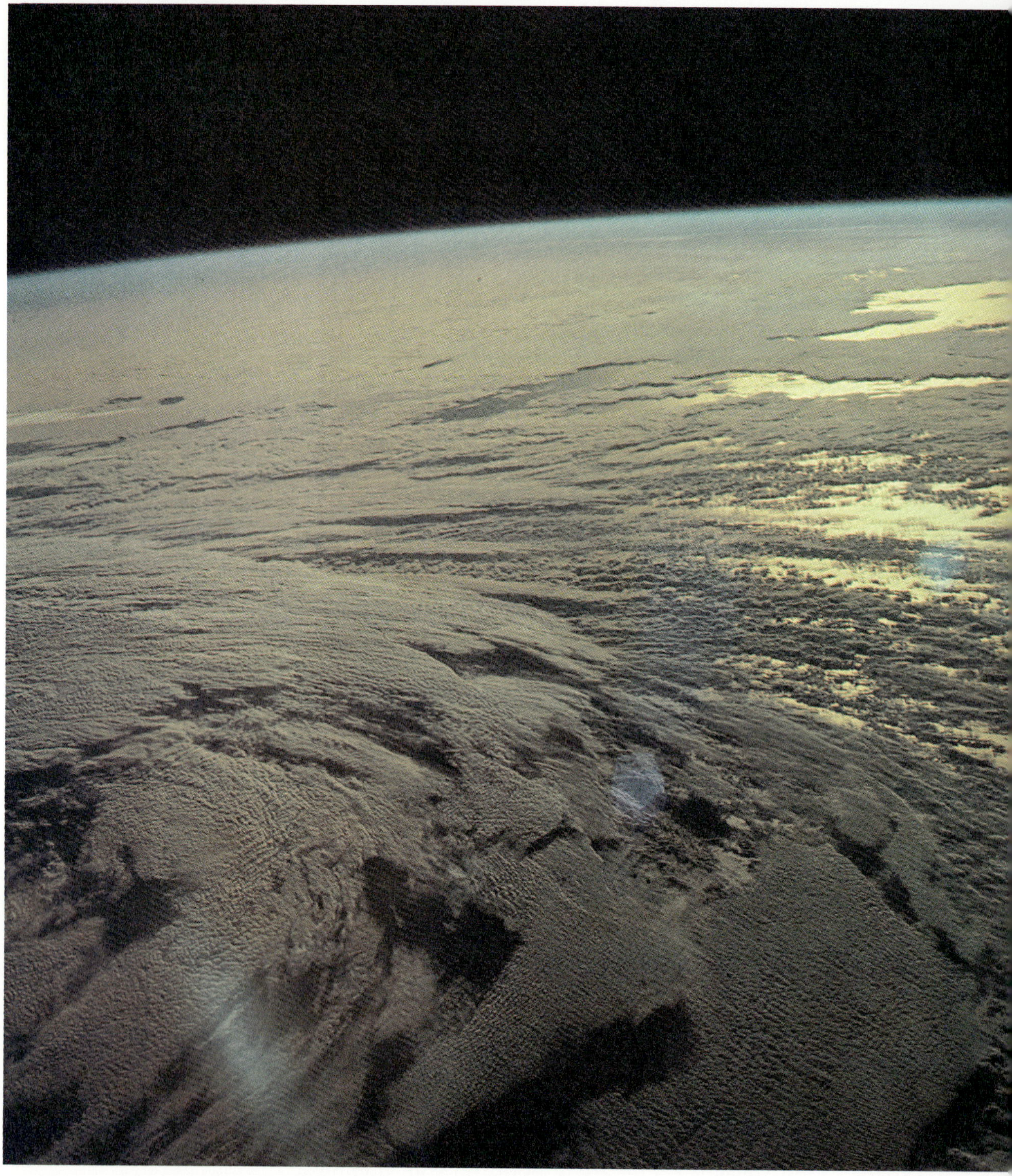

UNIT TWO

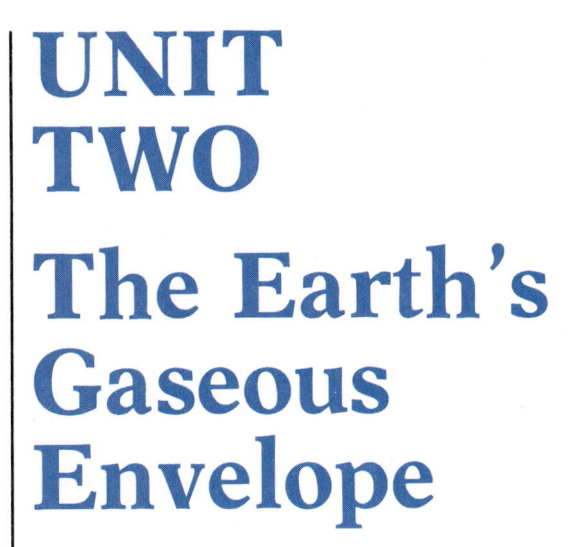

The Earth's Gaseous Envelope

Chapter 6
The Atmosphere and Its Movement

Chapter 7
Water in the Atmosphere

Chapter 8
Weather

Chapter 9
Climate

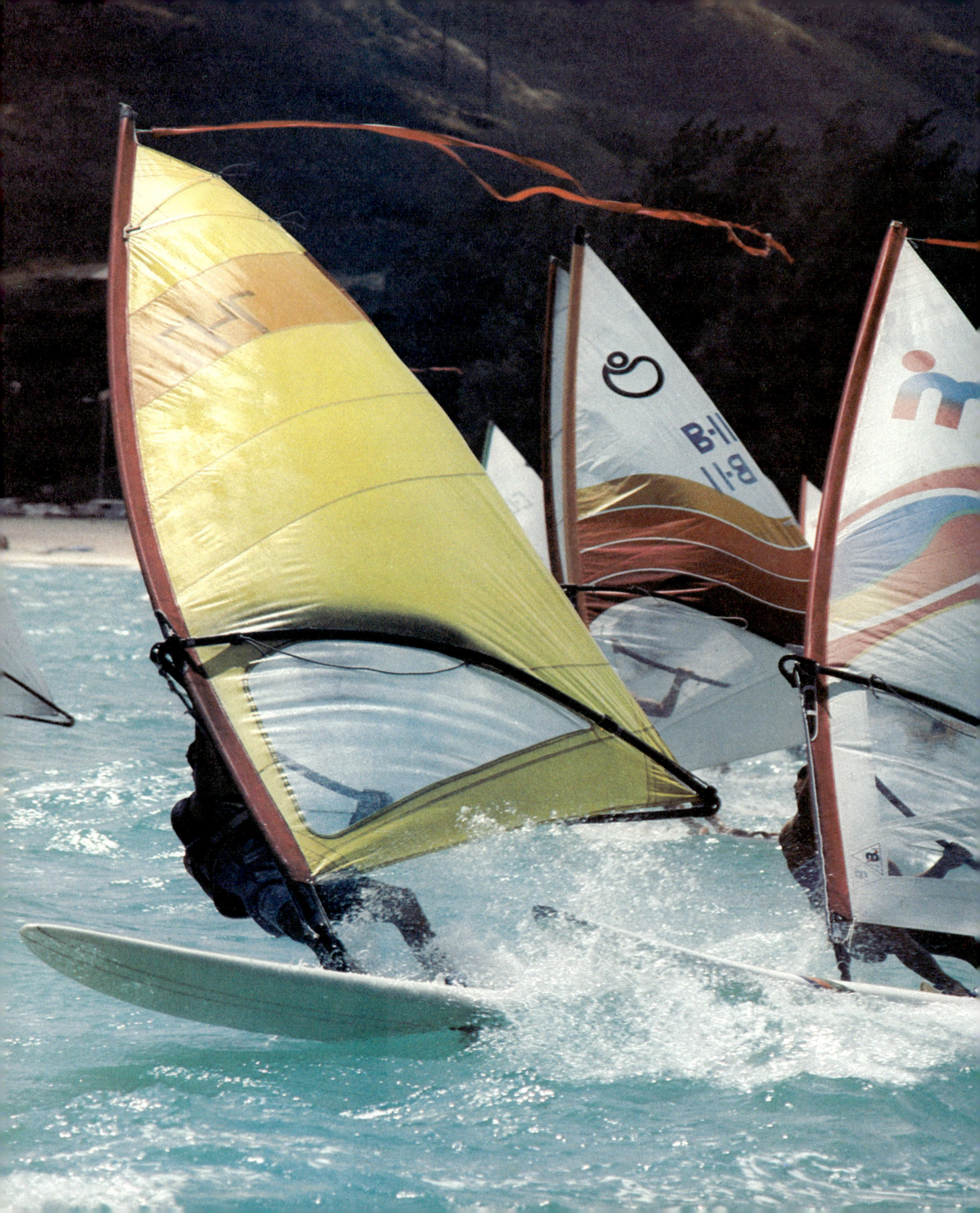
B-11

Chapter 6
The Atmosphere and Its Movement

Lesson Titles
6.1 The Air around You
6.2 Warming the Atmosphere
6.3 Wind
6.4 Global Wind Patterns

As you continue on your journey from outer space, you head for planet Earth. This planet is surrounded by an ocean of air. The surface of the earth lies at the bottom of the ocean of air.

Without air, life could not exist. Air is everywhere, always moving, and it is invisible. Though you cannot see the air, you know it exists because you can feel it. It fills the sails of a boat, and its force moves the boat across the water.

To understand this ocean of air, you must ask some questions. What is air made of? How deep is it? How does it move? And how does it affect you? Each answer to one of these questions is like finding a piece to a puzzle. The more you understand, the more pieces of the puzzle you can fit together.

In this chapter you will find the answers to some of these questions. You will also see how the air and the sun work together to make the weather.

There are still many pieces to the puzzle that are missing. Maybe one day you will find one of them.

Figure 6.1 *opposite:* Windsurfers ride the wind to ride the waves.

6.1 The Air around You

You will find out
- what gases make up the air around you;
- how air exerts pressure;
- how pressure exerted by the air is measured.

What is air? You know you can feel air if something moves. You feel it if you wave your arm back and forth. You feel it when you are in a moving car. Air moves through an open window of the car and moves your hair. Moving air can also turn the blades of a windmill. Since you can feel air and it can move things, air must be "stuff," or material. This is one piece of your puzzle.

The material called air is all around the earth. You live in an invisible sea of air. This sea of air is called the **atmosphere** [air sphere]. The atmosphere is a mixture of gases. The gases are invisible, have no color, and have no odor. Nitrogen (78 percent), and oxygen (20.9 percent) make up most of the mixture. Argon (0.9 percent), carbon dioxide (0.03 percent), and traces of many other gases complete the mixture. Near the earth's surface these gases are mixed with water vapor.

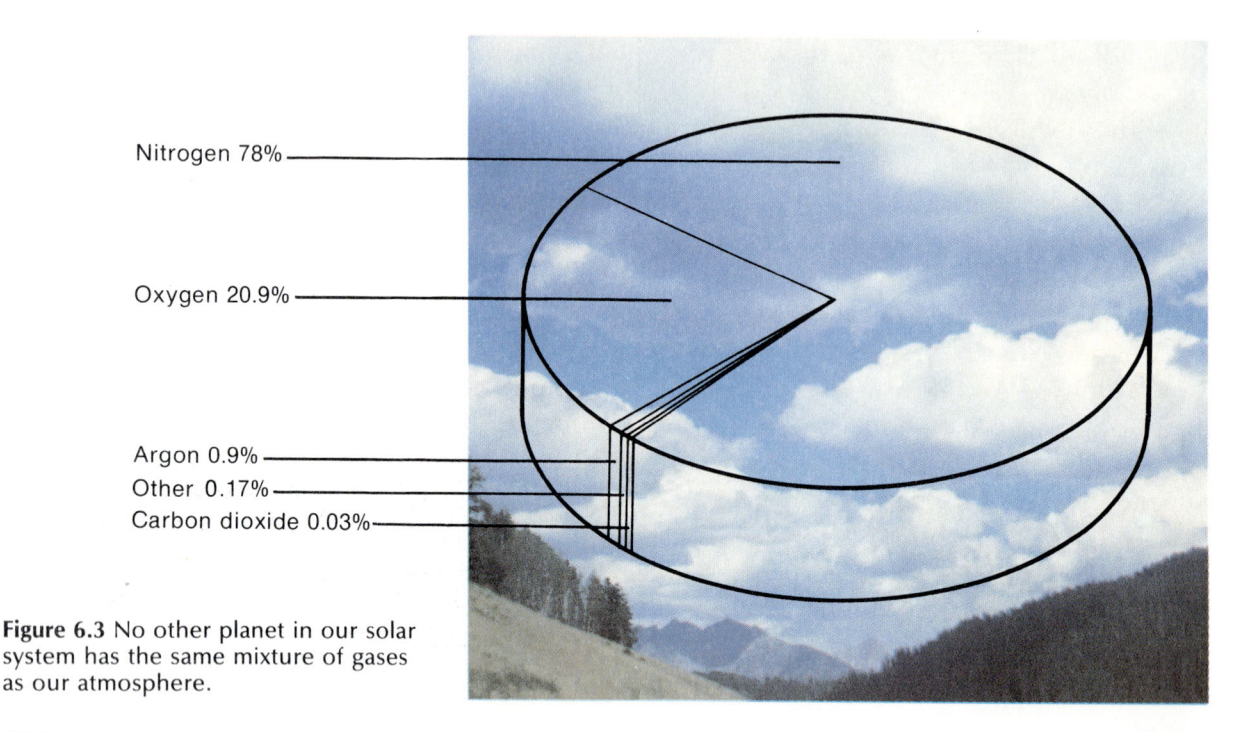

Figure 6.2 Air turns a weathervane, indicating the direction of wind.

Nitrogen 78%
Oxygen 20.9%
Argon 0.9%
Other 0.17%
Carbon dioxide 0.03%

Figure 6.3 No other planet in our solar system has the same mixture of gases as our atmosphere.

104   6 / The Atmosphere and Its Movement

How can you feel something that is invisible? The atmospheric gases are thought to be made of tiny particles called **molecules** [MAHL-uh-kyools]. Molecules are so very tiny that you cannot see them. Yet, even though you cannot see them, the molecules are materials. It is these tiny particles of materials that you feel when you move your arm through the air.

The gas molecules that make up air move about freely. They also move rapidly. Would you believe that they may move as much as 800 m a second or more? There are billions of gas molecules moving rapidly about and banging into one another. This is taking place all around you this very moment. This movement is also another piece of your puzzle.

There are two results of gas molecules moving rapidly about. One result is that the atmosphere is spread out. If the molecules were not moving, they would all be on the earth's surface. They would be like grains of sand on a beach. You would not be able to breathe! But the molecules are moving so they are found higher than just on the surface. They spread outward and upward. Because of the pull of gravity, however, more are found near the surface than higher up. The atmosphere is not a layer such as the skin on a peach. The atmosphere thins out as you go up from the surface. It gradually merges with the near-emptiness of space.

Figure 6.4 The movement of air causes these flags to flutter.

Do You Know?
If people were the size of molecules, it would take everyone in the United States standing in line to make a line 2.5 cm long.

6 / The Atmosphere and Its Movement

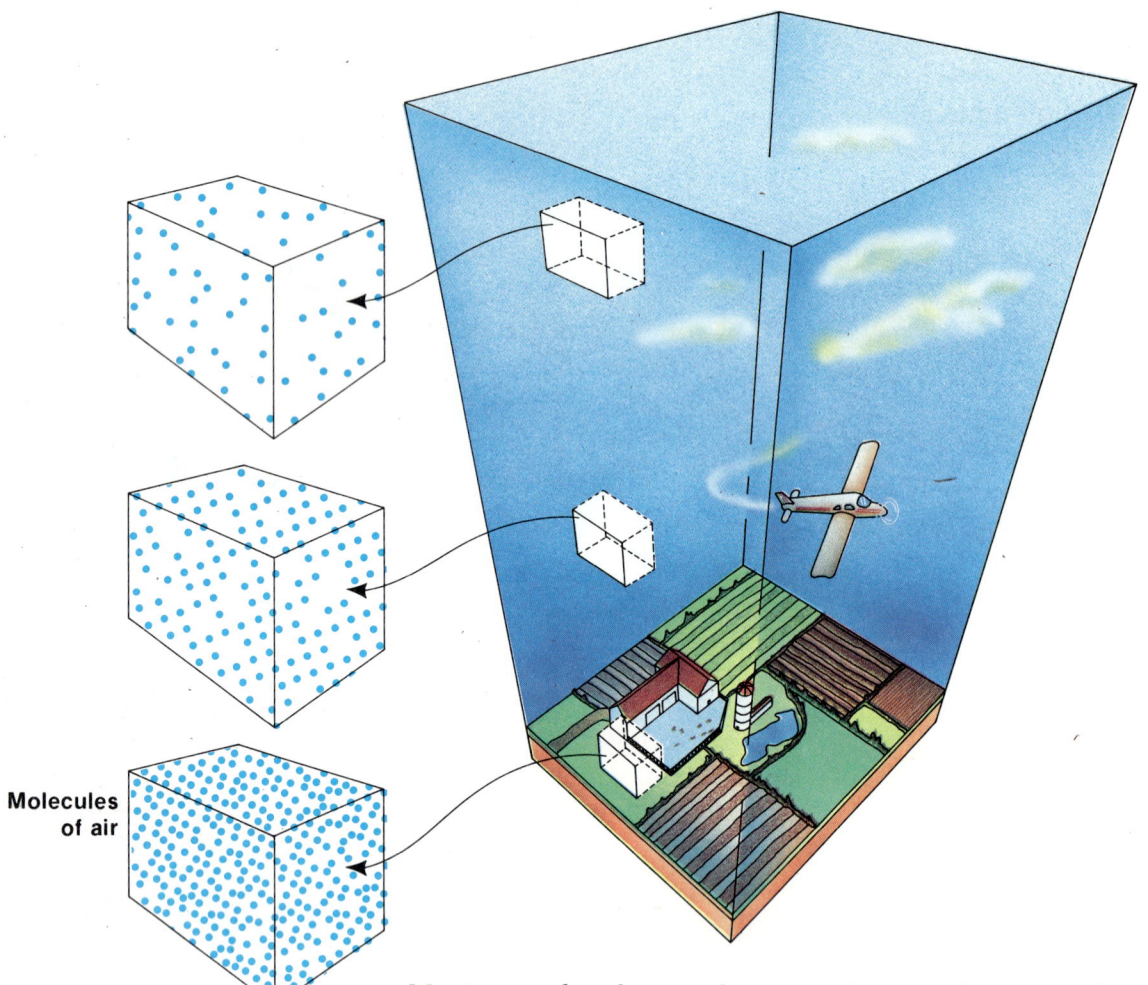

Figure 6.5 At greater heights, the same volume of air contains fewer molecules of gas.

Molecules of air

Do You Know?
Have your ears ever popped when riding in an elevator or in a car in the mountains? The pop is caused by a tube behind your eardrum adjusting to changes in the atmospheric pressure.

Moving molecules produce another result. When the molecules hit a surface they exert a pressure on it. **Atmospheric pressure** is produced by the molecules hitting a surface. Since more molecules are found near the surface, the pressure is greatest there. Higher up, there are fewer and fewer molecules so the pressure becomes less and less. The pressure decreases as you go away from the earth's surface. Atmospheric pressure is a big piece in your puzzle.

Atmospheric pressure on the surface can be measured. One way of measuring it is by using a 10.5-m length of tube that is closed at one end. You fill it with water and place the open end in a pan of water. When raised to an upright position, some of the water will come out of the tube, but not all of it. Atmospheric pressure will cause about 10.33 m of water to stay in the tube. If the atmospheric pressure becomes less, however, more water will come out of the tube. Suppose the atmospheric pressure increases. What will happen to the water in the tube? It will be pushed higher. By measuring the height of the water, you can measure the atmospheric pressure. Such a device that measures atmospheric pressure is called a **barometer** [buh-RAHM-uh-tuhr].

Imagine carrying around a 10-m tall water barometer. Of course it would not be useful. So mercury, which is much heavier, is used in place of water. Mercury is 13.6 times as dense as water. The height of mercury in a mercury barometer will be only 1/13.6 as tall as the height of water in a water barometer, or about 76 cm. A weather report stating that, "the pressure is 76 cm and is rising," is talking about the height of mercury in a mercury barometer. Now several of the pieces of your puzzle are beginning to fit together.

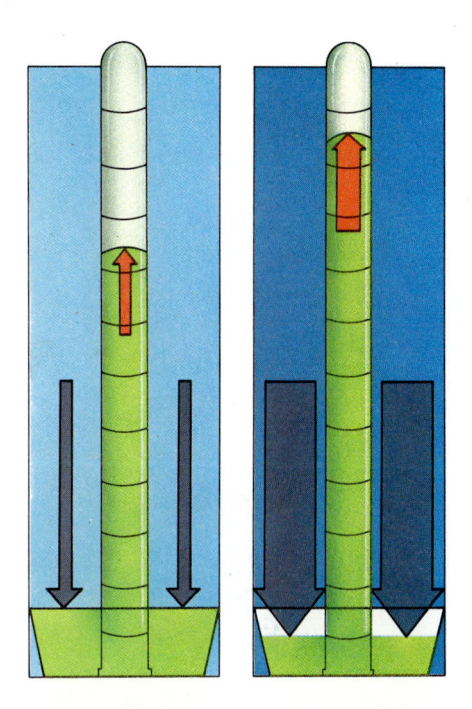

Figure 6.6 *above:* Arrows show the effect of atmospheric pressure on the barometer. Compare the effect of low atmospheric pressure (*left*) with that of high atmospheric pressure (*right*).

Figure 6.7 *left:* An aneroid barometer; *right:* A mercurial barometer.

Study Questions for 6.1

1. List four gases that make up our atmosphere and give their approximate percentage of the total.
2. What is the atmospheric pressure?
3. Explain how a mercury barometer measures atmospheric pressure.
4. Suppose you hear a weather report that the barometer is falling. What does this mean?

6.2 Warming the Atmosphere

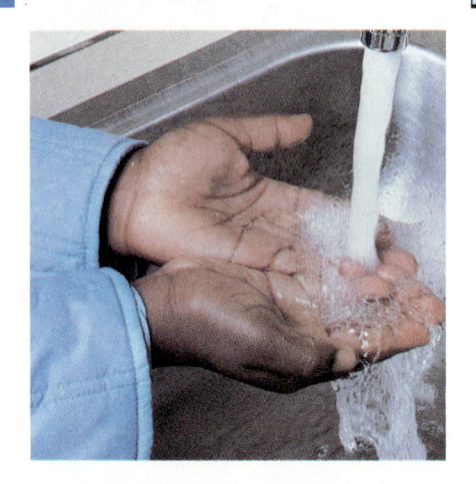

You will find out
- what temperature is;
- how the atmosphere is warmed.

Have you ever been tricked by snow? Have you ever had your hands in snow for some time and then washed your hands in cold water? The cold water feels warm. Since the snow made your hands colder than the water, you thought that the cold water was warm. You need a thermometer, since your body can be tricked. A thermometer measures the **temperature** of a material. Temperature is a measure of the average energy of motion of molecules. The higher the temperature, the faster the molecules move about. Warm air has rapidly moving gas molecules, and cooler air has slower moving gas molecules.

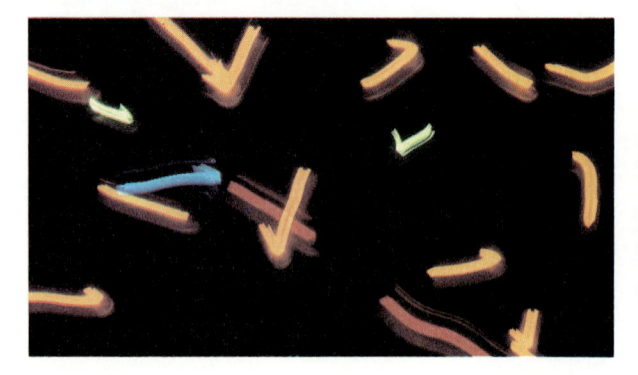

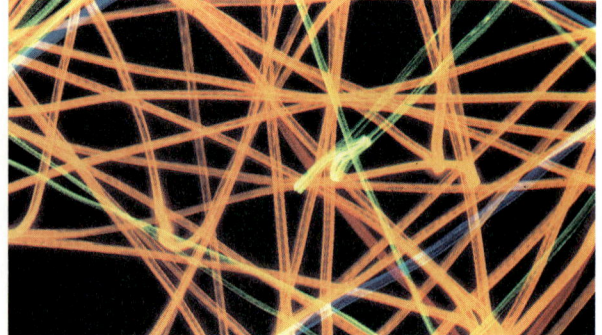

Figure 6.8 Your hands may not be an accurate way to measure temperature.

Figure 6.9 *left:* An illustration of the slow movement of cold gas molecules; *right:* Warm gas molecules move more quickly.

The atmosphere is warmed when the gas molecules gain energy, causing them to move about more rapidly. But where does the energy come from to make them move faster? It comes from two sources—the sun and the earth. Sunlight is energy that has traveled to you, from the sun to the earth. Such energy that travels through space is called **radiant energy.** When you are outside on a bright, hot summer day, you feel the sun's energy. The atmosphere absorbs some of the sun's energy, but much more is absorbed by the earth. The earth then radiates the energy back to the atmosphere. That is the kind of energy you feel coming from warm sand or hot pavement.

You learned in Chapter 2 (pages 30-31) that visible light, which you see is really only a small part of radiant energy. Infrared and ultraviolet are also forms of radiant energy, but you can't see these forms.

For example, consider the heating element of an electric range. When you turn the electric range on to a low setting, the element becomes warmer. You can feel radiant energy from the warm element if you hold your hand close to it. But you cannot see anything from the element, even if the room is dark. The element gives off infrared radiant energy. You cannot see infrared radiation, but you know it is there because you can feel it.

At higher temperatures not only do you feel radiant energy from the element but also you can see some of it. At higher temperatures the element begins to give off shorter wavelengths of radiant energy. These shorter wavelengths are the red light that you can see. Look at Figure 6.10. What color light would the range element give off if it became even hotter?

If the range element became as hot as the sun, you would see the short wavelengths as bright sunlight. Does the earth radiate long or short wavelengths of energy? From what you have learned, you should see that the earth gives off radiant energy at invisible longer wavelengths. The heat you feel from the warm sand at the beach or the hot pavement is infrared radiation.

Do You Know?
Animals can see parts of the radiant energy spectrum that humans cannot. Some snakes (sidewinders) can see infrared. Certain insects (bees, moths) can see ultraviolet.

Figure 6.10 *top:* No light is visible on a low heat setting. *bottom:* Radiant energy is visible at a high setting.

Figure 6.11 An infrared photo taken by satellite of San Francisco Bay; the warmest areas (those giving off more infrared radiation) show up as red.

6 / The Atmosphere and Its Movement

Here is an atmospheric puzzle piece you may think does not fit. You have probably seen pictures of mountains with snow on the tops. Did you ever wonder why the snow is on top of the mountain and not the bottom? After all, isn't the top of the mountain closer to the sun? One reason for this is the fact that sunlight passing through the atmosphere does not warm it very much.

Figure 6.12 Mountaintops are cooler than the ground below them.

Figure 6.13 Sunlight, shown in yellow, is absorbed by soil and plants. They radiate the energy as infrared rays, shown in orange.

If this is so, how does the atmosphere get warmed? Think about it this way. The warming of the atmosphere is similar to what happens in a greenhouse. Sunlight shines through the glass into a greenhouse. This energy is absorbed by the soil and plants. The soil and plants radiate energy, infrared radiation. Infrared radiation cannot escape through the glass and is absorbed by water and carbon dioxide molecules in the air. The temperature of the air is thus increased by the radiation of longer wavelengths. This is called the **greenhouse effect.**

6 / The Atmosphere and Its Movement

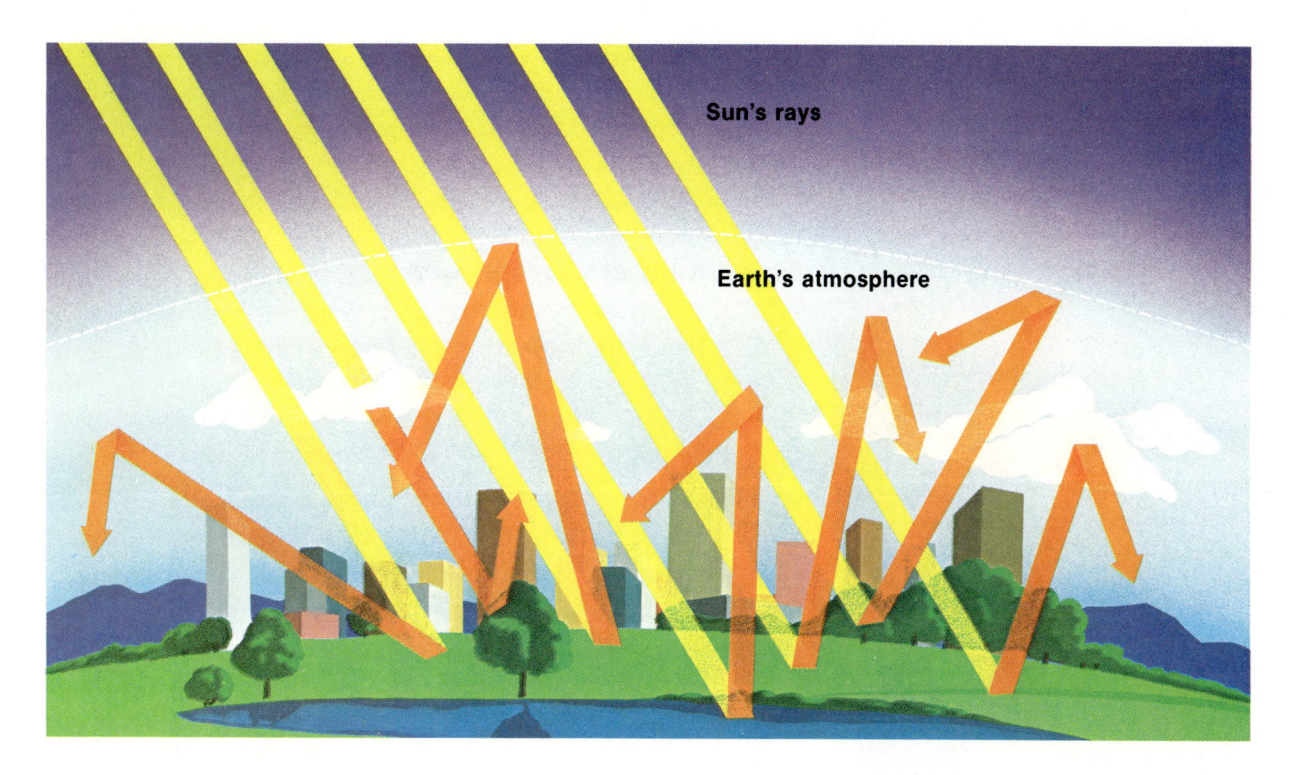

The earth's atmosphere is warmed in much the same way as the inside of a greenhouse. The radiant energy from the sun that reaches the earth's surface is mostly absorbed. Buildings, plants, water, and the ground become warmer as the energy is absorbed. All these materials radiate this absorbed energy as infrared energy. On their outward journey the longer wavelengths are absorbed by water and carbon dioxide molecules in the atmosphere. The main heating source of the atmosphere is the radiation of longer wavelengths that are then absorbed by the gases in the lower parts of the atmosphere.

Figure 6.14 The greenhouse effect of the atmosphere; sunlight is absorbed by objects on the earth's surface and then released as infrared radiation.

Do You Know?
If the year-round average radiant energy received by the earth's surface were not reradiated, it would become 1.5°C warmer each day. How much warmer would it be after one month?

Study Questions for 6.2

1. What happens to the air temperature as the gas molecules that make up air move about more rapidly?
2. What is radiant energy?
3. Explain the greenhouse effect and how it warms the atmosphere.

6 / The Atmosphere and Its Movement

111

6.3 Wind

You will find out
- that warm air is less dense than cold air;
- how changes in air temperature make the air move;
- what makes the wind blow.

The air around you is almost always moving. Sometimes the air moves slowly, gently rustling tree leaves. At other times the movement is faster, perhaps moving the whole tree top back and forth. Gentle or strong, the horizontal movement of air is usually called **wind.** What makes the wind blow?

Have you ever stood barefoot in front of an open refrigerator? You could feel cold air pouring onto your feet. Where do you hold your hands when warming them at a fire or heater? Warm air can be felt rising above the heat source.

There is a relationship between temperature and the movement of air. Cold air moves downward. Warm air moves upward. This happens because air expands as it is warmed, becoming less dense. Cooler air is more dense than warmer air. The cooler air flows beneath the warmer air and forces it upward. Now you have another piece for your atmospheric puzzle.

Figure 6.15 These socks will dry more quickly because warm air rises from the fire.

Activity

How Does Temperature Affect Air Density?

Materials
two large jars
safety goggles
candle
matches
refrigerator

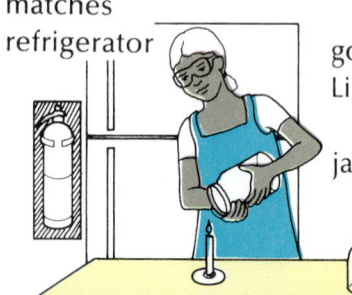

Procedure

1. Place a large jar in the freezer for 15 minutes. Leave a second jar at room temperature.
2. CAUTION: Put on safety goggles and tie back loose hair. Light a small candle on a table.
3. Pour the air from the cold jar onto the candle flame.
4. Repeat with the warm jar.

Questions

1. What do you see happening when you pour air from the jars?
2. How does cooling change air density? How do you know?

Convection cell

Warm surface

Cold surface

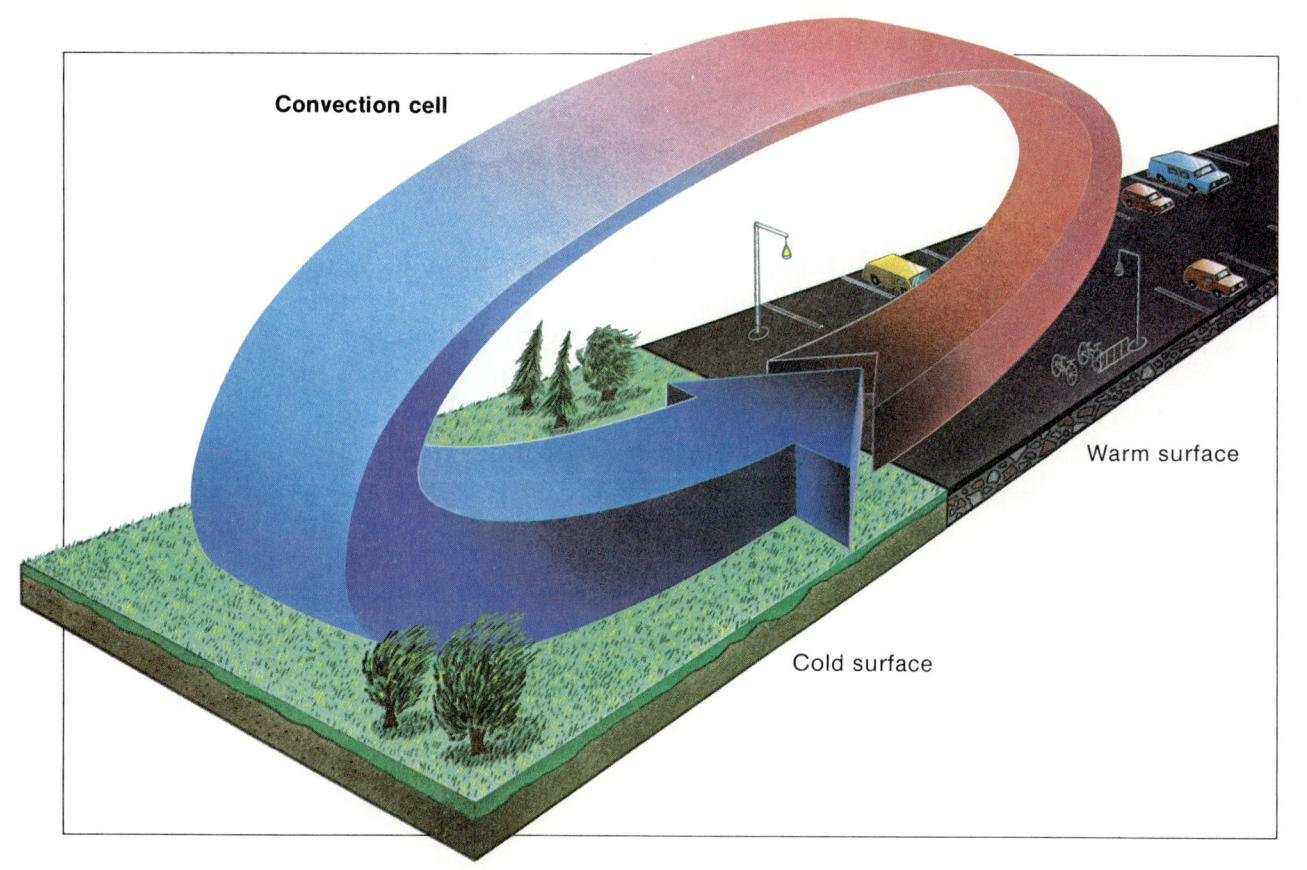

Earlier you noted that buildings, plants, and the ground become warmer when they absorb sunlight. However, not all materials are warmed the same by the sun. You can notice this difference if you walk barefoot across grass, concrete, asphalt, and dry sand on a hot summer day. These materials all receive the same amount of sunlight, but they are warmed to different temperatures. As a result, on a calm, sunlit day, wiggly currents of air can be observed rising over a hot asphalt street. Cooler, more dense air moves from a nearby cooler surface, such as grass. Figure 6.16 shows the movement of air from a patch of cool grass to a warmer asphalt street. The cooler, more dense air moves from the grass to the asphalt. It pushes the warm, less dense air upward. This process of warmer air being pushed upward is called **convection.** If the warmer air rises then moves back down onto the cooler surface, we say that a **convection cell** has been formed.

Figure 6.16 *above:* A visual model of a convection cell; blue represents cool, dense, air; red represents warm, less dense air. Cool air pushes warm air upward.

Figure 6.17 *below:* Unusual images result when objects are viewed through convection currents rising from hot ground.

6 / The Atmosphere and Its Movement

Earlier you learned that the air pressure decreases as you go higher into the atmosphere. You may expect the air pressure to be the same at the same altitude everywhere above the surface. If so, an air pressure model would look like Figure 6.18. The white lines you see represent equal pressure. Everywhere along the same line, the pressure is the same. Notice that in this model the pressure lines are straight. They will be straight if the entire surface is one temperature.

How does temperature change affect this air pressure model? Pressure is lower in warm air than in cold air. This is because air molecules move faster in warm air and are spaced farther apart than they are in cold air.

Look at Figure 6.19. Notice how the equal pressure lines are curved. The lines are closer together over the cold surface where the pressure is high. The lines are farther apart over the warm surface where the pressure is low. This arrangement of lines means that the air pressures are not equal at the same heights everywhere above the surface. Instead, equal air pressures occur at different heights when surface temperatures vary. Wind

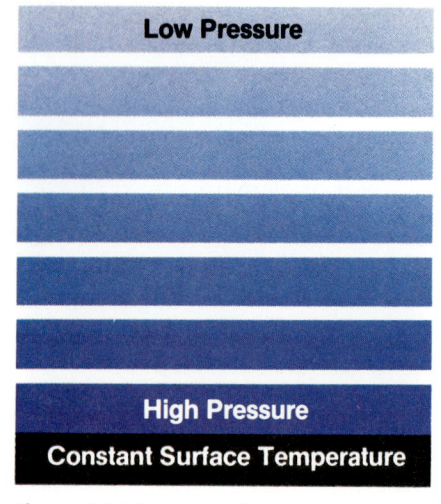

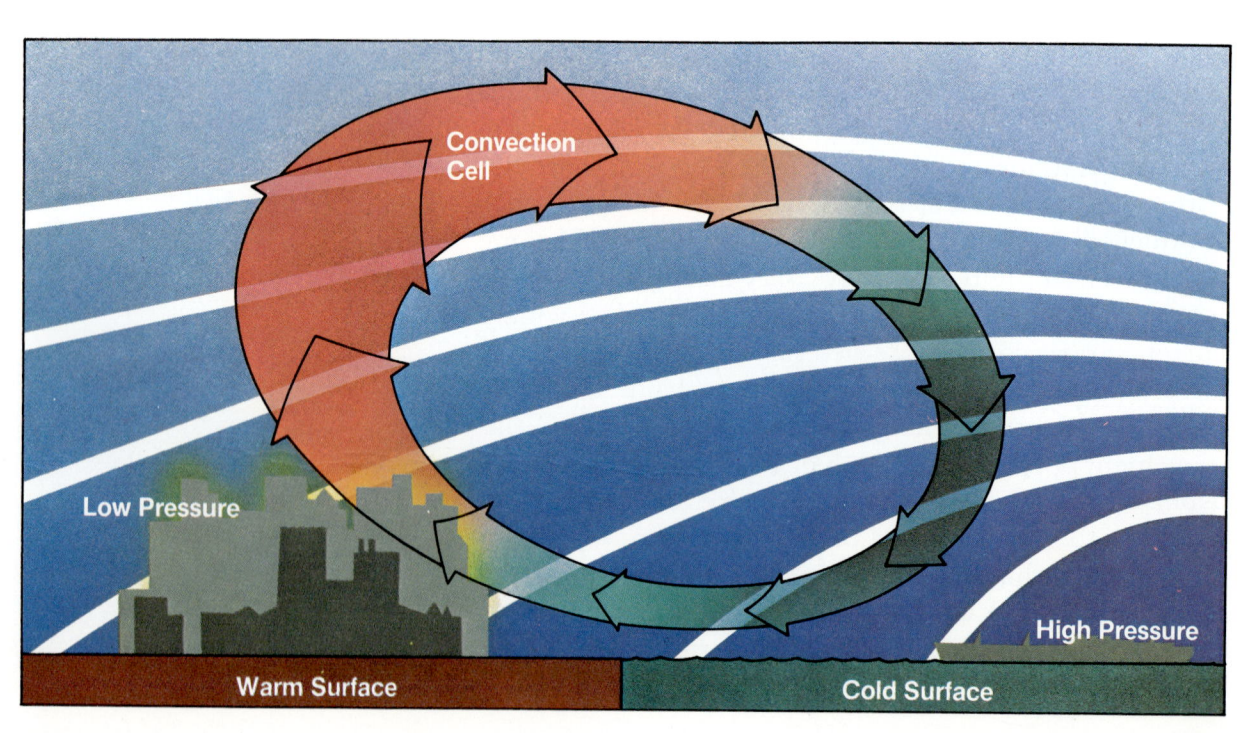

Figure 6.18 Pressure lines are straight when over a surface of constant temperature. The lines represent air pressure that is equal at equal altitudes. No air movement occurs.

Figure 6.19 When surfaces have different temperatures, air pressure varies. Equal pressure lines occur at different altitudes. Wind blows as air moves from areas of high to low pressure.

Activity

What Makes Air Move?

Materials
plastic food wrap
masking tape
cardboard box
knife
pan of ice cubes
black paper
smoking punk

Procedure

1. Make a smoke box as shown. CAUTION: Be careful when using the knife. Always point the blade away from your body.

2. Position a pan of ice, a smoking punk, and a sheet of black paper in direct sunlight. Place the box over them so the sunlight shines directly on the paper and ice.

3. Look through the side window. Observe how the air moves in the box for 10 to 15 minutes.

Questions

1. Do you see any evidence that the air is moving?

2. Where does the air move upward?

3. Why did the air move as observed?

4. Explain an afternoon, on shore breeze at the beach. Use a diagram to aid your explanation.

blows because air moves from areas of high pressure to areas of low pressure. Factors such as temperature and altitude can cause pressure changes and so produce wind.

Study Questions for 6.3

1. Is warm air more or less dense than cold air?
2. What is a convection cell? Diagram one.
3. What makes the wind blow?

6.4 Global Wind Patterns

You will find out
- why the equator is warmer than the poles;
- why the earth's large convection system appears to be deflected;
- that the whole earth has large-scale air movements.

Figure 6.20 Indirect sunlight at the poles results in cold temperatures.

The sun is shining on half the earth at all times. Different regions of the sunlit earth, however, have very different temperatures. For example, the equator receives more direct sunlight than the poles, so it is much warmer. Since the equator is warmer than the poles, you would expect a huge convection cell to form. The cooler, more dense air from the poles should move across the surface toward the equator. Warm, less dense air at the equator should be forced upward and should move in the upper atmosphere to the poles. You should find a belt of lower pressure around the equator and an area of higher pressure at the poles. Measurements have shown that these pressure areas do exist. If this is all there is to the model, the wind on the surface should always blow from the north in the northern hemisphere. In the southern hemisphere the wind on the surface should blow from the south. But how does this model test out?

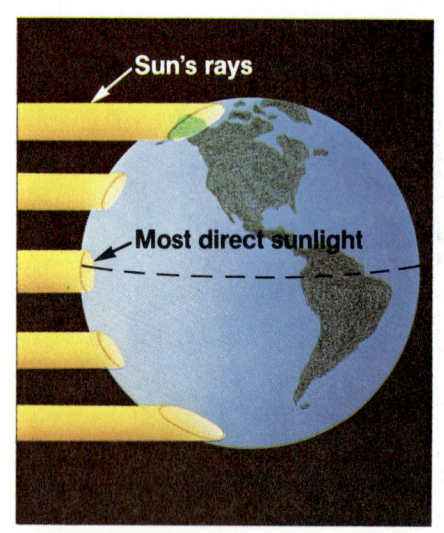

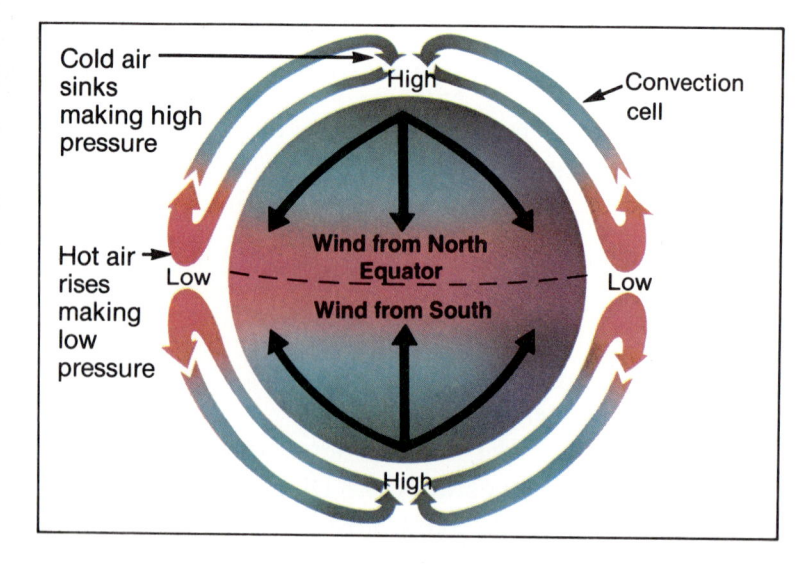

Figure 6.21 *above:* The sun's rays striking Earth's surface; *right:* If the earth did not rotate, convection currents, or winds, would behave like this model.

116

6 / The Atmosphere and Its Movement

For one thing you know that the wind does not always blow from the north in the northern hemisphere. You also know that the wind does not always blow from the south in the southern hemisphere. It would if the earth were not spinning on its axis. The rotation of the earth has an important effect on large-scale movements of air. Except at the equator all objects moving in the northern hemisphere tend to turn or curve to the right as seen by a ground observer. The moving object may actually be moving in a straight line but appears to be turning because the earth is moving under it. The turning is called the **Coriolis** [kawr-ee-OH-lihs] **effect.** When viewed from a polar position, moving things in the northern hemisphere appear to turn to the right when moving away from you. In the southern hemisphere they appear to turn to the left.

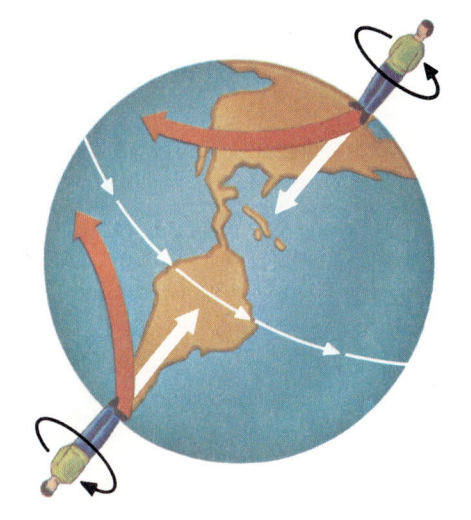

Figure 6.22 People at opposite poles experience the Coriolis effect differently.

Activity

Can You Go Straight?

Materials
globe
paper
pencil

Procedure
1. Place the paper on the globe to cover the route from St. Louis to New Orleans.
2. Practice making an air flight with your pencil point from St. Louis straight down to New Orleans.
3. Now have your partner slowly turn the globe counter-clockwise (looking down on the North Pole) as you move the pencil straight south from St. Louis.

Questions
1. Did you land in New Orleans? To the east or to the west of it?
2. Did your air flight path turn to the right or left (remember, you are inside the aircraft)?
3. Why does the Coriolis effect appear to make moving objects drift to the right or left?

6 / The Atmosphere and Its Movement

Do You Know?
Global wind belts push against the surface, actually slowing the earth's rotation rate. Scientists have measured these tiny effects and found the length of a day varies less than one millisecond because of the winds.

Air is heated at the equator, becomes less dense, and moves upward and poleward above the earth. This forms a low-pressure belt around the equator. As the poleward moving air gets to 10° latitude north or south, it is influenced by the Coriolis effect. By the time it reaches 30° latitude north or south of the equator it tends to sink and pile up. Some of the air sinks toward the earth's surface. The piling up of air forms a warm high-pressure belt. Air moving away from the high-pressure belt produces two global wind belts, the **trade winds** and the **prevailing westerlies.** These wind belts are near the surface. Some of the upper air continues on to the poles. Over the poles it sinks toward the surface. It then moves toward the equator. This produces a third global wind belt, the **polar easterlies.**

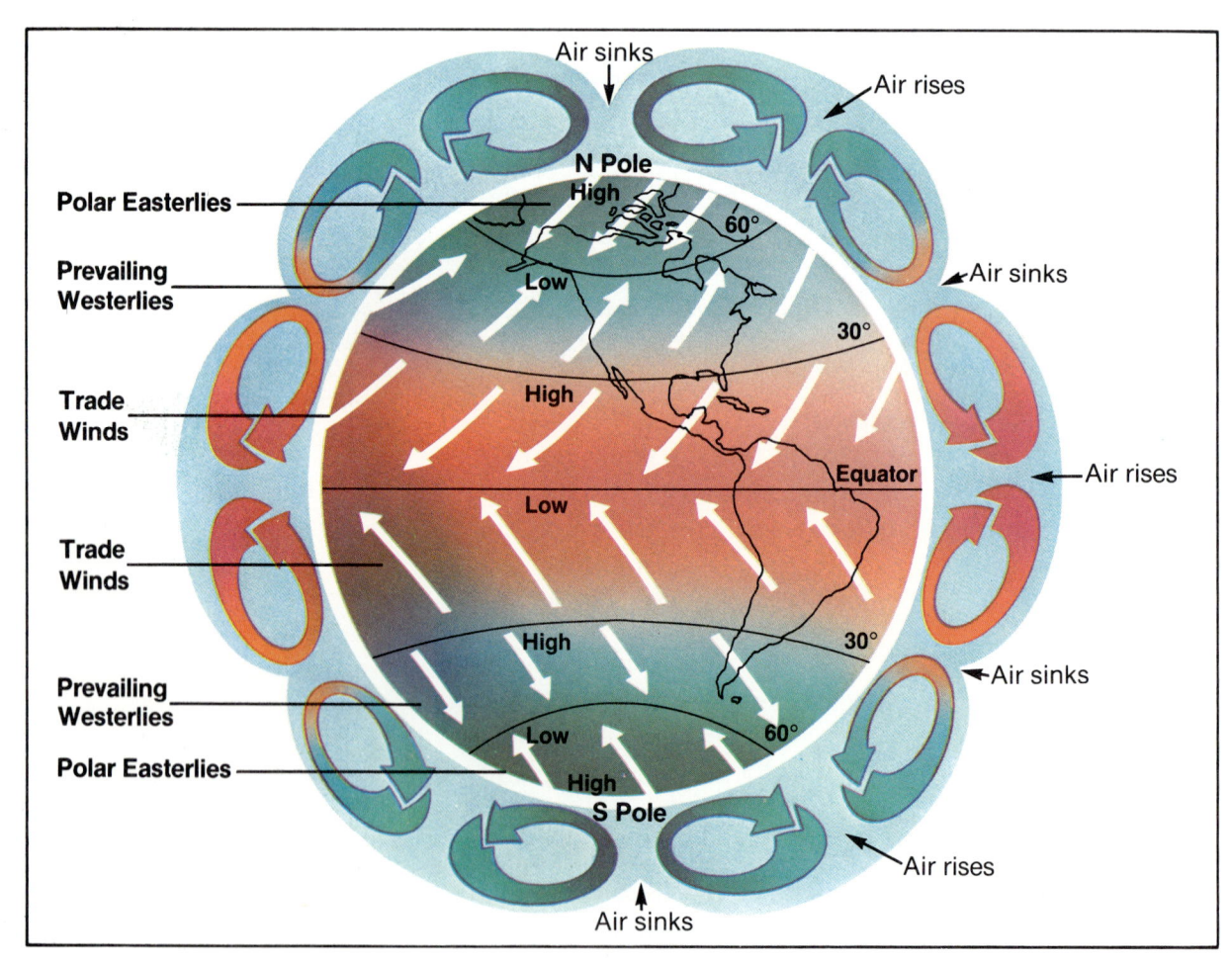

Figure 6.23 A model of the global winds that result from the Coriolis effect and convection

118

6 / The Atmosphere and Its Movement

This is a simplified model of atmospheric air movement. It shows a zone of high pressure to the north and a zone of high pressure to the south of the United States. Since air moves from high pressure to low pressure, we would expect to find cold air moving from the north. We would expect warm air to move from the south. Most of the United States is in a "battle zone," where warm and cold air encounter each other and push back and forth. It is in this battle zone that rapid and frequent weather changes occur.

Figure 6.24 High-pressure zones at 30° and at the polar region cause air movement toward the region of low pressure near 60°. These opposing wind belts create the battle zone of changing weather patterns over North America.

Study Questions for 6.4

1. Why is the equator warmer than the poles?
2. What is the Coriolis effect?
3. Why is most of the United States in a battle zone between cold air from the north and warm air from the south?

Science and Technology

An Hourglass and the Greenhouse Effect

Do you know what an hourglass is? You've probably seen one. An hourglass measures time by having sand trickle through it. If you happen to own an old hourglass, you may be able to help earth scientists in their study of the greenhouse effect.

The greenhouse effect is the process by which Earth's atmosphere is heated. Carbon dioxide is a factor in the greenhouse effect. An increase in the amount of carbon dioxide in the atmosphere increases the greenhouse effect and may lead to a warming of the atmosphere.

A warmer atmosphere may not sound like a bad problem to you, especially if you live in a cold northern climate. But think about some other things that may happen. If the air became warmer worldwide, the vast ice sheets that now cover our polar regions might melt. That would cause the sea level to rise. How would you feel about a warmer climate if it caused your city to slowly drown? Or if the farmland on which you depended for food became the floor of an ocean?

Another effect of a warmer climate may be an increase in the size of the world's deserts. In fact, that change may have already begun. Some scientists think that it is one of the causes of the continuing famine in Africa.

Scientists are certain that the worldwide carbon dioxide level has increased over the past few years. The major source of carbon dioxide in the air is the burning of any substance that contains carbon. This includes such things as oil, gasoline, kerosene, and even wood. As the burning of these substances increases, the amount of carbon dioxide in the air increases.

In order to compare the level of carbon dioxide today with levels from the past, scientists need samples of air from the past. That is where your hourglass comes in! When that hourglass was made, it was tightly sealed. That means that the air now in it is a sample of air from the past. Measuring the amount of carbon dioxide in your sample of air may help scientists to see how fast the amount of carbon dioxide in the air is changing. It may also help us to learn how to closely monitor carbon dioxide levels in the atmosphere.

CHAPTER REVIEW

Main Ideas

- The atmosphere is mostly nitrogen (78 percent), plus oxygen (20.9 percent), argon (0.9 percent), and carbon dioxide (0.03 percent).
- The atmosphere exerts a pressure as the result of molecular bombardment. This atmospheric pressure is measured with a barometer.
- Temperature is a measure of the average energy of motion of molecules.
- Radiant energy is energy that travels through space. Hotter objects give off shorter-wavelength radiant energy than cooler objects.
- The lower atmosphere is warmed from below because of the greenhouse effect.
- Cool, more dense air moves under and pushes warmer, less dense air upward. This movement is called convection.
- Horizontal movement of air is called wind. Wind blows from areas of high pressure to areas of low pressure.
- The equator receives more direct sunlight than the poles, so it is warmer.
- The atmosphere and things moving through it appear to turn because of the Coriolis effect.
- The atmosphere of the earth moves as a huge convection cell that is turned by the Coriolis effect. This produces pressure zones and global winds.

Using Vocabulary

On a separate paper, write a sentence for each word listed below. Each sentence should give a *clue* as to the meaning of the word.

atmosphere
molecule
atmospheric pressure
barometer
temperature
radiant energy
greenhouse effect

wind
convection
convection cell
Coriolis effect
trade winds
prevailing westerlies
polar easterlies

6 / The Atmosphere and Its Movement

Remembering Facts

On your paper, write the word or words that best completes each sentence.
1. The atmosphere is composed mainly of (oxygen, nitrogen, carbon dioxide) gas.
2. Atmospheric gases are thought to be made of tiny particles called (radiant energy, molecules, argon).
3. Normally, molecules of gases in the atmosphere are moving about (rapidly, slowly, not at all).
4. As you move up from the earth's surface, atmospheric pressure (increases, decreases, remains the same).
5. Molecules of a cooler gas move about (faster than, slower than, the same as) those of a warmer gas.
6. The warmth you feel from a hot wall is from (ultraviolet, visible, infrared) radiation.
7. Earth's atmosphere is heated mainly by the (sun, moon, earth).
8. Warm air has (greater, less, the same) density than/as cold air.
9. The process of warmer air being pushed upward by cooler air is called (conduction, convection, radiation).
10. Objects moving in the area above the Northern Hemisphere would appear to (curve right, curve left, go straight).
11. The (trade winds, westerlies, easterlies) move air directly to the equator.
12. The greenhouse effect causes an increase in (air pressure, winds, temperature).
13. The earth's surface gives off (infrared, visible, ultraviolet) radiation.
14. The curving of the path of an object moving through the atmosphere is called the (greenhouse, convection, Coriolis) effect.
15. Atmospheric pressure is measured with a (thermometer, barometer, radiometer).

Understanding Ideas

On your paper, answer each question in complete sentences.
1. What temperature changes would you expect if you went away from the earth's surface? Why?
2. Would you expect the Coriolis effect to be greater at the equator or at the poles? Why?
3. Why does the inside of an automobile become so hot on a sunny day when the windows are closed?

Applying What You Have Learned

1. Explain how a hot-air balloonist is able to go up and down in the atmosphere at will.
2. Sometimes people open a window and let cold air into a room when trying to start a fire in a fireplace. How would this help start a fire?
3. Why does weather in the prevailing westerly wind belt change more rapidly than elsewhere?
4. Suppose you are growing fruit trees that are sensitive to cold air. Would it be better to plant the trees in a valley or on the slopes leading to the valley? Why?

Challenge

This diagram shows, on the average, how 100 units of short-wave radiation from the sun interact with the earth's atmosphere and its surface.

1. Use the information in the diagram to show that the average loss and gain of energy is in balance for (a) the earth's surface, (b) the atmosphere, and (c) the earth's surface and the atmosphere combined.
2. During what hours of the day do the three energy-exchange processes take place?
3. Suppose something happened and the atmosphere no longer radiated energy to the earth's surface. What effect would this have on the earth's energy balance? On the average temperature of the earth?

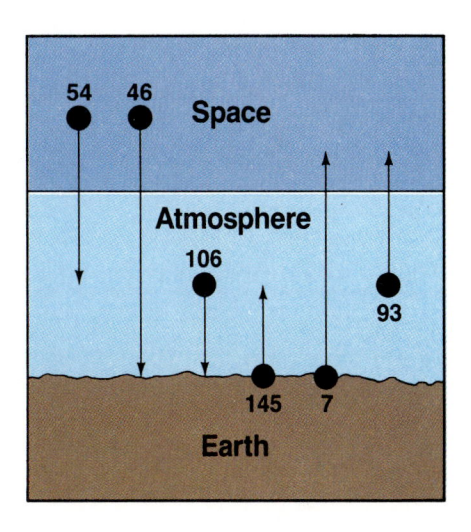

Research and Investigation

1. Investigate wind patterns where you live. Obtain helium-filled balloons. Attach to each balloon a stamped postcard that is addressed to you. Ask the person finding the card to write when and where it was found and to mail the card to you. Note on a map when and where each balloon was found. Prepare a report.
2. An altimeter is a barometer that is calibrated to show altitude instead of pressure. Obtain an aneroid barometer. Measure the pressure at different heights in a building. Make an altitude scale for the barometer and measure the heights of hills, valleys, and other places.
3. Find out if weather balloons are used to study the weather in the area where you live.

6 / The Atmosphere and Its Movement

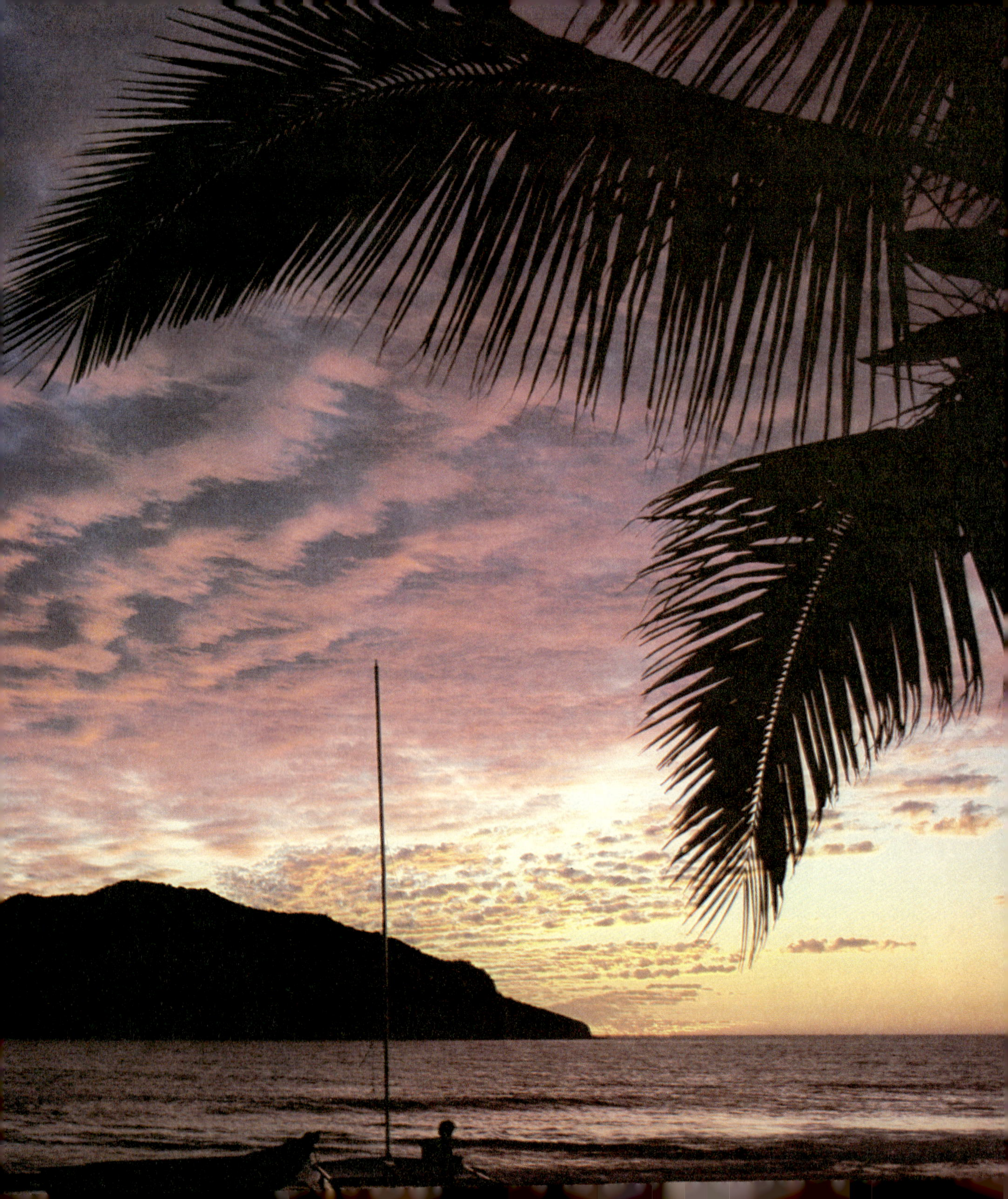

Chapter 7
Water in the Atmosphere

Lesson Titles
7.1 Water on the Move
7.2 Condensation
7.3 Fog and Clouds
7.4 Precipitation and the Hydrologic Cycle

When will it rain? What causes storms? When will a storm occur? People have tried to answer questions like these throughout history. A long time ago people had to rely on their memories and experiences for answers. They sometimes told others of their experiences through weather proverbs. Here are some of the proverbs:

> *Mackerel sky and mare's tails*
> *Make tall ships carry low sails.*

> *A rainbow in the morning is the shepherds' warning;*
>   *a rainbow in the afternoon is the shepherds'*
>   *delight.*

> *When the grass is dry at morning light,*
> *Look for rain before the night.*
> *When dew is on the grass,*
> *Rain will never come to pass.*

These proverbs all refer to a sequence of weather events. All are related to some form of water. This chapter is about water in the atmosphere. After you finish the chapter, return to these proverbs. Will they help you predict when it will rain?

Figure 7.1 *opposite:* A mackerel sky, named for its speckled texture of cirrocumulus clouds

7.1 Water on the Move

You will find out
- how water moves into and out of the atmosphere;
- how the amount of water in the atmosphere is measured;
- how the amount of water in the atmosphere can be increased.

You know about water. You use it all the time. You use it as a liquid when you wash in it or drink it. You use it as a solid when you skate on ice or eat a snow cone. Water also occurs as a gas called **water vapor.** Water is different from most substances on the earth. It is different because it can occur naturally as a solid (ice), a liquid (water), and a gas (water vapor).

Water is always on the move. Liquid water moves across the land in streams and rivers. Water moves through the atmosphere as tiny droplets called clouds. It also moves through the atmosphere as invisible vapor. There is more water vapor moving through the atmosphere than there is water in all the rivers on land. The study of water on and within the earth, and in the atmosphere, is called **hydrology** [hy-DRAHL-uh-jee].

Water is also moving in other ways. It moves back and forth between liquid water and water vapor. How are water vapor and liquid water different? For your model you can think of water vapor as single molecules of water moving about. They move about freely in the air. Liquid water can then be thought of as many molecules being held together. They are held together by forces between the molecules. These forces are like springs. They let the water molecules move back and forth but hold them in the liquid form.

Water molecules on the earth are always moving. How fast they move depends on the temperature. As the temperature goes up, they move about more rapidly. As the temperature goes down, they slow down. Molecules have more energy at higher temperatures.

Water molecules in liquid form can obtain enough energy of motion to escape into the air. This happens when the energy of motion is great enough to break the

Figure 7.2 Some water molecules in the waterfall have enough energy of motion to escape into the air as vapor.

force holding the molecules together. If more molecules are leaving the liquid state than are returning, it is said that the water is **evaporating** [ee-VAP-uh-rayt-ihng]. These water molecules going into the air are water vapor. Water vapor goes into the air through evaporation. Evaporation from the mirror in your bathroom after your shower is a good example of this.

Water vapor molecules in the air slow down when cooling occurs. If they slow down enough so that molecular forces grab them, they again form liquid water. When more molecules are returning to the liquid state than are leaving, it is said that water vapor is **condensing** [kahn-DENS-ihng]. Water vapor leaves the air through condensation. A good example is water on a kitchen window on a cold winter day.

As you can see, there is a relationship between evaporation, condensation, and the temperature. If the temperature is decreased, the average energy of motion of the molecule is decreased. Water vapor molecules condense into the liquid state when they slow down enough so that molecular forces grab them. Faster molecules are therefore less likely to be captured. As the temperature increases, there is less tendency for water vapor to return to the liquid state.

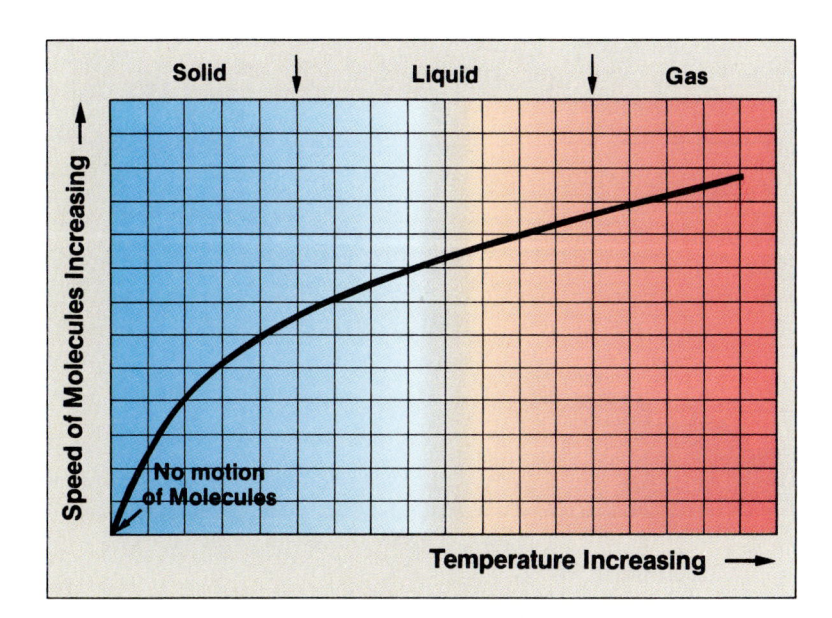

Figure 7.3 *top:* Water vapor molecules condense on the cool mirror. *middle to bottom:* Evaporation gradually returns water molecules to the air.

Figure 7.4 Average energy of motion of molecules increases at higher temperatures.

7 / Water in the Atmosphere

127

Warm air can therefore hold more water vapor than cooler air. In fact, warm air on a summer day can hold five times as much water vapor as cold air on a winter day. The amount of water vapor in the air is called **humidity** [hyoo-MIHD-uh-tee].

Air at the same temperature can have different amounts of water vapor in it. The amount of water vapor in the air may be referred to as low humidity or high humidity. Humidity, or the amount of water vapor in the air at a certain temperature, can be stated as a percentage.

One hundred percent humidity means that the air has all the water vapor it can hold at that temperature. Fifty percent humidity means that the air is holding half of the water vapor it can at that temperature. These percentages of humidity readings are called the **relative humidity.** The relative humidity tells you how much water vapor is in the air compared to the total that could be in the air at a certain temperature.

Relative humidity can be increased two ways. Adding more water vapor to the air increases the relative humidity because it increases how much water is in the air. Cooling increases the relative humidity because it

Figure 7.5 This bar graph illustrates that air at higher temperatures contains more water when at 100-percent humidity than air at lower temperatures.

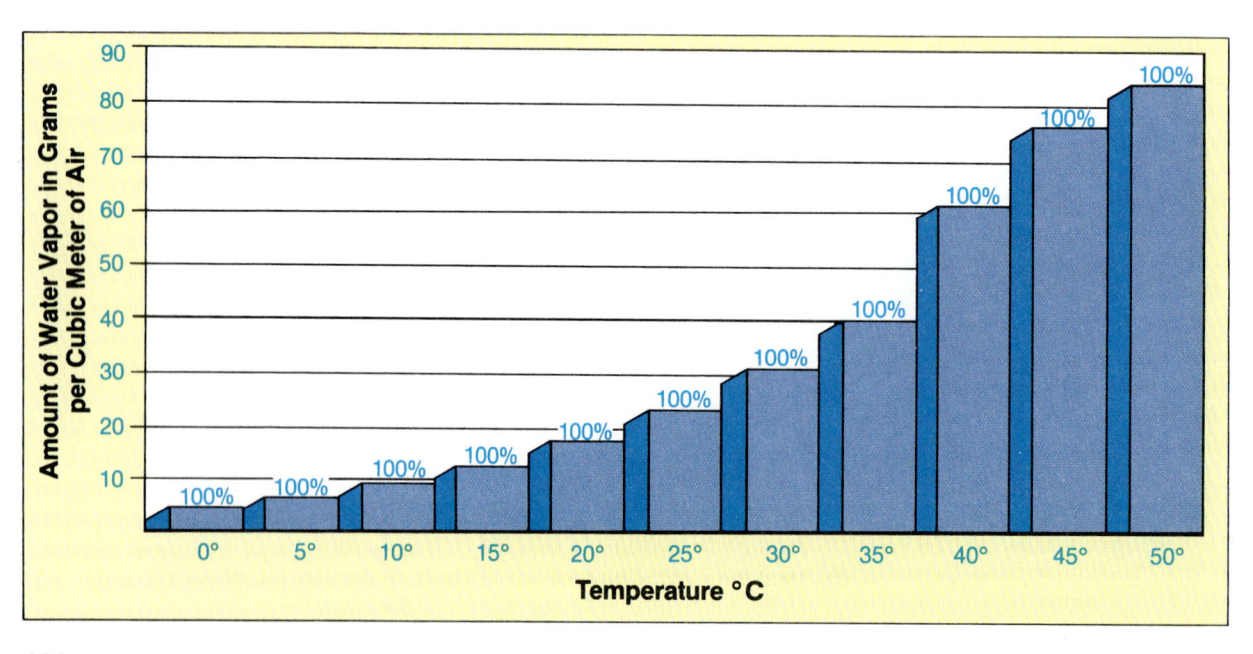

128

7 / Water in the Atmosphere

reduces the amount of water vapor that can be in the air. Have you heard a weather report lately? What is happening to the relative humidity?

Do You Know?
Cold air cannot hold much water vapor so the saying "It's too cold to snow" has meaning.

Activity

How Wet Is the Air?

Materials
cotton shoelace
index card
two thermometers

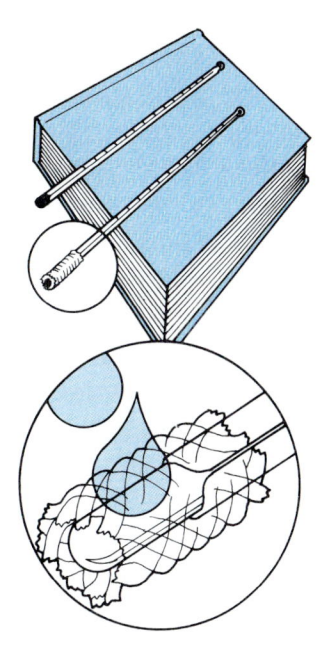

Procedure

1. Make a wet-bulb thermometer. Slip a short piece (3 cm) of shoelace over the bulb of a thermometer. Wet the shoelace with water.

2. Place the wet-bulb thermometer beside a dry-bulb thermometer on a book as shown.

3. Fan the bulb end of the thermometers with an index card. Note the temperature of the wet-bulb thermometer.

4. Continue to fan the thermometers until the wet-bulb thermometer registers its lowest reading. At this time, record the wet-bulb and the dry-bulb temperatures.

5. Subtract the wet-bulb reading from the dry-bulb reading. Use this difference and the dry-bulb temperature on a relative humidity chart (page 515) to find the relative humidity.

6. Measure the humidity in your classroom, outside, and in other locations.

Questions

1. What data did you obtain about the humidity in the different locations?

2. What would explain any differences you may have found?

Study Questions for 7.1

1. Describe how water moves into and out of the atmosphere.
2. What is meant by the "humidity is 50 percent"?
3. What are two different ways that the humidity can increase?

7 / Water in the Atmosphere

7.2 Condensation

You will find out
- how condensation occurs;
- the relationship between relative humidity and condensation;
- how to predict when dew or frost will form.

Figure 7.6 Water vapor exhaled in warm breath condenses in cold air.

Figure 7.7 A spider's web looks like a jeweled necklace as dew condenses on it.

Have you ever seen your breath on a cold day? You can see your breath because your exhaled air is warm and contains much water vapor. Your breath forms a small pocket of air with a high amount of water vapor. As this pocket of air is cooled, its relative humidity increases. The humidity reaches 100 percent and condensation takes place, forming tiny water droplets. What you see is a small cloud with thousands of tiny water droplets. As the condensed droplets spread into the surrounding air with lower humidity, they evaporate and disappear.

In the atmosphere large amounts of air can also be cooled. Air near the ground cools during the night by contact with the cooling earth surface. It sometimes cools until the relative humidity reaches 100 percent. Further cooling then results in condensation. The temperature at which condensation occurs is called the **dew point.** If the dew point is above 0°C, the water vapor will condense on surfaces as a liquid, called **dew.** If the temperature is at or below 0°C, the vapor will condense on surfaces as a solid, called **frost.**

Dew or frost forms on *C* nights—clear, calm, cool nights. Let us see why dew or frost forms on *C* nights. Here is how it works. The earth is warmed by radiant energy from the sun and gives off infrared radiation (page 109). The surface warms during the day as more energy is received than is given off. The surface cools during the night because no energy is received, but the surface continues to give off infrared radiation. This infrared radiation passes back into space. If there are clouds they serve as blankets, keeping the radiation in. This keeps the temperature above the dew point. *C* nights favor dew or frost formation because there is nothing to keep the heat from the radiation in the area.

130

7 / Water in the Atmosphere

Activity

What Is the Dew Point?

Materials
shiny metal can
crushed ice
thermometer

Procedure

1. Fill a shiny metal can about half full with tap water.

2. Place a thermometer in the water. Add a *small* amount of ice. Watch the sides of the can as you stir the water.

3. Continue adding small amounts of ice and stirring until dew begins to form on the can. The dew point of the air will be the temperature of the water in the can when dew begins to form on the can.

4. Repeat steps 1 through 3 outdoors. Compare the dew point of the air in your classroom to the dew point of the air outside.

Questions

1. What is the dew point inside your classroom?

2. What is the dew point outside your classroom?

3. Find out the predicted low temperature for tonight. Will the dew point be reached?

Fruit growers have developed special means to prevent frost in their orchards. Stack heaters are sometimes used to warm the air in the orchard. Other times large fans are used to mix the air being cooled near the surface with warmer air above the surface as another way of preventing frost.

When conditions are favorable, condensation occurs on surfaces as the dew point is reached. Note that dew or frost forms on, under, and on the sides of objects. People used to believe that frost and dew fell out of the air. But frost and dew really condense on cool objects, just as water vapor condenses on a glass of ice water.

Figure 7.8 Stack heaters protect orchard trees from damaging frost.

Study Questions for 7.2

1. The weather reporter states that "the dew point is 10°C." What does this mean?
2. What is the relative humidity when the dew point is reached?
3. Under what conditions does dew form?
4. Under what conditions does frost form?

7 / Water in the Atmosphere

7.3 Fog and Clouds

You will find out
- how a cloud is formed;
- the three basic cloud shapes.

Are there clouds where you are now? Some people watch clouds for clues about the weather. They call clouds "billboards of the sky" because clouds advertise the coming weather. Do you think clouds can tell you that much about coming weather?

What are clouds? Clouds are mostly tiny droplets of water. These droplets have been condensed on small particles that are present in the air. The particles are called **condensation nuclei** [NOO-klee-eye]. Particles of salt (from evaporating sea spray), smoke particles, and dust in the air all serve as condensation nuclei.

After water vapor molecules stick to a condensation nucleus, other water molecules will join and the droplets will grow larger. It may take several minutes to form the tiny water droplets that make up a cloud. It may take several hours for drizzle droplets to form. Compare the size of the water droplets in Figure 7.10.

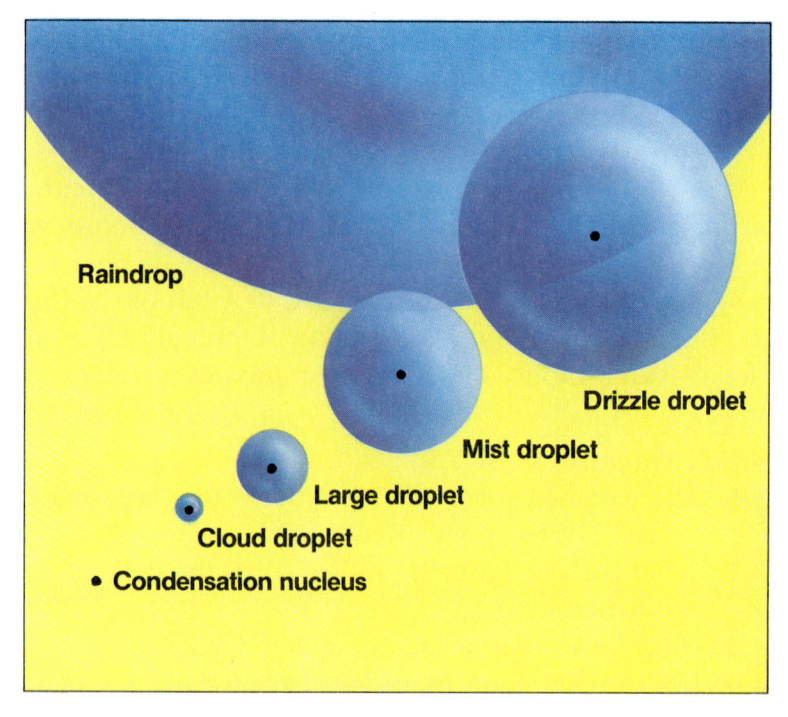

Figure 7.9 *top:* A clear sky has few condensation nuclei. *bottom:* A dirty sky has many.

Figure 7.10 Relative sizes, enlarged 500 times, of water droplets and a condensation nucleus.

Do You Know?
Volcanic dust travels all the way around the earth and can stay in the atmosphere for years.

132

7 / Water in the Atmosphere

Three things are needed for a cloud to form. Water vapor and condensation nuclei are needed, of course, but cooling must also take place. For example, convection may create a cloud. A pocket of air near the ground is moved upward by a convection current. The pocket of air cools as it travels upward. It soon reaches a height where it is cooled to the dew point. Condensation then takes place on condensation nuclei. Water droplets are formed, making a cloud.

The water droplets making up a cloud are very small. They fall to the earth very slowly. In calm air, droplets may fall less than 0.5 m per second. A very slight upward movement of the air will overcome this small falling speed. This is why clouds appear to float in the sky.

Fog is also a cloud. It's at or near the earth's surface. It is made up of very small water droplets that fall very slowly. Fog often forms under the same conditions favorable for dew or frost to form—C nights. Coastal fogs are usually fogs that form over the ocean and then move inland.

Do You Know?
Water vapor from the engines of high-flying jet airplanes sometimes forms clouds. These clouds may be affecting the weather.

Figure 7.11 The development of cumulus clouds

Figure 7.12 Ground fog looks like a cloud upon the earth.

7 / Water in the Atmosphere

Career

Meteorologist

People often need to know future weather conditions. Builders need to know if it is going to rain before they pour concrete. Farmers need to know future weather conditions to plan crop planting and harvesting. You need to know about future weather to plan what you will wear to school or will do during the weekend. Information about future weather conditions comes from a meteorologist, a scientist who studies the weather.

June Bacon-Bercey is a meteorologist. As a meteorologist, she has been a weather analyst, a radar meteorologist, and then a chief forecaster, predicting the weather for New York, Connecticut, Pennsylvania, and New Jersey, including Long Island Sound and Cape May to Block Island. She has also been a television weather caster (WGR-TV in Buffalo) and an aviation operations meteorologist. She is presently a public information specialist with the National Oceanic and Atmospheric Administration (NOAA). As you can see, a meteorologist can do more than gather information about temperature, wind speed, pressure, and humidity.

June Bacon-Bercey became the first woman recipient of the Seal of Approval of the American Meteorological Society for television weather casting. She has received many awards for her work. Her present job is to inform people about weather. She makes films to prepare people for weather disasters. These films are shown on television. She says that the United States needs more and better scientists and a public that understands science. She says that in her present job she can encourage people to consider careers in meteorology and earth science. She means what she says. In 1977 she won $64,000 on a TV quiz show. She used it to set up a scholarship assistance program for women wanting a career in meteorology.

CHAPTER REVIEW

Main Ideas

- Water enters the atmosphere through evaporation and leaves by condensation.
- Relative humidity is the ratio of the amount of water vapor that is in the atmosphere to the amount that could be in the atmosphere at a particular temperature.
- Relative humidity is increased when more water vapor is added to the air or when the air is cooled.
- The dewpoint is the temperature at which water vapor condenses on a surface.
- Dew or frost forms on C nights—clear, calm, cool nights.
- Fog and clouds are made of tiny droplets of water. These droplets form on condensation nuclei when air with 100-percent humidity is cooled.
- The basic cloud shapes are cirrus, cumulus, and stratus.
- Precipitation forms from small cloud droplets that collide and join together or from ice crystals that grow heavy and fall from a cloud.
- Precipitation that falls to the surface of the earth is solid or liquid, depending on the temperature in different layers of air.
- The earth's hydrologic cycle is evaporation, condensation, and precipitation of water—a never-ending process.

Using Vocabulary

Use the Glossary to define each of the words below. Write the definitions on a separate piece of paper.

water vapor	dew	cumulonimbus
hydrology	frost	altostratus
evaporating	condensation nuclei	cirrostratus
condensing	fog	precipitation
humidity	cirrus	cycle
relative humidity	cumulus	drought
dew point	stratus	

7 / Water in the Atmosphere

Remembering Facts

Number your paper from 1 to 15. Match each term in column **A** with a phrase in column **B**.

A	B
1. water vapor	a. solid or liquid water that falls to the earth's surface
2. frost	b. evaporation, condensation, and precipitation
3. condensation nuclei	c. a cloud on the surface
4. dew	d. water in the gaseous state
5. fog	e. percent of water vapor in the air at a temperature
6. cirrus	f. a piled-up storm cloud
7. evaporating	g. air temperature at which condensation occurs
8. cumulonimbus	h. water vapor that condensed as a solid
9. precipitation	i. water vapor molecules returning to the liquid state
10. dew point	j. feathery fiber clouds
11. stratus	k. water vapor that condensed as a liquid
12. condensing	l. a piled-up cloud
13. hydrologic cycle	m. a spread-out cloud
14. cumulus	n. water vapor molecules leaving the liquid state
15. relative humidity	o. particles water vapor condenses on in the air
16. hydrology	p. period when there is not enough rainfall
17. drought	q. clouds made of tiny ice crystals
18. humidity	r. study of water
19. cloud droplets	s. the amount of water vapor in the air
20. cirrostratus	t. form around condensation nuclei

Understanding Ideas

On your paper, answer each question in complete sentences.
1. Explain why some air pollution is needed for the hydrologic cycle to function.
2. Would you expect rain to fall from cirrus clouds? Why or why not?
3. Is the process of dew forming more like the process of cloud droplets forming or the process of raindrops forming? Why?
4. Under what atmospheric conditions would you expect dew to form?

Applying What You Have Learned

1. Explain why relative-humidity readings are often lower in the afternoon than they were in the morning.
2. Describe an imaginary trip of a water molecule from the time it evaporates until it returns as a raindrop. Include the conditions for each event in the trip.
3. Warm air holds more water vapor than cold air. What does air temperature have to do with the amount of water vapor in it?
4. What is wrong with making the statement "a heavy dew fell last night"?

Challenge

Use the graph and your understanding of relative humidity to answer the following questions.

1. How much water vapor can a cubic meter of air at 40°C hold?
2. Suppose a cubic meter of air is 40°C with 100-percent humidity. How much water would condense from the cubic meter if the air was cooled to 10°C?
3. Consider a cubic meter of air at 25°C with 35-percent relative humidity. How much water vapor is in this air?
4. To what temperature would you cool a cubic meter of 25°C, 35-percent-relative-humidity air to cause condensation?

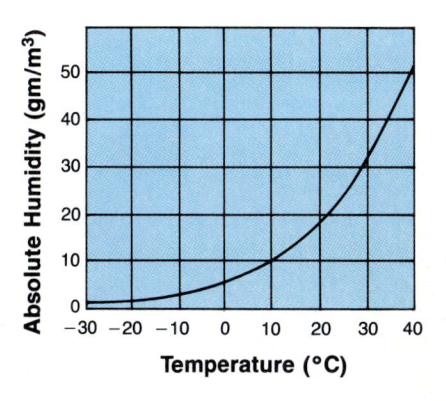

Research and Investigation

1. Set up a weather watch. See if you can find relationships between cloud types, wind speed, wind direction, humidity, and coming weather. Will identifying cloud types alone enable you to predict coming weather?
2. How large is a raindrop? Fasten some cloth material such as nylon hose over the opening of a small box. Smooth flour over the cloth. Hold the cloth horizontally for a few seconds in a rainfall. Drops passing through the cloth will leave their mark, which can be measured. What is the diameter of an average raindrop? Find out how to figure the volume of an average raindrop. Write a report and present your findings to your class.

7 / Water in the Atmosphere

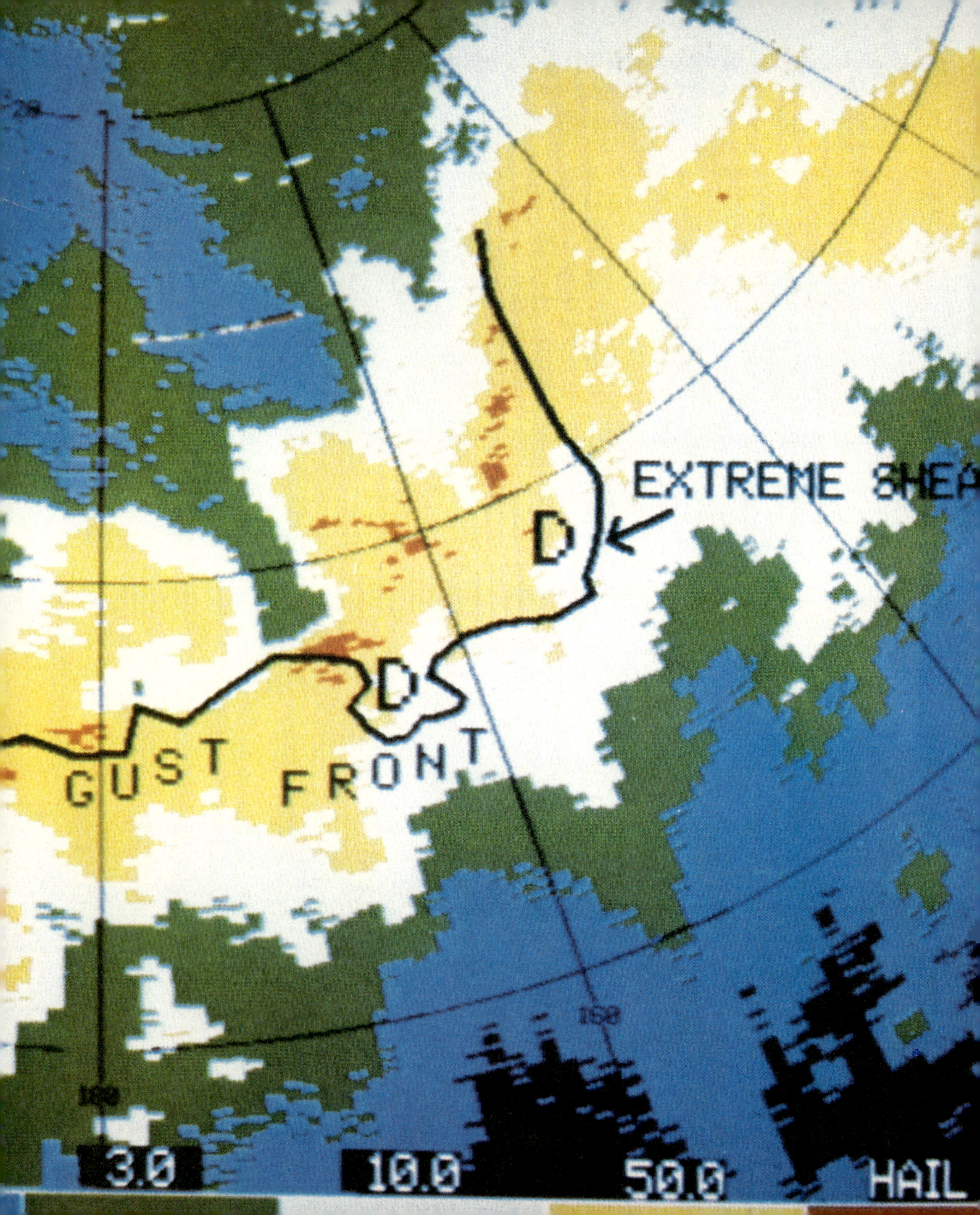

EXTREME SHEA
D
D
GUST FRONT
3.0
10.0
50.0
HAIL

Chapter 8
Weather

Lesson Titles
8.1 Air Masses
8.2 Weather
8.3 Forecasting
8.4 Major Storms

The weather is a common topic of conversation. Nearly everyone has some interest in knowing what weather changes will occur from day to day.

People have used observations such as wind direction, cloud types, and temperature changes to make weather forecasts. Sometimes even an amateur meteorologist is able to make accurate predictions about daily changes in the weather. But long-range forecasting is a far more complex problem.

Making accurate long-range forecasts requires a great deal of information and experience. Professional meteorologists realize that local weather is often affected by atmospheric changes that occur hundreds or even thousands of miles away. Therefore, modern forecasters try to show you the "big picture" when they explain their forecasts.

Modern technology has changed the science of weather forecasting dramatically. Weather balloons, satellites, precise modern instruments allow meteorologists to collect data worldwide. Computers are used to gather and organize all of the data. This allows meteorologists to put together a forecast quickly and accurately. They are able to warn us about most types of storms hours or even days before the storm arrives. In this chapter you will learn what causes changes in the weather and how scientists study those changes.

Figure 8.1 *opposite:* Modern equipment allows scientists to track storms that are moving across the country.

8.1 Air Masses

You will find out
- what an air mass is;
- that air moves across the country;
- the three things an air mass depends on.

Figure 8.2 These toes feel the draft of cold air flowing downward.

Every time you open the refrigerator door, cold air pours out onto the floor. The cold air that leaves the refrigerator is replaced by warm air from the kitchen. When you close the door, the warm air is cooled by the cooling coils of the refrigerator. The next time you open the door cold air will again pour out.

Much the same thing happens to air outdoors. Large sections of the atmosphere near the ground become "air conditioned." That is, the air takes on the same temperature as the earth's surface it is over. It also becomes almost as moist or dry as the surface. When such a body of air over thousands of square kilometers has uniform temperature and moisture, it is called an **air mass.**

How do air masses form? They form mostly in high-pressure belts. Recall the model developed in Chapter 6 of air movement of the earth's atmosphere. There are two zones of high pressure in the northern hemisphere. In both places air piles up, sinks, and spreads out slowly across the surface. The air slowly becomes changed by its surroundings. An air mass is formed. Air masses can be very large, thousands of square kilometers across. But they may be only a few kilometers deep.

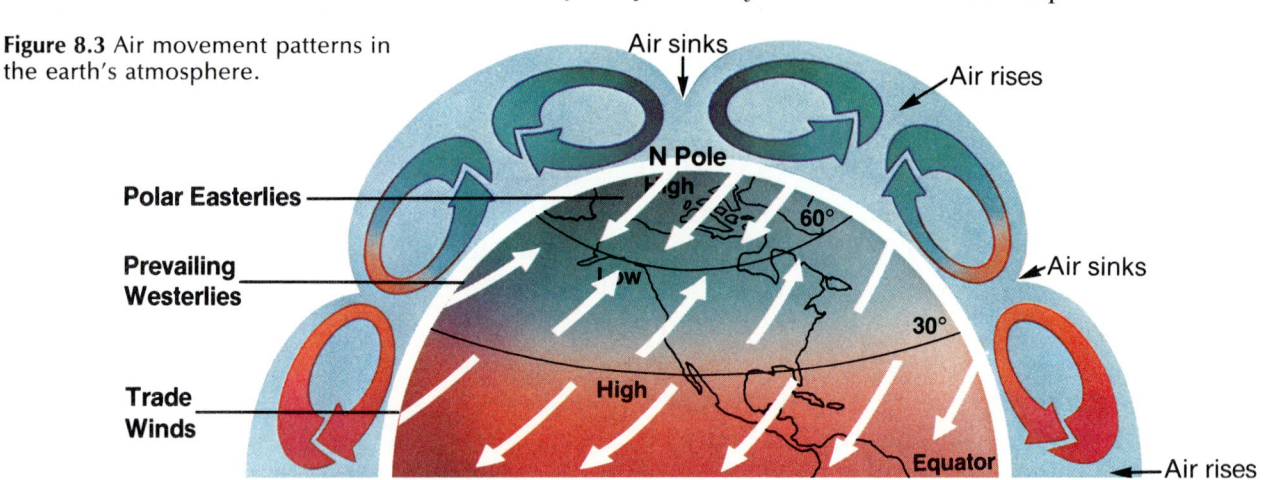

Figure 8.3 Air movement patterns in the earth's atmosphere.

144

8 / Weather

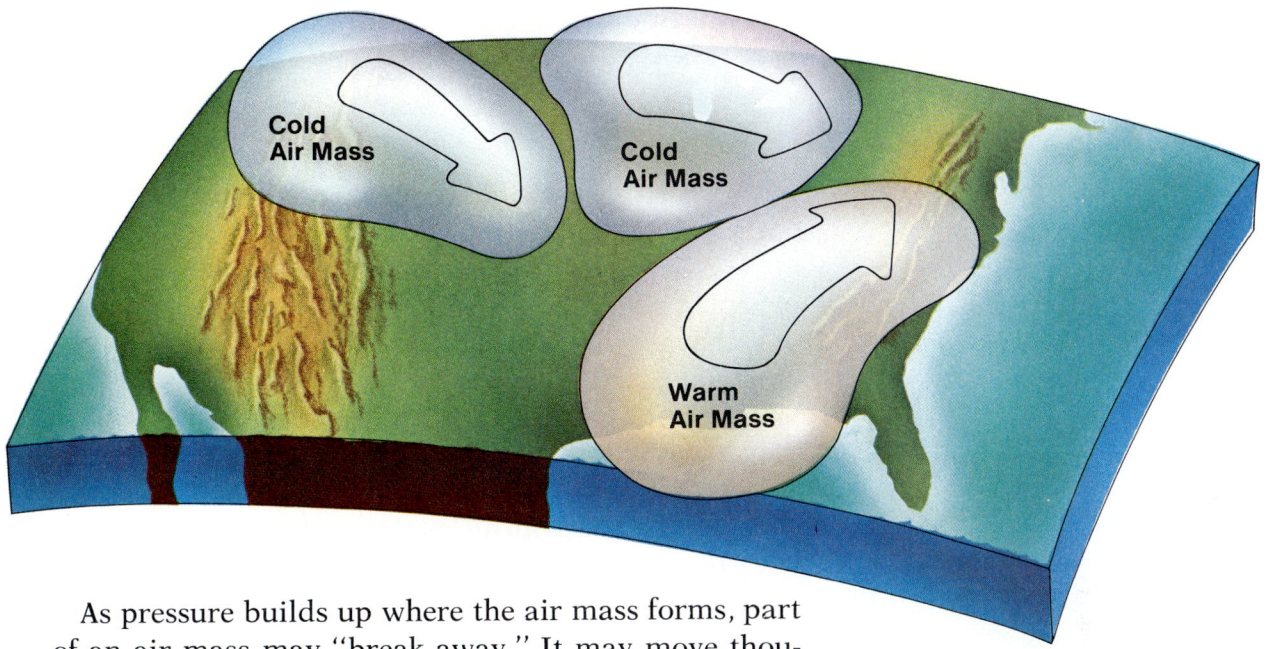

As pressure builds up where the air mass forms, part of an air mass may "break away." It may move thousands of kilometers. A moving air mass is like a large, flattened bubble of air. As the air mass moves across the surface, it may keep nearly the same temperature and moisture conditions. Since this bubble is so large, days may be required for it to move past your location. During this time, your weather is controlled by the conditions of the air mass that you are currently in.

If the moving air mass begins to slow or stop over your area, however, the conditions of the air you are in begin to change. The weather in the air mass depends on three things. These are (1) the temperature and moisture conditions of the air mass, (2) the temperature and moisture conditions of the area over which it has moved, and (3) how fast it has moved. Meteorologists keep close track of moving air masses. This tracking gives them important information for weather predictions.

Figure 8.4 Air masses as they may be located over the continental United States

Study Questions for 8.1

1. What is an air mass?
2. How does an air mass form?
3. What three things does the weather in an air mass depend on?

8.2 Weather

You will find out
- how air masses affect the weather.

The weather can be full of surprises for you. One day can be hot and humid with drizzling rain. The very next day can be clear and dry with a fresh clean smell in the air. It is as if something changed all the outside air. In fact, that is exactly what happens. A new air mass arrives and pushes the hot, humid air away. In its place comes a cool, dry air mass. But air masses must come from some place. In fact, air masses develop in a number of places.

The birthplace of an air mass is called a **source region.** One source region includes almost all of Canada and part of the northern United States in winter. Air masses formed here are cold and dry. They are called **continental polar** air masses. When a continental polar air mass arrives in the winter, the meteorologist reports a cold wave. The arrival of a continental polar air mass in the summer often provides relief from a heat wave. After a continental polar air mass arrives, your day may begin with crisp, clear air and blue skies. As the sun warms the surface, you see cumulus clouds start to form. By afternoon the sky may be covered with cumulus clouds. After sunset the clouds evaporate. Another source region is the hot and dry area of southwest United States. This air mass is called **continental tropical** and brings hot dry weather with it.

Another source region includes the mid Atlantic, the Caribbean, and the Pacific near the high-pressure areas found at about 30° north latitude. Air masses formed here are called **maritime tropical.** A maritime tropical air mass is warm and moist because it formed over subtropical waters. Maritime tropical air masses typically bring hot, humid weather. Clouds are more of the stratus type.

Still another source region for air masses is the cool northern Atlantic and northern Pacific oceans. What will these air masses be like? The moist, cool air masses

Figure 8.5 Four types of air masses

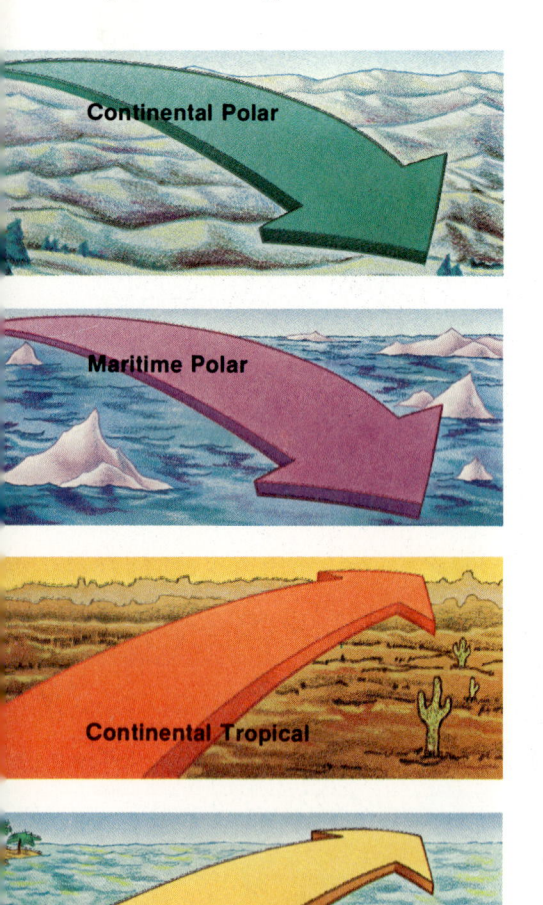

Continental Polar

Maritime Polar

Continental Tropical

Maritime Tropical

146

8 / Weather

formed here are called **maritime polar** air masses. Maritime polar air masses that form over the northern Atlantic Ocean may move into eastern Canada and the northeastern United States. They may be part of a storm called a "nor'easter" (northeaster). Maritime polar air also forms over the Pacific Ocean. It brings precipitation to the western states and to the Rocky Mountains.

Air masses are moved across the United States by the prevailing westerlies which you learned about in Chapter 6. Higher pressure to the north may send a bubble of continental polar air south into the United States. At other times pressure differences send a bubble of maritime tropical air northward into the United States and Canada. The different air masses tend to alternate and are moved eastward by the prevailing winds.

Figure 8.6 Air masses moving across North America create changing weather patterns.

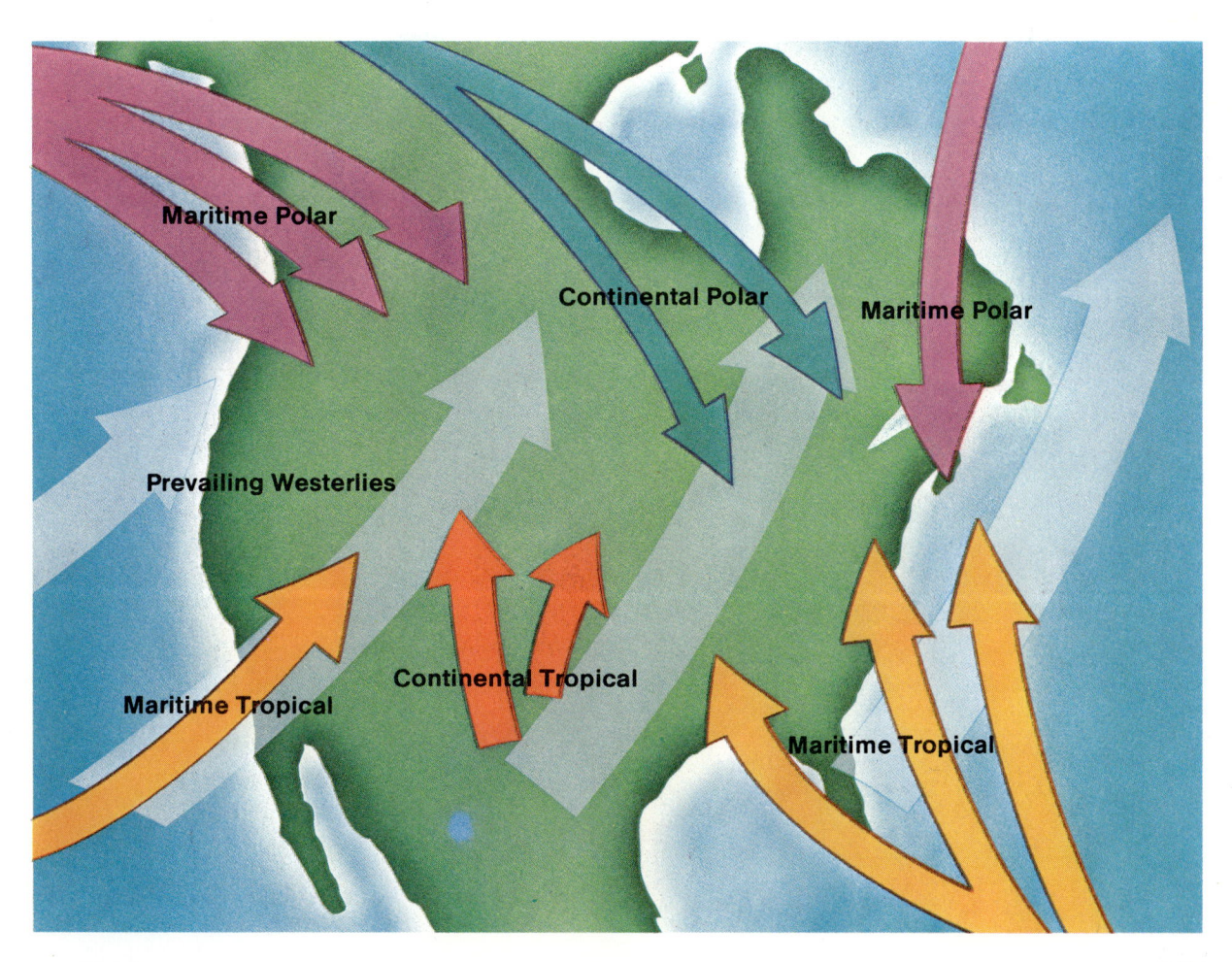

8 / Weather

Because air masses are so large, it may take days for one to move past one location. During this time you have **air mass weather.** Air mass weather is about the same from day to day with slow, gradual changes. Weather changes usually occur as one air mass is being moved out and replaced by the leading edge of another air mass.

The leading edge of a moving air mass is actually a zone from 5 to 80 km thick. This zone is called a **front.** There are different kinds of fronts. A **cold front** is at the front of a moving cold air mass. A **warm front** is at the

Activity

How Does an Air Mass Change the Weather?

Materials

A series of at least six newspaper weather maps. The maps should show a moving front passing some city on the second day.

Procedure

1. Study six weather maps that show a moving front. Identify a city that the front passes on the second day.

2. For a six-day period, make a list of the daily high temperatures, the low temperatures, any precipitation, wind speed, and direction.

Questions

1. Describe the weather before and after the front moved past the city. How did the low and high temperature change? Was there precipitation? What else changed?

2. What kind of air mass moved over the city?

3. What was the air mass weather like on the fourth, fifth, and sixth day? How did the low and high temperatures change? Was there precipitation? Were there any other changes?

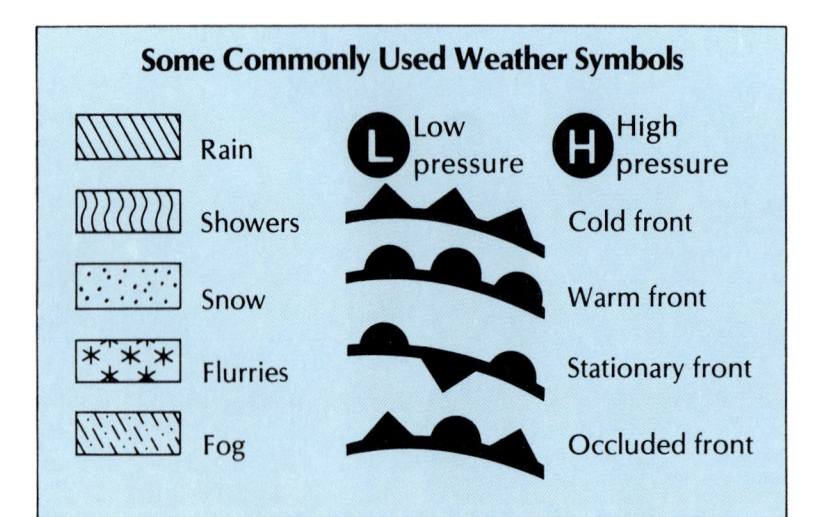

Some Commonly Used Weather Symbols

	Rain
	Showers
	Snow
	Flurries
	Fog
L	Low pressure
H	High pressure
	Cold front
	Warm front
	Stationary front
	Occluded front

148

8 / Weather

front of a moving warm air mass. Sometimes air masses stop and do not move. An unmoving zone or boundary between two air masses is called a **stationary front.**

Figure 8.7 Weather fronts bring changes in local weather as they pass.

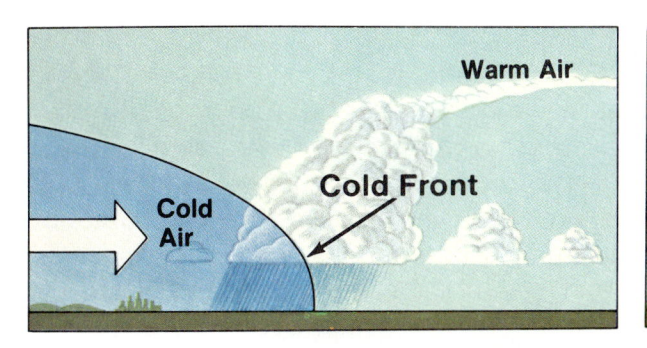

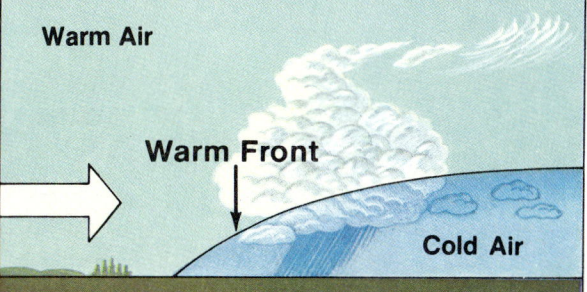

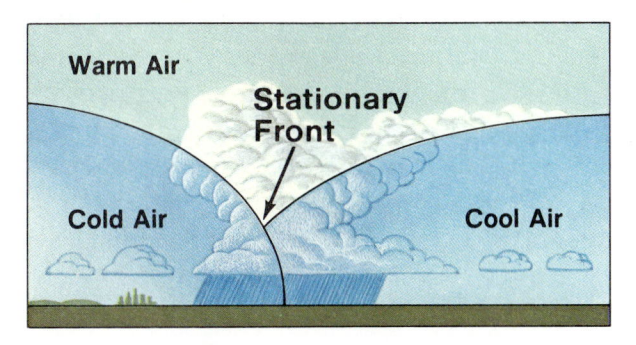

Fronts are shown as lines on a weather map. Different symbols are used to represent the different kinds of fronts. A symbol represents the place where the leading edge of a huge, flattened bubble of air touches the surface. When a front moves by, it may cause rapid and major weather changes. The changes caused by a front moving by are called **frontal weather.** Look at Figure 8.7 to see how a cold and warm front may change the weather. What type of weather are you having right now—air mass weather, cold front, or warm front?

Study Questions for 8.2

1. Name the source regions that produce the air masses that generally affect continental United States weather.
2. What is a cold front and what kind of weather follows it? A warm front?
3. What are the characteristics of "frontal weather"?

8.3 Forecasting

You will find out
- what is meant by highs and lows on a weather map;
- how a weather forecast is made.

You may have looked outside this morning before leaving for school. You looked to see if it was sunny, if it was raining, or if it was windy. Perhaps you listened to the radio to see what to expect later in the day. If so, you were listening to a weather **forecast.** It tells you about the coming weather. Did you use the forecast to decide what to wear? You could also use it to plan what to do after school.

Sometimes a weather forecaster will say something about high pressure or low pressure. Or sometimes just the words *high* and *low* are used. When barometric pressure is marked on a map, areas of high and low pressure are found. These pressure areas are important to meteorologists because certain kinds of weather can be expected with each kind of pressure area.

Figure 8.8 This map shows one possible pattern of high- and low-pressure areas over the United States.

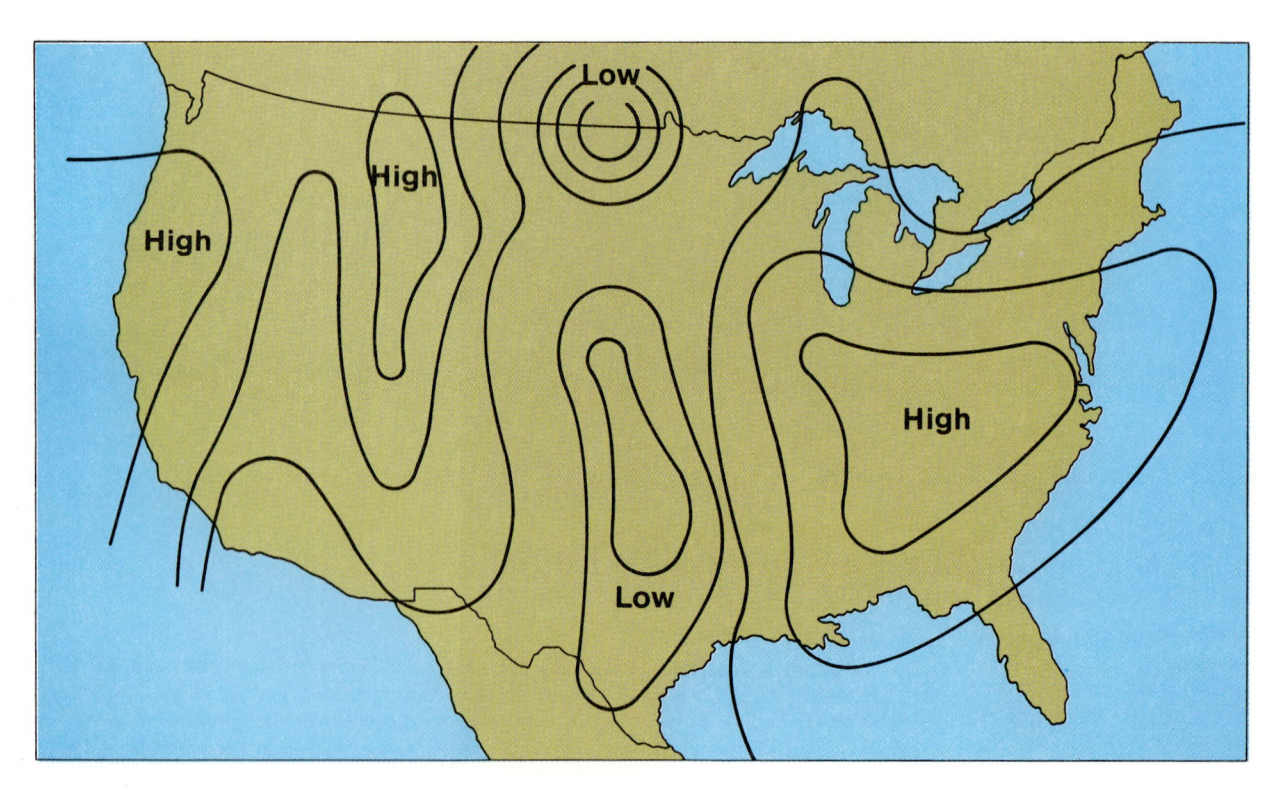

Suppose that a cold air mass moved over where you are. If you were watching a barometer, you would notice that the pressure goes up. Usually you are in a high-pressure area when you are in a cold air mass. The cold air produces a higher pressure because it is more dense than the warm air. The dense colder air sinks and spreads out. The downward movement of air is not very fast. It is usually not more than a few centimeters per second. It is enough, however, to warm the air some. This makes a clear sky. The air mass weather in a high-pressure area is usually fair. Most of the time high pressure means no clouds and fair weather.

Figure 8.9 *left:* The effect of a low-pressure air mass; *right:* The same location in a high-pressure air mass.

On page 148 you learned that when a cold air mass meets a warm air mass you have a front. Sometimes a wave occurs in the front. As a result, some cold air might move under part of the warm air, lifting it up. Upward moving air makes a lower pressure. The upward movement cools the air due to its expansion. This makes clouds. The weather in a low-pressure area is usually cloudy with precipitation. Most of the time, low pressure means bad weather.

8 / Weather

Figure 8.10 The prevailing westerlies help to push low-pressure areas east over the country.

Low-pressure areas and their associated bad weather usually follow certain tracks across the country. You can see some of the major tracks in Figure 8.10. According to Figure 8.10, where should you look to find out what kind of weather is moving toward Kansas?

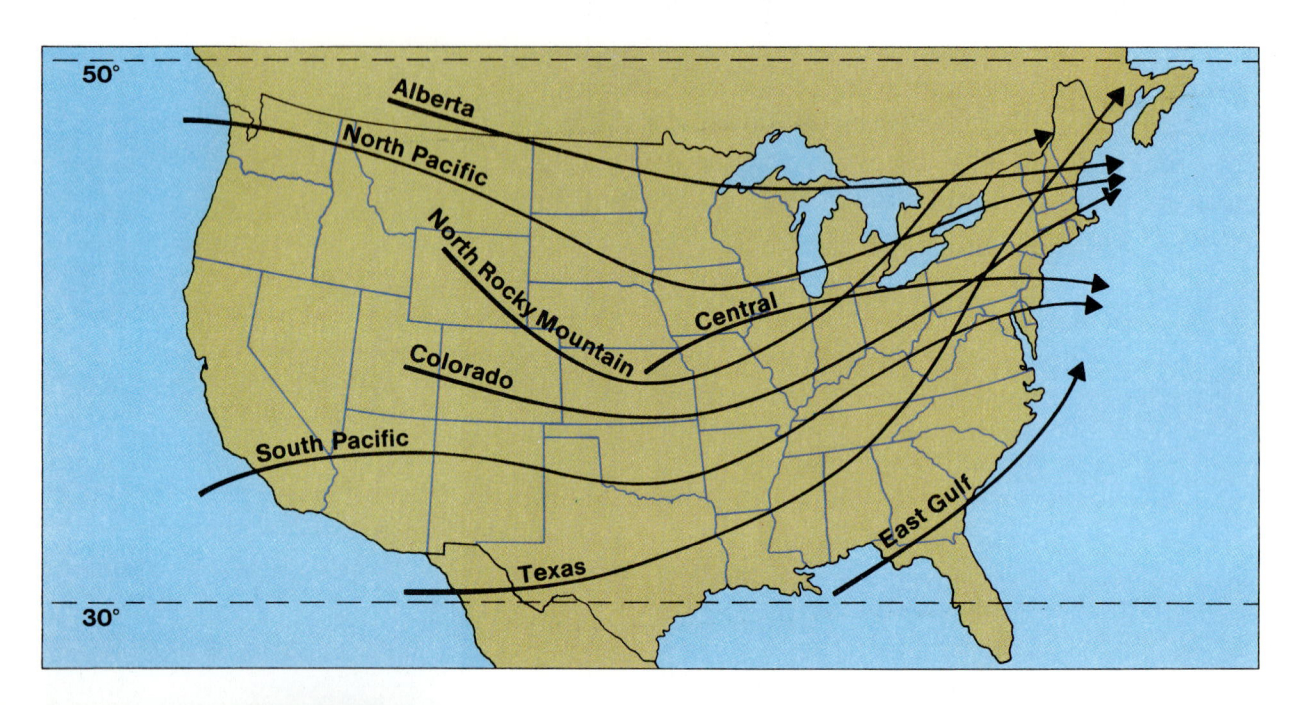

Figure 8.11 This meteorologist is recording data that are coming from other weather stations.

Weather forecasts begin with reports from the various weather stations. There are thousands of weather stations all across the country. People at the stations observe, measure, and report weather conditions. They describe the kinds of clouds over their stations. There are instruments to measure the temperature, relative humidity, pressure, wind, and precipitation. These observations and measurements are sent to regional offices of the National Weather Service. Meteorologists use the weather station information and information from weather satellites, radar, and their own instruments. They make a map that shows the location, size, and strength of high- and low-pressure areas. Fronts are then located and drawn on the map. Such a map and charts are used to determine the present state of the atmosphere. After all this is done, the meteorologists then must decide where the high- and low-pressure

152

8 / Weather

areas, air masses, and fronts will be tomorrow. From this, they can forecast where the clouds will be and if there will be precipitation. They also decide what the temperature will be and the kind of precipitation, if any. With all this information they then make a forecast. Such a forecast may state that there is a "30 percent chance of rain tomorrow." This means that when the conditions (air mass, front, pressure, etc.) are like they believe will occur, it is likely to rain three times out of ten. Three times out of ten is 30 percent. So the forecast is for a 30 percent chance of rain. With such a low chance for rain you can plan to have your picnic.

Do You Know?
The pressure difference between a high-pressure area and a low-pressure area is usually less than the pressure difference between the top floor of a skyscraper and the ground.

Activity

How Do Highs and Lows Help the Forecaster?

Materials
daily newspaper
weather maps

Procedure
1. Study daily weather maps showing a high-pressure area and a low-pressure area.
2. Read the daily weather forecasts for the days before and after each pressure area goes by.
3. Study the daily weather maps until it looks like a high- or low- pressure area is approaching where you are. Make your own forecast.

Questions
1. Describe the National Weather Service forecast that was made after the high-pressure area arrived.
2. Describe the National Weather Service forecast that was made as the low-pressure area arrived.
3. Describe the forecast you made. Was your forecast correct?

Study Questions for 8.3

1. A weather forecast mentions high- and low-pressure areas. What are these and what do they mean about the weather?
2. How is a weather forecast made?

8.4 Major Storms

Figure 8.12 Cumulonimbus clouds such as these are also known as thunderheads.

You will find out
- what the characteristics of a thunderstorm are;
- what is considered to be the most violent kind of storm;
- what a hurricane is and the major kinds of damage it causes.

The passage of many air masses, fronts, and pressure areas may go unnoticed. But they are sometimes accompanied by rapid and violent weather changes which are called **storms.** A snowstorm, for example, is a rapid change that a low-pressure area may bring. The three most violent kinds of storms, however, are thunderstorms, tornadoes, and hurricanes.

What is a **thunderstorm?** As the name suggests, it is a storm with thunder. The storm is an intense rainstorm with thunder, lightning, often strong winds, and sometimes hail.

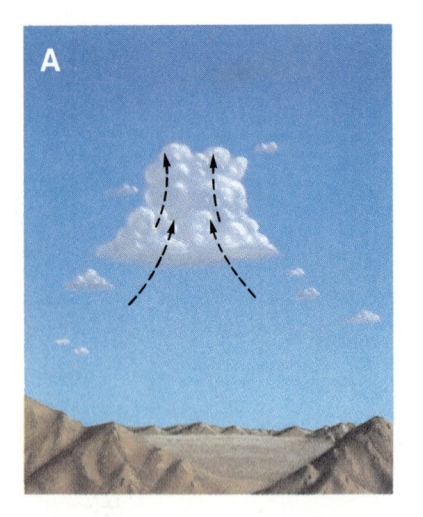

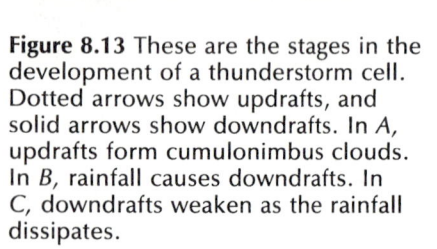

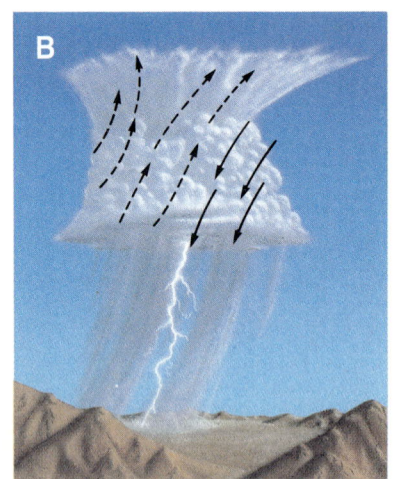

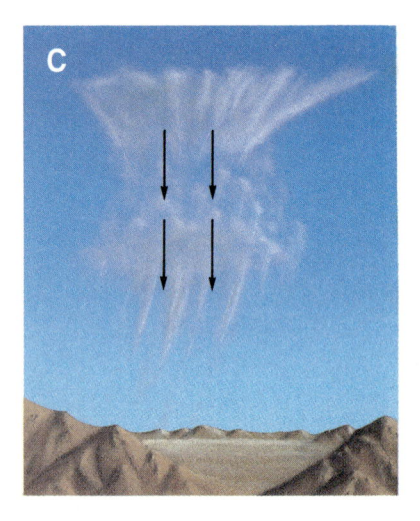

Figure 8.13 These are the stages in the development of a thunderstorm cell. Dotted arrows show updrafts, and solid arrows show downdrafts. In *A*, updrafts form cumulonimbus clouds. In *B*, rainfall causes downdrafts. In *C*, downdrafts weaken as the rainfall dissipates.

The updrafts and downdrafts in thunderstorm cells are responsible for hailstones and intense rainfall with large drops. The updrafts keep returning the hailstones and raindrops upward above the freezing level. When the rain and hail finally become too heavy for the updrafts, they fall to the ground. The result is a downdraft that produces a strong, cool wind that often arrives before the storm.

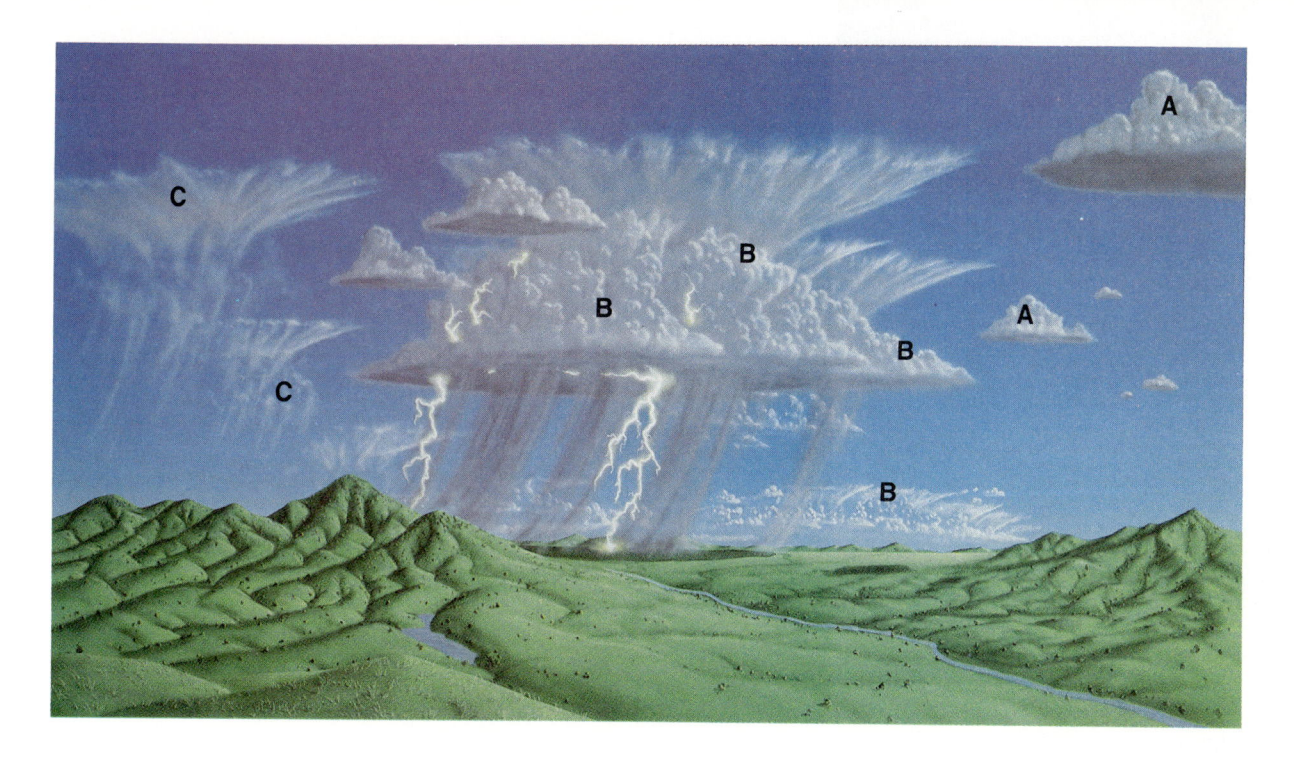

A thunderstorm is made up of one or more cells. Each cell is about 2 to 8 km in diameter. In Figure 8.13 you can see the three stages in the life of each cell. It usually takes less than an hour for a cell to go through all three stages. A thunderstorm, however, may last longer than an hour because new cells are formed as old ones die.

Air mass thunderstorms are the most common. More air mass thunderstorms occur in July than in any other month. These develop in warm, moist air from convection currents. They form mostly in the afternoon. Frontal thunderstorms can occur at any time of the day during any month. These develop as warm, moist air is lifted by a cold front as the front moves through.

Damage from a thunderstorm is usually caused by its lightning, wind, or hail. Lightning is really a giant electrical spark. The spark jumps between clouds, from a cloud to the ground, or from the ground to a cloud. Lightning heats the air, expands it, and produces a sudden pressure wave which you hear as thunder.

Figure 8.14 A thunderstorm moves over the land. The cells shown by letters here correspond to the stages of thunderstorm development in Figure 8.13.

Figure 8.15 Contrary to popular belief, lightning can strike the same place any number of times.

8 / Weather

155

Figure 8.16 Luckily this tornado is over open land. Sometimes tornadoes are called twisters.

Do You Know?
Hurricanes are given names that alternate between boys' and girls' names. The first hurricane of the season receives a name that begins with the letter *A*, the second hurricane one with a *B*, and so forth.

Figure 8.17 Common paths followed by hurricanes in the Atlantic Ocean and the Caribbean Sea

A **tornado** is the most violent storm that occurs on the earth. It is smaller but more violent than a thunderstorm or hurricane. A tornado often looks like a funnel or rope-shaped cloud that dips down from a cumulonimbus cloud. The diameter of the tornado is usually less than 400 m. It is a small low-pressure area around which air swirls violently up to speeds of 650 km per hour or more. If this swirling low-pressure area contacts the ground, it acts like a huge vacuum cleaner and causes considerable damage. It moves across the countryside at about 40 to 65 km per hour toward the northeast, and it may last up to an hour.

Most tornadoes occur in the afternoons of late spring or early summer. They are common in Kansas, Iowa, Arkansas, Texas, Mississippi, and Oklahoma. About 700 tornadoes occur in the United States each year.

A **hurricane** is a large, violent circular storm that is born over tropical bodies of water between the latitudes of 5 and 15 degrees. Hurricanes form from colonies of cumulonimbus clouds during late summer and fall when the bodies of water are the warmest. Once formed, they usually move to the northwest. If they reach north of 30° latitude, they usually start moving toward the northeast. Why do they move in this manner? How do the winds generally move north and south of 30° latitude?

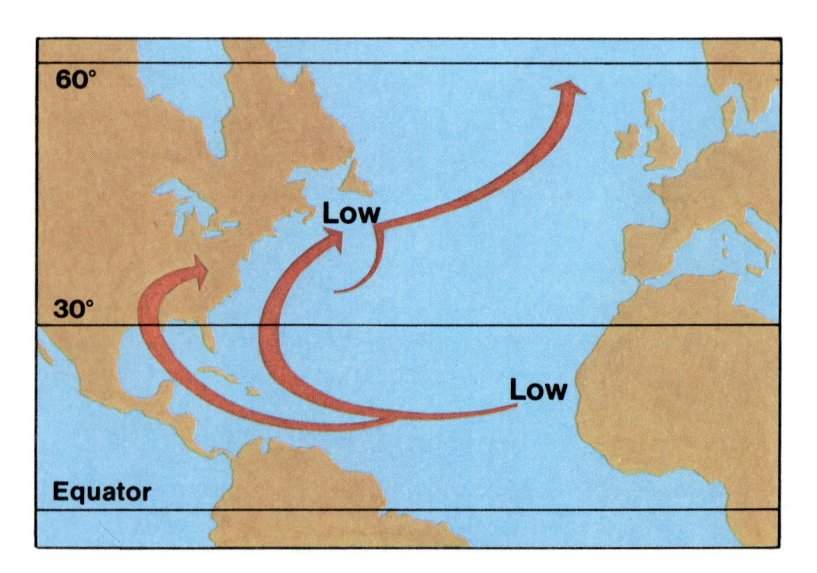

Figure 8.18 This man is watching the track of a hurricane with radar.

Figure 8.19 This is a computer radar picture of a hurricane. The calm blue area at the center is called the eye.

A hurricane may be from 150 to 650 km wide. In the northern hemisphere the wind blows around the center of the storm counterclockwise. These winds are greater than 120 km per hour and may reach 230 km per hour. The center or core of the system is called the eye of the storm. Little wind occurs in the eye and few clouds are present. The eye is usually about 15 to 30 km wide. As the eye of the storm passes an area it is calm for a short period of time.

Hurricanes may last up to nearly two weeks as they move across the ocean. They move at a rate of 15 to 50 km per hour. Most of the damage from hurricanes results from winds and flooding. Strong winds cause a "pileup" of water along the coast. Increases in sea level can be 4 to 6 m above normal. When storm waves of 10 to 15 m pile up above this raised sea level, large inland areas can be flooded. Hurricanes have caused extensive property damage and loss of life.

Now the National Weather Service can provide early hurricane warnings. Based on information from weather satellites, these early warnings have greatly reduced loss of life from hurricanes. Property damage, however, can be very large depending on the track of the storms. Hurricanes sometimes have thunderstorms with tornadoes that add to the overall damage.

Study Questions for 8.4

1. List the major characteristics of a thunderstorm.
2. What are tornadoes? Where do they form?
3. Describe a hurricane. How does one cause damage?

Science and Technology

Weather Radar

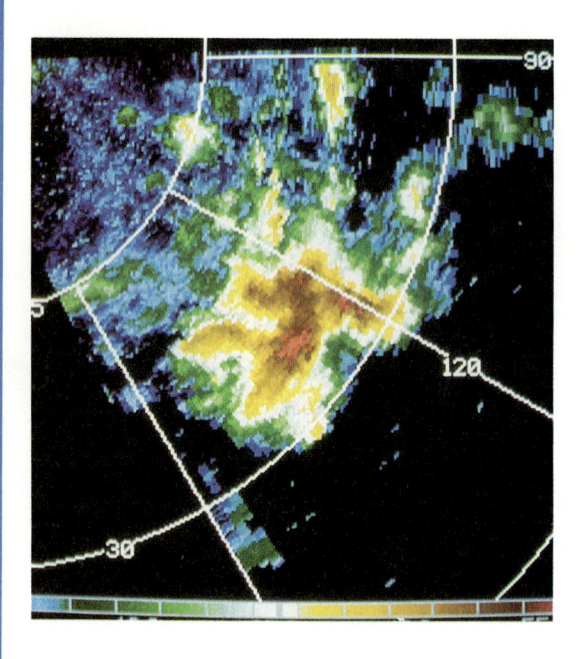

Weather scientists, or meteorologists, use many kinds of tools to help them predict weather. One of the most useful tools is radar. You may already know that radar works by sending out a thin beam of radio signals. If the signal "hits" an object in the sky, it bounces off the object and returns to a receiver. This "echo" can then be seen on a radar screen.

Radar is the only weather tool that can "see" inside clouds. You can see clouds and you can watch their changing patterns, but you cannot see what is inside them. Radar allows meteorologists to see into clouds and to find out which clouds contain dangerous weather.

Meteorologists have been using radar to see into clouds for many years. The early weather radar systems, however, could do little more than locate clouds that held large amounts of moisture. The newest weather radar systems can do much more.

One of the new radar systems, called Doppler radar, uses the Doppler effect. The Doppler effect is the change in wavelength that occurs in sound, light, and other waves as objects move toward or away from each other. In Doppler radar, the wavelength of the returning signal is compared with the wavelength of the radio signal that was sent out. If the wavelength of the returning signal is longer, the storm is moving away from the radar station. If the returning wavelength is shorter, the storm is moving toward the station.

With Doppler radar, meteorologists can learn far more than just which clouds contain storms. They can also find out the direction a storm is moving in, and they can measure how hard the winds in the storms are blowing.

Recently, a new kind of Doppler radar has been developed. It is called dual-polarization radar. With this system, radio signals are sent out from several sources at the same time. The data that result from the echoes are then given to a computer. The computer can draw cloud maps and provide other information about the clouds.

CHAPTER REVIEW

Main Ideas

- An air mass is a large part of the atmosphere that has much the same temperature and moisture conditions as the earth's surface it is over.
- Air masses form where air sinks and spreads out slowly across the surface.
- Air masses form in source regions, where they acquire conditions of temperature and moisture similar to the region.
- Air masses can leave the region where they formed and move across the surface of the earth.
- Air mass weather is what you experience while inside an air mass. Changes are slow and gradual.
- A front is the leading edge of a moving cold- or warm-air mass. Frontal weather is what you experience when the edge of a front passes.
- High atmospheric pressure is associated with dry air masses and fair weather.
- Low atmospheric pressure is associated with fronts and cloudy weather with precipitation.
- Weather forecasts are made from information about movement of air masses, fronts, and high- and low-pressure areas.
- Storms are rapid and violent weather changes.
- Thunderstorms and tornadoes are short-lived, small-area storms from a cumulonimbus cloud.
- A hurricane is a large circular storm that forms over tropical waters and moves to the northwest, then northeast after passing latitude 30° N.

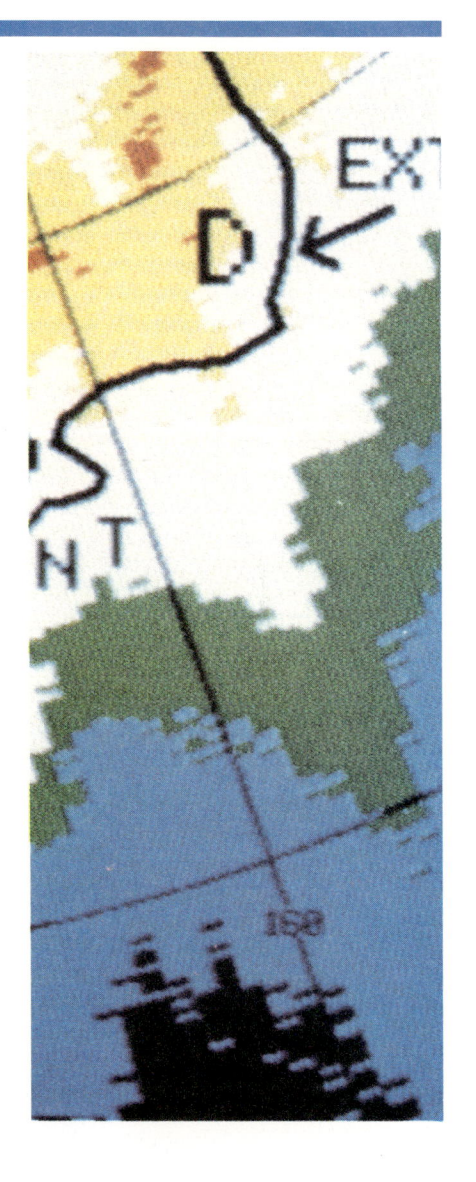

Using Vocabulary

Make up a matching-column quiz. On a separate piece of paper, list the words below in one column and describe each word in another. Exchange quizzes with a classmate.

air mass	maritime polar	warm front	storm
source region	air mass weather	stationary front	thunderstorm
continental polar	front	frontal weather	tornado
continental tropical	cold front	forecast	hurricane
maritime tropical			

Remembering Facts

On your paper, write the word or words that best complete each sentence.
1. Rapid and major weather changes caused by a moving front are called _____ weather.
2. A _____ _____ air mass forms over the northern Atlantic or Pacific Ocean. It is wet and cold.
3. A _____ _____ separates two stationary air masses.
4. The leading edge of a moving air mass is a zone that is called a cold or warm _____.
5. The location where an air mass develops is called the _____.
6. A _____ _____ air mass is cold and dry.
7. The most violent of all storms is a _____.
8. A _____ is an intense rainstorm with thunder, lightning, strong winds, and sometimes hail.
9. A large body of air that has uniform temperature and moisture conditions is called a(an) _____ _____.
10. A weather _____ tells you about the coming weather.
11. The leading edge of a moving warm-air mass is called a _____ _____.
12. _____ _____ weather is about the same from day to day, with slow, gradual changes.
13. The leading edge of a moving cold-air mass is called a _____ _____.
14. A _____ is a large, violent, circular storm that forms over tropical waters.
15. A warm, moist air mass formed over water at about latitude 30° N is described as _____ _____.

Understanding Ideas

On your paper, answer each question in complete sentences.
1. Two passing cold fronts can bring very different weather with them. Explain why this is possible.
2. Suppose you heard that it was raining in a nearby city. How could you predict the weather where you live without listening to any forecasts?
3. Why do both cold and warm fronts usually have clouds associated with them?
4. Why do hailstones fall only from thunderstorms?
5. Why do tornadoes do so much damage?

Applying What You Have Learned

1. Would an early-morning thunderstorm be more likely to occur in air-mass weather or frontal weather? Why?
2. Explain why the weather proverb, "When the dew is on the grass, rain will never come to pass," is usually true.
3. Explain why air masses, their fronts, and low- and high-pressure centers all move eastward or northeastward.
4. How do hurricanes do their damage?
5. Explain how a weather forecast is made.

Challenge

Thunderstorms occur frequently in some parts of the United States. In other areas, they are rare. The occurrence of these storms is not a random event. Patterns can be seen in the map on the right. This map shows the annual geographic distribution of thunderstorms in the United States. The lines on the map connect areas where these storms occur with the same frequency.

1. What two locations have the greatest number of thunderstorms?
2. Which location has the fewest thunderstorms?
3. What two factors seem to influence thunderstorm formation?
4. Why do states like Arizona and Colorado get so many thunderstorms even though they are on the eastern side of the Rocky Mountains?

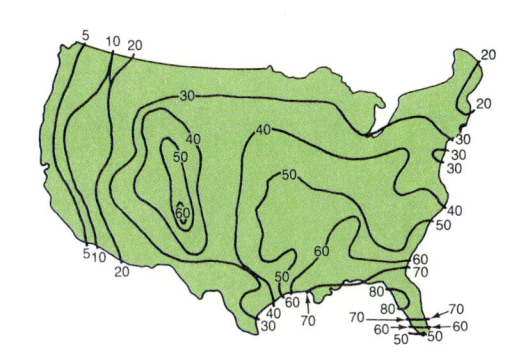

Research and Investigation

1. Track a thunderstorm. Obtain a compass, a city map, and straight pins. Use the compass to determine the direction of a lightning flash. Judge the distance of the flash by timing how long it takes for the thunder to reach you after you see the lightning. Count "1001, 1002, 1003," etc., at a normal speed to count seconds. It takes about 3 seconds for sound to travel 1 km. Stick pins in the map to trace the path of the thunderstorm. Prepare a bulletin-board report showing your map.
2. Plan a field trip to a weather observing station. What instruments are used? Find out what happens to the measurements that are made.

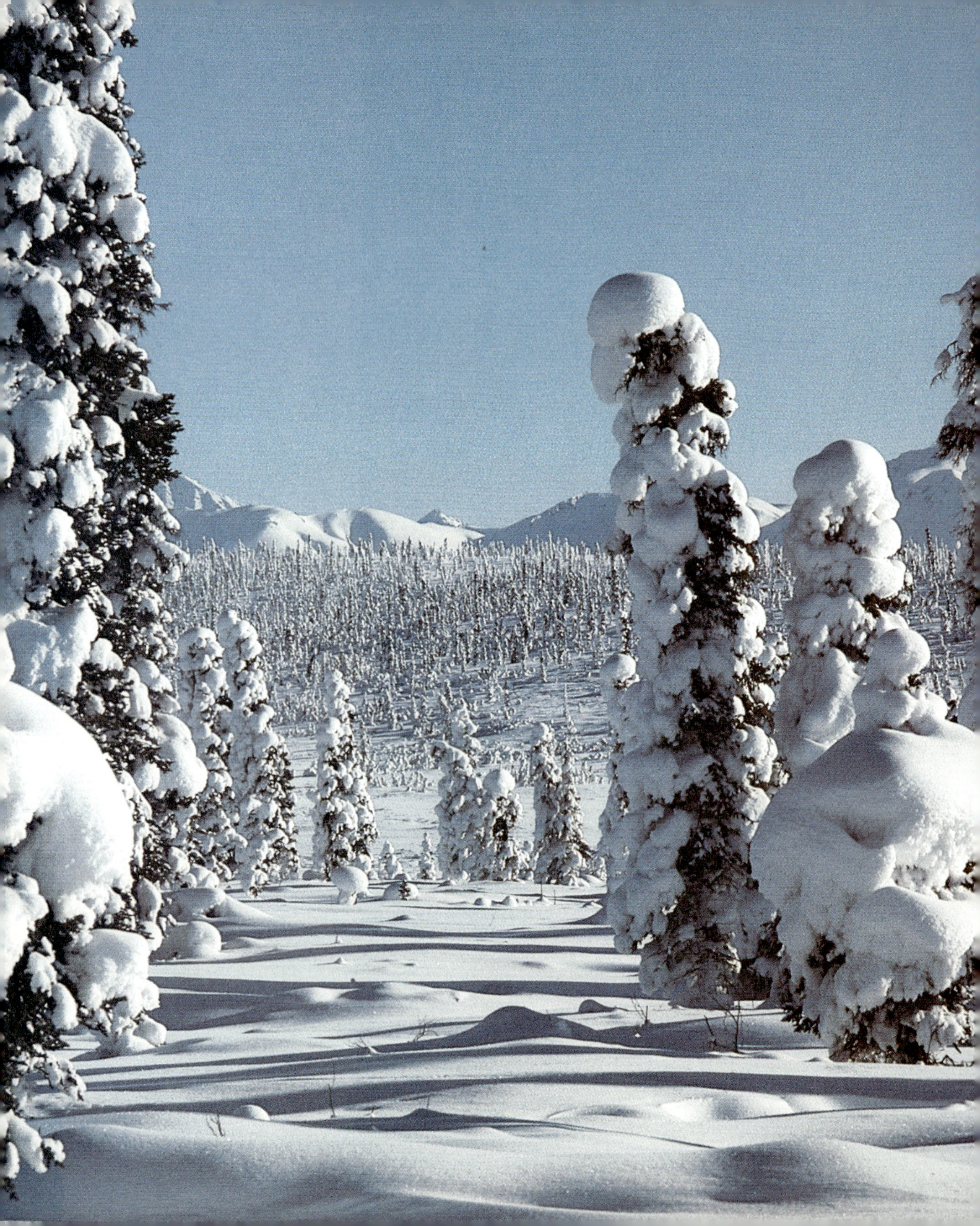

Chapter 9
Climate

Lesson Titles
9.1 Sunlight and Precipitation
9.2 Climate: Local Influence
9.3 Describing Climates

You know that the weather may change from day to day. The weather this week is probably different from the weather last week. Some months are colder than other months. But suppose you look at the temperature averages for a location. You will find a pattern each year. This pattern does not change much. The location where oranges grow, for example, has warm average monthly temperatures throughout the year.

Different monthly temperature and precipitation patterns occur in different locations. These determine the kinds of plants and animals that live in the locations. The patterns also determine what kinds of houses are built. The patterns even determine what people do for recreation. Consider skiing, for example. Would you expect to find a ski resort close to the area where orange trees grow? What kinds of weather patterns would you expect in places where a ski resort is located?

This chapter is about weather patterns that occur in different locations. You will find out what causes these patterns.

Figure 9.1 *opposite:* In some climates, deep snowfalls are a very common occurrence.

9.1 Sunlight and Precipitation

You will find out
- the difference between weather and climate;
- how sunlight makes temperature patterns;
- how atmospheric movement makes precipitation patterns.

Figure 9.2 What tells you that the moose, the forest, and the rafters share the same climate? The clue is the abundant amount of water.

Suppose two of your best friends move to two different places. Before they leave, both promise to write and send you pictures. Several months later, their letters arrive at the same time. Someone opened the letters, however, and the pictures were mixed up. Which of the pictures go together?

It looks as if your friends moved to very different places. How are the places different? Would you say that they have different weather? That might be true, but on any given day the weather in both places could be the same. The major difference in the two places is their average weather measured over a long period of time. The average weather over a long period of time is called **climate.** The two places have a different climate.

Do You Know?
Weather may change from day to day. The climate we have is here to stay.

164

9 / Climate

Weather changes from day to day and from week to week. The weather this winter may be very different from the weather last winter. But the climate of a location does not change so much. Climate describes the averages, totals, and the extremes for weather factors over long periods of time. Table 9.1 compares some of these weather factors for the places where your two friends moved. How would you describe the climate of the places where your friends live?

As you can see, climate is really weather considered over a long period of time. The two most important climate factors are temperature and precipitation. Let's see what determines these two climate-making factors. First, let's find out about temperature.

Table 9-1 Climatic Data for Two Locations					
Temperature	**Site 1**	**Site 2**	**Precipitation**	**Site 1**	**Site 2**
Average January High Temperature	18 °C	-3.3°C	Average Rainfall - Wettest month	2.5 cm	14.4 cm
Average January Low Temperature	1.6°C	-14.4°C	Average Rainfall - Driest month	0.2 cm	6.6 cm
Average July High Temperature	41 °C	30 °C	Average Rainfall for Year	18.2 cm	124.9 cm
Average July Low Temperature	24 °C	13 °C	Seasonal Average for Snow and Sleet	0.0	190.5
Average Temperature for Year	21 °C	6 °C	Percent of Yearly Possible Sunshine	84%	50%
Record Highest Temperature	47.8°C	37 °C	Number of Days with Thunderstorms per Year	26	43
Record Lowest Temperature	-8.8°C	-49 °C	Number of Days with Fog per Year	1	21

Temperature, as you know, is determined by how much sunlight is received. You learned in Chapter 6 (page 116) that different parts of the earth receive different amounts of sunlight. The greatest amount is received near the equator. The least amount is received at the poles. The yearly average temperature should therefore decrease as you move from the equator to the poles. In general, the temperature does decrease in this way.

9 / *Climate*

Figure 9.3 The locations of the three major climate regions on the earth

Figure 9.4 Vegetation in the three types of climate varies greatly. *top:* Polar; *middle:* Temperate; *bottom:* Tropical

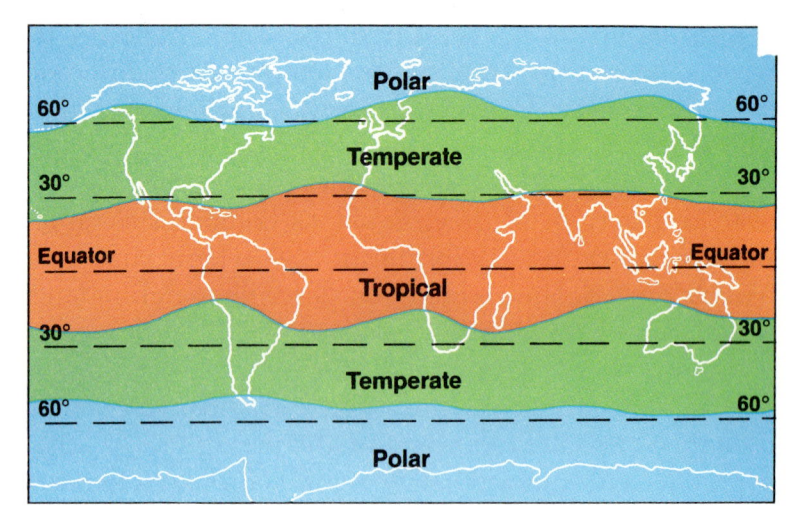

There are three major groups of climates that are based on yearly temperature averages. These occur in broad zones, or regions, as shown in Figure 9.3. They are (1) the **tropical** climate zone, (2) the **polar** climate zone, and (3) the **temperate** climate zone. There are subdivisions that occur within each of the three major zones. These will be discussed later.

The tropical climates are near the equator and receive the most direct sunlight all year. The average monthly temperatures are hot, staying above 18°C.

The polar climates are near the poles. The poles receive a lot of sunlight in the summer. In fact, the sun never sets during part of the summer. However, it never rises during part of the winter. Overall, the polar climates are cold. The average monthly temperatures are 10°C or less, even during the warmer months.

The temperate climates are between the polar and tropical climates. Temperate climates are neither very cold nor very hot. The average monthly temperatures during the year are between 10°C and 18°C.

The distance from the equator also determines precipitation patterns. See the model of atmospheric pressure air movement on page 119. The model has air moving upward near the equator. This moist air cools and forms clouds, which result in rain. On the other hand, air is slowly sinking near 30° latitude north or south, which makes it dry all season. Most of the great deserts of the world are near 30° north or 30° south latitude for this reason. There is another wet zone near 60° latitude and another dry zone near the poles.

These wet and dry zones move north, then south during the year. The wet and dry zones move in this way because the sun's rays hit the earth at different angles during different seasons. The sun's rays are received at the most direct angle in the northern hemisphere on June 21 or 22. They are received at the most direct angle in the southern hemisphere on December 21 or 22. After December 21 or 22 the wet and dry zones are moving toward the north. Then, after June 21 or 22, they start to move toward the south. This results in different precipitation patterns in each season. Figure 9.6 shows where the wet and dry zones are in winter and in summer. Imagine these zones moving north, then south, between two places. You see how the atmospheric movement produces precipitation patterns that change with the seasons.

Figure 9.5 The angle of the sun's rays striking Earth changes throughout the year. The northern and southern hemispheres have opposite seasons.

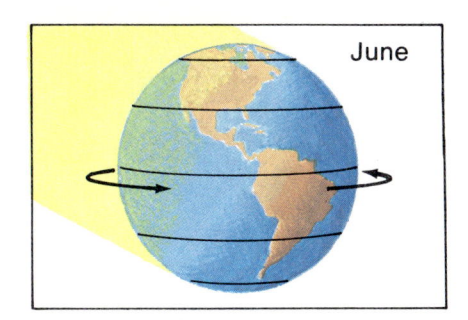

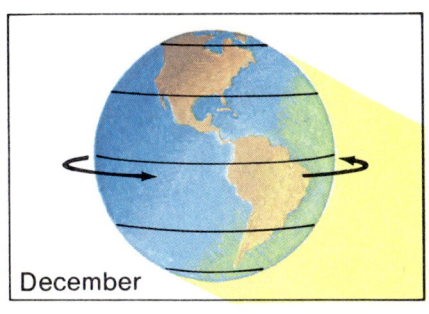

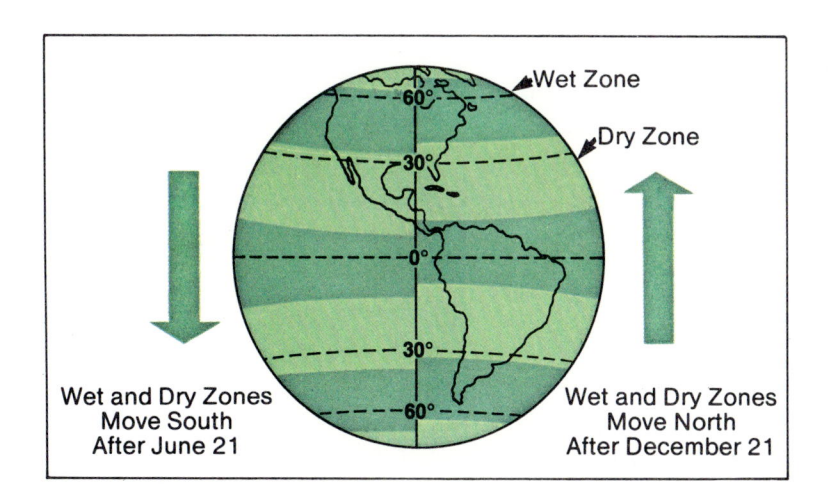

Figure 9.6 Compare the positions of the wet and dry zones at different times of the year.

Study Questions for 9.1

1. What is climate? How is it different from weather?
2. Name three major groups of climates that are based on yearly temperature averages.
3. Why would you not expect to find a tropical climate that is dry all year?
4. Why would you not expect to find a polar climate that is wet all year?

9.2 Climate: Local Influence

You will find out
- why mountains are climate makers;
- how climate changes with altitude;
- why large bodies of water are climate makers;
- how ocean currents influence climate.

So far you have looked at the kinds of climates caused by large zonal factors. These included such factors as tropical areas, polar areas, wet areas, dry areas. There are also four local influences that affect nearby climates. These are (1) altitude, (2) mountains, (3) large bodies of water, and (4) ocean currents. Let's find out why.

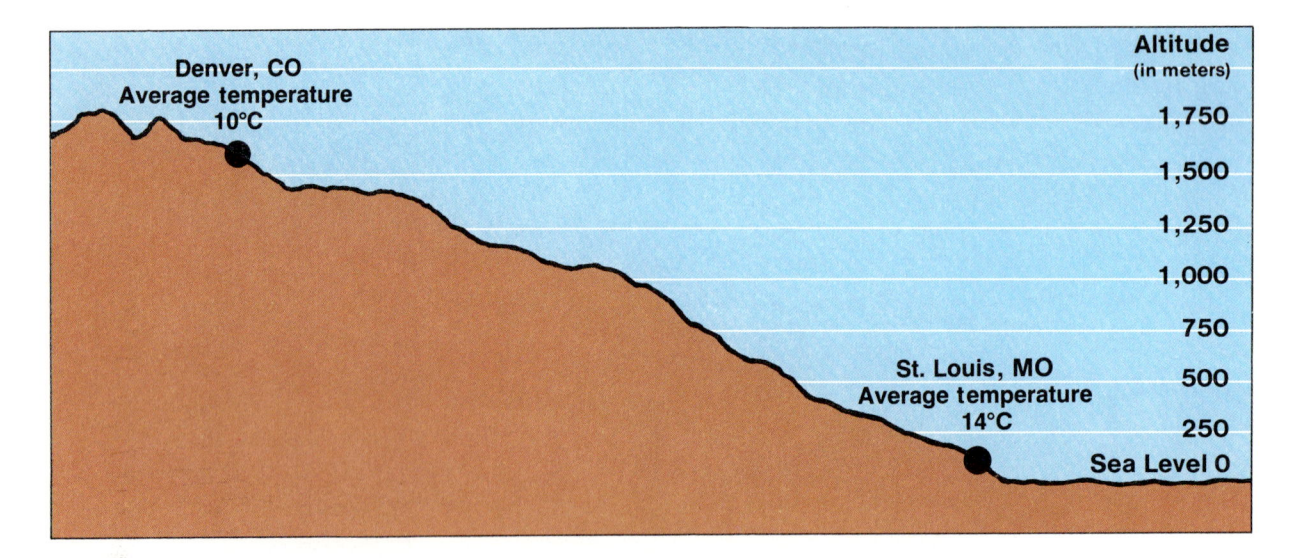

Figure 9.7 The difference in altitude between St. Louis and Denver is one reason their climates are different.

The first of the four local climate makers is altitude. As you go to higher altitudes, places will have lower average temperatures. Denver, Colorado, and St. Louis, Missouri, for example, are both in the temperate climate zone. They are almost at the same latitude. You would expect the two cities to have about the same average temperature. Denver, however, has an altitude of 1,609 m, and the altitude of St. Louis is 140 m. The average yearly temperature for Denver is about 10°C, and for St. Louis it is about 14°C. Altitude makes the difference. In fact, the temperature decreases about 3°C for each 450-m rise in altitude.

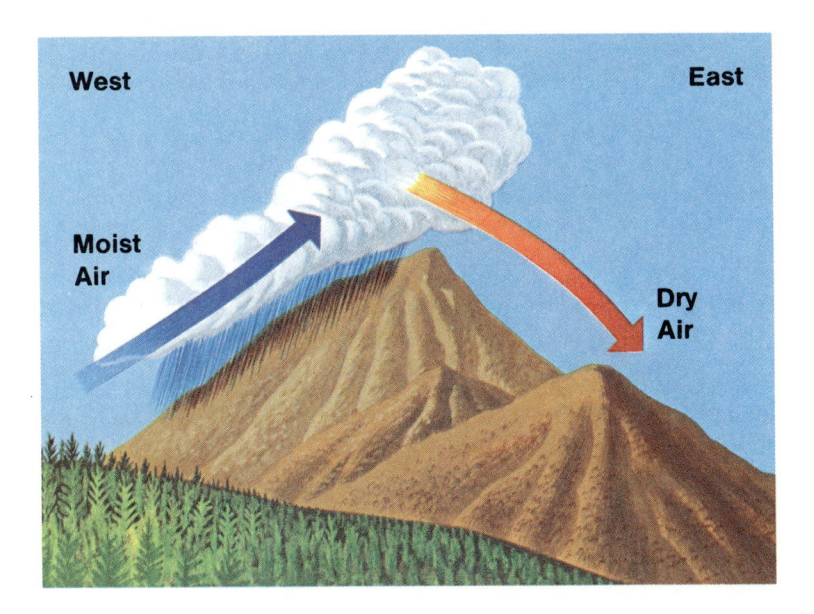

Figure 9.8 *left:* Wet air rising up the western side of the mountain produces rain. There is little moisture left in the air as it moves down the eastern slope.

Figure 9.9 *top:* Pear orchards grow well on the moist, western side of mountains in Oregon. *bottom:* The eastern slope has only desert grasslands.

The second of the local climate makers is mountains. You can be in the snow on a mountaintop even though you are near the equator. In addition to the temperature change caused by the altitude of the mountain, mountains influence the climate another way. Look at a map of North America. There are mountains on the west coast that run north and south. The western side of these mountains receives much precipitation. There are farms and fruit trees there. On the eastern side there is a desert. Only plants such as cactus can live on the eastern side.

Why is this so? You learned earlier that the earth has prevailing wind belts. The United States is in the prevailing westerly wind belt. These westerly winds move maritime air inland. This causes the west coast to have cooler summers and warmer winters than the east coast. The winds also bring moisture from the Pacific Ocean.

Moist air from the Pacific is forced up the mountain slopes by the prevailing westerlies. As the air moves up the slopes, it expands and cools. Water vapor condenses, clouds form, and precipitation forms. The precipitation falls on the western side of the mountains, the side that the wind pushes against. Air moving down the eastern slope is compressed. It becomes warmer and dryer, and deserts are found here.

9 / Climate

The third of the local climate makers is a large body of water. The climate of a seacoast is influenced by a large body of water, the sea. Large bodies of water increase the humidity. Nearness to a large body of water influences the temperature as well. If it is hot inland, the coast will not be so hot. If it is cold inland, the coast usually will not be so cold. San Diego, California, and Dallas, Texas, for example, are at about the same latitude. Dallas, however, is inland, and San Diego is at the seacoast. The average summer temperature is 7°C cooler in San Diego. San Diego has 5°C warmer average winter temperature than Dallas. Nearness to water keeps the temperature more even at San Diego. In general, nearness to large bodies of water tends to prevent extreme or rapid changes in weather.

The fourth of the local climate makers is ocean currents. Ocean currents can transport warm water northward or cool water southward. These currents will influence the temperatures of the air mass over the area. As this air mass moves inland, it also affects the areas near the seacoast. Look at Figure 9.11. What ocean currents are influencing the east and west coasts of North America?

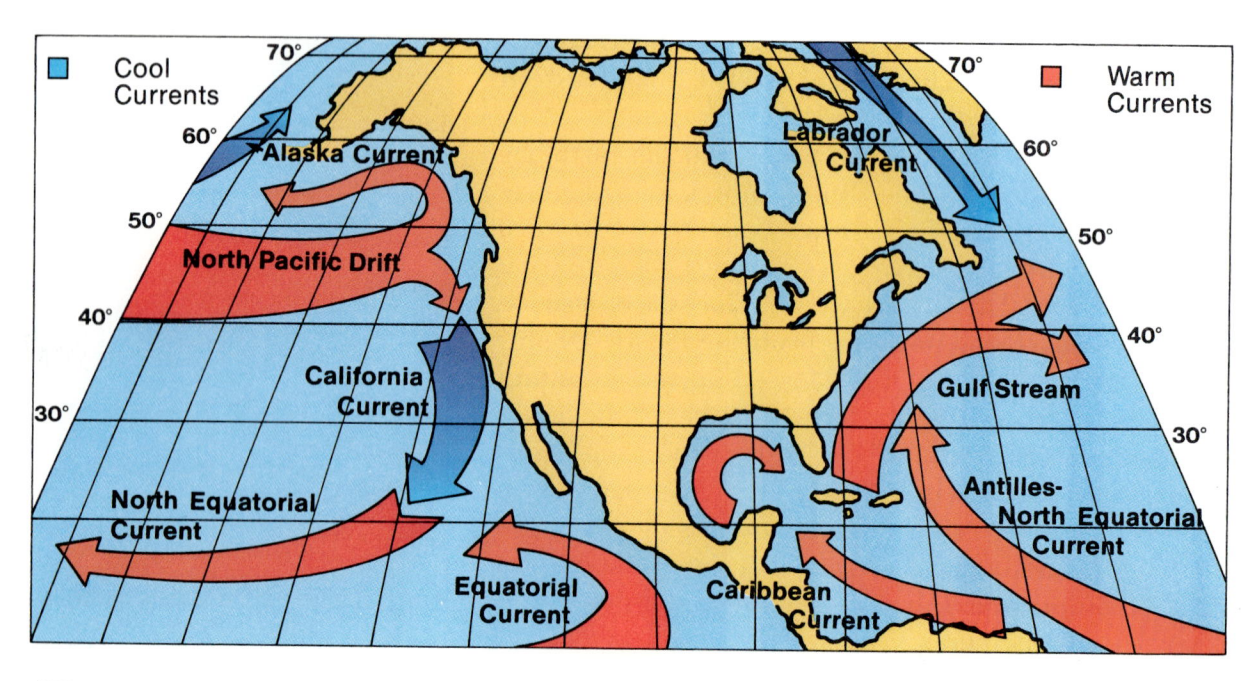

Figure 9.10 *top:* San Diego; *bottom:* Dallas

Figure 9.11 Major ocean currents that influence climate in North America.

170

9 / Climate

Activity

Materials
map of the United States
World Almanac, Information Please Almanac, or *National Atlas*

What Influences Your Climate?

Procedure

1. Find where you live (or a nearby large city) on a United States map. Estimate and record the latitude.

2. Identify another large city at about the same latitude that has the opposite climate-making influences to your location. For example, if you live near a seacoast, identify a city that is inland. Also find an opposite city for (1) northern United States and southern United States and (2) high and low altitude.

3. Find (1) the average yearly temperature, (2) the average high temperature in the summer, and (3) the average low temperature in the winter for each location. Record the information in a table like the one shown.

Questions

1. What is the latitude where you live?

2. Does altitude influence the climate where you live? What evidence can you give for your answer?

3. Does nearness to a large body of water influence the climate where you live? What evidence can you give?

City	Latitude	Average yearly temperature	Average high temperature	Average low temperature	Altitude	Nearest large body of water

Study Questions for 9.2

1. What happens to the climate at higher altitudes?
2. Describe how mountains are climate makers.
3. What are two influences that a large body of water has on climate?
4. How do ocean currents modify climates?

9 / Climate

9.3 Describing Climates

You will find out
- how to describe climates;
- what description to give the climate where you live;
- what a microclimate is.

How can you describe the climate where you live? First, you have learned that there are three major climate zones on the earth. The polar, temperate, and tropical zones are based on temperature. Second, you have learned that certain precipitation patterns occur because of atmospheric movement. Some places are wet all year, and others are dry because of the movement. Third, you studied the additional influence of mountains, large bodies of water, altitude, and ocean currents. Now, let's see how all this information is used to describe a climate.

Figure 9.12 Which of these climate types appeals to you? Look at the chart below.

Climate Type	Description	Location in North America
Polar	very cold, long winters, cold summers – dry	Northern Canada, Alaska, Greenland
Humid Continental (Sub-arctic)	long cold winters, cool summers – moderate precipitation	Most latitudes of Alaska, Canada
Humid Continental (Middle Latitudes)	cold winters, moderate summers – moderate precipitation	East of the Rockies in Northern U.S., south Canada
Humid Continental (Low Latitudes)	mild winters, hot summers – moderate precipitation	Inland U.S., east of the Rockies to Atlantic Coast
Humid Sub-tropical	short, mild winters, humid summers – moderate precipitation	Southeastern U.S.
Tropical Wet	hot and humid all year – heavy precipitation	Hawaii, eastern Mexico
Tropical Wet/Dry (sub-tropical)	hot all year – alternating wet and dry seasons	Hawaii, south Florida, coasts of Mexico
Semi-Arid	varying temperatures – low rainfall	U.S. Great Plains, parts of Canada
Desert	hot with cold nights – arid	Inland southwestern U.S.
Marine	mild winters, rainy summers, moderate temperatures	Northwestern coast U.S., western coast of Canada
Mediterranean	short, mild, moist winters, hot dry summers	Southwestern coastal U.S.
Highlands	temperature and precipitation vary with altitude and latitude	Mountainous regions in U.S., Canada, Mexico

In addition to the three major climate zones of polar, temperate, and tropical, certain areas between these zones are classified as subpolar or subtropical. A subpolar zone is between the temperate and polar zones. A subtropical zone is between the tropical and temperate zones.

There are subdivisions within each of the three major world climate zones. Within a major zone, for example, there may be an area near the ocean. This area may be influenced by air masses from the oceans. If so, the area has a **marine** climate. As you learned earlier, the ocean makes temperatures more even. Areas with a marine climate are cooler in the summer and warmer in the winter than farther inland.

Also within a major zone there may be an area that is far from an ocean. This area may be influenced mostly by air masses from large land areas. If so, the air has a **continental** climate. The land heats and cools rapidly. Summers are hot and winters are cold. A continental climate does not have as even temperatures as marine climates.

Climates can also be classified as either **arid,** meaning "dry" or **humid,** meaning "moist." Arid climates receive less than 25 cm of precipitation a year. Humid climates receive 50 cm or more of precipitation a year. If an area receives between 25 and 50 cm of precipitation, it is called **semiarid.**

Figure 9.13 Examples of vegetation types in the four major climate areas of North America.

9 / Climate

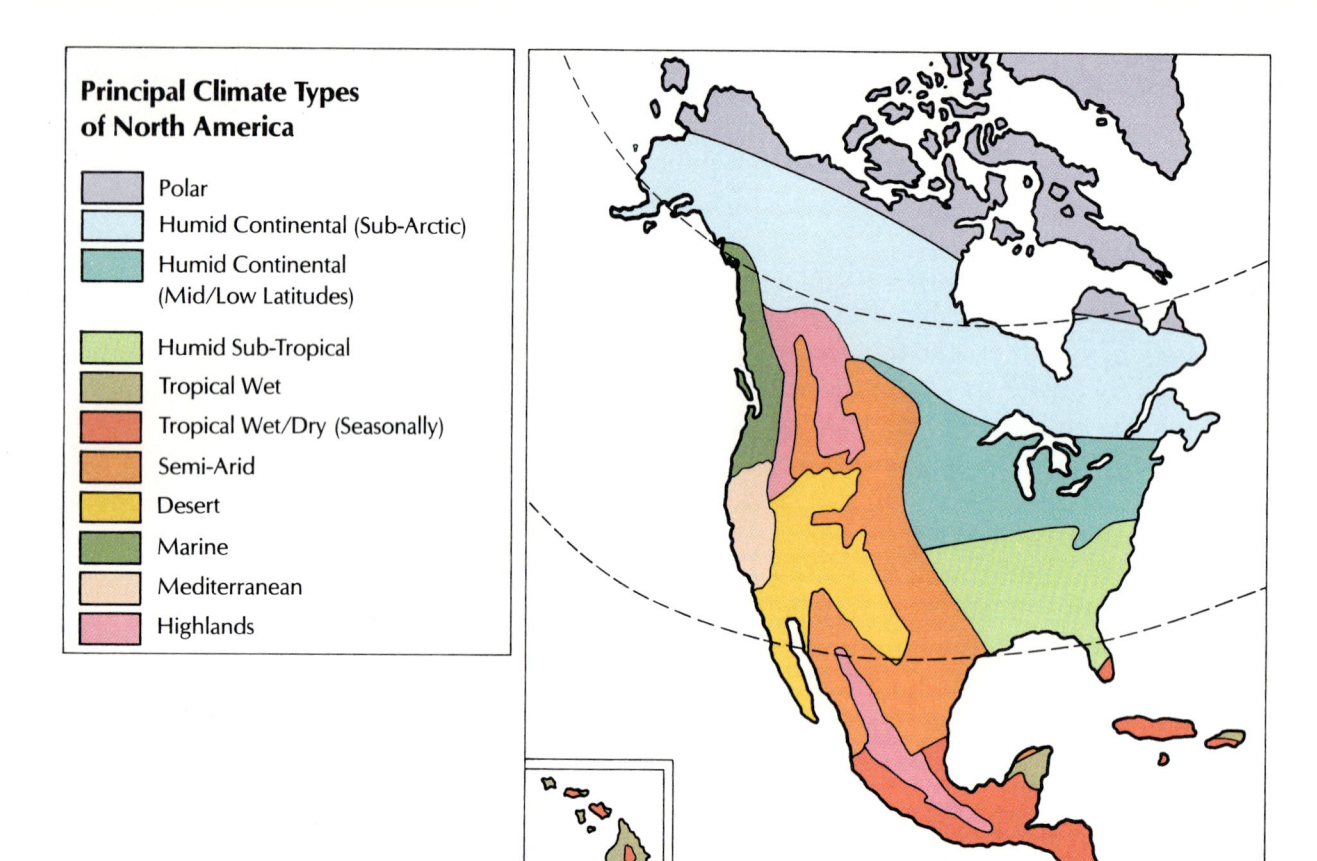

Principal Climate Types of North America

- Polar
- Humid Continental (Sub-Arctic)
- Humid Continental (Mid/Low Latitudes)
- Humid Sub-Tropical
- Tropical Wet
- Tropical Wet/Dry (Seasonally)
- Semi-Arid
- Desert
- Marine
- Mediterranean
- Highlands

Figure 9.14 Refer to Figure 9.12 for descriptions of these climate types.

The map in Figure 9.14 shows the different climate areas of the United States. This is a generalized picture of the different climate areas according to temperature and precipitation patterns as determined by latitude and local influences. The areas are said to be generalized because some other feature close by may change the local climate. Also the climate really doesn't change all of a sudden if you move across one of the lines. The climates really blend into each other. Find your location on the map. What is the climate called where you live? Whatever the climate is called in your area, remember that the two basic determiners of climate are the amount of precipitation and the average temperature. The name given to the climate generally relates to conditions that influence one or both of these. For example, nearness to an ocean, an inland location, altitude, latitude, or mountains all have an influence on climate.

Another way to describe climate is shown in Figure 9.15. This map is based on a **moisture index.** A moisture index is a measure of the moisture gained by precipitation minus the moisture lost by evaporation and plant use. This way of describing climate has meaning for the type of soil that is developed, the landscape, and the type of plants that will grow. Forests grow in areas of greater moisture than those areas where grasslands are. Only grasses and desert plants can grow in areas that are dry or semi-arid. Study Figure 9.15 for your location. What kinds of plants are shown where you live? How do they relate to the amount of rainfall in your area?

Do You Know?
Since the kind of plant life in an area is related to its climate, fossil pollen can provide information about climates of the past.

Figure 9.15 This map highlights the natural vegetation zones of North America.

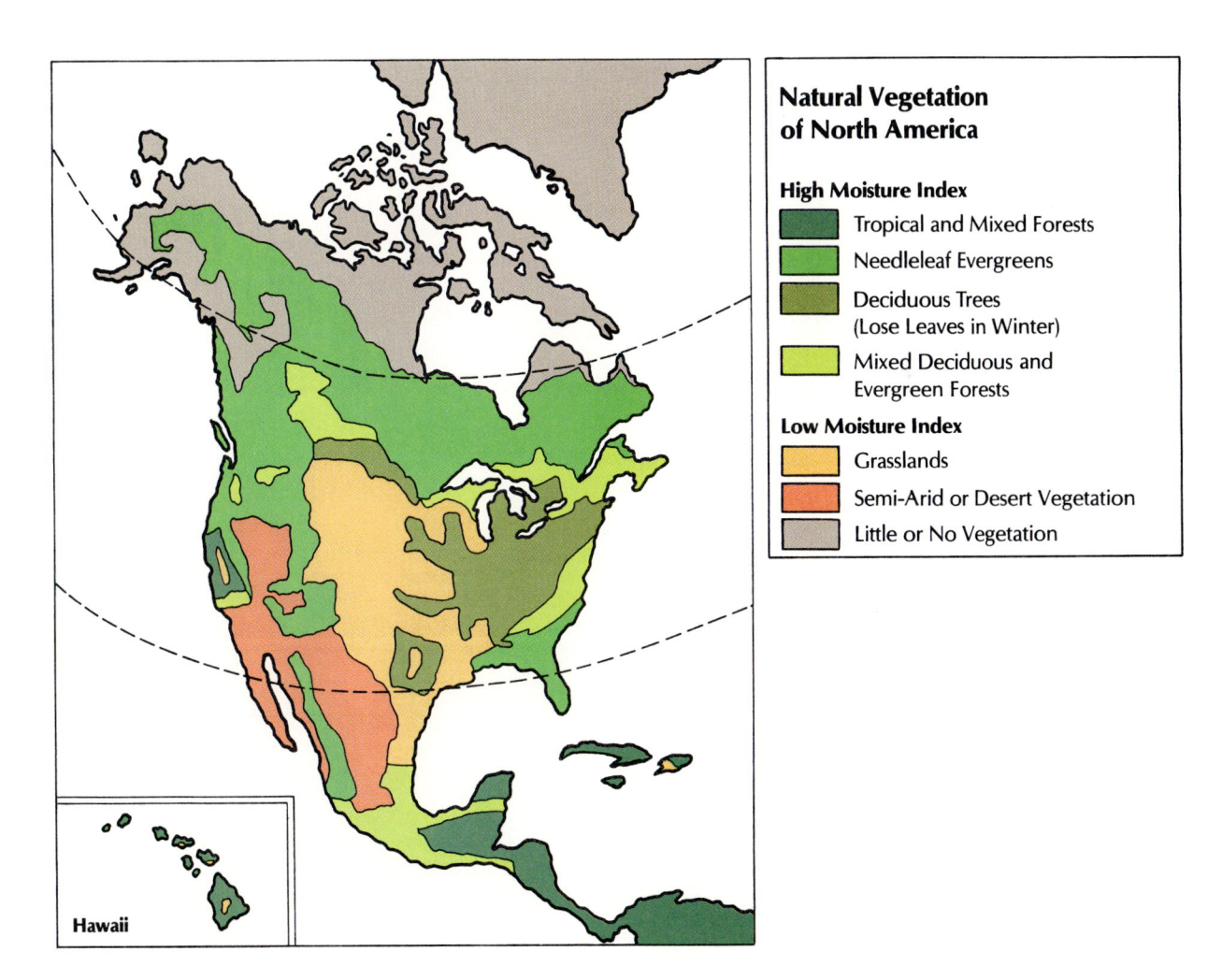

Natural Vegetation of North America

High Moisture Index
- Tropical and Mixed Forests
- Needleleaf Evergreens
- Deciduous Trees (Lose Leaves in Winter)
- Mixed Deciduous and Evergreen Forests

Low Moisture Index
- Grasslands
- Semi-Arid or Desert Vegetation
- Little or No Vegetation

9 / Climate

Do You Know?
The 1883 volcanic eruption of Krakatoa threw dust in the atmosphere which circled the earth with the result that summers were cooler for about five years afterward.

Once you describe the climate of a region, do you think the climate would be the same throughout the region? In general your answer should be yes, but the climate of any specific location in a region may change. New types of vegetation, buildings, roads, and water reservoirs can change the local climate. Local patterns of climate are called **microclimates.** A microclimate usually exists, for example, between the north and south side of a building. Certain plants may grow in one microclimate but not in the other. On a larger scale,

Activity

Where Is a Microclimate?

Materials
thermometer
wet bulb thermometer
water

Procedure

1. Choose two areas in which you can make measurements. One area should have nearby buildings, asphalt streets, and parking lots. The other area should have grass, trees, and plants, such as a park.

2. Measure and record the temperature and relative humidity (see page 128) in both locations. Report and record representative measurements on five separate days. Remember that representative measurements require that you follow the same procedure each day.

Questions

1. What were the temperature and relative humidity in the two areas on each day?
2. What were the average temperature and relative humidity for the two areas?
3. What did your data tell you about the two areas?
4. What would cause any differences you may have found?

Day	Grassy Area		Building Area	
	Temperature	Relative Humidity	Temperature	Relative Humidity
1				
2				
3				
4				
5				
Total				
Average				

trees are sometimes planted to break the force of the wind, called a windbreak. This makes a microclimate. The trees not only slow the wind but also may make the land warmer in the winter and cooler in the summer. They also increase the relative humidity. Many people are now considering microclimates when they build new buildings. How would people benefit from considering microclimates?

Have you read or heard a weather forecast that predicts a different temperature for a city and for its suburbs? Cities create microclimates. The asphalt, concrete, and bricks of a city absorb and radiate energy differently from soil and plants. Temperatures are therefore usually higher in cities than in the country.

Cities also change the climate in other ways. Rainfall collects and runs off sidewalks, buildings, and streets. In the country, the rainfall soaks into the ground. Cities have less grass and trees. The humidity is usually lower in cities than in the country.

Factories and automobiles pour gases and small particles into the atmosphere. These particles serve as condensation nuclei, increasing the amount of fog that forms. When the fog combines with exhaust gases and smoke, it is called **smog.** Smog helps to change the climate of a city. It makes the city warmer at night. It also reflects radiation during the day, making the high temperatures cooler. This makes the smog last longer.

Figure 9.16 *left:* The tree creates a natural microclimate in which moss can grow. *right:* Trees are grown around this farm to create a microclimate.

Figure 9.17 Smog can change the climate of a city.

Study Questions for 9.3

1. What are the two basic determiners of climate?
2. What is the climate where you live?
3. What is a microclimate? What causes it?

Career

Climatologist

Climate is weather considered over a long period of time. But there is more to climate than average temperature, rainfall, and snow depth measurements. There are questions about the climate. Is the climate changing? Is the earth's climate becoming warmer? If so, by how much? And if it is changing, what is causing the changes? These are some of the questions that climatologists, scientists who study climates, try to answer.

Kristina Katsaros is a climatologist with a university. As a research professor, she can choose the questions about the climate that she wants to investigate. She then tries to obtain the money to pay for the equipment, supplies, and computer time that she needs to investigate her question. Then she works with her students to collect the information that will help to answer her question about the climate. Kristina Katsaros says it is exciting to think up a question, conduct an experiment, and then find out answers. She says that her work never becomes dull and is always changing.

One of her questions is about how sunlight, the atmosphere, and the oceans interact. She uses ships, airplanes, and satellites to measure sea surface temperature, wind speed, and humidity. This work deals with the energy transfers which move both the atmosphere and the ocean. What she finds out, for example, will make it possible for other scientists to verify or reject theories about climates.

Kristina Katsaros says, that as a working scientist, there are prices to be paid in sacrifices and discipline, but the rewards are worth it.

CHAPTER REVIEW

Main Ideas

- Climate is the average of the many kinds of weather that occur at a given place over a period of time.
- The two most important factors that determine climate are temperature and precipitation.
- The major groups of climates of the earth are tropical, temperate, and polar.
- Worldwide atmospheric movement makes precipitation patterns at different latitudes.
- Climates are modified by mountains, large bodies of water, ocean currents, and altitudes.
- Mountains in prevailing wind belts are climate makers. As warm, moist air rises along the western side of the mountain, it expands and cools. Water condenses and precipitation forms. Little moisture is left in the air as it moves down the eastern side of the mountain.
- Large bodies of water modify climates by making the temperature more even.
- Ocean currents bring warmer or cooler water to a coastal area.
- Climates can be described by seasonal temperatures and precipitation patterns.
- Climate can also be described in terms of precipitation and moisture lost by evaporation.
- Climate can be changed by local influences. A local climate is called a microclimate.
- Cities can create microclimates. Cities are usually warmer, less humid, and foggier than the country.

Using Vocabulary

On a separate piece of paper, use the following words to make a crossword puzzle. Exchange puzzles with a classmate.

climate	marine	semiarid
tropical	continental	moisture index
polar	arid	microclimate
temperate	humid	smog

9 / Climate

Remembering Facts

On your paper, write the word or words that best complete each sentence.
1. A moisture index describes a climate on the basis of (precipitation, precipitation and evaporation, ocean currents).
2. A (marine, continental, arid) climate is influenced by an ocean.
3. Local patterns of climate are called (macroclimates, climates, microclimates).
4. (Altitude, Mountains, Water) help(s) to make temperatures more even all year around.
5. Pollution and fog make (low humidity, smog, high temperatures).
6. A climate with more than 50 cm precipitation a year is (humid, arid, semiarid).
7. The difference between the three major climates is based on (temperature, altitude, rainfall).
8. (Forecast, Climate, Weather) describes the temperature and precipitation in an area over time.
9. (Tropical, Temperate, Polar) climates are neither very hot nor very cold.
10. An area that receives 25 cm to 50 cm of precipitation a year is (humid, arid, semiarid).
11. An area influenced mostly by air masses from large land areas is (continental, marine, temperate).
12. A hot climate is (tropical, polar, temperate).
13. The driest climate is classified as (semiarid, humid, arid).
14. The sun never sets during part of the summer in areas with a (tropical, polar, temperate) climate.
15. The average temperature decreases with an (increase, decrease) in altitude.

Understanding Ideas

On your paper, answer each question in complete sentences.
1. Which type of major climate would you expect for an area near the equator with an altitude of over 3,000 meters? Why?
2. Explain how the North Pole could be covered with ice but have a dry climate.
3. What climate would you expect to find along a coastal area bathed in warm ocean currents and located at latitude 60° N?
4. How do convection cells contribute to the large amounts of precipitation in tropical areas?

Applying What You Have Learned

1. Is giving the temperature of an area a good way to describe the climate of that area? Why or why not?
2. Why does the kind of plant life change as the altitude increases?
3. Compare the different microclimates that might exist on a wooded hill in the country and in a valley in the city.

Challenge

Earth's climate has undergone dramatic changes over time. Ice ages lasting from 20,000 to 100,000 years have come and gone. At other times in the earth's history, tropical plants and animals were living as far north as Greenland. What would cause such drastic changes in climate? One model used by scientists involves the slow wobble in the earth's axis. This wobbling action alters the angle of tilt of the earth's axis every 40,000 years. It also causes the direction of the angle to change every 20,000 years. A wobbling axis would vary the amount of summer sunlight received at high latitudes. Variations in temperature over time can be seen in graph A. The geological evidence of past ice ages is shown in graph B.

1. What is the main idea of the paragraph above?
2. Does the geologic evidence of past ice ages support the axis wobble model? Why or why not?
3. What do the peaks in graph A and the peaks in graph B mean? Is there a direct correlation between them? Why or why not?
4. Graph A predicts a coming ice age. What factors could change this?

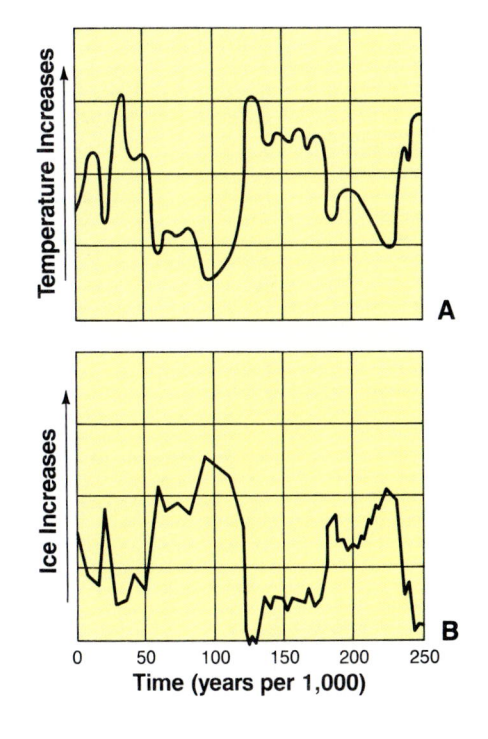

Research and Investigation

1. Report on how the climate influences gardening in your location. Find out the date of the last killing frost in the spring. How long is the growing season? What can be grown during this period? Consult weather data from a meteorological office.
2. Investigate the climate data for your location. Find the average maximum and minimum temperatures for each month. What are the averages for rainfall, snow, and sleet? What are the average wind speeds for different months?

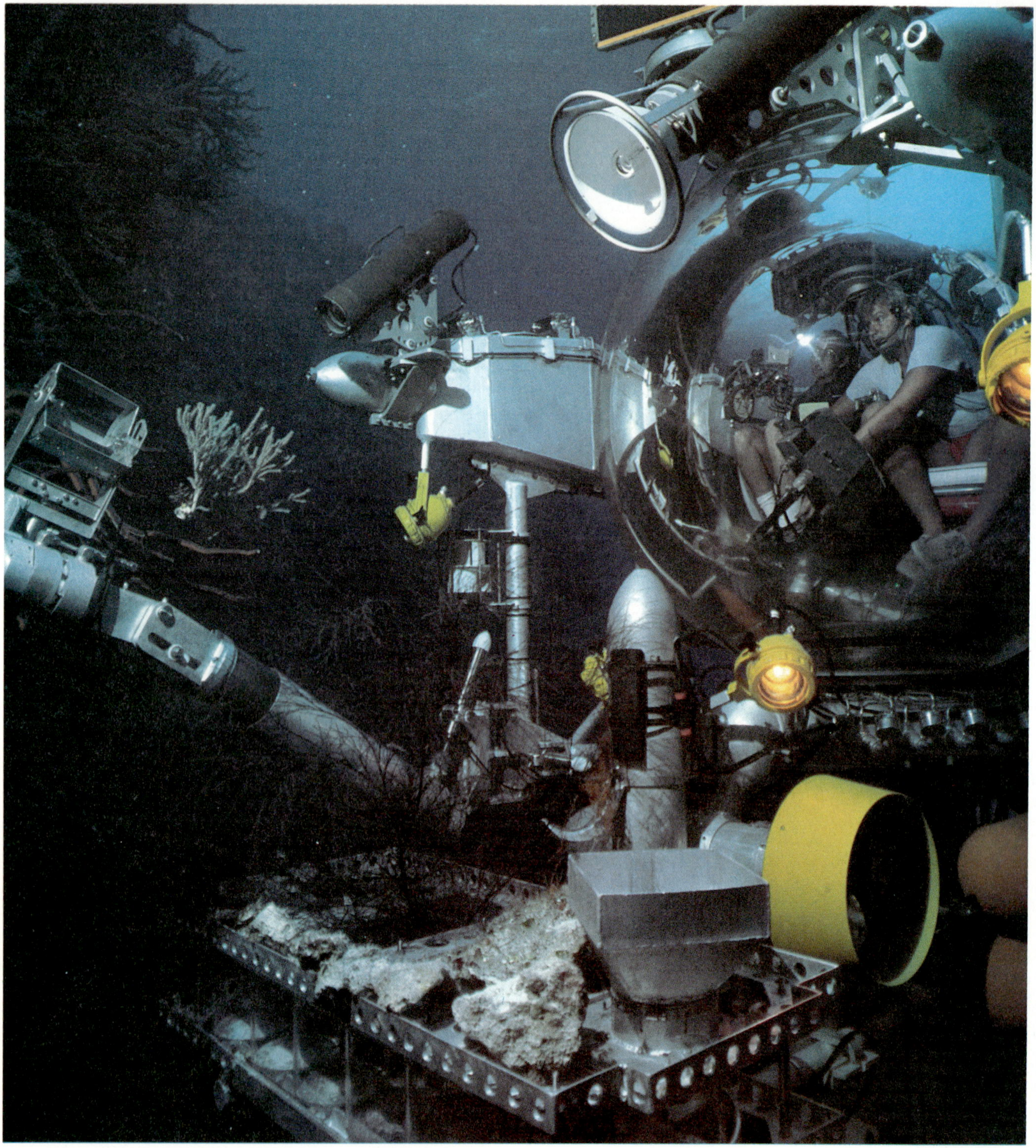

UNIT THREE

The Waters of the Earth

Chapter 10
Fresh Water

Chapter 11
Oceanography

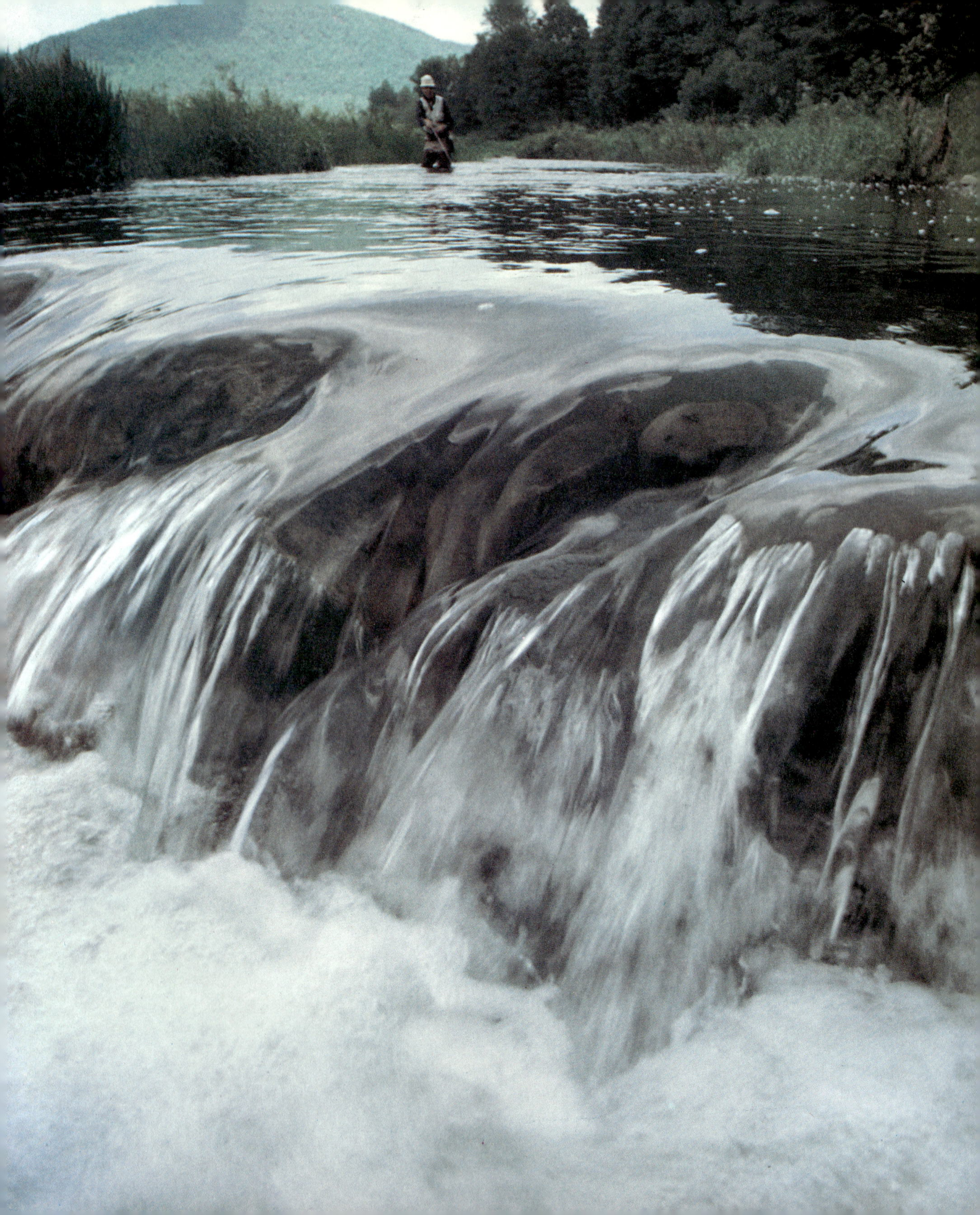

Chapter 10
Fresh Water

Lesson Titles
10.1 Earth's Water
10.2 Fresh Water on the Surface
10.3 Fresh Water below the Surface
10.4 Fresh Water as a Limited Resource

What do you think about when you look at a stream? Do you wonder where it came from or where it's going? Will it run out of water?

Not all people look at a stream and see the same thing. A park manager might see the stream as a place for boating. A city engineer might see the stream as a source of water for drinking, cooking, and washing. A farmer might see the stream as a source of water for thirsty crops. An electric utility planner might see the stream as a source of power. Many streams can provide all these things and have even other uses. The water in a stream is an important resource that can be used many ways.

Will there be enough water for all these uses? If there is not enough water for all these uses, which uses are more important? In this chapter you will learn where water comes from, where it goes, and some new ways to add to the available water supply.

Figure 10.1 *opposite:* A freshwater river has many potential uses.

10.1 Earth's Water

You will find out
- how much of the earth's water is fresh water;
- why only one third of the earth's fresh water is available for use;
- how the hydrologic cycle replaces fresh water.

The earth appears to have plenty of water. In fact, astronauts looking at the earth from space have called it the blue planet. One reason it appears blue is the large amount of water on it. The oceans cover about 70 percent of the earth's surface. The oceans also contain more than 97 percent of all the water on the earth. However, ocean water is salty. You cannot drink it.

This leaves only about 3 percent of all the water found on the earth that you can drink. This water, which is not salty, is called **fresh water**. About two thirds of the world's fresh water is locked up in ice, mainly in Greenland and the Antarctic. What remains, then, is less than 1 percent of all the water on the earth as the available fresh water. This fresh water is found underground, in rivers, in lakes, in ponds, and in the atmosphere. Most plants and animals that live on land need fresh water to survive. Since such a small percentage of the earth's water is fresh, you may think there is really not enough fresh water. Most places have enough, however, because the supply is frequently replaced by a natural cycle.

The atmosphere doesn't hold much water at any given time. Suppose all the water vapor in the atmosphere fell to the earth. How deep a layer of water would be made? The entire earth would be covered by only a few centimeters of water. But remember that water is continually evaporating, condensing, and falling as precipitation in what is called the hydrologic cycle. Because of the hydrologic cycle, enough precipitation falls each year to cover the entire surface of the earth 85 cm deep in water.

The amount of water that evaporates, condenses, and returns as precipitation is not the same over the oceans as over the land. This is due to the wind patterns. Look at Table 10-1.

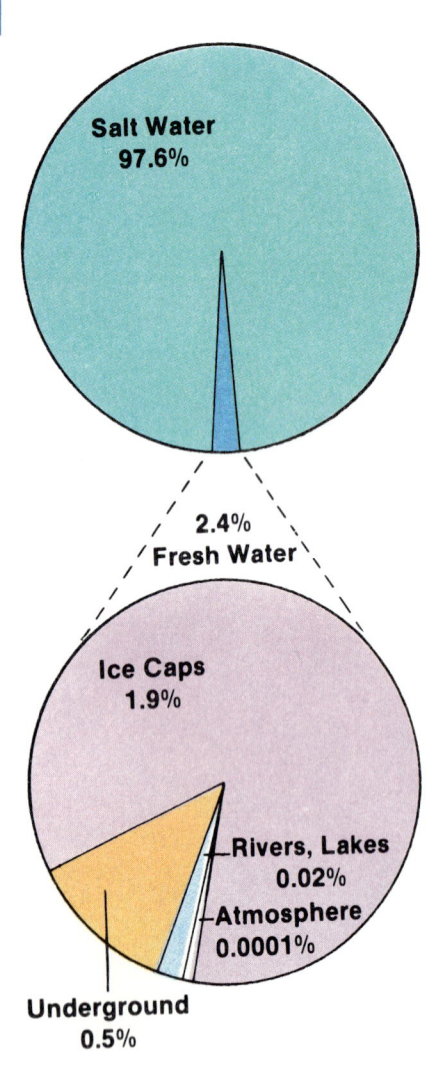

Figure 10.2 *top:* Compare the amounts of salt water and fresh water found on the earth. *bottom:* The distribution of the 2.4% of fresh water on the earth

Table 10-1 Worldwide Evaporation and Precipitation

Evaporation		Precipitation	
From Oceans	84%	On Oceans	77%
From Land	16%	On Land	23%
Total	100%	Total	100%

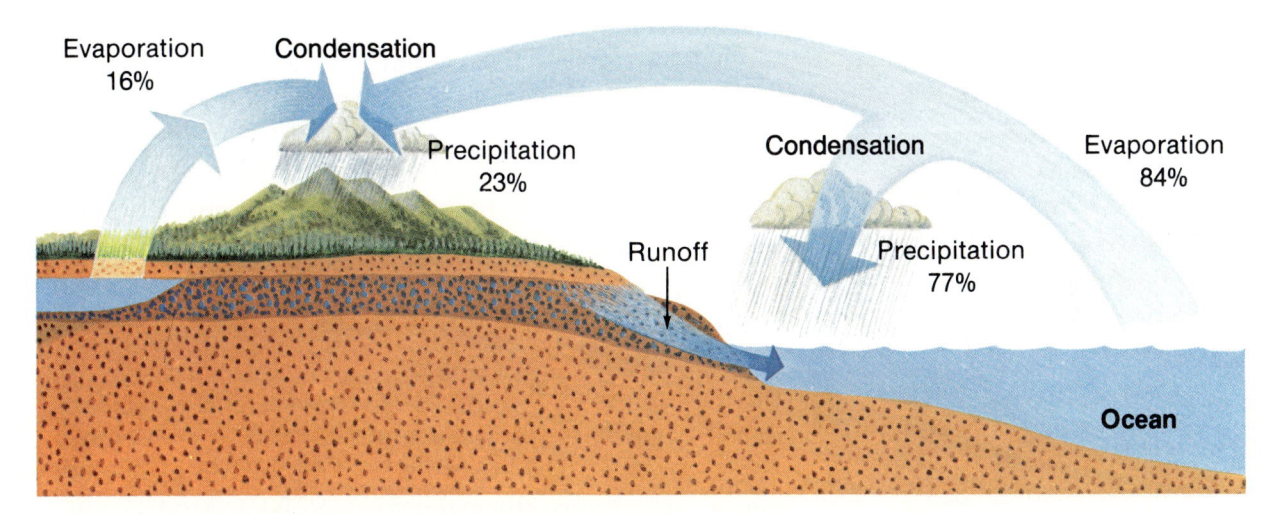

Notice that more water evaporates from the oceans than falls on the oceans as precipitation. Notice also that more water falls on land than evaporates from the land. Some of this rainwater soaks into the ground, and some of it flows across the land. Eventually the water returns to the oceans, balancing the cycle. As you can see, the hydrologic cycle is continuously replenishing the fresh water on land from the vast supply of water in the ocean.

Figure 10.3 The hydrologic cycle

Study Questions for 10.1
1. How much of the water on the earth is salt water?
2. Why is only one third of the earth's fresh water available for use?
3. Construct a pie graph to compare evaporation and precipitation over the oceans to evaporation and precipitation over the land. What happens to the difference?

10.2 Fresh Water on the Surface

You will find out
- what happens to water that falls on the land;
- what kind of soil holds more water;
- what makes rock layers permeable;
- what surface runoff is.

What happens to rain after it falls? Rain falling on a sidewalk or street forms many puddles. If the rain is heavy enough, the street may become flooded. After the rain stops, the puddles gradually disappear as the water evaporates, returning to the atmosphere. Much of the water that falls as rain evaporates back into the atmosphere.

Basically three things happen to water that falls as rain. As much as two thirds of any rainfall may evaporate back into the atmosphere. Of the remaining one third of the rainfall, some soaks into the ground, and the rest flows across the surface of the land.

The amount of water that soaks into the ground depends on how dry the ground is and what kind of soil is there. Some kinds of soil have more space between the soil particles than others. This space between soil particles is called the **pore space.** The more pore space a soil has, the more water it will hold.

Figure 10.4 *above:* Puddles that remain after rain can be a minor inconvenience.

Figure 10.5 When rain hits the soil's surface, water is absorbed into available pore space.

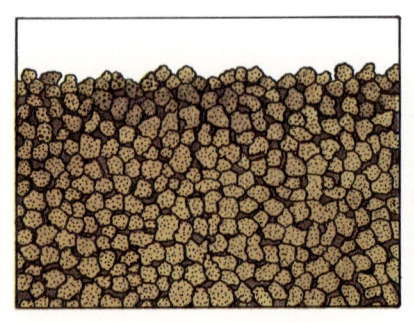

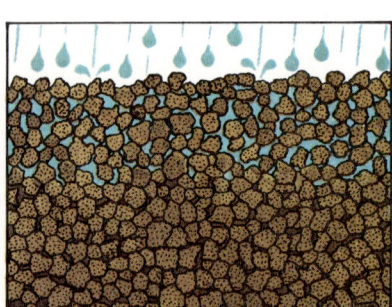

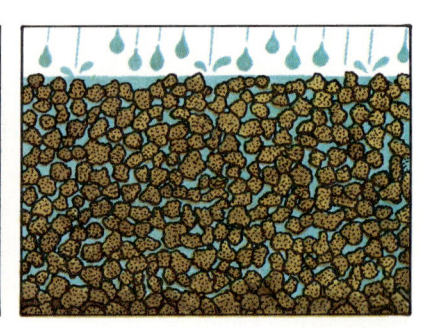

188

10 / Fresh Water

The total amount of pore spaces in a volume of materials is called **porosity.** For example, if there is 25 mL of pore space in 100 mL of matter, the porosity is 25 percent. The porosity of rock layers is an important property to consider when studying groundwater.

Another important property of rock layers is their **permeability.** Permeability is a measure of how well water flows through the pores and cracks in rock layers. Water can flow quickly through some materials, such as sand. Materials that water flows through quickly are said to have high permeability. The amount of permeability depends on the size and shape of the pore spaces and how they are connected. Highly permeable rock layers are able to transport groundwater over great distances.

Do You Know?
Dry soil with a lot of pore space can soak up to 10 cm of water an hour.

Activity

How Much Pore Space?

Materials
sand
clay
gravel
garden soil
4 glass containers of equal size
graduated cylinder
water

Procedure

1. Fill four glass containers with sand, clay, gravel, and garden soil.

2. Use a graduated cylinder to add measured amounts of water slowly to each container. Add enough water to fill all available pore space.

3. Record how much water each container of soil material will hold.

Sand	__ mL
Clay	__ mL
Soil	__ mL
Gravel	__ mL

Questions

1. How much water were you able to add to each container?

2. What does this mean about the pore space in sand? Clay? Gravel? Garden soil?

3. Which would soak up the most rainfall?

4. Which would have the most surface water at first?

10 / Fresh Water

189

Figure 10.6 This runoff will eventually drain into a lake or pond or a river that empties into the ocean.

The water moves down into the soil as the pore spaces fill. If rain falls faster than the water can move through the soil, the water begins to collect on the surface. This water may move downhill across the surface of the land. When water moves across the surface, it is called **surface runoff.**

Surface runoff moves on the land from high places to lower places. It collects in small streams. A **stream** is a body of water that is moving. Small streams carry the water to a few larger streams, and the larger streams drain into major rivers. The area of land drained by a river is known as the river's **watershed.** Figure 10.7 shows three large watersheds. The Columbia River watershed and the Colorado River watershed drain water into the Pacific Ocean. The Mississippi River watershed drains water into the Atlantic Ocean.

Between every two watersheds is a line called the **divide.** A divide separates regions that drain into one

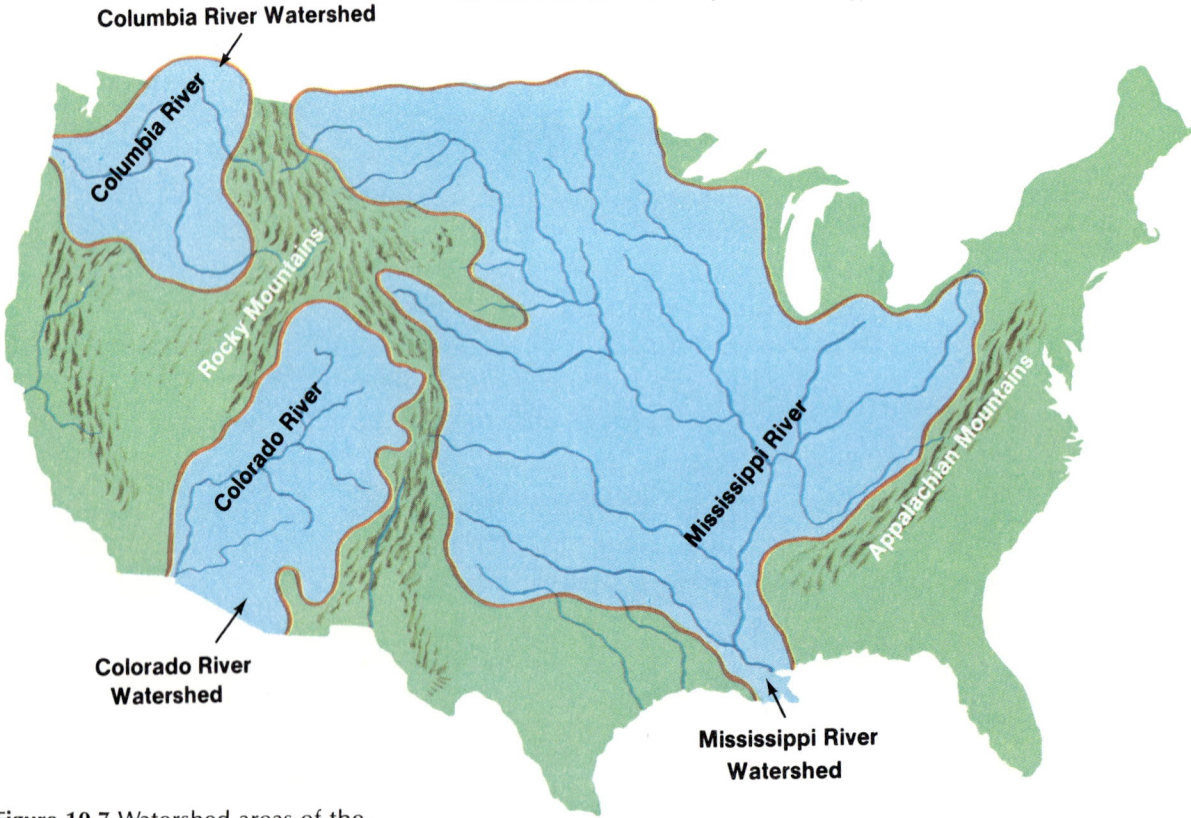

Figure 10.7 Watershed areas of the continental United States.

190   10 / Fresh Water

watershed from those that drain into another. The Continental Divide separates rivers that drain into the Atlantic Ocean from those that drain into the Pacific Ocean.

Within a watershed, some of the runoff may be caught in a low place. This forms a standing body of fresh water. This body of water is called a **pond** or **lake**, depending on its size. To be called a lake, the water must be deep enough in some places so that sunlight does not reach the bottom. Some lakes and ponds, however, must have been named before people knew how deep they were. Sometimes lakes are called ponds and some ponds are called lakes. Do you know of any that are misnamed? The water found in all the rivers, streams, lakes, and ponds is also called surface water.

A lake can be created by building a dam on a stream or river. A lake formed in this way by a dam is called a **reservoir.** Dams are built and reservoirs are created for three different purposes: (1) water storage, (2) flood control, and (3) generating electricity. Water storage is used to make a new water supply or increase a supply that is already there. This supply can be used to provide water for cropland and cities. Flood-control reservoirs catch heavy runoff and hold the water, preventing flooding downstream. In many areas it is possible to store water in huge reservoirs for the generation of electricity. However, a reservoir cannot be used for all three purposes at the same time. For example, you cannot store water and release water to generate electricity at the same time. To generate electricity, water must be drawn from the reservoir to turn the turbines. What problem can you see if you tried to use a reservoir for both water storage and flood control? Consider where the flood water can go if the reservoir is already full.

Figure 10.8 Glen Canyon Dam in Arizona

Do You Know?
Straddling the equator and receiving 1.5 m to 2.5 m of rainfall every year, the Amazon River basin contains fully two thirds of all the river water on earth.

Study Questions for 10.2

1. Describe what happens to rain when it reaches the earth's surface.
2. What kind of soil holds more water?
3. Name one watershed. Describe how rain falling on this watershed ends up in the ocean.

10.3
Fresh Water below the Surface

You will find out
- what the water table is;
- how water moves under the ground;
- what are some problems related to using groundwater.

Have you ever visited a seashore or lakeshore? If so, perhaps you have dug a hole in the sand. You did not have to dig very deep before the lower part of the hole filled with water. You reached a depth where all the pore spaces in the soil were filled with water. Water from such a water-filled underground zone is called **groundwater.**

If you look down into the hole, you will see the surface of a tiny pond. Below the surface level of this tiny pond the surrounding ground is full of groundwater. The level of the water in the tiny pond and the surrounding ground is called the **water table.** A hole dug or drilled to the water table to get water is called a well. Near a large body of water the water table is not very deep, and wells can be quite shallow. In other places you may have to dig deeper, perhaps hundreds of meters deeper, to find the water table.

In a moist climate region the water table is close to the surface. In fact, it might even come right up to the surface and form a swamp, a lake, or a spring.

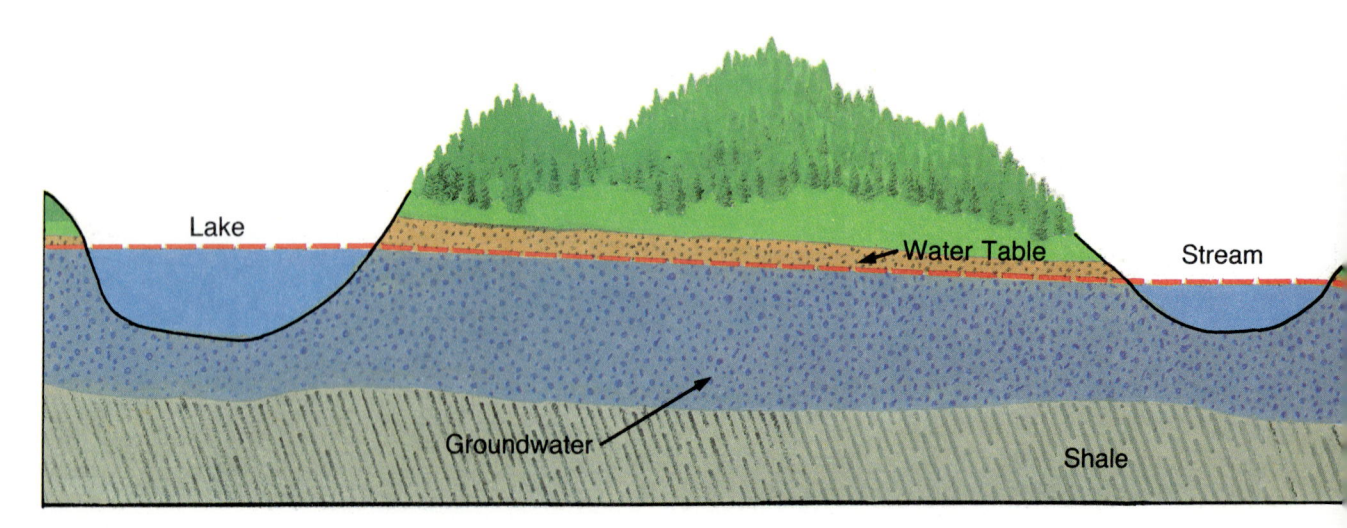

Figure 10.9 Groundwater can be easily reached in some areas but not in others.

Figure 10.10 This illustration shows some of the characteristics of the water table.

192

10 / Fresh Water

Figure 10.11 Rivers that flow through underground caverns can sometimes be reached by visitors.

Where does groundwater come from? Almost all of it was once precipitation. Some of the precipitation soaks into the soil and is used by plants. The rest of the precipitation continues to move slowly downward until it reaches the water table. Then it will generally move downward underground. It continues flowing underground until it finds an opening to the surface at a lower level. Such an opening forms a spring as in Figure 10.10 There the groundwater may join a stream and flow back to the ocean. This trip may be short, or it may take thousands of years. In some places groundwater moves only a few meters a year. In other places it may move several meters a day.

Do You Know?
There is 30 times more groundwater than water in all the streams, rivers, and lakes of the world. We can pump out a volume of this equal to the amount of precipitation that falls in 10 years.

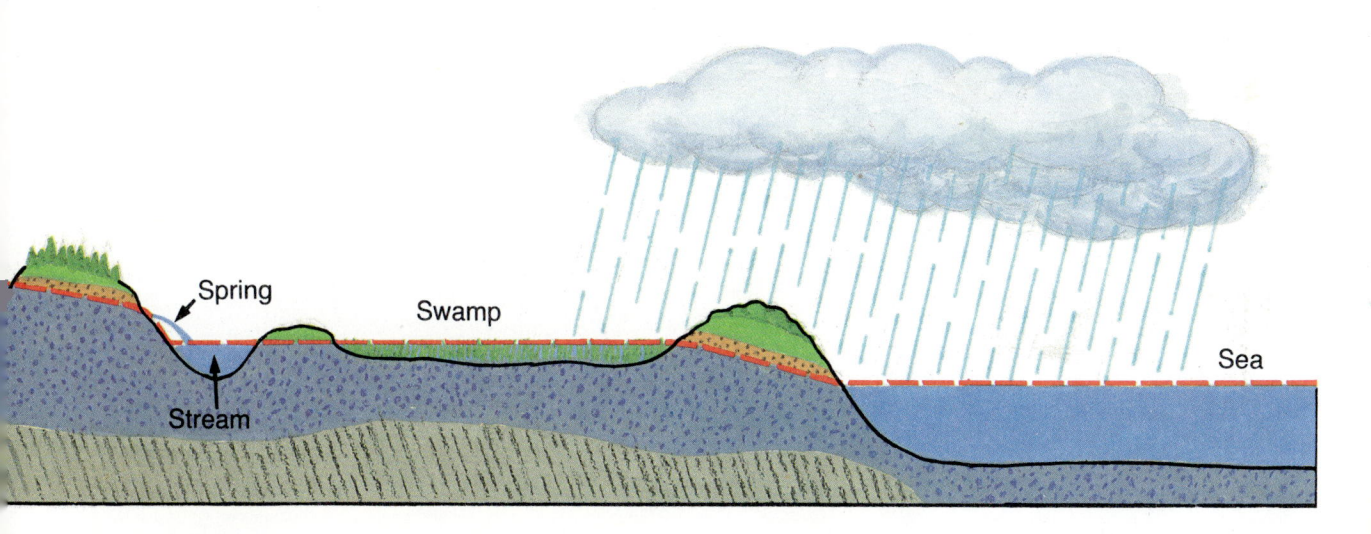

10 / Fresh Water

Figure 10.12 *top left:* Shale does not permit water to move through it. *top right:* An outcrop of shale

Figure 10.13 *bottom left:* Sandstone is permeable. *bottom right:* A sandstone landscape.

Groundwater also moves through rocks that have connected cracks and through rocks and materials that have openings through them. You have learned that rocks that allow water to move through them are permeable. Sandstone is an example of a permeable rock. Shale is an example of nonpermeable rock. These rocks are usually found in layers. Often a layer of sandstone that contains water may be trapped between two layers of shale. In this case the sandstone with the groundwater in it is called an **aquifer** (AH-kwih-fuhr). An aquifer forms when any permeable rock containing water becomes trapped between two layers of nonpermeable rock. An aquifer may also form when soil saturated with groundwater is located above a layer of nonpermeable rock.

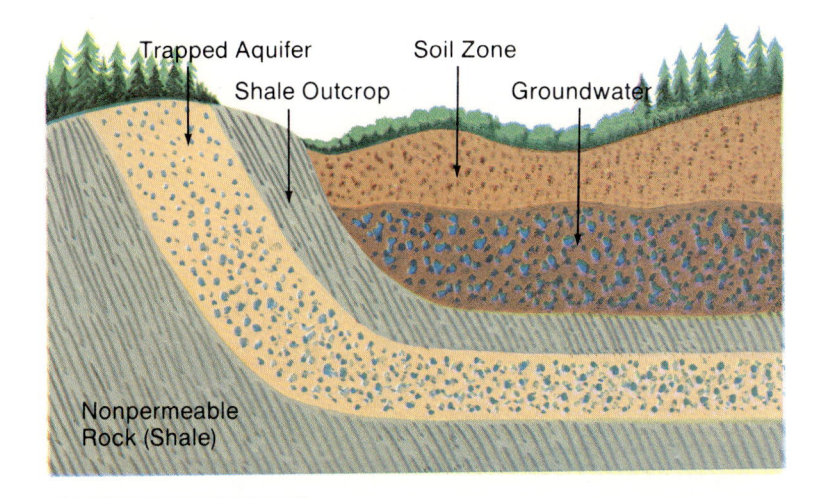

Do You Know?
It takes 200 years for a drop of water to move through one aquifer from Wisconsin to Chicago.

Figure 10.14 Water becomes trapped by layers of nonpermeable rock, creating an aquifer.

Activity

How Much Water Can a Rock Hold?

Materials
egg-sized pieces of sandstone, shale, and other rocks
water
containers
balance

Procedure
1. Find and record the mass of each rock sample.
2. Soak the rocks in a container of water overnight.
3. Remove the rocks from the water. Again find and record the mass of each rock sample.

Questions
1. What data did you obtain about the rocks?
2. Which rock would make the best aquifer?
3. How would this rock compare to sand as an aquifer (see data from the activity on page 189)?

Rock sample	Mass before soaking	Mass after soaking	Difference
1			
2			
3			

10 / Fresh Water

195

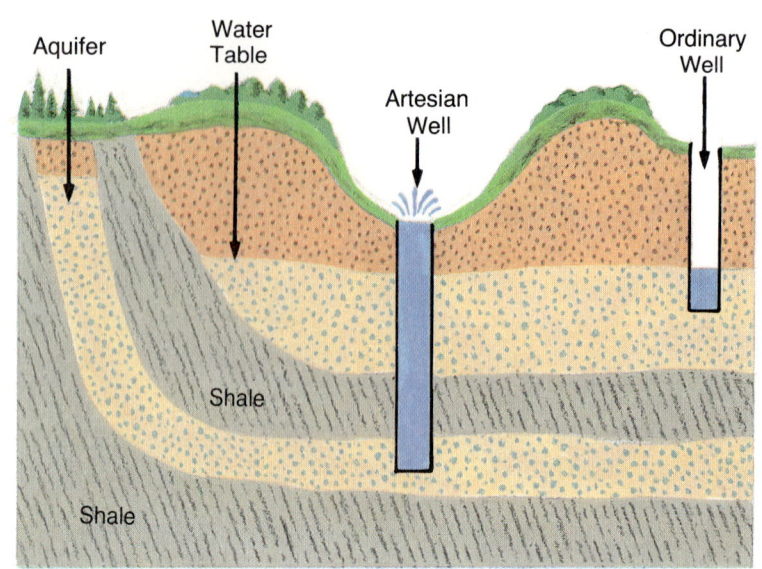

Figure 10.15 *right:* Underground water sources can be tapped for use through wells that bring the water to the surface.

Figure 10.16 *below:* A diesel pump brings underground water to the surface for irrigation.

Aquifers are a source of groundwater. A well can be drilled into an aquifer. Groundwater then moves into the hole forming a pool of water. The level of the pool of water is the same as the water table. As water is pumped from the well to the surface, more water moves into the hole through the aquifer. Since the water table rises in wet seasons and falls in dry seasons, the well hole often must go some distance below the water table to provide water all the time. About one third of all cities in the United States obtain water from wells. Does your city or town use surface water or groundwater?

In some places an aquifer carries water from a higher altitude to a lower altitude. If the aquifer has nonpermeable rock layers above and below it, pressure may build up at the lower altitude. Water may flow without pumping from a well drilled into such an aquifer because of the pressure. Wells from which water flows without pumping are called **artesian** [ahr-TEE-zhuhn] **wells.** The amount of water that flows from an artesian well depends on the pressure and how much water is in the aquifer. Some people called any deep-drilled well an artesian well. This is incorrect. To be a true artesian well, confined water under pressure must rise above its aquifer.

Do You Know?
Water in some aquifers is in the same place it was 25,000 years ago.

196

10 / Fresh Water

Groundwater that is pumped out is replaced by rain and melted snow. But this is a slow process because it takes time for melted snow and rain to soak into the ground. In some places groundwater is being removed faster than it is being replaced. As the level of the water table is lowered by excessive pumping, wells must be drilled deeper and deeper. In some areas it is possible that the groundwater could be used up.

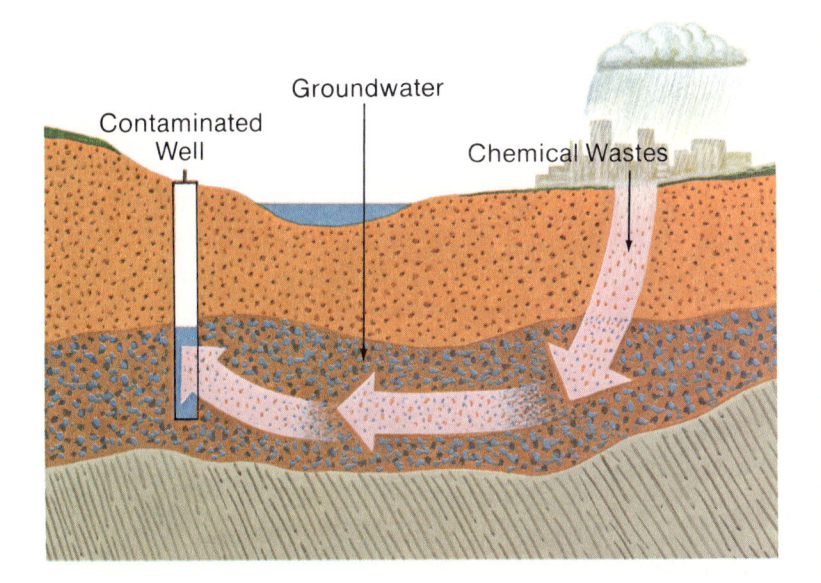

Do You Know?
If all the groundwater within 30 meters of the surface were placed on the surface, it would make a layer 5 meters deep across all of the United States.

Figure 10.17 *left:* Chemical wastes from one area may contaminate groundwater that is then drawn to the surface somewhere else.

Figure 10.18 *below:* Contaminated water is a problem people must learn to solve.

Wastes from cities and industries can also affect groundwater. They can seep into the ground just like the water. In some areas groundwater has been polluted with waste chemicals. When this happens, people can no longer use this groundwater, and the wells have to be shut down.

Study Questions for 10.3

1. Where does groundwater come from and what is the upper level of groundwater called?
2. What is the property of a rock that allows water to move through it?
3. What are underground rock formations that hold water called?
4. What are two problems that can happen when using a well for a freshwater supply?

10 / Fresh Water

197

10.4
Fresh Water as a Limited Resource

You will find out
- why fresh water is a limited resource;
- possible new sources of fresh water.

All of the water you use comes from precipitation. If your supply is from surface water, the precipitation probably occurred within the last year. If your supply is from groundwater, the water may be from precipitation that occurred a long time ago. Whatever your supply, enough precipitation falls in the United States each year to supply 21,570 L of water a day for each person. Do you use that much water?

The average daily use of water per person in the United States is about 6,500 L per day. Of course, each person does not use that much water. Less than 10 percent of the water is used for your home water supply. Farmers and ranchers use about 40 percent of the supply for crops and animals. Industry uses the other 50 percent. Even with evaporation, it seems that there is plenty of water. All of the uses together consume an amount that is less than a third of the yearly average precipitation.

Figure 10.19 *above:* One of the many vital uses for water

Figure 10.20 *right:* The use of freshwater in the United States

Industry 50%

Farming 40%

Home 10%

198

10 / Fresh Water

Even though there appears to be enough water, problems do develop with the supply. One problem for users of surface water is that it depends on precipitation. If precipitation does not fall for a long period of time, a drought occurs. Rivers and lakes become low, and there is not enough water in that area. One solution to this problem is to build large reservoirs that will store enough water to be used during a drought. Another solution is to use other water sources.

Another problem relates to the climate. Because of climatic differences not all areas of the country share equally in the total precipitation. In some areas of the United States all of the surface water is already being used. Even the groundwater is being pumped from the ground faster than it is being replaced. In these areas water may be brought in from long distances.

As the population grows, more and more demands are placed on the limited water supply. New industries develop. People want more food. Should farmers give up their share of the water to the city dwellers? Should city dwellers give up their water so new industries can develop? Should an upstream city or irrigation project take so much water that downstream cities will not have any? Who has the right to use the water when there isn't enough for everyone? For people in some places these questions are very difficult to answer.

Do You Know?
Some parts of Arizona, California, Florida, and Texas are withdrawing groundwater up to 20 times faster than it is being replaced. This causes the ground to sink in these areas.

Figure 10.21 *above:* This aqueduct in California helps transport water from where it is stored to where it is used.

Figure 10.22 *left:* Aqueducts now bring Colorado River water into central Arizona.

Figure 10.23 You can see why some people would object to an intentional increase in precipitation.

Figure 10.24 By using purified waste water, this power plant helps conserve fresh water for use elsewhere.

Water supply problems related to climate could be solved by increasing the water supply. Some possible ways to increase water supplies are (1) increasing the rainfall, (2) recycling waste water, (3) moving large icebergs from the polar oceans, and (4) desalting ocean water.

There have been attempts to increase precipitation in the Rocky Mountains. Devices were placed in the mountains and operated during the winter. The devices made billions and billions of snowflake-forming nuclei that were carried into clouds. These nuclei caused water droplets in the clouds to form snowflakes, which fell to the ground. Snowfall was increased 10 to 15 percent as a result. Many people who lived in mountain towns objected to the increased snowfall. They did not want more snow to shovel from walks and to drive through. Do you think they should have to put up with more snow so other people can have more water?

Another way to increase the water supply is to recycle waste water. This is already happening in some places. A nuclear power plant uses treated sewage water from Phoenix, Arizona. The power plant purifies the treated sewage water and then uses it for cooling. Part of the increased demand for water can be met by more recycling of water.

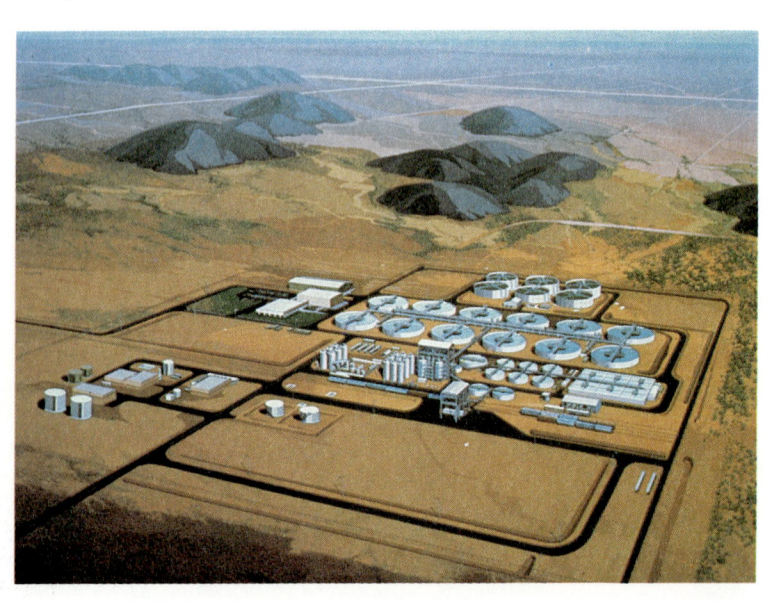

Remember that two thirds of the earth's fresh water is trapped in ice. In the polar regions, these huge masses of ice break away and float in the ocean as icebergs. They are made of fresh water, since they formed from snow. Some people have discussed using ships to push or tow these icebergs to coastal cities for use as a water supply. What problems do you think might develop when attempting to push icebergs to Los Angeles or New York City for a water supply?

Still another supply of fresh water could come directly from the oceans. Salt can be removed from ocean water. Desalting factories would produce a limitless supply of fresh water for areas near the ocean. But the cost of removing salt from seawater by evaporation or by chemicals is very high. So far it is cheaper to build pipelines that carry fresh water hundreds of kilometers than it is to build a factory to remove salt from ocean water.

Can you think of other new sources of fresh water? The greatest amount of water used is not by farming, industry, or people. A much greater amount of water is lost by evaporation from lakes and rivers. In fact, evaporation and growing green plants use up nearly three fourths of all precipitation that falls. Yet, few ways have been found to prevent this loss. Perhaps in the future you may be the one to find a new way to slow water loss by evaporation.

Figure 10.25 *top:* Do you think icebergs will be a source of fresh water in the future?

Figure 10.26 *bottom:* In the future, scientists may find a way to collect and use water that is released by growing plants.

Study Questions for 10.4

1. How does the amount of fresh water used in the United States each year compare to the yearly average precipitation?
2. What problems can develop in some places with the water supply?
3. Discuss four possible *new* sources of fresh water.

Career

Hydrologist

Some cities use streams and lakes as a source of water. Other cities use groundwater. How do the cities know about the water quality and how much water is available? They ask a hydrologist, a scientist who measures the amount and quality of fresh water.

Do you know anyone who started in one career but later changed to another one? Judy D. Fretwell, who started as an elementary school teacher, did that. She taught school for four years. She found doing research for science projects very exciting. But she also wanted to work outside, and she enjoyed writing.

Judy Fretwell left her teaching job and went back to college. There she studied science, mathematics, and computers. Two years later, she found work that included all the things she enjoyed doing. She was hired as a hydrologist by the U.S. Geological Survey. As a hydrologist, Judy Fretwell measures the water levels in lakes, streams, and wells. She also evaluates the water quality. After collecting this and other information, she writes reports. The reports tell other people about possible threats to their water supply.

Judy Fretwell wants other people to know about their surface water and groundwater supply and not to take it for granted. She states that water is our most valuable resource.

CHAPTER REVIEW

Main Ideas

- Of all the water on the earth, 97 percent is salt water and 3 percent is fresh water.
- About 2 percent of the earth's water is fresh water frozen in ice. Less than 1 percent of all water on the earth is fresh water that is available for use.
- Over the oceans, evaporation is greater than precipitation. Over the land, precipitation is greater than evaporation.
- About two thirds of precipitation finds its way back into the atmosphere. About one third soaks into the ground or flows across the land.
- Soil with more pore space holds more water.
- Permeability is a measure of how well water flows through the pores and cracks in rock layers.
- Water moving across the surface is called surface runoff. Runoff forms streams and rivers as it moves from high places to low places.
- Standing bodies of fresh water are called ponds or lakes, depending on their size. A lake formed by a dam is called a reservoir.
- The water table is the surface of a water-soaked underground zone. Precipitation that soaks into the ground moves downward to the water table, then moves toward a lower elevation.
- Problems may develop when groundwater is pumped out faster than it is replaced or when the groundwater becomes polluted.
- Fresh water is a limited resource.

Using Vocabulary

On a separate piece of paper, write a paragraph or two describing the water supply. Use and underline each term listed below.

fresh water	surface runoff	pond	water table
pore space	stream	lake	aquifer
porosity	watershed	reservoir	artesian well
permeability	divide	groundwater	

Remembering Facts

Number your paper from 1 to 15. Match each term in column **A** with a phrase in column **B**.

A
1. water table
2. salt water
3. lake
4. watershed
5. pore space
6. reservoir
7. groundwater
8. nonpermeable
9. pond
10. well
11. permeable
12. fresh water
13. aquifer
14. surface runoff
15. artesian well
16. divide
17. stream
18. porosity

B
a. space between soil particles
b. hole drilled to below the water table
c. kind of rock that water moves through
d. water from a water-soaked underground zone
e. water that moves on the land
f. a lake created by building a dam on a stream or river
g. water found on the earth that you can drink
h. kind of permeable rock with groundwater in it
i. standing body of fresh water shallow enough for sunlight to reach the bottom
j. area of land drained by a river
k. more than 97 percent of all water on the earth
l. well from which water flows without being pumped
m. level below which the ground is full of groundwater
n. kind of rock that water cannot move through
o. standing body of fresh water so deep that sunlight does not reach the bottom
p. total amount of pore space available in a given volume of material
q. body of water that is moving
r. separates regions that drain into one watershed from those that drain into another

Understanding Ideas

On your paper, answer each question in complete sentences.
1. Is it possible to increase the supply of groundwater in just a few years? Why or why not?
2. What variables determine how much rainfall evaporates, runs off, or becomes groundwater?
3. How is it possible to have a water well in the Rocky Mountains, thousands of meters above sea level?
4. What type of underground rock layers are most likely to contain groundwater?

Applying What You Have Learned

1. Describe the factors that would affect the depth of a water table.
2. In cold climates, less water enters the ground during the winter than in any other season. Why?
3. How could your town increase its supply of water if surface runoff was the only source of water?

Challenge

A major river receives most of its water from two sources. Surface runoff can double the volume of water in a river. This source of water, however, is inconsistent. The steady supply of groundwater is what maintains the normal volume of water in a river. The graph shows the volume of water in a river before and after a rainfall. Rainwater has not yet reached the river between points A and B. The river is being supplied by groundwater. From B to C, the volume rises rapidly as the rainwater arrives. From C to D, the volume decreases gradually as rainwater slowed down by vegetation begins to arrive. From D to E, the surface runoff has stopped and the river is once again being fed by groundwater.

1. What are the sources of river water?
2. How does a river continue to flow after a long dry spell?
3. Why does the amount of water supplied to a river by surface runoff and groundwater vary so dramatically?

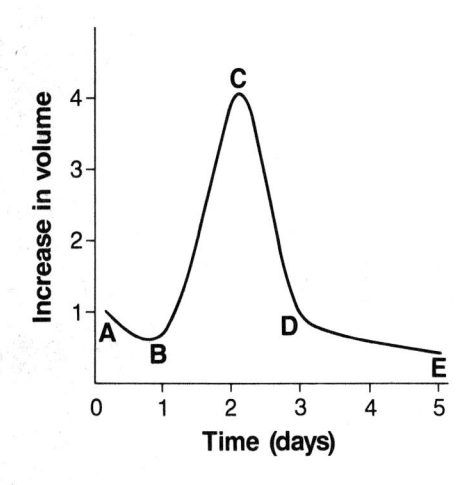

Research and Investigation

1. Investigate the amount of water used by industrial processes, farming, and homes in your area. Make a pie graph to show your findings. Compare your results to the national averages. Report your findings to the class.
2. Plan a field trip to a local water-treatment plant. What is the source of water in your area? How does water arrive at the treatment plant? What processes are used to treat the water? How does treated water get to your house?
3. Investigate the water table in your area. How deep is the water table? What aquifer supplies the water? Make a drawing to show the water table in your area. Also show the location of any streams, lakes, springs, or swamps in your area.

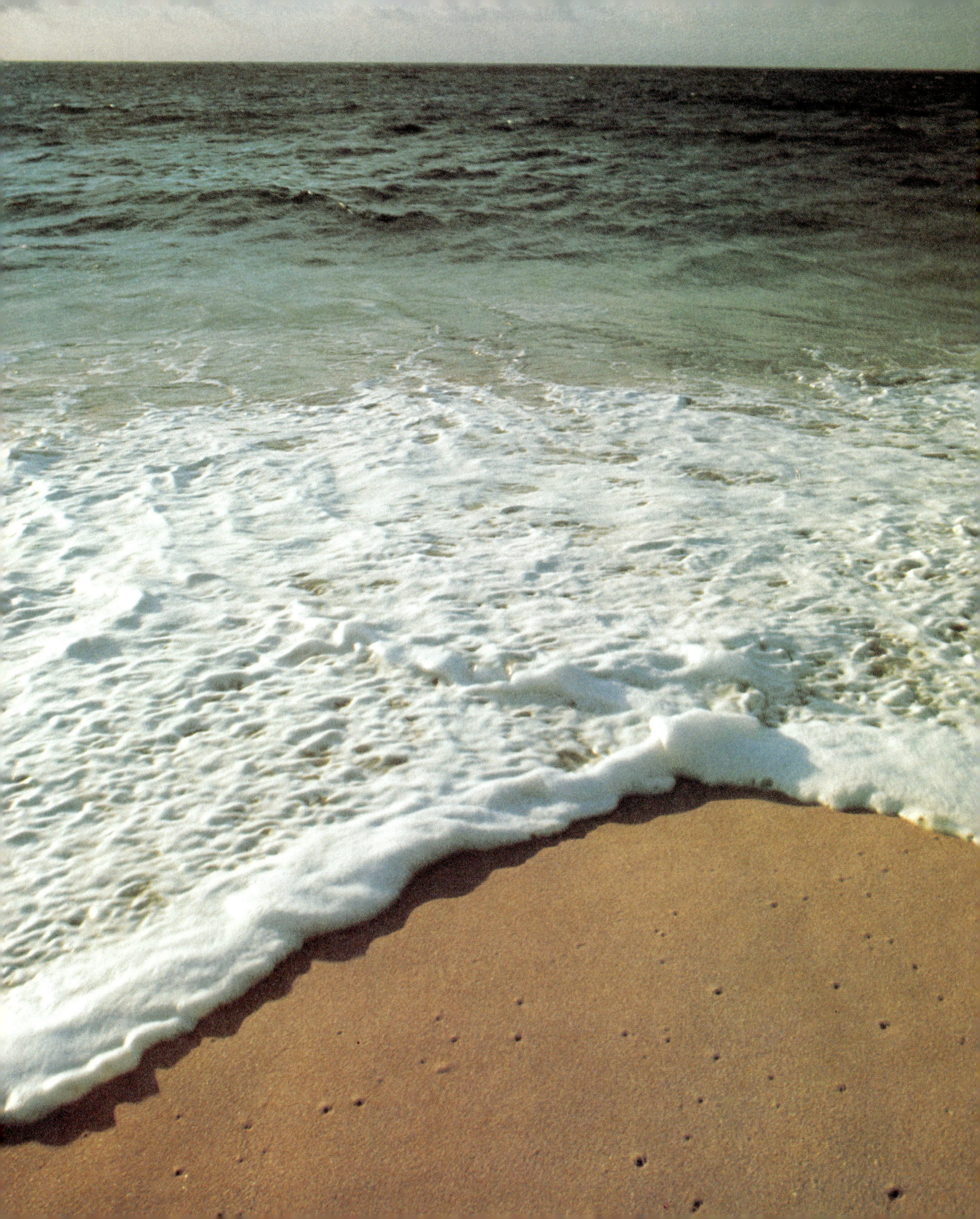

Chapter 11
Oceanography

Lesson Titles
11.1 Waves and Currents
11.2 Beaches and Shorelines
11.3 The Ocean Floor
11.4 Composition of Seawater
11.5 Life in the Ocean

Have you ever walked along a sandy beach at the ocean? Perhaps you walked just out of reach of the waves that crashed onto the beach. Each wave pushes a surge of churning water and foam across the sand. The water hesitates and then rushes back toward the ocean only to be swallowed by the next crashing wave. What makes these waves? Where do ocean waves come from?

If you have ever explored a beach, you probably have found rocks and seashells of all shapes and colors. Where do these interesting, wondrous things come from? As you look out over the vast, watery surface of the ocean, do you wonder what lies beneath that surface?

People have always wanted to know more about the ocean. Some of the most exciting things about the earth are being discovered in the depths of the ocean. Scientists are studying the ocean in many different ways. In this chapter you will study the ocean and the strange but exciting world beneath the ocean surface.

Figure 11.1 *opposite:* A sandy beach on the island of Kauai, Hawaii

11.1
Waves and Currents

You will find out
- what makes waves on the ocean;
- what determines how big a wind-made wave becomes;
- what makes currents in the ocean.

On their first trip to the ocean many people quickly notice the vast, watery surface. Water as far as they can see! Then they notice something else. The surface of the ocean is rarely, if ever, still. The water's surface rises and falls, forming **waves.** On some days small waves tumble and surge on the shore. On other days large waves, topped with foam, thunder and crash onto the shore, threatening boats and buildings with disaster. Waves are in many ways the most destructive part of the ocean. They erode and shape the coast. They are always a threat to ships and buildings near the shore. One after another, the waves keep coming. What causes waves and where do they come from?

Figure 11.2 Wave action always brings change and sometimes causes destruction.

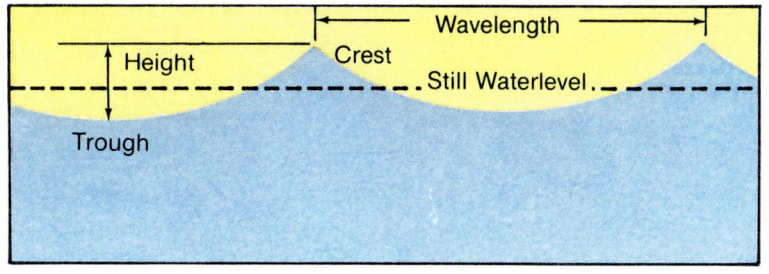

Figure 11.3 *left:* A profile of a wave

Figure 11.4 *below:* Rough seas are familiar to most ships. Would you like a ride such as this boat is getting?

You have made waves if you have thrown a rock into a pool of water. The rock made wrinkles on the surface that moved away from the disturbance. These moving wrinkles are called waves. A simplified sketch of a wave is shown in Figure 11.3. The highest part of a wave is the **crest.** The lowest part is the **trough** [trawf]. The horizontal distance between two crests is defined as the **wavelength.** The vertical distance between a crest and a trough is the **wave height.** A wave can have various wavelengths and wave heights. Ocean waves to a height of 165 m have been observed. The wavelength usually ranges from 65 m up to 6,500 m.

Activity

How Does a Wave Move?

Materials
rope about 15 meters long
10-cm piece of colored yarn or string

Procedure

1. Tie a 10-cm piece of colored yarn or string to the center part of a 15-m rope.
2. Have someone hold one end of the rope still while you shake the other end up and down.
3. Observe what happens to the yarn as waves move down the rope.

Questions

1. Make a sketch of the wave formed along the rope.
2. What was the motion of the colored yarn?
3. What evidence do you have that a wave moves forward, not the material that the wave is in?

11 / Oceanography

What causes waves? Wind, earthquakes, and the attraction of the moon and sun are the most important wave makers. Most ocean waves are made by winds.

When the wind begins to blow over calm water, first, areas of ripples appear and then disappear as they become waves. As the wind continues to gust, the waves become larger. How large the waves become depends on (1) the wind speed, (2) the length of time the wind blows, and (3) the **fetch,** the distance the wind blows over the water.

If the winds are strong, they might topple the wave, making foam. These foam-topped waves are called whitecaps. If you see whitecaps, you know that the wind is blowing at 30 km an hour or more.

Wind-caused waves can travel thousands of kilometers from where they were formed. The waves that travel such a distance are long, wide waves that are not very high. These waves are called **swell.**

As a wave moves from open water and nears the shore, it starts to change. The wave slows as the lower part drags on the ocean bottom. The wave height starts to increase. Then the wave top bends forward and finally breaks, forming foamy **breakers.** The zone where the breakers occur is called **surf.** It is swell that forms breakers in the surf along the shore. The breakers are caused by the ocean bottom near the shore, the long gentle slope. Here the waves begin to build up far from the shore. They travel a long distance before breaking.

Figure 11.5 *top:* The ocean surface is calm when there is little wind. *bottom:* Seas become rough when winds are strong.

Figure 11.6 *below:* This illustration represents the pattern of a swell as it reaches a gently sloping beach.

Passing Wave →

Swell

210

11 / Oceanography

Wind-made waves are easy to see because they happen often. Wind-made waves have short wavelengths. Waves made by gravitational attraction or earthquakes have large wavelengths.

Tides can also be thought of as waves. They have a wavelength of nearly 22,000 km. It takes about 12 hours for the water to go up and down from such a wave. Tides are made by gravitational attraction of the sun and the moon. More information about tides can be found on page 69.

A wave made by an undersea earthquake is called a **tsunami** [tsoo-NAH-mee]. The tsunami is the largest of all ocean waves. It may have a 200-km wavelength and move across the ocean at hundreds of kilometers per hour. When this wave reaches the shore, a huge breaker forms. In some cases this breaker has been over 66 m tall, causing much damage as it moves on shore. The Hawaiian Islands average a tsunami every four years.

Almost all of the water in the ocean is always moving. Probably only the water in the bottom of some deep basins does not move. Wind moves the water on the surface. Below the surface, the water is moving in a way you can't see. It is moving in streams called **currents.** A current is a moving stream of water in a body of water. Perhaps you have felt a current in a swimming pool. Water pumped through the filter returns to the pool through small pipes in the side. This makes currents in the pool. You can't see a current, but you can feel it.

Do You Know?
The world's greatest tide occurs in the Bay of Fundy and is over 16 m.

Table 11-1 The Beaufort Scale

Force	Wind Speed*	Description
0	0	Calm
1	2	Calm
2	5	Light
3	9	Light
4	13	Moderate
5	18	Moderate
6	24	Strong
7	30	Strong
8	37	Gale
9	44	Gale
10	52	Storm
11	60	Storm
12	68	Hurricane

* (knot-speed of one nautical kilometer, 1.852 km per hour)

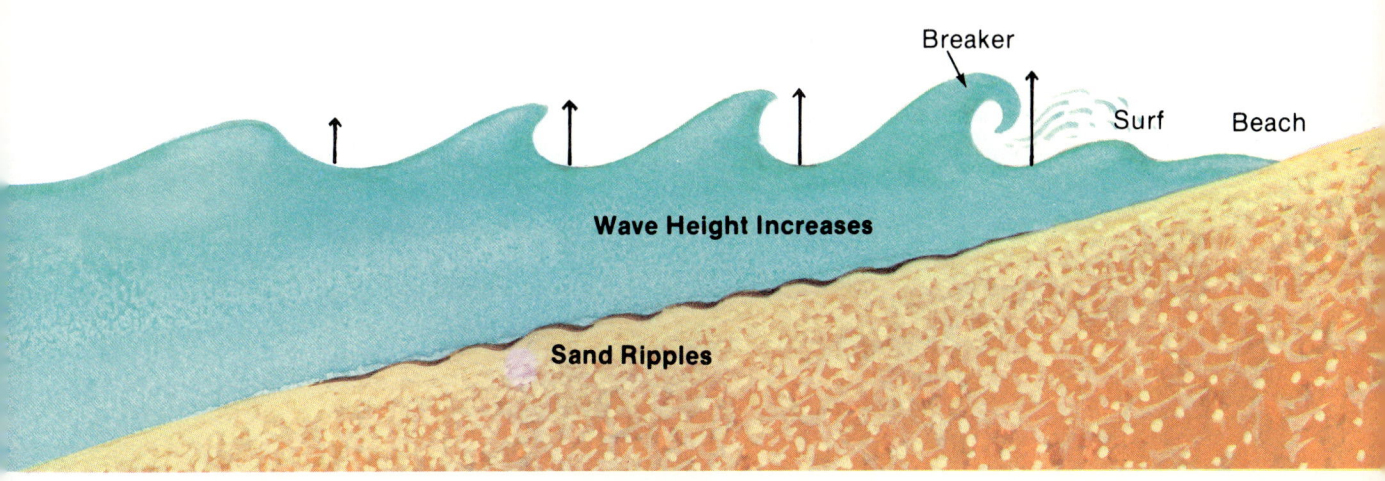

Figure 11.7 *top:* Sediments suspended in the water show the direction of longshore and rip currents.

Figure 11.8 *bottom:* The shape of the shore bottom may cause a longshore current to turn and become a rip current.

Ocean currents are made by (1) waves, (2) wind, and (3) differences in water density. The density of water is changed by temperature and by its salt content. Evaporation, fresh water from rivers, and melting ice change the salt concentration and thus the density.

Currents made by waves occur in a small area near a shore. There is not much forward movement of water by waves in the ocean. It is different near the shore. Breakers pile up water near the shore. This water divides into two currents. One current is pushed along by waves, producing a **longshore current.** This current moves along the shore until it finds a place where it can head out to sea. When it does, it produces a second current called an **undertow** or a **rip current.** There is usually no surf where a rip current occurs. The current usually occupies a channel in this place. A rip current continues for a kilometer or two out to sea. Rip currents are strong and can carry a swimmer far from the shore. You should swim across a rip current rather than try to swim against it. The movement of sand and mud along the ocean floor can create another type of current, called a **turbidity current.** Turbidity currents are powerful agents of erosion. They often reshape the slope of the ocean floor.

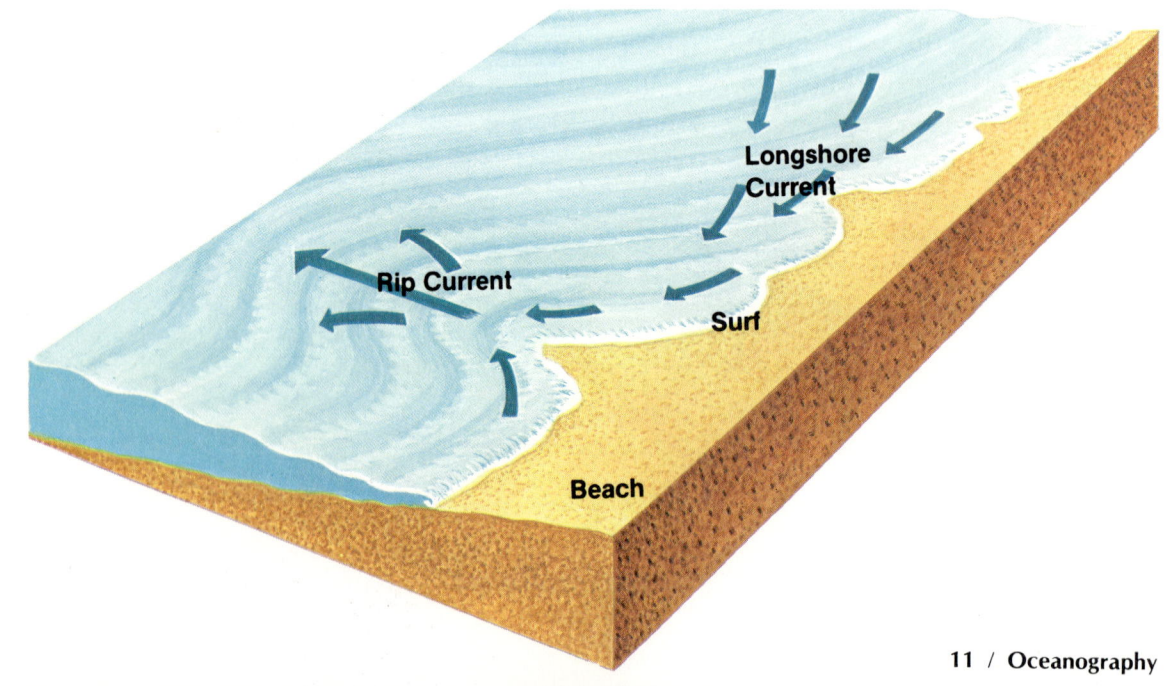

212

11 / Oceanography

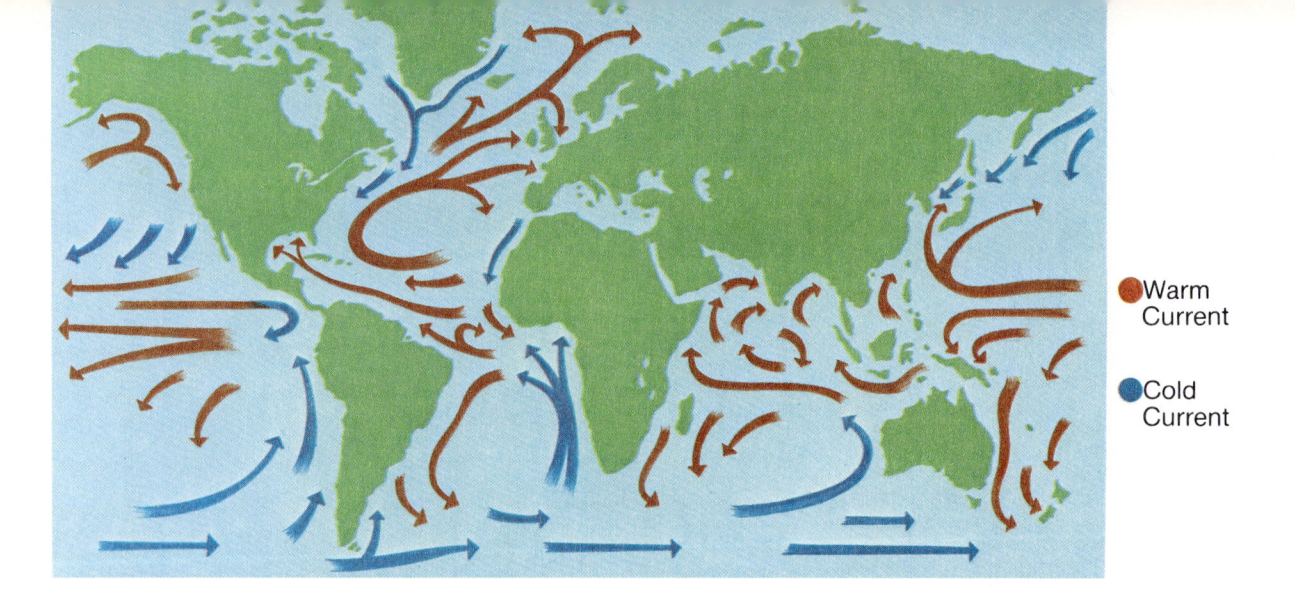

Figure 11.9 The major ocean currents of the world

● Warm Current
● Cold Current

There are also currents that move over long distances in the ocean. These are shown in Figure 11.9. These currents are started by density differences and then pushed by prevailing winds. These currents are also influenced by the Coriolis effect (see page 117) and the shape of the ocean bottom. They are like giant rivers of water in the ocean. The Gulf Stream, for example, is a stream of water that is moving up to 120 km per day. It is about 150 km wide and may extend to a depth of a thousand meters. Some of the currents are even larger and move more slowly. The California current is broader, but it is moving at only up to 7 km per day. Both the Gulf Stream and California current, however, carry huge volumes of water great distances.

Since all of the oceans are connected, all of the major currents are related. Just as the atmosphere has a worldwide circulation pattern of air, the ocean currents make up a worldwide circulation pattern of water.

Do You Know?
The volume of water moving in ocean currents is about 10,000 times greater than the flow of all large rivers.

Study Questions for 11.1
1. Name three things that make ocean waves.
2. What determines how big a wind-made wave becomes?
3. What is a current?
4. Name one ocean current that is near the shore and one current that is far from shore.

11 / Oceanography

11.2 Beaches and Shorelines

You will find out
- how beaches are formed;
- what beach sand is made of;
- how sand-deposited shore features are formed.

Figure 11.10 Examples of shorelines include a rocky shoreline (*top*), a sandy beach (*bottom left*), and a tidal marsh (*bottom right*).

Suppose you want to go to a place on the earth where you can see the most obvious and ongoing change in the land. Where would you go? The place where you should go is where the land and the ocean meet. The waves and currents never stop. They are very good at changing land, as you will see.

The place where the land and water meet is called the **shoreline.** The **shore** is the area where waves are active. Most of the shores of the earth are covered with beaches. A beach is a deposit of sand or gravel that covers the shore. Other shores are rock cliffs with no sand deposits at all. The constant pounding and grinding action of waves slowly wears these cliffs away. On the other hand, shores in sheltered bays have mud that has been deposited by tides and longshore currents. Eventually, a shallow bay could fill to form a broad, flat muddy area called a **tidal marsh.** Many tidal marshes are located on the eastern coast of the United States because of the low flat terrain and many rivers.

214　　　　　　　　　　　　　　　　　　　　　　　　　　　11 / Oceanography

Waves and currents not only grind up rock cliffs and deposit mud marshes but also move sand around. In fact, waves and currents moving sand around are what form beaches. Most all the sand making up a beach has been moved there from the ocean floor. Sand was brought to the ocean by rivers. Sand can also be small pieces of coastal rocks that have been ground up by waves. These sands were deposited on the ocean floor and then moved onto the beaches by waves.

Figure 11.11 A sandy beach can be made of quartz (*top left*), grains of shells and coral (*below left*), or volcanic rock (*below right*).

Most beach sand is made of many different minerals. The greatest amount is quartz, however, because quartz is very hard and weathers slowly. Beaches in tropical areas are sometimes made up of grains of shells or coral. Waves grind the shells and coral into grains and then deposit the grains on the shore. These beaches are usually white and softer than the hard, quartz-sand beaches. Along the east coast of Florida, you can see the beaches change from quartz sand to shell sand as you drive south. Some beaches in Hawaii are black. Black beaches are formed from grains of volcanic rock. You even have a choice in Hawaii, as some islands have a white beach on one side and a black beach on the other.

Figure 11.12 This photograph is a close-up of the grains of shells and coral composing some sandy beaches.

Figure 11.13 A sandbar

A beach is always changing. Wind, waves, and currents move the sand around. Some beaches grow larger during the summer and smaller during the winter. Small waves during the summer bring more sand to the beach. Winter storms with their high waves can carry much of the sand off the beach and out to sea. During the calmer summer months, waves and currents move the sand back onto the beach.

Moving sand is sometimes deposited by a longshore current. This could happen if something deflects the current or if the current moves into open water. The deposited sand could be moved again by waves. But if enough sand is gradually deposited over a period of time, certain shore features are formed. A **sandbar** is a shore feature. It is a long pile of sand that is under water. Sometimes a sandbar can be seen at low tide. If the sandbar is connected to the shoreline, it forms another shore feature called a **spit**. A spit may grow as storm waves toss more sand on it. Eventually it may grow higher than sea level.

Activity

How Many Different Materials Are in Sand?

Materials
beach sand
magnifying lens
sheet of paper

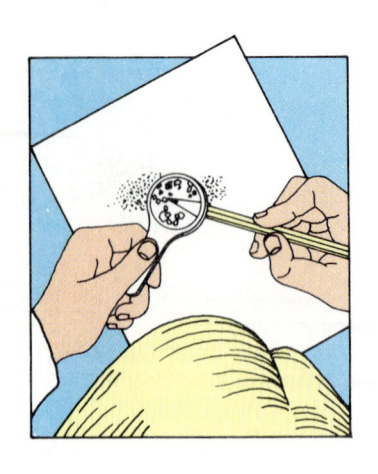

Procedure

1. Carefully pour about one-half teaspoon of beach sand in the center of a sheet of paper.

2. Record the overall color of the sand.

3. Use your pencil point to carefully spread the sand grains. Observe the grains with a magnifying lens.

4. Record your observations about the grains. How many different kinds of grains are there? Group the similar grains together.

5. Record other observations about the grains. For example, do they have corners or are they rounded?

Questions

1. How many different kinds of sand grains did you find?

2. Describe and sketch the different grains.

3. How many different types of grains did you find?

216   11 / Oceanography

Figure 11.14 *left:* A spit reaches out from the shore to the ocean.

Figure 11.15 *below:* A barrier bar and its long, straight beach

Another type of sand-deposited shore feature is found on the East Coast from Long Island to Florida, around the Gulf Coast, and in a few places along the West Coast. These features are long sandbars called **barrier bars.** Barrier bars are usually parallel to the coast and form a barrier between the coast and the ocean. They are separated from the coast by a relatively narrow body of water. Barrier bars accumulate sand to become **barrier islands.** Barrier islands have long, straight beaches on the seaward side. These beaches are popular recreational areas. Atlantic City, New Jersey, and Galveston, Texas, are both built on barrier islands.

Study Questions for 11.2
1. What is a beach?
2. How is a beach formed?
3. What are beach sands made of?
4. What shore features form from deposited sand?

11.3 The Ocean Floor

You will find out
- what the three main divisions of the ocean's floor are called;
- what the landforms of the ocean basin are.

Rock cliffs, beaches, and tidal marshes are familiar parts of the ocean shore because you can easily see them. But what is underneath all the ocean water? How deep is the ocean? Early attempts to answer these questions were made from ships. A long length of wire with a heavy weight attached was lowered from a ship. The length of wire needed for the weight to reach the bottom was measured. Not many measurements were made in this way, but some data were collected. The limited data gave people the wrong idea. They thought the ocean floor was smooth and flat like a gigantic cereal bowl.

A new way to measure the ocean floor changed people's ideas about the ocean bottom. This newer way is called **echo sounding.** It uses a device that sends a sound signal through the water. The sound signal hits the bottom and bounces (echoes) back up to the ship. The echo sounder measures the time required for the sound signal to reach the bottom and to return. Sound travels through water at about 1,460 m per second. Suppose the ocean floor is exactly 1,460 m below the ship. How long

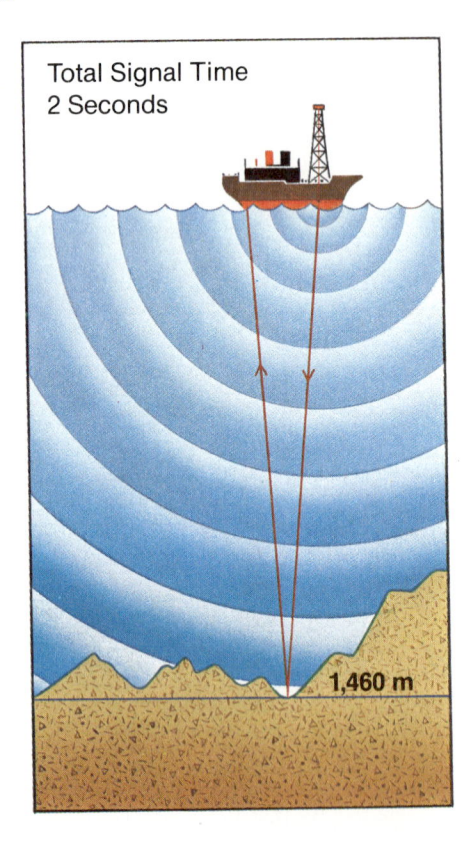

Figure 11.16 If a round trip for echo sounding signals takes two seconds, the one-way distance must be 1,460 meters.

Figure 11.17 A scientist studies echo sounding data returning from the ocean floor.

218   11 / Oceanography

would be required for the signal to reach the bottom and to return? One second would be required for the sound to travel to the floor and one second for it to return. Two seconds, then, would mean that the ocean floor is 1,460 m below the ship.

Some echo sounders draw a picture of the ocean floor. They make a continuous picture of the floor as the ship moves across the ocean. Much of what is known about the ocean floor comes from the use of such sounders.

Thousands of echo soundings have been used to gain an idea of what the ocean bottom is like. The bottom is no longer thought of as very smooth and flat. There are mountains underwater bigger than any on the land above water. There are canyons deeper than any canyon found on land. There are plains, hills, and valleys. Look at Figure 11.18. It shows what the earth might look like beneath the ocean. The ocean floor can be divided into three main areas: (1) the **continental shelf,** (2) the **continental slope,** and (3) the **ocean basin.** Let's take a closer look at each of these.

Do You Know?
If the tallest mountain on the earth (Mount Everest) were placed in the deepest trench (Mariana Trench), the mountaintop would still be about 2,850 m below the ocean's surface.

Figure 11.18 The features of the ocean floor are better understood because of echo sounding studies.

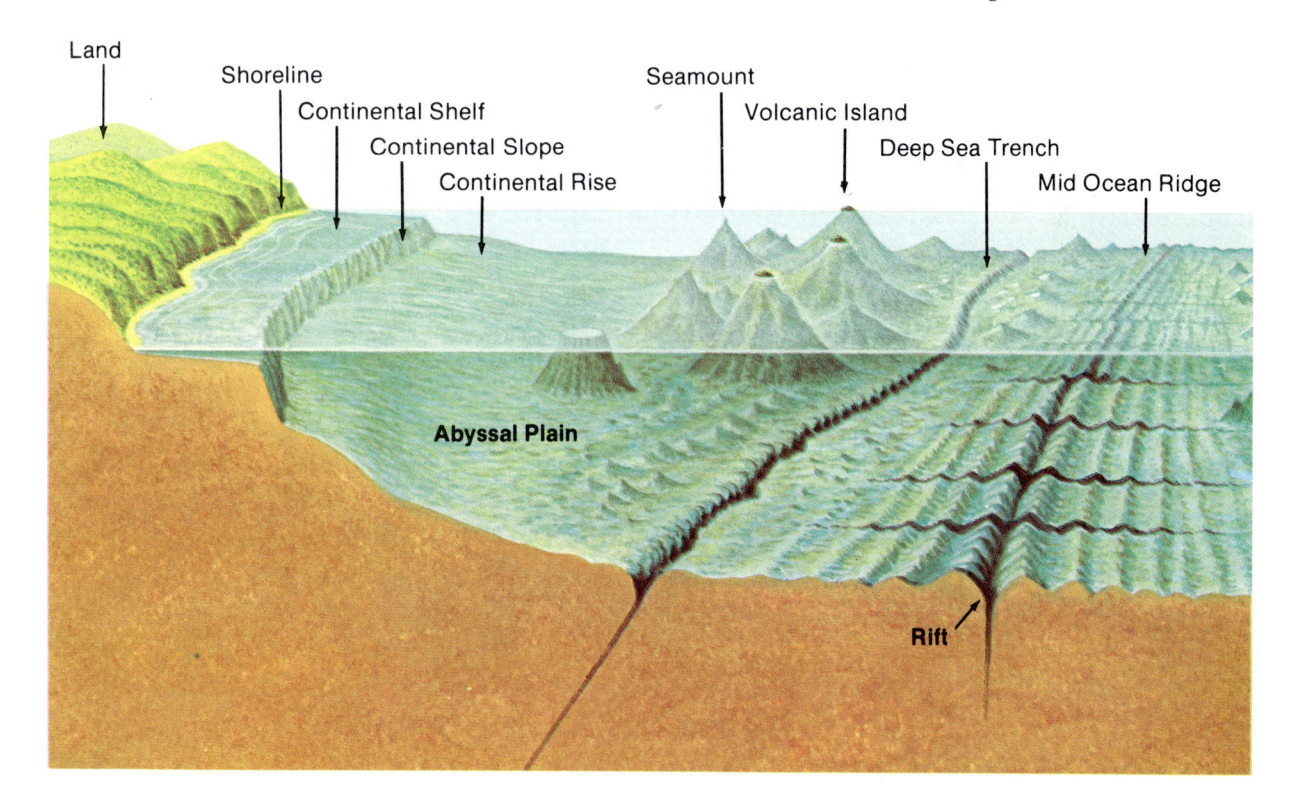

11 / Oceanography

Figure 11.19 A physical map of the earth's ocean floor shows the locations of the larger ridges and trenches.

Each continent is surrounded by a somewhat shallow area called the continental shelf. The water gradually becomes deeper as you move from the shoreline and out over the shelf. Eventually, it will reach a depth of about 130 m. In Figure 11.19, you will notice that the continental shelf is wider in some places than in others. The average width of a continental shelf is 75 km.

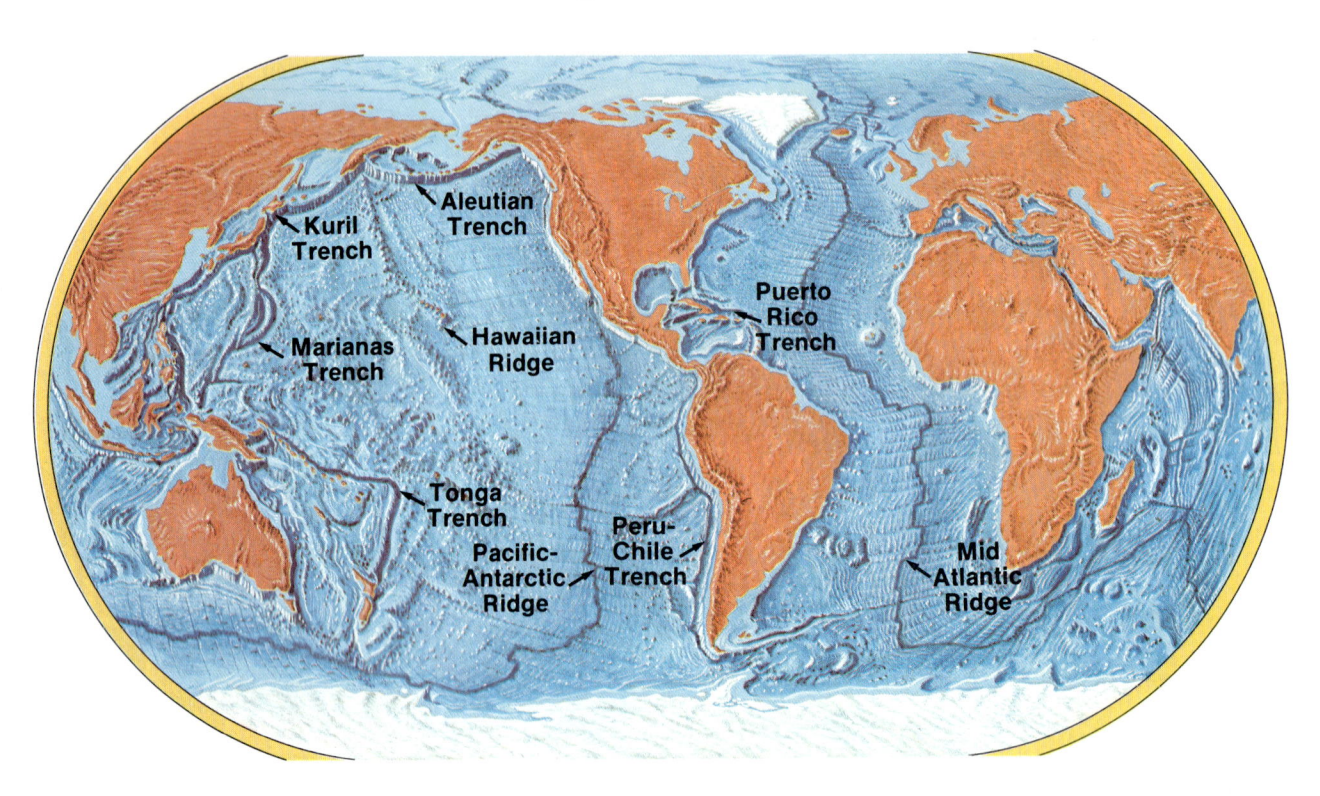

Beyond the continental shelf the depth starts to increase rapidly. This is the continental slope. The continental slope starts where the continental shelf ends and plunges rapidly down to depths of about 4,000 m. The slope is usually between 20 and 40 km wide. In many places the slope has gullies, valleys, and huge canyons. Some of these submarine canyons are larger than Arizona's Grand Canyon of the Colorado River. Submarine avalanches on the continental slope are thought to cause these valleys and canyons. It is not the shoreline but the outer edge of the continental slope that is the boundary of a continent.

Do You Know?
The *Glomar Challenger* in its cruises in 1970 and 1975 obtained conclusive evidence that the Mediterranean Sea has gone dry a number of times over the course of several million years.

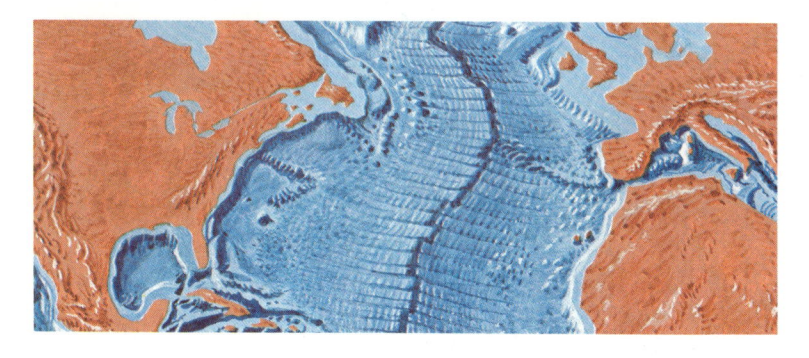

Figure 11.20 A closer look at the mid-Atlantic ridge

Beyond the continental slope is the ocean basin, the bottom of the ocean floor. The basins are 4,000 to 6,000 m deep. The basin does have landforms as you can see in Figure 11.19. The basin is not like a gigantic cereal bowl. It is somewhat flat, but there are many hills, mountains, and mountain ranges. The great mountain ranges are called **ridges.** The mid Atlantic Ridge rises above sea level in some places, forming islands. Submarine volcanoes have also occurred across the ocean basin. If the volcano does not make it to the surface, it is called a **seamount.** Volcanoes that do make it to the surface make islands. The Hawaiian Islands are islands formed by volcanoes. The ocean basin also contains **trenches.** Trenches are long, narrow, and deep with steep sides. Trenches are often found next to a chain of islands or offshore, close to a coastal mountain range. Earthquakes and volcanoes often occur near these trenches. The names and depths of some of these trenches are shown in Table 11-2.

More and more information about the ocean floor is being gathered by underwater cameras and deep-diving research vessels. Research vessels have been to the bottom of the trenches. Cameras have found strange new animals. Most of the ocean floor, however, is still unexplored. and there are still vast areas to be mapped.

Table 11-2

Trench	Maximum Depth(Meters)
Aleutian	8,100
Kuril	10,400
Japan	9,700
Marianas	11,034
New Britain	8,300
New Hebrides	9,000
Tonga	10,800
Kermadec	10,800
Peru-Chile	8,000

Study Questions for 11.3

1. Describe the continental shelf.
2. Describe the continental slope.
3. Describe the ocean basin.
4. Describe the landforms found in the ocean basin.

11.4 Composition of Seawater

You will find out
- why seawater is salty;
- what the composition of seawater is;
- how salty seawater is;
- what factors affect the salinity of seawater.

If you have ever been swimming in the ocean, you know that seawater is very salty. The large amount of dissolved materials in seawater gives the water its distinctive taste. These dissolved materials enter the ocean as a result of volcanic activity or through the hydrologic cycle. Seawater contains all of the elements that make up the minerals in the earth's crust.

The six most abundant elements making up the dissolved materials in seawater are listed in Table 11-3. These elements make up over 99 percent of all dissolved materials. Chlorine and sodium are the most abundant elements found in seawater. These two elements make up the familiar compound, table salt. Sulfur, magnesium, calcium, and potassium are also present in seawater. Elements such as silicon and bromine can be found in small quantities. Gases such as oxygen, carbon dioxide, and nitrogen are found in greatest abundance near the surface waters of the ocean.

How did all these elements get into the seawater? Volcanic activity on land and on the ocean floor releases elements such as chlorine and sulfur. Weathering and erosion wear away solid material from the earth's surface. Then the hydrologic cycle carries a great deal of solid and dissolved matter from the land into the sea. Gases also enter the water as a result of surface mixing between the atmosphere and water.

The measure of the amount of solid material dissolved in seawater is called **salinity** [suy-LIHN-uh-tee]. Scientists measure salinity by determining the mass of solids dissolved in 1,000 grams of water. The salinity of fresh water is usually less than 1 gram of salts per 1,000 grams of water. The average salinity of seawater is much higher. There are about 35 grams of salts per 1,000 grams of water.

Table 11-3 Dissolved Materials in Seawater	
Element	Percentage
Chlorine	55.04
Sodium	30.61
Sulfur	7.68
Magnesium	3.69
Calcium	1.16
Potassium	1.10

Figure 11.21 If 1,000 grams of seawater were evaporated, 35 grams of dissolved material would be left behind.

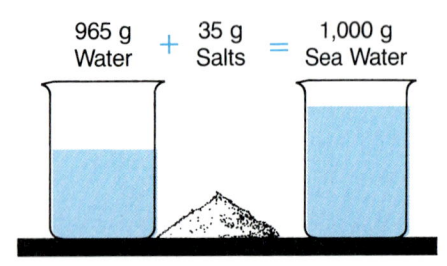

965 g Water + 35 g Salts = 1,000 g Sea Water

Local influences can affect the average salinity of the water in a given area. The salinity of seawater near the mouth of the river can be lowered by heavy rainfall or melting snow that has occurred upriver. The rate of evaporation can also affect salinity. Evaporation is high in ocean waters near the equator, and therefore the waters in tropical areas have a high salinity. Polar waters have low rates of evaporation and low salinity.

The salinity of the ocean has not changed much over the last 600 million years. Even though the salinity of seawater may vary in some places, the dissolved materials in seawater are always in the same proportion. At present, rivers carry about 4 billion tons of dissolved material to the ocean each year.

Why haven't the ocean basins been filled in by all the dissolved materials that arrive year after year? A balance is maintained by natural processes occurring within the ocean. Once dissolved materials are in the ocean, some of them are removed in various ways. Some elements are used by plants for growth and repair. Marine animals use elements such as calcium to make shells and bones. Some elements fall out of the water and form mineral deposits on the ocean floor. The rest of the dissolved materials remain suspended in seawater.

Figure 11.22 This large mound of salt was mined by evaporating seawater.

Do You Know?
If all the seawater in the oceans of the world were to evaporate, a layer of salt 60 meters deep would be left behind.

Study Questions for 11.4
1. Why is seawater salty?
2. What is the composition of seawater?
3. What is salinity?
4. What factors affect the salinity of seawater?

11.5
Life in the Oceans

You will find out
- how the ocean can support life;
- what plankton, nekton, and benthos are;
- how the sun-driven ocean food chain works.

The ocean supports a tremendous variety of living things. Plants and animals make up the largest groups of ocean-dwelling organisms. Plant and plantlike organisms live only in areas that receive sunlight. They can be found along the shoreline, in shallow water, and near or on the surface of the water. Animals can be found at any depth in the ocean. All living things require water, energy from the environment, and dissolved materials for survival. Currents keep an abundant supply of dissolved materials and gases circulating in the world's oceans.

Ocean-dwelling plants and animals can be categorized by how they move and where they live. Small, floating plants and animals that live near the surface are called **plankton** [PLANK-tuhn]. Plankton either drift or move along by ocean currents. The plantlike organisms of this group include diatoms and dinoflagellates. Diatoms make up the most important and most abundant group of organisms in the ocean. These plantlike protists provide the source of food for many animals in the sea. Animal plankton include larval fishes, jellyfish, radiolarian, and copepods.

Ocean-dwelling organisms can be further divided into two groups. Animals that swim freely are called **nekton** [NEHK-tuhn]. The nekton group includes fish, whales, octopuses, seals, and other animals. Some nekton can swim at varying depths in the ocean. However, most of them swim at a specific depth. Factors such as the temperature, the food supply, and the salinity of the water seem to determine at which depth a nektonic organism can live.

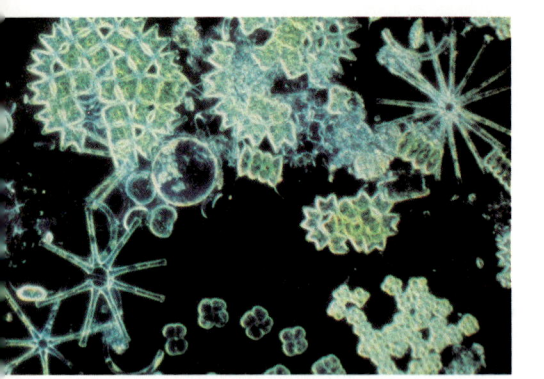

Figure 11.23 Tiny plankton floating in seawater provide food for larger organisms.

Figure 11.24 These streamlined fish swim freely in the open ocean.

Benthos [BEN-thohs] live within or on the ocean floor. This group includes oysters, starfish, kelp, sponges, and bacteria. The plants in this region live only in areas where sunlight reaches the ocean floor. Animals can live on any part of the ocean floor. These organisms feed on decaying material or on fish smaller than themselves.

The plankton, nekton, and benthos are all involved in one large food chain. The cycle starts with planktonic plants. In the presence of sunlight, the plants convert the dissolved elements into food. These plants are the food source for animal plankton. Both groups of plankton are eaten by many nektonic animals. Most of the smaller animals of the nekton are eaten by larger animals in the area. When nekton die, they sink to the bottom of the ocean. Benthos feed mainly on this decaying material. Bacteria are the final part of the cycle. They break dead material down into the essential elements. Ocean currents carry these elements up to the water's surface, where plankton use them as food. The cycle begins again.

Most ocean life is related through this sun-driven food chain. Recently, however, a separate food cycle involving organisms such as large clams, worms, and crabs was discovered near hot water vents in regions where the seafloor was spreading. This food chain is based on chemicals, not sunlight. This discovery may require new models about the life cycles and the chemical cycles of the ocean.

Figure 11.25 Snails, barnacles, and starfish live on the ocean floor. Most benthos-dwelling organisms eat dead matter that has settled on the ocean floor.

Figure 11.26 Sunlight provides the energy that starts the ocean food chain.

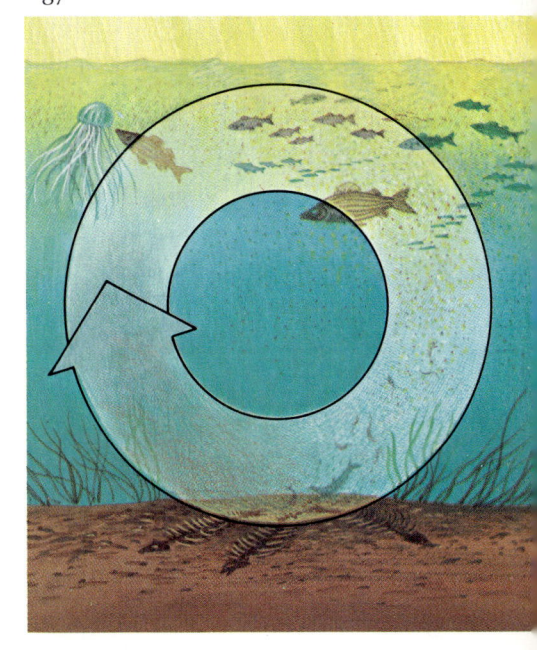

Study Questions for 11.5

1. What do all living things need to survive?
2. Describe the plankton, nekton, and benthos organisms.
3. Explain the sun-driven ocean food chain.

Science and Technology

Exploring the Seafloor

Can you swim under water? How deep could you go? Suppose you wanted to explore an area 1,000 meters deep. Could you swim down that far? Of course not! Oceanographers, however, want to explore the ocean to that depth and much deeper. How do they do it?

In recent years, a number of undersea vessels have been built that have made direct observations possible. One is a small submarine named *Alvin*. It can carry a pilot and two passengers to a depth of about 4,000 meters and move them safely around on the seafloor. But *Alvin* and other small submarines like it have a major drawback—oceanographers who use them must spend half their working time going down to the bottom and then returning to the surface. Only a small part of each dive can be spent in actually observing the seafloor.

Now a new kind of submarine vessel has solved that problem. Instead of carrying people to the bottom, these vessels carry television cameras. They are robot submarines. Using robot submarines, oceanographers can see the bottom without ever leaving the safety of a surface ship. Best of all, these submarines can, if necessary, stay on the bottom for long periods of time. Observations that used to take weeks to complete with research vessels like *Alvin* can now be done in a few days. That does not mean that *Alvin* should be retired. It will still be needed for direct observations of sea-floor features discovered by robot submarines.

One of the new robot submarines, *Argo*, has already become well-known. Although it was built to explore sea-floor features, *Argo* has been used to find the wreckage of the ocean liner *Titanic*. The *Titanic* was thought to be unsinkable until it rammed an iceberg and sank on its first voyage in 1912. Although many other ships had tried to locate the *Titanic*, *Argo* was the first vessel to find it and to take pictures of it. Discovering the *Titanic* made *Argo* famous around the world.

CHAPTER REVIEW

Main Ideas

- Wind, earthquakes, and gravitational attraction make ocean waves.
- How large wind-made waves become depends on the wind speed, the length of time the wind blows, and the fetch.
- An ocean current is a moving stream of water.
- Ocean currents are made by waves, wind, and differences in water density.
- Beaches are sand or pebbles that have been moved onto the shore by waves and currents.
- Most beach sand is made up of quartz and grains of shells and coral.
- Sand-deposited shore features are sandbars, spits, barrier bars, and barrier islands.
- The continental shelf, the continental slope, and the basin make up the ocean floor.
- Seawater contains about 35 grams of dissolved materials per 1,000 grams of seawater.
- The salinity of seawater is affected by the rate of evaporation and precipitation.
- Ocean-dwelling organisms are grouped according to how they move, and where they live.
- Plankton, nekton, and benthos are part of a food chain. The chain depends on the sun's energy.

Using Vocabulary

On a separate piece of paper, write a paragraph or two describing waves and currents. Use as many of the words listed below as possible.

waves	surf	shore	continental slope
crest	tsunami	tidal marsh	ocean basin
trough	current	sandbar	ridge
wavelength	turbidity current	spit	seamount
wave height	longshore current	barrier bar	trench
fetch	undertow	barrier island	salinity
swell	rip current	echo sounding	plankton
breaker	shoreline	continental shelf	nekton
			benthos

11 / Oceanography

Remembering Facts

On your paper, write the word or words that best complete each sentence.

1. _____ is a strong current that heads out to sea.
2. A _____ is a wave made by an undersea earthquake.
3. The shallow area of the ocean floor that surrounds a continent is the _____ _____.
4. The wave _____ is the vertical distance between the crest and the trough.
5. Small, floating organisms that live near the surface of the ocean are called _____.
6. _____ and _____ feed mainly on decaying material.
7. The zone where wave tops bend forward and break is called the _____.
8. A _____ is a moving stream of water in a body of water.
9. Animals that can swim at varying depths in the ocean are called _____.
10. The measure of the amount of solid matter dissolved in seawater is referred to as _____.
11. A _____ is a long, narrow, and deep part of the ocean basin, often located near an island chain or mountain range.
12. The _____ is the area where waves are active.
13. _____ and _____ are the most abundant elements found in seawater.
14. An ocean current that is pushed by waves near the shore is the _____ current.
15. The average salinity in a given area is affected by varying rates of _____ and _____.
16. All living things require _____, _____, and _____ _____, for survival.

Understanding Ideas

On your paper, answer each question in complete sentences.

1. Why don't the tropical oceans become warmer over time?
2. Describe how the various ocean currents affect humans and their activities.
3. Why are there so few benthos and so many plankton?
4. Describe the sun-driven food chain.

Applying What You Have Learned

1. Why does a floating object bob up and down?
2. Explain how barrier islands form.
3. If the time interval indicated by an echo sounder is 10 seconds, what is the depth of the water?
4. Describe three things that could happen to a sandbar in years to come.
5. Explain the processes that bring dissolved elements into the ocean and those processes that remove them.

Challenge

The movements of ocean and atmospheric currents seem to be dependent on each other. The most prominent current in the South Pacific Ocean is the Peru Current. It carries cold water from the Antarctic region northward along the coast of South America. This current moves in the same direction as the southeast trade winds. For some unknown reason, the southeast trade winds die down periodically. When this happens, the water in the western Pacific surges eastward. The Peru Current slackens and is rerouted seaward. This event is called an El Niño. What causes an El Niño is uncertain, but the ocean-atmospheric interaction seems clear.

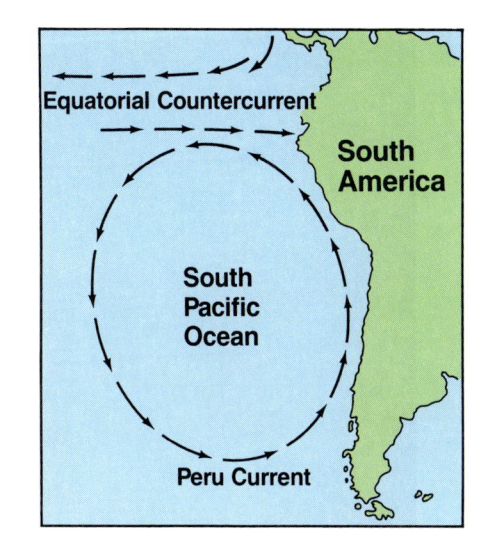

1. What is an El Niño event?
2. What effect would an El Niño have on the organisms living near the coast of South America?
3. What one question needs to be answered to determine the cause of an El Niño?

Research and Investigation

1. Use a large, shallow container to build a sand and gravel "shore" at one end. Move a small wooden block up and down in the water at the other end to make waves. Show how waves move the sand and make sandbars, etc. Change the direction of the waves to make longshore currents. Can you stop shore erosion with structures? Report your findings.
2. Investigate and prepare a report on the present and possible future use of the ocean as a source of mineral resources, fresh water, and a place for farming or ranching.

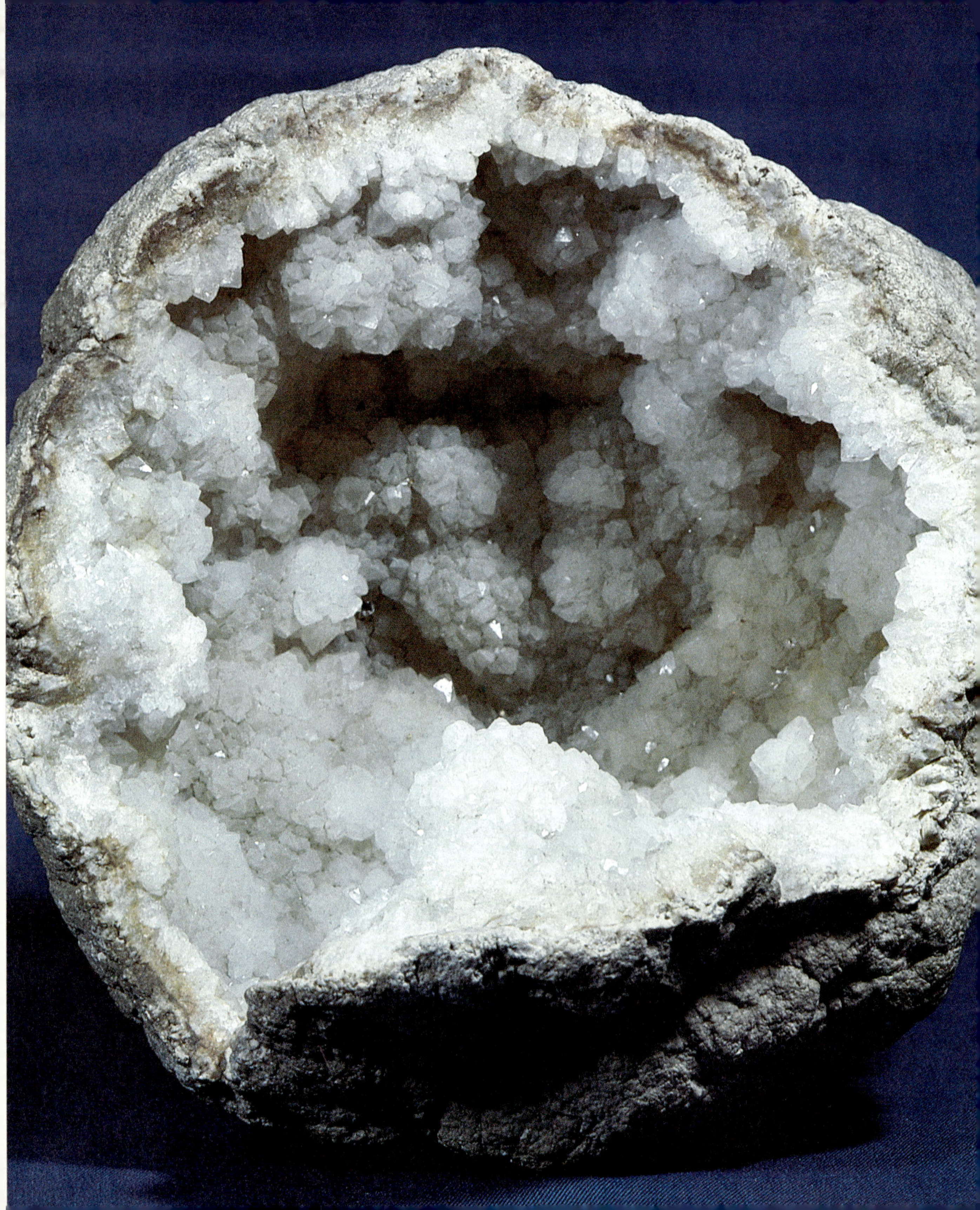

Chapter 12
Minerals

Lesson Titles
12.1 Atoms and Crystals
12.2 The Physical Properties of Minerals
12.3 Identification of Minerals

Look at the unusual shape and form of the objects inside the rock in this picture. If you look in the right places, you can find many attractive and unusually shaped objects with beautiful colors. Why did these objects form in this shape? What material are they made of? Does that material always form in this interesting shape?

In trying to answer these questions scientists have made some interesting discoveries. The earth's crust is made from about 92 different building blocks. It is the combination in many different ways of these 92 building blocks that make up all the materials found in the earth's crust. In fact, there are about 2,500 different kinds of materials in the earth's crust. Each is unique in color, shape, and composition because of what it is made of and how it formed. In this chapter you will learn about these materials in the earth's crust and their importance to you.

Figure 12.1 *opposite:* This hollow rock contains many colorful and irregular objects.

12.1 Atoms and Crystals

You will find out
- what the parts of an atom are;
- what model of atoms most scientists accept;
- why crystals have their shape.

More than 2,000 years ago a Greek scholar named Democritus had a good idea. He thought that all solid substances were made of small indivisible particles. They were supposed to be something like very tiny balls. Somehow the particles held firmly together to form different substances.

Have you ever hit a stone with a hammer to break it into smaller pieces? If you break a stone into very, very small pieces and then look at the pieces through a microscope, you begin to see what the stone is made of.

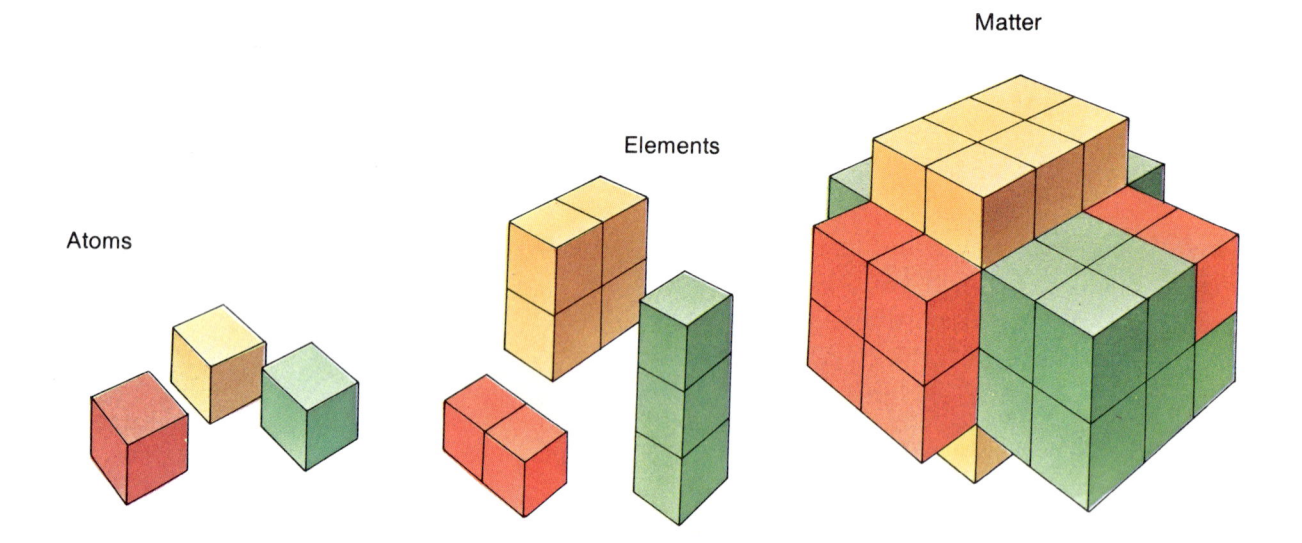

Figure 12.2 *top:* A close-up of granite shows small pieces that are meshed together.

Figure 12.3 *bottom:* The building blocks of matter

Do You Know?
Democritus was the first person to propose the word *atom*.

If you kept breaking a stone, you'd eventually find the building block of all material, an **atom.** There are 92 naturally occurring atoms. An atom is the smallest unit of an **element.** An element is made of only one kind of atom. Atoms of elements exist alone, or they can combine. When atoms combine, they form **matter.** Atoms are the building blocks of matter. Matter is anything that takes up space and has mass.

234

12 / Minerals

If atoms are the building blocks of all matter, what are atoms like? It turns out that Democritus was almost right, but not quite. What, then, is today's model of an atom? Since atoms are so small you can't see them, you must imagine what an atom looks like. Think of a tiny sphere in which, at the center, is a still smaller inner sphere, called the **nucleus** [NOO-klee-uhs]. The large sphere is very small, but even so, it is more than 600,000 times the size of the inner sphere. Yet, in the nucleus are still smaller particles! These smaller particles are of two kinds, called the **proton** [PROH-tahn] and the **neutron** [NOO-trahn]. They are defined by their electric charge.

Protons have a positive charge. Neutrons have no electrical charge. Each atom of an element has a certain number of protons. The simplest atom has one proton in the nucleus. The naturally occurring atom with the highest number of protons has 92. Outside the nucleus is another kind of particle that carries a negative charge. It is called the **electron** [ee-LEK-trahn]. The electrons really fly around. Even though the electrons are moving rapidly around the nucleus, they are believed to move in a kind of pattern. Figure 12.5 shows a model atom.

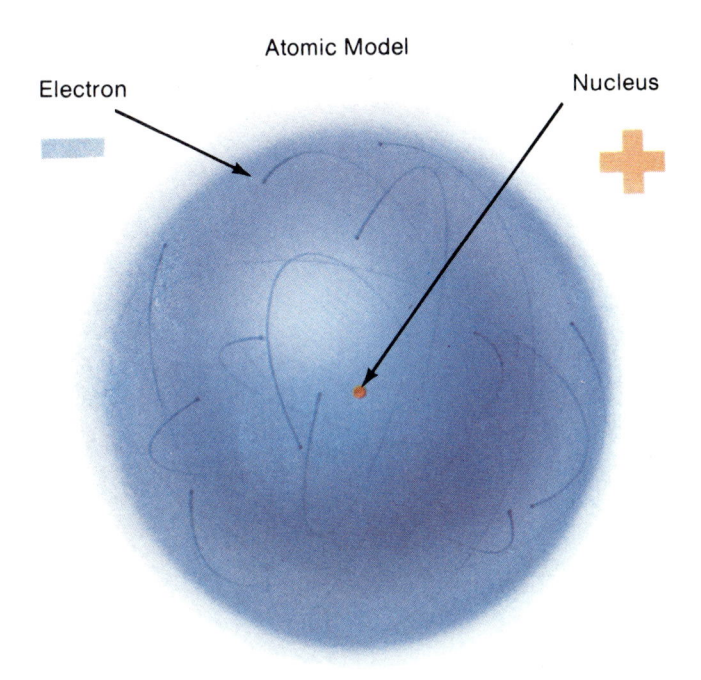

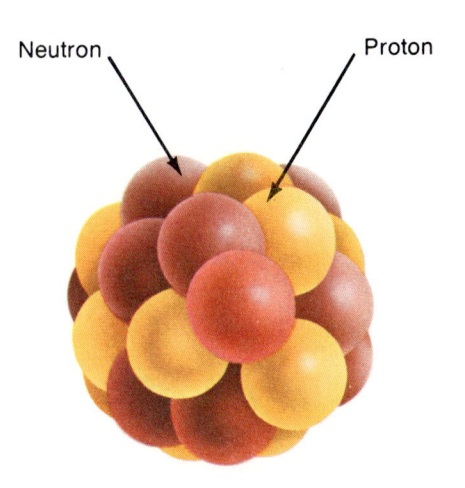

Figure 12.4 The nucleus of an atom is made of protons and neutrons.

Figure 12.5 Scientists believe the modern model of an atom includes a tiny nucleus surrounded by rapidly moving electrons. The number of electrons equals the number of protons in any one atom.

12 / Minerals

The way an atom behaves is largely determined by the number of its electrons and protons. Some atoms easily gain electrons from neighboring atoms, and others easily lose electrons. When this occurs, the atoms become electrically charged and are called **ions** [EYE-uhns]. Unlike electrical charges attract one another. Thus an ion that has a positive electrical charge will stick tightly to an ion that has a negative charge.

Ions do not join together in just any old way. As you see in Figure 12.6, they pack together in a special arrangement. It is the way ions pack together that determines the form or special shape matter will take. Notice the geometric shape and smooth surfaces of the solid shown in Figure 12.7. The reason for the shape of this solid is that ions making up the solid are packed together in special repeating patterns. Solids with repeating patterns of packed ions are called **crystals** [KRIS-tuhls]. Each different kind of crystal has a special shape because of the way its ions are packed together in these repeating patterns. Crystals can be made up of one or of many different types of ions.

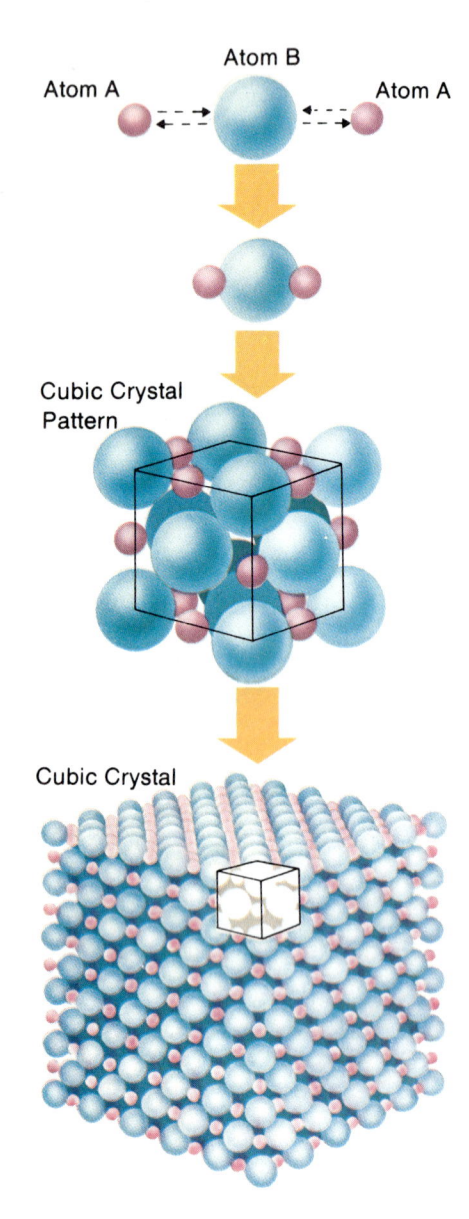

Figure 12.6 *above:* Ions often join in specific patterns that produce regularly shaped crystals.

Figure 12.7 *right:* The cubic shape of these halite crystals results from the way the ions join together.

236

12 / **Minerals**

Figure 12.8 Two examples of the many shapes that different crystals can have

Do You Know?
Since 1912, X-ray methods have been used to study the pattern arrangement of atoms in crystals.

Activity

What Will the Crystal Look Like?

Materials
safety goggles
ring stand
250-mL beaker
Bunsen burner
copper sulfate or
   potassium alum
water
stirring rod
small glass jar with lid
thread

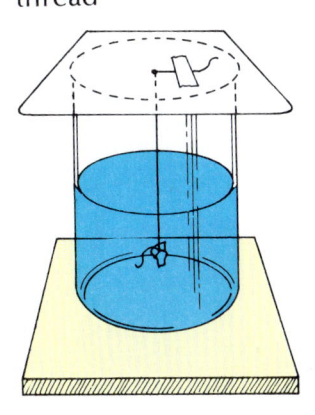

Procedure

1. Collect your materials. Put on safety glasses.

2. Fill the beaker about half full with water. Heat to boiling. CAUTION: Hot water can cause severe burns.

3. Remove the beaker and add the chemical slowly. Stir constantly. Try to dissolve all of the chemical.

4. Pour a little of the solution into the jar lid (about 4 mm deep).

5. Let the solution cool overnight.

6. Select a "seed" crystal from the jar lid.

7. Tie a thread around the seed crystal.

8. Pour the solution from the beaker into the glass jar.

9. Suspend your crystal as shown.

10. Place your crystal where it will be safe for a week.

Questions

1. Draw a sketch of your crystal.

2. Did your crystal have the same shape as the crystals in the chemical you started with?

Study Questions for 12.1

1. Draw a sketch of a model of an atom and label the parts.
2. Describe the model of an atom that most scientists accept.
3. How is a crystal formed?

12 / Minerals

12.2
The Physical Properties of Minerals

You will find out
- what a mineral is;
- what are some physical properties of minerals;
- how to test for some physical properties of minerals.

Do You Know?
A mineral is named by the person who discovers it. It can be called anything he or she wishes.

Do You Know?
Snow is a mineral.

Crystals have an important place in any study of the earth's crust. In Figure 12.9 you can see four different crystals in a piece of the earth's crust. These four different crystals are also called **minerals.** Generally you find minerals as crystals. In addition to their crystalline structure, minerals are also naturally occurring substances, and they have never been a living organism.

Figure 12.9 The large piece of granite at the top of the picture is made of the four minerals shown at the bottom. *left to right:* quartz, hornblende, feldspar, mica

The minerals making up the earth's crust are usually found as solids. Each mineral solid has its own set of physical properties. The differing properties make it possible to tell one mineral from another. There are about seven major properties that are useful in identifying minerals. They are color, streak, luster, hardness, cleavage, fracture, and density.

Figure 12.10 *left:* These are some examples of the many colors of quartz.

The **color** of a mineral is obvious, but it is not very useful for identification. Some minerals are always the same color. Other minerals, though, may vary in color. For example, quartz may be clear, milky, rose, or yellow.

A more accurate test of a mineral is to rub it across an unglazed tile called a streak plate. The color of the line of finely crushed mineral left on the plate is called a **streak**. The streak of the same minerals usually shows the same color even though the minerals themselves sometimes have a different color. Hematite may vary from steel gray to black in color, but it will always show a red-brown streak.

Luster [LUHS-tuhr] is the way light looks coming from a mineral's surface. Minerals looking like metal are called metallic. Others have a nonmetallic look, like silk, pearls, grease, glass, resin, and diamond. Luster is helpful for identification, but it must be used along with other properties.

Figure 12.11 *below:* The streak color of a specific mineral is always the same.

Figure 12.12 *left to right:* Metallic, silky, glassy, and greasy are examples of some mineral lusters.

12 / Minerals

Figure 12.13 Scratch tests help determine the hardness of minerals.

Do You Know?
An Austrian mineralogist named Friedrich Mohs (1773–1839) in 1822 proposed the hardness scale we use today.

Table 12.1 Mohs' Hardness Scale

Hardness	Mineral	Test Material
1	talc	fingernail
2	gypsum	fingernail
3	calcite	penny
4	fluorite	knife
5	apatite	knife
6	feldspar	will
7	quartz	scratch
8	topaz	glass
9	corundum	↓
10	diamond	

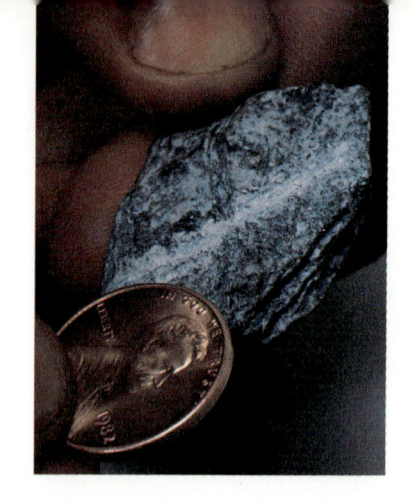

Hardness is the resistance of a mineral to being scratched. It is a good test to use in identifying minerals. You will use a relative scale in making hardness tests. If your fingernail can scratch the mineral, it is softer than 2.5. Your fingernail has that hardness. A penny is about 3; a piece of glass, about 5 to 5.5; a knife, about 5.5; and a file, nearly 7. The test is made by trying to scratch the mineral or by using the mineral to try to scratch the test substance. If the mineral can scratch the test substance, the mineral is harder than the test substance. If the mineral is scratched by the test substance, the mineral is not as hard as the test substance. Table 12-1 is the scale used by mineralogists.

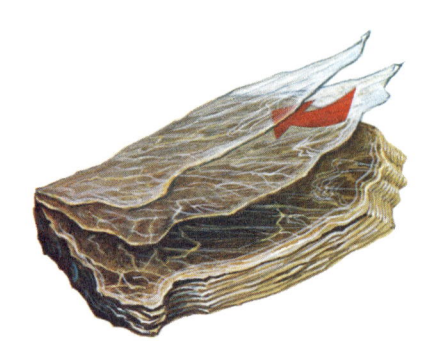

Figure 12.14 *above:* Parallel cleavage occurs in mica. *above right:* Minerals such as halite cleave in three directions.

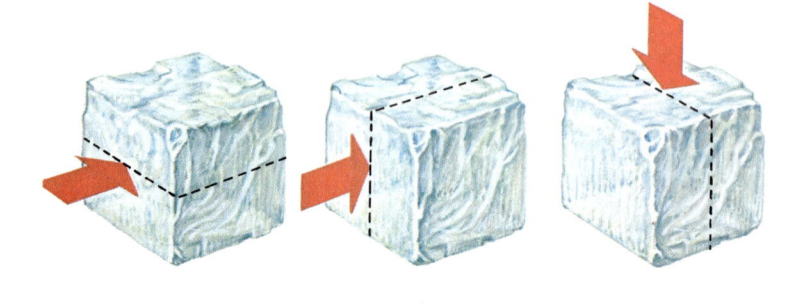

Cleavage [KLEE-vuhj] is the ability of some minerals to break along smooth planes that are parallel to each other. Cleavage is determined by how the atoms are located in the minerals. Mica will split into very thin sheets. Calcite and halite will break in three directions.

If you strike a piece of either mineral, it will shatter into little pieces shaped like the big one. Cleavage is a good test to use in identification.

Fracture is the way the mineral breaks if it doesn't have cleavage. Different minerals fracture, or break, in different ways. *Conchoidal fracture* breaks along smooth curved surfaces like a shell. *Fibrous fracture* breaks along fibers. Most other fractures are rough, jagged, and irregular.

Figure 12.15 Two examples of fracture are obsidian (*far left*) and asbestos (*left*).

Figure 12.16 *below:* The heft test is a simple way to compare densities.

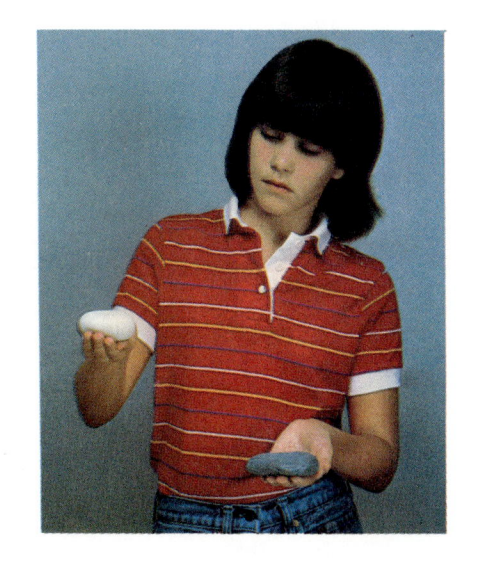

Density is the comparison of how heavy something is to the space it occupies. Imagine a piece of cotton and a piece of iron the same size. Which is denser? You know the iron is denser. Some minerals are denser than others. Take two minerals about the same size and put one in each hand. Which is heavier? The heavier one of the same size is also the denser one. This kind of hand test is useful only as a general comparison of the density of the minerals.

Some other properties and tests that can be used for a few minerals are salty taste, greasy feel, ease or difficulty of melting, and responses to a magnet.

Study Questions for 12.2

1. Name three characteristics of a mineral.
2. Define *luster, cleavage,* and *fracture.*
3. Describe how to test for streak, hardness, and density.

12.3 Identification of Minerals

You will find out
- that each of the many minerals found in the earth's surface has its own set of properties;
- what methods are used in identifying minerals.

There are more than 2,500 different minerals found in the earth's crust. How can you tell which mineral is which? Pick up a mineral. Look at it carefully. Even though each mineral has its own set of properties, choosing the correct mineral out of more than 2,500 does not seem easy. The mineralogist has a system to do this. Often what the mineralogist does is eliminate all the minerals it cannot be. The mineral that remains then is what it is. Sound confusing? Here's how it works.

Figure 12.17 Common minerals

242

12 / Minerals

You have a mineral you want to identify. Suppose you first make a hardness test and find it has a hardness of 7. That eliminates all minerals with a hardness other than 7. You then make a streak test and find it is white. That eliminates all minerals that do not have a white streak. By making two tests you have eliminated about 1,900 minerals that do not have both of these properties. You can eliminate many more with a few more tests. Then at last you have a good idea of what you are holding. In other words, you determine the mineral by showing what it cannot be.

Activity

What Is the Name of These Minerals?

Materials
minerals
test equipment for hardness and streak
luster set

Procedure
1. Copy the physical properties chart.
2. Select one mineral.
3. Determine its properties.
4. Record the properties on the chart.
5. Determine its name from the list of minerals and their properties on pages 244–245.
6. Repeat steps 1 through 4 for the other minerals.

Questions
1. List the minerals you identified.
2. How did you identify each mineral?
3. List the minerals in your set in order of hardness from softest to hardest.

Mineral Number	Color	Streak	Luster	Hardness	Cleavage	Fracture	Estimate of Density	Mineral Name
1								
2								
3								

Study Questions for 12.3
1. Tell why you can identify each of the many minerals found in the earth's surface.
2. Describe the system used to identify a mineral.

Mineral Chart

Material Name	Composition	Hardness	Specific Gravity	Color	Cleavage	Luster	Streak	Uses
Albite	Al, Na, O, Si	6	2.62	Grayish White	2/93°, 87°	Glossy	White	Ceramics
Apatite	Ca, Cl, F, H, O, P	5	3.2	Green, Brown	Poor	Glossy	White	Fertilizer, Jewelry
Augite	Al, Ca, Fe, Mg, O, Si	5–6	3.3	Green	None	Glossy	Greenish Gray	Rock-Forming Mineral
Barite	Ba, O, S	3.0–3.5	4.5	Clear, White, Reddish	1 Good 2 Poor	Glossy to Earthy	White	Drilling Mud
Bauxite	Mixture of Clays	—	2.0–2.5	Gray, Brown	None	Dull to Earthy	Colorless	Ore of Aluminum
Biotite	Al, Fe, H, K, Mg, O, S	2.5–3.0	2.8–3.2	Black, Green, Brown	1 Very Good	Glossy, Pearly	Colorless	Rock-Forming Mineral
Bornite	Cu, Fe, S	3	5.0	Bronze, Purple, Blue, Black	None	Metallic	Grayish Black	Ore of Copper
Calcite	Ca, C, O	3	2.72	White, Gray, Yellow, Colorless	3/not 90°	Glossy	Colorless	Cement, Fertilizer
Copper	Cu	2.5–3.0	8.9	Copper Red	None	Metallic	Metallic	Wire, Jewelry
Fluorite	Ca, F	4	3.2	Lt. Green, Blue, Yellow, Purple	4 Good	Glossy	Colorless	Flux in Steelmaking
Galena	Pb, S	2.5	7.5	Lead Gray	3/90°	Metallic	Lead Gray	Ore of Lead
Garnet	Variable	7	3.5–4.3	Red, Brown, Green, Black	None	Glossy to Resinous	Colorless	Abrasives, Jewelry
Graphite	C	1–2	2.3	Black	1 Very Good	Metallic to Earthy	Black	Lubricant, Pencils, Electrodes, Rubber

Mineral	Composition	Hardness	Specific Gravity	Color	Cleavage/Fracture	Luster	Streak	Uses
Gypsum	Ca, H, O, S	2	2.3	Colorless, White, Gray, Yellow	1 Good	Glossy to Pearly, Silky	Colorless	Plaster, Wallboard
Halite	Cl, Na	2.5	2.2	White, Colorless	3/90°	Glossy to Dull	Colorless	Nutrient, Chemical Industry
Hematite	Fe, O	5.5–6.5	5.26	Reddish Brown to Black	None	Metallic	Reddish Brown	Ore of Iron
Hornblende	Al, Ca, Fe, H, Na, Mg, O, Si	5–6	3.25	Dark Green to Black	2/56°, 124°	Glossy to Silky	Colorless	Rock-Forming Mineral
Limonite	Fe, H, O	5–5.5	3.3–4.7	Yellow Brown to Brown	1 Very Good in Crystals	Dull to Vitreous	Yellow to Brown	Pigment
Magnetite	Fe, O	6	5.2	Black	None	Metallic	Black	Ore of Iron
Muscovite	Al, H, K, O, Si	2–2.5	3.0	Colorless, Shades of Green, Gray, or Brown	1 Very Good	Glossy, Silky, Pearly	White, Colorless	Electric Insulation
Olivine	Fe, Mg, O, Si	6.5	3.2–4.4	Olive Green, Grayish Green	None	Glossy	White, Gray	Gemstone
Potassium Feldspar	Al, K, O, Si	6	2.6	White, Gray, Pink	2/90°	Glossy, Pearly	White	Ceramics, Porcelain
Pyrite	Fe, S	5	4.3	Brassy Yellow	None	Metallic	Black	Source of Sulfur
Quartz	O, Si	7	2.7	Colorless, White, Varied	None	Glossy to Dull	White	Glass, Gemstones
Serpentine	Fe, H, Mg, O, Si	2–5	2.2	Green, Yellow	None	Greasy, Waxy, Silky	White	Source of Asbestos
Talc	Fe, H, Mg, O, Si	1	2.7–2.8	Pale Green, White, Gray	1 Very Good	Pearly, Greasy, Dull	White	Talcum Powder, Lubricant
Topaz	Al, F, H, O, Si	8	3.5	Clear, Yellow, Blue, Pink	1 Very Good	Glossy	Colorless	Gemstone

Key
Al = Aluminum
Ba = Barium
C = Carbon
Ca = Calcium
Cl = Chlorine
Cu = Copper
F = Fluorine
Fe = Iron
H = Hydrogen
K = Potassium
Mg = Magnesium
Na = Sodium
O = Oxygen
P = Phosphorus
Pb = Lead
S = Sulfur
Si = Silicon

Science and Technology

Imaging Spectrometry

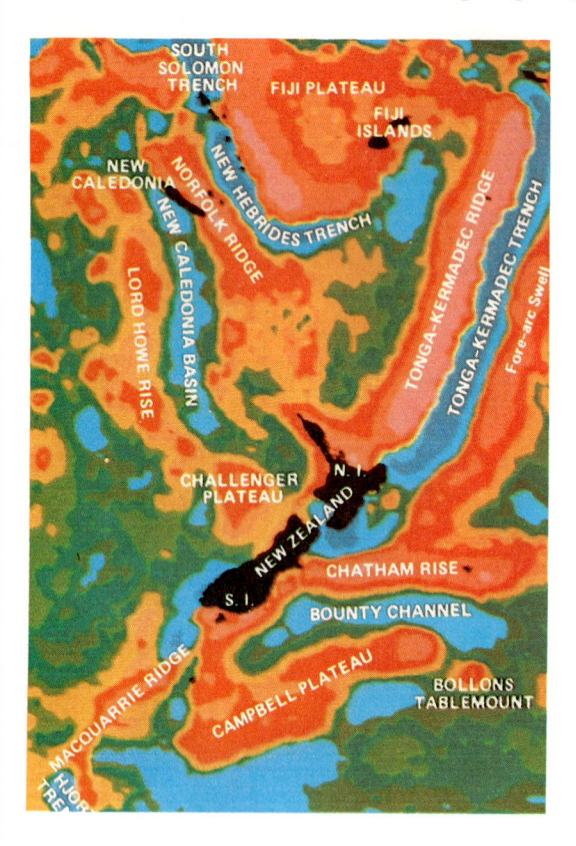

In Chapter 2, you read about an instrument called the spectroscope. It is a tool used by astronomers to study the light from stars. With a spectroscope, astronomers can find out what each star is made of. Now earth scientists are using a spectroscope too. Instead of using it to learn about stars, they are using it to locate new mineral deposits on Earth. The new method is called imaging spectrometry.

Unlike the spectroscope in Chapter 2, this spectroscope is not attached to a telescope looking toward space. Instead, it is attached to an airplane or spacecraft looking back at Earth's surface. It collects data on the energy that Earth's surface reflects back to space. But it does not study all the energy reflected back; it studies only a very special part.

Different kinds of energy occur in different wavelengths. (See pages 30 and 31.) Scientists using the imaging spectrometer study wavelengths of visible light and infrared light. The wavelengths are collected in widths called bands. Each band is about 10 micrometers wide. Usually from 100 to 200 separate bands of data are collected for each piece of ground surface the imaging spectrometer flies over. This results in an enormous number of data. A computer is necessary to help collect and sort out the data.

How do all of these data identify a mineral? Each mineral that occurs at Earth's surface reflects light in a different way. Other minerals each produce their own unique pattern. Once the computer has plotted the pattern for each wavelength, the mineral that causes the pattern can be identified.

This technology has provided a great deal of information about the features and makeup of the earth's crust. Scientists hope to extend the technology to find out more about what is happening beneath the crust.

246

12 / Minerals

CHAPTER REVIEW

Main Ideas

- Atoms are the building blocks of matter. The nucleus of an atom contains protons and neutrons and is surrounded by rapidly moving electrons.
- Atoms that gain or lose electrons are called ions. Ions are electrically charged.
- Solids with repeating patterns of ions are called crystals.
- Minerals are naturally occurring substances with a crystalline structure.
- The major physical properties of minerals are color, streak, luster, hardness, cleavage, fracture, and density.
- Streak is the color of the crushed mineral as seen on a streak plate.
- Hardness is a measure of the resistance of the mineral to being scratched.
- Cleavage is the ability of some minerals to break along smooth planes.
- Fracture is the way a mineral breaks when it does not have cleavage.
- Density is the ratio of an object's mass to the space it occupies.
- There are more than 2,500 different minerals found in the earth's crust. Each mineral has its own unique set of physical properties.
- One way of determining the identity of a mineral is to show what it cannot be.

Using Vocabulary

Use the Glossary to define each of the words below. Write the definitions on a separate piece of paper.

atom	electron	luster
element	ion	hardness
matter	crystal	cleavage
nucleus	color	fracture
proton	mineral	density
neutron	streak	

12 / Minerals

Remembering Facts

On your paper, write the word or words that best complete each sentence.
1. The colored mark left by a mineral when it is rubbed on a tile is (luster, streak, color).
2. (Minerals, Crystals, Elements) have only one kind of atom.
3. A mineral that has (fracture, cleavage, luster) breaks into irregular shapes with jagged edges.
4. Naturally occurring substances with a crystalline structure are called (elements, matter, minerals).
5. (Protons, Electrons, Neutrons) are atomic particles that have a positive electrical charge.
6. (Weight, Density, Mass) is the comparison of how much mass something has compared to the space it occupies.
7. The tiny inner part of an atom is the (ion, neutron, nucleus).
8. Solids with a geometric shape and repeating patterns of ions are called (crystals, elements, rocks).
9. (Density, Cleavage, Hardness) is the resistance of a mineral to being scratched.
10. (Protons, Electrons, Neutrons) are outside the nucleus.
11. (Atoms, Electrons, Neutrons) are the smallest units of matter.
12. The *least* useful property in identifying a mineral is (color, streak, luster).
13. A mineral that breaks along smooth parallel planes has the property of (hardness, cleavage, fracture).
14. Atoms that become electrically charged by gaining or losing electrons are called (crystals, ions, soft).
15. Minerals that look like metals are said to have metallic (luster, streak, color).

Understanding Ideas

On your paper, answer each question in complete sentences.
1. What do you think determines the physical properties of minerals, such as hardness, cleavage, and fracture?
2. Coal and a diamond are both made of carbon. Why is a diamond considered a mineral, but not coal?
3. What physical properties of minerals make some of them valuable as gemstones?
4. How would you compare the density of two mineral samples that are the same size?

Applying What You Have Learned

1. Suppose you find a clear shining object in a streambed. How can you determine whether you have found a diamond, a piece of glass, or a quartz pebble?
2. Synthetic diamonds, rubies, and sapphires can be made in a laboratory. Are they minerals? Why or why not?
3. Suppose you have three different minerals and nothing else. Call the minerals A, B, and C. Describe how you could find which is the hardest and which is the softest.
4. Arrange the following from the softest to the hardest: penny, file, fingernail, glass, knife.

Challenge

When light strikes a mineral crystal, some of it bounces off the surface and some of it enters the crystal. Light that enters a crystal slows down and changes direction, as if it had been bent. This slowing and changing of direction is known as refraction. Minerals that have less refraction, such as quartz, have the luster of glass. The higher refraction of a diamond gives it a hard, brilliant luster.

Fluorite

Diamond

1. At what angle is light striking the minerals in the diagram?
2. According to the diagram, does fluorite or diamond refract light more? Explain your answer.
3. Would you predict that fluorite would have metallic luster or the luster of glass? Why? Use the mineral chart to name another mineral that has properties that are similar to those of fluorite.

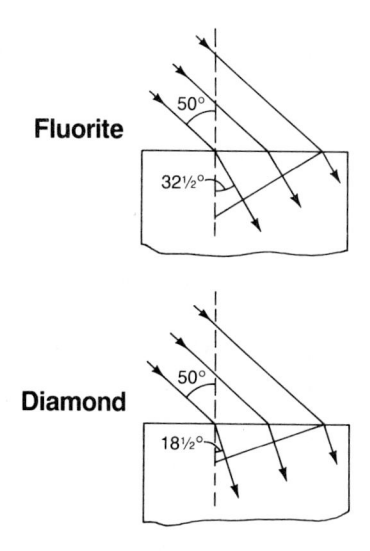

Research and Investigation

1. Start a collection of minerals. Mount and label samples of minerals and crystals that are found locally. Display your mineral collection in the school library, along with library books, paperbacks, and magazine articles on minerals and gems.
2. Investigate the six basic crystal systems. Make a series of models out of paper and wire, cardboard or any other materials to illustrate each system. Identify minerals that belong to each system.
3. Invite a mineralogist to visit your classroom.

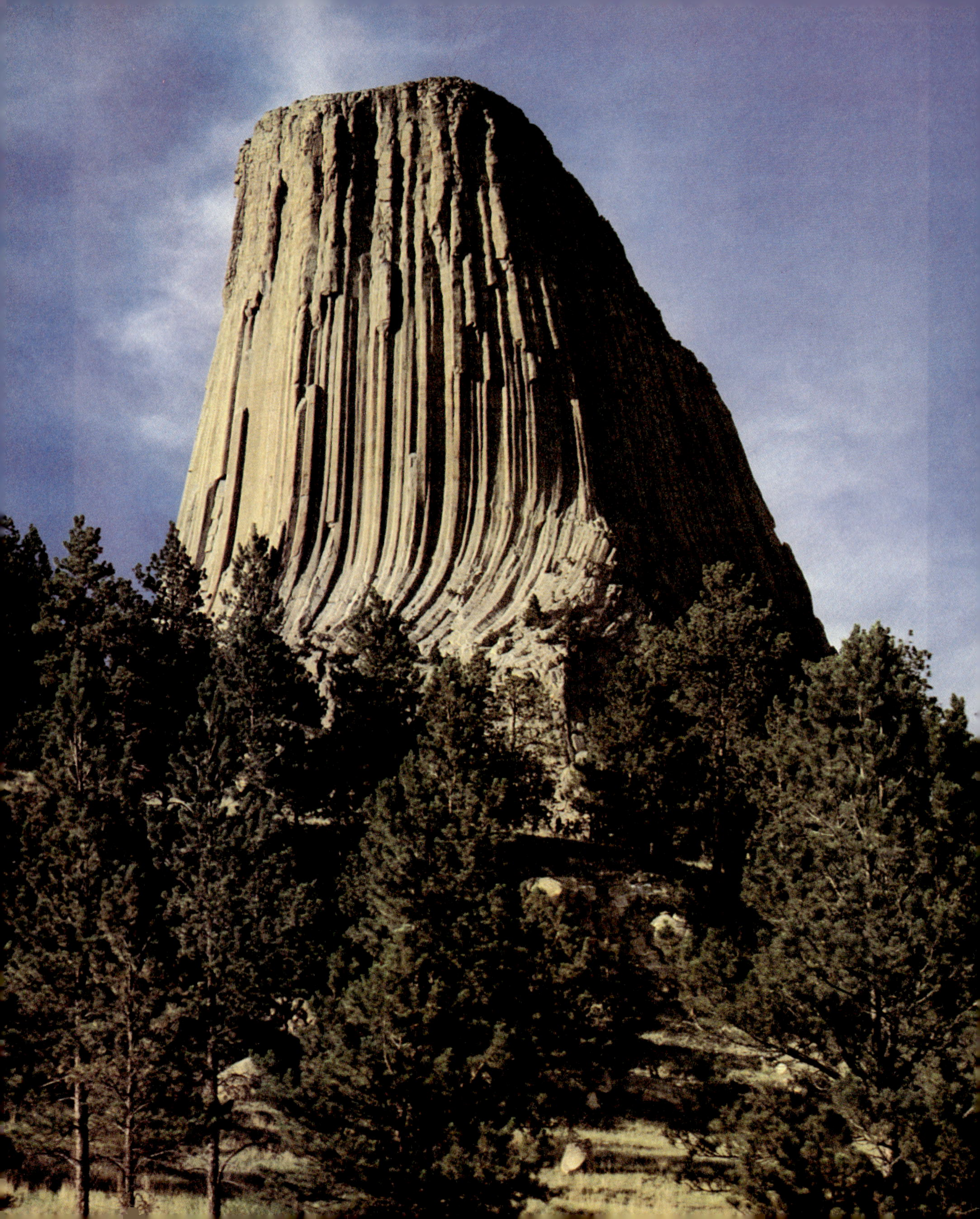

Chapter 13
Rocks and the Rock Cycle

Lesson Titles
13.1 How Rocks Form
13.2 Igneous Rocks
13.3 Sedimentary Rocks
13.4 Metamorphic Rocks

How did this gigantic mass of rock get to be in this location? Did some beings from another planet build it here? Notice the long lines that divide the rock mass into columns. Even the Indians once had a legend about this rock. They said a huge bear made these lines by trying to climb the rock.

What you are seeing was at one time liquid rock in the center of a volcanic mountain cone. The surrounding cone is gone, carried away by wind and water leaving only the harder rock core. The lines were formed when the liquid rock cooled. The lines are cracks that formed as the rock shrank during cooling, creating the huge columns in the rock. The name of this huge mass of rock is Devil's Tower, and it is located in Wyoming.

The rock you now see in Devil's Tower formed from cooling liquid rock. But not all rocks look like this, nor are they all formed from hot liquid rock. What are some other types of rocks you can find and how did they form? This chapter focuses on how to identify a rock and read its history.

Figure 13.1 *opposite:* Devil's Tower in Wyoming is an example of a volcanic neck.

13.1 How Rocks Form

You will find out
- what the three types of rocks are;
- what processes form rocks;
- what is meant by the rock cycle.

What is a rock? Although you may think this is a simple question, it is not so simple as it seems. Rocks are identified by the minerals in the rock and how these minerals came together. But the task of learning about rocks isn't very difficult. About 92 percent of the rocks are made of one group of minerals, the silicates. In addition, there are only three basic types of rocks. Each type is named by the way it was formed.

Figure 13.2 Half Dome, Yosemite National Park, is made of granite, an igneous rock.

Figure 13.3 *right:* The eruption of Heimaey volcano in Iceland

Have you ever seen a rock being formed? Most people say no. But if you've seen a stream of liquid rock coming from a volcano, your answer should have been yes. Some rocks are formed by the process of cooling liquid rock. These rocks are called **igneous** [IHG-nee-uhs] **rocks.** The word *igneous* comes from the Latin word meaning "fire."

Do You Know?
Geologists believe igneous rocks are the ancestral material from which all other rocks are made.

252

13 / Rocks and the Rock Cycle

Figure 13.4 *left:* Sedimentary rocks are exposed by the wearing action of a river.

Figure 13.5 *below:* This muddy river is carrying sediments that will eventually settle on the ocean bottom.

Igneous rocks exposed on the surface of the earth slowly break apart. When exposed to air, water, and changing temperature, some of the minerals in the rocks begin to crumble. This loose rock is pulled downhill whenever possible by gravity. At times wind, water, and ice move some of the pieces along. Eventually these tiny pieces of igneous rock are carried to the ocean by rivers and glaciers. Over millions of years the bits and pieces settle to the bottom of the ocean. Solid materials that settle out of the water are called **sediments**. Variations in the color or makeup of the sediments result in layers called **strata**. In time, the sediments in the strata become pressed and cemented together. Rocks that are formed from these settled bits and pieces of other rocks are called **sedimentary** [sehd-uh-MEHN-tuh-ree] **rocks**. *Sedimentary* comes from a Latin word meaning "to settle." Most sedimentary rocks are formed on the shallow sea floor near the shore.

Do You Know?
Some chalk, or limestone, is sedimentary rock. It contains microscopic shells of plankton that accumulated on the ocean bottom millions of years ago.

13 / Rocks and the Rock Cycle

A third type of rock is called **metamorphic** [meht-uh-MAWR-fihk] **rock.** *Metamorphic* comes from Latin and French words meaning "change." And that is just what has happened to these rocks. They are rocks that were once igneous or sedimentary rocks, but they have been changed. These changes are caused by heat and pressure. The ideal conditions for these metamorphic changes are generally deep in the ground. At depths of 12 to 16 km beneath the surface, temperatures may range from 200°C to 800°C. Under these conditions the existing rock is changed, often without melting. It may undergo a change of the mineral grains, a change in or an enlargement of crystals, or a change in the chemical composition.

Figure 13.6 *above:* One rock resulting from metamorphic change is quartzite which is made from sandstone.

Figure 13.7 *right:* The altered patterns of layers in this metamorphic rock result from extreme forces of heat and pressure.

The distinction between rock types is often shady, not clear or sharp at all. Look at Figure 13.8. This is a model of the changes that rocks undergo through time. No one has ever seen one rock change into another. Geologists believe that changes do occur, and also that they occur over and over. There is no such thing as the eternal hills or the unchanging mountain. In time—a long, long time—the rocks change. Over and over they change from one kind of rock to another. These endless changes are part of a cycle that is called the **rock cycle.** The sedimentary rocks you see were once igneous or metamorphic or other sedimentary rocks. Someday they will again be forced deep into the earth where they will melt. The rock cycle is endless.

Do You Know?
Geologists estimate that the time it takes for a rock to turn to sediment and back to rock again is a few hundred million years or less. The earth is over 4 billion years old. It is unlikely that any large block of the earth's first rock could exist.

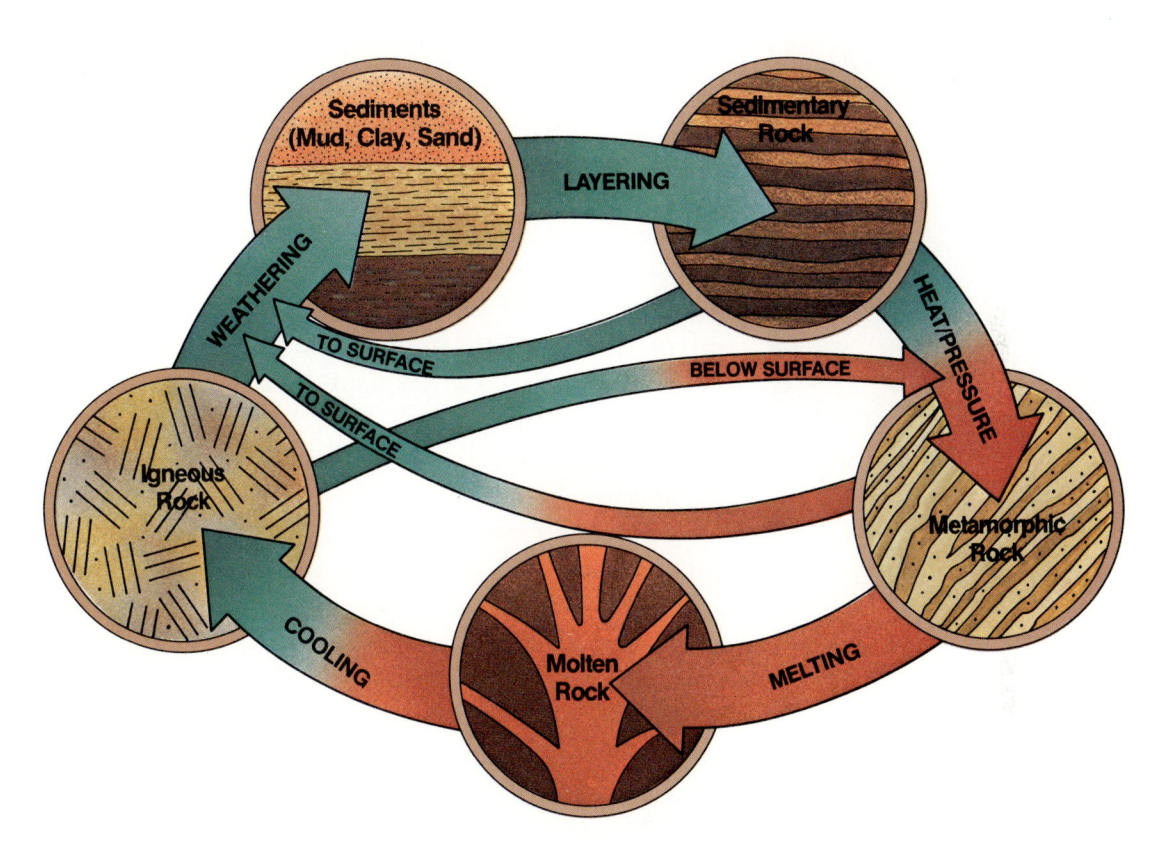

Figure 13.8 The rock cycle

Study Questions for 13.1

1. What are the major types of rocks?
2. List the processes that form the three types of rocks. Are the names given each type appropriate?
3. Describe what is meant by the rock cycle.

13 / Rocks and the Rock Cycle

13.2 Igneous Rocks

You will find out
- how igneous rocks form;
- why igneous rocks have different sizes of crystals;
- what the color of an igneous rock means.

Figure 13.9 *above:* Porphyry is an igneous rock with large crystals surrounded by small ones.

Do You Know?
Most of the rocks returned from the moon were igneous rocks.

Figure 13.10 *right:* Large and small crystals in igneous rocks

Because of the intense heat and pressure inside the earth, some of the rock inside the earth is in a liquid state. This liquid rock inside the earth is called **magma**. When magma cools, it forms igneous rock.

One important property of an igneous rock is the size of its crystals. This is determined by where the magma cooled and hardened. Magma that forces its way, or intrudes, into or between overlying rock layers forms **intrusive** rock. This magma cools very slowly underground. It may take thousands of years to cool. This gives the atoms enough time to form large crystals. Intrusive igneous rocks have a coarse-grained texture because of the large crystals.

Magma that flows out onto the surface of the earth is called **lava**. Lava cools quickly on the earth's surface. The rock that forms from lava on the earth's surface is called **extrusive** rock. The atoms of the elements do not have enough time to form large crystals. Therefore, many extrusive igneous rocks have a fine-grained texture. You may need a microscope to see the particles in these fine-grained rocks.

Another important property of igneous rocks is texture. Textures of igneous rocks may vary a great deal. Glassy textures are formed when the rock cools very fast. Fragmented textures occur when volcanic ash and dust are cemented together. Bubbly textures develop when gas bubbles are trapped in a rock as it cools. Sometimes this kind of igneous rock, called pumice, is so filled with gas bubbles it will float on water.

Figure 13.11 *left:* Examples of textures of igneous rocks are (1) glassy obsidian, (2) fragmented basalt, and (3) bubbly tuff.

Figure 13.12 *below:* Granite was used to construct many large buildings.

The color and density of igneous rocks is determined by what elements were in the magma. Not all magmas have the same makeup of elements. Magma that is rich in aluminum, potassium, and sodium forms light-colored igneous rocks. Granite (coarse-grained) and rhyolite (fine-grained) are good examples.

Magma that is rich in iron and magnesium forms dark-colored igneous rocks such as gabbro (coarse-grained) and basalt (fine-grained). Compare the colors and textures of the igneous rocks shown in Figure 13.11.

How are igneous rocks identified? The process is similar to how you identified minerals. By examining the properties of a rock you can decide what it isn't. Each property examined will eliminate whole groups of rocks. By elimination you come to the only rocks possessing the properties of the rock in your hand.

Do You Know?
Igneous rocks comprise 93 percent of the outer 10 km of the earth's crust.

Activity

What Are the Names and Cooling Histories of These Igneous Rocks?

Materials
igneous rock set
magnifying glass
safety goggles

Procedure
1. Select a rock from your set.
2. Look at your rock chart. Ask the first question. If the question is appropriate, record the names of the rocks with that physical characteristic.
3. Ask the second question. Record the answer.
4. Determine the amount of light or dark mineral in your rock.
5. Continue until you know what kind of rock you are holding.
6. Repeat this procedure with the other rocks in the rock set.

Questions
1. What are the names of your coarse-grained rocks? What is their cooling history?
2. What are the names of your fine-grained rocks. What is their cooling history?

Igneous Rock Classification Chart

	Obsidian	Granite	Rhyolite	Diorite	Andesite	Gabbro	Basalt	Pumice	Porphyry	Tuff
Is the rock fine-grained?			●	●	●		●	●		
Is it coarse-grained?		●		○	●			●		
Is it glassy?	●							○		
Does it contain quartz?		●	●	○	○			○		
How much quartz?		>10%	>10%	0–10%	0–10%					
Is it mostly dark mineral?				○	○	●	●			
Is it mostly light mineral?		●	●	○	●			○		
Does it have bubbles?						○	●			
Will it float in water?							●			
Is it large and small crystals?					○				●	
Is it made of broken pieces?										●

Key:
● Always present
○ Sometimes present

13 / Rocks and the Rock Cycle

1. Granite   2. Andesite   3. Basalt   4. Tuff   5. Diorite
6. Gabbro   7. Porphyry   8. Obsidian   9. Rhyolite   10. Pumice

Figure 13.13 Common igneous rocks

Study Questions for 13.2

1. Explain the difference between intrusive and extrusive igneous rocks.
2. Why do igneous rocks have different textures?
3. Why do igneous rocks have different colors?

13 / **Rocks and the Rock Cycle**

13.3 Sedimentary Rocks

You will find out
- what the sources of sediments are;
- how sediments become sedimentary rocks;
- how to identify sedimentary rocks.

Figure 13.14 Sedimentary rock

Do You Know?
One kind of sedimentary rock stands out as the most valuable: oil shale. Found in the western United States, oil shale contains enormous quantities of oil. It has been estimated that more than 12 trillion barrels of oil are contained in this oil shale.

Unlike igneous rocks, sedimentary rocks form from matter that originates on the earth's surface. As time passes, moving water and wind free small particles from rocks and soil on the earth's surface. Some of the matter is dissolved in water on or below the earth's surface. But most of the matter is carried away and then deposited in another location as layers of sediment. Older layers are buried by new layers of sediments. Eventually, the bottom layers of sediments harden to form layers of sedimentary rock. Unless the layers have been disturbed, the oldest layers are always on the bottom. Today, about two thirds of the rocks at the earth's surface are sedimentary rocks.

There are three main sources for the sediments that become sedimentary rocks. These include (1) rock fragments, (2) dissolved materials, and (3) plant and animal matter.

Rock fragments are pieces of rock that are in various stages of being broken down. These fragments are the source of sediments that range in size from gravel down to microscopic bits of dust. Table 13-1 lists the sizes of various types of fragments.

Table 13-1 Particle Sizes		
Size	Name	Type of Sedimentary Rock
2 mm–64 mm	Gravel	Conglomerate or Breccia
1/16 mm–2 mm	Sand	Sandstone
1/256 mm–1/16 mm	Silt	Shale
1/256 mm or less	Clay	Shale

Sedimentary rocks that are composed mainly of rock fragments are classified as **clastic** sedimentary rocks.

These rocks are identified by the sizes and types of fragments that they contain.

As time passes, two main processes harden the sediments into layers of sedimentary rock. First, sediments are pressed together into a solid mass. This process is called **compaction.** As compaction occurs, the bottom layers of sediments are tightly squeezed together by the weight of overlying layers of sediments. The result is that fragments in the bottom layers are pressed closer to one another.

The other process that contributes to the formation of clastic sedimentary rocks is **cementation.** In cementation, the spaces between the sediment particles are filled with chemical deposits. The most common cements are silicon dioxide, calcium carbonate, and iron oxide. When these chemical deposits harden, the fragments are cemented together into a solid mass. The clastic rock in Figure 13.14 shows the results of cementation.

Sedimentary rocks that are formed from chemical deposits are called **nonclastic** sedimentary rocks. As minerals and rocks are broken down on the earth's surface, some of their matter dissolves in surface water and groundwater. The dissolved materials are then transported to lakes or oceans.

The dissolved materials become sediments in the form of chemical deposits. Chemical deposits occur through **precipitation,** a process in which dissolved matter settles out of solution. These deposits form when water evaporates. As the volume of water decreases, the water is able to hold less solid matter. Rock salt and gypsum are examples of sedimentary rocks that have a chemical origin.

Sediments that contain plant and animal matter form another type of nonclastic sedimentary rock. One example is coal. Coal deposits consist of layers of decayed plant matter that have been compacted. Another example of nonclastic sedimentary rock is limestone. Limestone deposits contain the mineral calcite. Calcite comes from dissolved shells of shallow-water animals like the clam.

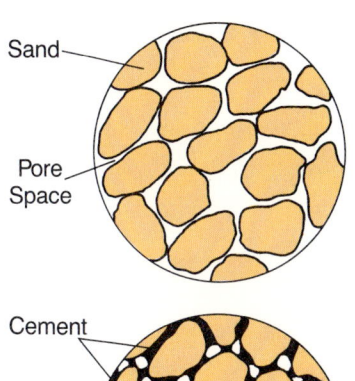

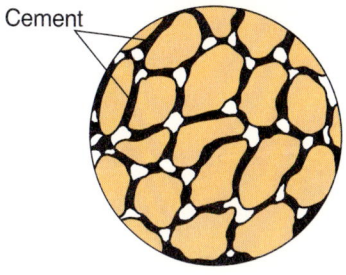

Figure 13.15 Sediment grains are cemented by chemical precipitates that enter the pore spaces.

Figure 13.16 The salt formations at Mono Lake in California are chemical deposits that formed as the lake water evaporated.

13 / Rocks and the Rock Cycle

Activity

What Are the Names and Histories of These Sedimentary Rocks?

Materials
sedimentary rock set
magnifying glass
dilute acid
knife
eyedropper
safety goggles

Procedure
1. Select a rock from your set.
2. Look at the chart. Ask the first question. If the question and answer are appropriate, record the rock names with that physical characteristic.
3. Ask the second question. Record the answer.
4. Repeat this procedure until you have identified the rock. CAUTION: Use care when working with acid. Be sure to wash your hands and the rocks after doing the acid test.
5. Repeat this procedure with the other rocks in the rock set.

Questions
1. What are the names of your sedimentary rocks made of fragments? What are their histories?
2. What are the names of your sedimentary rocks made from precipitation from sea water? What is their history?

Sedimentary Rock Classification Chart

	Conglomerate	Breccia	Sandstone	Shale	Limestone	Dolomite	Chert	Coquina	Coal
Contains fragments?	●	●	●	●	○		●		
Round fragments?	●		○						
Angular fragments?		●	○		○		●		
Bubbles when acid applied?	○	○	○	○	●			●	
Bubbles only when acid applied to powder?						●			
Harder than a knife blade?							●		
Black color?				○					●
Scratches limestone?						●	●		○
Contains plant material?									○

Key:
● Always present
○ Sometimes present

How are these characteristics used in identifying sedimentary rocks? Look carefully at the rock and at the pieces making up the rock and again use the process of elimination. Each identified characteristic will eliminate other rocks without that characteristic. This will help you select its name and describe its history.

Figure 13.17 Common sedimentary rocks

1. Conglomerate   2. Breccia   3. Sandstone   4. Siltstone   5. Shale
6. Limestone   7. Dolomite   8. Gypsum   9. Coquina   10. Coal

Study Questions for 13.3

1. What are sediments? Where do they come from?
2. What three main processes are involved to change sediments into sedimentary rocks?
3. Explain how the properties of a sedimentary rock are used in identification.

13.4 Metamorphic Rocks

You will find out
- why a metamorphic rock is different from the rock that it formed from;
- where metamorphic rocks are formed;
- how metamorphic rocks are classified and identified.

All metamorphic rocks start out as something else and end up as metamorphic rocks. Most processes bringing about this kind of change take place deep inside the earth's crust. In Figure 13.18 you can see layer upon layer of sedimentary rock. This continuous piling up of layer upon layer over a large area increases pressure on the bottom layers. As the layers increase, tremendous pressure and heat develop. Changes are occurring at all levels. But in the lower levels the changes are greatest. Heat, pressure, and contact with mineral-rich liquids act to change one kind of rock into another. Geologists can read the changes that have taken place by looking at the arrangement of minerals in the rock.

Figure 13.19 shows a picture of a metamorphic rock. Try to read its history. This rock formed on the surface. In time it was buried five to ten km under rocks of the earth's crust. You can see that pressure and heat have flattened the fragments, and some material recrystallized around the fragments. Over much time the rock was forced upward to the surface. This cycle may be repeated more than once for the same rock.

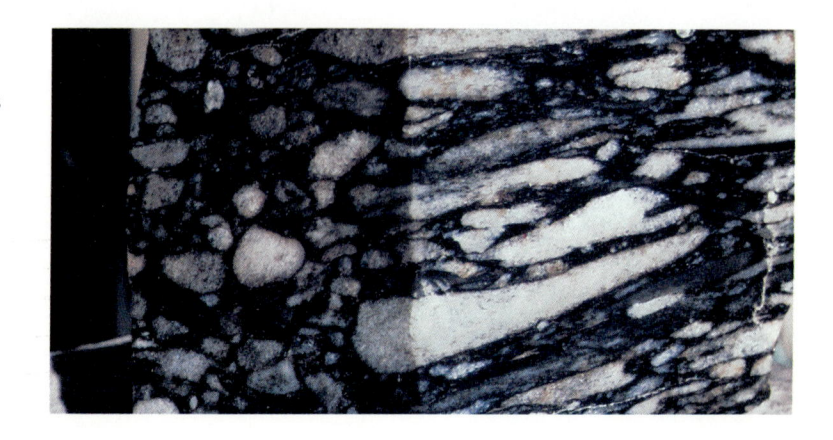

Figure 13.18 *above:* The formation of metamorphic rock

Figure 13.19 *right:* Flattened fragments are clearly visible in this example of metamorphic rock.

13 / Rocks and the Rock Cycle

Figure 13.20 is a model of metamorphic change. In general, the degree of change in a rock depends upon its depth in the earth and how long it stays at that depth. The model of metamorphic change can also be applied to the way minerals arrange themselves during metamorphism. In a low-grade change the minerals re-

Figure 13.20 The change to metamorphic rock varies with the type of rock, depth, and time.

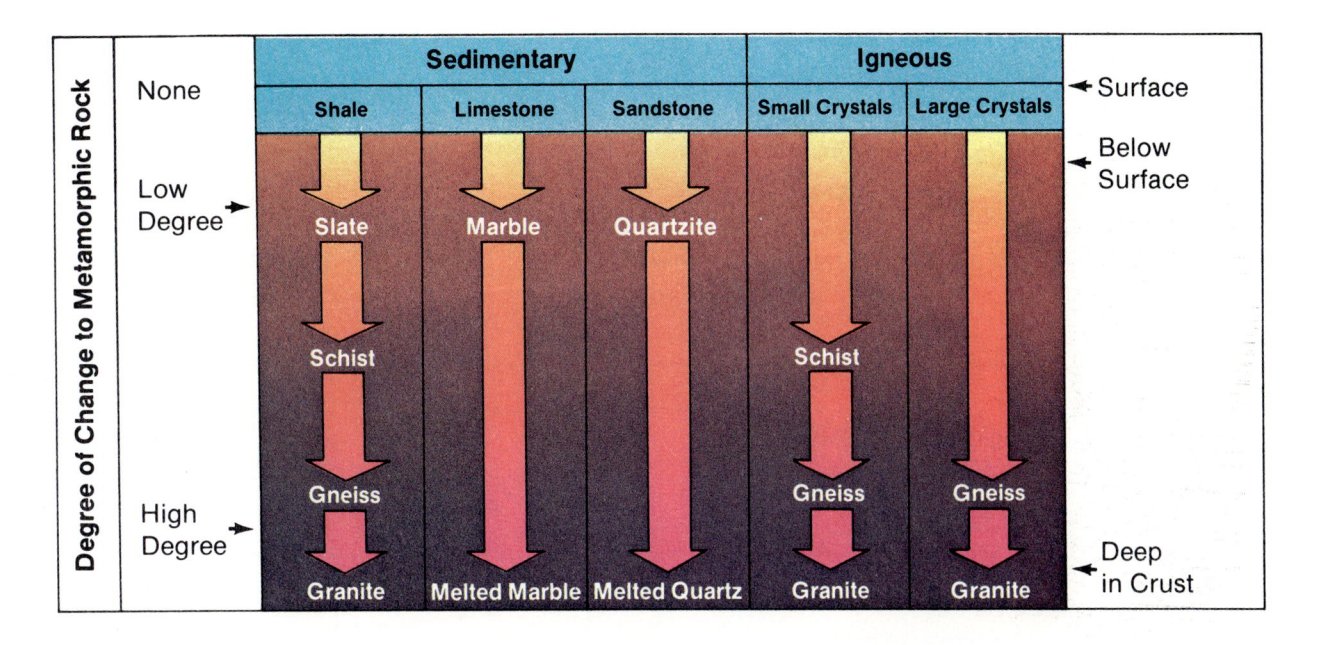

crystallize in flat or long slender shapes that line up in the rock. In high-grade change the minerals recrystallize to form bands of light- and dark-colored minerals. The way the minerals are arranged determines whether or not the rock will break in layers.

The arrangement of mineral crystals in parallel layers, or bands, is called **foliation.** Metamorphic rocks are classified as foliated or nonfoliated. Foliated metamorphic rocks, such as gneiss, display foliation by their banded appearance. Other rocks, such as slate, display foliation by the way they break apart in layers. Nonfoliated metamorphic rocks, such as quartzite and marble, are more uniform in texture and appearance. Compare the textures of the rocks in Figure 13.22. Metamorphic rocks are identified using physical properties such as texture.

Figure 13.21 Marble was used for the statue of Abraham Lincoln at the Lincoln Memorial in Washington, D.C.

13 / Rocks and the Rock Cycle

Activity

What Are the Names of These Metamorphic Rocks?

Materials

metamorphic rock set
magnifying glass
safety goggles
eye dropper
knife
dilute acid

Procedure

1. Select a rock from your set.
2. Look at your rock chart. Ask the first question. If the question is appropriate, record the names of the rocks with that physical characteristic.
3. Ask the second question. Record your answer.
4. Repeat this procedure until you have identified the rock. CAUTION: Use care when working with acid. Be sure to wash your hands and the rocks after doing the acid test.
5. Repeat this procedure with the other rocks in the rock set.

Questions

1. What are the names of your layered metamorphic rocks? What is their degree of metamorphism?
2. What are the names of your nonlayered metamorphic rocks?

Metamorphic Rock Classification Chart	Slate	Schist	Gneiss	Quartzite	Marble
Is the rock layered?	●	●	●		
Can you see large mineral grains?			●		
Can you see medium sized grains?		●			
Is the rock fine grained?	●				
Does it break into layers?	●	●			
Is it banded?			●		
Does it sparkle like sugar?					●
Does it bubble with acid?					●
Will it scratch a knife blade?				●	
Does it contain quartz?				●	

Key:
● Always present

266

13 / Rocks and the Rock Cycle

How many different minerals are found in metamorphic rocks? Table 13.1 shows that most metamorphic rocks are made from seven minerals. With the exception of garnet the same minerals are also abundant in igneous rocks. Sedimentary rocks are made primarily of only four minerals. The great variety of rocks you find is due to different arrangements and different amounts of these minerals.

Table 13.1 Mineral Type	Igneous	Metamorphic	Sedimentary
Olivine	Abundant	Rare	Rare
Garnet	Rare	Abundant	Rare
Augite	Abundant	Common	Rare
Hornblende	Abundant	Abundant	Common
Muscovite	Abundant	Abundant	Common
Biotite	Abundant	Abundant	Common
Kaolinite	Rare	Rare	Abundant
Potassium Feldspar	Abundant	Abundant	Common
Sodium Feldspar	Abundant	Abundant	Common
Quartz	Abundant	Abundant	Abundant
Calcite	Rare	Common	Abundant
Dolomite	Rare	Common	Abundant

Key: 🟢 Rare 🔵 Common 🟠 Abundant

1. Schist   2. Gneiss   3. Slate   4. Quartzite   5. Marble

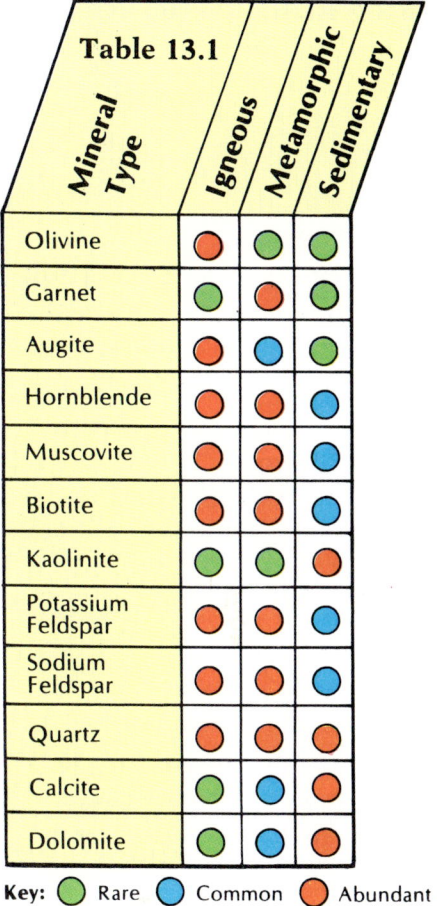

Figure 13.22 *left:* Common metamorphic rocks.

Study Questions for 13.4

1. What causes rocks in the earth's crust to change into metamorphic rocks?
2. What determines the degree of change in metamorphic rocks?
3. How are metamorphic rocks classified?

Career

Geochemist

Geochemists study the chemical composition of and the actual or possible chemical changes in the crust of the earth. To do this work requires advanced study in the fields of mathematics, chemistry, and geology.

Dr. Rosemary Vidale, a geochemist, works at Los Alamos National Laboratory and lives in Los Alamos, New Mexico. She earned a B.A. degree in chemistry from Oberlin University in Ohio and a Ph.D. from Yale University. When she's not working on her field of special interest, the transport and concentration of chemical elements in the earth's crust, Dr. Vidale enjoys several hobbies. These include photography, hiking, reading, camping, and music. She regularly gives geology travelogues and talks to school groups and the public on such topics as hot springs, volcanoes, and mineral and rock identification. She leads local geology field trips for interested groups.

Her research findings are useful in determining a safe disposal method for chemically dangerous wastes.

CHAPTER REVIEW

Main Ideas

- Igneous rocks are firm, hard rocks that cooled from hot melted rock.
- Sedimentary rocks are formed from sediments that have been pressed and cemented together.
- Metamorphic rocks are formed from igneous and sedimentary rocks.
- The rock cycle is a model showing the changes rocks undergo through time.
- Magma is an underground pocket of melted rock.
- Magma that cools underground forms coarse-grained intrusive rocks.
- Magma contains different mixtures of elements that result in light- or dark-colored igneous rocks.
- Sediments come from rock fragments, dissolved materials, or plant and animal matter.
- Sedimentary rocks that form from the compaction and cementation of rock fragments have a clastic texture.
- Sedimentary rocks that form from chemical deposits or from deposits of plant and animal matter are nonclastic.
- Metamorphic rocks form from heat and pressure generated from rock folding, mountain building, or magma intrusions.
- Metamorphic rocks are classified as foliated or nonfoliated.

Using Vocabulary

Make up a matching-column quiz. On a separate sheet of paper, list the words below in one column and describe each word in another column. Exchange quizzes with a classmate.

igneous rock	magma	cementation
sediments	intrusive	nonclastic
strata	lava	precipitation
sedimentary rock	extrusive	foliation
metamorphic rock	clastic	
rock cycle	compaction	

13 / Rocks and the Rock Cycle

Remembering Facts

On your paper, write the word or words that best complete each sentence below.

1. _____ is the process of pressing materials together in making sedimentary rocks.
2. The layered texture of some metamorphic rocks is called _____.
3. Solid materials that settle out of water are called _____.
4. The process of filling spaces between sediments with chemical deposits is called _____.
5. _____ rocks were once igneous or sedimentary rocks that became changed.
6. _____ are layers of different kinds or colors of sediments.
7. Magma cooling deep in the ground forms _____ igneous rocks.
8. _____ is a coarse-grained, light-colored igneous rock.
9. Chemical deposits are dissolved materials that become sediments through _____.
10. _____ metamorphic rocks have a uniform texture and appearance.
11. An extrusive rock with no crystals has a _____ texture.
12. Sedimentary rocks with rock fragments have a _____ texture.
13. Rocks are broken apart and new rocks are formed in as part of the _____ _____.
14. The size, shape, and arrangement of particles give a rock its _____.
15. _____ is a fine-grained, dark-colored igneous rock.
16. The three major types of rocks are _____, _____, and _____.

Understanding Ideas

On your paper, answer each question in complete sentences.
1. What is the difference between minerals and rocks?
2. Compaction alone will not form a sedimentary rock. What else is necessary to form a sedimentary rock?
3. Granite has been classified as an igneous rock, a metamorphic rock, and sometimes a combination of both. Which rock category do you think granite falls under?
4. Will all rocks eventually become sedimentary rocks? Why?
5. What does the formation of metamorphic rocks indicate about conditions deep within the earth's crust?

Applying What You Have Learned

1. Why are fossils found only in sedimentary rocks?
2. Density is a property useful in identifying minerals but not rocks. Why is this true?
3. Of the three kinds of rocks on the earth's surface, igneous rocks are the oldest and also the youngest. Explain how this could be.
4. Describe the process by which sandstone is changed into quartzite.

Challenge

Sedimentary rocks can be made up of a wide range of fragment sizes. Rock fragments form wherever rock meets the air. These fragments are carried off by winds, waves, rivers, and glaciers. The size of a fragment often depends on how far it has traveled from its source.

Since the size of fragments tells so much about the origins of a rock, the names used to describe rocks are critical. A sedimentary rock made of very fine mud particles is called shale. Another sedimentary rock, siltstone, has fine-sized particles (silt). Sandstone is made of medium-sized grains (sand). Some sedimentary rocks contain a mixture of these grain sizes. Study the diagram and answer the following questions.

1. What is the least amount of sand that a rock must contain to be considered a sandstone?
2. How much silt must a rock have before it can be called a siltstone?
3. What name would be given to a sedimentary rock which had a shale to sand ratio of 3:1?

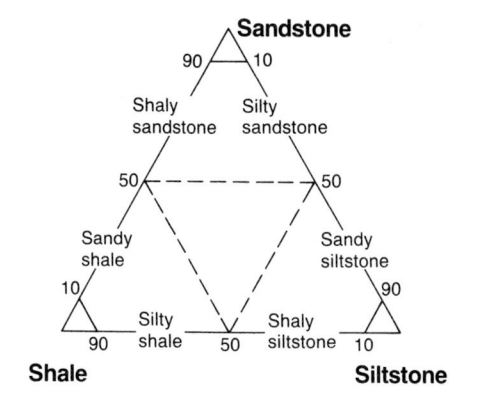

Research and Investigation

1. Find out whether any homes and buildings in your community have been built using rock. Survey the buildings to see how many kinds of rocks can be identified.
2. Investigate the bulk materials used in the construction industry. Interview someone in the construction industry to find out how much rock is used to build a typical house. Find out how bricks, cement, and concrete are made, what raw materials they are made from, and where? Prepare a bulletin board report for your class.
3. Find out how much sand and gravel are required to build a block of sidewalk.

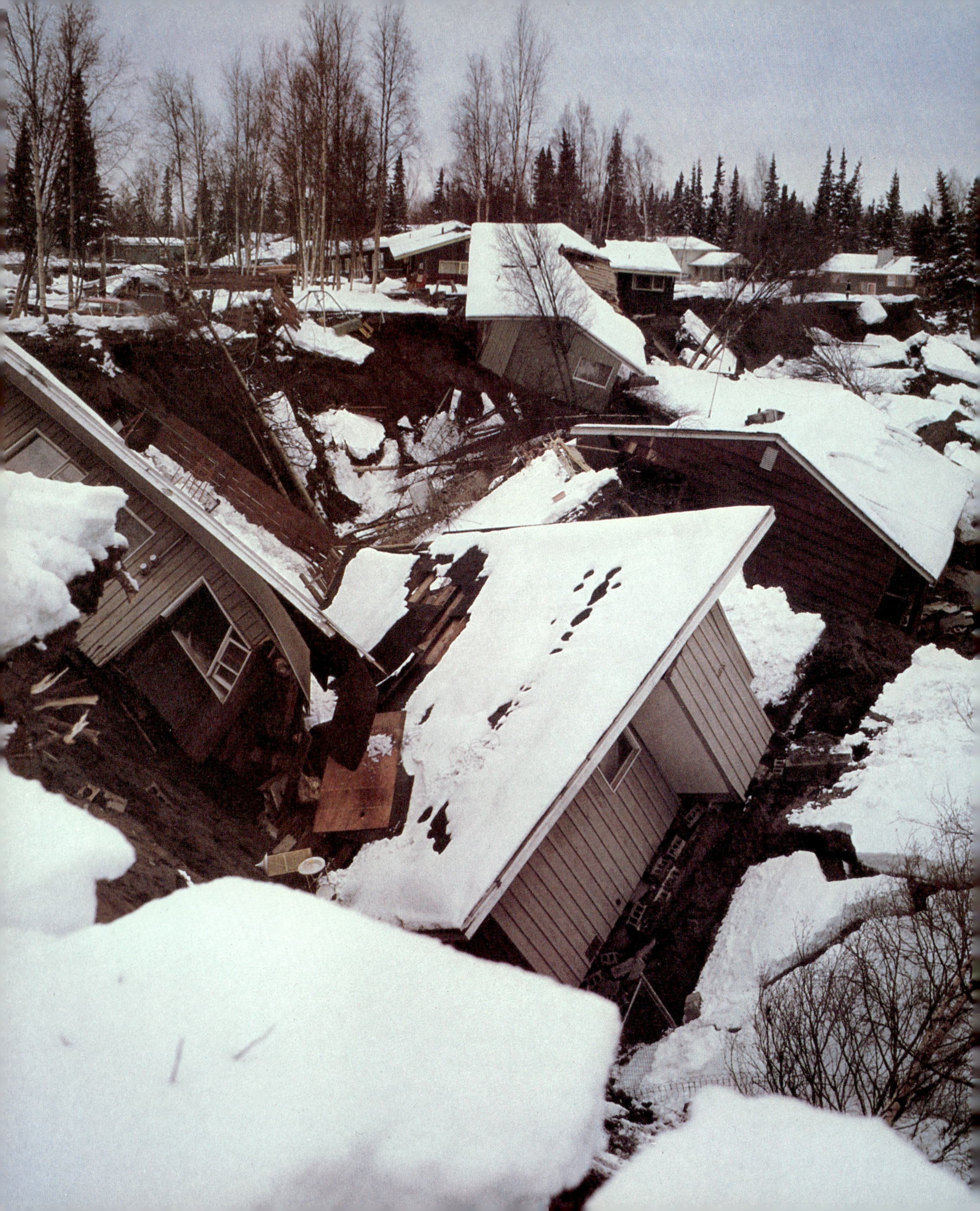

Chapter 14
Internal Structure of Earth

Lesson Titles
14.1 A Model of the Earth's Interior
14.2 Indirect Evidence from Space
14.3 Earthquakes and Seismic Waves
14.4 Evidence from within the Earth

In this picture you see the terrible destruction caused by the earthquake in Anchorage, Alaska, on March 27, 1964. What caused the earth's surface to move with such destruction? Possibly something happened to squeeze or stretch the earth's outer layer. Some people in the past thought that perhaps the earth was growing larger. This growth would stretch and crack the rocks in the earth's outer layer. Others have suggested that the earth was a cooling molten planet with a shrinking and crackling surface. Now scientists have constructed a model of the internal structure of the earth to answer some of these questions. How they obtained the information they used to make their model is developed in this chapter.

Figure 14.1 *opposite:* Sudden destruction comes from forces within the earth.

14.1 A Model of the Earth's Interior

You will find out
- what the three main layers of the earth are;
- what the characteristics of these layers are believed to be.

What do you think of when you hear that something is "as big as a mountain"? The size of a mountain is hard to understand. When you see a mountain from a distance, it looks big. Yet when you are on the mountain, you see only small boulders and rocks. It is difficult to look at all the small rocks and understand the size of the mountain. Scientists had this same problem when they tried to understand the whole earth. They couldn't see the whole earth. They could only see bits and pieces of information about the earth. But over a long period of time these bits and pieces of information helped the scientists build a model of the earth. According to this model, shown in Figure 14.2, the earth is made of three main layers.

The outside layer of earth is called the **crust**. It is a relatively thin layer of solid rock made of sedimentary, metamorphic, and volcanic rocks. You cannot see the crust because it is mostly covered with small particles of rocks, soil, and sand. The seas and oceans also cover the crust.

The crust is not the same thickness everywhere. Its thickness varies from 20 to 50 km across continental United States. The average thickness is 32 km. The crust is thinner beneath the oceans, averaging less than 8 km thick. The crust makes up 1 percent of the earth's volume but only 0.4 percent of its mass.

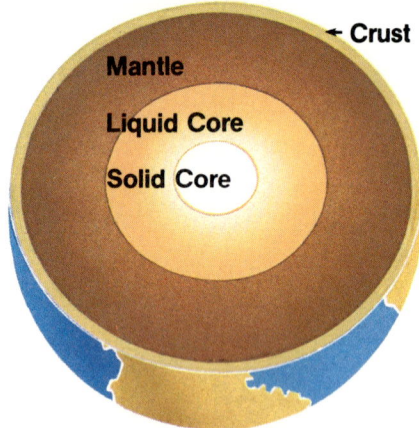

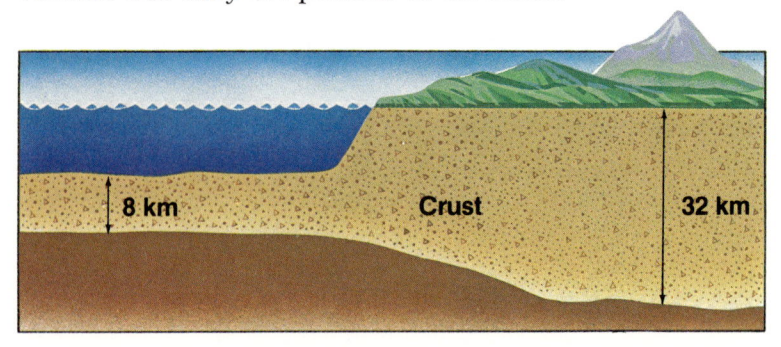

Figure 14.2 The main layers of the earth

Figure 14.3 The thickness of earth's crust varies at different locations. The average thickness across the continental United States is shown in this diagram.

274

14 / Internal Structure of Earth

The layer below the crust is called the **mantle.** It is a very thick layer that goes from the bottom of the crust down to about 2,900 km. The mantle is made of solid rock. But the rocks in the mantle are different from the rocks in the crust. The mantle itself consists of layers. It has rigid upper and lower parts surrounding a middle layer that is able to move slowly like very thick syrup. The mantle makes up 84 percent of the earth's volume and about two thirds of the earth's mass.

The center part of the earth is a large, dense core. The core begins below the mantle and continues the remaining 3,400 km to the center of the earth. The core is believed to be made of a solid inner part surrounded by a liquid outer layer. Both are thought to be made of iron and nickel. The core makes up 15 percent of the earth's total volume and about one third of its mass.

As you can see, the model of the earth's interior has three basic parts. It is like a huge soft-boiled egg. The model has a center core (the yolk), a middle part (the white), and a thin outer layer (the shell).

How do scientists know so much about the earth's interior? No one has ever traveled more than a few kilometers beneath the earth's surface. Even the deepest wells have not been drilled much more than 12 km deep. Yet the center of the earth is over 6,000 km from the surface. How can scientists make a model of something they cannot see? To make a model of the earth's interior, it has been necessary for scientists to collect and fit many bits and pieces of evidence together.

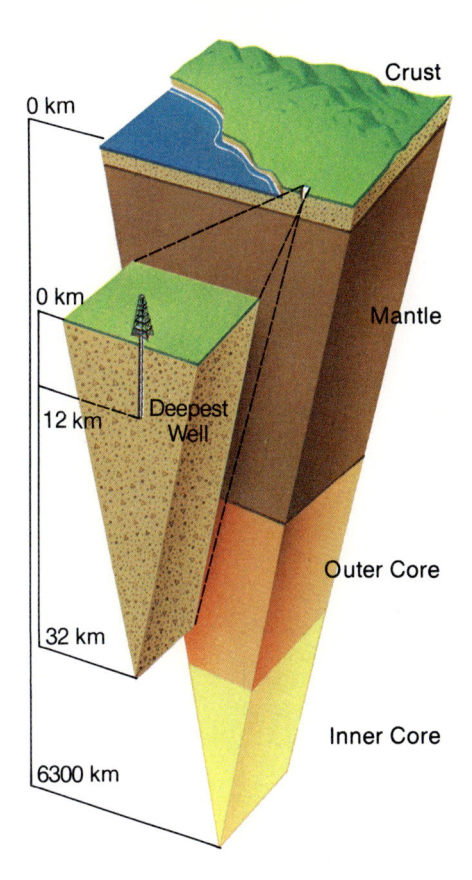

Figure 14.4 The deepest wells of 12 km barely pierce the earth's surface.

Study Questions for 14.1

1. Name the three main parts of the earth.
2. Describe each of the main parts of the earth.
3. Explain how the model of the earth is like a soft-boiled egg.

14.2 Indirect Evidence from Space

You will find out
- what evidence the moon provides about the earth's interior;
- how meteorites provide evidence about earth.

Nearly all of the information scientists have used to make their model of the earth's interior has been learned indirectly. The first evidence about the earth's interior came from a study of the earth's moon.

The moon's path around the earth depends on several factors, one of which is the mass of the earth. Remember that gravitational attraction is related to mass. Using information they knew about the moon's motion and distance from the earth, scientists were able to determine the mass of the entire earth.

Knowing the earth's mass alone did not tell scientists much about the earth's interior. But now the scientists were able to determine the average density of the earth by comparing its mass with its volume. Surprisingly, the earth's density was found to be more than 5 grams per cubic centimeter. This was a surprise because scientists knew that rocks on the earth's surface had an average density of less than 3 grams per cubic centimeter. The whole earth's average density, then, is almost twice the density of the rocks on the surface. This must mean that the earth's interior is much more dense than surface rocks.

Figure 14.5 Studying the earth by studying the moon helped scientists determine the mass of the earth.

Table 14-1. Volume, Mass, and Density of the Earth				
	Average Radius (km)	**Volume** (millions of km³)	**Mass** (g X 10²⁴)	**Average Density** (g/cm³)
Total Earth	6,371	1,083,230	5,976	5.52
Oceans	3.8	1,370	1.41	1.03
Glaciers	1.6	25	0.023	0.9
Continental crust	35	6,210	17.39	2.8
Oceanic crust	8	2,660	7.71	2.9
Mantle	2,883	899,000	4,068	4.5
Core	3,471	175,500	1,881	10.71

Metal Meteorite **Rock Meteorite**

Figure 14.6 *left:* Earth is believed to have the same composition as meteorites like these.

Figure 14.7 *below:* Earth's core matter weighs more than an equal volume of crustal matter because the core is more dense.

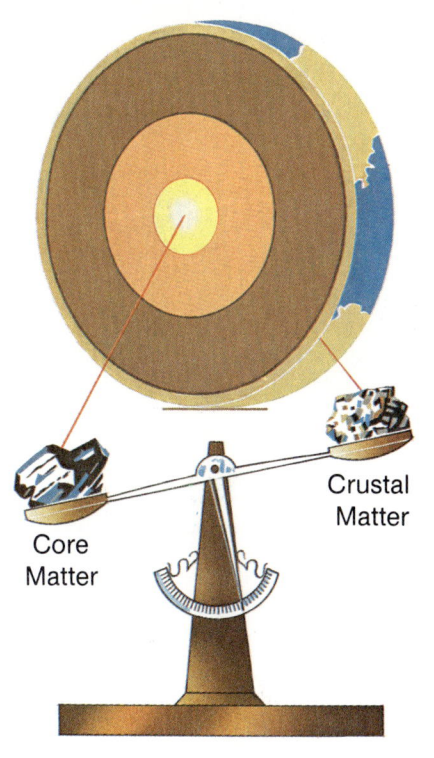

More evidence about the earth's interior came from a study of meteorites, which sometimes fall to the earth's surface from space. Meteorites that have been recovered are mainly of two types, rock and metal. The rock meteorites are made of silicate minerals. The metal meteorites are mostly made of iron and nickel. Meteorites are believed to be mostly odds and ends which were left over from the time when the solar system was formed. It is reasonable, therefore, to assume that meteorites and the earth are largely made of the same materials.

As the earth was formed, scientists believe that the earth passed through a molten stage. During this molten period heavier metal materials would have settled to the earth's center, or core. Lighter silicate materials would have risen to the surface and eventually formed a crust. Since iron and nickel are found in the metal meteorites, it appears these metals were present when the earth was formed. An iron and nickel core would greatly increase the average density of the earth. This hypothesis fits nicely with what has also been learned about the earth's density from the moon. Thus, meteorites indirectly provide a second piece of evidence about the earth's interior.

Core Matter   Crustal Matter

Do You Know?
About 500 meteorites that are the size of an orange or larger strike the earth's surface each year.

Study Questions for 14.2

1. How did the moon provide indirect evidence about the earth's interior?
2. Why do scientists believe that the earth has a center part made of iron and nickel?

14.3 Earthquakes and Seismic Waves

You will find out
- what causes most earthquakes;
- how earthquake waves are measured;
- what the three kinds of seismic waves are.

You have learned that meteorites and the moon provide indirect evidence about the earth's interior. Evidence comes from within the earth too. Have you ever felt the earth vibrate? A passing truck or train can cause vibrations to move through the ground. These vibrations move through the ground much like the ripples you see move across a bowl of water if you tap the bowl with a pencil. Sometimes there are much larger vibrations or waves in the earth's surface. These vibrations are caused by a sudden release of energy within the earth. Vibrations can cause the ground in some places to roll like waves on the ocean. These sudden waves in the earth are called **earthquakes.**

Figure 14.8 *above:* A disturbance causes vibrations to move through matter in waves.

Figure 14.9 *right:* An explosion of dynamite starts vibrations moving through the earth.

The energy released by some earthquakes is small and just rattles windows. However, the energy released by other earthquakes is large enough to alter major landforms on the surface of the earth. Small or large, an earthquake is the result of a disturbance in the earth.

What causes a disturbance in the earth? Relatively small disturbances can be produced by a passing train, an explosion, or a landslide. Larger disturbances, though, are produced by a movement deep in the earth's crust or mantle. Various pressures cause part of the crust or mantle to be pushed together or pulled apart. A section breaks along a huge crack and moves, releasing energy in the process. The place where the movement happens is called a **fault**. At a fault, rocks can break and move past one another, causing a disturbance that results in an earthquake.

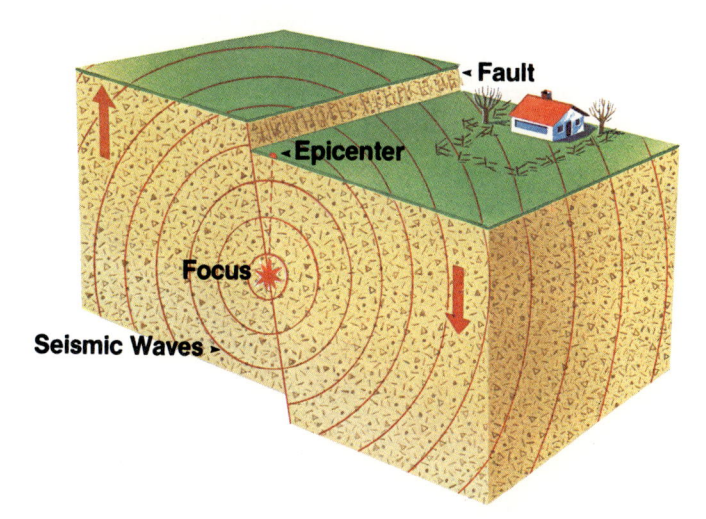

Do You Know?
Each year, on the average, there are 10 earthquakes with widespread destruction, 100 with local destruction, 1,000 that do some damage, 100,000 that can be felt, and about 1,000,000 that are detected only by sensitive instruments.

The place along a fault where an earthquake begins is called the **focus** [FOH-kuhs] of the earthquake. Energy moves outward from the focus causing the earth's surface to vibrate. These vibrations are called **seismic** [SIZE-mihk] **waves**. Measurements of seismic waves have shown that the focus of most earthquakes is in the crust and top part of the mantle down to about 75 km. But the focus of some earthquakes has been measured as deep as 700 km.

Seismic waves move outward in all directions from the focus of an earthquake. Traveling downward, some of the seismic waves can travel all the way through the earth. Traveling upward, some of the waves reach the surface. The place on the surface directly above the focus is called the **epicenter** [EHP-uh-sehn-tuhr]. News reports usually identify the epicenter of an earthquake.

Figure 14.10 *above left:* Rocks break and move along a fault. The Richter scale is a numerical system that measures the amount of energy released during an earthquake.

Figure 14.11 *above:* The San Andreas Fault in California

14 / Internal Structure of Earth

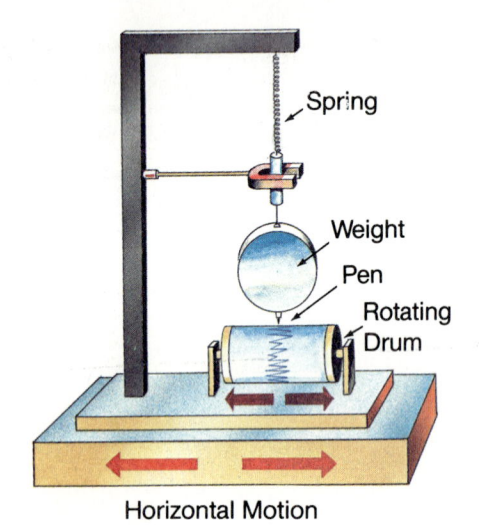

Figure 14.12 This seismograph measures horizontal movement of the earth's crust during an earthquake.

Do You Know?
Some seismic waves travel at 24 times the speed of sound, or 30,000 km per hour, through the earth.

Figure 14.13 This is a model of how seismic waves move through the earth.

Scientists measure seismic waves with an instrument called a **seismograph** [SIZE-muh-graf]. One type of seismograph has a massive object suspended from a spring. Since the object is not attached directly to the earth, it tends not to vibrate much even as the earth vibrates under it. A pen is attached to the relatively stationary massive object so that it will mark on a sheet of paper on a slowly turning drum. Since the pen does not move but the drum vibrates with the movement of the earth, a wavy line is made on the paper. Thus, a record is made of how much of the ground is vibrating.

Scientists have found that there are three kinds of seismic waves. These are the **primary waves,** the **secondary waves,** and the **surface waves.** The primary waves, or *P* waves, are vibrations that cause a material to vibrate back and forth. A clap of thunder is a sound wave in the air that is like *P* waves in the earth. They move in the direction the waves are traveling as shown in Figure 14.13. *P* waves are the fastest seismic waves and can travel through any material. In addition, *P* waves speed up as the density of the material they pass through increases. Denser materials have closer molecules, which let the waves pass through more rapidly. The changing density of materials also causes the waves to curve or change direction just as light waves are refracted when passing from air to water.

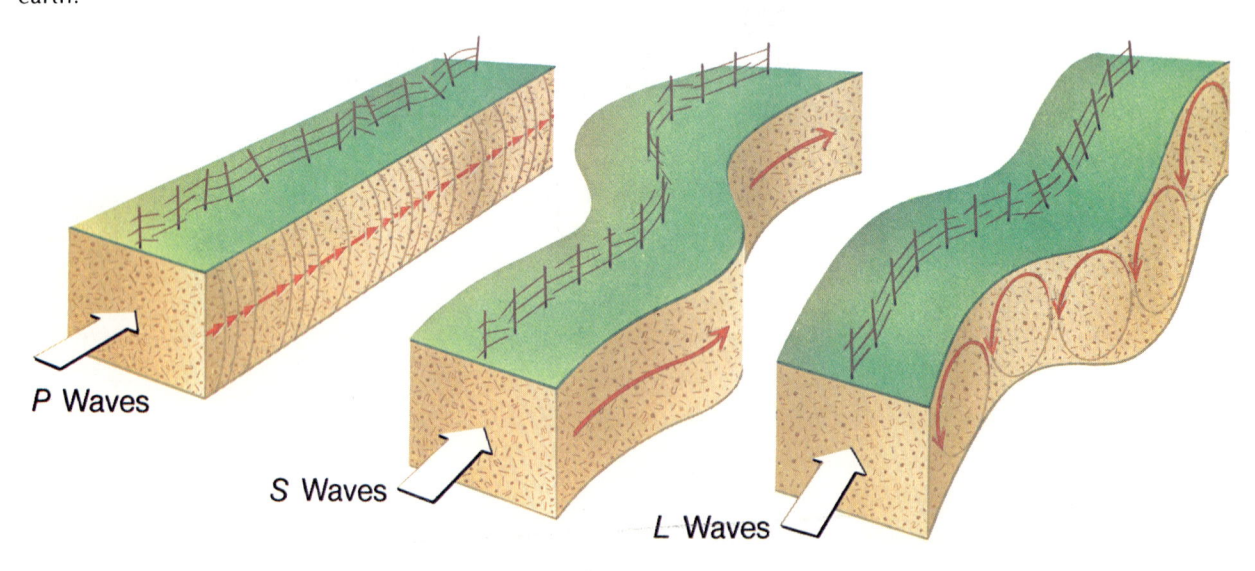

14 / Internal Structure of Earth

The secondary waves, or *S* waves, are vibrations that cause a material to move from side to side. They move at right angles to the direction the waves are traveling. *S* waves are slower than *P* waves, and they cannot pass through liquid. The molecules in a liquid can move by each other easily, so the *S* waves just cause some molecules to slip back and forth.

The surface waves, or *L* waves, are the slowest of the seismic waves. *L* waves move along the earth's surface much like waves on the ocean. As the surface of water rises and falls with each passing wave, the earth's surface moves up and down as each *L* wave passes. The *L* waves cause most of the damage from an earthquake.

The amount of energy released during an earthquake can be measured using the *Richter scale*. Each number on the scale indicates an increase in strength that is 10 times greater than the previous number. An earthquake measuring 3 on the scale is 10 times stronger than an earthquake measuring 2.

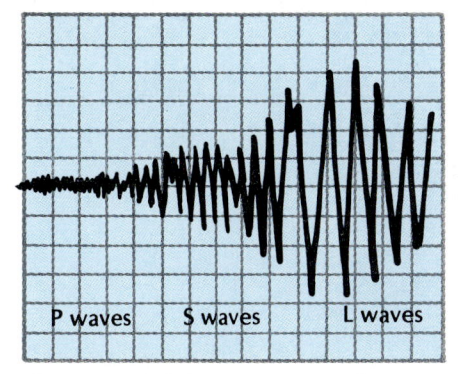

Figure 14.14 Seismic waves as they would look on a seismographic record

Activity

How Do Earthquake Waves Move?

Material
Slinky toy

Procedure
1. Place the Slinky on the floor. Hold one end while your partner stretches the other end about three meters across the floor.
2. Pull about 15 of the coils together and then let them go.
3. When the Slinky is still, move one end of the Slinky rapidly from side to side.

Questions
1. What did you observe when you pulled the coils together and then released them?
2. What type of earthquake waves move like this?
3. What did you observe when you moved one end of the Slinky from side to side?
4. What type of earthquake waves move like this?
5. Which wave form moved faster through the Slinky?

Study Questions for 14.3
1. What is the cause of most earthquakes?
2. How are earthquake waves measured?
3. What are three types of seismic waves?

14.4 Evidence from within the Earth

You will find out
- how the crust was discovered;
- what the structure of the mantle is;
- why scientists believe the core has a solid center surrounded by a liquid outer layer.

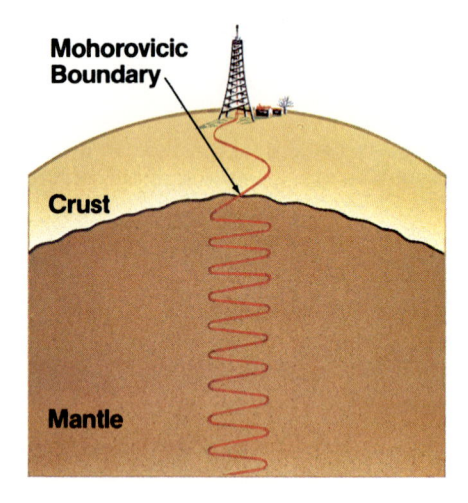

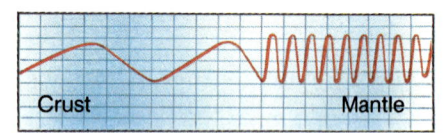

Figure 14.15 By studying seismic waves, scientists discovered the Moho boundary between the crust and the mantle.

Figure 14.16 Some places on the earth are rising. This led scientists to wonder about the nature of the mantle.

When you open a soft-boiled egg, you know what to expect. But no one has ever "opened" the earth or visited the interior. Yet scientists know a great deal about the earth's interior. They have used indirect evidence from the seismic waves to develop their information.

The earth's crust, for example, was discovered early in the history of seismic-wave studies. Andrija Mohorovicic [MOH-hoh-ROH-vuh-sihk] found that seismic waves suddenly increase in speed below a certain depth. This increase could be accounted for by a change in the density of the rocks. There seems to be a boundary with a different kind of rock below it. The boundary where the seismic waves increase in speed is now called the **Moho** [MOH-hoh]. The Moho boundary marks the bottom of the crust and the top of the mantle.

Recent evidence indicates that part of the mantle acts like a thick syrup. During the Ice Age, huge amounts of ice accumulated in some places. The weight of this ice caused the crust and upper mantle to sink. The ice has now melted, of course, and the crust and upper mantle are moving back up. Some of these places are still rising today at about one centimeter per year. It is as if the weight of the ice squeezed part of the mantle away like toothpaste in a tube, causing the land to sink. After the ice melted, the mantle part started slowly moving back. With increasing or decreasing weight the crust and upper mantle sink or rise as if they are floating on a thick syrup layer.

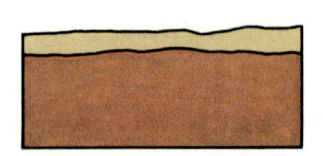

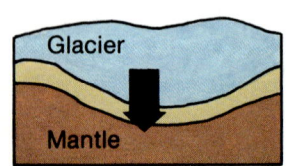

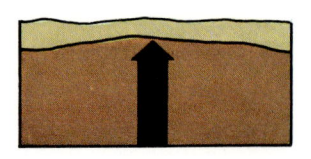

282

14 / Internal Structure of Earth

There is seismic evidence, however, that the mantle is a solid, not a liquid. *S* and *P* waves move all the way through it. Since *S* waves do not move through liquid, it must mean that the mantle is solid.

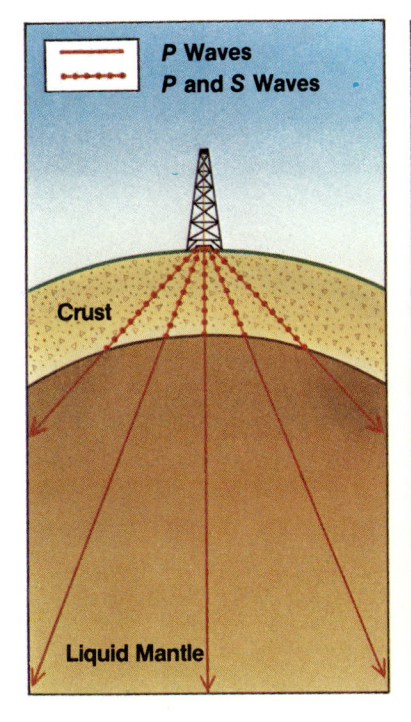

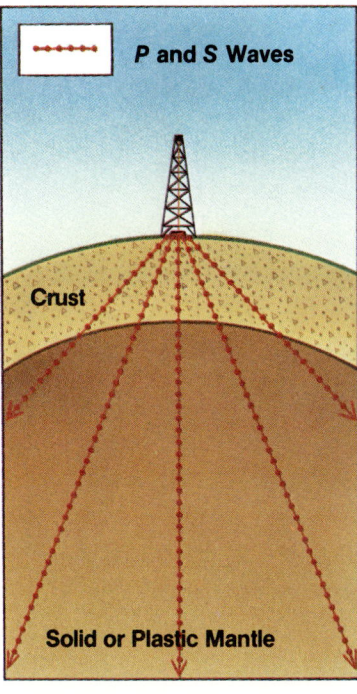

Figure 14.17 *left:* Evidence from seismic waves implies that the mantle is not a liquid but rather has the solid and liquid properties of a plastic.

Figure 14.18 *below:* The mantle seems to have properties like some plastics. *top:* Solid and brittle; *bottom:* Soft and stretchable

How can the mantle act like both a solid and a liquid? Perhaps it is a **plastic** material. Plastic here does not mean a material such as a plastic bag. A plastic material is one that is a solid but can flow over a long period of time.

Since rocks in the mantle are subjected to high pressure and high temperature, that fact could account for their having plastic-like properties. The mantle would then be able to flow slowly, adjusting to stresses such as the weight of ice. *S* waves could also move through a mantle that responds like a plastic.

More studies of seismic waves suggest that not all of the mantle is plastic. Below the solid crust is a zone of plastic, easily-flowing material. The plastic layer is from 75 to 250 km below the surface, and it goes all around the earth. Below this plastic layer, the rest of the mantle is a dense solid.

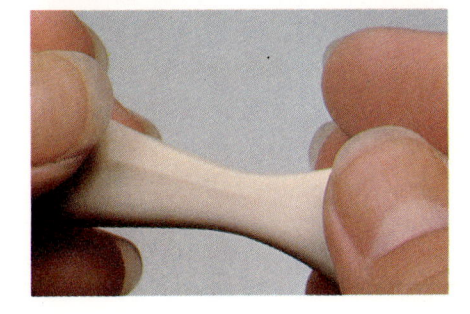

14 / Internal Structure of Earth

Seismic-wave evidence also points to something unexpected in the earth's core. When scientists study records of seismic waves that have passed through the earth, they find a pattern. The pattern forms three zones on the earth's surface. See Figure 14.19. No matter where the earthquake occurs, the same pattern is observed. One zone receives S waves and P waves that have curved and increased in speed. Another zone receives no waves and is called a shadow zone. The third zone receives P waves only.

Do You Know?
The earth has a magnetic field that causes compasses to point north. The magnetic field is believed to originate from the liquid outer core.

Activity

How Does a Plastic Substance Act?

Materials
dish or container
paper cup
plastic spoon
cornstarch
water
metal, wood, and plastic objects
plastic mixing bowl

Procedure

1. Place one tablespoon of cornstarch in a plastic mixing bowl. Add water a few drops at a time and stir the mixture. Stir until a thick paste is formed.

2. Pour the mixture onto a dish. Give it time to pour. Remember that a plastic flows over a long period of time. If it will not pour at all after 5 minutes, add a few drops of water and stir. Repeat until the mixture will slowly pour. Record your observations.

3. Place metal, wood, and plastic objects on the mixture. Record your observations.

4. Remove a large piece of the mixture from the dish. Can you bend it? Can you break it? Record your observations.

Questions

1. In what ways did the mixture appear or act like a liquid?

2. In what ways did the mixture appear or act like a solid?

3. In what ways did the mixture appear or act like a plastic material?

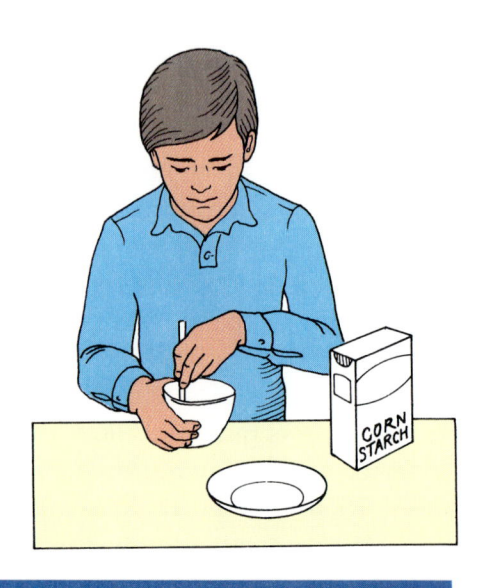

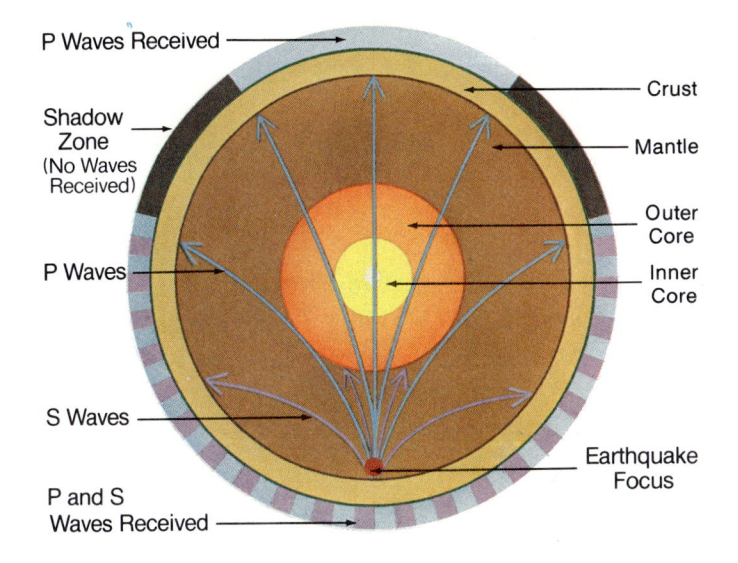

Figure 14.19 *left:* The patterns followed by seismic waves support the model of solid, plastic, and liquid layers within the earth.

Figure 14.20 *below:* This profile of the earth's interior is based on the latest information from seismic studies

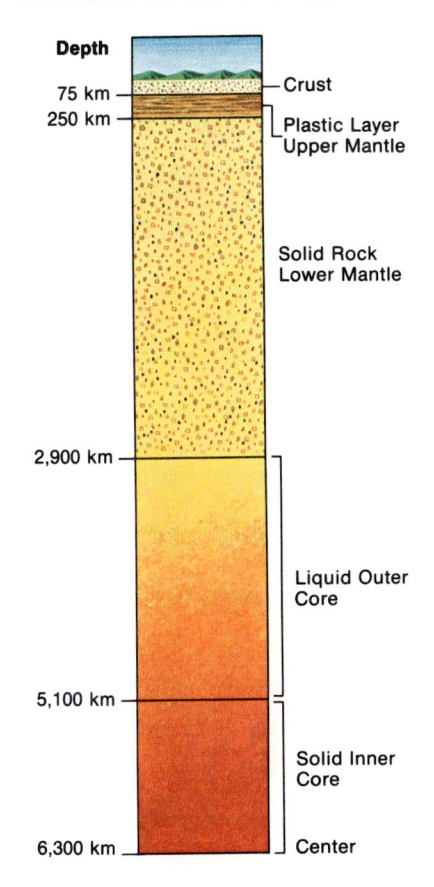

How can this pattern be explained? First, the direction of travel of *P* waves is changed when they reach a material that is less rigid, such as a liquid. This occurs at a depth of 2,900 km, bending the waves to produce a shadow zone on the surface. Second, no *S* waves appear in or beyond the shadow zone. Since *S* waves are stopped by liquid, it must mean that at least part of the core is liquid. Finally, the *P* waves that pass directly through the earth gain speed and arrive on the opposite side sooner than they would if the core were all liquid. This leads to the possibility that there is a solid inner core surrounded by a liquid outer core. A solid inner core would cause *P* waves to increase their speed. Thus, the evidence suggests that the earth has a core with a solid inner part and a liquid outer part.

Study Questions for 14.4

1. How was the presence of the earth's crust discovered?
2. What is a plastic substance?
3. What evidence points to a layer in the mantle that acts like a plastic substance?
4. What is the evidence that points to a liquid and solid inner core?

14 / Internal Structure of Earth

Science and Technology

CAT Scans and Earthquake Waves

Have you ever heard of a CAT scan? *CAT* stands for Computer-Aided Tomography, a method of making X-ray pictures of the human body.

CAT-scan pictures are different from ordinary X-ray pictures. To make an ordinary X-ray picture, the X-ray waves are sent through a body in only one direction. To make a CAT scan, X rays are sent in many different directions. This results in many more data. In fact, it provides so many data that a computer is needed to sort them all out. The computer then draws a three-dimensional picture that shows the inside of a human body much more clearly than an ordinary X ray can.

What does all this have to do with earth science? The answer is that earth scientists now have their own kind of CAT-scan method. Instead of using X rays, however, these scientists, called seismologists, use seismic waves made by earthquakes. The method is called seismic tomography and it is providing a new picture of the earth's interior.

Like the medical CAT scan, seismologists must have data from many waves that have traveled in many different directions. Since thousands of earthquakes occur around the world each year, there are plenty of waves to record. Some of the data come from the standard seismograph stations that record primary and secondary waves from every earthquake. The rest of the data come from a worldwide network of special seismographs that record just surface waves. These waves are important because they travel through the upper part of the mantle.

Once the data are collected, they must be sorted out. A computer then draws a three-dimensional picture of the mantle. These pictures have provided new information about Earth's mantle. This information has also helped in our understanding of the motions of Earth's crust.

CHAPTER REVIEW

Main Ideas

- The three main layers of the earth are the crust, mantle, and core.
- The crust is the thin outer layer of solid rock. It averages 32 km thick beneath the land and 8 km thick beneath the ocean.
- The mantle is a thick layer beneath the crust and extends down to the core at 2,900 km.
- The mantle has rigid upper and lower parts with a plastic layer between. The mantle makes up 84 percent of the earth's volume and about two thirds of its mass.
- The core makes up 15 percent of the earth's volume and about one third of its mass.
- Information about the moon's motion and distance from the earth has been used to determine properties of the earth's interior. Scientists know that the earth's interior is very dense.
- Indirect evidence from meteorites indicates that the earth's interior contains iron and nickel.
- Most earthquakes are caused by rocks breaking and sliding past each other on a fault.
- The three major types of seismic waves are primary (*P* waves), secondary (*S* waves), and surface (*L* waves). They are measured with instruments called seismographs.
- Indirect evidence from seismic-wave patterns supports a plastic layer in the mantle and a liquid outer core surrounding a solid inner core.

Using Vocabulary

On a separate piece of paper, write a paragraph describing the earth's interior. Use each of the words listed below.

crust	seismic wave	*L* wave
mantle	epicenter	Moho
earthquake	seismograph	plastic
fault	*P* wave	
focus	*S* wave	

Remembering Facts

Number your paper from 1 to 15. Match each term in column **A** with a phrase in column **B**.

A
1. core
2. mantle
3. *S* waves
4. seismograph
5. *L* waves
6. Moho
7. focus
8. crust
9. seismic waves
10. fault
11. metal meteorite
12. earthquake
13. plastic
14. epicenter
15. *P* waves

B
a. boundary between the crust and the mantle of the earth
b. vibrations or waves in the earth
c. vibrations that cause materials to move back and forth
d. the plane along which rock breaks and slips
e. vibrations that cause the earth's surface to move up and down
f. a solid that can flow over time
g. center part of the earth
h. something that provides indirect evidence about the earth's interior
i. instrument that measures seismic waves
j. layer of the earth below the crust
k. place on the surface of the earth located directly above the focus of an earthquake
l. vibrations that cause materials to move from side to side
m. place along a fault where an earthquake begins
n. outside layer of the earth
o. vibrations that move outward from the focus of an earthquake

Understanding Ideas

On your paper, answer each question in complete sentences.
1. Describe the motion of a long row of trees as each kind of seismic wave moves along and under the row.
2. Why do some seismic stations receive both *P* and *S* waves from an earthquake, while other stations receive only *P* waves?
3. Suppose seismic-wave records showed that *S* waves and *P* waves that had increased in speed were received everywhere. What would that indicate about the interior of the earth?
4. Where would you be more safe during an earthquake, inside a building or outside in an open space? Explain your answer.

Applying What You Have Learned

1. The term *solid earth* is often used to describe our planet. Explain how evidence from each of the earth's layers proves that the earth is not completely solid.
2. How does the shape of the shadow zone provide evidence that the earth's core is shaped like a ball?
3. *P* waves from a deep focus travel faster than *P* waves from a shallow focus. What does this mean?

Challenge

Seismic waves from earthquakes have revealed a model of the earth's interior. New technologies are now adding detail to the model. One new technology has made it possible to drill down into the earth to depths of over 12 km. Measurements from such depths will help improve the accuracy of seismic records. The graph shows pressures at depths that were derived from previous seismic-wave measurements and the actual pressures found in the 12-km well.

1. What is the main idea in the paragraph above?
2. Does the information from new technologies mean that the previous model of the earth's interior was wrong? Why or why not?
3. Look at the graph. List at least three questions about the actual pressures found at depths that you think scientists should seek answers for.

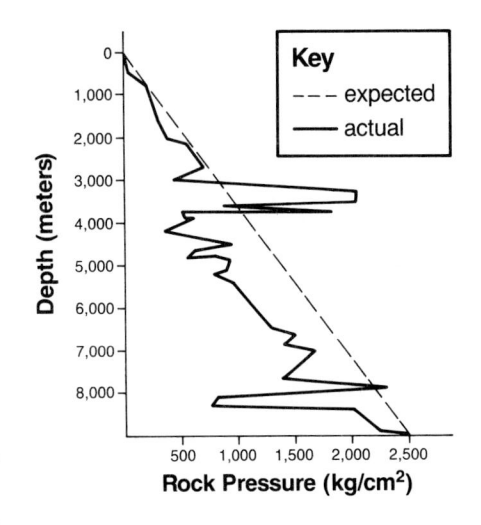

Research and Investigation

1. There have been several attempts to drill through the earth's crust into the mantle. This would provide *direct* evidence about the earth's interior. Use the resources in your library to find out about some of these projects. Investigate *Project Mohole* and prepare a report for your class.
2. Attempts are being made to predict earthquakes. Some predictions have worked, but most have not. Use your library to research the problems related to earthquake prediction. Find out about the latest technology used to study seismic waves and movements in the earth's crust.
3. Find out what is meant by the term "shadow zone."

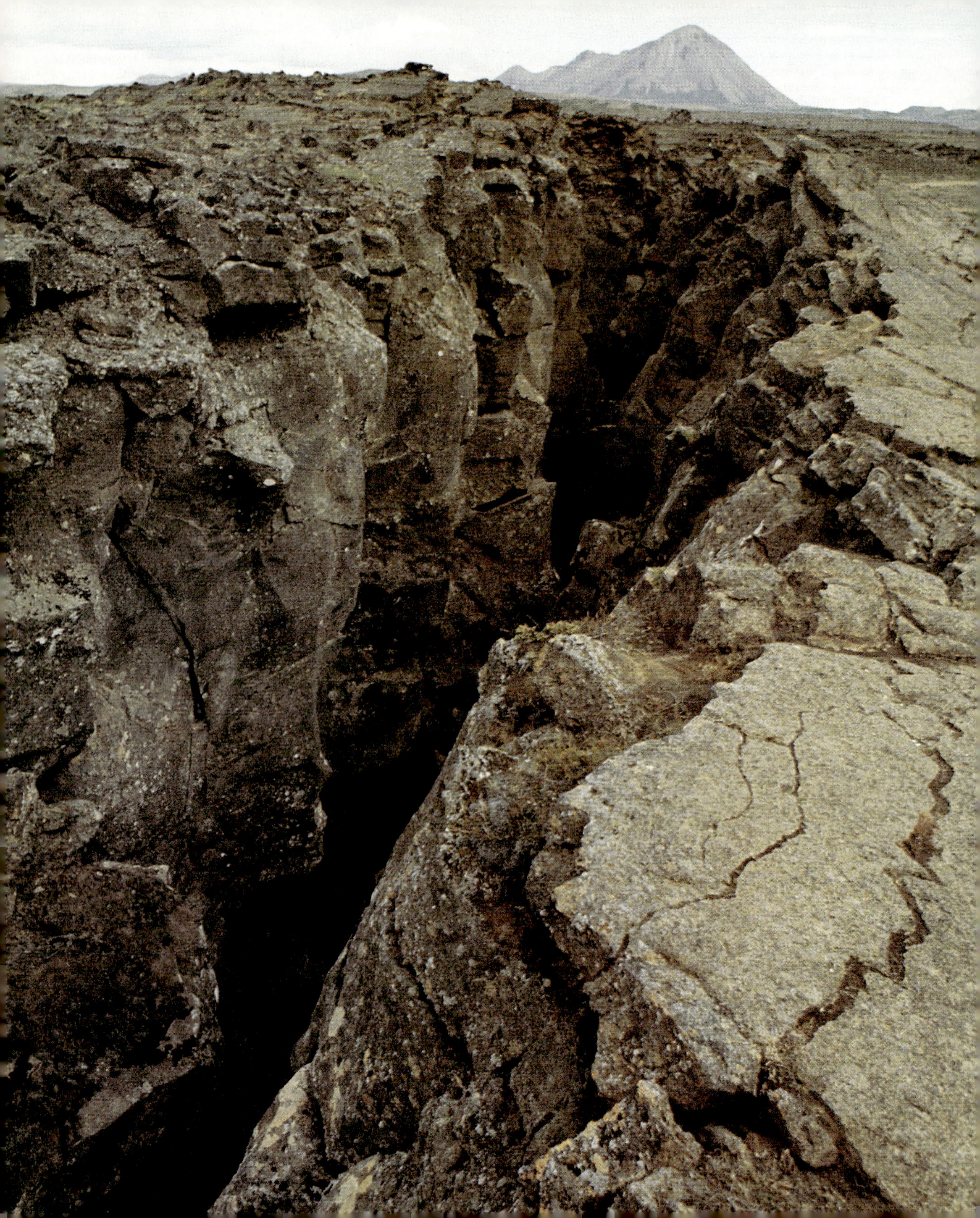

Chapter 15
Plate Tectonics

Lesson Titles
15.1   Continental Drift
15.2   The Rock Record
15.3   Evidence for Plate Movements
15.4   Unanswered Questions

Something quite amazing is happening along this ridge. The two sides of the ridge are moving apart. Of course, the movement is only a few centimeters each year. Nevertheless, these huge pieces of the earth's surface are moving. Scientists have collected data from around the earth in order to determine why changes like this are taking place. In this chapter, you will have an opportunity to review the data and examine the conclusions that scientists have come up with so far.

The plot is simple enough. All the continents were once joined together in a supercontinent. The supercontinent then broke up into big pieces. Some pieces became ocean floor. Some pieces became continents and ocean floor combined. Even today pieces are still moving. In 50 million years our world will look very different.

Can solid rock drift across the earth's surface like a raft on water? Many people have said "No." What does the evidence show? You will have to study the evidence and decide for yourself.

Figure 15.1 *opposite:* Scientists who study plate tectonics are very interested in changes along the mid-Atlantic ridge.

15.1 Continental Drift

You will find out
- that the earth's crust is made up of plates that drift or move about;
- the types of plate boundaries;
- where different types of plate boundaries are found.

Pangaea

Figure 15.2 *above:* Pangaea is believed to have been a massive combination of today's separate continents.

Figure 15.3 *below:* These are the positions of the continents as they appear today. The red line outlines the Pacific Plate.

The world map you see below is familiar. That map will look the same for the rest of your life. But did the world always look this way? What did the world look like 300 million years ago?

Imagine the continents were at one time all joined together. Some of the continents look like they would fit together. For example, North America, South America, and Africa would fit together. If all the continents were attached there would have been a supercontinent. The world would have one large landmass and one large ocean. This supercontinent is called **Pangaea** [Pan-JEE-ah].

Pangaea broke into huge pieces. Each piece drifted across the earth's surface to its present location. The movement of these pieces is called **continental drift.** The way the pieces fit together now makes our current picture of the world.

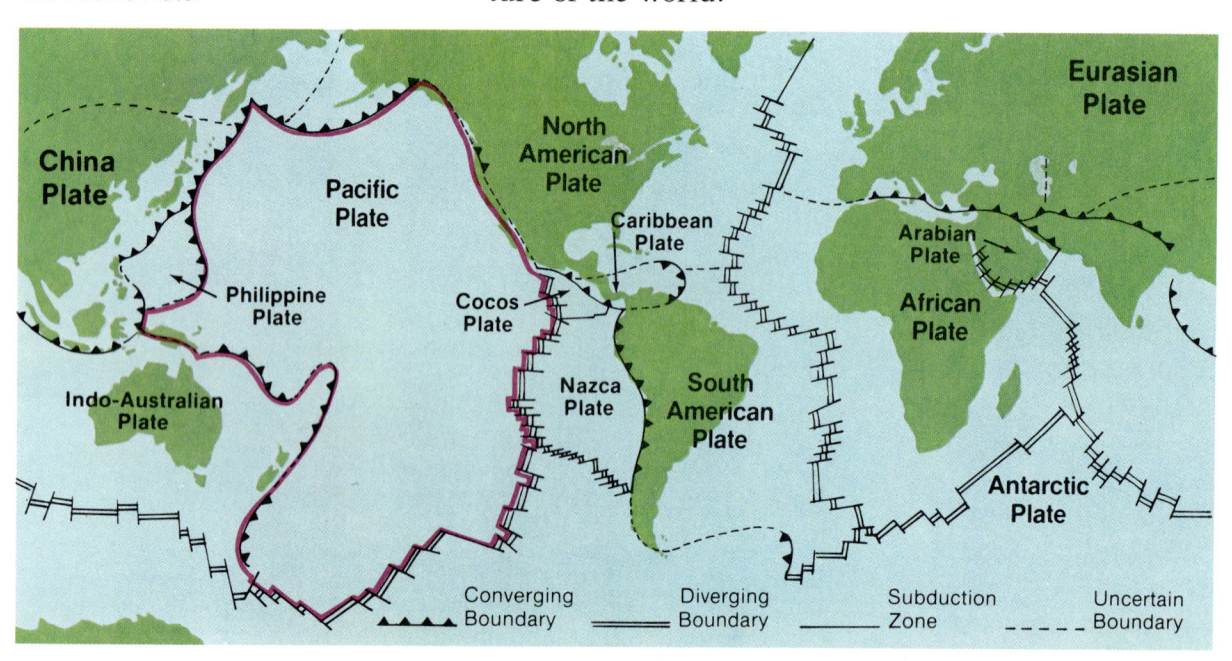

How fast do continents drift? On the average they drift about 5 cm a year. In your lifetime—or about 72 years—some of the continents will have drifted about 360 cm or 3.6 m. The world changes so slowly that most people think of it as unchanging.

Activity

Did These Two Continents Fit Together?

Materials
scissors
plastic tape
colored pencils

Procedure

1. Copy the two map sections. Carefully label and color each section as it appears in the original.

2. Carefully cut out the two continents you have copied.

3. Try to fit the two continents together. Tape them in place.

Questions

1. Do the two continents fit together?

2. Is there a best fit? How do you know?

3. What new information did you use?

4. The age of
rock G is __?__ years old.
rock H is __?__ years old.
rock X is __?__ years old.

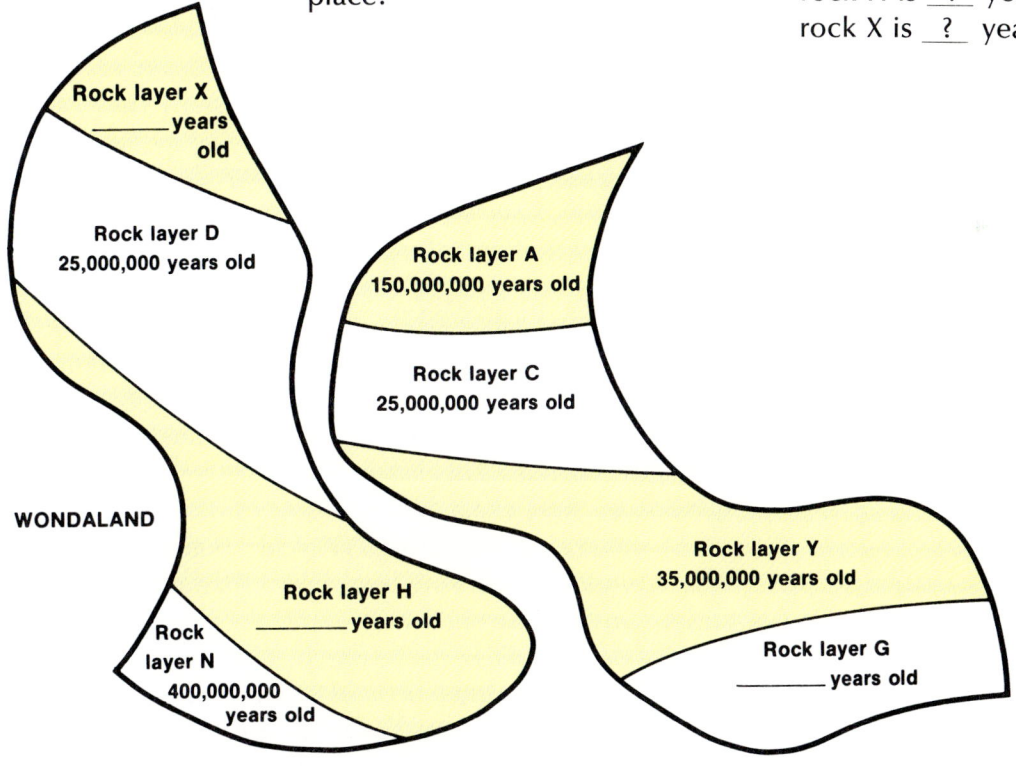

Rock layer X _____ years old

Rock layer D 25,000,000 years old

Rock layer A 150,000,000 years old

Rock layer C 25,000,000 years old

WONDALAND

Rock layer H _____ years old

Rock layer N 400,000,000 years old

Rock layer Y 35,000,000 years old

Rock layer G _____ years old

15 / Plate Tectonics

293

Figure 15.4 *right:* The interaction of moving crustal plates produces a variety of effects at the plate boundaries.

Figure 15.5 *below:* Diverging boundaries lead to the appearance of new crustal material.

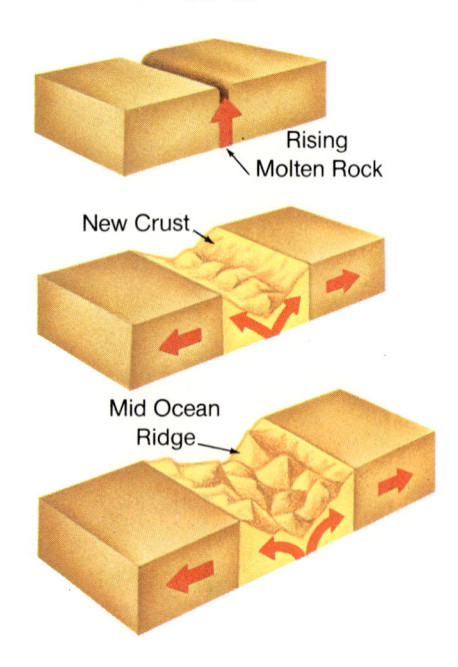

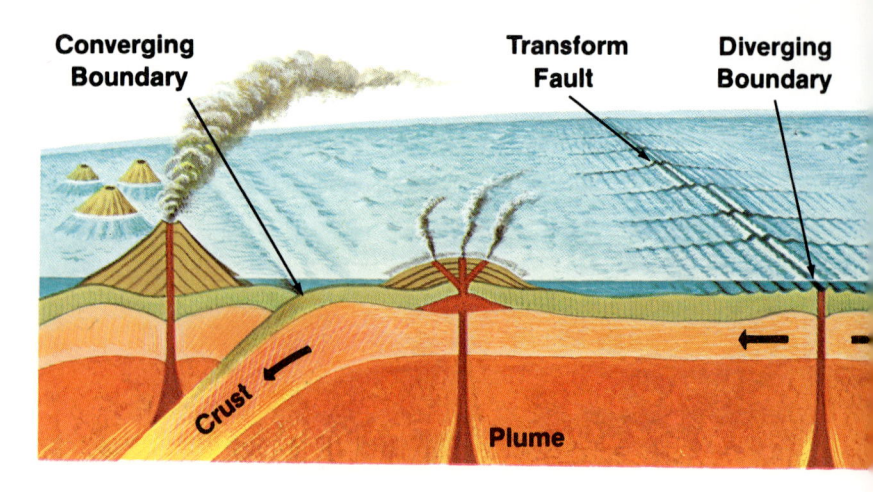

Take another look at the world map. Run your finger along the red line. Notice that your finger traced around a big area—the Pacific Ocean. It is one of the larger pieces of earth's crust that move across the earth's surface. Such big blocks are called **plates.** Plates are rigid sections of the earth's crust. Plates are hundreds or even thousands of kilometers across and about 100 kilometers thick. **Plate tectonics** [tehk-TAHN-ihks] is the model for the study of plate formation, movement, interaction, and destruction.

Plates come together at a **boundary.** Along the boundaries some exciting things happen. For example, earthquakes and volcanoes frequently occur along plate boundaries. There are three types of plate boundaries.

1. **Diverging** [dy-VUHR-jing] **boundaries,** occur between plates that are separating. New molten rock material rising from below forms a mid ocean ridge on the ocean floor. The rock hardens and is pushed outward from the ridge. This movement is called **sea-floor spreading.** New crust forms at the mid ocean ridges.

2. **Converging** [kuhn-VUHR-jing] **boundaries** occur where plates are coming together. When an ocean plate and a continental plate collide, the ocean plate usually buckles downward into the earth. This type of boundary is called a **subduction** [suhb-DUHKT-shuhn] **zone.** Along the boundary there are high mountains, earthquakes, volcanoes, and deep ocean trenches. Deep trenches are found in the oceans at these places where one plate

15 / Plate Tectonics

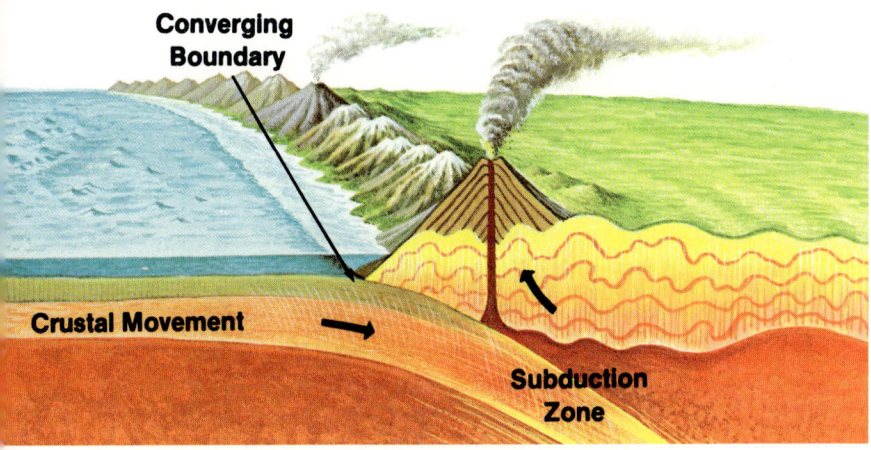

Figure 15.6 *below:* Changes at a transform fault.

is being pushed under another. Crustal material is returned to the earth's interior at boundaries of this type. At other places plates of continental crust may collide with each other. High mountains are formed at this boundary.

3. **Transform fault** boundaries occur where plates slide past each other. Notice how the ocean ridge is offset in Figure 15.6. Many such offsets occur along mid ocean ridges. These offsets are called transform faults.

Can you find each type of plate boundary on the world map? What type of boundary is found along the mid Atlantic Ridge? Along a trench? Along the coast of California? Along the border of India and Asia?

Before learning more about the plot of this incredible detective story, take one more look at the world map. There are six major plates. They are the African Plate, the Eurasian Plate, the American Plates, the Pacific Plate, the Indo–Australian Plate, and the Antarctic Plate. Some of the minor plates are the Philippine Plate, the Cocos Plate, the Nazca Plate, and Caribbean Plate.

Study Questions for 15.1

1. Describe what is meant by a plate in the term *plate tectonics*.
2. Name the types of plate boundaries.
3. Describe the kinds of plate movements along each plate boundary. Give at least one location for each type.

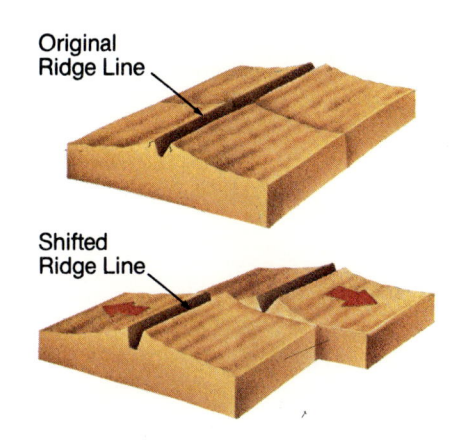

15 / Plate Tectonics

15.2
The Rock Record

You will find out
- how fossils support the theory of plate movements;
- why the age of the ocean floor is important;
- what is meant by magnetic stripes.

Do You Know?
The fossil record shows that India drifted alone about 50 million years.

Figure 15.7 The locations of fossil remains of *Lystrosaurus (top left)* and *Glossopteris (bottom left)* are shown on the world map *(right)*.

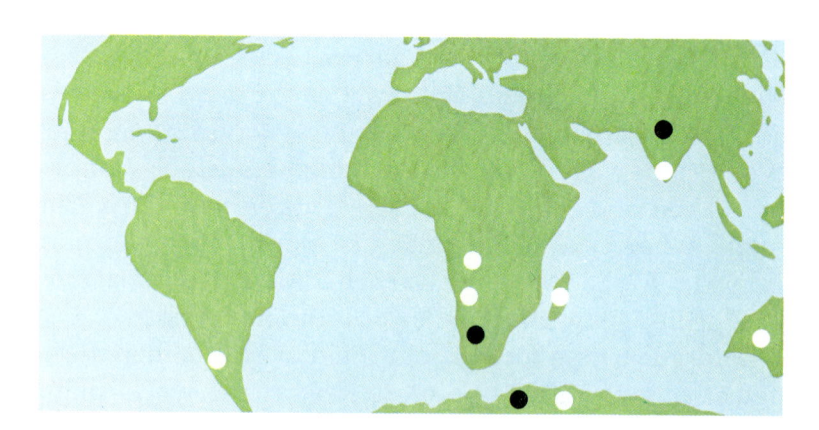

Lystrosaurus

Glossopteris

No one has ever directly measured continental drift. We infer the speed and direction of movement based on information stored in the rocks. Events that have happened to the earth in the past are recorded in the rocks. By studying the record you can infer what has happened. No one can see what the earth looked like 100 million years ago. But scientists can get an idea of what it looked like from the evidence they collect. Although the evidence may be clear, people can interpret the data differently. That is why scientists often disagree with each other.

Both plant and animal **fossils** can be used as supporting evidence for plate tectonics. A fossil is any trace of a plant or animal preserved in rock. Two fossils *Glossopteris* [glahs-SAHP-tur-us] and *Lystrosaurus* [li-struh-SAWR-us], provide strong supporting evidence for plate tectonics. Fossil remains of *Glossopteris*, a plant, are found in rocks that are the same age on five continents and some islands in between. The continents are South America, Africa, Antarctica, India, and Australia. Notice that *Lystrosaurus* is found on the same continents as *Glossopteris* with the exception of Australia and South America.

Do You Know?
Lystrosaurus was a heavily built reptile. It lived on plants and was amphibious. Its size was about 1.2 m.

Isn't that strange? Part of the evidence would require the continents to be together. Another part of the evidence seems to indicate that the continents were not together. You don't have all the evidence you need to prove the incredible story. The fossil evidence is strong, but not conclusive. What can you believe? Perhaps not all the rocks have been looked at.

More evidence for plate tectonics is found in the rock record of the ocean floor. Scientists are studying the age of rocks in areas where sea-floor spreading has occurred. They collect rock samples by drilling into the ocean floor. Then they compare the ages of rock samples taken from different locations.

This procedure has been carried out by the ship *Glomar Challenger*. This ship has a complete research laboratory and drilling rig for collecting rock samples. Some of the results of the research are shown in the graph below.

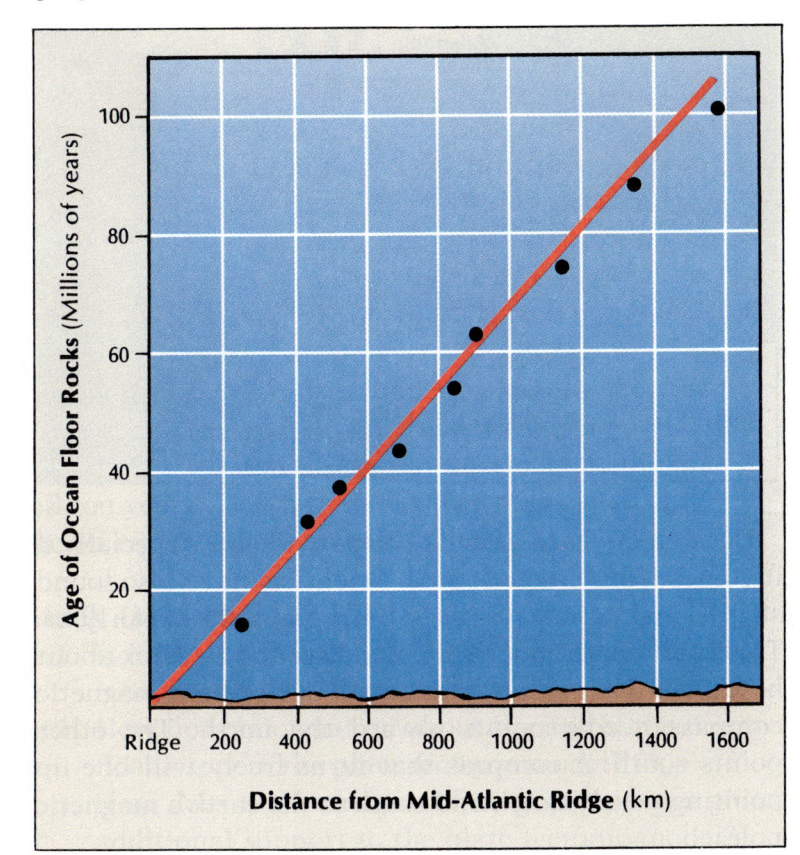

Do You Know?
The *Glomar Challenger* is 120 m long with 10,000 tons displacement. A 43 m high drilling derrick is amidships.

Figure 15.8 *below left:* The farther rocks are from the mid-Atlantic ridge, the older they are. Such evidence supports the model of plate movement.

Figure 15.9 *below:* Out at sea aboard the *Glomar Challenger*

15 / Plate Tectonics

297

15.3 Evidence for Plate Movements

You will find out
- the location of volcanoes and earthquakes is related to plate movements;
- mountain ranges are the result of plate movements;
- how glaciers indicate that plates have drifted apart.

Earthquakes and volcanoes provide additional evidence that directly supports the plate tectonic model. Although volcanoes and earthquakes are two different things, they are sometimes related. For example, the movement of hot, liquid rock underground can cause earthquakes. But most earthquakes have no direct association with volcanoes.

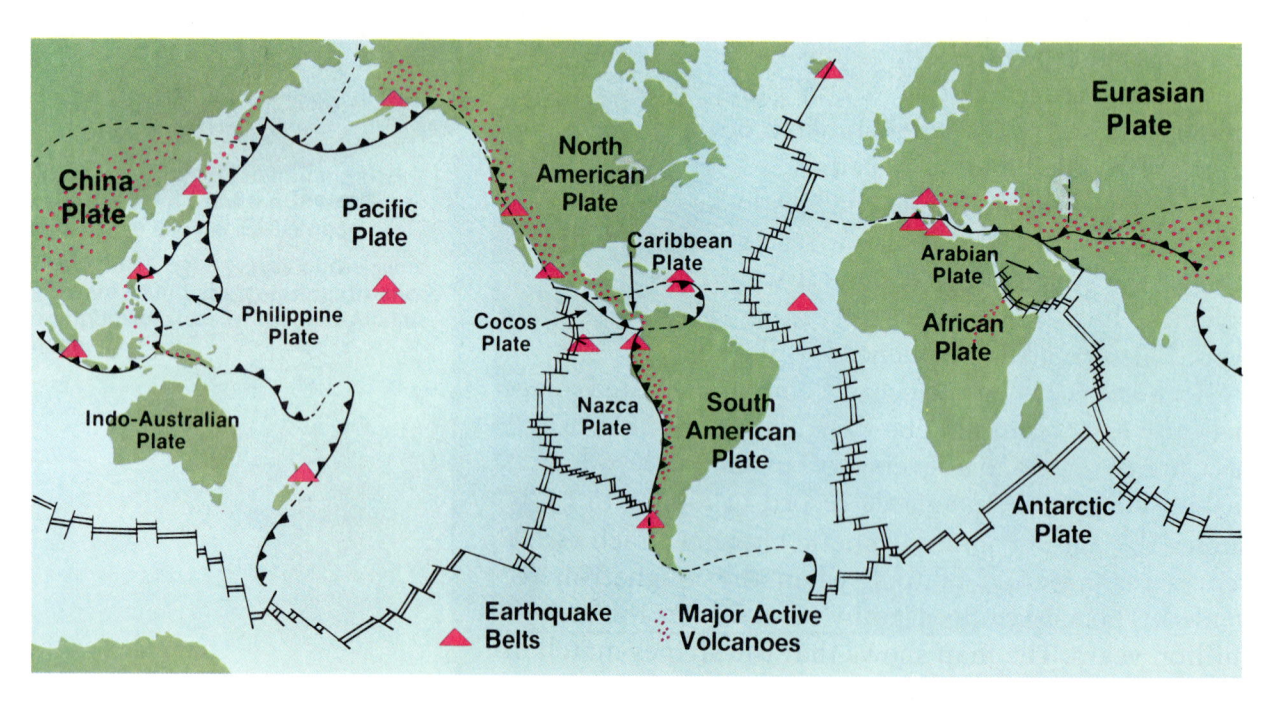

Figure 15.14 Compare areas of frequent earthquake and volcanic activity with the location of major plates.

Volcanoes frequently occur along subduction zones. Since earthquakes also occur with great frequency along plate boundaries, both may be found in nearly the same place at times. But earthquakes along plate boundaries are usually not directly associated with volcanoes. A careful study of the map shows that many earthquakes are found in areas unrelated to volcanic action, such as ocean ridges and transform faults.

In general, volcanoes and earthquakes are located where something is happening in the earth's crust. Volcanic and earthquake activity can release large amounts of energy. The most activity in the crust occurs along boundaries. A careful study of volcanic and earthquake activity then tells where plate boundaries are found. It appears that worldwide geologic activity supports the plate tectonic model.

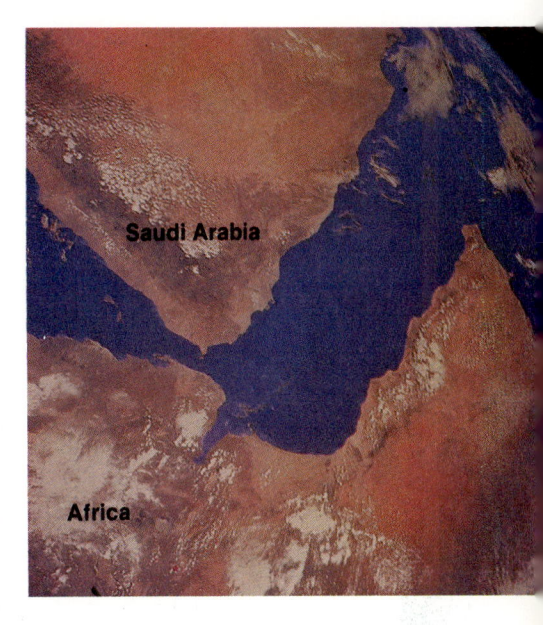

Figure 15.15 *left:* This man is measuring a widening rift at the boundary of the North American and Eurasian plates in Iceland.

Figure 15.16 *above:* A satellite picture of the Arabian peninsula may support the model of plate movement.

15 / Plate Tectonics

301

There is still more worldwide geologic activity supporting plate tectonic theory. Think of the big mountain ranges—the Himalayas, the Rockies, the Alps, the Andes, and the Appalachians. All of these mountain ranges show evidence of being squeezed and pushed into their present shapes. Some parts of the Appalachians now occupy a width of 96 km. If you stretched out these same folded rocks, they would extend to 288 km. What could squeeze the rocks from 288 km down to 96 km wide? Plate collisions are one explanation. The origin of the Appalachian Mountains is explained by the diagrams in Figure 15.18.

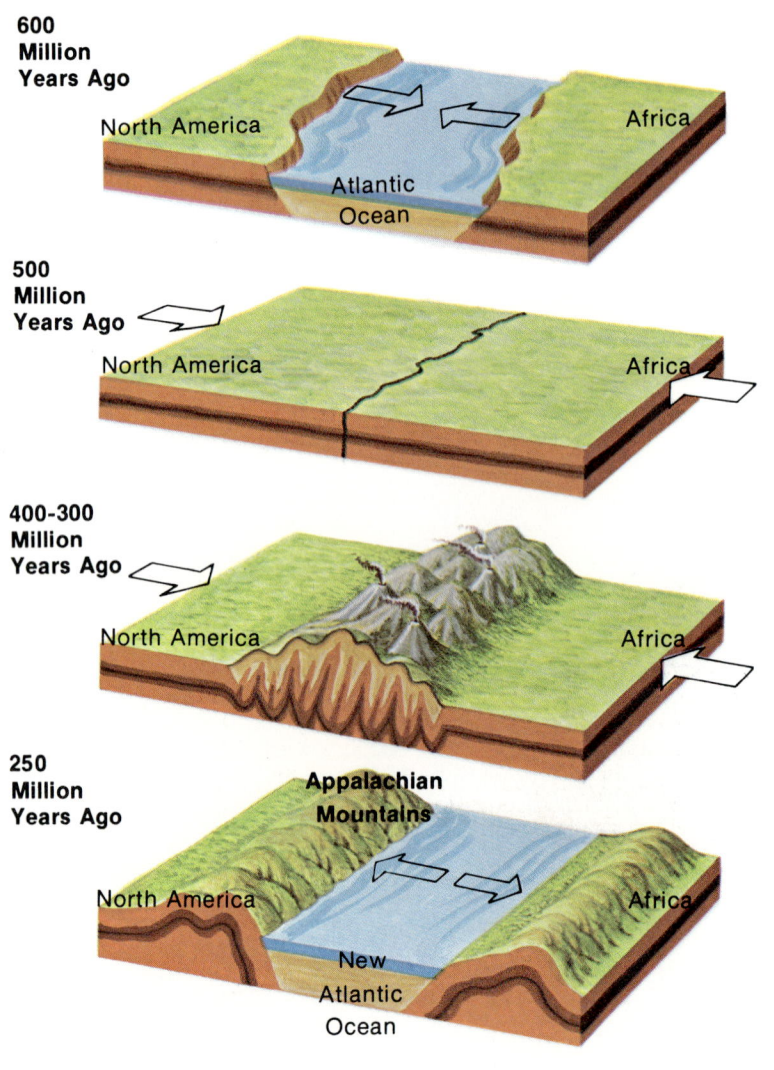

Figure 15.17 *above:* The Blue Ridge Mountains of the Appalachians

Figure 15.18 *right:* The story of the Appalachians is an example of massive folds in the earth's crust being produced by plate collisions.

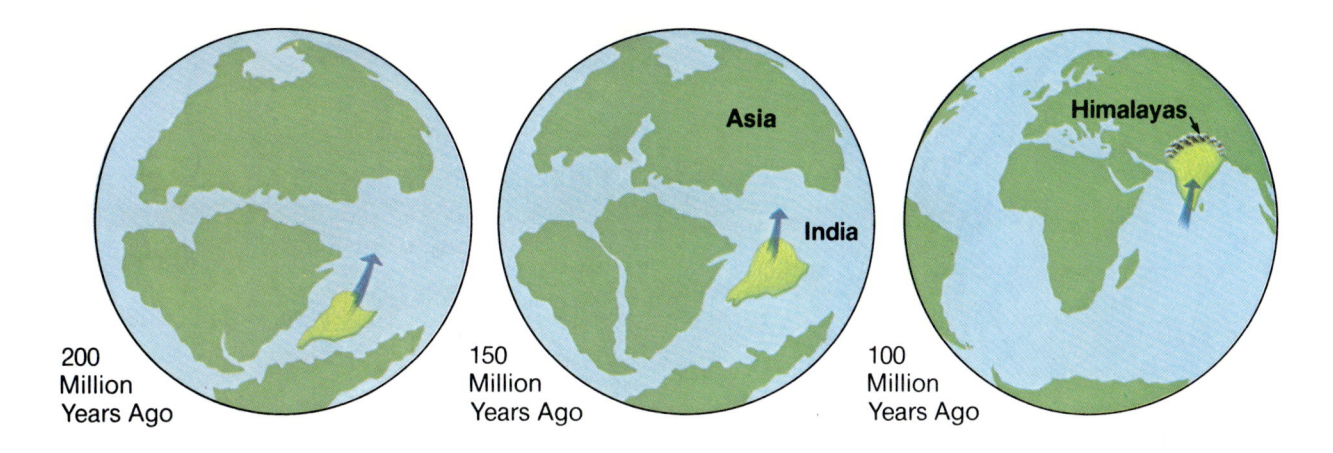

| 200 Million Years Ago | 150 Million Years Ago | 100 Million Years Ago |

In Figure 15.19, you see how the Indian Plate collided with Asia to form the Himalayas. Collisions between plates are thought to be the major cause of the Appalachians, the Himalayas, the Alps, and the Andes. In the case of the Rockies, however, the evidence is not so strong. The Rocky Mountain Range is too complex. Its origin cannot be explained solely by plate boundary collisions.

Figure 15.19 *above:* India is believed to have moved northward, colliding with Asia to produce the Himalayas.

Figure 15.20 The Himalayas are still being forced upward as India continues to push against the Asia Plate.

15 / Plate Tectonics

Activity

What Kind of Plate Boundary Is This?

Material
pencil

Procedure

The chart shows the location and depth of 11 earthquakes that occurred near South America. These earthquakes were selected from thousands in that area. They appear to be on a plate boundary.

1. Make a copy of the graph in your notebook or on a sheet of graph paper.
2. Plot the earthquakes on the graph.
3. Draw a line on the graph that represents the data. This would be a smooth line passing through or near the data points.

Questions

1. Suppose that you had been given 1,000 earthquakes for this area. Where on the graph would they likely plot?
2. These earthquakes lie on a plate boundary. What type of boundary is this one?

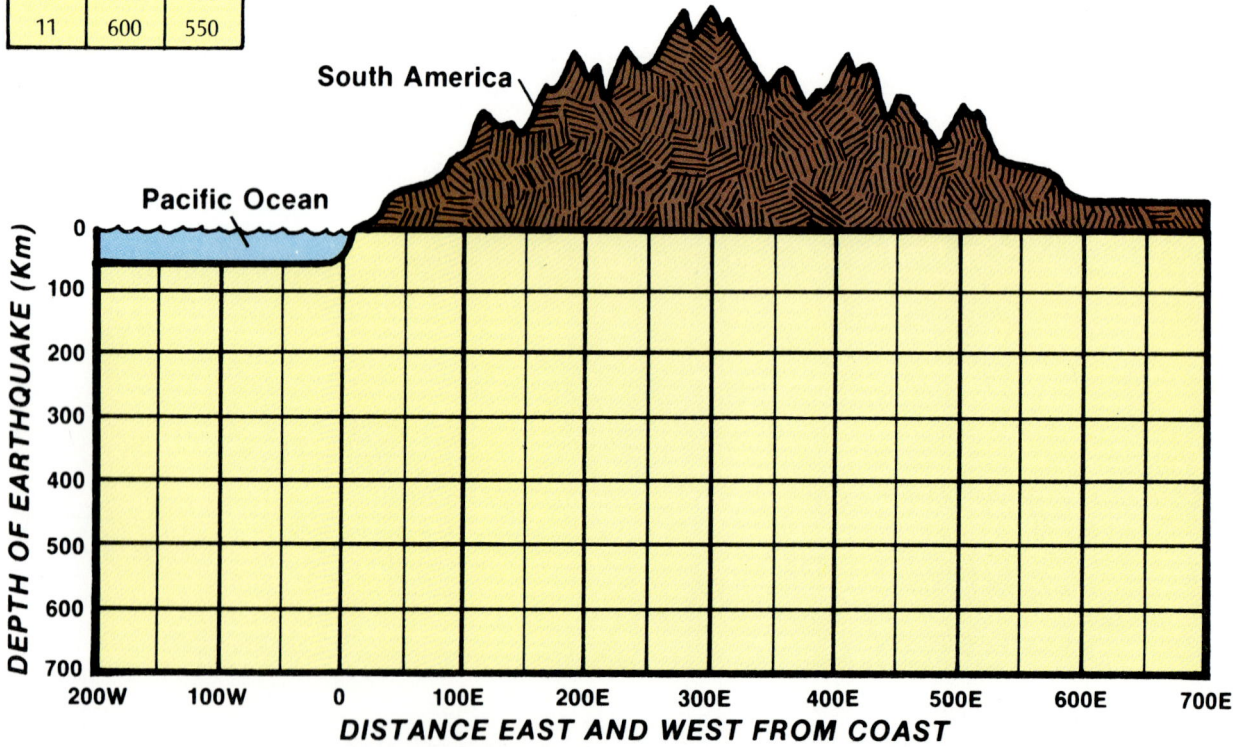

Earthquake Number	Distance East (km)	Depth (km)
1	400	230
2	80	50
3	450	320
4	220	120
5	10	15
6	480	400
7	250	150
8	500	500
9	150	60
10	300	175
11	600	550

15 / Plate Tectonics

There is another bit of evidence supporting continental drift. It is found in the study of the large masses of ice called **glaciers.** In the past, glaciers covered enormous amounts of land area. The glaciers left a clear record of where they had been. A thick glacier scrapes across the rocks as it moves. This makes deep scratches in the rocks. Glaciers also carve deep valleys in the earth. Rocks carried by the glacier are deposited when the glacier melts.

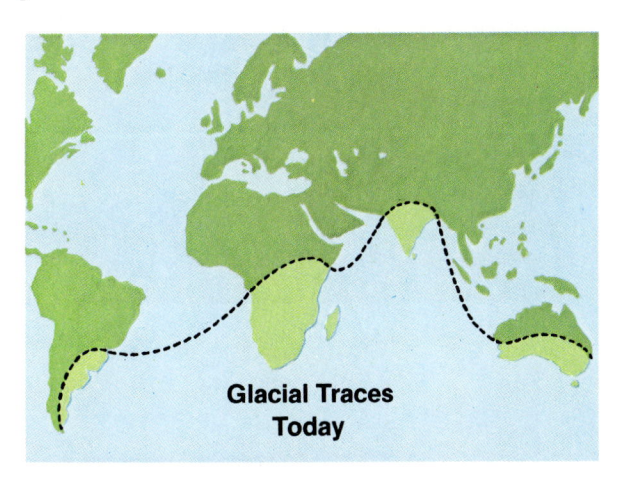

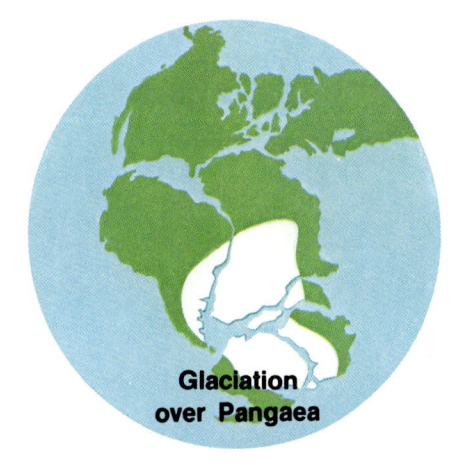

Traces of glaciers in South America, Africa, India, Australia, and Antarctica were found to have a related pattern. These traces were left on the continents about 300 million years ago. Glacial traces that appear to match up have been found on five continents separated by long distances today. Why? Look at the map that shows the glacial covering of Pangaea. Then look at the map that shows the same glaciated regions, but as they are today. Are there any other explanations for such worldwide glaciation than continental drift?

Figure 15.21 Glacial traces found on the continents today provide some evidence that the continents were connected in the past.

Study Questions for 15.3

1. Along which kind of plate boundaries are volcanoes and earthquakes generally found?
2. Name four mountain ranges whose origin may be related to plate movements.
3. A glacier covered part of Pangaea. Which continents did the glacier partially cover?

15 / Plate Tectonics

15.4 Unanswered Questions

You will find out
- three reasons for questioning the plate tectonic model.

Not everyone accepts the model for plate tectonics. What are some of the observations people have made that cause them to doubt? First, there is no known mechanism within the earth to make the plates move. Many ideas have been proposed, but all seem to need additional supporting information. Look carefully at Figure 15.22 as you consider this problem.

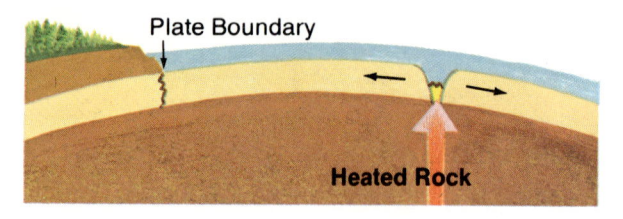

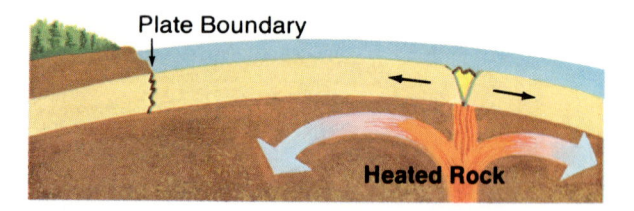

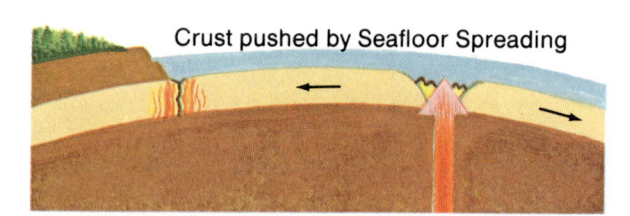

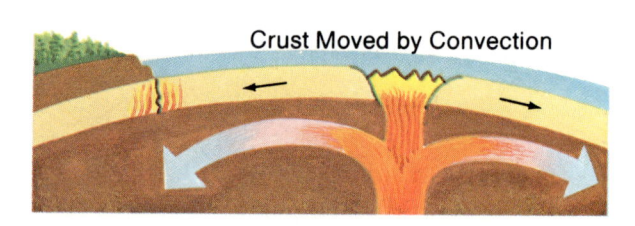

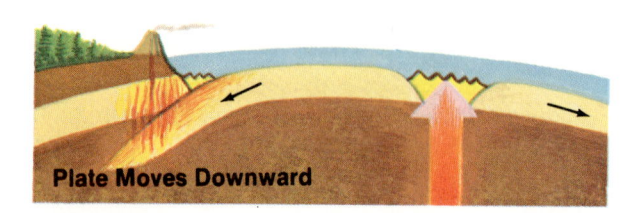

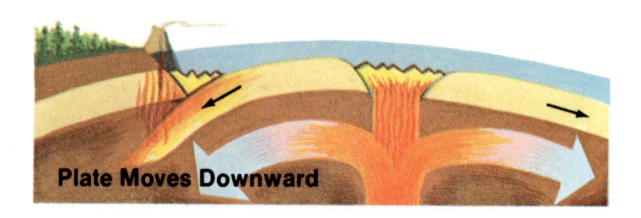

Figure 15.22 *left:* Are crustal plates pushed sideways by pressure from heated rocks that are rising to the surface and spreading? *right:* Do crustal plates move by floating on the convection currents of moving, heated rocks? Neither model explains why the plates move downward at their other boundaries.

Scientists think they have found evidence that heated rocks rise up in the sea-floor ridge. This heated rock may push sideways on the crustal plates. But that still leaves the question of why a plate would move downward under another plate. Another theory holds that the heated rock moves in a convection current. But even if the crustal plates floated along on the current, again, what moves them down? As yet there is no satisfactory explanation for this motion.

15 / Plate Tectonics

Second, what causes earthquakes to occur in the middle of a plate? The greatest earthquakes to hit the United States occurred near New Madrid, Missouri, in 1811 and 1812. New Madrid is near the center of a plate. If earthquakes occur because of moving plates, what causes earthquakes in the interior of a continent?

Third, some people believe that the Hawaiian Islands are formed over a **plume**. A plume is a localized hot spot of material rising from the earth's interior. Figure 15.24 shows how a plume might have formed the Hawaiian Islands. But is there another answer? For example, what happens if you have a stationary crust and a moving plume?

There are some good reasons to support the plate tectonic model. There are also good reasons to question the model. Think about the things that the model doesn't explain. Could it be that the continents don't drift? Further discoveries and study will be needed to answer this question fully.

Figure 15.23 *above:* New Madrid is nowhere near a plate boundary.

Figure 15.24 Some scientists wonder whether the crust moves over a plume (*left*) or a plume moves beneath the crust (*right*).

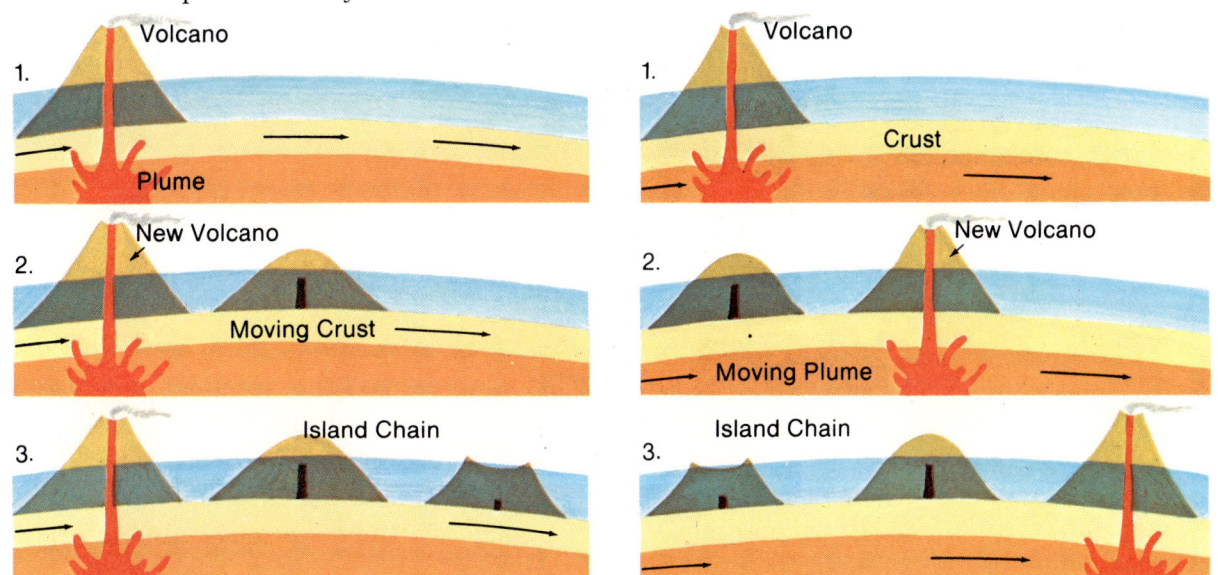

Study Questions for 15.4

1. List three reasons to question the plate tectonic model.
2. Which of the three reasons do you think raises the strongest arguments against the plate tectonic model? Explain your answer.

Science and Technology

Seismic Reflection Profiling

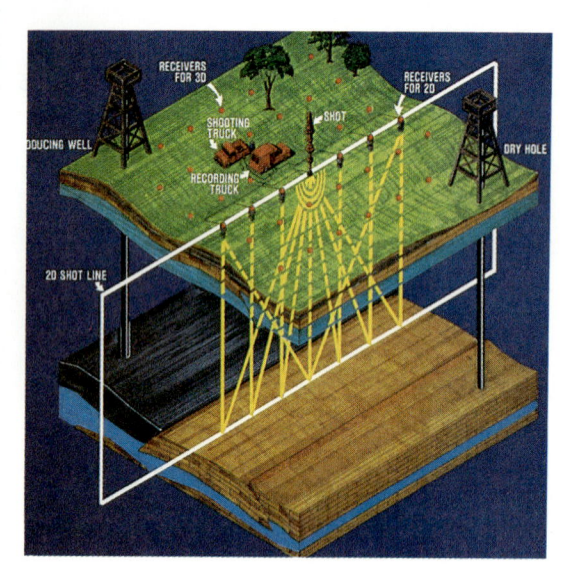

When someone draws your profile, the result is a side view of your head. Geologists draw profiles too. Their profiles, however, are often side views of rock layers. Sometimes the rock layers can't be viewed directly. If the rock layers to be profiled are hidden deep underground, special methods are needed to make the drawing. One method is called seismic reflection profiling. This method was first used by oil companies searching for oil. Now it is used to study the rock layers deep within the crust of the continents. Geologists are using these profiles to add to our understanding of plate tectonics.

Before seismic reflection profiling can be done, an area must be found away from superhighways, railroads, or other structures that might cause the ground to vibrate. Then several of specially designed trucks are parked, one behind the other, at about 13-meter intervals. The number of trucks used is usually about five. Each truck contains a device that can vibrate at several speeds. A platform is lowered under each truck. Its purpose is both to jack up the truck and to give the vibrator a solid contact with the ground surface. Then the vibrators are started up. They make small, earthquakelike waves that travel into the rocks beneath the trucks. As these waves strike different rock layers, they are reflected back to the surface. There, many small seismographs record the reflections. Later, a computer studies the seismograph records and draws the profile.

One area that has been studied using seismic reflection is the southern Appalachian Mountains. You learned in this chapter that the Appalachians are folded mountains that formed about 300 million years ago when North America and Africa collided to form Pangaea. To the surprise of almost all geologists, the profiles showed flat-lying rocks beneath the folded rocks of the mountains. The geologists concluded that the plate collision had pushed a thin sheet of folded rock over the flat-lying rocks.

CHAPTER REVIEW

Main Ideas

- The earth's crust consists of large pieces called plates that are moving across the earth's surface.
- The area between plates is called a plate boundary. There are three types of plate boundaries—diverging, converging, and transform fault.
- Diverging boundaries occur where plates are moving apart.
- Converging boundaries occur where plates are coming together.
- Transform fault boundaries occur where plates slide past each other.
- Fossil remains on five continents support the plate tectonic model.
- The age of the ocean floor is older as you move away from the sides of a mid-ocean ridge.
- Magnetic stripes are rock records of the earth's magnetic field.
- Volcanoes occur frequently at converging plate boundaries. Earthquakes occur frequently at all plate boundaries.
- Mountain ranges show evidence of having formed as a result of plate collisions.
- Traces of glaciers on five now separate continents support the plate tectonic model.
- Not all the geologic evidence supports the plate tectonic model.

Using Vocabulary

On a separate piece of paper, write a sentence for each of the words below. Each sentence should give a *clue* as to the meaning of the word.

Pangaea
continental drift
plates
plate tectonics
boundary
diverging boundary
sea-floor spreading

converging boundary
subduction zone
transform fault
fossil
magnetic reversal
glacier
plume

Remembering Facts

On your paper, write the word or words that best complete each sentence.
1. Plates move away from each other at a _____ boundary.
2. The movement of huge pieces of Pangaea to their present location is called _____ .
3. A _____ is a localized, hot spot of material rising from the earth's interior.
4. Plates come together at a _____ boundary.
5. The original supercontinent when all of the continents were attached is called _____ .
6. Both plant and animal _____ can be used as evidence to support the plate tectonic model.
7. The area between two plates is called a _____ .
8. High mountains, earthquakes, volcanoes, and deep ocean trenches occur along a _____ zone.
9. Plates slide past each other at _____ boundaries.
10. Traces of _____ on five continents separated by long distances today appear to match.
11. New crust forms on the ocean floor as a result of _____ .
12. The magnetism of the earth's magnetic poles trades places when there is a _____ .
13. Big blocks of crust that move across the earth's surface are called _____ .
14. The model that describes the movement of plates across the earth's surface is called _____ _____ .
15. A _____ might have formed the Hawaiian Islands.
16. Sea-floor spreading occurs at _____ plate boundaries.

Understanding Ideas

On your paper, answer each question in complete sentences.
1. Describe at least five reasons that support the existence of Pangaea.
2. What is the most important thing that is yet to be explained in the plate tectonic model?
3. How do the locations of earthquakes and volcanoes support plate tectonics?
4. What kind of plate movement causes volcanoes like Mount St. Helens to form?

Applying What You Have Learned

1. According to Figure 15.8, how far has a rock moved from the mid-Atlantic Ridge if it is 60 million years old?
2. How far apart will the continents drift in 50 years according to the average rate of drift?
3. Suppose you were to find fossils of seashells along a mountain ridge. How could you explain your finding in terms of the plate tectonic model?

Challenge

A plume is a spot where a slender column of hot rock rises continuously from deep inside the mantle. Volcanoes and earthquakes are produced when a plume reaches the surface. This can occur far away from a plate boundary.

Satellite measurements show that the earth's crust bulges above a plume. Chemical studies show that the material inside a plume comes from deep within the earth. Further analysis has shown that this material contains radioactive decay products. This evidence seems to suggest that plumes are stationary. As a crustal plate moves over a plume, a trail of identifiable features is left. Look at the map of plume trails and answer the following questions.

1. What do you think causes a plume to form? Explain.
2. In what direction has North America moved in the last 50 million years? Explain.
3. In what direction have Africa and South America been moving since they separated from Pangaea?

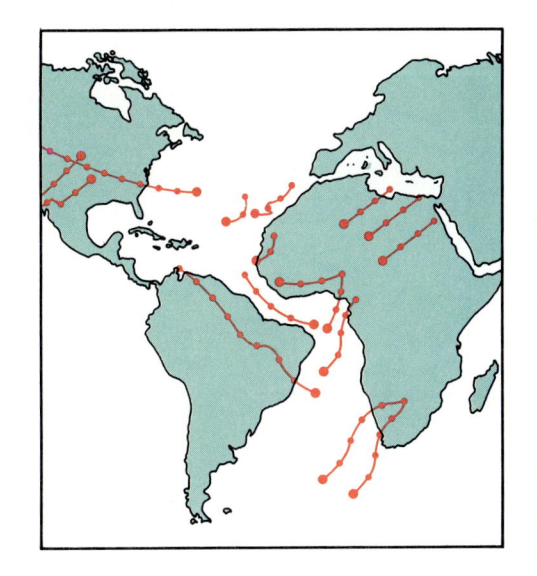

Research and Investigation

1. Design a 10-item questionnaire about plate tectonics. Use this questionnaire to survey how much the students in your school know about this subject. Then write an article for the school paper on the model of plate tectonics and the results of your questionnaire.
2. Select one of the following people and write a paper describing what contribution that person made to the theory of plate tectonics: H. Benioff, Robert Dietz, H. Hess, D. Matthews, F. Vine, Alfred Wegener.

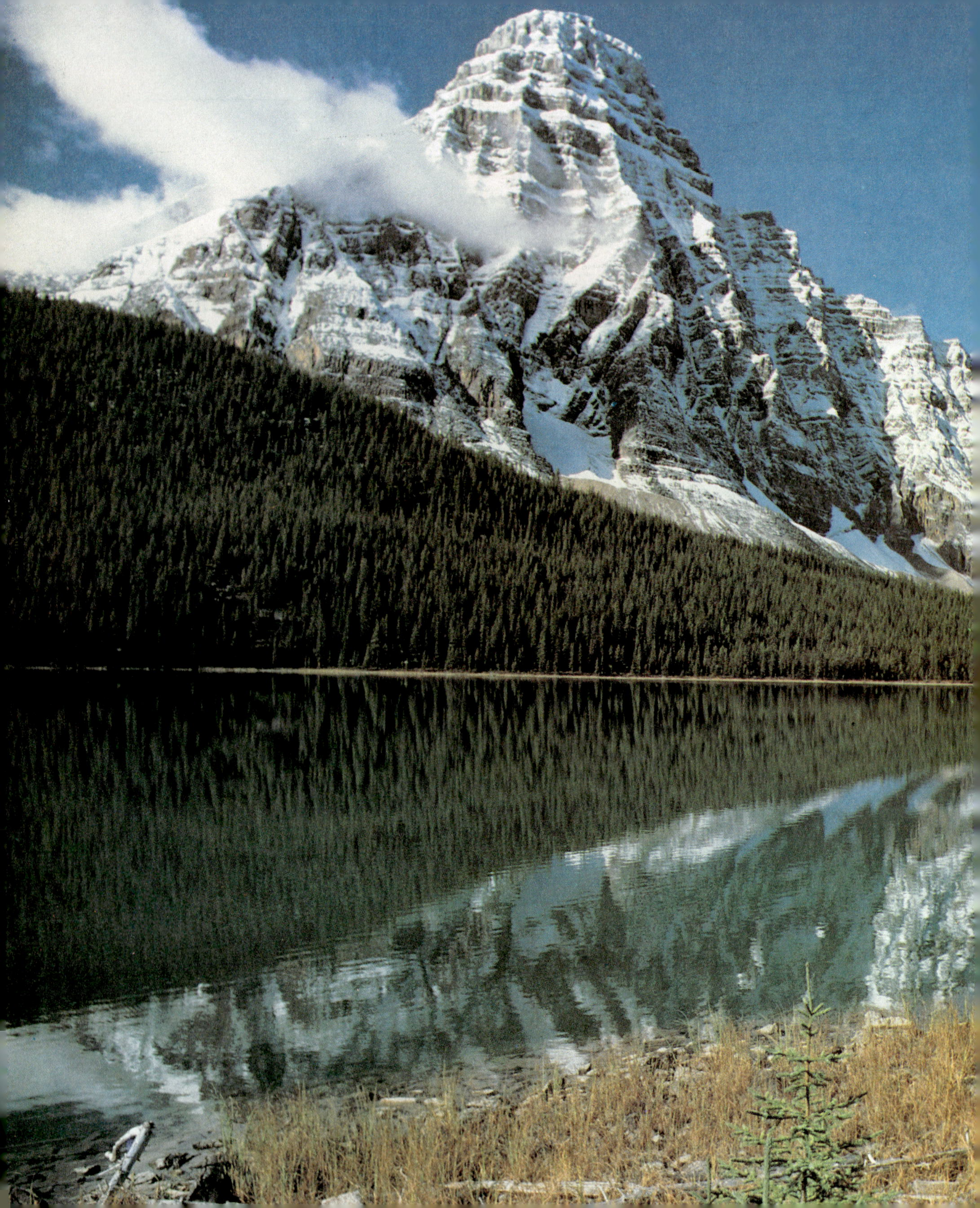

Chapter 16
Mountains and Crustal Movement

Lesson Titles
16.1 Folding and Faulting
16.2 Volcanic Mountains
16.3 Other Mountain-Forming Processes
16.4 The Distribution of Mountain Ranges

You live on an earth that is constantly changing. This remarkable mountain scene may have been the bottom of a seafloor eons ago. It could have been a mountain twice as high as the one you see in the picture. How does the hard, rocky crust of the earth move up and down? Why are some mountains so high? Why are they where they are? What do geologists know about mountain building?

This chapter is about the types of mountains found on the earth and the processes that formed them. Mountains vary in size and shape. In Chapter 15 you learned that there is a relationship between mountains and movement in the earth's crust. But how are mountains formed and how long does it take to make them?

Answers to questions like these are the focus of this chapter. You'll find that learning to recognize clues to mountain building is an exciting challenge.

Figure 16.1 *opposite:* A part of the Canadian Rockies in Banff National Park, Alberta

16.1 Folding and Faulting

You will find out
- what a mountain is;
- how to identify two kinds of folds;
- what a fault is;
- how to identify different types of faults.

A **mountain** is any part of the earth's surface that stands much higher than its surroundings. The highest mountain in North America, Mount McKinley in Alaska, is more than 6,100 m high. Pikes Peak is one of 14 peaks in Colorado that are more than 4,300 m high. Mount Whitney in California, the tallest mountain in the continental United States, is 4,418 m high.

Geologists find that most of the highest places on the earth are igneous or metamorphic rocks. You may have read in Chapter 13 that granite is a rock that cools slowly deep in the earth. If that is so, then these mountaintops must have once been deep in the earth's crust. Even if the highest rocks are sedimentary, they too started far below the place where they are now found. Sedimentary rocks form in the bottom of a sea. What could cause rocks from deep inside the earth or below the sea to be moved to such high places? **Folding** is one way mountains are produced. The easiest folds to recognize are those found in sedimentary rocks. Since these rocks are usually laid down as flat layers, any bending appears as a fold. Two easily spotted kinds of folds are **anticlines** [AN-tih-klyns] and **synclines** [SIN-klyns]. An anticline forms when the layers of rocks are bent upward into an arch. A syncline occurs when the layers of rocks are bent downward to form a trough. Both of these kinds of folds are shown in Figure 16.3. Whenever rocks are folded, the earth's crust is squeezed together or shortened.

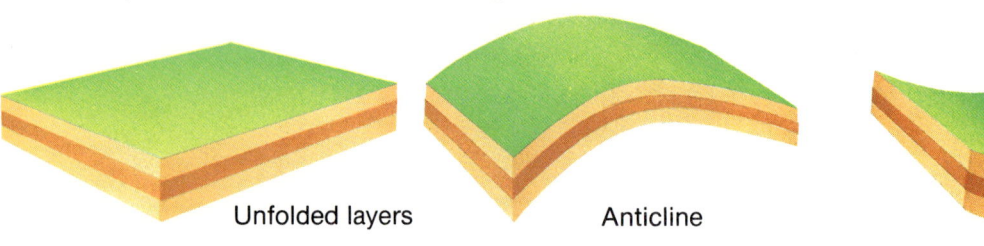

Figure 16.2 Mount McKinley

Figure 16.3 Types of folding found in sedimentary rock

Unfolded layers   Anticline   Syncline

16 / Mountains and Crustal Movement

You can't fold a hard, brittle rock. But if the rock was flexible, somewhat like warm wax, it could be bent. Where would you find such rocks? The answer is deep in the earth's crust. Here high pressure and temperature turn rock into a flexible state. This occurs over a long period of time. If the rock is squeezed, it folds and wrinkles like a piece of cloth.

Folds are easily seen from a cross-sectional view. A cross-sectional view is like cutting a cake and looking at the cut side to count the layers. If you looked down on a fold, you might see a striped pattern of rock layers as shown in Figure 16.5B. If the fold is tilted and dips into the earth, you might see a curved pattern of rock layers on the surface as shown in Figure 16.5C. The zigzag ridges found in Pennsylvania are caused by folds that have been tilted like this.

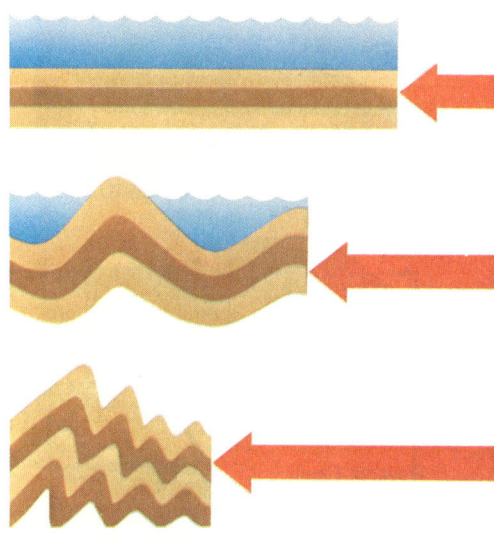

Figure 16.4 *above:* The arrows show how pressure may force rocks to fold.

Figure 16.5 *top left:* This cross section of a fold shows an anticline and a syncline. *bottom left:* The exposed layers of a tilted fold. *bottom right:* An aerial photo shows the erosion of tilted layers in Pennsylvania. The dotted lines show zigzag ridges caused by this erosion.

Do You Know?
In anticlines the oldest rocks are found in the center of the fold. In synclines the youngest rocks are found in the center of the fold.

16 / Mountains and Crustal Movement

315

16.2 Volcanic Mountains

You will find out
- how volcanic mountains are made;
- what features can be found in volcanic areas.

There is a great deal of heat and pressure along plate boundaries. Often the heat and pressure are so great that pockets of rock are melted. This liquid rock deep within the earth is called magma.

At subduction zones, the heat and pressure force magma upward through cracks in the earth's crust. In some locations, magma bursts through the earth's crust with a cloud of gases and ash. This opening in the earth's crust that allows magma, gases, and ash to escape is called a **volcano.**

Magma that reaches the earth's surface is called lava. Sometimes lava pours onto the earth's surface like a glowing river. At others it explodes onto the surface with a huge cloud of ash. When lava cools, it hardens to form igneous rock. In time, as layers of rock and ash pile up, a volcanic mountain is formed.

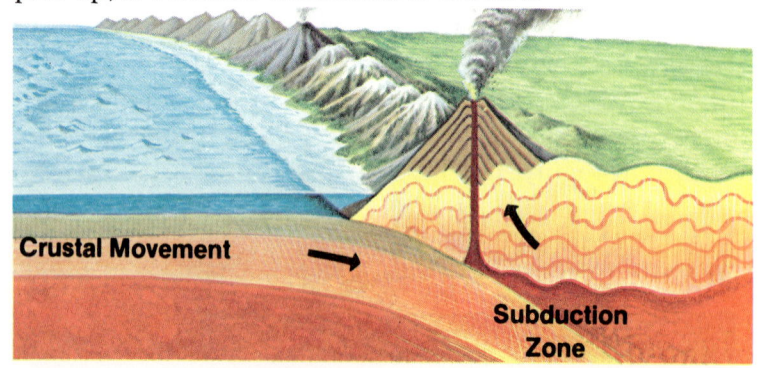

Figure 16.10 *above:* Mount St. Helens
Figure 16.11 *right:* The formation of a volcano at a subduction zone.

Mount St. Helens is a volcanic mountain located in the state of Washington. It erupted in 1800 after remaining quiet for 150 years. It erupted on and off for about 55 years, and then remained quiet until 1980.

On May 18, 1980, Mount St. Helens erupted again. About 4 cubic km of rock and ash were hurled as high as 20 km into the air. Trees were flattened within a fan-shaped area 12.8 km long and 24 km wide. This was followed in 1982 with a great avalanche of mud.

Mount St. Helens is one of a series of volcanoes extending from California to Canada that are located over a subduction zone. The volcanoes in this region have a record of long calm periods followed by short periods of eruptions.

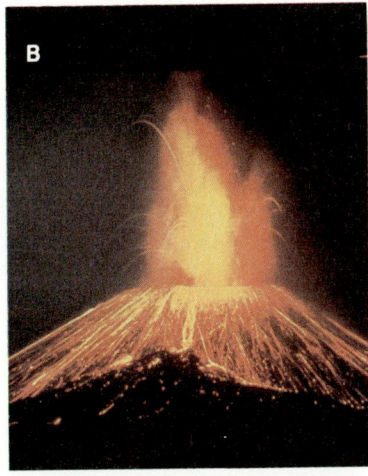

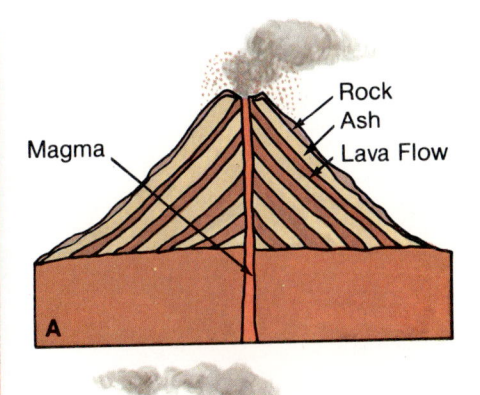

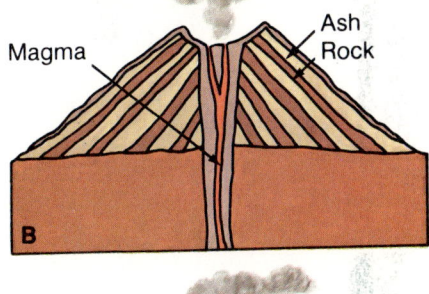

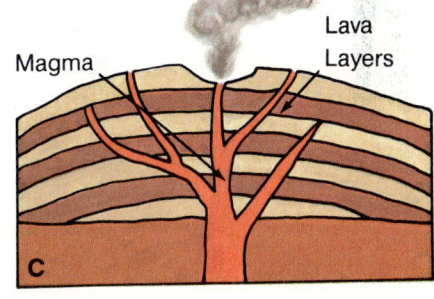

Figure 16.12 shows three basic types of volcanoes. **Composite** or **stratovolcanoes** are built up from a combination of lava, solid rock, and ash. Mount St. Helens is a stratovolcano. **Cinder cones** are built of rock and ash. Parícutin in Mexico is a cinder cone. **Shield volcanoes** are built by a series of lava flows which pile one on top of another. The best known shield volcanoes are the Hawaiian Islands.

Figure 16.12 Photographs of (A) Mount St. Helens, a stratovolcano; (B) Parícutin, a cinder cone; and (C) Mauna Kea, a shield volcano. Matching diagrams show the structure of each type of volcano.

16 / Mountains and Crustal Movement

Figure 16.13 *left:* The formation of a lava flow; *right:* The lava field of the west wall of Grand Coulee Valley, Washington

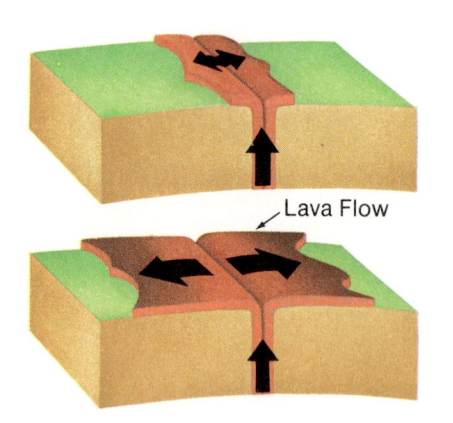

There is still another kind of volcanic activity. In eastern Washington, Oregon, and southern Idaho, geologists have found evidence of multiple lava flows. The accumulated lava is as much as 2 km thick, but there is no volcanic mountain. These flows came from huge cracks in the earth's crust. The flows cover an enormous area of at least 51,000 square km in size.

Activity

What Volcanic Eruption Was the Greatest?

Materials
pencil
graph paper

Procedure
1. Make a bar graph of the data in the table.
2. Label the vertical axis *Amount of Ejected Material*.
3. Label the horizontal axis *Date and Volcano*.
4. Enter data on the graph.

Questions
1. Which volcano ejected the greatest amount of material?
2. What is the total amount of material ejected from Mount St. Helens?
3. How does the total amount of ejected material from Mount St. Helens compare with that from Tambora?

Table

Volcano	Dates of Eruptions	Amount of Material Ejected (cubic kilometers)
Mazama	4600BC	40
St. Helens	1900BC	3.3
Vesuvius	79AD	2.7
Hekla	1104AD	2.0
Fuji	1500AD	1.3
St. Helens	1707AD	0.9
Tambora	1815AD	80.0
Krakatoa	1883AD	20.0
Pele	1902AD	0.3
Katami	1912AD	30.0
St. Helens	1980AD	4.0

What of the magma inside the earth that doesn't come to the surface? Look at Figure 16.14 and follow the movement of magma from deep in the earth.

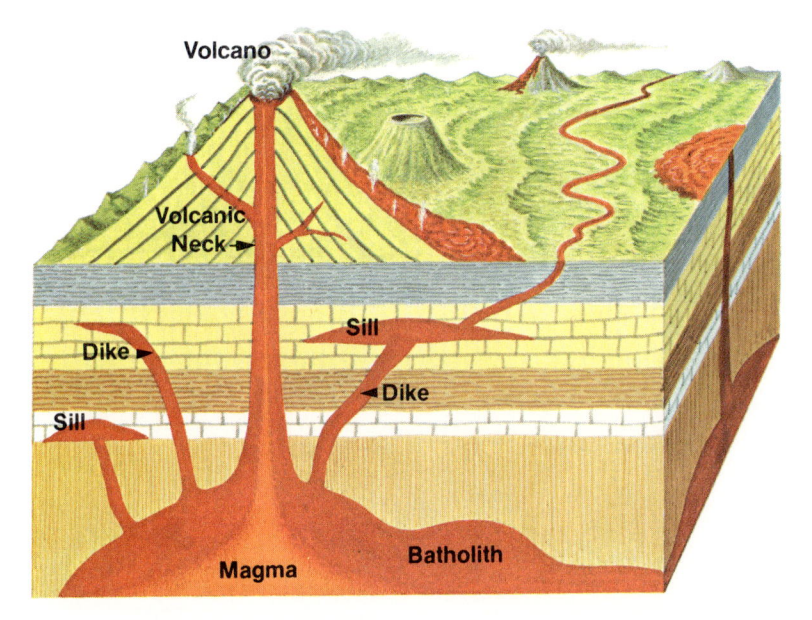

Figure 16.14 *left:* Magma formations beneath the earth's surface

Figure 16.15 *below:* The volcanic neck of Ship Rock is all that remains of a onetime volcano.

Deep in the earth the magma may lie in a huge pocket. These huge pockets of magma may cool and harden, forming a huge mass of rock called a **batholith** [BATH-uh-lith]. The magma may also force its way upward cutting through overlying layers of rock. The magma that cools and hardens in these vertical cracks forms **dikes.** Magma that spreads out in horizontal cracks between rock layers and cools and hardens forms **sills.** These features cannot be seen until erosion later exposes them to view. Sometimes a volcanic cone is completely removed by erosion, leaving a mass of igneous rock that hardened inside the mountain. This feature is called a **volcanic neck.** Ship Rock in New Mexico is a near-perfect example of a volcanic neck.

Study Questions for 16.2

1. What is a volcano and name the three types of volcanic mountains.
2. What features may be produced by magma inside the earth?

16 / Mountains and Crustal Movement

321

16.3
Other Mountain-Forming Processes

You will find out
- what processes form fault-block mountains;
- how complex mountains are formed;
- how the Rocky Mountains were formed.

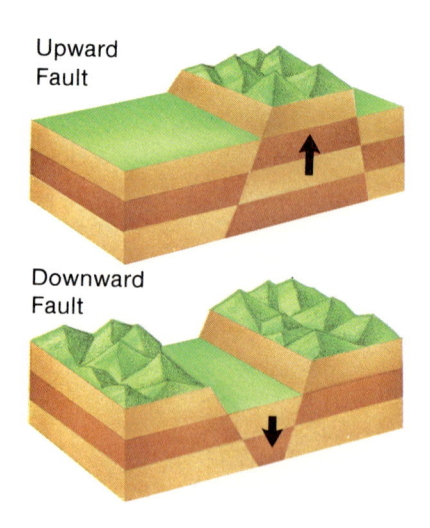

Figure 16.16 *left:* Fault-block mountains may result when land is uplifted or when land sinks. *right:* Frenchman Mountain in Nevada

Upward Fault

Downward Fault

Do You Know?
The fault-block mountains in Nevada have no streams running through them.

If the formation of all mountains is related one way or another to movements of plates in the earth's crust, what about mountains that are not located near plate boundaries? This is a puzzling question because the internal processes that make mountains are not well understood.

An example of mountains that do not appear to be related to a plate boundary is the **fault-block mountains** in Nevada. A fault-block mountain is a landmass noticeably higher than its surroundings and bounded by one or more faults. You can see a photograph of a fault-block mountain in Figure 16.16. The faults aren't visible, but they're there alongside the blocks. Some movement of magma and hot gases from the earth's interior is also associated with the fault-block mountains in Nevada.

Geologists believe that this region of the plate, although not on a boundary, was once over an enormous plume, or hot spot. Heat coming from the interior of the earth warmed the crust under a large area. This caused

322

16 / **Mountains and Crustal Movement**

the crust to bulge upward. As the uplifting continued, it cracked the crust. Volcanic rocks on the surface indicate there was some volcanic activity. Later the volcanic activity decreased. The area gradually cooled off when it moved from the hot spot or when the hot spot became inactive. Cooling rocks shrink in size. The uplifted land then slowly collapsed and broke into many blocks. The blocks settled at angles to each other, sliding along normal faults.

Figure 16.17 How fault-block mountains develop

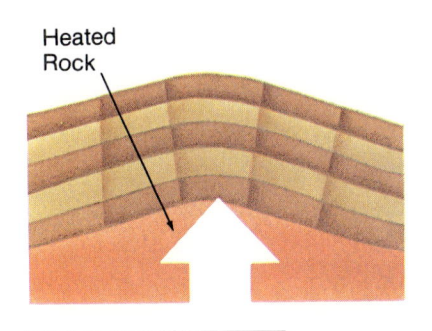

Activity

How Are Fault-Block Mountains Formed?

Materials
a piece of file folder
ruler
plastic tape
colored pencils
scissors

Procedure

1. Copy the pattern of faults and rock layers shown onto the piece of file folder.
2. Cut along the faults.
3. Make a normal faulting of about 2 cm along fault number 1. Make normal faulting of 2 cm along the other faults.
4. Now tape your model together.

Questions

1. Which of the blocks are mountains?
2. How would you describe a highway built across this area?
3. Why is *fault-block mountains* a good name for land that is shaped this way?

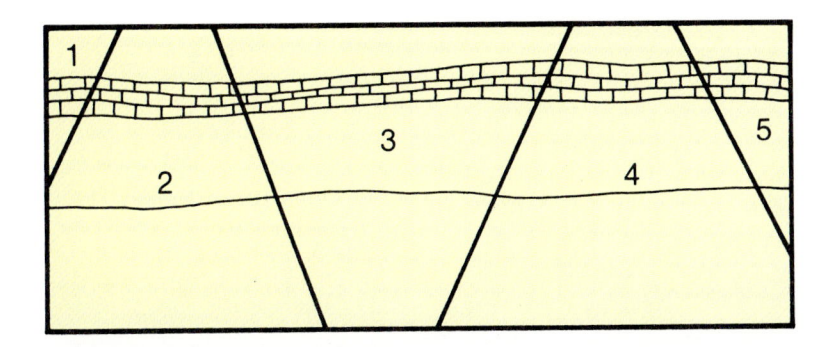

16 / Mountains and Crustal Movement

Geologists also recognize that a combination of building processes sometimes occurs. You can see evidence of this in the Appalachians, the Alps, and the Himalayas. For example, they each have long narrow zones of folded sedimentary rock alongside a region of metamorphic and igneous rocks. Mountain ranges that have this kind of structure were formed by a combination of mountain-building processes. These mountains are called **folded** or **complex mountains.**

What on earth would cause all this folding, faulting, and igneous activity? Remember that all mountains are related to crustal plate movements. Folded or complex mountains occur along boundaries where plates are moving toward each other. Figure 15.18 shows the model that explains the formation of folded or complex mountains. Notice that in this model the plates collide and press on each other. Slowly over time the crust folds and faults. In some cases such as the Appalachians there has been more than one collision.

The Rocky Mountains in western United States are different from any other mountain region of North America. The Rockies did not form along a plate boundary either. They occupy a region located between stable continental crust on the east and a less stable crust on the west. The Rockies are long, extending more than 4,800 km from Mexico through the United States into Canada. This region has a long history of mountain building. It is believed that several different processes, as shown in Figure 16.19, contributed to the formation of today's Rockies.

Figure 16.18 The Colorado Rockies

1. Ancestral Rocky Mountains

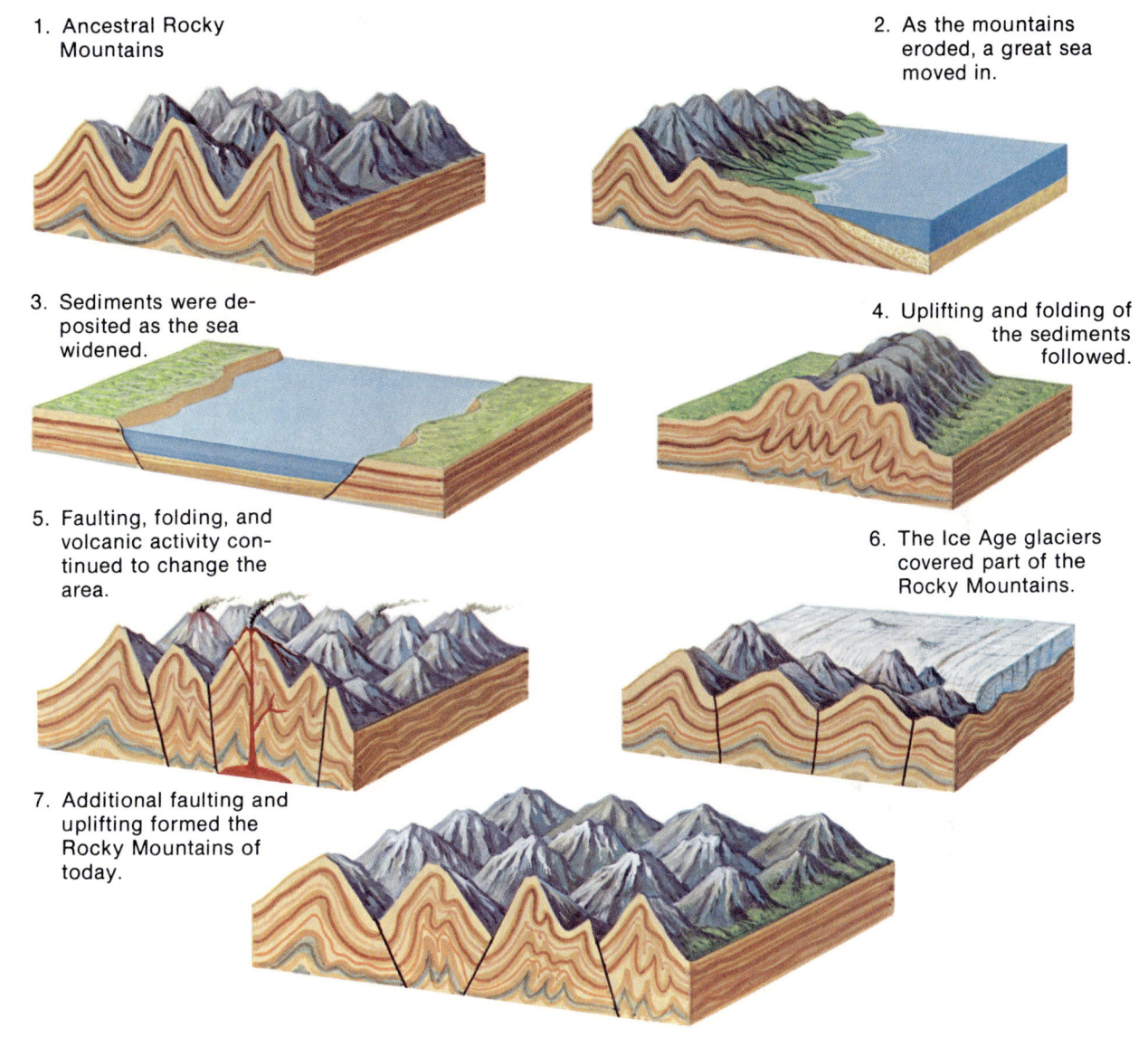

2. As the mountains eroded, a great sea moved in.

3. Sediments were deposited as the sea widened.

4. Uplifting and folding of the sediments followed.

5. Faulting, folding, and volcanic activity continued to change the area.

6. The Ice Age glaciers covered part of the Rocky Mountains.

7. Additional faulting and uplifting formed the Rocky Mountains of today.

Figure 16.19 Repetitions of the geologic changes shown in this model produced the modern Rocky Mountains.

Study Questions for 16.3

1. Describe how fault-block mountains may have formed.
2. Describe the stages in forming folded or complex mountains.
3. On a time line indicate the major events in the history of the Rocky Mountains.

16 / Mountains and Crustal Movement

16.4 The Distribution of Mountain Ranges

You will find out
- where the major mountain ranges are located on land;
- where the major mountain ranges are located in the ocean;
- what is the geologic cycle.

A series of mountains makes a **mountain range.** The Sierra Nevada mountains in California are an example of a mountain range. These mountains extend from southern California to northern California and appear to belong to a single geologic unit. A **mountain system** is made of a series of mountain ranges. The Rocky Mountains extending from Mexico to Canada are a mountain system made of different ranges.

Figure 16.20 The Sierra Nevadas

Now look at the map on page 328 and notice that there appears to be one continuous system of mountain ranges after another from the tip of South America to Alaska. All these mountain ranges and systems connected together are called a **mountain chain.** Where are the mountains in this mountain chain located relative to a plate boundary? You were right if you answered that the mountains are located on or near the boundary. In fact, the cause of most all mountains can be traced to some kind of movement of the earth's crust.

For example, volcanic mountains such as the Pacific Cascades occur along subduction zones. Folded or complex mountains occur along converging plate boundaries. Here sediment is trapped between the colliding plates, forcing some sediment upward and some downward to make a mountain range like the Appalachians. Fault-block mountains are formed by movements and adjustments of the earth's crust even though they are not always located near a plate boundary. The Sierra Nevadas in California and the Grand Tetons in Wyoming are fault-block mountains.

Wherever mountains occur, geologists consider their presence as part of the **geologic cycle.** This cycle, or model, is built on the idea that the earth's crust is constantly changing. Refer to Figure 16.21 as you read the following description of the geologic cycle.

Do You Know?
A spectacular movie could be made if the earth's surface could be photographed with one frame for every 1,000 years. If this happened for 50 million years, it would make a movie one hour long. What you would see is the rise and erosion of several folded or complex mountain ranges.

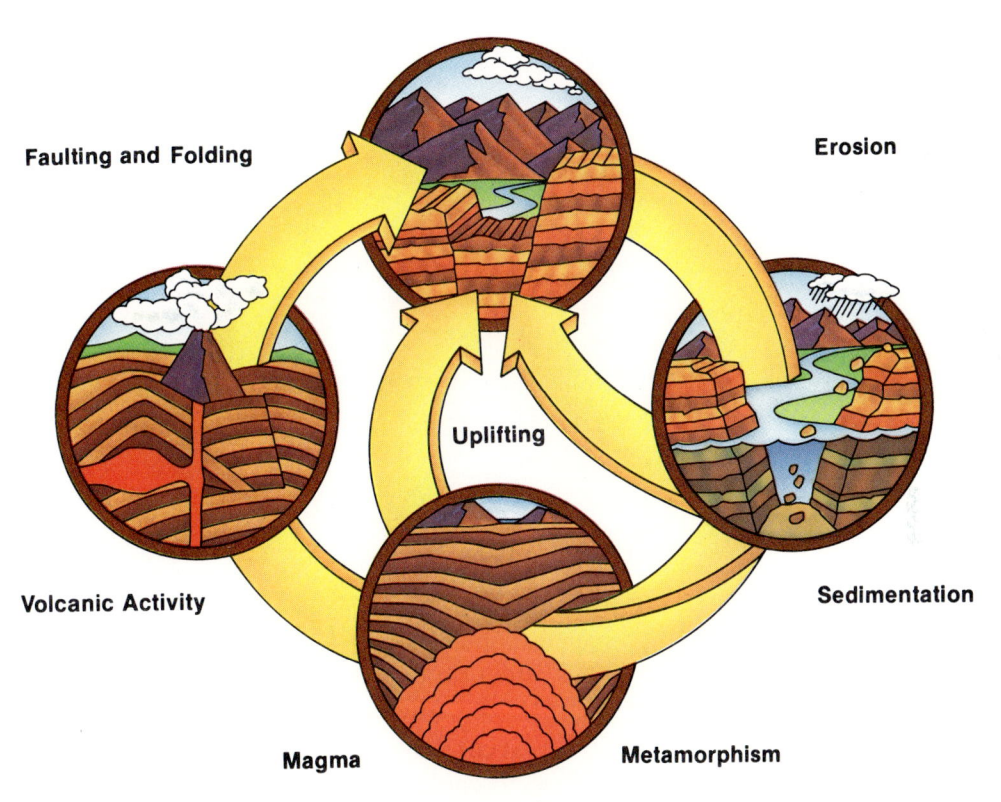

Mountains wear away to become sedimentary rocks. These rocks may be uplifted to form mountains or may be changed to metamorphic rocks. These metamorphic rocks may be uplifted to form mountains or in some cases melted to become igneous rocks later. Igneous rocks can be uplifted to form mountains. The processes continue through time.

Figure 16.21 The geologic cycle

16 / **Mountains and Crustal Movement**

327

Mountain Ranges
1. Alps
2. Urals
3. Andes Mountains
4. Himalayas
5. Carpathians
6. Great Dividing Range
7. Rocky Mountains
8. Appalachians

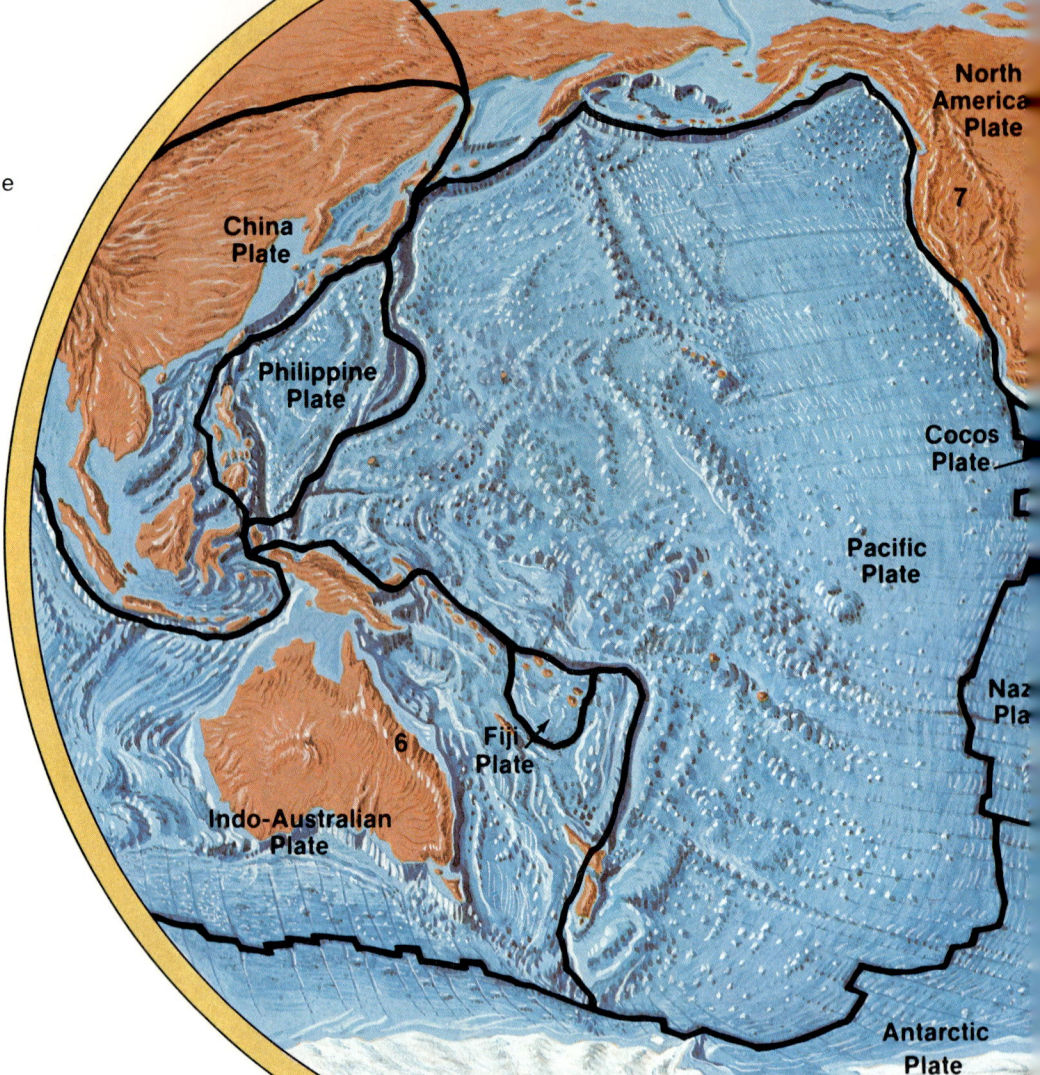

Figure 16.22 Mountain ranges and plate boundaries are closely related.

Look for mountain ranges on the map. Find the Alps, the Urals, the Andes, the Himalayas, the Carpathians, and the Great Dividing Range. What plate boundaries are close to each?

The longest and most recently discovered mountain ranges in the world can't be seen. They lie on the floor of the ocean. The mid ocean ridges on diverging plate boundaries form the longest and highest mountain ranges found on the earth. You can see that these mountains stretch almost unbroken nearly 64,000 km through the ocean basins. Some approach the height of Mount

328   16 / **Mountains and Crustal Movement**

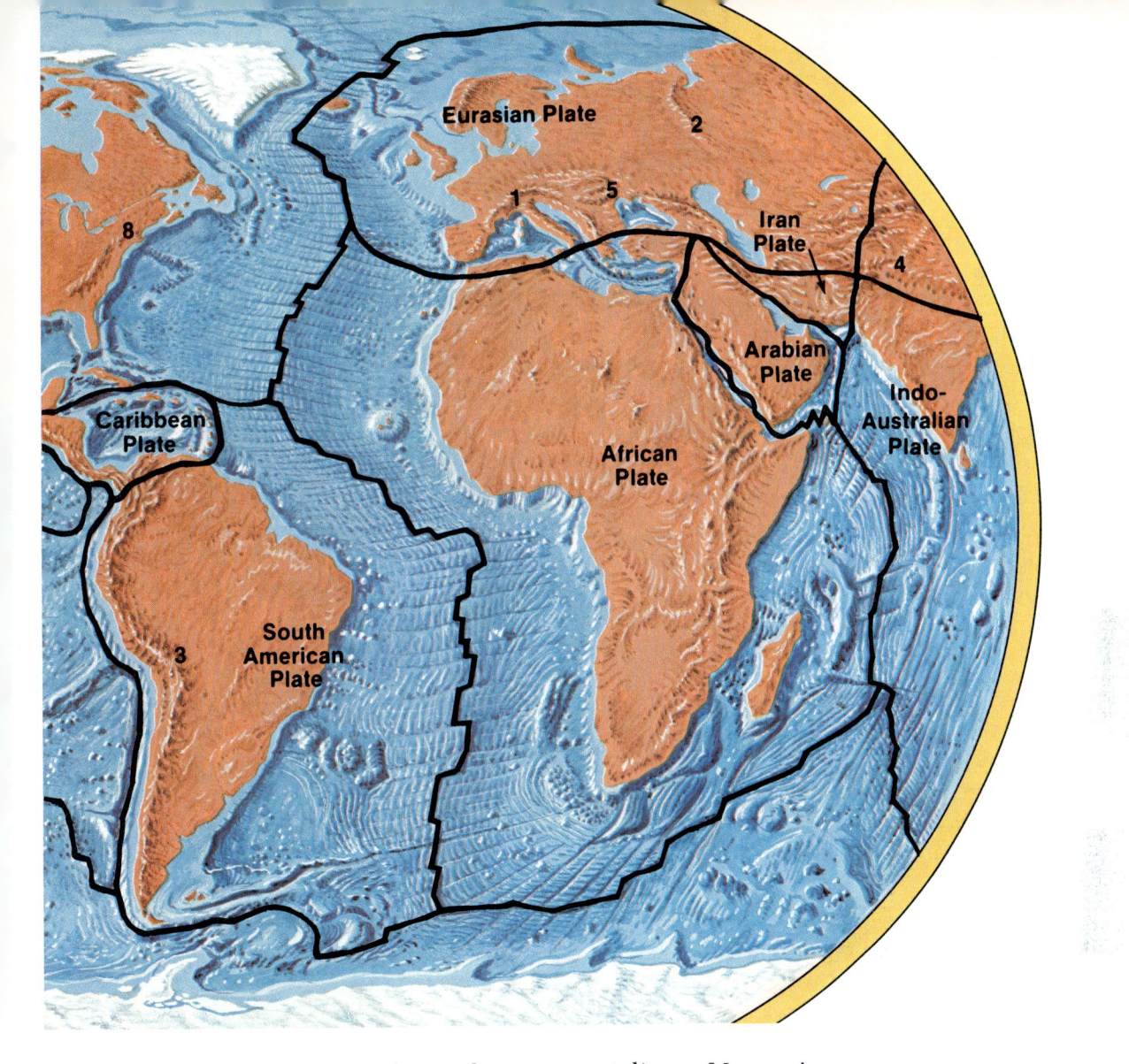

Everest, 8,850 m above their surroundings. Mountain building on the ocean floor or on the land is a worldwide geologic activity that continues through time.

Study Questions for 16.4
1. What mountain ranges are found in North America, South America, Asia, Europe, and Australia?
2. Where are oceanic mountains located?
3. What are the major geologic processes making the geologic cycle?

16 / Mountains and Crustal Movement

Biography

Dr. Marie Morisawa

Dr. Marie Morisawa, a Japanese–American, is a professor of geology at the State University of New York, Binghamton. How she got to that position is as interesting as what she does as a geologist.

Dr. Morisawa started as a math major with a chemistry minor, graduating with honors from Hunter College. She discovered geology when a friend twisted her arm to take an introductory geology course. Although she liked the course and took several more courses after graduation, she entered Union Theological Seminary. After earning an M.A. degree, she taught two years in Hawaii before accepting a job as the director for geology laboratory work and equipment at Hunter College. This experience led her to pursue graduate studies in geology at the University of Wyoming and Columbia University.

At the time she received her Ph.D., women were not so well accepted in geology as they are today. She encountered a number of interesting experiences as her career developed, such as waiting aboveground while her male students went underground at a mine because women were not allowed to go into mines. She summarizes her experiences by saying, "I discovered that those who like you and respect you as a person are more numerous and more important than those who do not. It is one's inner self that determines success or failure, whether one is a man or woman."

Dr. Morisawa is currently pioneering a new field of aesthetics and environmental geology.

CHAPTER REVIEW

Main Ideas

- A mountain is any part of the surface that stands much higher than its surroundings.
- An anticline forms when rock layers are folded upward into an arch. A syncline forms when rock layers are folded downward.
- Rocks move along a plane called a fault. Three types of fault are reverse, normal, and horizontal faults.
- A volcano is an opening in the earth's crust that allows lava, ash, and gases to reach the earth's surface. Lava and ash may pile up around the opening to form a volcanic mountain.
- Underground pockets of magma harden to form dikes, sills, batholiths, and volcanic necks.
- Fault-block mountains form when the crust is uplifted and then settles as uneven blocks bounded by faults.
- Complex mountains form from a combination of processes: folding, faulting, and volcanism.
- Mountain ranges on land are located at or near plate boundaries.
- The geologic cycle is a model of the processes that build mountains and wear them down.
- Mountain ranges in the ocean are located along diverging plate boundaries.

Using Vocabulary

Make up a matching-column quiz. On a separate piece of paper, list the words below in one column and describe each word in another. Exchange quizzes with a classmate.

folding	volcano	volcanic neck
anticline	composite volcano	fault-block mountain
syncline	cinder cone	folded mountain
fault	shield volcano	mountain range
reverse fault	dike	mountain system
normal fault	sill	mountain chain
horizontal fault	batholith	geologic cycle

16 / Mountains and Crustal Movement

Remembering Facts

On your paper, write the word or words that best complete each sentence.
1. Magma that cools and hardens in horizontal cracks between rock layers forms a (batholith, dike, sill).
2. A series of individual mountains makes a mountain (chain, range, system).
3. A (mountain, hill, volcano) is any part of the earth's surface that stands much higher than its surroundings.
4. Hot, liquid rock inside the earth is called (batholith, lava, magma).
5. (Anticlines, Synclines, Reclines) form when rock layers are bent upward into an arch.
6. Magma that hardens in vertical cracks between rock layers forms a (batholith, dike, sill).
7. Mountains formed from lava and ash are called (complex, volcanic, folded) mountains.
8. Rock layers bent downward into a trough are called (anticlines, synclines, declines).
9. Mountains occur in the (water, rock, geologic) cycle.
10. An anticline occurs when rocks are (faulted, folded, melted).
11. Rocks break and slip along a (fold, fault, sill).
12. The crust moves sideways in a (normal, reverse, horizontal) fault.
13. Mount St. Helens is a (cinder cone, shield volcano, composite volcano).
14. The Appalachians are (folded, faulted, volcanic) mountains.
15. A batholith forms from (faulting, lava, magma).
16. The Grand Tetons in Wyoming are (volcanic, fault-block, folded) mountains.

Understanding Ideas

On your paper, answer each question in complete sentences.
1. Why is the word *volcano* used to describe a cinder cone but not a batholith?
2. Would larger mineral cyrstals be found at the bottom of a sill or at the bottom of a dike? Why?
3. Why do the processes of weathering and erosion wear down an anticline faster than a syncline?
4. What is the difference between magma and lava?
5. What type of rock is found in underground formations such as batholiths, dikes, and sills?

Applying What You Have Learned

1. Why do anticlines and synclines form when rock layers are folded?
2. What determines whether a reverse fault or a normal fault will occur in a particular location?
3. Is it possible for a sill to become a shield volcano? Explain your answer.
4. Explain why the faults that form fault-block mountains are normal faults.

Challenge

Volcanoes occur in three main geologic settings: (1) at converging plate boundaries along a subduction zone; (2) at diverging plate boundaries; and (3) over rising hot plumes. Subduction zone volcanoes tend to be explosive, throwing ash and rock pieces high into the air. Diverging boundary volcanoes are usually quiet, as they release flowing molten rock. Plume volcanoes flow quietly when they penetrate the ocean crust, but are explosive if they penetrate continental crust. Use the map on the right to answer the following questions.

1. Mount St. Helens exploded in 1980. Over which geologic setting could Mount St. Helens possibly be located?
2. What information is needed to find out whether the mountains between Lassen Peak and Mount Rainier are part of a northward-moving plume trail?
3. If Mount Rainier and Mount Hood were found to be the same age, in which geologic setting would Mount St. Helens be located? Explain your answer.

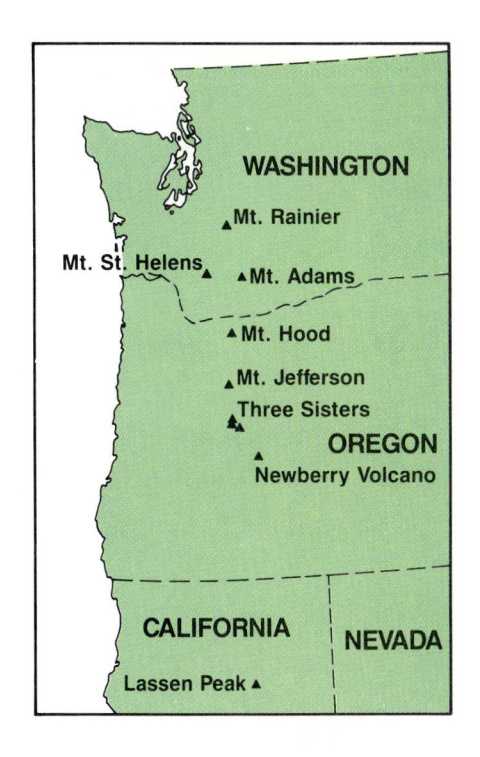

Research and Investigation

1. Visit a city or town planning office to find out whether any faults run through the area in which you live.
2. Use resources in your library to prepare a report on any mountain-building features in your area.
3. Divide the class into groups. Each group should organize and present a travelogue about a mountain range. A geologic history and a pictorial review of the mountain range should be included in each travelogue.

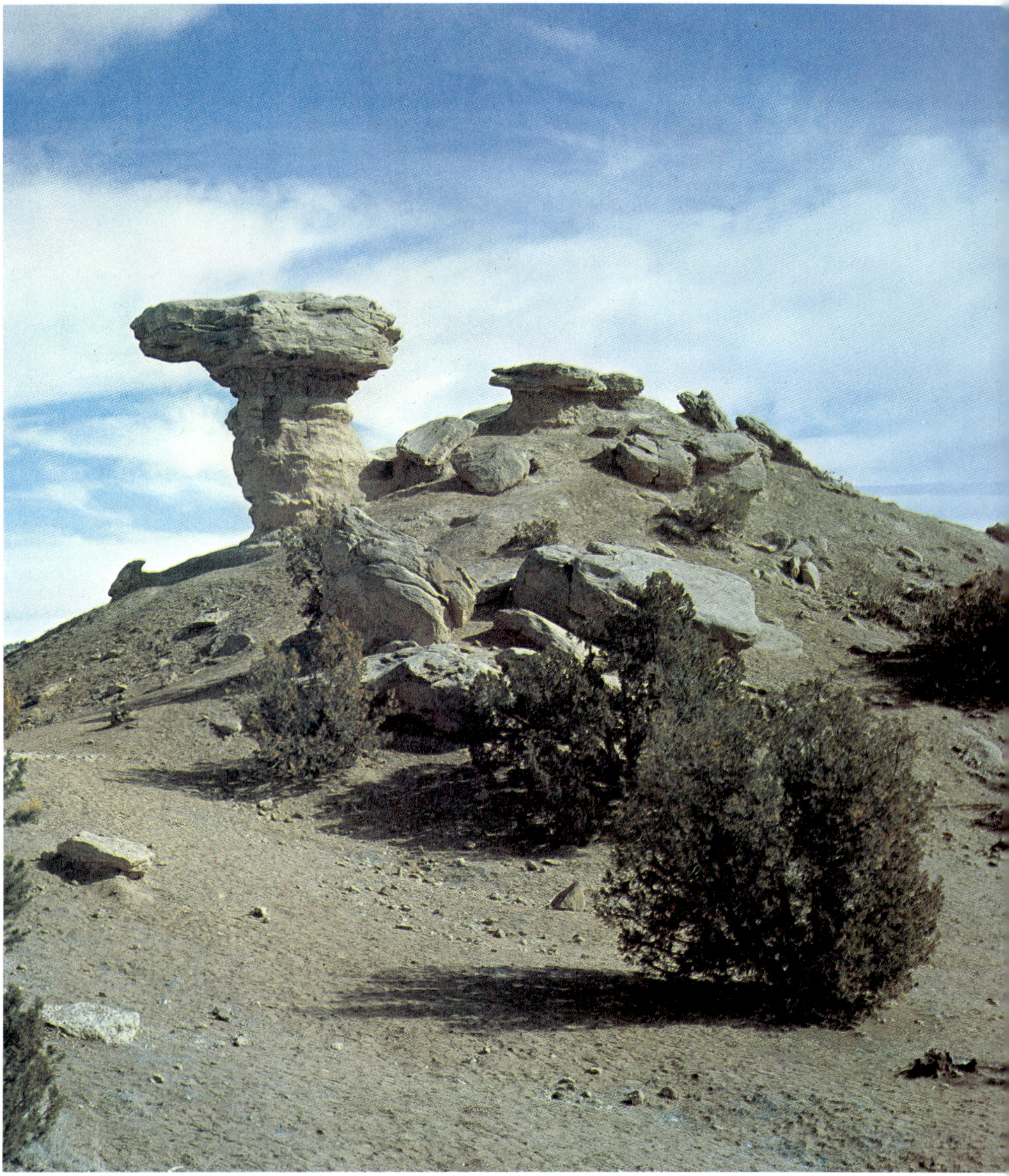

UNIT FIVE

The Rock Story

Chapter 17
Mapping the Earth's Surface

Chapter 18
Weathering and Erosion

Chapter 19
The Rock Record

Chapter 20
Dating and Geologic Time

Chapter 21
The Fossil Record

Beech Hill
Hurricane Hill
Dark Pd
Dublin Pond
Dublin
Spaulding Hill
DUBLIN GOLF CLUB
Francis Ch
Stone Pd
Sunset Hill
D U B L I N
Hinds Bk
Mountain
Gleason Bk
Brook
FARMERS TRAIL
PUMPELLY TRAIL
CASCADE LINK
MARLBORO TRAIL
MONADNOCK MTN
FIRE LOOKOUT
WHITE DOT TRAIL
WHITE ARROW TRAIL
RED CROSS TRAIL
HARLING TRAIL
Halfway House
Gilson Pd
Thorndike Pond
Woodbury Hill
Frost Pond
Garfield Pd
Mills Brook
Stanley
Bigelow Hill
Jenkins Pd
Fassett Brook
Poole Res
Tyler
J A F F R E Y
Whites Pd
Cummings Meadow
Mead Brook
Jaffrey Center
Mountain Brook
Quarry
Gap Mtn
Fern Hill
Potters Pd
Cubleigh Hill
Gilmore Pond
Bowkerville
Bowker Pond
Jock Page Hill
Hodge Pond
Dead Swamp
Peabody Hill
Carter Hill
LINE

Chapter 17
Mapping the Earth's Surface

Lesson Titles
17.1 Models of the Earth's Surface
17.2 Topographic Maps
17.3 Major Landform Regions of the United States

Have you ever been lost in a strange place? Perhaps this has happened to you during a visit to an unfamiliar town or city. Chances are that when you realized you were lost, you looked for a map to help show you the way around. Many people have relied on maps to help them find their way around unfamiliar locations.

If you have ever made a long trip by automobile, then you probably used some type of road map. This map showed the names of cities and landmarks in a given area. It also included information regarding distances between places on the map. If you were lucky, the map even showed the location of a good place to stop for a bite to eat.

Another kind of map, like the one on the opposite page, provides much more detail than an ordinary map. This map shows the natural features found on the earth's surface. It even includes the location of landmarks created by people. In this chapter, you will learn how people make and use these and other kinds of maps. In addition, you will learn about several of the major surface features found in the United States.

Figure 17.1 *opposite:* This is a topographic map. This type of map includes specific details of many features of the earth's surface.

17.1
Models of the Earth's Surface

You will find out
- what kinds of information are included on maps;
- what a map projection is;
- how locations are pinpointed on a map.

An airplane flight presents a surprising view of the earth's surface. Highways look like straight lines running across the surface. Streams look like narrow ribbons winding through patches of green. Farmland looks like neatly divided squares and rectangles. If you could make a drawing of the highways, streams, and farms as they appear from high above the earth, you would have a map. A map is a reduced likeness of part of the earth's surface.

Figure 17.2 An aerial view of the earth's surface reveals distinct patterns in the use of the land.

What features would you include if you were drawing a map? The answer depends on why you are making the map. Different kinds of maps are used for different purposes. A road map shows the relationship between roads and towns. A relief map shows land features and indicates elevations with colors. Geologic maps are concerned with kinds of rocks and their arrangement. Using any of these maps can be like traveling to new and interesting places. All you need is an understanding of different kinds of maps and how they are made.

To use a road map, you must study direction and distances between points on the map. Finding direction is quite simple. Usually the top of a map is north, the right is east, the left is west, and the bottom is south. However, to measure distance, you use the **map scale.** The map scale tells you how a distance on the map compares to the actual distance on the earth's surface. For example, if the map scale is 1 cm = 5 km, then every centimeter of distance on the map represents 5 km of actual distance. If the distance between two points on the map is 2 cm, then the actual distance is 10 km; 3 cm = 15 km; 4 cm = 20 km; and so on.

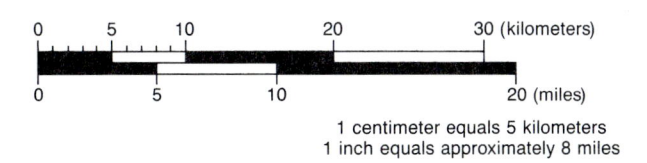

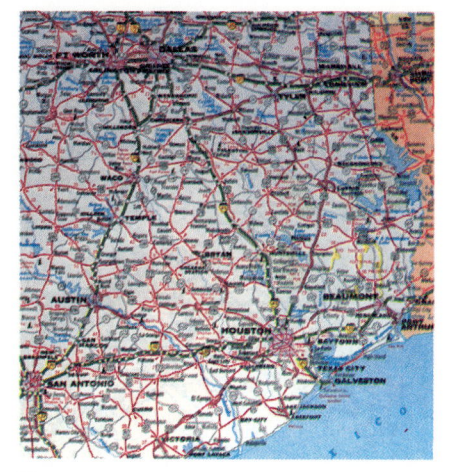

Figure 17.3 Have you ever used a road map?

1 centimeter equals 5 kilometers
1 inch equals approximately 8 miles

Maps are always much smaller than the pieces of land they represent. The more closely the map approaches the land in size, the larger its scale is said to be. A map of the United States on a sheet of paper would have to use a very small scale. On the other hand, a large wall map of the same area would use a larger scale.

Maps include other kinds of information, such as locations of landmarks, patterns, and what the earth's surface looks like in a specific area. In order to make all this information useful, these details are simplified by the use of symbols and colors. The key to reading a map is understanding what each symbol and color represents. The symbols and colors on a map are explained on the **map legend.** Symbols are used for roads, towns, streams, and other features. Colors and lines are used to show areas with something in common. This could be something that people have decided, such as city or state boundaries. Colors and symbols are also used to represent other information about a location, such as soil type, climate, or mineral resources. All this information is summarized in the map legend.

Figure 17.4 By using a map scale you can estimate the distance between points on a map.

17 / Mapping the Earth's Surface

A globe is a fairly accurate representation of what the earth's surface looks like. It is accurate because it is curved like the earth. But imagine trying to fit a sheet of paper on a globe without wrinkling or tearing the paper, then drawing a map on the paper. Try this yourself. It is impossible to do without distorting the map.

In order to reduce distortion, a technique called **map projection** is used to show the earth's curved surface on a flat map. Imagine that you have a transparent globe with a light inside. The features on the globe will make shadows on a sheet of paper held against the globe.

Three kinds of map projection are shown in Figure 17.6. The polar projection is made on a flat piece of paper. The mercator projection is made on a cyclinder. The conic projection is made on a cone. In each case, the map is most accurate where the paper touches the globe, but distorted away from that point.

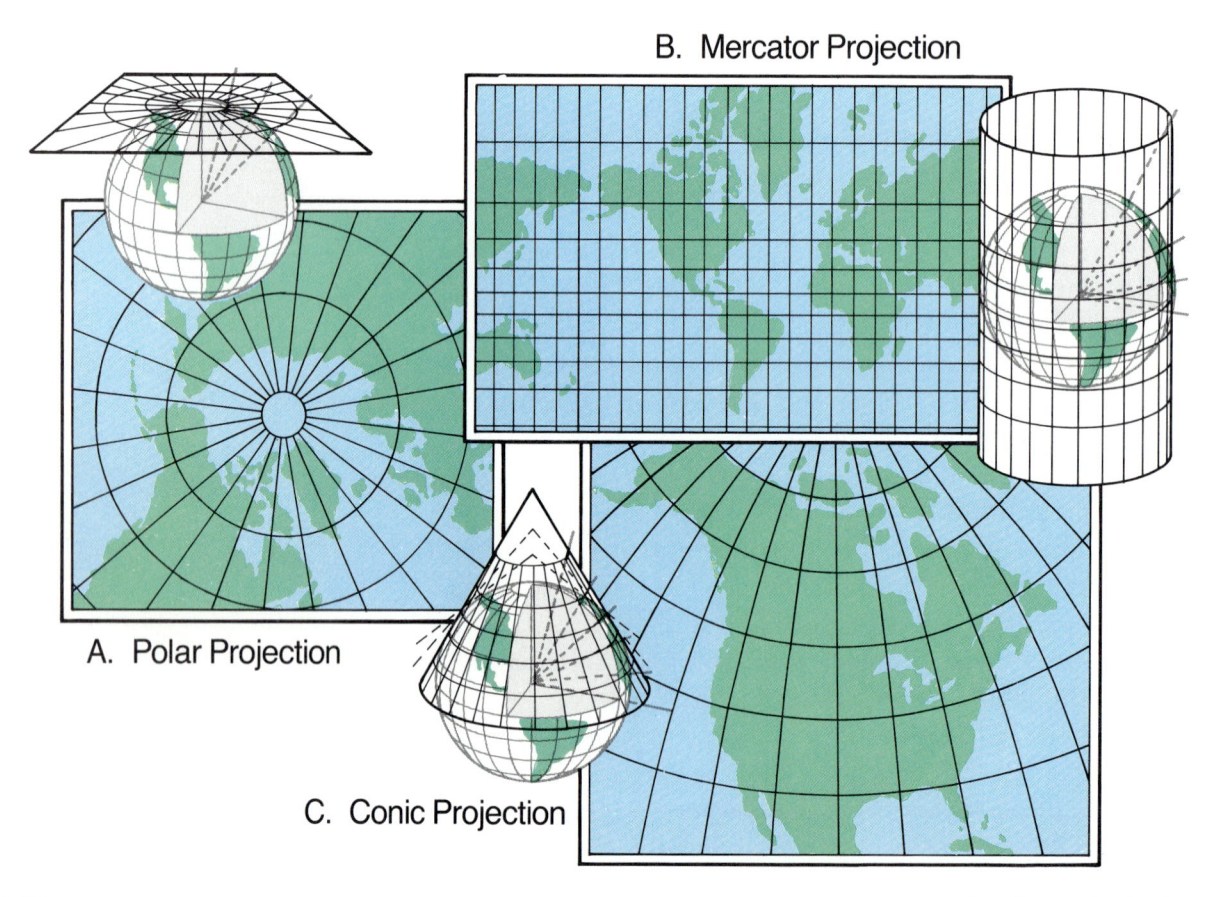

Figure 17.5 A globe is a fairly accurate representation of the earth's shape and surface features.

Figure 17.6 Map projections are used to show the curved earth on a flat surface.

A. Polar Projection

B. Mercator Projection

C. Conic Projection

340　　　　　　　　　　　　　　　　　　　　　　　17 / Mapping the Earth's Surface

Locations on the earth's surface are pinpointed using two sets of imaginary lines. One set of lines, called **parallels,** help identify the position of a place north or south of the equator. The north-south distance of a point on the earth's surface is called **latitude.** Latitude is described in degrees north or south of the equator. If you are at a latitude of 40°N, you are located 40° north of the equator.

The second set of lines, called **meridians,** runs from pole to pole. These help you find the east-west position of any point on the earth's surface. Since there is no natural place to start the 0° meridian, the **prime meridian** was chosen by agreement. It is a line that passes through Greenwich, England. East-west distances from the prime meridian are called **longitude.** On the opposite side of the earth from the prime meridian is the international date line. As you travel east or west from the prime meridian, longitude increases from 0° to 180° east or 180° west.

Understanding longitude helps to avoid confusion over time changes as you travel around the earth. Time zones are roughly the width of 15° of longitude.

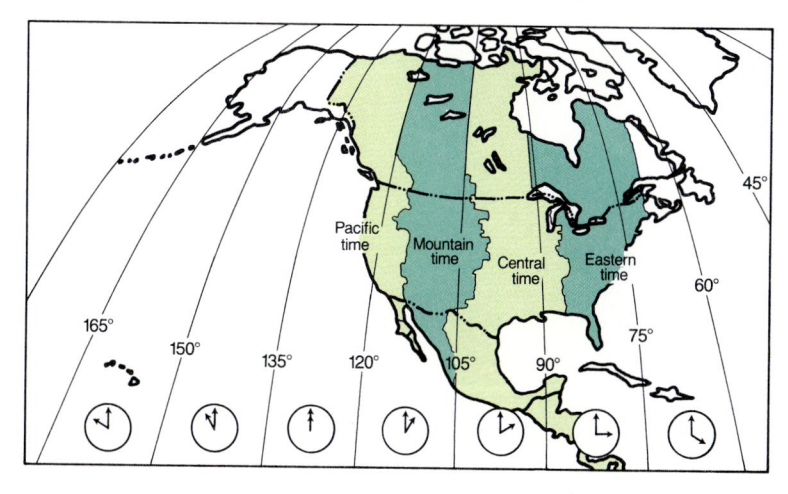

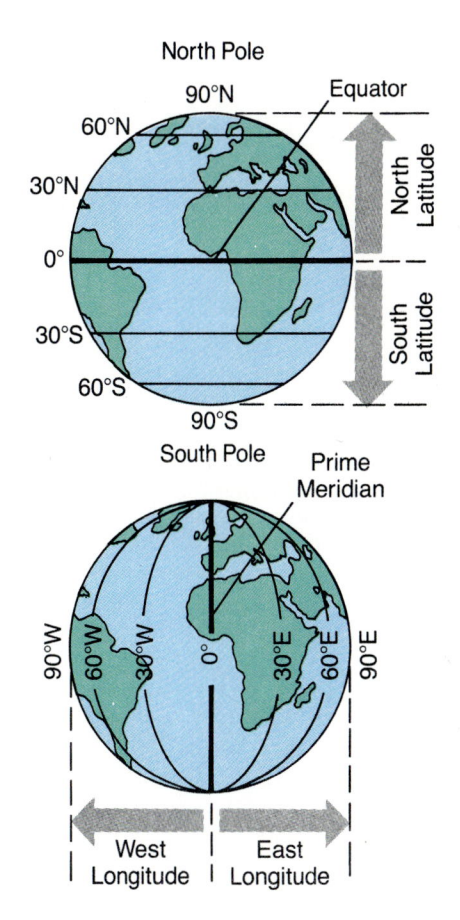

Figure 17.7 Latitude is measured in degrees north or south of the equator. Longitude is measured east or west of the prime meridian.

Figure 17.8 *left:* The world's time zones are closely related to lines of longitude.

Study Questions for 17.1

1. How are distances represented on a map?
2. What is a map projection?
3. Define the terms latitude and longitude?

17 / Mapping the Earth's Surface

17.2 Topographic Maps

You will find out
- what a topographic map is;
- what a contour line is;
- what kinds of information are included on a topographic map.

Geologists show the shape and features of the land by using **topographic** [TAHP-uh-GRAF-ihk] **maps**. A topographic map shows the contour and elevation of the land. It also shows special features of the land, such as streams. On a topographic map, points of the same elevation are connected with a **contour** [KAHN-toor] **line**. The contour lines are repeated at regular intervals.

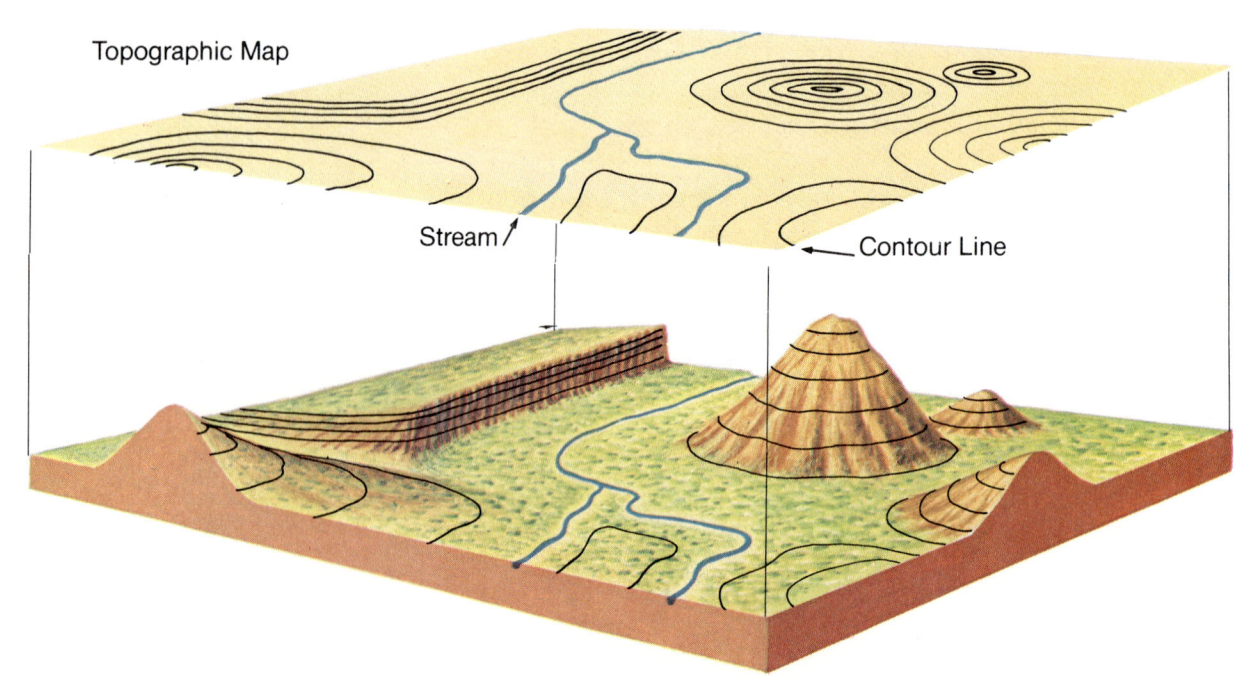

Figure 17.9 Compare this illustration of a land area *(bottom)*, with its topographic map *(top)*. Notice how the contour lines are spaced to correspond with the slope of the land.

Compare the sets of contour lines on the topographic map in Figure 17.9. By understanding the patterns of contour lines on a topographic map, you can describe the land surface of a particular area. Contour lines that are close together mean steep slopes. Widely spaced contour lines indicate a gentle slope. Some topographic maps show elevation with colors and different kinds of shading. But the most accurate maps use contour lines.

17 / Mapping the Earth's Surface

On many topographic maps, only every fifth contour is labeled. It is usually a heavy brown line, while the other lines are lighter brown. When you look at contour lines on a map, remember that

(1) the distance between the lines indicates the slope of the land.
(2) a contour line that crosses a stream vees in an upstream direction.
(3) contours do not cross, but many come together at a straight up-and-down cliff.
(4) closed contour lines indicate a hill. If the closed contour has short lines like teeth, it means a depression, or a hollow area.

Figure 17.10 The spacing and direction of contour lines help describe the physical appearance of the earth's surface in a particular area.

Figure 17.11 Examples of some of the symbols used on topographic maps.

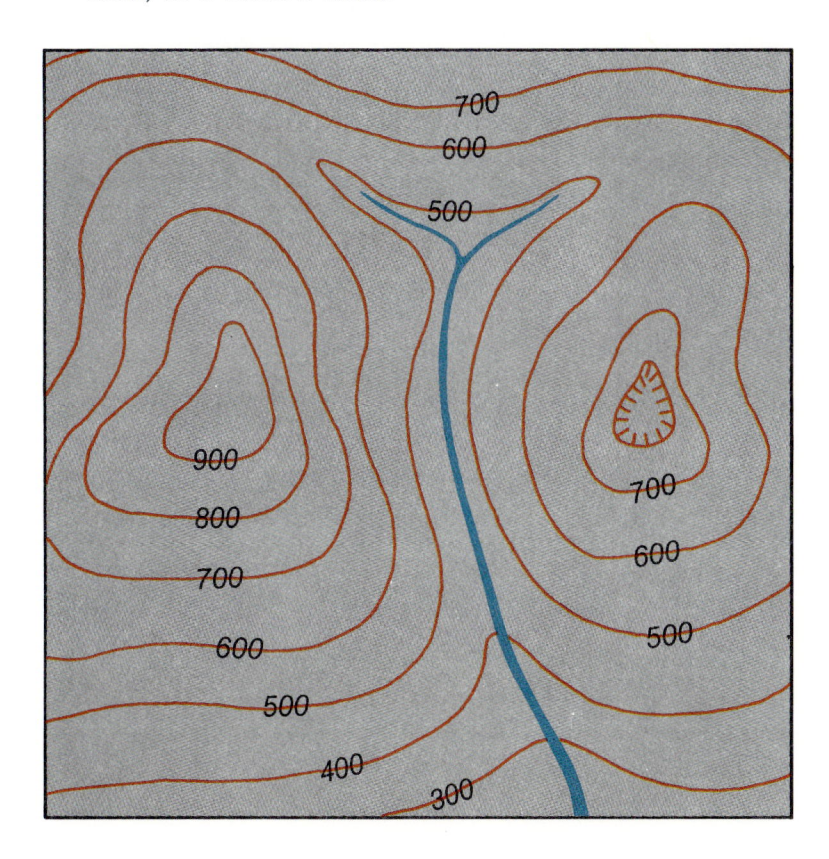

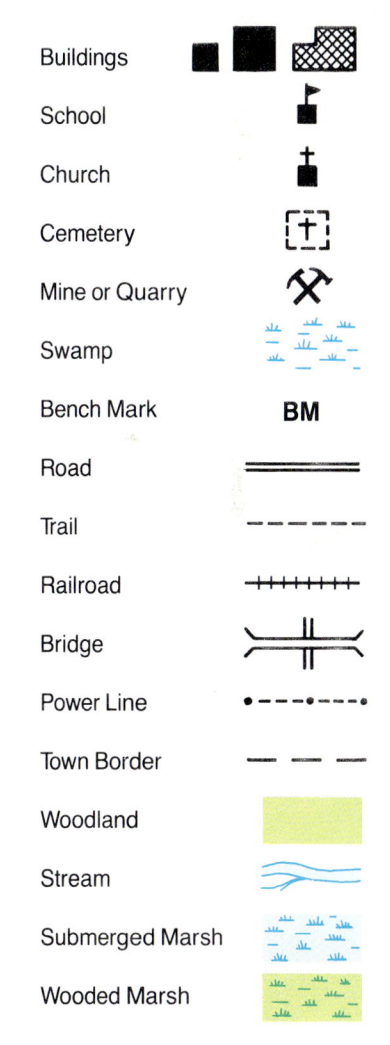

Buildings	
School	
Church	
Cemetery	
Mine or Quarry	
Swamp	
Bench Mark	BM
Road	
Trail	
Railroad	
Bridge	
Power Line	
Town Border	
Woodland	
Stream	
Submerged Marsh	
Wooded Marsh	

In addition to contours, a topographic map uses symbols to show streams, highways, buildings, and other features of interest. Figure 17.11 lists several of the kinds of symbols that you would expect to find on a topographic map like the one on the next page.

17 / Mapping the Earth's Surface

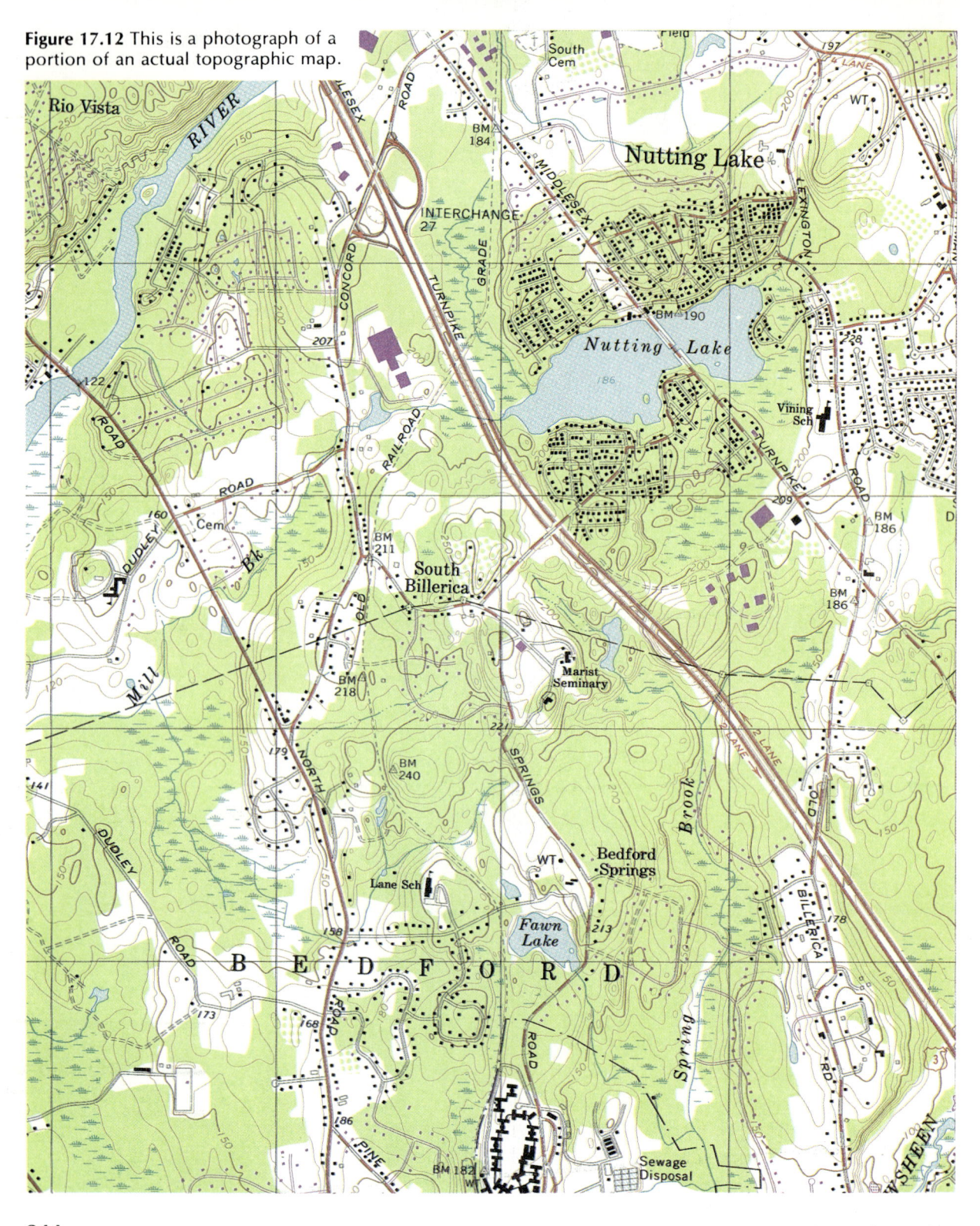

Figure 17.12 This is a photograph of a portion of an actual topographic map.

344　　　　　　　　　　　　　　　　　　　　　　　　　17 / Mapping the Earth's Surface

Activity

How Can You Make a Contour Map?

Materials
clear plastic container with cover
modeling clay
tracing paper
wax pencil
sharp pencil
metric ruler

Procedure

1. Mark the outside of one side of your container with lines spaced at 1-cm intervals.

2. Build a cone-shaped clay mountain. Make sure your mountain is not taller than your plastic container.

3. Place your mountain in the container and add water to the level of the first centimeter mark. Use the point of your pencil to make a line around the mountain at the level of the water. Repeat the procedure for every centimeter of elevation until the top of the mountain is reached.

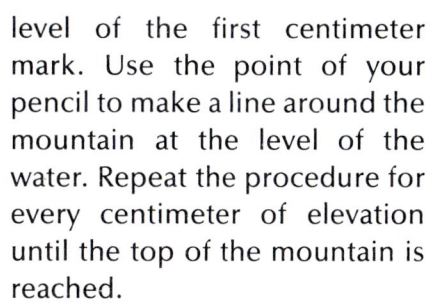

4. Fasten the cover to the container and place the tracing paper on the cover.

5. Looking down through the cover, trace each contour line, beginning with the line at the base of your mountain. The result will be a contour map of your mountain.

Questions

1. Which side of the mountain has the most widely spaced contours?

2. Which side of the mountain has the most closely spaced contours?

3. How do the lines show your mountain's shape? How does your mountain's shape compare to the shape of mountains made by your classmates?

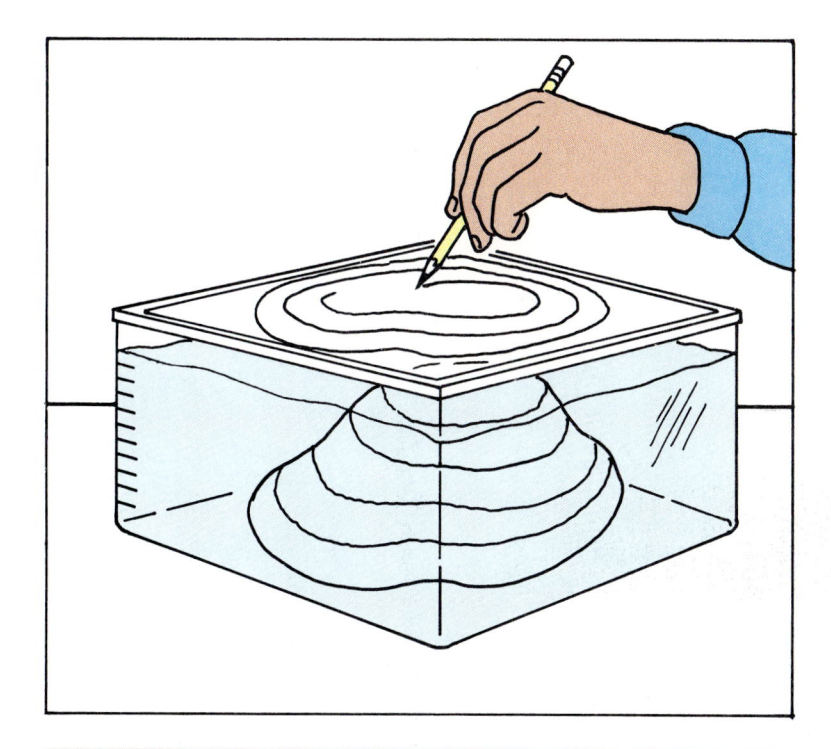

Study Questions for 17.2

1. What is shown on a topographic map?
2. How are elevations represented on topographic maps?
3. Besides elevation, what kinds of information are included on topographic maps?

17.3 The Major Landform Regions of the United States

You will find out
- what makes a major landform region;
- what the major landform regions of the United States are.

The United States can be divided into eight major **landform regions.** A major landform region is a large area which contains similar or related landforms, soils, rock types, and rock structures. The eight regions of the continental United States are the Coastal Plain, Appalachian Highlands, Central Plains, Rocky Mountains, Colorado Plateau, Basin and Range, Columbia Plateau, and Pacific Mountains.

Figure 17.13 The major landforms of the continental United States

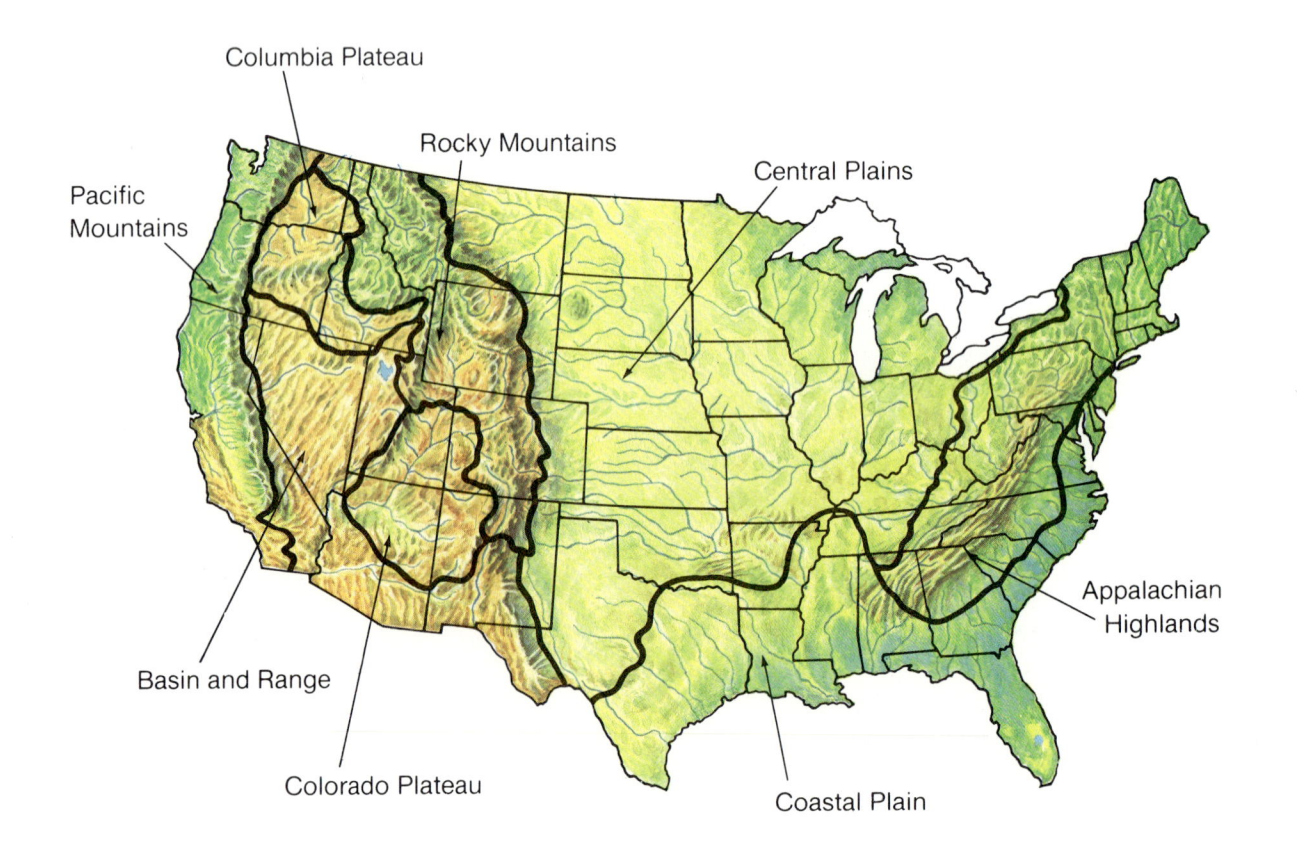

346

17 / Mapping the Earth's Surface

The major landform region in the United States in which the most people live is called the Coastal Plain region. A section of the Coastal Plain region is photographed in Figure 17.14. The Coastal Plain is low in elevation and, in general, consists of a gently sloping surface of rocks dipping toward the ocean. The rock types are sedimentary and 135 million years old or younger. The land is favorable for farming and supporting large populations. Many large rivers run parallel courses across the Coastal Plain to the ocean, where they form large deltas.

West and north of the Coastal Plain lies the Appalachian Highlands. See Figure 17.15. Included in this region are the Appalachian Mountains and the land next to those mountains. In general, the land has been heavily eroded by streams. Rivers are numerous and large, and many lakes exist. Many different rock types of many different ages are associated with the Appalachian Mountains.

The Central Plains is another major landform region. This is the largest region, and part of it is photographed in Figure 17.16. It has low elevation. Most of the rocks in this area are sedimentary rocks. It has great rivers and large lakes. Soils are thick, and the farmland is rich. It is the major agricultural area of the United States.

Figure 17.14 A typical section of the Coastal Plains

Figure 17.15 *left:* The Appalachian Highlands

Figure 17.16 *right:* The Central Plains region

17 / Mapping the Earth's Surface

Figure 17.17 The San Juan Mountains in the Rocky Mountain Region

Figure 17.18 *left:* Part of the Colorado Plateau region

Figure 17.19 *right:* The east side of the Sierra Nevada in the Basin and Range region

Further west is the Rocky Mountain landform region, such as that shown in Figure 17.17. Here are some of the highest elevations of the United States. Igneous, metamorphic, and sedimentary rocks are found. The region is the principal headwaters for many rivers. Soils are thin, and there are large areas of barren rock.

South and west of the Rocky Mountain region lies the Colorado Plateau, as you see in Figure 17.18. Here are found extensive areas of nearly horizontal sedimentary rocks, with some igneous rocks occurring as volcanic rocks. The whole region is high in elevation and has a shortage of water.

The region photographed in Figure 17.19 is the Basin and Range region. This region has high mountain ranges and broad, flat basins. Many of the mountains have large, fan-shaped deposits called **alluvial** [uh-LOO-vee-uhl] **fans.** Some of the basins do not have rivers that flow out. The Salton Sea and the Great Salt Lake are in two such regions.

North of the Basin and Range region is the Columbia Plateau. Part of this area, shown in Figure 17.20, is covered by great thicknesses of lava flow. Except for a few areas, soils are poorly developed. The better soil areas are from windblown deposits. The Columbia River and the Snake River canyons are found in the Columbia Plateau.

To the west and south of the Columbia Plateau is the Pacific Mountain region, shown in Figure 17.21. This area has a great variety of landforms, rock types, and rock structures. In the north are volcanic mountains; the mountains somewhat in the center are the Sierra Nevada granites; near the ocean lies the Coast Mountain range. The great valley of the Pacific Mountain region, the San Joaquin, is a vast farmland.

In which region do you live? Would you like to live in one of the other regions?

Figure 17.20 *left:* Lava flows in the Columbia Plateau region

Figure 17.21 *right:* The northern Casades in Washington, part of the Pacific Mountain region

Study Questions for 17.3
1. Define a major landform region.
2. Name the eight major landform regions of the United States.
3. In which landform region do you live? In general, what is this region like?

17 / Mapping the Earth's Surface

Career

Exploration Petroleum Geologist

An exploration petroleum geologist studies surface and subsurface rocks in search for petroleum. The work involves the evaluation of potential areas as a source of petroleum and the analysis of the rock material that is removed when a well is being drilled. The exploration petroleum geologist is the first to know whether or not drilling is successful.

Marsha Findlay is an exploration petroleum geologist. She attended Walt Whitman High School in Huntington, New York. Later she studied geology and earth science at Vassar College. Her master's degree was earned at the University of South Carolina. Her thesis study on the effects of tectonic events on carbonate sediments of the Jurassic Period provides her with the kind of information that helps her locate potential sources of petroleum.

Her interest in geology began in elementary school when she learned about the glacial features near her home on Long Island. In the ninth grade she took an earth science course that she liked very much. This interest has continued and led to her present position.

An exploration petroleum geologist must be able to interpret surface landforms and how they relate to subsurface rock formations that may hold petroleum. The scale of events that must be studied range from the microscopic to global. Marsha Findlay finds the study of geologic changes in surface and subsurface rocks exciting and the challenge of using this knowledge in the search for petroleum important.

Marsha Findlay is a member of the Scholarship Committee for the American Geological Institute's Minority Participation Program. This group encourages minority students to study the geologic sciences.

CHAPTER REVIEW

Main Ideas

- There are many kinds of maps. Each map represents some of the features of the earth's surface.
- A map scale tells you how a distance on a map compares to the actual distance on the earth's surface.
- The colors and symbols used on a map are explained in the map legend.
- A map projection is an attempt to show the earth's curved surface on a flat surface.
- Latitude describes a location on the earth's surface north or south of the equator.
- Longitude describes location on the earth's surface east or west of the prime meridian.
- A topographic map shows the contour and elevation of the land.
- Contour lines connect points on the map that have the same elevation.
- Topographic maps use different symbols to represent features of interest in a particular area.
- The major landform regions of the contiguous United States are the (1) Coastal Plain, (2) Appalachian Highlands, (3) Central Plains, (4) Rocky Mountains, (5) Colorado Plateau, (6) Basin and Range, (7) Columbia Plateau, and (8) Pacific Mountains.

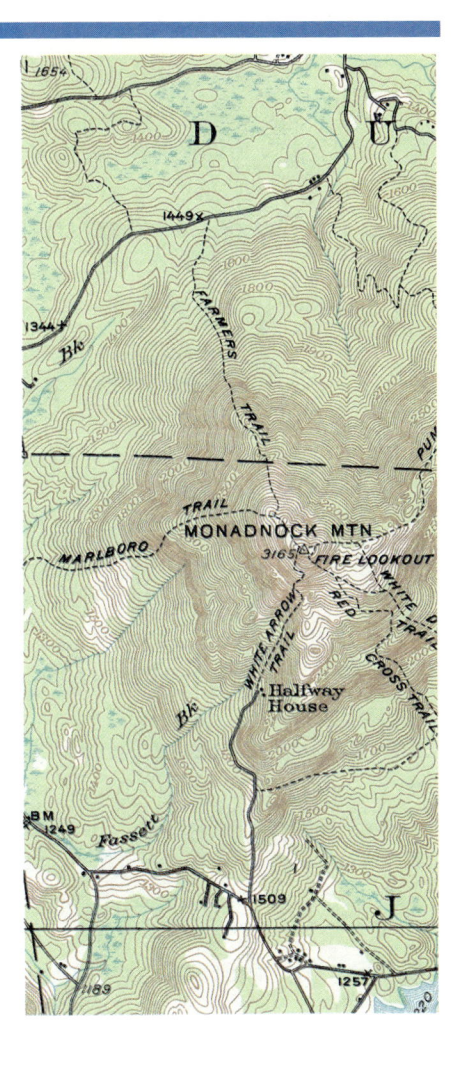

Using Vocabulary

On a separate piece of paper, write a sentence for each of the words below. Each sentence should give a *clue* as to the meaning of the word.

map scale
map legend
map projection
parallels
latitude
meridians
prime meridian

longitude
International Date Line
topographic map
contour lines
landform regions
alluvial fan

17 / Mapping the Earth's Surface

Remembering Facts

On your paper, write the word or words that best complete each sentence.

1. A large land area with related landforms, soils, and rock types is called a _____ .
2. A _____ is a reduced likeness of the earth's surface.
3. A _____ line connects points on a map with the same elevation.
4. An east-west location on the earth's surface is called the _____ of that place.
5. A _____ map shows the contour and elevation of the land.
6. The north-south position of a place is called _____ .
7. _____ are imaginary parallel lines that lie north and south of the equator.
8. Closely spaced contour lines mean a _____ slope.
9. A _____ is an attempt to show a curved surface on a flat map.
10. Longitude is measured east or west of the _____ .
11. A map _____ compares distance on a map to the actual distance between two points.
12. You change the date when you cross the _____ .
13. Latitude is measured north or south of the _____ .
14. _____ maps show rocks and their arrangement.
15. Closed contour lines indicate a _____ .
16. Mercator is a type of _____ _____ .
17. _____ _____ are roughly the width of 15° of longitude.
18. Latitude at the equator is _____ .
19. Plateau landforms are found in the _____ United States.
20. The _____ _____ is a major agricultural area.

Understanding Ideas

On your paper, answer each question in complete sentences.

1. What does the land surface look like in northeastern Iowa? How do you know?
2. How would you expect the contour lines on a topographic map from the Central Plains to compare to the lines on a map from a mountainous area? Perhaps a simple sketch would help explain your answer.
3. Give two reasons why the Coastal Plain region has parallel river drainage but the Colorado Plateau does not.

Applying What You Have Learned

1. What does the expression 40° N, 74° W mean?
2. When using a topographic map with contours, explain how you could determine the height of a hill.
3. The Grand Canyon is in the Colorado Plateau region. Could a second Grand Canyon ever develop in the Coastal Plain region? Explain.
4. How can the information on topographic and geologic maps be combined to tell you the position of rock layers in a given area?

Challenge

Topographic maps show the features of the earth's surface in a particular area. Use the map below and your understanding of contour lines to answer the following questions.

1. What letter on the map is close to a cliff? Give a reason for your answer.
2. What letter on the map is on a gentle slope? Again, give a reason for your answer.
3. What is the elevation of the highest point on the map?
4. Describe the landform that this map shows.

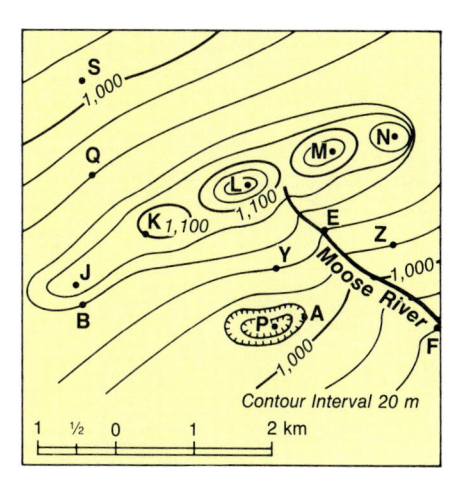

Research and Investigation

1. Find a map of your state. Lay a piece of tracing paper over it. Try to divide your state into landform regions. Start by locating mountainous areas and low, flat areas. Then subdivide the state into areas of similar landform character.
2. Determine the major landform region you live in. Use the library to find out what landforms, rock types, and rock structures are found in your region.
3. Have a "plan a trip" contest with your classmates. The trip must start and end at your school but must go through each of the major landform regions. The winner will be the one whose trip has the most interesting geological features (count them) *and* the fewest miles traveled.
4. Find out the name of the topographic area, or quadrangle, that you live in. Perhaps your teacher can order a map for your area from the United States Geological Survey.

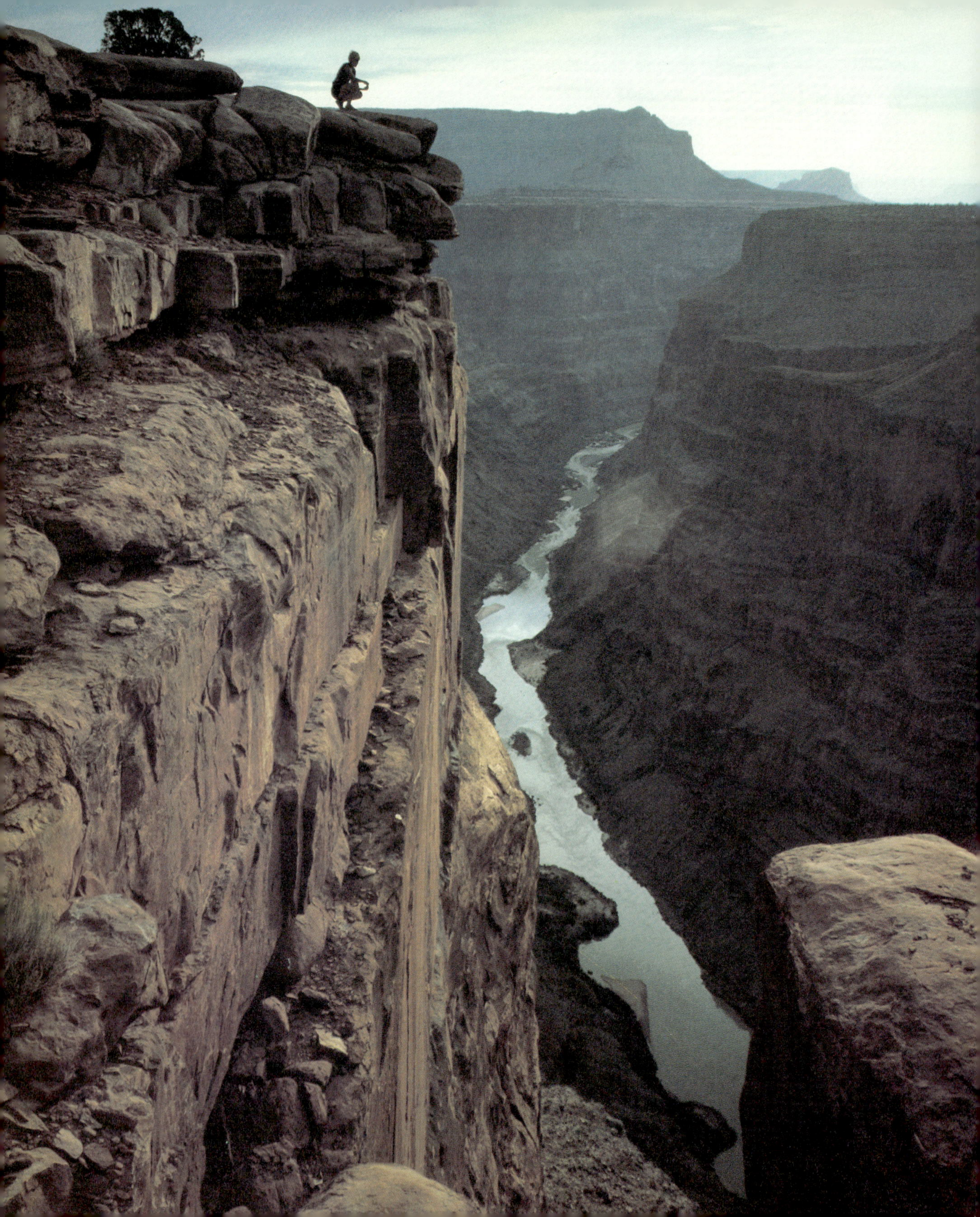

Chapter 18
Weathering and Erosion

Lesson Titles
18.1 Weathering and Erosion of Rocks
18.2 Erosion by Running Waters
18.3 Erosion by Wind
18.4 Erosion by Ice

The Grand Canyon is an awesome sight.

Imagine a gorge in the earth 1.6 km deep, more than 16 km wide in some places, and 450 km long. Cutting through thick beds of colorful rock, the canyon is a monument to erosion by the Colorado River. If you were standing on the canyon's rim, wouldn't you wonder about the events that formed this great canyon? Could that little river at the bottom really cut that great big canyon? Do streams carve their own valleys or are valleys formed separately in other ways?

If the only process working were the stream, valleys would be only as wide as the streams that formed them. Other earth processes must have helped the stream. This chapter is about the processes that break up and move rock.

Figure 18.1 *opposite:* The incomparable Grand Canyon

18.1 Weathering and Erosion of Rocks

You will find out
- what weathering is;
- what three processes cause weathering;
- what erosion is;
- how gravitation moves weathered rocks and soil.

Figure 18.2 Few things escape the effects of weathering.

Figure 18.3 This sinkhole formed when underground limestone dissolved and collapsed.

Exposed rocks on the earth's surface are continuously being broken down into smaller bits and pieces. This process of being broken down is called **weathering.** But rocks are not the only things that weather. Buildings, fences, bridges, highways, and automobiles also weather. Weathering can be caused by several different processes depending upon the conditions. The three basic weathering processes are **chemical weathering, mechanical weathering,** and **biological weathering.**

In the process called chemical weathering, substances in the atmosphere combine with materials on the earth and slowly change. You see the results of this process every time you see a rusty nail. Oxygen in the air combines with iron in the nail to form rust. The combination of a substance with oxygen is called **oxidation** [AHKS-uh-DAY-shuhn]. Carbon dioxide in the air combining with water to form a weak acid can also cause weathering. The acid dissolves some of the minerals in the rocks. Chemical weathering gradually changes the materials in rocks to something else. Often the new material is more easily dissolved by water and is slowly carried away.

Chemical weathering sometimes occurs underground where you cannot see it. Rainwater, which is a weak acid, dissolves some of the limestone rock as the water seeps downward. Caves are formed where the limestone has been dissolved and carried away. In some places the roofs of these caves and underground passages collapse. **Sinkholes** are funnel-shaped depressions caused by the collapse of underground caves. In central Florida many of the lakes are really large sinkholes which have filled with water.

In mechanical weathering, rocks are broken apart. They are not changed into something new. Mechanical weathering occurs when water freezes in cracks of rocks. The freezing water expands and opens the crack even further. If you live where it is cold, you've seen this process at work in the street pavement. Large holes develop because repeated freezing and thawing of water breaks up the pavement. In Figure 18.4 you can see that this same thing happens to rocks.

Plant material and organisms can also break up rocks. This process is called biological weathering, and it is really a little of both chemical and mechanical weathering. The roots of plants weather rocks by reacting chemically with the rock. Roots also mechanically weather rocks by enlarging the cracks in which the roots are growing. Every time you see something growing in the crack of a rock or on its surface, you know biological weathering is occurring.

Figure 18.4 *above:* Water expands when it freezes, causing rocks to crack and crumble over time.

Figure 18.5 *left:* Over long periods of time, plants like these will weather the rock away.

Do You Know?
At times weathering extends deep into the earth. Mining operations have exposed thoroughly weathered bedrock to depths of 100 m.

18 / Weathering and Erosion

Activity

What Happens When Something Weathers?

Materials
steel wool
vinegar
jar with water
moist sand
container
paper towels
3 beakers, 250-mL

Procedure

1. Wash the protective coating from the steel wool with the vinegar.
2. Blot the steel wool with paper towels.
3. Divide the steel wool into 3 pieces.
4. For 24 hours place one piece in water with little pieces sticking out, and another piece in the air outside, and bury the third piece in moist sand.

Questions

1. What evidence do you see of weathering?
2. Which piece of steel wool weathered the most?
3. Do you see any stains from weathering?
4. If you found a rock that contained iron, what weathering features might you see?

The rate at which rocks weather depends upon three factors: the kind of rock, the climate, and the surface area exposed to the atmosphere. Hard rocks weather more slowly than soft rocks. A climate that has much freezing and thawing increases the rate of weathering. The more area of a rock that is exposed, the faster weathering can take place. In Figure 18.7 you can see why rocks tend to weather faster at their corners and edges than on their flat faces. A good place to see this effect is in very old graveyards. You can see the rounded-corner effect caused by weathering as well as which kinds of rocks weather most rapidly.

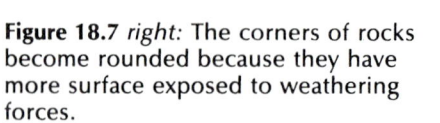

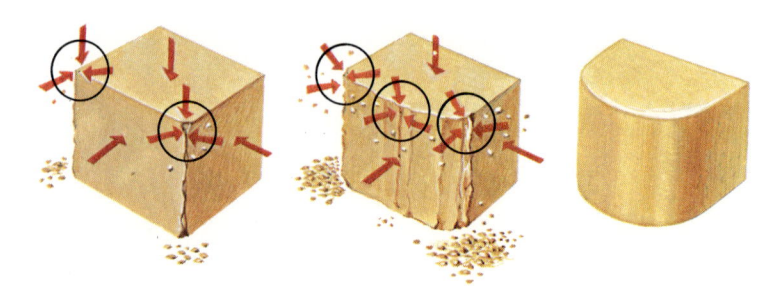

Figure 18.6 *above:* Sometimes weathering causes the outer surface of a rock to flake off in layers.

Figure 18.7 *right:* The corners of rocks become rounded because they have more surface exposed to weathering forces.

18 / Weathering and Erosion

Figure 18.8 *left:* Landslides and mudflows cause quick and severe changes in local surface features.

Figure 18.9 *below:* Soil creep occurs gradually but can do damage over time.

In addition to the breaking down and decomposition that occurs in weathering, materials on the surface are also loosened and carried away by the action of water and wind. This process of loosening and of carrying away the material is called **erosion** [ee-ROH-zhuhn]. But before you look closely at what causes erosion, you should understand what happens to weathered and loosened rock materials.

In general, weathered rock materials move downhill because of gravity. This downward movement of earth materials is called **mass movement.** You've heard about mass movement when the news reported a **landslide** or **mudflow.** Landslides occur when there is a mass movement of sliding rock materials. A mudflow exists when the mass movement is composed of much finer material and usually occurs after heavy rainfall. In Figure 18.9 you can see evidence of very slow mass movement. A slow mass movement such as this is called **soil creep.**

Gravity also can cause the rock materials to fall vertically. Whenever a stream undercuts a bank, the materials fall into the stream. Sometimes rocks fall from cliffs and collect around the base of the cliff. Whenever there are loose rock materials, gravity will act to move them downhill.

Study Questions for 18.1

1. Describe what is meant by weathering.
2. List three basic kinds of weathering.
3. Tell what causes mass movement.
4. What is meant by erosion?

18.2
Erosion by Running Water

You will find out
- ways that running water erodes the land;
- what some of the landscape features produced by running water are.

Figure 18.10 The features of a streambed can reveal many things about the action of the stream.

Do You Know?
Rivers carry off enough sediment to lower the whole surface of the United States about one meter every 27,000 years.

To see how water can cause erosion, you need to look at what happens to the water that falls on the earth. Think about what happens in your backyard. The first rain that falls is taken up by the soil and plants. The next thing you notice is water collecting in low spots, and some water may even be running off in mini streams across the yard. You also see that the runoff water is dirty. It is carrying material that it is eroding away.

If the rain is coming down hard, larger pieces of material begin to move as the mini stream grows and runs faster. The streambed of your mini stream may even curve back and forth as it crosses the yard. If you look closely, you can see that the water in the mini stream doesn't always move at the same speed. Drop a small stick in your mini stream, and you'll see it swirl, twist, speed up, slow down, and sometimes get hung up on an obstruction. Notice that the water flows fastest where the mini stream is narrowest. The more you study this mini stream, the more you learn. Your backyard mini stream is almost a perfect scale-down model of a large stream. This mini stream does a lot of the same things a large stream does as it moves along.

Large streams cut streambeds and pick up material loosened by the rolling, sliding, and bumping of pieces of rock along the streambed. Also the materials carried by the stream rub against the channel and against each other. You can think of these materials carried by the stream as cutting or grinding tools. As the water moves along, it uses these tools to carve and shape the earth. Some material such as soil and clay are transported as fine solid particles in the water. Other materials such as salts are dissolved and then carried away.

18 / Weathering and Erosion

The amount of material carried by the stream changes as the stream slows down or picks up speed. As a stream slows down, it deposits heavier material. A faster-moving stream picks up material and erodes its bed more rapidly. During floods, part of the streambed is carried away. As the stream slows again, sandbars and gravel beds are deposited.

Drainage patterns are one of the landscape features produced by streams. Drainage patterns are distinctive forms of streams and tributaries as viewed on a map. As you can see in Figure 18.11, different drainage patterns can provide you with clues to the kind of land the stream flows over. A branched pattern like a tree generally occurs in flat areas, and the branches are very random in their location. If the drainage pattern appears to radiate in all directions, then there is usually a central high point such as a mountain peak. Sometimes the branches in the pattern appear to be long and run parallel to the main stream. In these cases the land usually consists of parallel ridges or folded mountains. Stream patterns can tell you much about how the land looks.

Figure 18.11 These are drainage patterns produced by streams. *left:* Branched, *above:* Radiating, and *below:* Parallel.

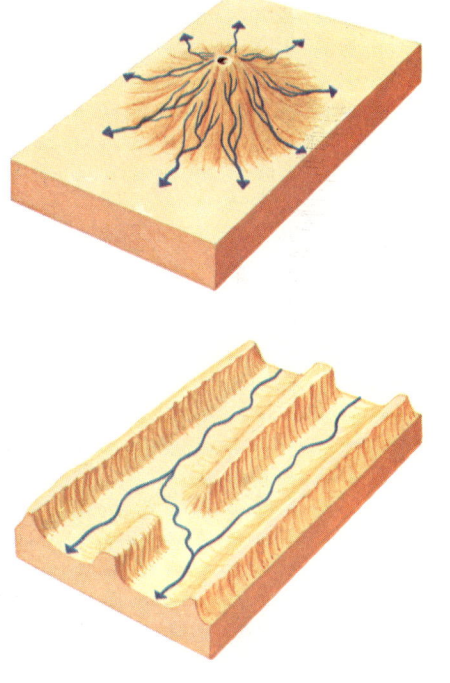

18 / Weathering and Erosion

361

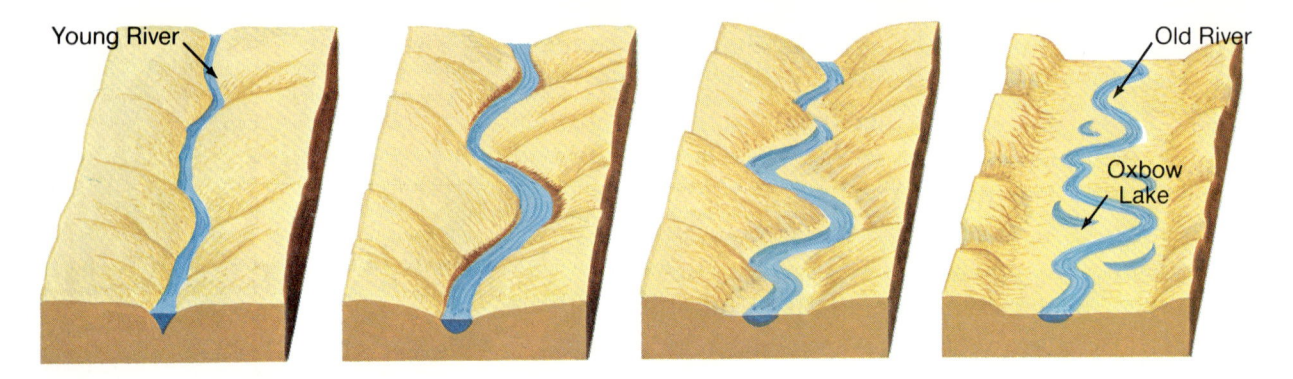

Figure 18.12 *above:* Compare the sizes of the valley floor cut by a meandering stream as time passes.

Other drainage pattern features also develop as streams wear down the land. In level areas streams often wind back and forth in many S curves or bends. These bends in a stream are called **meanders** [mee-AN-duhrs]. Streams widen the floor of the valley through which they run by cutting away on the outside of their bends or meanders. The cut-away material is then deposited on the inside of another bend downstream. In this way the stream works its way slowly across the land. Sometimes one bend in the stream meets another bend and cuts off a meander leaving a long curved lake called an **oxbow lake.**

Streams, along with mass movement, develop valleys. If the land is slowly uplifted, the stream cuts into the earth, leaving terraces like those in Figure 18.13. Within the channel itself streams sometimes develop waterfalls and rapids. In extreme cases the stream meanders cut a deep gorge like the Grand Canyon.

Figure 18.13 *right:* Terraced streambeds usually occur over large, flat surfaces which are gradually uplifted.

362

18 / Weathering and Erosion

Where a stream flows into a lake or ocean, it deposits material. These deposits at the opening of a stream to a lake or ocean are called **deltas** [DEL-tuhs]. Large rivers such as the Mississippi have large and extensive deltas. Streams also deposit material on land. For example, in the dry regions streams may come rushing out of a mountain range as a flash flood after a heavy rain. As the stream spreads out and slows down, it deposits the material it has been carrying in a large fan. As you learned in Chapter 17, this fan-shaped deposit is called an alluvial fan. Alluvial fans are most noticeable in dry regions even though there is no water flowing at the time, but they are also found in other regions.

Do You Know?
The Mississippi Delta began forming near Cairo, Illinois, and has advanced nearly 1,600 km to the south. A section of the delta near New Orleans, Louisiana, has been built in the last 500 years.

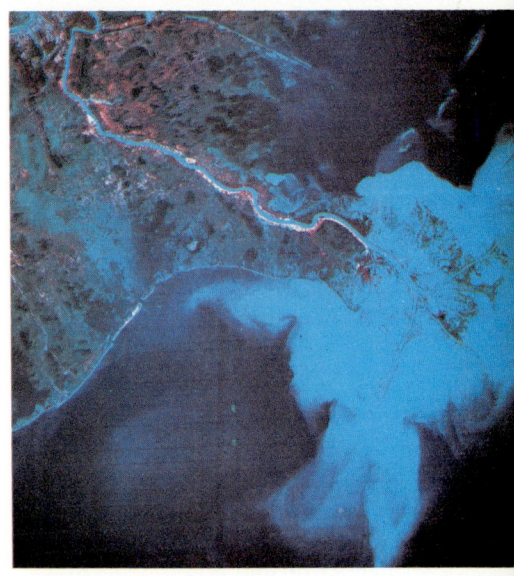

Figure 18.14 *above:* The Mississippi River delta extends into the Gulf of Mexico.

Figure 18.15 *left:* What do alluvial fans such as this one tell you about water flow in an area?

Study Questions for 18.2

1. Explain how a stream erodes the land.
2. Name six landscape features developed by running water.

18.3 Erosion by Wind

You will find out
- how the wind erodes the land;
- what landscape features are produced by the wind;
- why loess is an important wind deposit.

Figure 18.16 This sand dune will change shape and position when wind patterns change.

Do You Know?
Winds blowing over the Mississippi basin have over 1,000 times the transporting power of the river itself.

Figure 18.17 The shallow bowls left from wind deflation are called blowouts.

As the wind moves across the surface, small hard pieces of sand may be moved with it. The sand particles are really small pieces of rock and minerals. These sand pieces moving with the wind at speeds of as much as 100 km per hour or more tear into buildings, cars, rock formations, and people. Over long periods of time the small pieces literally blast and tear away paint, dig holes in rocks, and shape the land. With the exception of dust storms the wind moves sand-sized or smaller particles in an area close to the ground. As with water, when the speed of the wind is slowed, materials being carried along stop moving and are left in a deposit.

The best-known wind deposits are **sand dunes** found in desert and semiarid areas or near beaches. The sand accumulates in piles that shift and flow with each change in wind direction.

Two major processes that make up wind erosion are called **deflation** [dee-FLAY-shuhn] and **abrasion** [uh-BRAY-zhuhn]. Deflation occurs when the wind picks up material and moves it. Sometimes deflation makes shallow bowl-like features on the earth's surface. See Figure 18.17. Abrasion occurs when the particles carried along by the wind polish or break up the things hit by the particles. Deflation and abrasion are the work of the wind. One process picks things up, and the other process polishes and breaks up the things hit.

Figure 18.18 *left:* Flat faces are sculpted onto rock by wind erosion.

Figure 18.19 *right:* Unusual rock sculptures result as wind erodes materials in the rock unevenly.

Figure 18.20 *below:* Dust storms can deposit large amounts of loess but can also blow it away.

Some of the landscape features produced by wind are unusual forms or land sculptures. Some rocks in the desert, as in Figure 18.18, show flat faces almost like you see on a gemstone. Another way wind shapes rock formations is shown in Figure 18.19. When the wind-blown particles strike rock formations, the particles remove the softest material first.

The most important wind deposit is called **loess** [LOH-uhs]. Loess is fine dust deposited by winds over a large area. These deposits can be several meters thick and cover enormous areas. The fertile soil that develops on loess is rich in nutrients needed by grain crops. Rich farmland in parts of Nebraska, Kansas, Iowa, Illinois, and Missouri are loess deposits. Figure 18.20 shows a dust storm in New Mexico that deposited fine material over thousands of square kilometers in the Southwest. Storms such as this can travel for several hundred kilometers.

Study Questions for 18.3

1. Name the two processes of wind erosion.
2. Name three landscape features developed by wind action.
3. Where are loess deposits found and why are these deposits important?

18 / Weathering and Erosion

18.4 Erosion by Ice

You will find out
- what a glacier is;
- how glaciers erode the land;
- what landscape features are produced by glaciers.

In some high mountains and in the polar areas there are places where the snow does not completely melt in summer. The edge of these places where the snow accumulates is called the **snow line.** The snow line moves back and forth with the seasons. The ice and snow that accumulate above the snow line make up a glacier.

The ice in the glacier is not like the ice in your freezer. Glacier ice forms gradually through a change from snow to granular snow and ice. As the granular ice gets buried deeper and deeper, the weight of the snow and ice above causes the bottom granules to recrystallize. This glacial ice is tough, is hard, and melts slowly.

Glaciers are born in areas always covered by snow. Those glaciers that cover a large area of a continent are called **continental glaciers.** If the ice is confined to valleys, it is a **valley glacier.**

Figure 18.21 *above:* A continental glacier spans flat areas.

Figure 18.22 *right:* Valley glaciers are common in high mountain areas.

Continental glaciers form in regions of high latitude. They cover a region completely. These glaciers cause uniform erosion. They smooth out the terrain by wearing down the high peaks and filling in lower regions. Antarctica and Greenland are buried under continental glaciers.

Valley glaciers occur in all parts of the world where mountains stretch above the snow line. Erosion caused by this type of glacier makes the terrain more rugged. The largest valley glaciers are found in southern Alaska. The world's largest mountain region, the Himalayas, is also a source region for valley glaciers.

Gravitation constantly acts on valley glaciers, causing them to move downhill. As the glaciers are pulled through V-shaped valleys, the walls of the valleys are scoured. The valleys are made deeper and wider. Curves in the path of the valley are straightened. Later, when the glaciers recede, these V-shaped valleys will have been transformed into U-shaped valleys.

Figure 18.23 *left:* This U-shaped valley was cut by the powerful forces of a glacier.

Figure 18.24 The Matterhorn

The scouring action of glaciers has produced spectacular peaks and valleys in mountain regions around the world. These glaciers filed away the sides of mountains as they moved through an area. The Matterhorn is the highest mountain peak in the Pennine Alps of Europe. Its pyramidlike shape is the result of such glacial filing.

18 / Weathering and Erosion

It's hard to visualize how glaciers move. They don't slide along as one mass. The lower part of the glacier flows and continuously changes its shape by recrystallization. The upper part of the glacier acts like a brittle solid and cracks and slides over the lower layer.

Glaciers do a lot of work as they move along. Freezing ice breaks loose chunks of rocks. These rock chunks become part of the glacier and move along with it. Over a long period of time the chunks of rock are scattered throughout the glacier, but more rocks are near the bottom. As rocks are pushed along by the glacier, they erode the land underneath. These rocks polish or make huge grooves or scratches in the land under the glacier. At the same time the rocks inside the glacier are also grinding against each other. This grinding puts scratches on the rocks and makes rock powder.

Figure 18.25 *right:* Rocks moved by glaciers easily make grooves in surfaces they pass.

Gravitation is continuously moving the ice and the rock material to the lower end of the glacier. There the rock material is deposited as the ice melts. This deposit of rock at the farthest point the glacier reached is called a **terminal moraine** [TUR-mih-nuhl muh-RAYN]. Long Island in New York is a terminal moraine that was built up many meters from the seafloor by debris dropped from melting ice.

Do You Know?
If the Antarctic ice sheets were melted at a suitable rate, the melted ice could keep the Mississippi River flowing for 50,000 years or all the rivers in the United States for about 17,000 years.

The rocks carried by the glacier and deposited in an unsorted way when the glacier melts are called **till**. Glaciers also make deposits that are layered. Large depressions on a glacier may accumulate meltwater. In these pools the rock material settles in layered deposits. At times the meltwater develops huge tunnels that wind their way along the bottom of a melting glacier. Layered deposits then form a snakelike ridge of land in the tunnels. The snakelike ridge shown in Figure 18.26 is called an **esker** [ES-kuhr].

Glaciation is continuously at work changing the landscape in many places today. But the glaciation that formed the landscape features in Yosemite National Park took place thousands of years ago during earlier periods of glaciation. Geologists have found evidence of four major ice ages. The first of these advances of ice took place perhaps more than one million years ago. Figure 18.27 shows the maximum extent of the four ice advances. Following each advance of the ice came a warm period. Will another ice age cause a glacier to cover the northern United States? Nobody can tell for sure.

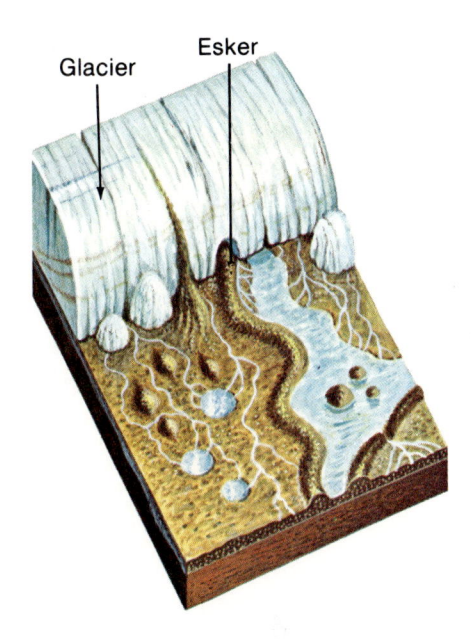

Figure 18.26 *above:* An esker marks the place where meltwater tunneled under a glacier.

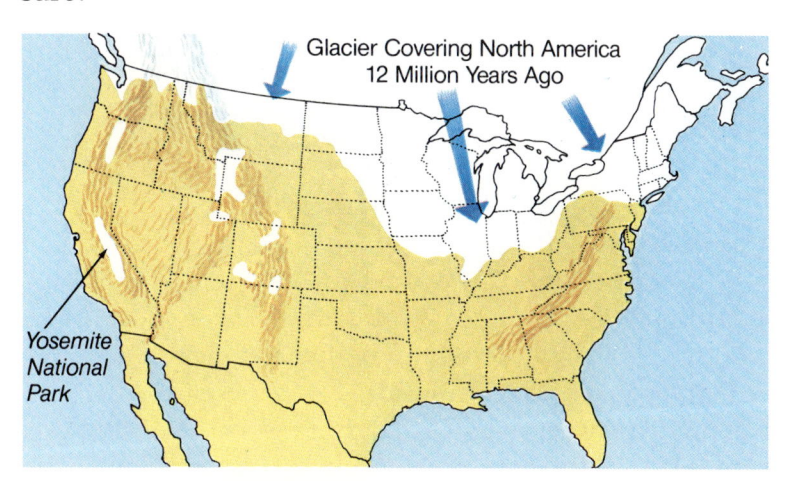

Figure 18.27 *left:* The combined southern limits reached by all glacial movement over North America.

Study Questions for 18.4

1. Explain what a glacier is and why glaciers are found where they are.
2. Tell how a glacier works.
3. Name three landscape features developed by glaciers.

18 / Weathering and Erosion

Career

Geomorphologist

A geomorphologist is a person who makes a study of surface landforms and the processes that cause them. Geomorphologists are also interested in the changes in landforms over time. Geomorphologists recognize that every landform is in the process of becoming something else. Hills that are worn down and V-shaped stream valleys that become flatter and wider are two examples of changes in the land surface that geomorphologists study.

Dr. A. Wesley Ward is a geomorphologist working for the United States Geological Survey in Flagstaff, Arizona. Currently he is working on a large-scale map showing the geology in the San Juan Basin. This region is located in northwest New Mexico. Dr. Ward is studying the surface features, soils, and climate relationships involved in the development of landforms in this area. When completed, the map will be used in the search for oil, gas, and coal that are thought to exist in this region.

To make such a map requires a great deal of training. Dr. Ward took many courses in geology, chemistry, physics, engineering, atmospheric science, and mathematics.

Geomorphologists usually have a great interest in and love of the outdoors. Dr. Ward's love of the outdoors began as a child when he collected frogs, turtles, and other living creatures with his grandfather in Michigan. When asked why he liked his work, Dr. Ward replied, "Because it is like solving a great big puzzle. I like the outdoors. I observe the surface and then try to figure out how it got to be that way. I like this kind of detective work."

CHAPTER REVIEW

Main Ideas

- Weathering is the mechanical, chemical, or biological breakdown of rocks.
- Erosion is the process of loosening and carrying away earth materials. Gravity, wind, water, and ice contribute to the process of erosion.
- The downward movement of loose earth materials by gravity is called mass movement.
- Running water grinds and transports rocks and rock materials.
- Landscape features formed by moving water include meanders, oxbow lakes, terraces, deltas, and alluvial fans.
- Wind erodes the land by deflation and abrasion.
- Landscape features formed by wind include sand dunes, loess, rocks with flat surfaces, and shallow bowl-like features.
- Loess is a fine dust deposited by winds that develops into a fertile soil.
- A glacier is a large mass of ice that formed from an accumulation of snow above the snow line.
- Glaciers erode the land by splitting off rocks and moving them, and by scraping the land.
- Two types of glaciers are continental glaciers and valley glaciers.
- Landscape features formed by glaciers include moraines, tills, and eskers.

Using Vocabulary

On a separate piece of paper, write a paragraph describing erosion. Use as many of the words listed below as possible.

weathering	mass movement	delta	valley glacier
chemical weathering	landslide	sand dune	terminal moraine
mechanical weathering	mud flow	deflation	till
biological weathering	soil creep	abrasion	esker
oxidation	drainage pattern	loess	
sinkholes	meander	snow line	
erosion	oxbow lake	continental glacier	

Remembering Facts

Number your paper from 1 to 15. Match each term in column A with a phrase in column B.

A
1. mechanical weathering
2. terminal moraine
3. weathering
4. delta
5. erosion
6. meander
7. valley glacier
8. deflation
9. glacier
10. oxbow lake
11. sinkhole
12. landslide
13. sand dune
14. mud flow
15. oxidation
16. loess
17. soil creep
18. till
19. abrasion
20. esker

B
a. stream deposit in lake or ocean
b. s-shaped bends in a stream
c. accumulated ice and snow
d. that which results from the collapse of underground caves
e. accumulated ice and snow in a valley
f. making shallow bowl-like features on the surface
g. example of chemical weathering
h. mass movement of fine material after heavy rainfall
i. a cut-off meander
j. rapid mass movement of rock and earth material
k. rock deposits found at the farthest point that a glacier moves to
l. breaking down and dissolving rocks
m. the loosening and carrying away of pieces of rock and earth material
n. a wind deposit
o. breaking rocks apart
p. the polishing of objects by wind-carried particles
q. snakelike ridge formed by a glacier
r. unsorted rocks deposited by a glacier
s. fine dust deposited by winds over a large area
t. slow mass movement

Understanding Ideas

On your paper, answer each question in complete sentences.
1. Why do rocks found along the shores and river bottoms rarely have sharp edges?
2. Which agent of erosion is the most effective in each of the three major climate zones? Explain your answer in each case.
3. Explain how mechanical weathering helps chemical weathering and how chemical weathering helps mechanical weathering.
4. What do an alluvial fan and a delta have in common? Why are alluvial fans more common in dry regions than in wet regions?

Applying What You Have Learned

1. What environmental factor helps cause a glacier to move forward or to recede?
2. What two factors influence the ability of wind to erode the land?
3. Would you expect to find an oxbow lake in a mountain region? Explain your answer.
4. When do you think a glacier deposits rock material?

Challenge

The rate at which chemical and mechanical weathering takes place depends to a large degree on climatic conditions. The graph shows the intensity of physical and chemical weathering on the earth's surface with respect to average yearly rainfall and temperatures. Study the graph and answer the following questions.

1. Under what conditions does strong chemical weathering take place? Why?
2. According to the graph, describe the climate where the least weathering takes place.
3. Soil is produced by the processes of chemical weathering. Describe the earth's surface in an area where the average yearly temperature is −5°C and the yearly precipitation is 50 cm. Give reasons for your description of such an area.
4. Why is the upper left part of the graph blank?

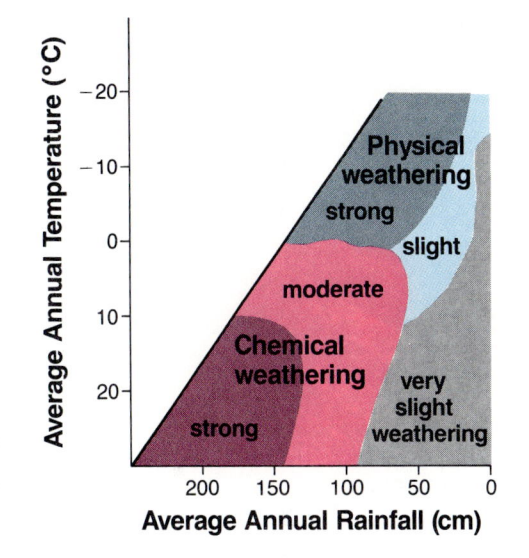

Research and Investigation

1. Make a picture collection of landscape features near the area in which you live. Label and describe evidence of the processes of weathering found in each picture.
2. Use the resources in your library to learn more about one of the national parks. Give an oral report on the natural land features unique to that park. Describe the weathering and erosion of the past that have shaped the features of the park. Compare the weathering and erosion of the past to what is occurring today.
3. There may be evidence of glaciation in your local landscape. Find out whether the area you live in was once covered by a glacier.

19.1 The Rock Record

You will find out
- what the law of superposition is;
- why the law of crosscutting relationships is useful in determining what event occurred first;
- why the principle of uniformity is important.

The last time you were watching an old black-and-white movie on TV, did you try to guess when it was made? If so, what did you look for? Was it how the cars looked? the clothes the people were wearing? the hair styles? or some other clues? A clue is something that aids in the solution of a problem. Clues can help you learn about the ages of the rocks you see.

The position of the rock layers is one clue to look for. In Chapter 13 you learned that layers of sediment are deposited (laid down) in horizontal layers. These layers form sedimentary rock in time. If the rock layers have not been turned over, the oldest layer will be at the bottom. The youngest layer will be on top. This relationship of youngest layer on top and oldest layer on the bottom is called the **law of superposition.**

Figure 19.2 *above:* Sedimentary rock layers follow the law of superposition.

Figure 19.3 *right:* The law of crosscutting relationships can be applied to this sedimentary rock. The rock was faulted after the layers were formed.

What's another clue to look for in the rock record? Look for faults in rocks or magma features that cut across other rocks. Figure 19.3 shows a layer of sedimentary rock cut by a fault. Which came first, the layer of rock or the fault? The layer of rock had to come first because the rocks had to be there before the fault could occur. The fact that younger features cut across older features is called the **law of crosscutting relationships.** Faults, for example, are younger than the rocks they cut.

Geologists believe that the laws of nature that are recognized today have always existed. Water has always flowed downhill and carried sand and silt to the sea. The rock cycle worked the same millions of years ago as it does today. Rocks have weathered and eroded in the same manner throughout geologic time. Earth features formed long ago were made by the same processes operating in the same way as they do today. This is called the **principle of uniformity.**

Figure 19.4 Ripples in ancient sandstone (*left*) were formed by the same process that made the new ripples in the sand (*right*).

Is the principle of uniformity ever questioned? Some geologists believe the rate at which the earth processes work may differ over time. Volcanism may have been more frequent at certain times in the past. There may even have been earth processes operating in the past that are not apparent today. The earth's atmosphere may have been different a long time ago. This would cause different chemical reactions in the weathering process. But one thing seems certain. The physical and chemical laws of nature are unchanging. The earth processes that these laws of nature caused in the past continue to happen today. By studying the present, you can infer the behavior of these processes in the past.

Study Questions for 19.1

1. Name two geologic laws used in reading the rock record.
2. Make a sketch illustrating the two geologic laws.
3. Describe the principle of uniformity.

19.2 Gaps in the Rock Record

You will find out
- what is meant by an unconformity in the rock record;
- how to use correlations to determine if rock layers are related in age.

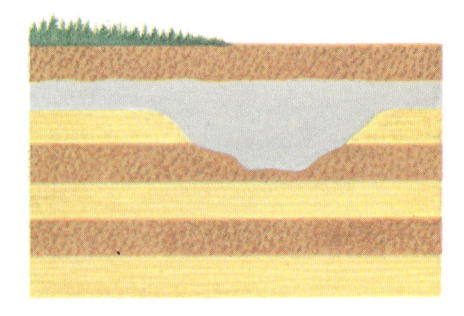

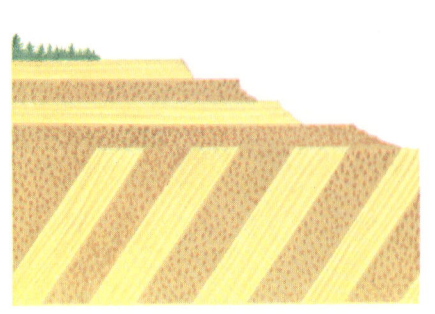

Figure 19.5 These are examples of unconformity. *top:* Sedimentary layering interrupted by erosion, *middle:* A break between igneous rock and sedimentary rock of different ages, and *bottom:* A change in tilt between sedimentary layers.

By now you may think that reading the rock record is an easy process. You just apply the geologic laws. This would be true if the rock layers in each area were a complete story. Why isn't the story complete? The principle of uniformity gives you some clues about why the story is incomplete. Remember that according to this principle the earth processes that are going on now have probably always been occurring. If rocks are being eroded away today, they were also eroded away millions of years ago. The erosion wore away the rock layers and deposited the rock material somewhere else. As the rock layers eroded away, that part of the rock record also disappeared.

After a period of time new layers of sediments may again have been deposited on top of the eroded area. These sediments in time became sedimentary rock. But an examination of the layers shows a time lapse between the top of the eroded layers and the new layers. These time lapses are breaks in the rock record. You no longer can read a complete story. Something is missing.

When geologists find such a break in the rock record, they say an **unconformity** [uhn-kuhn-FOHR-mih-tee] exists. Unconformities then represent a lapse of time. During that time, the rock record was not recorded or was being destroyed by erosion, creating an unconformity. An unconformity may occur within rocks of the same kind or between different kinds of rocks.

The easiest unconformity to spot is an **angular unconformity**. An angular unconformity is one in which the older layers slope at a different angle from that of the younger layers. In Chapter 18, you learned that there are pressures in the earth's crust that can fold the layers of sedimentary rock. In time the top of a fold or an anticline is worn away, leaving only the sloping layers.

With more time this area may again be covered with a sea, and new sedimentary deposits may be formed. The new rock layers are laid down horizontally on the sloping lower layers. The result is an angular unconformity. In Figure 19.6 you can see how this happened.

Figure 19.6 The four stages in the formation of an angular unconformity.

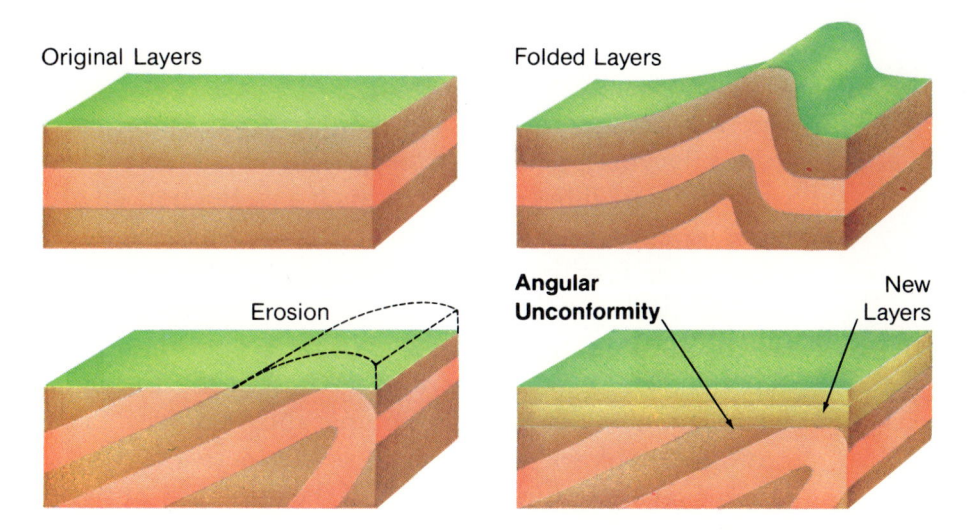

Original Layers

Folded Layers

Erosion

Angular Unconformity — New Layers

By now you can see that sometimes there are problems in reading the rock record. If you are trying to compare the rock records in two different areas, these problems can make the task very difficult. But geologists have developed some ways of comparing rock layers in different places. One way is to walk along a rock layer and trace it from place to place. You can walk along a rock layer and follow it from location A to location B without a break in the layer. What would you think? The rock layer is obviously the same rock formation in both location A and location B. The rock must be the same age in each location.

Another way is to note the sequence of distinctive rock layers. Examine the rock layers in Figure 19.7. Suppose that 100 km away in another area you also find the same distinctive layers. You find the red shale, gray limestone, and yellow sandstone are laid down in the same order. You can infer that both areas contain rock layers that were laid down at the same time. They were probably joined together in the past.

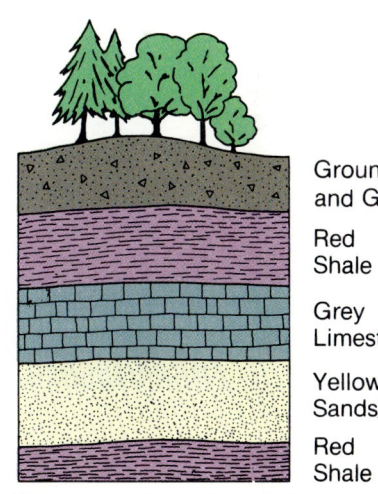

Ground and Gravel
Red Shale
Grey Limestone
Yellow Sandstone
Red Shale

Figure 19.7 If you found these same rock layers in another area, what would they tell you about the age of each area?

19 / The Rock Record

A third way uses a **marker layer.** Marker layers provide an even more distinctive characteristic. A volcanic-ash layer can be a marker layer. It would cover a wide area and be deposited at one time. Wherever this layer is spotted, you'll find rocks of a similar age.

A fourth way is the location of **index fossils.** If rock layers in two different locations contain the same groups of fossils, they are thought to be about the same age. Sometimes there is a very distinctive fossil that lives only a brief geologic time. Yet this fossil is found in rocks in many different places. Such a distinctive, single fossil is called an index fossil. Rocks containing the same index fossil are related by age.

When geologists compare the ages of rocks in two different locations, they use a process called **correlation.** In a correlation they compare the rocks in the different locations by looking for comparable features. The geologists look for such things as distinctive layers, a marker layer, and index fossils. If they find any of these in both areas, they have a correlation. The geologists can then say the rocks are related in age. Correlations are much easier to do with rocks separated by only a few kilometers. Yet correlations have been done with rocks separated by oceans.

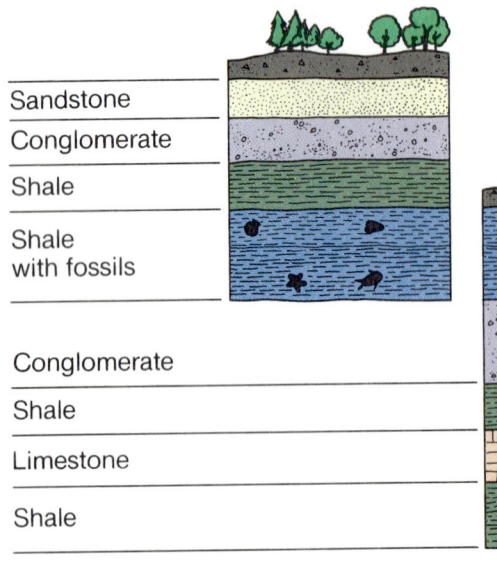

Figure 19.8 Fossil remains of this organism make it a valuable index fossil. The organism is related to the chambered *Nautilus,* which still exists.

Figure 19.9 Examine the correlation clues shown in the diagram. Can you pick out the related rock layers?

380

19 / The Rock Record

Activity

Which of These Rock Layers Are Related?

Materials
pencil
paper
colored pencils
scissors

Procedure

The rock layers in four different places were identified as shown below. (Fossil symbols represent groups of fossils.)

1. Copy the rock layers and mark each layer as shown.
2. Cut out the columns of rock layers.
3. Arrange the columns of rock layers side by side by matching layers of the same age.

Questions

1. Which rock layer(s) correlates with layer 2? With layer 3? With layer 4? With layer 9?
2. How many different rock layers are shown?

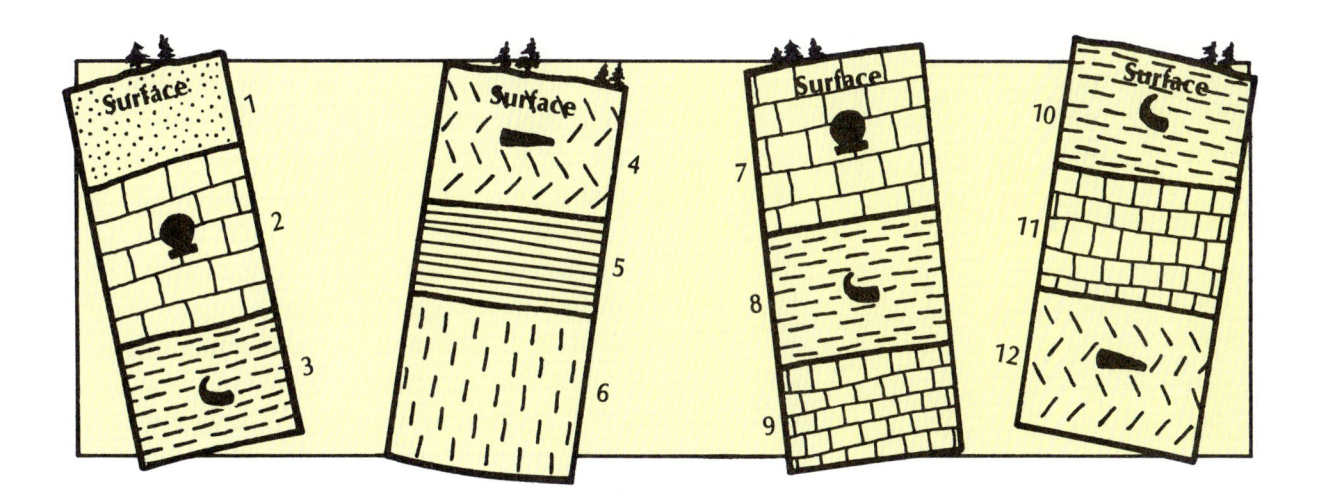

Just as reading the rock record has its problems, correlations are sometimes difficult to make. The same fossil may be found in different kinds of rocks. Geologists must use as many clues as possible when they correlate rock layers.

Study Questions for 19.2

1. What is the name of the geologic feature that indicates part of the record is lost?
2. Describe what it means to correlate rock layers. How are index fossils and marker layers used in correlations?

19 / The Rock Record

19.3 Clues in Sedimentary Rocks

You will find out
- what sedimentary structures are;
- how rock layers indicate a change in sea level.

Figure 19.10 *right:* The imprints of lightly falling rain are preserved in sandstone. What do they tell you?

Figure 19.11 *below:* Four sedimentary structures that give geologists clues about past conditions: (a) ripple marks, (b) crossbedding, (c) graded bedding, (d) mud cracks.

In learning how to read the earth's history, you must look everywhere for clues. Remember, a clue is something that helps you find a solution to a problem. What clue do you see in Figure 19.10? What could make these circular imprints in this piece of sandstone? What you see in the sandstone are raindrop imprints. These imprints tell you that the sand was above water and a light rain was falling when the imprints were made. From the raindrop imprints the geologist also knows which side of the rock layer is the top side. The imprints were made more than 100 million years ago. They are a reminder of the principle of uniformity. The same earth processes have operated throughout time. Rain fell upon the earth 100 million years ago as it does today.

You can find many clues to the conditions that existed when sedimentary rocks were deposited. Figure 19.11 shows four **sedimentary structures** that are good clues. Sedimentary structures are patterns formed in the sediment before it becomes solid rock. Ripple marks are formed in the sand, which later becomes rock. They indicate that water or wind flowed back and forth or in one direction. Crossbeds show shifting water or wind currents flowing in one direction. Graded bedding indicates rapid settling of particles of different sizes in still water. What conditions exist when mud cracks form? Mud cracks when it is exposed to air and dries out. Each clue in a sedimentary structure helps us to learn the conditions existing at the time the sediments accumulated.

By using clues, geologists can usually tell land deposits from ocean deposits. Most land deposits occur in the beds of streams, on the flat areas of valleys, in lakes, in swamps, and in deserts. Each kind of deposit will contain clues that help in reading the earth's history. For example, the roundness of pebbles is usually related to how far they have traveled.

Ocean deposits occur below sea level. Since the level of the sea changes because of tides, there is a transition zone between land and ocean deposits. When you go to the beach, you play in this zone. The next time you go to the beach, look carefully and you'll see both land and ocean deposits.

Figure 19.12 Notice the order of deposits of sediment shown here. Compare the pattern with those in Figure 19.13.

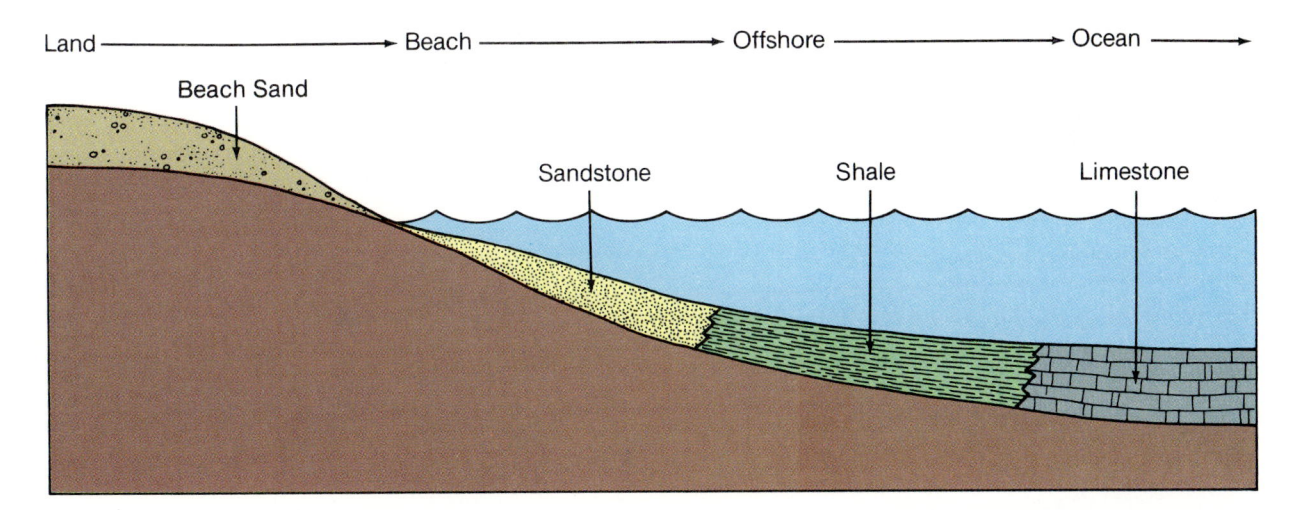

Figure 19.12 is a model of the near-shore land and ocean pattern of deposits. This model shows that in general the sediment particles get finer as you go out to sea. On land there is a wide variety of deposits. In the ocean you find more uniform deposits and finer particle sizes. As you see, the sediments change as you go from shore out to sea. Deposits near shore are mostly sand and form sandstone. Farther out to sea the fine deposits of silt form shale. In the deeper seawater the deposits form limestone. If you live in an area that is largely limestone, you know it was once under a sea. If your area is largely shale, you can guess that it was an area nearer shore than the limestone area was.

Do You Know?
The total thickness of all sedimentary rock has been used to estimate the age of the earth. If the average rate of deposition was 3,000 years per meter, 128 km would require at least 384,000,000 years to accumulate. Geologists believe this figure is far too low.

19 / The Rock Record

How do geologists use this information? By examining the layers of rock, they can tell that an area was submerging and the sea was moving onto the land. They can also tell if the land was rising and the shoreline was moving outward. In Figure 19.13A you can see how layers were formed in a submerging area. As the land submerged, the shoreline with its deposit of beach sand moved in over the former land area. The fine silt that would form shale was deposited over sand deposits. Farther at sea, deposits that would form limestone were laid over the area that was shale. If the water rose even higher, you would find these patterns repeated again farther toward land. Suppose you are looking at three layers of rock with limestone on top and then shale with sandstone on the bottom. This pattern of deposit tells you that the land submerged or the sea level rose. This caused the shoreline to move inland.

Figure 19.13 *top:* A submerging land area; *bottom:* An emerging land area

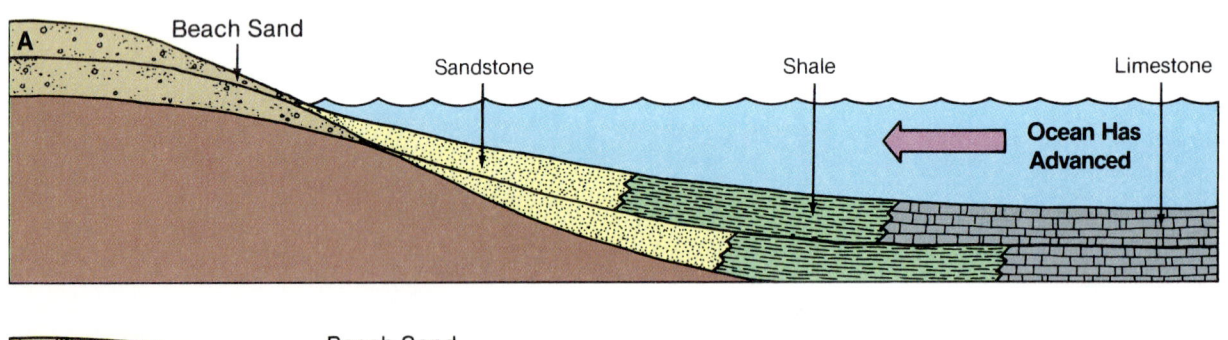

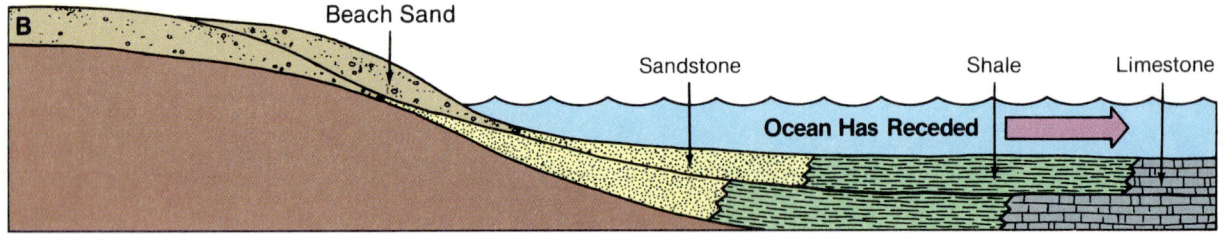

Suppose the three layers were in this order—sandstone (top), shale, and limestone (bottom). Does that change the earth's history at that spot? Geologists would say that sea level had been falling when these layers were deposited. You can see how this occurred in Figure 19.13B.

Figure 19.14 Exposed rock layers like these provide clues about sea level changes.

The next time you see some rock layers, look for the order of the sandstone, shale, and limestone layers. The order of deposits in an area indicates changes in sea level.

By now you should have learned the rock record is not always clear and easy to read. Sometimes it is necessary to look for more clues and the interpretation becomes more difficult. In fact, you may not be able to interpret the earth's history as well as you would like. This is true for geologists as well.

Study Questions for 19.3

1. What is a sedimentary structure?
2. What conditions produced the following clues: ripple marks, mud cracks, and graded bedding?
3. What sequence of sedimentary layers would indicate a sea moving over the land?

19 / The Rock Record

19.4 Interpreting What You See

You will find out
- how geologists use cross sections to read the earth's history;
- what information can be found on a geologic map.

Interpreting what has happened in the earth's past is somewhat like deciding what happened in building your school. You see the finished building, but what was the first event in building it? What were all the events in between the first and the last event? In what order did these events occur? These are the kinds of questions geologists ask about the earth's history.

Figure 19.15 Can you read the history written in this road cut? The illustrations below show the order of events that happened before the road cut.

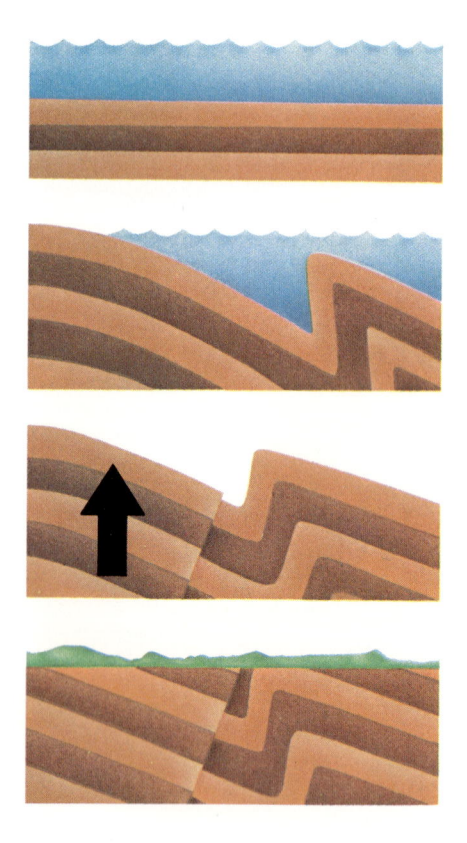

In Figure 19.15 you see a road cut. You can think of it as a **geologic cross section.** There are several sedimentary layers, and the layers have been cut by a fault. Now think about what happened and in what order. What evidence do you have? There is evidence of (1) folded sedimentary rock layers, (2) a fault, (3) a period when this place was underwater, (4) a period when it was above water, (5) erosion of the surface, and (6) a recent road cut. In what order did these things occur?

386

19 / The Rock Record

The first thing to occur was that the region was underwater. While the region was underwater, the sedimentary rock layers were deposited and folded. The next event was the faulting. Remember the law of cross-cutting relationships? Geologists then assume that the uplift of the land, or the fourth event, which raised the land out of water, occurred during faulting. The last natural event was the surface erosion, followed by the event of the road cut being made by people. In interpreting the earth's history, then, geologists look for geologic features and the sequence in which these features occurred.

Activity

What Is the History of the Rocks in These Geologic Cross Sections?

Materials
pencil
paper

Procedure

1. Make a list of the things that occurred in cross section A.
2. Write down the order in which these things occurred.
3. From the evidence you should have found these things:
    two sets of sedimentary layers
    area underwater two times
    angular unconformity
    erosion two times
    uplift two times
    tilting

You should have listed the order in which things happened as (1) area underwater; (2) sedimentary layers C, D, E, F; (3) tilting; (4) uplift; (5) erosion; (6) underwater; (7) sedimentary layers K, J, I; (8) uplift, (9) erosion.

4. Now repeat steps 1 and 2 for cross section B.

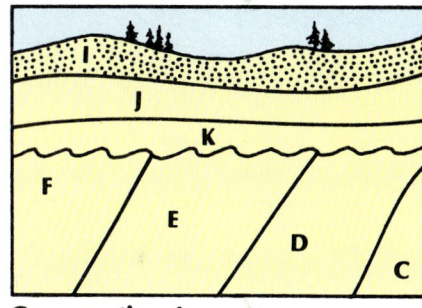

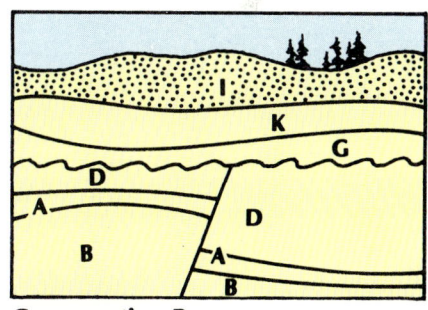

Cross-section A

Cross-section B

Questions

1. List the evidence you find.
2. In what order did these things occur (first to last)?

Road cuts or exposed cross sections are not always available. Geologists must rely on other sources for the information they need. For many areas special maps have been prepared. These are maps that show rock types on the surface, ages of rocks, topography, and how the rocks lie. A map showing geologic features of the land is called a **geologic map.** Geologic maps show a vertical look at the land as if you were looking straight down from an airplane.

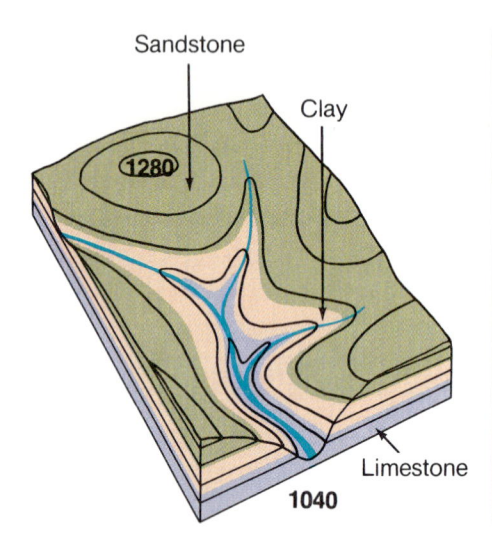

Figure 19.16 The geologic features of an area (*left*) are shown on the geologic map with contour lines added (*right*).

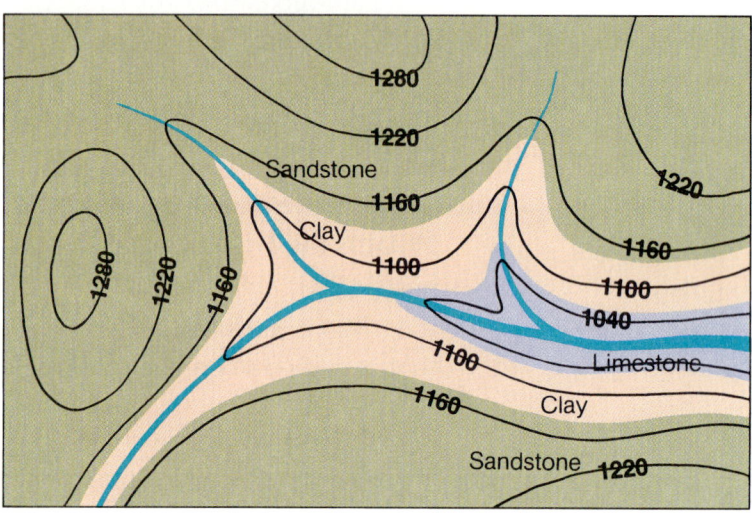

In Figure 19.16 you see a part of a geologic map. It shows three different kinds of rock. You can also see that there is a creek. The direction of the stream flow can also be determined. Where is the highest land? Where is the lowest land? The contour lines tell you how high the land is in each area. Now look at the rock layers. Which layer is the oldest? Remember what the law of superposition tells you. Which layer is the youngest? The rock layers are also horizontal. What on the map tells you that? Did you notice that the contour lines and rock layer lines run side by side?

You can read the history of the earth in this area from the map. Remember what you have learned about what the sequence of deposits tells you. Since there are sedimentary rocks, the area was once underwater. The sequence of sandstone, clay bed, and limestone tells you that the area was uplifted. As the area rose, the shoreline moved out away from this area. Finally, from the contours and the stream flow, you know the area has been eroded. You can read this history because you now understand the earth-shaping processes.

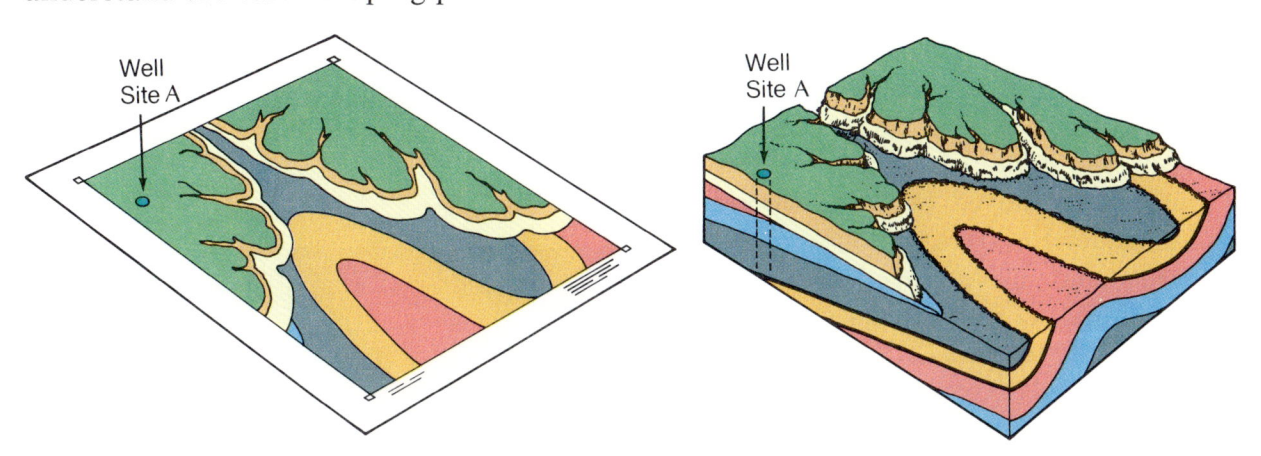

Geologists also use geologic maps to tell them what rock layers are found underground. Look at the geologic map shown in Figure 19.17. You can see the pattern of the rocks on the earth's surface. Suppose you are going to drill a well at location A. What rock formations will you find when you drill the well? Now look at Figure 19.18. This figure shows the surface and an underground view. This view is based on the geologist's interpretation of the geologic map. A geologic map shows the patterns of the rocks on the earth's surface. From these patterns a geologist usually can interpret what rock layers are underground and how the rock layers lie. By now you should be able to see that there are many clues in the rock record that are used to interpret the earth's history. You must be able to use them all.

Figure 19.17 *left:* A geologic map showing surface features of an area.

Figure 19.18 *right:* A cross section of the same area based on the surface patterns.

Study Questions for 19.4

1. What two things should you look for in making an interpretation of a geologic cross section?
2. What are some features shown on a geologic map?
3. Draw a geologic map showing three horizontal rock layers. What is the earth's history of the place you have drawn?

19 / The Rock Record

Biography

Dr. David Lopez (1949–   )

Dr. David Lopez, a field geologist, was born in El Rito, New Mexico, in 1949. While he was still a small child his family moved to Grand Junction, Colorado. He grew up loving the outdoors and has enjoyed fishing and hunting all of his life. His mother says he was a great rock collector as a child.

He started his career in geology when a college advisor suggested that he change from a forestry major to a geology major. He did very well in his studies in the new area. However, a summer job in the field really convinced him that work in geology was to be his future. Dr. Lopez was an outstanding student and received a number of scholarships during his college years. He completed his Ph.D. in 1981 at the Colorado School of Mines, Golden, Colorado.

Dr. Lopez's work experience includes several years as a field geologist doing research for the United States Geological Survey in Idaho and Montana. This work was primarily a mapping study that included an appraisal of the mineral and petroleum potential in this area. Currently he is working for Montana Power Company, Billings, Montana, exploring for petroleum in southwest Montana, Idaho, and northern Utah.

His love of field geology is based on a desire to know how things fit together. He enjoys figuring out the three-dimensional relationships between and within rock formations. He says that he has to develop a model of how things fit together before he feels right.

CHAPTER REVIEW

Main Ideas

- Geologists believe that the sediments that formed sedimentary rock layers were deposited in horizontal layers.
- The law of superposition is that the oldest sedimentary rock layer is always on the bottom if the rock layers have not been disturbed.
- The law of crosscutting relationships is that younger features always cut across older ones.
- The principle of uniformity is that the geologic processes of the past are the same as those you see happening today.
- An unconformity is a part of the rock record that is missing.
- Unconformities represent a time when the rock record was unformed or destroyed by erosion.
- Geologists correlate rock layers by comparing the ages of rocks in different places. Index fossils and marker layers are used in correlations.
- Sedimentary structures are patterns formed in the sediment before it becomes rock. These include ripple marks, crossbeds, graded bedding, and mud cracks.
- The order in which sedimentary layers appear indicates how the shoreline has moved.
- A geologic cross section is an interpretation of the rock layers found underground.
- The earth's history can be interpreted from geologic cross sections and geologic maps.

Using Vocabulary

Use the Glossary to define each of the words below. Write the definitions on a separate sheet of paper.

law of superposition
law of crosscutting relationships
principle of uniformity
unconformity
angular unconformity

market layer
index fossil
correlation
sedimentary structures
geologic cross section
geologic map

19 / The Rock Record

Remembering Facts

On your paper, write the word or words that best complete each sentence.

1. Patterns formed in sediments before they become rock are called _____ structures.
2. _____ fossils are used to correlate rock layers that are found in different locations.
3. _____ show that currents have flowed in one direction across sediments.
4. Sedimentary rock layers are laid down in a _____ direction.
5. The geologic feature that cuts across other geologic features is _____ in age.
6. The principle of _____ says that the laws of nature are unchanging.
7. Finding age relationships between rock layers is called _____.
8. Older rock layers are sloped differently than younger rock layers in a(an) _____ unconformity.
9. The deeper the ocean, the _____ sedimentary particles become.
10. A distinctive layer of sedimentary rock is called a _____ layer.
11. A(An) _____ represents a part of the rock record that is either missing or was never formed.
12. The law of _____ states that the oldest sedimentary rock layer is usually on the bottom.
13. If you live in an area where the sedimentary rock is mainly _____, then your area was once covered by an ocean.
14. A road cut provides us with a geologic _____ _____.
15. _____ _____ indicate that water flowed back and forth or in one direction over the sediments before they became rock.

Understanding Ideas

On your paper, answer each question in complete sentences.

1. How would you interpret the presence of an unconformity between similar layers of sandstone?
2. A geologic cross section has a bottom layer of shale, followed by layers of sandstone, shale, limestone, and finally another layer of shale. Explain what may have happened to the shoreline during the formation of these rock layers.
3. Describe the history of rock layers containing two similar layers of sandstone with a layer of salt sandwiched in between.

Applying What You Have Learned

1. When would the position of ripple marks in a sedimentary bed be used to prove that rock layers had been overturned?
2. What methods can a geologist use to determine how long ago a geologic event occurred?
3. Suppose you find a sequence of rock layers that is upside down when compared to another rock sequence that is 100 km away. Both sequences contain marker layers and index fossils. Describe how you could determine which is right side up and which is upside down.

Challenge

Study the cross section and geologic map below. Use these diagrams to answer the following questions.

1. Describe the geologic events that would make the cross section. List them from oldest to most recent.
2. What is probably missing from the diagram on the left because of the unconformity? Explain.
3. Describe the geologic events that would create the situation shown in the geologic map.
4. Does the diagram on the right show an eroded anticline or syncline? Explain.

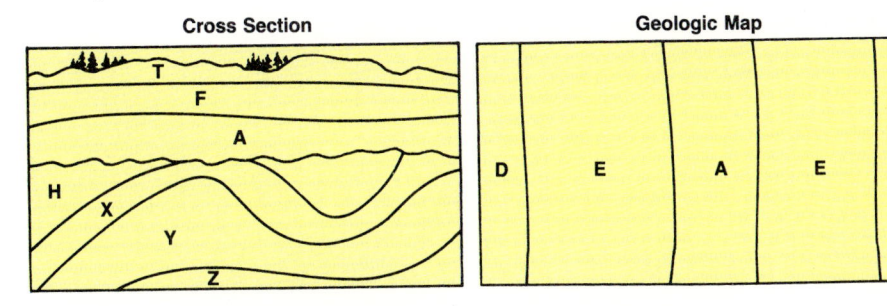

Research and Investigation

1. Use references in the library to find a description of the earth's history in the area where you live. Obtain a geologic map of your community. Make a list of the rock layers that lie under your school and your home. Describe how the rock layers correlate with the history.
2. If you live in an area of sedimentary rocks, try to find a sequence of sedimentary layers in your community that indicates the movement of the sea toward or away from land.

20.1
The Concept of Geologic Time

You will find out
- what the requirements for a geologic clock are;
- how the age of the earth has been estimated in the past;
- how the age of the earth is estimated today.

Figure 20.2 There are 21 sedimentary layers exposed in the Grand Canyon. Stacked one above the other, these strata give a view of the earth that stretches back a billion years.

A key difference between geologists and other scientists is their attitude toward time. Physicists and chemists make measurements in their laboratories over fractions of a second, a few minutes, or a few weeks. Geologists make measurements of the earth processes that take up to millions and even billions of years. For example, assume that the Colorado River deepens its channel one tenth of a centimeter per year. In 1,000 years it would cut down one meter. To cut the Grand Canyon (1.7 km deep), it would take only about two million years. Even that is only a brief instant in geologic time. In reality it is believed the Colorado River began its task about 6 million years ago. How do you measure time over millions and billions of years? What kind of clock would you use?

This was the kind of problem facing early geologists. They wanted to know the age of the earth and the length of time for a given geologic event. For example, how long did it really take for the Colorado River to make the Grand Canyon in Arizona? How could these early geologists determine geologic time? They wanted a clock for geologic events.

In a large clock you can see certain things happening. The pendulum swings back and forth with great regularity. The hands of the clock count the number of swings to tell how much time has passed. Geologists have looked for things that have happened with regularity on the earth. This regularity would compare with the pendulum in the clock, and each occurrence could then be counted to measure geologic time. The search for such a clock focused on finding a series of actions or happenings that met certain requirements. First, the actions had been operating since the earth began. Second, the actions had never varied in their rate of operation. Third, the rate of the actions had to be measurable. Early geologists thought of three earth processes that could meet each of these requirements. The processes were (1) the rate at which salt was added to the oceans, (2) the rate of deposition of sediments in the sea, and (3) the rate the earth loses heat.

In 1899 John Joly estimated the age of the earth by using the rate at which salt was being added to the ocean. He estimated the amount of salt in the ocean and the rate salt was being added to the ocean each year. He divided the amount of salt in the ocean by the rate it was being added. From this he obtained an age for the earth of about 90 million years. But really all he was measuring was the age of the ocean. Most scientists today do not think that the ocean salt is a good clock for measuring the true age of the earth.

The rate at which sediments were being deposited was another process used for determining the age of the earth. In the late 1800's five scientists made estimates of the age of the earth using this method. Each of these scientists estimated the total thickness of sedimentary rock found on the earth. Each used his experience and knowledge to estimate the rate of deposition. By dividing the total thickness by the rate of deposition, each estimated the age of the earth. There were wide differences in their estimates, ranging from 17 million years to 1,584 million years. The differences occurred because there was no accurate way to measure maximum thickness or rate of deposition.

A third idea for a clock to estimate the earth's age was based on the rate the earth was losing heat. Lord Kelvin, a physicist, assumed the earth had been losing heat from its beginning. He measured the rate at which the earth was losing heat. He also estimated how hot the earth had to be for rocks to be melted. Using these two estimates, Lord Kelvin calculated how long it would take the earth to cool. His estimates for the age of the earth ranged from 20 to 100 million years.

Do You Know?
Lord Kelvin was very interested in many areas of science. He published 661 papers on a variety of science topics. He also had patents on 70 inventions!

Figure 20.3 *below:* One half of the amount of radioactive material present will decay when the half-life passes.

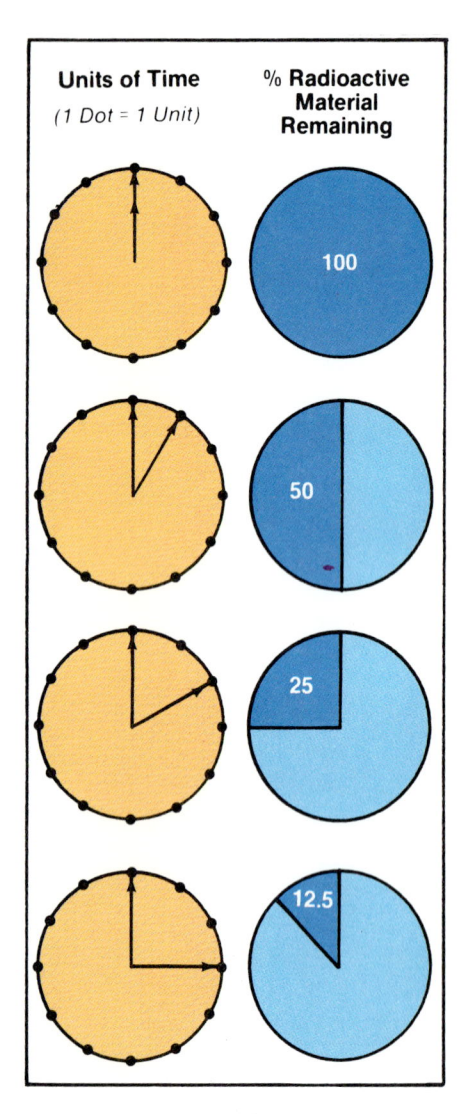

Units of Time (1 Dot = 1 Unit)	% Radioactive Material Remaining
(clock, full)	100
(clock)	50
(clock)	25
(clock)	12.5

Geologists now use **radioactive decay** [ray-dee-oh-AK-tihv dee-KAY] processes to estimate the age of the earth. Radioactive decay is a natural, regularly occurring process in which certain radioactive elements change into different elements. This happens as their atomic nuclei break down and simpler atoms are formed. The rate of change for different elements varies. Scientists base their measurements on the length of time it takes half the atoms in a sample to change. The amount of time it takes for half the atoms in a sample to change into simpler unchanging atoms is very regular. This period of time is called the **half-life** for that element. The half-life of a radioactive element, then, because it is always the same, is like a clock. It is an atomic clock that can be used to measure the age of rocks and also the age of the earth. Atomic clocks are not affected by changes in temperature, by weathering, or by erosion.

How an atomic clock works is shown in Table 20-1. This table shows that the number of atoms of A and B changes through time. Compare the amount of A atoms to the amount of B atoms. Study the changes taking place in the ratios. Which type of atom is decreasing in number? By how much is it decreasing? What is happening to the A atoms? They change to B atoms. This process could continue for a long time.

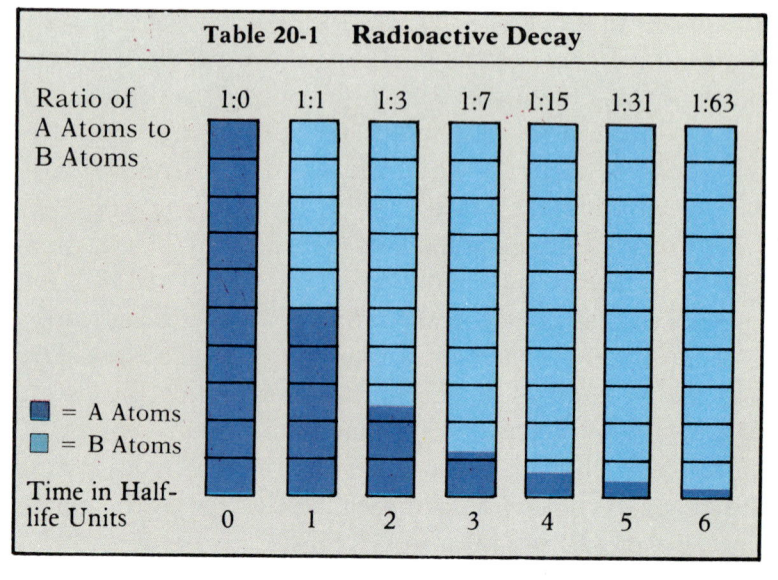

Table 20-1   Radioactive Decay

Ratio of A Atoms to B Atoms	1:0	1:1	1:3	1:7	1:15	1:31	1:63
Time in Half-life Units	0	1	2	3	4	5	6

■ = A Atoms
□ = B Atoms

20 / Dating and Geologic Time

To see how the age of a rock is estimated, imagine a rock which contains both uranium-238 and lead-206. The numbers 238 and 206 refer to forms of these elements. It takes 4.5 billion years for half of the uranium-238 atoms to turn to lead-206. If a rock has equal amounts of uranium-238 and lead-206, how old is it? It is 4.5 billion years old. If a rock contains three quarters of uranium-238 and one quarter of lead-206, how old is it? The answer is marked on Figure 20.5. Since only one quarter of the uranium-238 has changed to lead-206, the age is one half of the half-life, or about 2.25 billion years. The regular rate of decay of radioactive elements in a sample has provided geologists with the accurate geologic clock they were looking for.

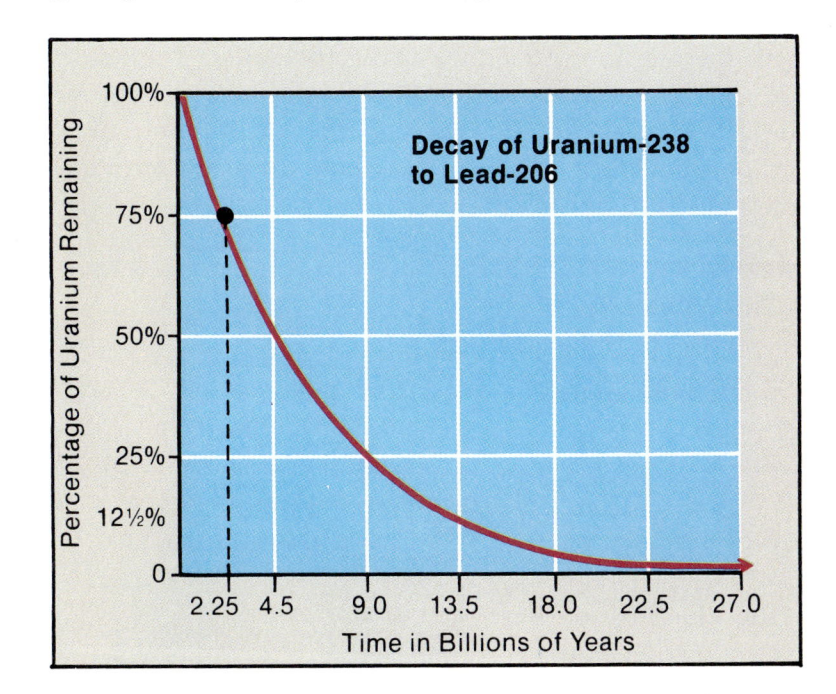

Figure 20.4 *above:* The radioactive decay of uranium-238 into lead-206

Figure 20.5 *left:* During radioactive decay, uranium-238 changes to lead-206 in the ratios shown here.

Do You Know?
Antoine Henri Becquerel discovered radioactivity in 1895. It wasn't until 10 years later in 1905 that Ernest Rutherford suggested that radioactive minerals could be used to date rocks.

Study Questions for 20.1

1. What three requirements must be met by an earth process before it can be used as a geologic clock?
2. List three ways the age of the earth has been calculated in the past.
3. What method is used today to estimate the age of the earth?

20.2 Geologic Dating

You will find out
- what methods are used today to date rocks;
- what the difference is between relative and radiometric, or absolute, dating.

Figure 20.6 Atomic measurements indicate that this rock is over 3.9 billion years old. It is one of the oldest earth rocks ever found.

How can you measure the age of the earth? One way geologists use is to treat the whole earth as a great big rock. Estimates of the present ratio of uranium-238 to lead-206 is about 1 to 1. In other words, about half of all the uranium-238 atoms have changed to lead-206 atoms. From Figure 20.5 you can see that the time it would take for this to occur is 4.5 billion years. This is one half-life of uranium-238 and makes the age of the earth about 4.5 billion years old. How does this age of the earth compare with the age found by measuring the salt in the seas? The earth's sediments? The heat loss? Since the age of the oldest rock found so far on the earth is about 4 billion years old, the atomic clock seems to provide more accurate information.

Activity

How Old Is This Model Rock?

Materials

boxes labeled *model rock*, each containing 80 pieces of paper (some of the pieces of paper are marked *atom A*, some *atom B*)

pencil

Procedure

1. Select one of the model-rock boxes.
2. Count the number of A atoms.
3. Count the number of B atoms.
4. Divide the number of B atoms by the number of A atoms. This is the ratio of B atoms to A atoms.
5. Use Table 20-1 to find the estimated age of your model rock.

Questions

1. How many atoms A and atoms B do you have?
2. What is your ratio of B atoms to A atoms in step 4?
3. How old is your rock?

When you determine the age of a rock using an atomic clock, you are using **radiometric** [ray-dee-oh-MET-rihk] **time.** For example, if you find that the amount of radioactive decay of atoms in a rock would require 100,000 years, then the rock has existed for 100,000 years of radiometric time. When you place a date or length of time on an event by using an atomic clock, it is called radiometric, or absolute, dating.

Do You Know?
Radiometric dating of rocks from the moon range from 3.1 to 4.5 billion years old. There are none younger.

Kauai 5.6–3.8 m.y.
Oahu 3.4–2.7 m.y.
2.5–2.2 m.y.
1.8 m.y.
1.5–1.3 m.y.
1.3–1.15 m.y.
Molokai 0.8 m.y. and younger
Maui
Hawaii Less than 1 m.y.

The most widely used atomic clock is the potassium-40–argon-40 clock. Small amounts of potassium-40 are found in many rocks. It takes 1.3 billion years for half of the potassium-40 atoms to change to argon-40 atoms. In other words, the half-life of potassium-40 is 1.3 billion years. The amount of potassium-40 atoms that have changed can be used to date rocks as young as a few thousand years as well as the oldest rocks known. The potassium-40–argon-40 atomic clock was used to determine the age of the rocks making up the Hawaiian Islands in Figure 20.7.

Figure 20.7 The Hawaiian Islands formed individually as their crustal plate gradually drifted northwest over a hot plume. The islands in the northwest erupted first.

Figure 20.8 *above:* Radiometric dating can identify how long ago once-living organisms existed.

An atomic clock for determining the age of material that was once part of a living organism is called **radiocarbon** [ray-dee-oh-KAHR-buhn] **dating.** Radioactive carbon-14 is created in the atmosphere. Carbon-14 atoms enter into all living things and slowly decay to nitrogen-14 atoms. As long as life exists, there is a ratio maintained in the organism between carbon-14 atoms and ordinary carbon-12 atoms. New carbon-14 atoms are added as fast as some of the old ones decay to nitrogen-14 atoms. When death occurs, carbon-14 atoms are no longer added and the clock is started. Then the ratio between unchanging carbon-12 atoms and carbon-14 atoms begins changing. In 5,730 years, the half-life of carbon-14 atoms, one half of the carbon-14 atoms will be changed to nitrogen-14 atoms. During this time carbon-12 atoms do not change. The amount of carbon-14 remaining in a dead object can be compared to the amount of carbon-12. If you find one half the ratio of carbon-14 to carbon-12, then half of the carbon-14 has changed to nitrogen-14. You then know that 5,730 years, the half-life of carbon-14, have passed since the organism died.

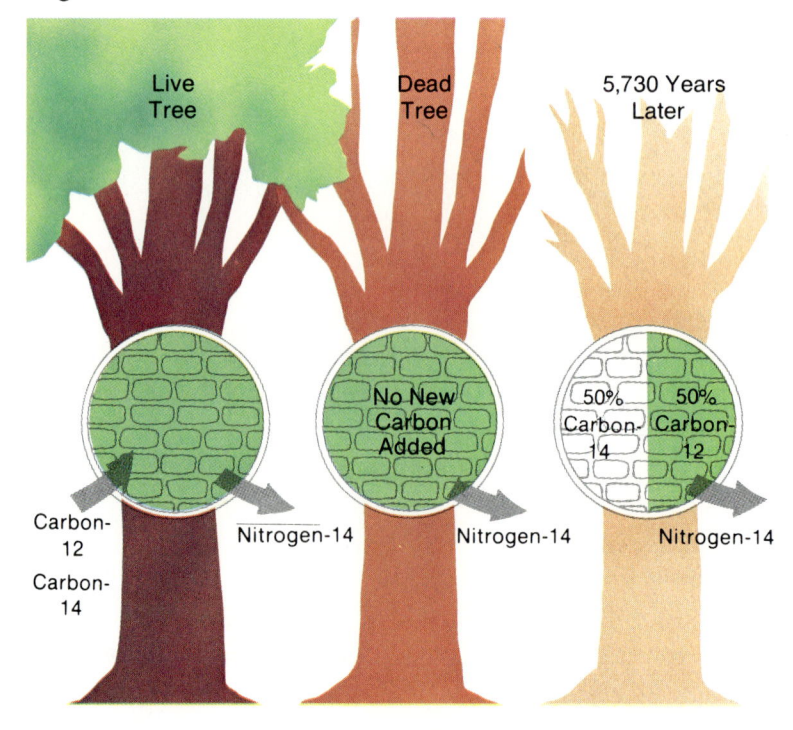

Figure 20.9 *left:* In a live organism, carbon-14 decay is balanced by newly added carbon. *middle:* When the organism dies, carbon-14 continues to decay, but no new carbon enters the organism. *right:* The percentages of carbon-12 and carbon-14 remaining reveal the age of the organism.

Another way of looking at geologic time is to compare two events by asking which event came first. When you do this, you are thinking of **relative time** and relative dating. When you apply the law of superposition, you are using relative dating of events. You don't know when the events happened or how long they lasted, but you do know in what order they occurred.

Relative dating is used to find the "before" and the "after" time of a rock. Radiometric dating can be used to tell the age of a rock in years. In Figure 20.10 you can see how relative and radiometric time can be used to figure out the earth's history. You know the relative age of the rocks: first, rock A was deposited, and then rock B cut across it, followed by the deposition of rock C, and finally the deposition of rock D. Suppose your atomic clock has shown that rock B is 90 million years old and rock D is 15 million years old. How old are rock A and rock C? You won't know the age of rock A, but it must be older than 90 million years. Now you also know that rock C is younger than 90 million years and older than 15 million years. By using both radiometric time and relative time, you can add dates and time spans to the geologic history of that cross section.

Why couldn't the ages of rock layers C and A be measured by the atomic clock? Unfortunately, not all rocks contain radioactive substances. Sometimes too much of the radioactive substance has been lost since the rock first formed to permit atomic measurement. Atomic clocks work only if radioactive substances are present in the rock. You must use every clue you can find to make your interpretations of the rock record.

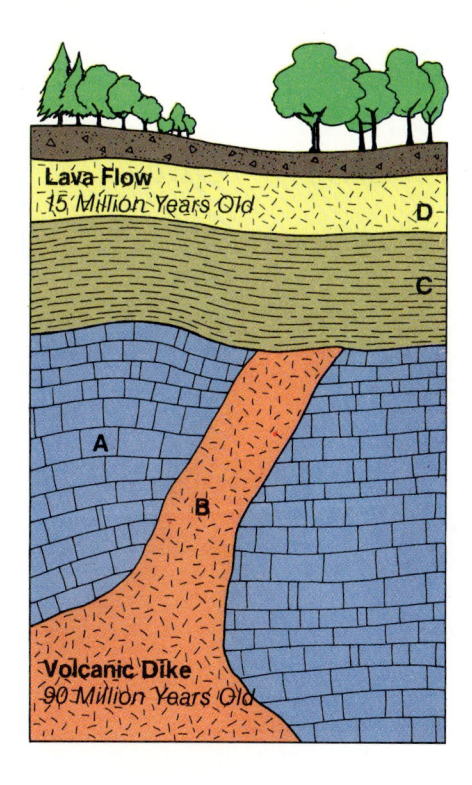

Figure 20.10 How do relative dating and radiometric dating help identify the history of this geologic sample?

Study Questions for 20.2

1. List the methods used to date rocks today.
2. Describe the difference between relative dating and radiometric, or absolute, dating.

20.3
Dimensions of Geologic Time

You will find out
- what a geologic column is;
- how the geologic time scale was developed;
- what the names of the eras in the geologic time scale are.

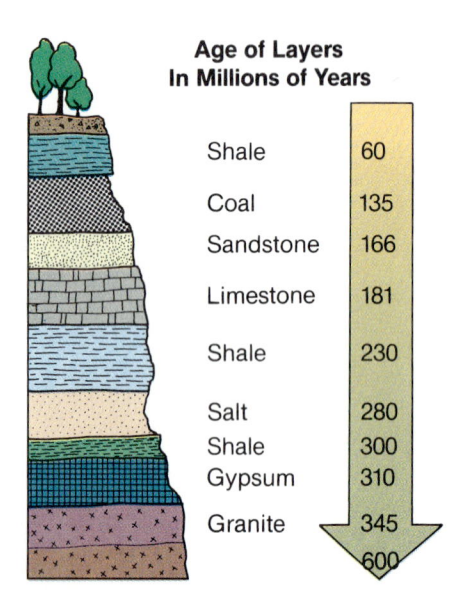

How long is geologic time? It has to be a long, long time, since it began when the earth formed. There is some evidence that it was at least 4.5 billion years ago. Geologic time encompasses such a vast interval that it's too much to comprehend fully. Humans can keep track of events in their lives for about 50 years. After that, they usually rely on some method of recording events to keep track of what happens around them. Geologists can use the information that is recorded in rocks. That is a record of events that have happened on the earth since the beginning of time.

The first relatively complete part of the geologic record was compiled by William "Strata" Smith. Smith made the first geologic map of England. He was able to place the rock layers into a sequence in order from oldest to youngest. Thus he made a type of relative time scale. Later, other geologists working in France, Germany, and Russia also began to order the rocks. At each place the relative time scale of the rock record was worked out. With the discovery that rocks containing similar kinds of fossils were the same age, the relative sequence of the rock layers in all of Europe was put in order. Geologists call such a sequence of layered rocks arranged in order a **geologic column.**

Many attempts were made to divide the geologic column into blocks of time. Finally, by international agreement, the rock record was divided into blocks of time, creating a relative geologic time scale. Later, by using radiometric dating, dates in years were added to the scale. Thousands of rocks were dated. This allowed geologists then to combine the relative geologic time scale with a radiometric, or absolute, scale. All this information has been used to make up the geologic time scale.

Figure 20.11 *above:* William "Strata" Smith

Figure 20.12 *below:* An example of a geologic column

Age of Layers In Millions of Years

Shale	60
Coal	135
Sandstone	166
Limestone	181
Shale	230
Salt	280
Shale	300
Gypsum	310
Granite	345
	600

20 / Dating and Geologic Time

The geologic time scale, as shown in Figure 20.13, is divided into **eras** [IHR-ruhs], **periods,** and **epochs** [EP-uhks]. Eras are the largest time blocks of the scale. There are four eras. They are in the left-hand column of the time scale. Periods are blocks of time within an era. The periods are in the middle column. Epochs are blocks of time within a period. The epochs are in the third column from the left. The eras were named to indicate the fossils they contained. **Cenozoic** [see-nuh-ZOH-ihk] refers to the time of recent life. **Mesozoic** [mez-uh-ZOH-ihk] refers to middle life. **Paleozoic** [pay-lee-oh-ZOH-ihk] is the time of ancient life. **Precambrian** [pree-KAM-bree-uhn] refers to the time before ancient life.

Do You Know?
If the geologic time scale was plotted alongside the Empire State Building (381 m high), a dime (1/8 cm thick) would more than equal the span of recorded history.

Figure 20.13 The divisions of the geologic time scale

Geologic Time Scale			Time* (Millions of years)	Duration (Millions of years)
Era	**Period**	**Epoch**		
Cenozoic	Quarternary	Holocene	last 10,000 years (approx.)	
		Pleistocene	— 2-3 —	1
	Tertiary	Pliocene	— 12 —	10
		Miocene	— 26 —	14
		Oligocene	— 37-38 —	11
		Eocene	— 53-54 —	26
		Paleocene	— 65 —	12
Mesozoic	Cretaceous		— 136 —	71
	Jurassic		— 190-195 —	54
	Triassic		— 225 —	35
Paleozoic	Permian		— 280 —	55
	Carboniferous	Pennsylvanian	— 320 —	40
		Mississippian	— 345 —	25
	Devonian		— 395 —	50
	Silurian		— 430-440 —	35
	Ordovician		— 500 —	70
	Cambrian		— 600 —	100
Precambrian				3,900

*Estimated ages of time boundaries

Figure 20.14 The still lifeless earth may have looked like this.

Another way of visualizing geologic time is to think of all the time since the earth formed at least 4.5 billion years ago compressed into a year. How would the rock record appear on that scale? If the earth began January

Activity

What Does a Time Line of the Geologic Scale Look Like?

Materials

5 m of adding-machine tape
pencil
metric ruler

Procedure

1. Place a mark labeled *today* near one end of the tape.
2. Place another mark labeled *beginning* at 4.5 m from *today*.
3. Using a scale of 1 m = 1 billion years, compute the scale distance for the beginning of each era and period. See Figure 20.13 for dates.

$$\text{Scale distance in meters} = \frac{\text{number of years ago}}{1,000,000,000}$$

4. Using the scale values, plot each era and period on the tape.
5. Label each era and period.

Questions

1. How long did the Precambrian Era last?
2. How long was the Devonian period?
3. How long was the Mesozoic Era?

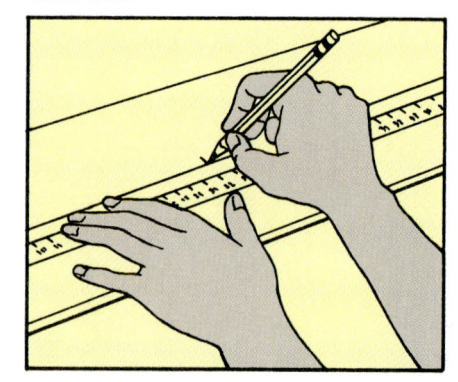

20 / Dating and Geologic Time

1, living things appeared in the sea in May. Land plants and animals showed up in the rock record in November. The swamps that formed most of the coal existed for about four days in early December. Dinosaurs appeared in mid-December and disappeared on December 26. This is about the time the Rocky Mountains were uplifted. On this scale, the first humans appeared during the evening of December 31. The last of the big glaciers receded about one minute and fifteen seconds before midnight on December 31. Rome ruled the world for five seconds. Columbus discovered America about three seconds before midnight.

This way of looking at geologic time is based on the best inference geologists can make with the evidence they now have. With each new piece of evidence geologists reexamine their models and inferences. Sometimes the new evidence confirms and supports their previous model. Other times new inferences and models are called for that can be supported by the new evidence.

Figure 20.15 *Tyrannosaurus rex* and a three-horned triceratops were two of the dinosaurs that roamed the earth.

Do You Know?
How long is 5 billion years? If you were to begin counting at the rate of one number a second and continued 24 hours a day for 7 days a week and never stopped, it would take two lifetimes (150 years) to reach 5 billion.

Study Questions for 20.3

1. What is a geologic column?
2. Describe the development of the geologic time scale.
3. List four eras of the geologic time scale.

Career

Research Engineer Scientist in Radiocarbon Dating

Persons working in radiocarbon dating use radiocarbon dating techniques to date archeological objects, antiques, charcoal samples, bones, shells, and wood samples. Radiocarbon dating techniques are usually applied to objects that are thought to be less than 40,000 years old. A research engineer scientist uses special chemical treatment techniques in preparing the samples for dating. This work requires at least a bachelor's degree in mathematics and chemistry.

Alejandra Gloria Varela is a research engineer scientist working at the Radiocarbon Dating Laboratory at the University of Texas in Austin. She attributes her interest in science and mathematics to her mother, who held daily classes with the children of the family in their early years. In this class her mother would teach the children to read, write, and do mathematics. Alejandra knew the multiplication tables before she entered first grade. In high school she had an outstanding biology teacher who helped develop her math and science talents by setting up special projects and extra assignments for Alejandra.

In college she took as much mathematics and chemistry as possible. This prepared her for dating archeological materials, antiques, charcoal samples, bones, shells, and wood. Each substance must be treated chemically before its age can be determined. Calculating the age of a substance requires the application of her mathematics.

Alejandra has had more than ten articles published in scientific journals. She finds a special reward when she learns that other scientists refer to her work.

CHAPTER REVIEW

Main Ideas

- To serve as a geologic clock, an earth process must (1) have been going on since the earth began, (2) never have varied in rate, and (3) have occurred at a measurable rate.
- In the past, the amount of salt in ocean water, the rate at which sediments were deposited, and the rate at which the earth cooled were used as geologic clocks.
- Today, the rate of radioactive decay is used as a geologic clock.
- Half-life is the time it takes for half the atoms of a radioactive element to decay into simpler, unchanging atoms of a different element.
- The age of rocks is based on the radiometric dating of uranium-238 or potassium-40.
- Relative dating is used to determine which event occurred before another. Absolute, or radiometric, dating is used to determine the age of a rock in years.
- A geologic column is a sequence of layered rocks arranged in order by age.
- A relative geologic time scale was developed from the geologic column. Dates were added from radiometric dating.
- Eras are the largest blocks of time on the geologic time scale. The eras are the Precambrian (before ancient life), Paleozoic (ancient life), Mesozoic (middle life), and Cenozoic (recent life).

Using Vocabulary

On a separate sheet of paper, use the following words to make a crossword puzzle. Exchange puzzles with a classmate.

radioactive decay　　relative time　　epoch　　Precambrian
half-life　　geologic column　　Cenozoic
radiometric time　　era　　Mesozoic
radiocarbon dating　　period　　Paleozoic

20 / Dating and Geologic Time

Remembering Facts

Number your paper from 1 to 15. Match each term in column **A** with a phrase in column **B**.

A
1. Paleozoic Era
2. era
3. epoch
4. Cenozoic Era
5. radioactive decay
6. Mesozoic Era
7. 4.5 billion years
8. radiometric time
9. geologic column
10. Precambrian Era
11. radiocarbon dating
12. relative time
13. potassium-40–argon-40
14. period
15. half-life

B
a. the part of the geologic time scale that is older than the Paleozoic
b. a comparison that determines which of two events came first
c. sequence of layered rocks arranged in order
d. largest time block on the geologic time scale
e. age determined with an atomic clock
f. block of time within an era on the geologic time scale
g. the breakdown of radioactive elements to form simpler elements
h. the time of recent life on the geologic time scale
i. widely used atomic clock
j. time required for one half of the atoms in a sample to decay
k. estimated age of the earth
l. the time of middle life on the geologic time scale
m. block of time within a period
n. atomic clock that uses carbon
o. the time of ancient life on the geologic time scale

Understanding Ideas

On your paper, answer each question in complete sentences.
1. What events are used to separate one era from another on the geologic time scale?
2. Compare the advantages and disadvantages of uranium, potassium, and carbon atomic clocks.
3. Which atomic clock would be used to determine the age of a fossilized fern?
4. Pretend that you have found an ancient bone. What procedure would you use to determine its age?
5. Why is radioactive decay more reliable for measuring time than rates of erosion and deposition?

Applying What You Have Learned

1. How old is a rock that contains 1/8 potassium-40 and 7/8 argon-40?
2. Explain how the application of the law of crosscutting relationships provides the geologist with information about relative time.
3. Why are the recent subdivisions of time in the geologist time scale much smaller than the early ones?
4. Describe how the age of the earth was estimated by using the salt content of the ocean.

Challenge

The cross section shows rock layers, structures that were formed from lava and magma, and buried objects. The absolute age has been determined for some of the structures and buried objects. These are shown on the cross section. Use the cross section and your understanding of geologic dating to answer the following questions.

1. What can you say for sure about the age of layer 1? Explain.
2. What is the approximate age of layer 2? Explain how you arrived at your answer.
3. What is the approximate age of layer 4? Are you more certain about the age of layer 4 or layer 2? Why?
4. What can you say about the approximate age of layer 5? Explain.

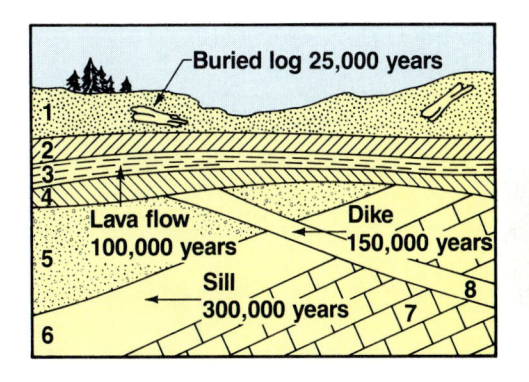

Research and Investigation

1. Study buildings in an older part of your community and in a new section of your community. Describe what you can use to establish a relative time scale for the buildings. Consider weathering, style, and so forth. Compare this to an absolute time scale as shown by dates at the top or on cornerstones.
2. Use the library to find out which rocks make up the geologic column in your area. Make a sketch of the geologic column like the one in Figure 20.13. Draw heavy lines across the column to identify the eras represented. Draw lighter lines to identify the periods represented within each era. Display the column on the bulletin board.
3. Assign an oral report on the problems of radioactive dating.

21.1
Types of Fossil Preservation

You will find out
- what the five types of fossil preservation are;
- what the most likely conditions are for making a fossil.

The record of life on the earth is preserved in fossil remains. A fossil is any evidence of past life. Fossils come in many different sizes. A fossil may be a piece of bone, a shell, a tooth, or a footprint. It can even be a piece of animal flesh frozen in ice. How can material that was once alive be preserved for millions and millions of years? How are fossils made?

Figure 21.2 Fossils provide pictures of living things as they looked long ago.

Fossils can be made in several ways. The five types of preservation are (1) preservation without change, (2) replacement by a mineral, (3) the filling of a hollow space in a shell or bone with a mineral, (4) formation of a thin carbon film, and (5) formation of an imprint or the filling of an imprint. How did each of these ways of preservation occur?

When an organism dies, parts of it may be preserved as a fossil without change. Bones, shells, and teeth are examples of such fossils. Sometimes the whole organism becomes a fossil. An example is an insect trapped in tree sap. As the tree sap ages and hardens, it forms a transparent yellow-orange fossil, which is called **amber** [AM-buhr]. The insect trapped in the tree sap is now clearly seen embedded in the transparent amber. These fossil insects often have nearly perfect forms. Animals that have been frozen in ice can also be preserved with hair and flesh intact. In some fossils even the food the animal was eating is preserved.

Sometimes the once-living organism is replaced by a mineral. **Petrified** [PET-ruh-fyd] **wood** is made in this way. The original wood parts of a tree are removed cell by cell, and the mineral silica is substituted. This process can preserve remarkable detail. Notice you can count the tree rings in Figure 21.4.

Figure 21.3 *below:* An insect is perfectly preserved in amber.

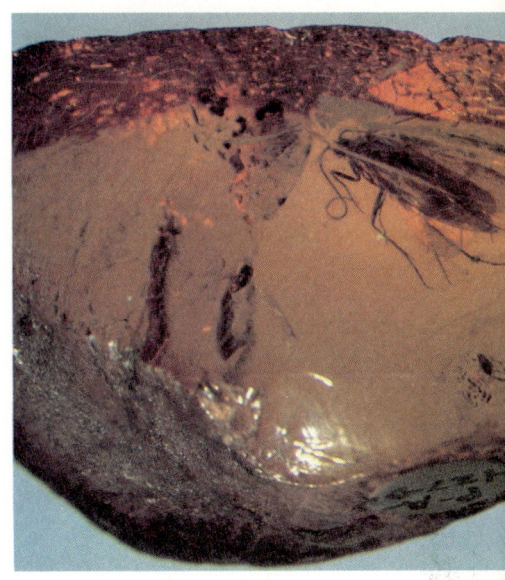

Do You Know?
Thomas Jefferson, in the spring of 1797, carried some bones from a cave floor in western Virginia to Philadelphia. There he wrote a memoir describing the specimens. The memoir, published in 1799, was the first study of American fossils by an American.

Figure 21.4 Wood can become petrified when conditions preserve the cell materials from rapid decay.

21 / The Fossil Record

415

At times small open spaces in a shell or bone are filled with a mineral. If you pick up a fossil bone, you'll notice it is heavier than you might expect because of the added mineral material. The mineral matter hardens and preserves the bone as a fossil.

Figure 21.5 *right:* A bone fossil preserved with added mineral matter

Some fossils appear as thin films of carbon in a rock. Fish, leaves, and insects are found preserved in this way. After the organism is buried, it is pressed by forces within the earth. Under this pressure the organism leaves a thin film of carbon in the rock. When the rock is cracked open, the thin carbon fossil is discovered. See Figure 21.6 and Figure 21.7.

Figure 21.6 *below:* A carbon fossil within this rock is a lucky find for a geologist.

Figure 21.7 *below right:* Another example of a carbon fossil

Traces of past life may be preserved as an imprint in rock or as a filling of an imprint. Footprints, shell imprints, and worm burrows are fossils of this type. **Molds** and **casts** are examples of these kinds of fossils. When water dissolves a shell or bone around which sand or mud has already hardened, a cavity is left in the rock. This cavity is called a mold. If the mold is later filled with mud or mineral matter, the filling is called a cast. A cast can be identified because it has no inner structure of the original organism.

Generally, fossils form best under certain conditions. First, hard parts of the plant or animal are more easily preserved. Second, the plant or animal should be buried or frozen soon after death. As a result, only a few of all the plants and animals living in the past have become fossils. After death the soft parts of plants and animals are removed by scavengers, bacteria, and chemical decay. The hard parts are not so easily destroyed and are more likely to become fossils. Shells, bones, teeth, and skulls are the parts of animals most likely to be preserved. An animal such as a clam has hard parts and lives in the mud or sand on the bottom of a lake or an ocean. When the clam dies, it is already buried. The soft parts may be destroyed, but the shell remains for a long time and may become a fossil.

Figure 21.8 *above left:* The imprint of a shell is a pretty reminder of a once-living sea animal.

Figure 21.9 *above:* The imprint on the left is the cast. The one on the right is the mold.

Study Questions for 21.1

1. What are the five types of fossil preservation?
2. What are the most likely conditions for making a fossil?

21.2 Recognizing and Identifying Fossils

You will find out
- how to recognize fossils;
- how to identify fossils.

In order to tell whether something you've found is a fossil, you must be able to tell whether or not it was alive. Look for pieces of bone or shell or for other evidence that tells you what you found was once alive.

Geologists sometimes say, "I know this is a fossil because it looks like . . ."—a whole or part of an organism that was once living. Geologists identify a fossil by the features it has. A fossil horseshoe crab looks much like the horseshoe crab living today. A fossil snail and a modern snail also have a similar appearance. The major key to whether or not something is a fossil is its appearance. Generally it looks like something you know that is living today. The more you know about living things, the easier it is to recognize a fossil.

Once you know something is a fossil, how do you find out what kind of fossil it is? How is it identified? In Figure 21.11 you see three fossils. Opposite shows three sketches of what the organisms these fossils came from are believed to have looked like. Can you match the fossils with the sketches? One way you can identify a fossil is by matching a fossil with a sketch of a once-living organism.

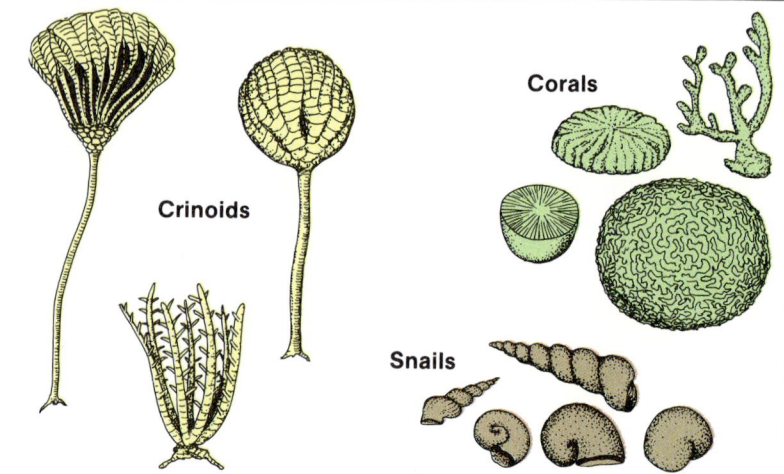

Figure 21.10 *top:* The modern horseshoe crab is sometimes called a living fossil. *bottom:* Compare its resemblance to an ancient horseshoe crab.

Figure 21.11 Geologists identify unknown fossils by matching them to organisms which are familiar.

418

21 / The Fossil Record

Activity

Which Molds Look like Once-Living Things?

Materials
plaster of Paris
plastic mixing bowl
water
two objects: something once alive and something that was never alive
petroleum jelly
paper towels
wooden spoon
aluminum tray

Procedure

1. Coat each object with petroleum jelly.
2. Make a thick paste of the plaster of Paris. Pour the plaster into an aluminum tray as shown in step A.
3. Place the objects in the plaster as shown in step B. Let them set for 24 hours.
4. Remove the objects, as shown in step C, and clean the molds that you have made.
5. Exchange your molds with another student's. Don't tell what your molds are.

Questions

1. Which mold looks like something that was once living?
2. What is it and how do you know?

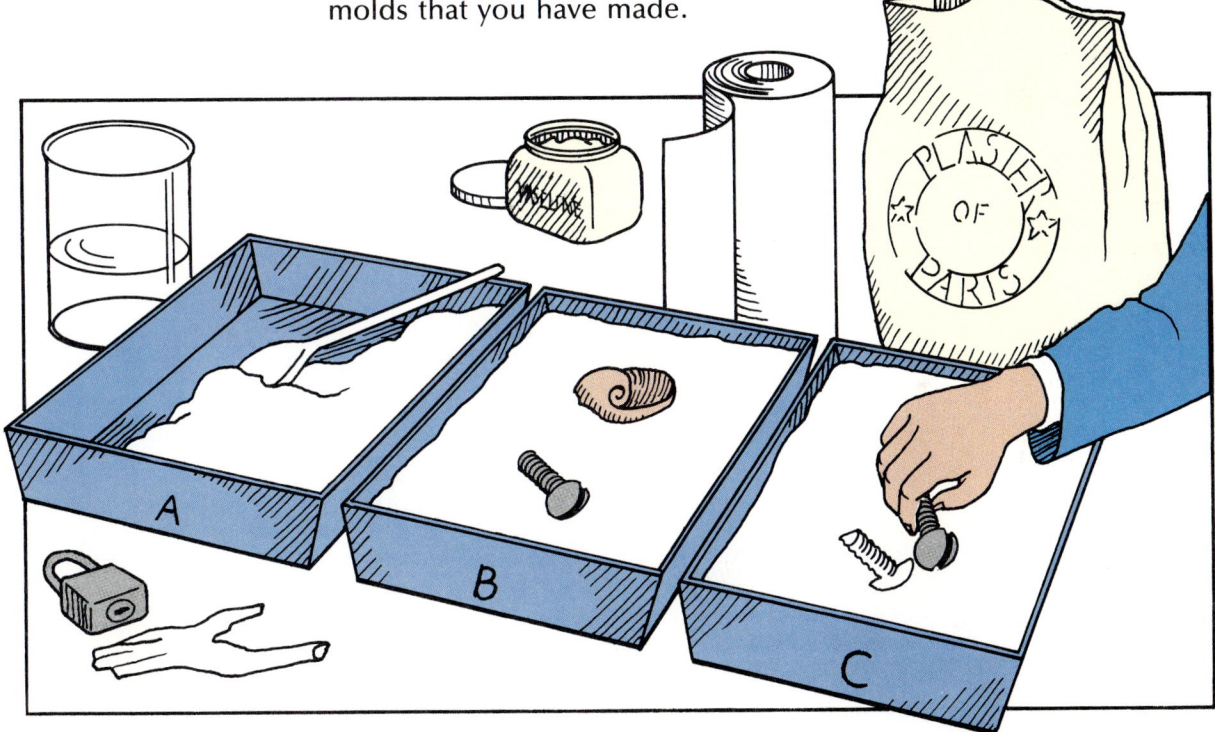

Study Questions for 21.2

1. What do you look for to tell whether you've found a fossil?
2. Describe a procedure for identifying a fossil.

21 / The Fossil Record

21.3 Dating Fossils

You will find out
- how groups of fossils can be used in dating another fossil;
- how index fossils are used in dating other fossils.

Figure 21.12 *top:* Can you determine when this cephalopod lived?

Figure 21.13 *bottom:* Match the unknown fossil in Figure 21.12 to one of these four cephalopod types.

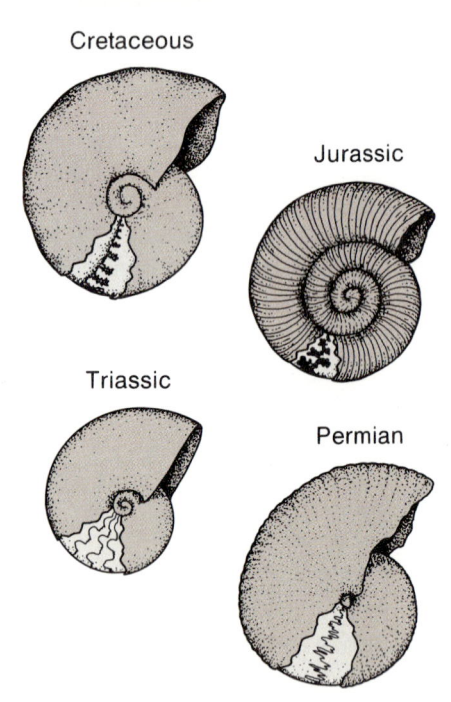

4 Kinds of Cephalopods

Cretaceous
Jurassic
Triassic
Permian

Fossils do not occur with any signs telling their ages. Yet paleontologists are able to determine the age of a fossil. How do they do it? They must rely on many pieces of related evidence. Even then, the age is an estimate and may be off by many millions of years.

Imagine looking at an old photograph of your family. You may recognize relatives, but they look somewhat different from how you know them. You may want to know when the photos were taken. Suppose your grandfather examines the photo carefully and then says it was probably taken at the 1952 family reunion. What evidence does he find in the picture for his answer? The ages of the people when the photo was taken may help identify the time. The styles of clothes, hair, and car may also help. Using the evidence in the picture, your grandfather can date it. Any other photos of the same group of people who look the same way must also have been taken at about the same time.

Paleontologists do almost the same thing. Whenever they find a group of fossils, they compare these fossils with other groups of fossils. If the fossils in one of the other groups are largely the same, they both probably lived about the same time. Each block of geologic time has its own set of plants and animals that lived at that time.

How can you use this information to date the fossil shown in Figure 21.12? The paleontologist would start by finding in which group of fossils it lived. In Figure 21.13 are four coiled, shelled animals called **cephalopods** [SEF-uh-luh-PODS]. Each of the cephalopods lived at a different period of time. Paleontologists guess this by the fossil groups with which each of these cephalopods has been found. After examining the fossil carefully, you can see that it is like the cephalopod that lived in the **Jurassic** [juh-RAS-ihk] age. Your fossil then is a

Jurassic cephalopod. Now you can determine its approximate age.

Geologists also look for other pieces of evidence called index fossils. Index fossils represent organisms that lived only a short time, but whose remains are found in many areas. Because index fossils are unusual, they are special markers to geologists. Figure 21.14 shows how index fossils can be used to date other fossils. If widely separated rock layers contain the same index fossil, the rock layers are probably the same age. Therefore, other fossils in the rock layer would also be the same age.

Figure 21.14 Notice how the rock layers shown below can be matched using index fossils.

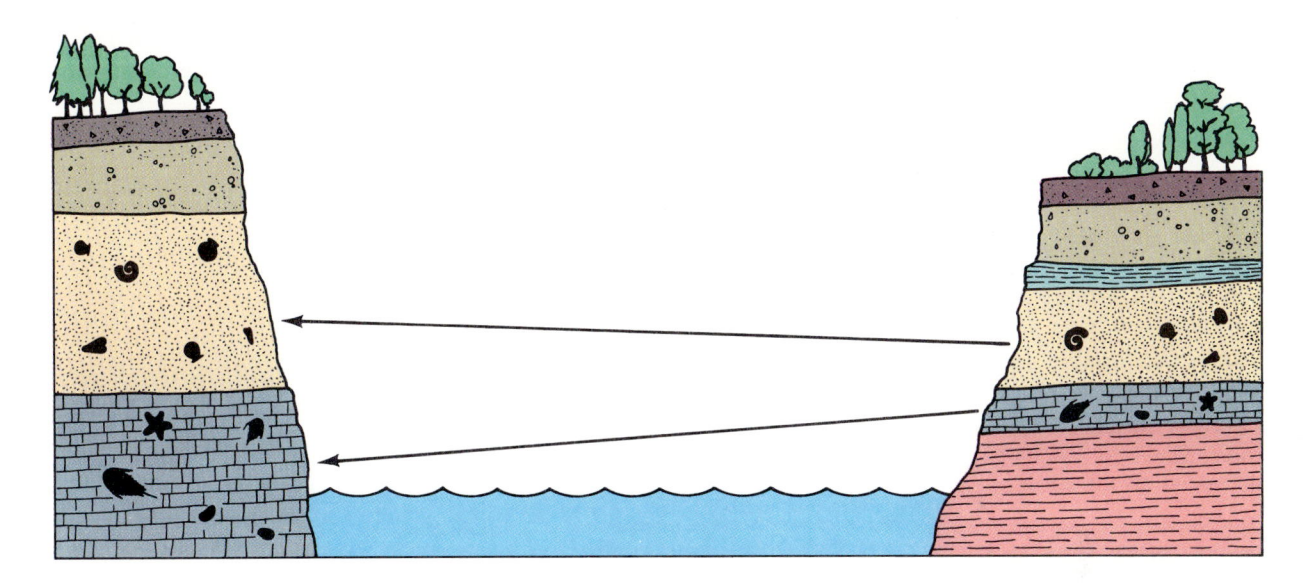

Study Questions for 21.3

1. Describe how the age of one fossil can be determined by using groups of other fossils.
2. Describe how index fossils are used in dating other fossils.

21 / The Fossil Record

21.4 The Fossil Record at Different Times

You will find out
- why the age of fossils and of the rocks they are found in is the same;
- what the dominant forms of life in the past were;
- why eras came to a close.

In Chapter 20 you learned about the geologic time scale and how rocks are dated. Figure 21.16 shows the record of life at different times on this scale. What do geologists believe about life that existed 600 million years ago? What is the source of their information?

Fossils can be dated by the rocks they are found in because the organisms were deposited at the same time the rock was laid down. Thus, the forms of life that existed in Cambrian time are revealed by the fossils found in rocks of Cambrian age. Not all forms of past life are found in the fossil record. The earliest life forms were largely soft-bodied. In addition, much of the fossil evidence may have been destroyed by heat and pressure in older rocks. However, the best evidence of what life existed at any time in the past is found in the fossil record. The fossils provide the best picture of life in the past, and finding new fossils adds to that picture.

Look carefully at the time span for each of the eras

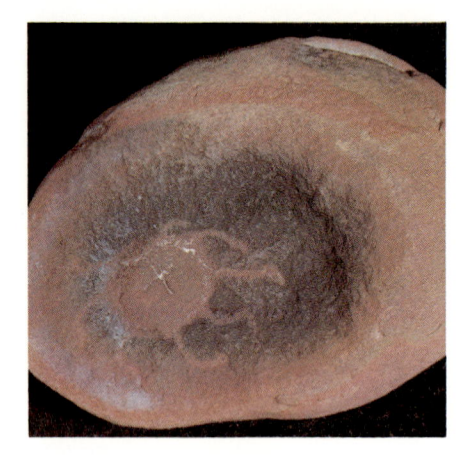

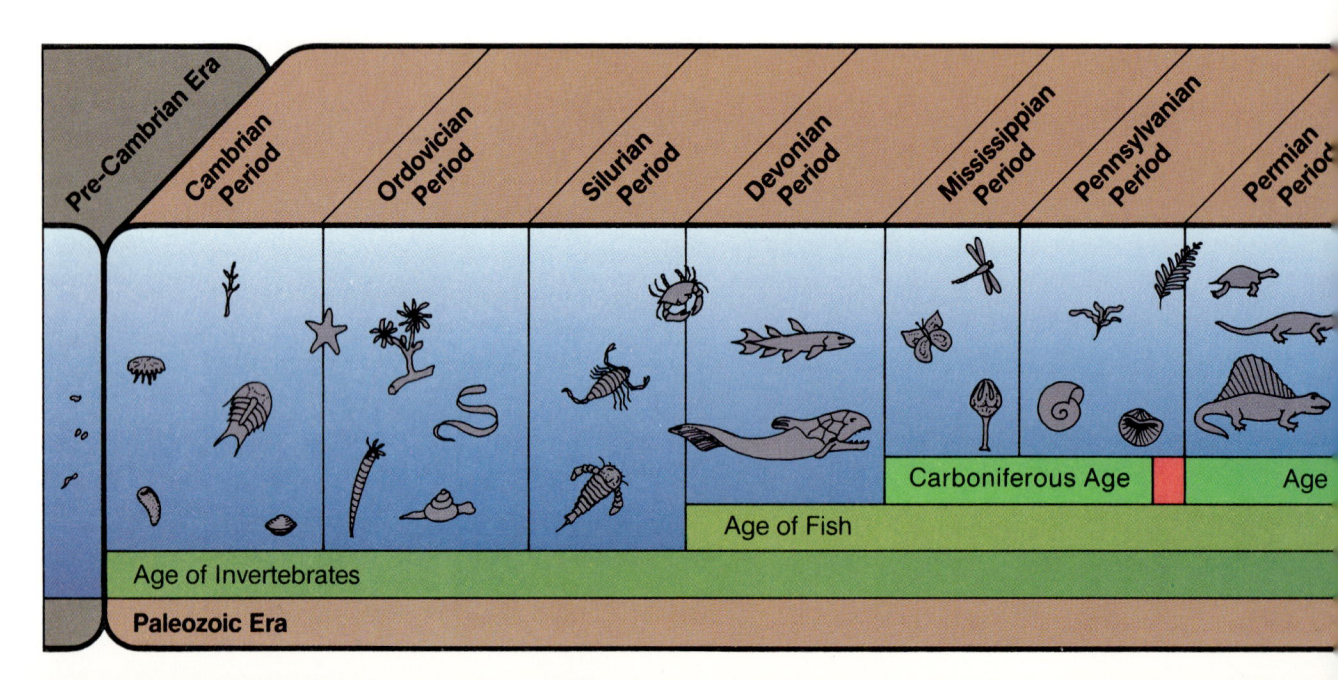

Figure 21.15 Soft-bodied fossils decay too quickly to leave fossil evidence.

Figure 21.16 The geologic time scale indicates when various life forms appeared on the earth.

Pre-Cambrian Era | Cambrian Period | Ordovician Period | Silurian Period | Devonian Period | Mississippian Period | Pennsylvanian Period | Permian Period

Carboniferous Age | Age

Age of Fish

Age of Invertebrates

Paleozoic Era

and periods of the geologic time scale. There seems to be no order or regularity to this system of dating the eras. What evidence did the geologists have for choosing such random dates? Why did they close out one era and begin another?

The evidence the geologists used is found in the fossil record. Although the record is incomplete, it is the best evidence available. Geologists have been able to make several inferences from this evidence. The first inference is that there were blocks of time when certain groups of animals and plants were the major groups then living. The second is that there were distinct times when many of the plants and animals disappeared. The boundaries of the geologic eras were set to correspond with those times when many of the plants and animals became extinct.

On the geologic time scale you see that the earliest fossils are from the Cambrian Period at the beginning of the Paleozoic Era. During the early periods of the Paleozoic Era nearly all animal types were without backbones. Animals without backbones are called **invertebrates** [in-VUR-tuh-bruhts]. Geologists call this time the Age of Invertebrates. Fossil **trilobites** [TRY-luh-byts] and **brachiopods** [BRAY-key-oh-pods] provide extensive evidence of these early invertebrates.

Figure 21.17 *top:* An ancient trilobite; *bottom:* A brachiopod

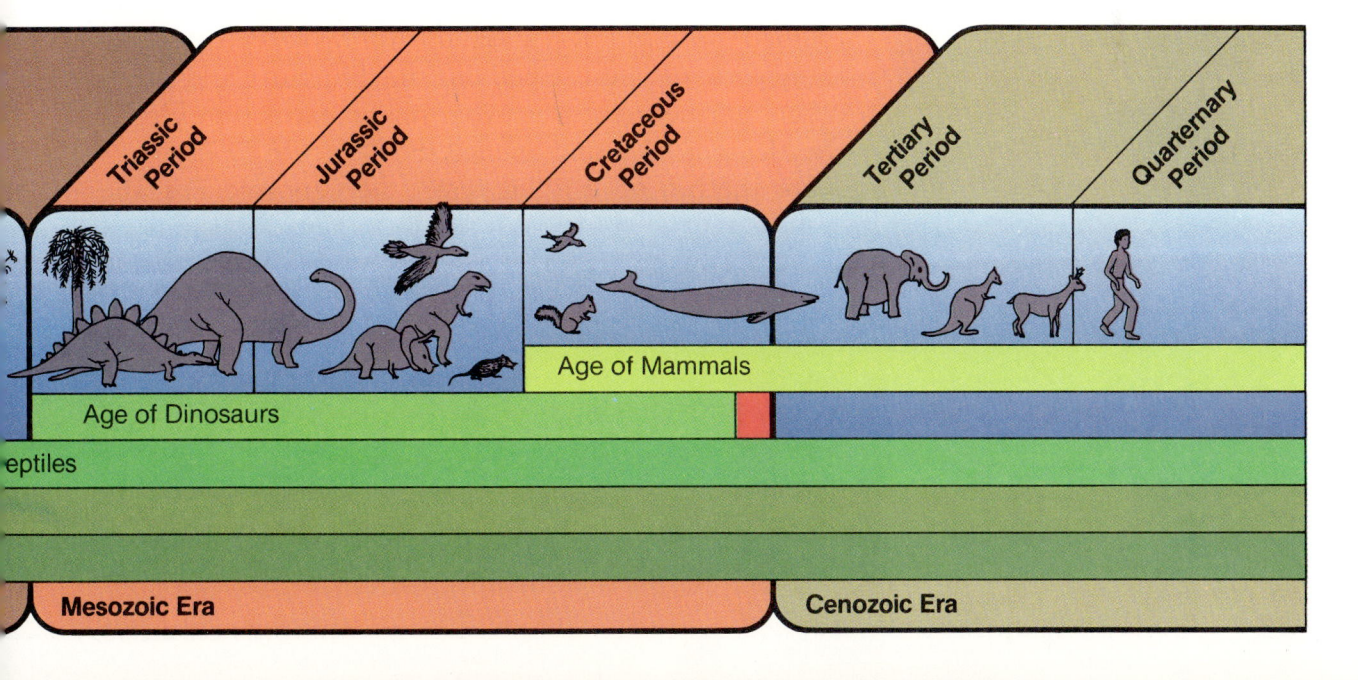

Figure 21.18 The structure of a once-living fish is clearly seen in this fossil.

Figure 21.19 *below:* Dinosaurs ruled the earth for 90 million years before being mysteriously wiped out.

The fossil record in the rocks of the Devonian Period shows that the major forms of life were fish. This period, lasting about 50 million years, is called the Age of Fishes.

The Mississippian Period and Pennsylvanian Period are called the Carboniferous Age. This is the time when plants lived that later became coal deposits. The Paleozoic Era concludes with what geologists call the Permian extinction. For some reason over 90 percent of the shallow-water animals died out.

For the next 160 million years, the Mesozoic Era, the dominant forms of life were the **reptiles** [REP-tyls]. Reptiles are cold-blooded, air-breathing animals that lay eggs. This era is known as the Age of Reptiles. The reptiles came in many sizes and many shapes. Most were plant eaters, but a few were meat eaters. It was during this era that the reptiles known as dinosaurs roamed the world. But about 65 million years ago something occurred that wiped out the dinosaurs and many other marine creatures. This major extinction closed the Mesozoic Era and opened the Cenozoic Era.

For the last 65 million years, the Cenozoic Era, the dominant form of life has been the **mammals.** Mammals are warm-blooded and have hair, and the females nurse their young.

Will the Cenozoic Era also be closed in time with a mass extinction of many organisms? The fossil record suggests this may happen. Geologists don't really know why the earlier eras ended. Why did those times of major extinctions occur? From geologists' knowledge of the earth's history, they can make some inferences. Perhaps the drifting crustal plates and continental changes

Activity

During Which Geologic Periods Did These Fossils Live?

Materials
pencil
paper
metric ruler

Procedure

1. Look at the shaded column *Late Cambrian time* on the chart. Note that fossil groups A and B lived at that time.
2. Now find the time when fossil groups A, B, C, and D lived together.
3. Find the time when fossil groups A and B, fossil groups C and D, and fossil groups A, C, and D lived together.

Questions

1. During which geologic time(s) did fossil groups A and B live together?
2. When did fossil groups C and D live together?
3. When did fossil groups A, C, and D live together?

Precambrian	Cambrian			Ordovician			Silurian			Devonian
	Early	Middle	Late	Early	Middle	Late	Early	Middle	Late	Early

caused major climatic changes. Perhaps a comet or an asteroid collided with the earth and caused the great change at the end of the Cretaceous Period. The fossil record leaves many questions yet to be answered. Perhaps you may be the one who solves the mystery of why the dinosaurs disappeared.

Study Questions for 21.4

1. Why is the age of a fossil and of the rock it is found in the same?
2. What were the dominant forms of life in each era?
3. What event caused the close of the Paleozoic and the Mesozoic eras?

Science and Technology

Unseen Fossils

Would it be possible to know about an animal that lived in the past without ever finding a fossil of the animal? Yes. In fact, this situation is not uncommon. For example, many more dinosaurs are known by their footprints than by their skeletons. After all, a single animal could leave hundreds of footprints, but only one skeleton.

Now consider the case of an animal that is known only because it drills holes into the shells of other animals. The fossil record shows many examples. But recently some new samples have been found. They are special because the shells with the drill holes are Devonian in age. That makes them nearly twice as old as any other shells with drill holes that have ever been found.

The Devonian drill holes have been found in brachiopods. You learned in this chapter that brachiopods were invertebrate animals that were abundant during the early periods of the Paleozoic Era. Brachiopods had two shells. They were similar but not related to the clams and scallops that you can find on some beaches today. They lived in shallow water near the shore.

The drill holes in the brachiopod shells are very tiny, usually about 0.20 millimeter across. Most of the holes slant inward as they deepen, and many have raised centers. Some of the holes have been drilled completely through the shells, but most have not. A single shell might contain several holes.

Scientists do not know what kind of animal drilled the boreholes in the brachiopods. Today, ocean-living snails may make drill holes in clamshells. But modern snails have hard shells. Whatever drilled into the Devonian brachiopods was not preserved, so apparently it did not have a hard shell.

Scientists do know some things about the animal that drilled the holes. Almost all of the drill holes are in the "meaty" part of the brachiopod's shell. This indicates that the animal used brachiopods as food and was drilling the holes in order to eat the brachiopods.

Many questions still remain about the hole-drilling animal. While the Devonian brachiopods push the record of drilled shells much farther back in geologic time, the animal that made the drill holes remains both unseen and unknown.

CHAPTER REVIEW

Main Ideas

- Fossils are traces or the preserved remains of organisms that once lived on the earth. Many kinds of fossils have been found in the earth's rocks.
- A fossil is most likely to form from the hard parts of an organism when the organism is buried or frozen soon after death.
- The key to recognizing a fossil is to identify a feature that is similar in appearance to something living today.
- One way to identify a fossil is to match it with a sketch of a once-living organism.
- Each block of geologic time had its own set of plants and animals that lived during that time.
- Index fossils are fossils of organisms that lived for a short period of time in many areas.
- Different rock layers with the same index fossil are the same age.
- Fossils and the rocks in which they are found are probably the same age.
- Invertebrates, fish, and plants were the dominant life forms during the Paleozoic Era. Plant remains later formed huge coal deposits.
- Reptiles were the dominant life forms during the Mesozoic Era.
- Mammals have been the dominant life forms during the Cenozoic Era.
- Each era ended with a major extinction of large numbers of organisms that lived in that era.

Using Vocabulary

On a separate piece of paper, write a sentence for each of the words below. Each sentence should give a *clue* as to the meaning of the word.

amber	cephalopod	brachiopod
petrified wood	Jurassic	reptile
mold	invertebrate	mammal
cast	trilobite	

Remembering Facts

On your paper, write the word or words that best complete each sentence.
1. (Rocks, Fossils, Minerals) are preserved evidence of past life.
2. Early invertebrates were (trilobites, reptiles, fish).
3. The Mesozoic Era was dominated by (fish, reptiles, mammals).
4. Animals without backbones are called (vertebrates, invertebrates, fossils).
5. Whole organisms have not been preserved in (amber, ice, petrified wood).
6. Index fossils represent organisms that lived (a short time, a long time, forever).
7. A (clam, bird, jellyfish) would not leave many fossils.
8. Fossilized (palm trees, fish, brachiopods) provide extensive evidence of early invertebrates.
9. A footprint is an example of a (mold, cast, carbon) fossil.
10. The dominant life form during the Cenozoic Era has been (fish, dinosaurs, mammals).
11. Fossils are (older than, younger than, the same age as) the rocks they are found in.
12. The Jurassic Period occurred during the (Paleozoic, Mesozoic, Cenozoic) Era.
13. A (mold, cast, petrified log) has no inner structure.
14. Fossils show that cephalopods (changed, did not change) over time.
15. Silica replaces once-living cells to form (amber, petrified wood, molds).
16. (Mesozoic, Paleozoic, Cenozoic) fossils are the least common, because invertebrates were the dominant life form in that era.

Understanding Ideas

On your paper, answer each question in complete sentences.
1. Why is Precambrian time not divided into periods as the other three eras are?
2. How do scientists distinguish between the end of the Paleozoic Era and the beginning of the Mesozoic Era?
3. What new form of animal life began to flourish in the Cretaceous Period? What would explain why this happened?
4. Why have only a small percentage of plants and animals living in the past become fossils?

Applying What You Have Learned

1. Why does petrified wood have a greater density than dead wood?
2. Describe why only a few of all plants and animals that lived in the past have become fossils.
3. How do paleontologists know what forms of life existed in the past?

Challenge

The rock record contains the fossils of many ocean-dwelling, clamlike animals that lived during the Paleozoic Period. The fossils show that the variety of animals increased and decreased with the passing of each period. One model proposes that the varieties correlated with a rise in sea level. Another model suggests that the variety was due to a drop in sea level. Use the graph and the geologic column to answer the following questions.

1. What changes occurred in the variety of animals from period to period?
2. What changes occurred in the rock column from period to period? Interpret your findings.
3. Which model does the fossil evidence support? Explain why this model seems to fit.

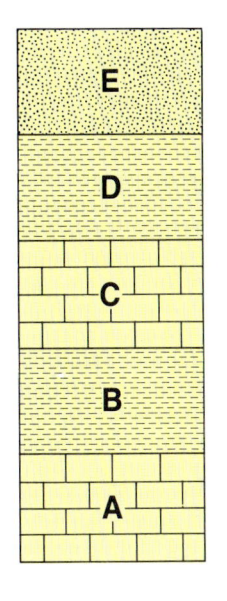

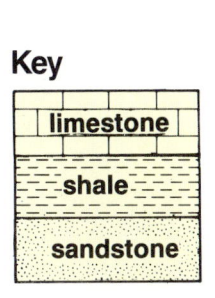

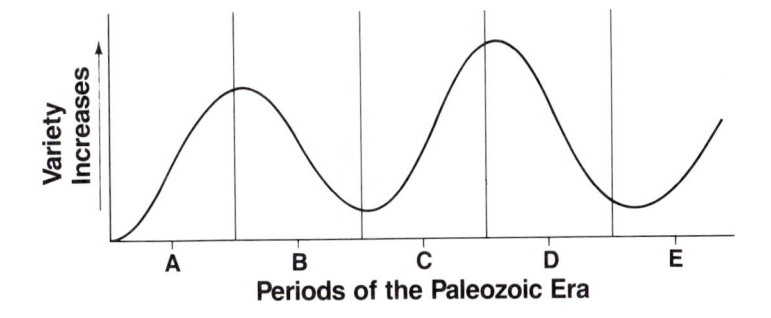

Research and Investigation

1. Make drawings of some of the fossils found in your area. Then make a geologic time scale like the one in Figure 21.16. Label each fossil and place it in its correct position on the time scale.
2. Use the library to learn more about the different theories developed by scientists to explain the disappearance of the dinosaurs. Choose the theory that you believe is correct. Explain why you think it is correct.

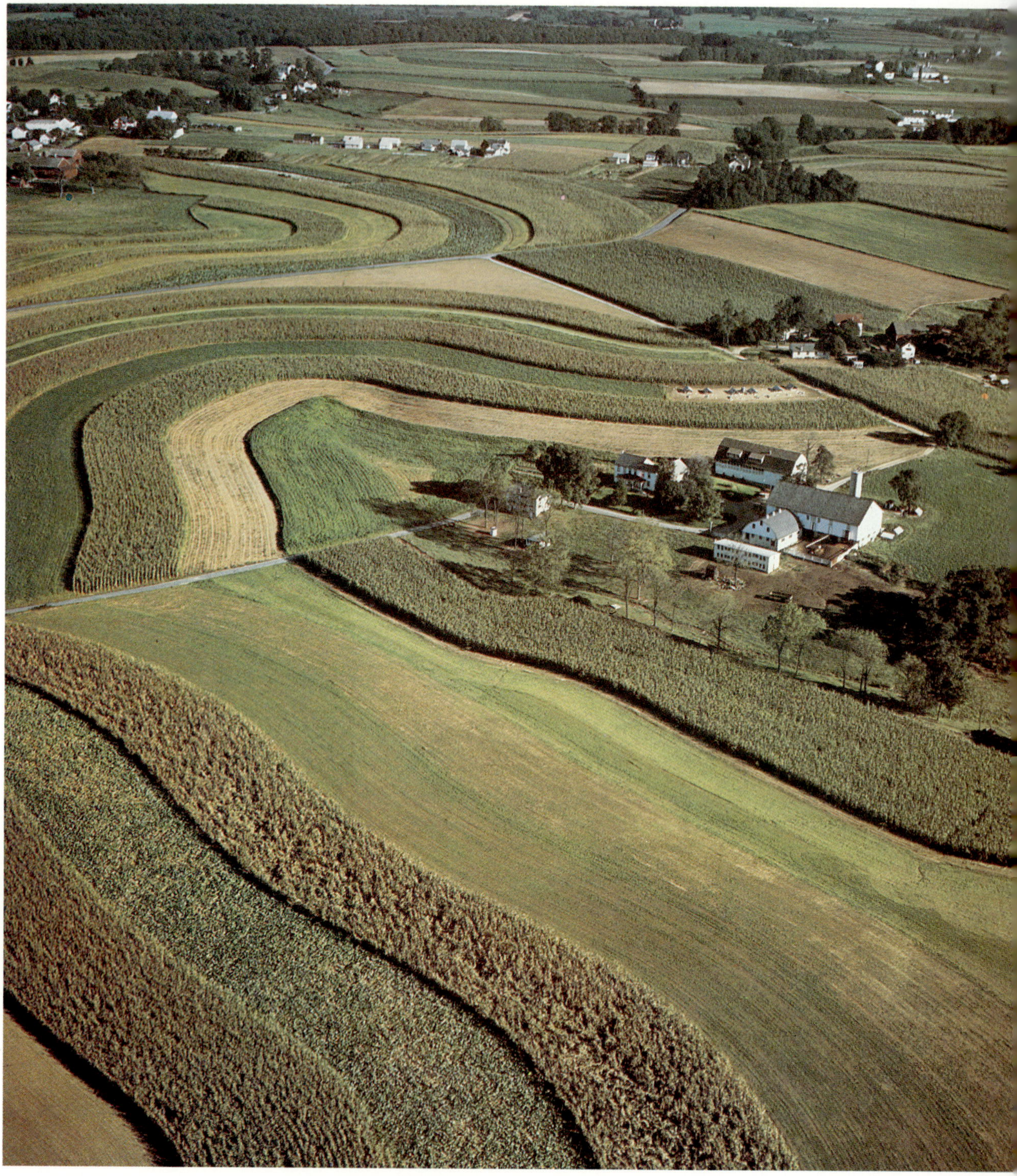

UNIT SIX

The Earth's Bounty

Chapter 22
The Earth's Resources

Chapter 23
Nonrenewable Energy Resources

Chapter 24
Renewable Energy Resources

Chapter 25
Your Environment, Earth

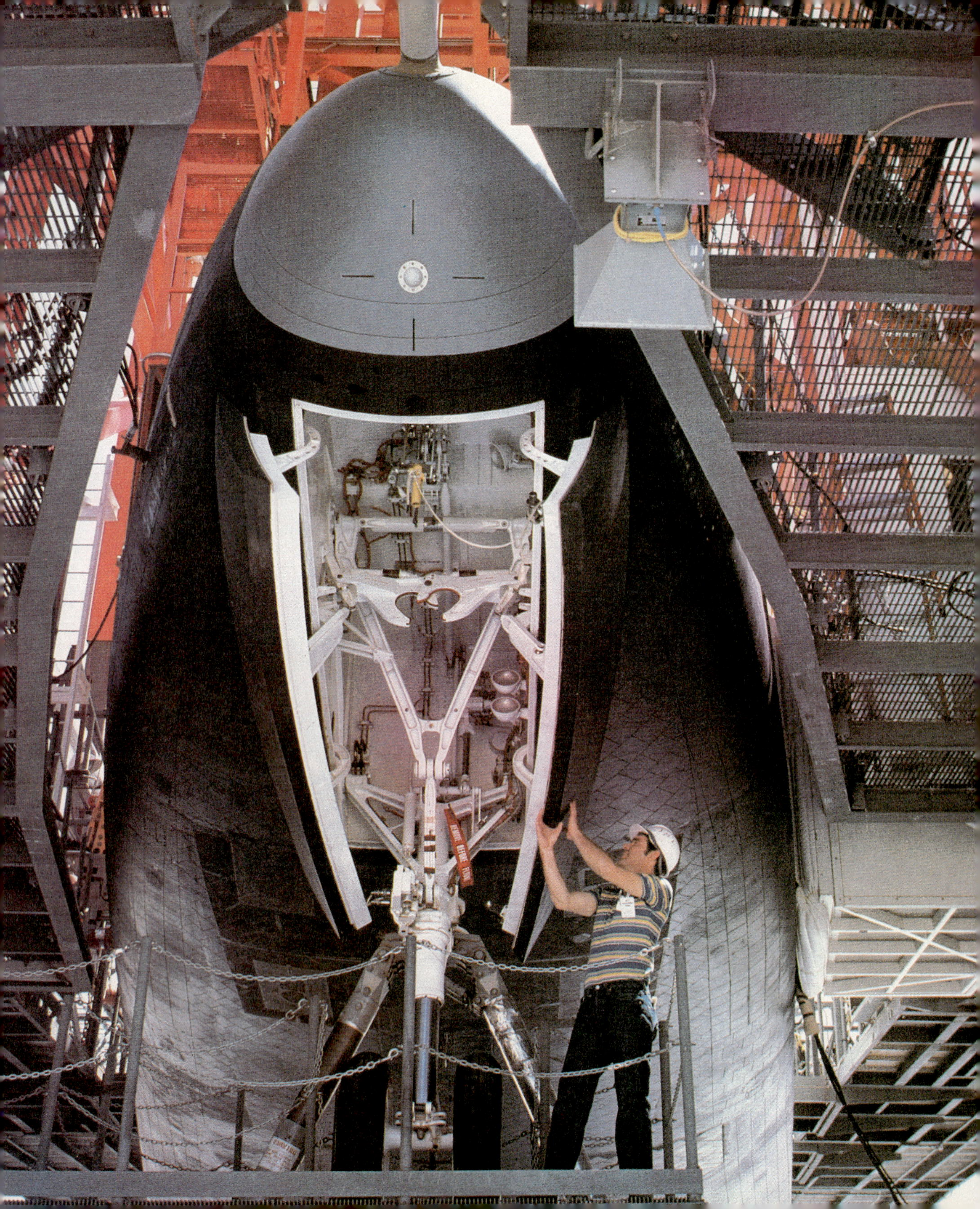

Chapter 22
The Earth's Resources

Lesson Titles
22.1 Metallic Resources of the Land
22.2 Nonmetallic Resources of the Land
22.3 Resources of the Ocean
22.4 Where the Resources are Found

The space shuttle is a marvel of engineering and science. But have you ever thought about all the different materials the space shuttle is made of? Many different kinds of materials were needed to make the computers and electric systems which help control the craft. Other materials were required for the special heat-resisting tiles to keep the craft from burning up upon reentry into the earth's atmosphere. Vast amounts of still other materials are burned in the rockets that lift the shuttle into space. Would you believe that all of the materials needed for the space shuttle come from the earth in some form? In fact, just about everything you use, wear, or eat comes directly or indirectly from the earth's crust. Till now the earth has been able to supply all the materials people have wanted. Will this always be true?

In this chapter you'll learn about some of the materials people take from the earth, where the materials are found, and how much of them there is.

Figure 22.1 *opposite:* Materials to build the space shuttle come from many of Earth's natural resources.

22.1 Metallic Resources of the Land

You will find out
- what a natural resource is;
- what some renewable resources are;
- what some nonrenewable resources are;
- what an ore is.

The earth has a large supply of materials people use. They are called **natural resources.** Natural resources are the supplies taken from the earth and include water, food, building materials, fiber for clothing, minerals, and energy.

Figure 22.2 A new crop will be planted to replace this one after it is harvested, but the machinery is made of resources that can be taken from the earth only once.

Natural resources fall into two types, renewable and nonrenewable. **Renewable resources** add a new supply each growing season or will become available again sometime soon in the future. Wood, food, and wool are examples of such resources. A **nonrenewable resource** is one that is not available again from the earth once it is taken and used. Examples of nonrenewable resources are metallic substances such as copper, iron, and aluminum. Nonmetallic substances such as oil, coal, clays, and chemical fertilizers are also nonrenewable resources. Although paper made from wood and many metals can be recycled, neither wood nor metals are considered to be renewable.

434

22 / The Earth's Resources

Metallic resources used for making things are found in the earth as the elements that make up minerals. **Ores** are minerals from which metals can be taken at a reasonable cost. Table 22-1 shows some of the widely used metals and their most common ore minerals.

Iron is the most widely used metal. It accounts for over 90 percent of all metals mined. The major ore minerals from which iron is taken are hematite and magnetite. These ores contain from 15 percent to 60 percent iron. In the United States the location of the major iron deposits is the Lake Superior region. Here the ore is found in huge sedimentary deposits. Other metals are added to iron to make special steels. The strength of iron may be increased by adding nickel, carbon, manganese, and other metals. Steel's resistance to rusting is due to the presence of added chromium.

Table 22-1 Ten Common Metals and their Ore Minerals

Metal	Ore Mineral
Iron	Magnetite Hematite
Copper	Native copper Chalcocite Chalcopyrite
Aluminum	Bauxite
Lead	Galena
Zinc	Sphalerite
Gold	Native gold
Silver	Native silver
Chromium	Chromite
Mercury	Cinnabar
Nickel	Pentlandite

Figure 22.3 Steel is one of the most important building materials used in modern industry.

The procedure for obtaining a metal from an ore is done in four steps. The first step is to extract the ore from the earth. Next, the ore must be enriched by removing waste materials found with the ore. The third step is to process the enriched ore to obtain the metal that is wanted. The fourth step is to use the metal to manufacture a final product.

Figure 22.4 *right:* A copper mine

Figure 22.5 *below:* Copper may be fashioned into a variety of useful forms.

Copper is another widely used mineral. You might think a copper ore would be rich in copper. That is not true. Most copper ores contain very little copper. They may have as little as 4 kg of copper for each metric ton of ore. That means for every metric ton mined there is 996 kg of waste material. Because a great deal of copper is used in the electrical industry, some copper mines are enormous.

One of the metals used for its lightness and strength is aluminum. It is used in many household products, in airplane and automobile construction, and in the electrical industry. Most new electrical transmission lines in the United States are made of aluminum. The number of different uses for this metal grows every day.

Gold is a desirable metal for its beauty and the fact that it is almost indestructible. It occurs in small amounts in deposits that are located in present or old stream channels. It is used in making jewelry, in electri-

Do You Know?
The United States is the world's leading producer of copper. Over half of this supply comes from the state of Arizona.

cal circuits, and in gold work by dentists.

Metals play an important role in your life. Imagine how your surroundings, your activities, and even your clothes would be different if there were no metals. Forms of transportation from bicycles to spaceships would be unknown. There would be no telephones, televisions, or stereos. Tools, modern appliances, jewelry, and some kinds of clothing would be impossible without metals. Metals are essential to your way of life.

Activity

What Happens When an Ore Is Smelted?

Materials
safety goggles
crucible
ring stand
galena (composed of lead and sulfur)
Bunsen burner
pliers
iron ring

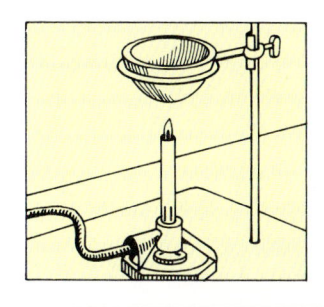

Procedure
Wear your safety goggles at all times and provide some ventilation in the room while heating this material.

1. Place a small amount of galena powder in the crucible. CAUTION: Wear your safety goggles.
2. Heat the galena as hot as possible.
3. Observe the changes.
4. When the galena has changed, remove the heat. Let the mass cool and then squeeze it with pliers. CAUTION: Do not handle the mass until it is completely cool.

Questions
1. Did you smell anything coming from the galena while it was being heated? What did you smell? Remove flame before testing for smell.
2. What happens when you squeeze the material remaining in the crucible with pliers?
3. What metal is in galena?

Study Questions for 22.1

1. Define *natural resources*.
2. Give three examples of a renewable resource. Explain why they are renewable.
3. What are three nonrenewable resources? Explain why they are nonrenewable.
4. What is an ore and what are the basic procedures followed to obtain metal from an ore?

22.2 Nonmetallic Resources of the Land

You will find out
- what some nonmetallic resources are;
- how nonmetallic resources are used.

Would you prefer to own a gold mine or an oil well? A coal mine or an iron mine? A copper mine or a clay pit? Most students say they would prefer to own a metal mine because they think metallic resources are more valuable than nonmetallic resources. More than 10 billion dollars yearly is spent on metals, but the amount spent on nonmetals is more than three times that amount.

What are the major nonmetallic resources that cost so much? The major nonmetallic resources are (1) the fossil fuels—petroleum, natural gas, and coal; (2) minerals for fertilizers; (3) minerals for the chemical industry—sulfur and salt; (4) abrasive minerals; and (5) building materials. Today's industry runs because there is a continuing supply of nonmetallic resources.

Figure 22.6 Which do you think is more valuable, an oil resource (*left*) or a sulfur resource (*right*)?

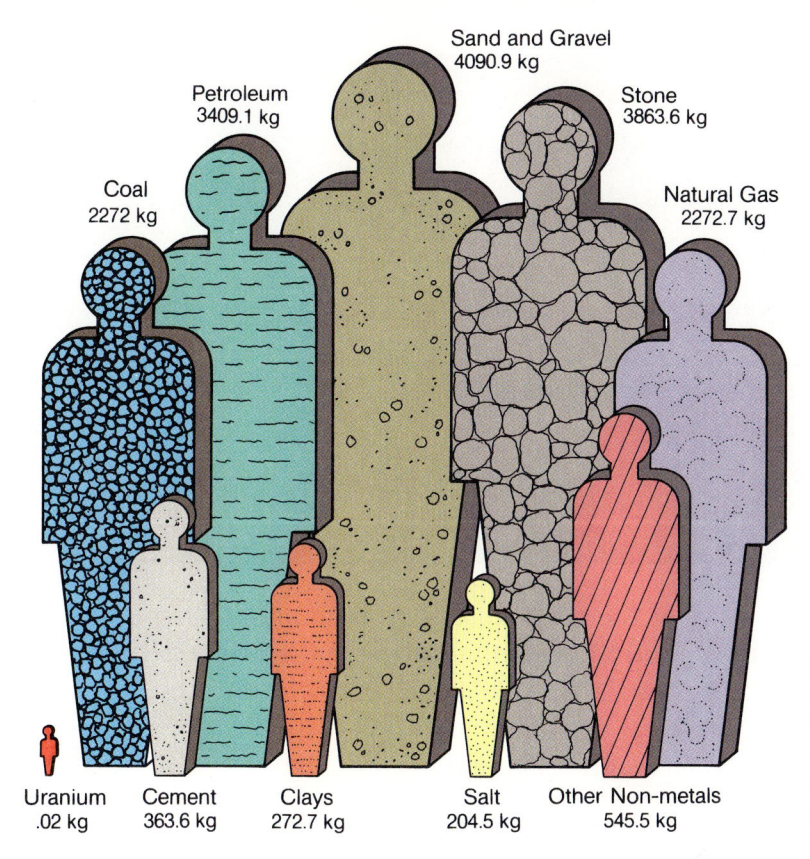

Figure 22.7 *left:* The consumption of nonmetallic resources in the United States per person

Figure 22.8 *below:* Fossil fuels are used to manufacture a wide variety of products. How many fossil fuel products do you use in one day?

Look at Figure 22.7. This figure shows the amount of some nonmetallic resources used for each person in the United States each year. The numbers were obtained by dividing the total amount of each nonmetallic resource used each year by the population of the United States. You probably didn't realize how much of the earth's crust you use each year. You use such a great amount of nonmetallic resources each year because they are used in so many different ways. Nonmetallic resources are used for fuels, fertilizers, chemicals, foods, medicines, abrasives, and building materials to name just a few of the ways.

The most valuable of the nonmetallic resources is the fossil fuels. Their primary use is to produce energy for power and heat, and lubricants. However, many other things can be made from the fossil fuels. Did you know that nylon, Styrofoam, polyesters, aspirin, and more than 3,000 other things can be made of chemicals obtained from fossil fuels?

22 / The Earth's Resources

One of the most necessary nonmetallic resources for the United States and the rest of the world is the fertilizer minerals. Fertilizers are essential for growing crops to feed the world's population. The big three in fertilizers are nitrogen, potassium, and phosphorus. The demand for these three elements doubles every ten years. Fortunately, there appear to be large reserves of these elements.

The chemical industry is a large user of nonmetallic resources. Sulfur is one of the most widely used chemical nonmetallic resources. Sulfur is used in making insect and weed killers. It is also used in making sulfuric acid, which is used in many manufacturing processes. Sodium chloride, or salt, is another chemical nonmetallic resource. It is used as a food, in medicines, as a food preservative, and in packing houses. Many other nonmetals are used by the chemical industry but, with the exception of the fossil fuels, only in relatively small amounts.

The abrasive minerals include substances that are hard. Diamond is the hardest natural substance and the most important abrasive. It is used in grinding wheels, as a powder, and on the tips of oil-drilling bits. Other abrasive materials are pumice—used in soaps and scouring powders—and garnets and quartz used to make sandpaper.

Figure 22.9 *top:* Crop-dusting enables farmers to use chemical, nonmetallic resources on large areas of crops.

Figure 22.10 *bottom:* What does a diamond have in common with these other materials?

Activity

Which Cleanser Contains Quartz? Which Contains Feldspar?

Materials
2 kinds of scouring powder (1 made of feldspar and another made of quartz)
4 glass microscope slides
gloves
water

Procedure
1. Put a small pinch of scouring powder near one end of a glass microscope slide.
2. Add a couple drops of water.
3. Place another glass microscope slide on top of the first slide and rub the powder between them. Wear your gloves while doing this.
4. Repeat steps 1–3 for the other scouring powder.
5. Carefully examine the surface of each set of slides.

Questions
1. Which powder scratched the glass slides?
2. Why didn't both powders scratch the glass slides?
3. Which powder contains quartz? Which contains feldspar? Explain your choices. *Hint:* Quartz has a hardness of 7; feldspar has a hardness of 6.

Building materials are another valuable nonmetallic resource. Stone is used for building structures and for ornamental display. Cement for buildings and roads is made from limestone and clay. Sand and gravel are widely used for roads. They are also mixed with cement to make concrete for roads and concrete buildings. Clay is used to make bricks used in the building industry. Pure quartz-sand is made into glass.

Look around your school to see how nonmetallic resources were used in building it. How many nonmetallic materials can you spot in your home? You'll be surprised how much use you make of these materials.

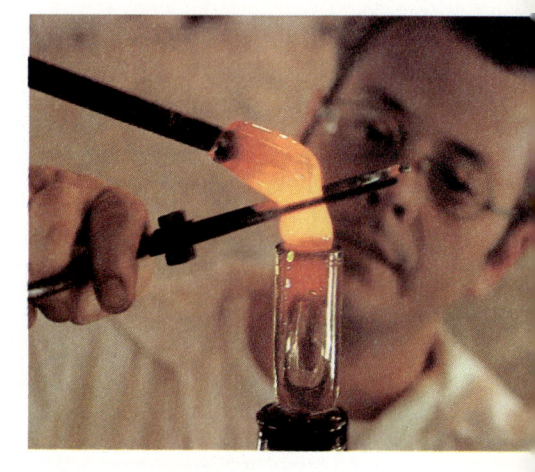

Figure 22.11 Ordinary quartz-sand is used to produce glass.

Study Questions for 22.2

1. List five major nonmetallic resources.
2. Select one of the major nonmetallic resources and describe its use.

22 / The Earth's Resources

22.3 Resources of the Ocean

You will find out
- what mineral resources are obtained from seawater;
- what some of the mineral resources are in or on the ocean floor;
- what some of the biological resources of the ocean are.

Figure 22.12 Common salt can be mined from sea water.

Do You Know?
The abundant elements formed in seawater are also abundant in rocks with the exception of chlorine, which is much more abundant in the ocean. Scientists are not sure why the ocean has so much chlorine.

Table 22-2 The seven most abundant elements in seawater

Element	Estimated value in combined form ($ per 4×10^6 liters)
Chlorine	$924
Sodium	$378
Magnesium	$4,130
Sulfur	$101
Calcium	$150
Potassium	$91
Bromine	$190

The thing that impresses everyone who has ever taken an ocean voyage is the ocean's vastness. There's a lot of it, more than 1,370,000,000 km³. This enormous volume contains more than just water. In every cubic kilometer there are 5×10^{12} metric tons of dissolved elements. The ocean is said to contain enough gold to make everyone a millionaire. Each cubic kilometer is worth about $1.6 billion if all the elements could be recovered and sold.

Seven elements found in seawater and their dollar values are shown in Table 22-2. The elements are worth a lot of money but are costly to remove. Imagine an industrial plant that could remove all of the elements from seawater flowing through it. At the rate of flow of one million liters per minute, it would take almost two years to process one cubic kilometer of seawater. It is worthwhile, however, to extract only a very few substances from seawater. The table salt you eat on your food may have come from the sea. Salt is made from a combination of two elements, sodium and chlorine. About 6 million tons of salt are taken from the seawater each year. Magnesium is also removed in useful amounts.

The most valuable thing taken from seawater is fresh water. Fresh water is the world's most important resource. Whether or not fresh water is available determines where people live, where they can farm, and what kinds of manufacturing can be done. The recovery of fresh water from seawater is important for countries that border on the ocean and have a desert climate. Figure 22.13 shows one type of plant used to obtain fresh water. The cost of such fresh water is as low as $.50 for 4,000 liters. Costs are expected to drop in the future as more efficient plants are developed. Fresh water from the sea could change many deserts into fertile farms.

Figure 22.13 Desalinization plants can recover large volumes of fresh water from the ocean.

Activity

How Will This Water Taste?

Materials
2 cups
plastic sandwich bag
3 soda straws
6 toothpicks
1 jar lid, 6.5 cm in diameter, painted black
plastic tape
water and salt

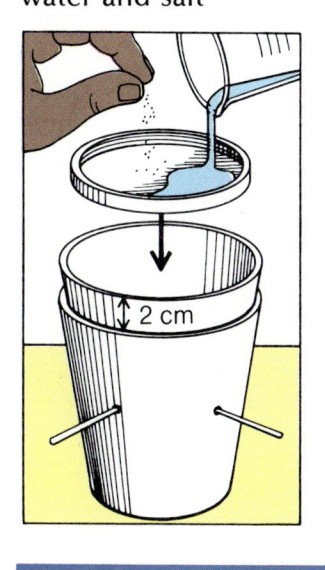

Procedure

1. Set up the apparatus by first placing one cup inside the other. The inside cup should be raised enough to give a 2-cm clearance between the two. Hold the inner cup in this position with four toothpicks.

2. Place the jar lid in the inner cup and fill halfway with water. Add a pinch of salt and stir. Now taste the water.

3. Fasten the soda straws together with tape to form a tripod and set into the jar lid.

4. Use two toothpicks to make a support at the top of the tripod.

5. Place a plastic bag over the tripod with the bottom edge inside the outer cup. Use plastic tape to secure the bag in place and hold it away from the inner cup.

6. Place the apparatus in sunlight for a day.

7. Dismantle the apparatus and taste the water that has collected in the outer cup.

Questions

1. Where did the water in the outer cup come from?
2. How did it taste?
3. Describe how you could make fresh water from seawater.

22 / The Earth's Resources

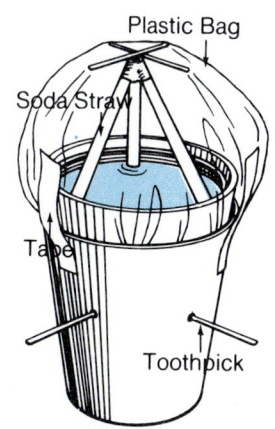

The ocean floor is also a rich source of minerals. Some of these minerals are found as small lumps called **nodules** [NAHJ-ools]. These nodules, found on the ocean floor, are rich in manganese, copper, nickel, and cobalt. These are important minerals that have wide use in manufacturing. Will the ocean floor ever be mined for these minerals? Some people believe it will. In Figure 22.15 you see the design of a device proposed to recover the nodules from the ocean floor.

Beneath the ocean floor is another mineral resource. Huge drilling platforms can be located offshore to drill through the ocean floor for oil and gas. Geologists expect that more and more of the oil you use in the future will be taken from the ocean floor.

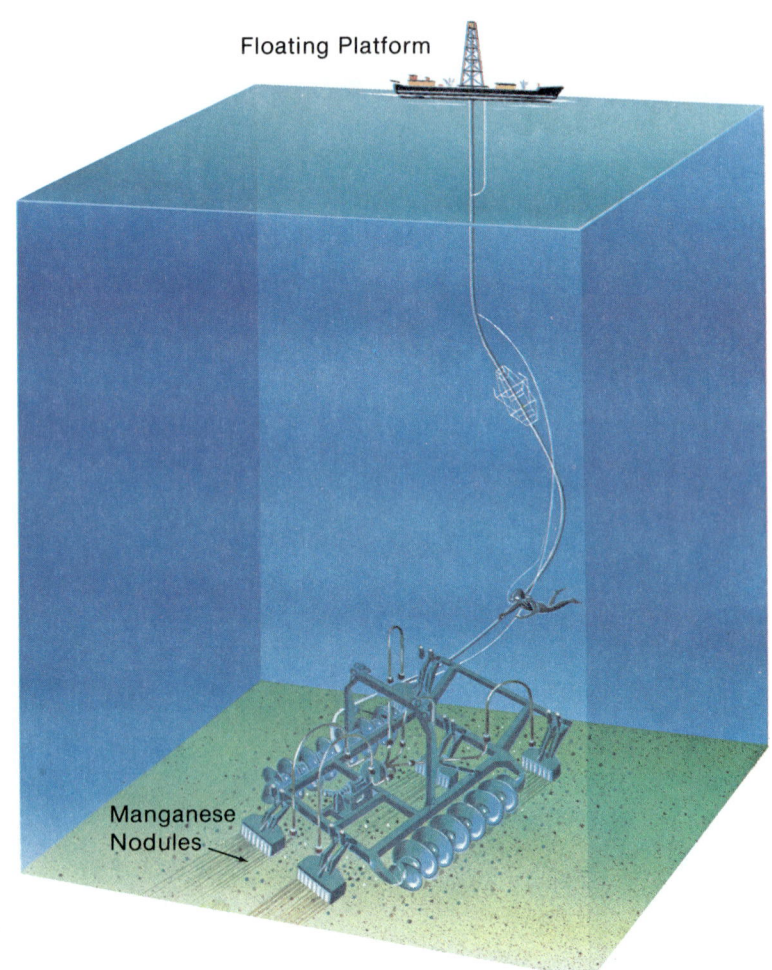

Figure 22.14 *above:* Manganese nodules on the ocean floor

Figure 22.15 *right:* Devices such as this one will be used for many sea-mining operations in the future.

Do You Know?
It has been estimated that more than 1.5 billion metric tons of manganese nodules lie on the Pacific Ocean floor.

444

22 / The Earth's Resources

An even more promising resource found in the ocean is biological. The ocean is an excellent source of food, especially **protein.** Proteins are substances that the body uses for the growth and repair of tissues. Fish are rich in proteins. About 90 percent of the ocean harvest is fish; the rest consists primarily of whales and shellfish.

Not all fish end up directly on someone's dinner table. About half of the fish landed in the United States go to feed animals in the form of fish meal. The poultry industry uses large amounts of fish in this form. Fish meal is rich in minerals that are essential to animal and plant growth.

Although fishing will continue to provide an important food resource from the ocean, it is believed by many that even more food can be obtained by farming the ocean. The process of farming the ocean is called **aquaculture** [AH-kwa-KUL-chur]. The Japanese grow seaweed, oysters, and shrimp under farming conditions in the sea. This makes the ocean an important resource because people can grow the kinds of things they like to eat. The ocean is one of the earth's treasures. In the future it will play an even more important role in supplying people with minerals and food.

Figure 22.16 These chickens are being fed a nourishing diet of fish meal. The chickens will then produce food for people.

Do You Know?
Farmers used powdered fish to feed their livestock as early as 325 B.C.

Figure 22.17 The ocean is becoming a rich resource for food because of modern techniques of aquaculture.

Study Questions for 22.3

1. Name the mineral resources taken from seawater.
2. What resources are found in or on the ocean floor?
3. How can the biological resources of the ocean be increased?

22.4 Where the Resources Are Found

You will find out
- where mineral resources are found and used worldwide;
- where fossil fuels are found and used;
- how future supplies of mineral resources will be met.

Everyone who studies about the uses of natural resources sooner or later asks the questions, "Are there enough? Will the earth's resources run out? What's going to happen in the future?"

The earth's natural resources are being used up faster than they are being produced in the earth. This might lead you to think that the earth's resources will someday be all used up. That's not exactly true. Instead, the materials that people use will just become increasingly difficult to obtain. They will cost more, and it will require more energy to take the material from the ore.

Figure 22.18 The location of the world's major mineral resources

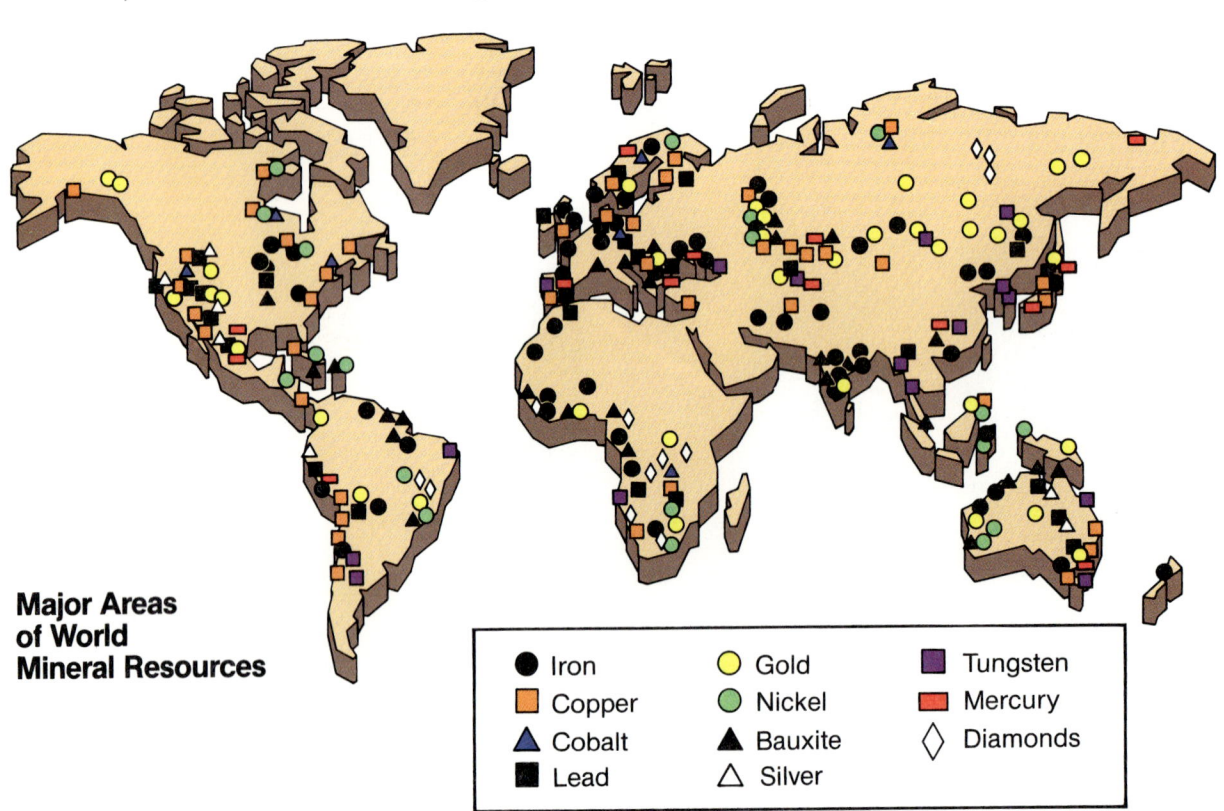

Major Areas of World Mineral Resources

- ● Iron
- ■ Copper
- ▲ Cobalt
- ■ Lead
- ○ Gold
- ● Nickel
- ▲ Bauxite
- △ Silver
- ■ Tungsten
- ■ Mercury
- ◇ Diamonds

446   22 / The Earth's Resources

One clue that the earth's natural resources will not run out all at once is shown in Figure 22.18. The main sources of minerals used by people and industry are shown in this figure. Each kind of mineral is found in many different places around the world. All of these places won't run out of ore at the same time, and some new sources of ore may be discovered.

Many of the earth's resources, however, are not found where they are used. It is necessary to move some of the minerals used in manufacturing long distances from where they are found. You will see why this is so if you compare Figure 22.20 with Figure 22.18. The industrial countries are big users of minerals. Some minerals, such as cobalt and nickel, are found in locations that are not highly industrial. That means these materials, which are important in making steel, must be moved from one part of the world to another. The buying and selling of mineral resources is part of international trade.

Figure 22.19 *above:* Mineral resources are necessary for manufacturing and industry.

Figure 22.20 The major manufacturing regions shown on this map draw their raw materials from the areas shown in Figure 22.18.

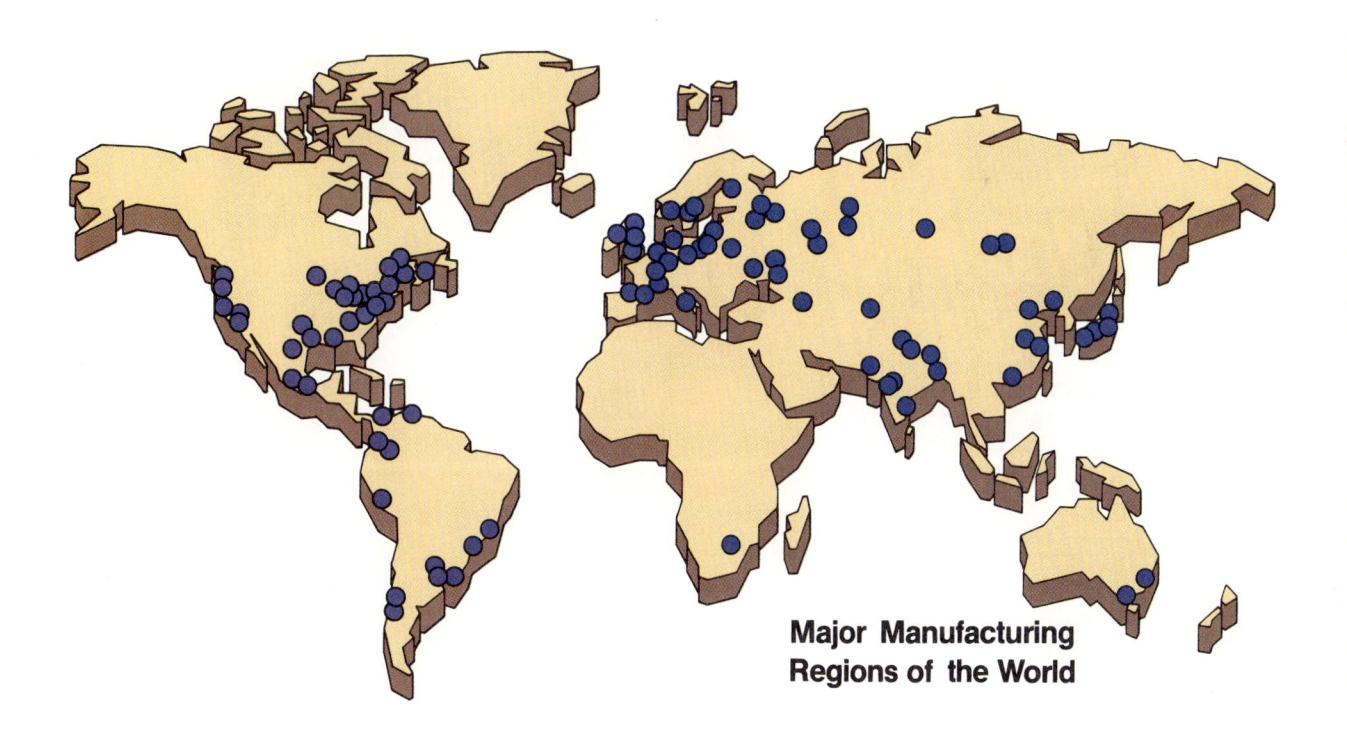

Major Manufacturing Regions of the World

22 / The Earth's Resources

Like minerals, fossil fuels and uranium are found in many places. The largest users of these fuels are also the industrial nations. Fossil fuels and uranium must be moved, like the minerals, from wherever they are found to wherever they are used. Petroleum is moved the farthest and in great amounts. Coal is moved to where it is used, but this is usually only a relatively short distance. Most of the uranium that is used in nuclear power plants must be moved long distances to the industrial countries. Figure 22.22 shows where most of the large fossil fuel and uranium resources are located in the world. Compare this map with Figure 22.23. You can see that the places where the fuels are used are often not the same as the places where they are found.

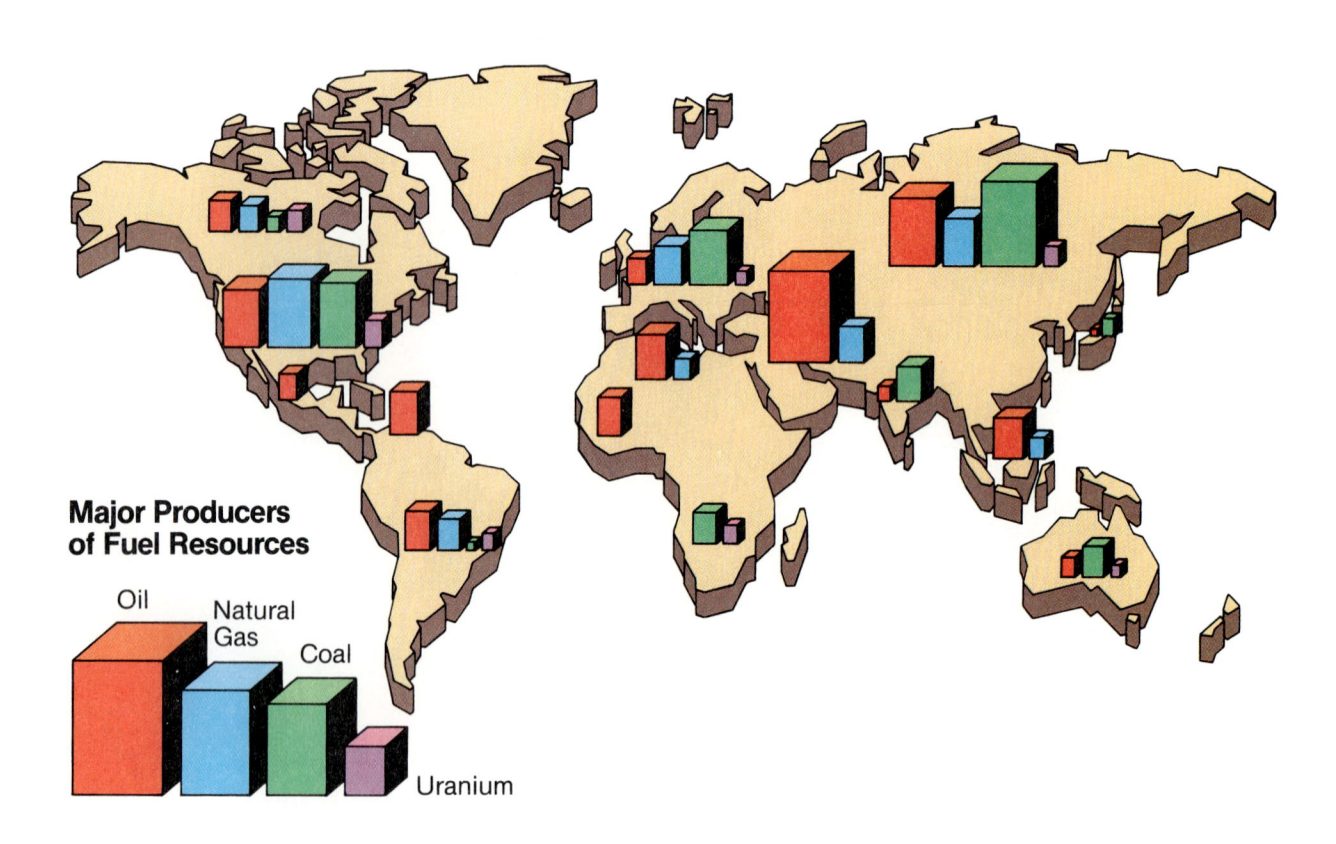

Figure 22.21 *above:* Oil freighter

Figure 22.22 The major areas of energy resources

Major Producers of Fuel Resources

Oil Natural Gas Coal Uranium

448

22 / The Earth's Resources

Major Consumers of Fuel Resources

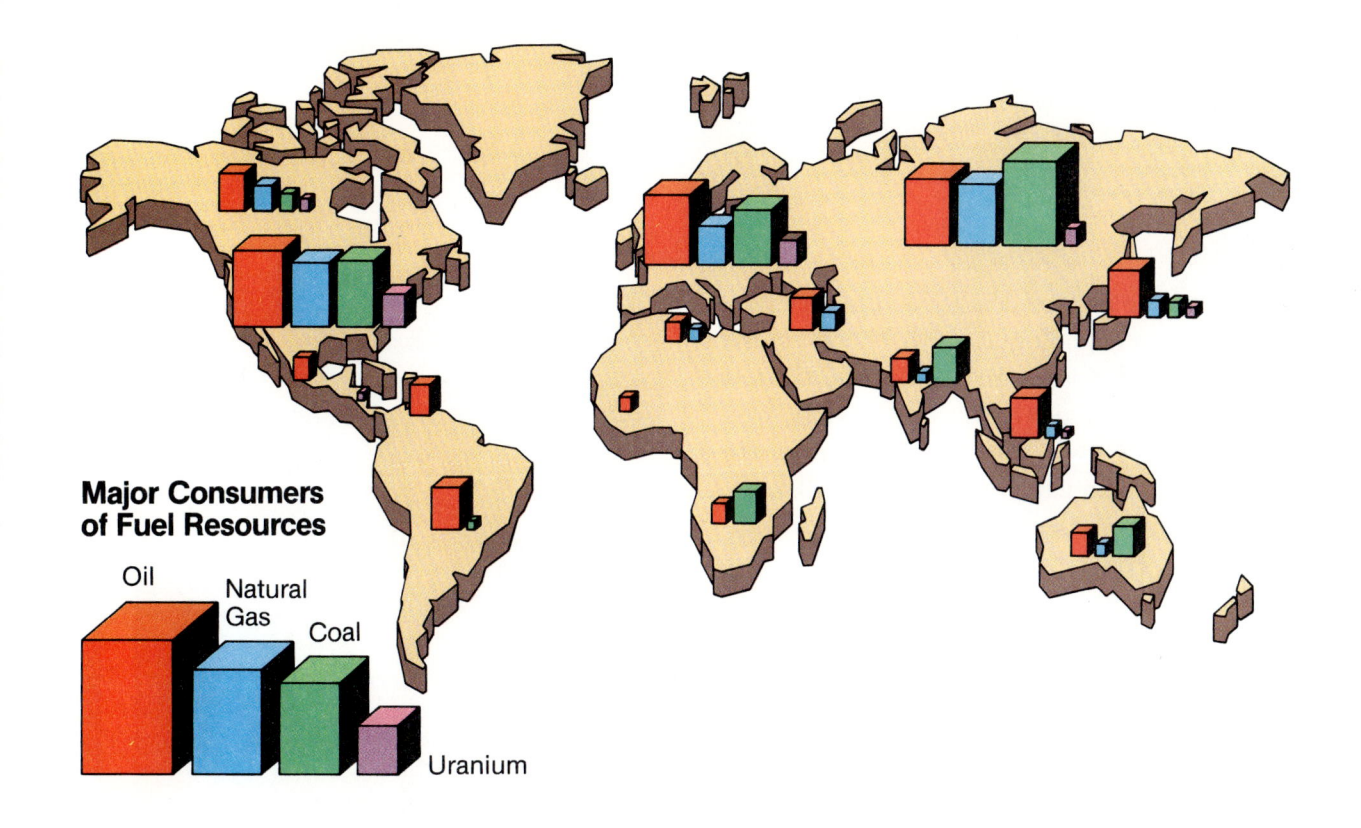

Oil • Natural Gas • Coal • Uranium

How will the expanding needs for mineral resources be met? One way will be to use machines that require less material in their construction and which require less energy to run. Another way is to recycle materials that are scarce and costly. Industry and people worldwide will also learn to conserve materials and reduce wastes. All of these efforts will greatly help to maintain adequate supplies of mineral resources in the future.

Study Questions for 22.4

1. Each continent is not equally rich in minerals. Which continent seems to have the most minerals? Which seems to have the least?
2. Which continent seems to have the most petroleum?
3. List four ways to meet the future needs for the earth's mineral resources.

Figure 22.23 the major areas of energy use

Do You Know?
The concentration of some metals in waste dumps is higher than the concentration of these metals in the earth's crust. Someday it may become profitable to mine the waste piles being made today.

22 / The Earth's Resources

Biography

Floyd Gray (1951–   )

On September 15, 1951, Floyd Gray, a research geologist with the Western Mineral Resource Branch of the United States Geological Survey (USGS), was born in New Orleans, Louisiana. He moved at an early age to Baton Rouge, Louisiana, where he attended public school. His early interest in science was encouraged by his father, who took him through the laboratories in the refinery where he worked. In the fourth grade Floyd's interest in science was sparked by a wonderful science teacher, and in the ninth grade he won a statewide science competition.

In college he started studying journalism, but a summer USGS geology job changed his life. The job took him to Hawaii, where he saw a volcanic eruption. In fact, he had the opportunity to gather data and make observations of that eruption.

Upon returning to the mainland, Gray enrolled in the University of California at Santa Cruz. His two bachelor's degrees were in earth science and anthropology. He earned a master's degree at the University of Massachusetts in Amherst. For his thesis he studied the magmatic ore deposits in southern Oregon.

Currently Gray is working for the USGS, evaluating the mineral potential of rocks of the ocean floor that have been forced onto the continental crust in northern California and southern Oregon. He does field mapping and lab petrology work and makes geochemical analyses of these rocks. He is looking for geochemical tracers to ore deposits.

Why does he like his work? He says, "I like outside work that is challenging. I'm interpreting nature and I like that. I enjoy traveling and the chance to do something rewarding."

CHAPTER REVIEW

Main Ideas

- Natural resources are the supplies taken from the earth and include water, food, building materials, fiber for clothing, minerals, and energy.
- Renewable resources will never run out because they are continuously being replaced.
- Nonrenewable resources will never again be available once they are used.
- An ore is a mineral from which a metal can be extracted at a reasonable cost.
- Nonmetallic resources are used for fuels, fertilizers, chemicals, foods, medicines, abrasives, and building materials.
- The most valuable of the nonmetallic resources are the fossil fuels.
- Table salt, magnesium, and bromine are mineral resources taken from seawater.
- Manganese nodules and petroleum are resources found on or under the ocean floor.
- Aquaculture is a way of farming the ocean.
- Many mineral resources must be transported from the place where they are found to the place where they are used.
- The earth's natural resources are being used up faster than they are being produced in the earth.
- Future needs for minerals will be met by reducing consumption, increasing efficiency, recycling, and conservation.
- The continents are not equally rich in mineral resources.

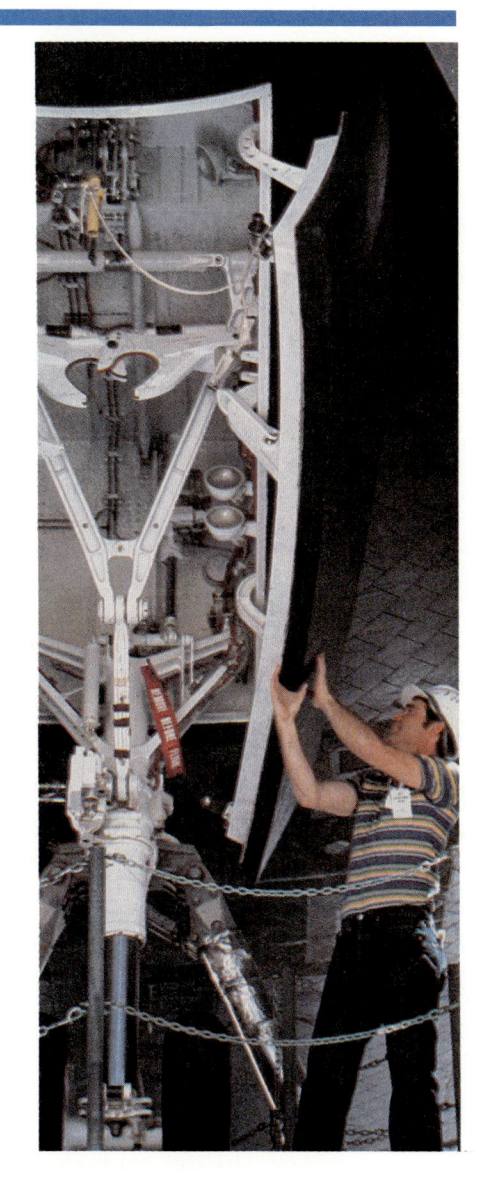

Using Vocabulary

On a separate piece of paper, write a paragraph explaining resources. Use each of the words listed below.

natural resource
renewable resource
nonrenewable resource
ore
nodule
protein
aquaculture

22 / The Earth's Resources

Remembering Facts

On your paper, write the word or words that best complete each sentence.
1. What determines whether a mineral will become an ore or not is the (source, composition, cost of removal).
2. Wood, food, and wool are examples of (nonrenewable, nonmetallic, renewable) resources.
3. Fish make up (10, 50, 90) percent of the ocean's harvest.
4. The most valuable thing removed from the ocean is (gold, table salt, fresh water).
5. The most important nonmetallic resource is(are) (diamonds, fertilizers, sulfur).
6. Oil, coal, and chemical fertilizers are (nonrenewable, metallic, renewable) resources.
7. Copper ores contain less than (90, 20, 1) percent copper.
8. The most valuable nometallic resource is (gold, diamonds, fossil fuels).
9. Farming the ocean is called (extraction, enrichment, aquaculture).
10. Supplies from the earth are (ores, natural resources, nodules).
11. The area with the greatest supply of and least demand for petroleum is (North America, Asia, Europe).
12. The most widely used metallic resource is (iron, aluminum, gold).
13. Mineral lumps on the ocean floor are called (ores, nodules, aquaculture).
14. An important new source of metals is (ores, recycling, oil).
15. Glass is made from (limestone, clay, sand).
16. A substance used by the body for growth and repair of tissues is (fresh water, protein, gold).

Understanding Ideas

On your paper, answer each question in complete sentences.
1. Explain why some people believe that the earth's resources will never be used up.
2. Which of the earth's resources are among the most valuable and cannot be recycled? Explain why they are valuable and why they cannot be recycled.
3. Land and its soil are considered to be renewable resources. What demands are being made by our society on these resources that could eventually turn them into nonrenewable resources?

Applying What You Have Learned

1. Describe how to calculate the amount of money spent per person per year for a resource.
2. Each cubic kilometer of seawater contains $150,000 worth of gold. If gold costs $14 per gram, how many grams of gold are there in 1 km³ of seawater?
3. If the supply of resources used in making chemical fertilizers is ever exhausted, what else could be used instead?
4. List the nonmetallic resources used in building your school.

Challenge

There are two main sources of the essential elements needed for plant growth: (1) chemical fertilizers that have been mined from the earth, and (2) organic fertilizers, such as decayed plant matter. Chemical fertilizers are required to supply a grade number, such as 10-20-10. The numbers show the percentages of nitrogen, phosphorus, and potassium in that order. The chart shows the average amount of these elements found in an organic fertilizer.

	Chemical Fertilizer	Decayed Plant Matter
Average Percent Nitrogen	10	2.5
Average Percent Phosphorus	20	0.75
Average Percent Potassium	10	1.5

1. How many kilograms of nitrogen are contained in a 100 kg bag of 10-20-10 chemical fertilizer?
2. How many kilograms of decayed plant matter would be needed to supply the same amount of nitrogen to an organic fertilizer as is found in a bag of 10-20-10?
3. Compare the advantages and disadvantages of using chemical and organic fertilizers.

Research and Investigation

1. Find out how table salt and other salts are obtained from seawater or lake water. Identify the places where this is done in the United States. If you can, find out which companies obtain table salt this way.
2. Prepare a written report on the uses of fish meal and the future uses of fish-protein concentrate.
3. Prepare an oral report on the mining of copper and how copper is removed from its ore minerals.
4. Find out about ongoing research projects that attempting to convert sea water to drinking water. What are the biggest obstacles to this research?

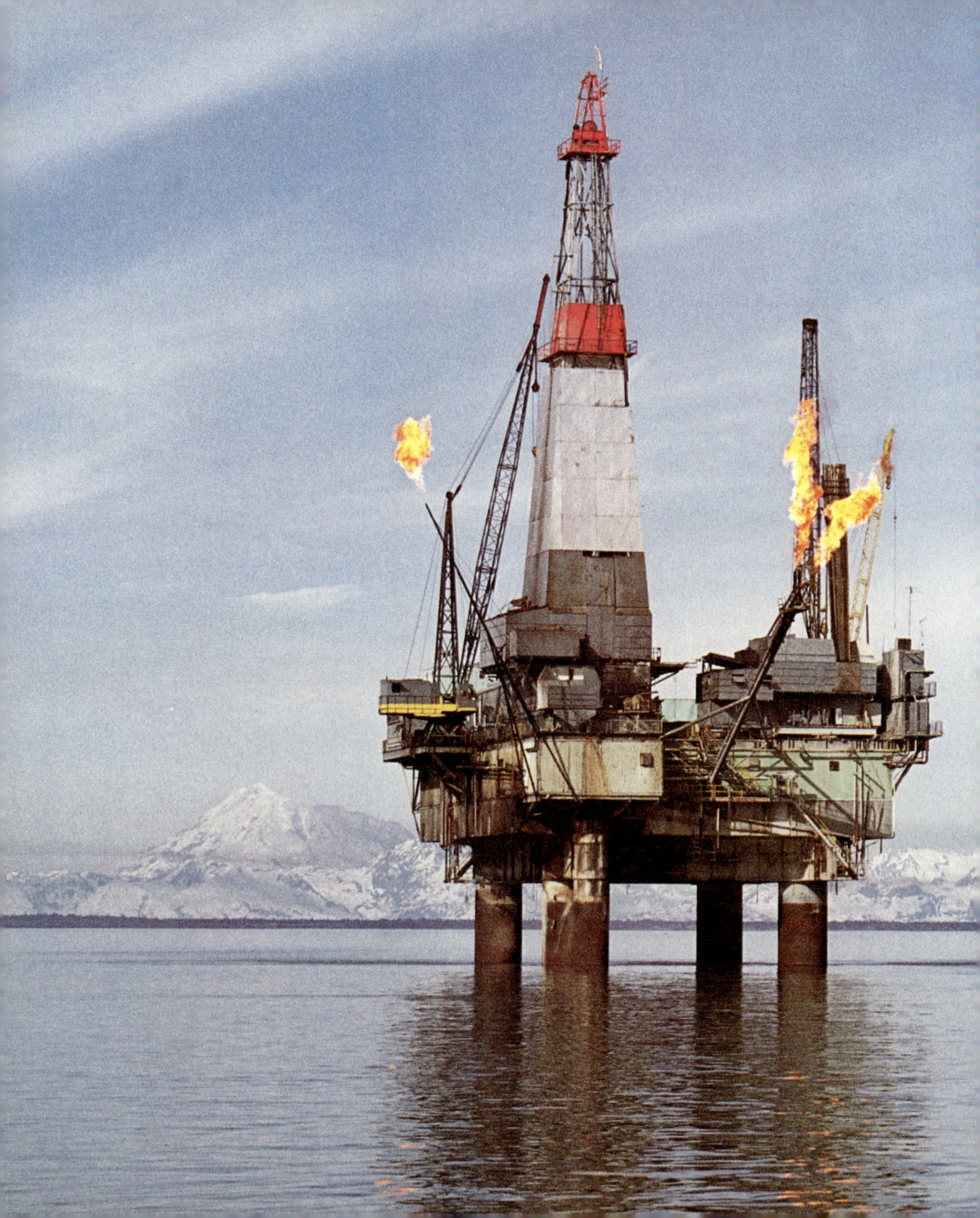

Chapter 23
Nonrenewable Energy Resources

Lesson Titles
23.1 Petroleum
23.2 Coal
23.3 Nuclear Fuel

Nothing can move or happen without energy. A bicycle will not move without energy. No light can be turned on without energy. No car can move, no plane can fly, no bell can ring, no breeze can blow without energy.

Where do moving things get their energy? You know that you need food. You know that an electric fan must be plugged into an electrical outlet. You know that cars need gasoline. You, fans, and cars need a source of energy. Food is your energy source. Gasoline is the energy source for a car. Electricity is the energy source for fans, lights, and toasters.

People have become very dependent on specific sources of energy. The major sources of energy used today are fossil fuels—petroleum and coal. However, in recent decades there has been an increase in the use of nuclear energy. In this chapter, you will learn where each of these sources of energy comes from and how they are used. You will also learn how long the supply of these nonrenewable energy resources is expected to last.

Figure 23.1 *opposite:* Offshore-drilling platforms have been built to provide access to petroleum deposits beneath the ocean floor.

23.1 Petroleum

You will find out
- what petroleum is;
- what the source of petroleum is;
- how petroleum is used;
- how much petroleum the United States has.

Gasoline is but one of many products made from a thick, smelly black liquid. This black liquid is called **petroleum** [puh-TROH-lee-uhm]. *Petroleum* literally means "oil that comes from rocks." For years people called petroleum rock oil. In fact, the first oil well was drilled by the Pennsylvania Rock Oil Company in 1859.

Petroleum is mostly **hydrocarbons** [HY-droh-kahr-buhnz]. Hydrocarbons are made of just two elements, hydrogen and carbon. Both hydrogen and carbon can burn and give off energy. They are the energy sources in petroleum. The hydrogen and carbon combine in hundreds of different ways, making many different hydrocarbons. Petroleum is a mixture of dozens of these different hydrocarbons.

Petroleum is believed to have formed over a period of millions of years. It formed from microscopic plants and animals that had been buried. Over long periods of time they decomposed. Petroleum is called a **fossil fuel**, since it formed from these plants and animals of such a long time ago.

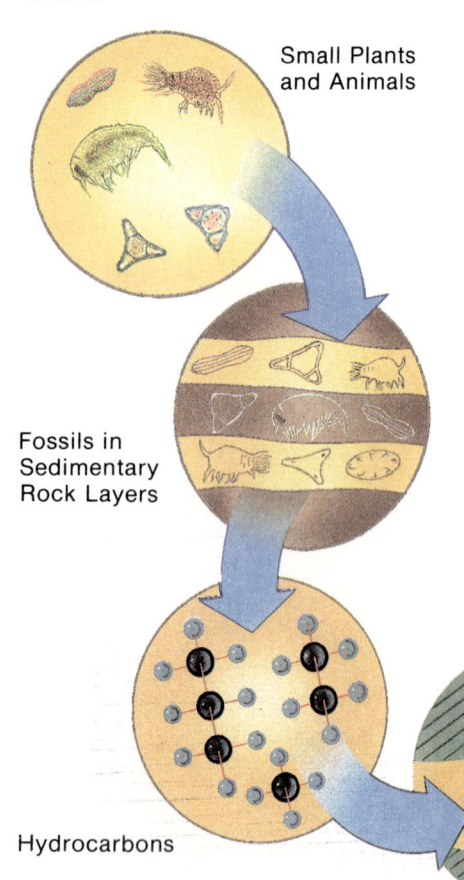

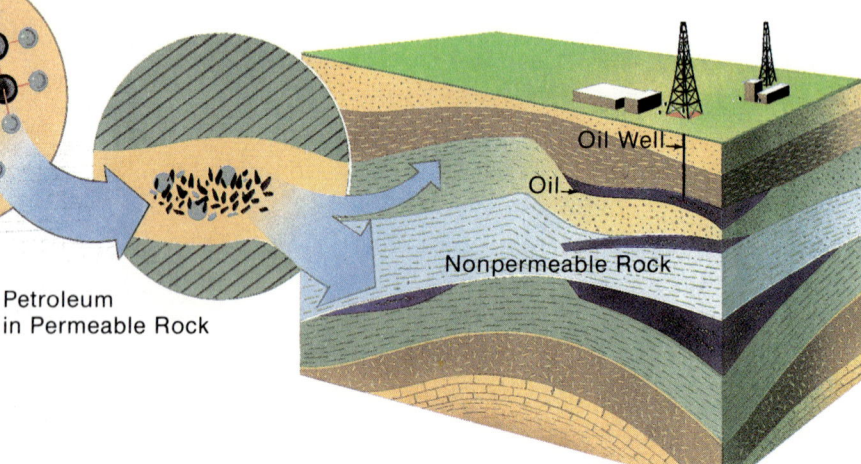

Figure 23.2 How fossil fuels are formed

- Small Plants and Animals
- Fossils in Sedimentary Rock Layers
- Hydrocarbons
- Petroleum in Permeable Rock
- Oil Well
- Oil
- Nonpermeable Rock

After the petroleum formed, it was forced through porous rock. It moved through the rock until it reached a rock type or rock structure it could not pass through. Here, in the rocks, it collected and formed a large oil pool called an **oil field**.

Petroleum is pumped from wells drilled into oil fields. The petroleum pumped from the wells is called **crude oil**. Oil can be dark or light, depending on the oil field. It also may contain various amounts of sulfur and other substances.

Many oil wells also produce petroleum gas in addition to liquid petroleum. Petroleum gas is a form of naturally occurring hydrocarbons of petroleum. It burns cleanly and can be transported easily by pipelines. Natural gas is widely used as a fuel for heating.

Figure 23.3 Shale may be a source of energy in the future.

Activity

How Much Oil Will a Pump Remove?

Materials
graduated cylinder
plastic bottle with spray pump
50-cm length of clear plastic hose
clean pebbles
100 mL of any motor oil
cold water
hot water
liquid detergent

Procedure

1. Assemble a model oil well as shown in the diagram. Pour 100 mL of oil into the well.

2. Pump out as much oil as possible. Record the amount recovered.

3. Add 50 mL of cold water to the well and again pump out all you can. Record the additional oil recovered.

4. Repeat step 3, but this time use 50 mL of hot water.

5. Repeat step 3, but this time add 50 mL of hot water with 15 drops of detergent.

Questions

1. How much oil was recovered by pumping?

2. How much oil was recovered by adding cold water, hot water, and detergent to the well?

3. Do you think oil wells are able to pump all the oil from an oil field? What evidence do you have for your answer?

4. Can you increase the amount of oil recovered from an oil field by adding water or detergents?

23 / Nonrenewable Energy Resources

Crude oil itself has little use. It must be separated into the different groups of hydrocarbons which make up gasoline, kerosene, and other products. Crude oil is separated into its many useful products at a **refinery** [ree-FYN-uhr-ee].

The first step in the refining process is to heat the crude oil. Crude oil vaporizes when heated. Since different hydrocarbons condense from the vapors at different temperatures, the hydrocarbons can be separated. Crude oil vapors are piped into a tall, slim tower like the one shown in Figure 23.5. As the vapors rise through the tower, different hydrocarbons condense at different levels and are drawn off. Heavy fuel oils collect in pans low in the tower. Above this, pans collect the kerosene, which has condensed. Still higher, gasoline condenses into pans. Pipes drain the pans. Each group of hydrocarbons, such as gasoline, is now processed further or sold as it is.

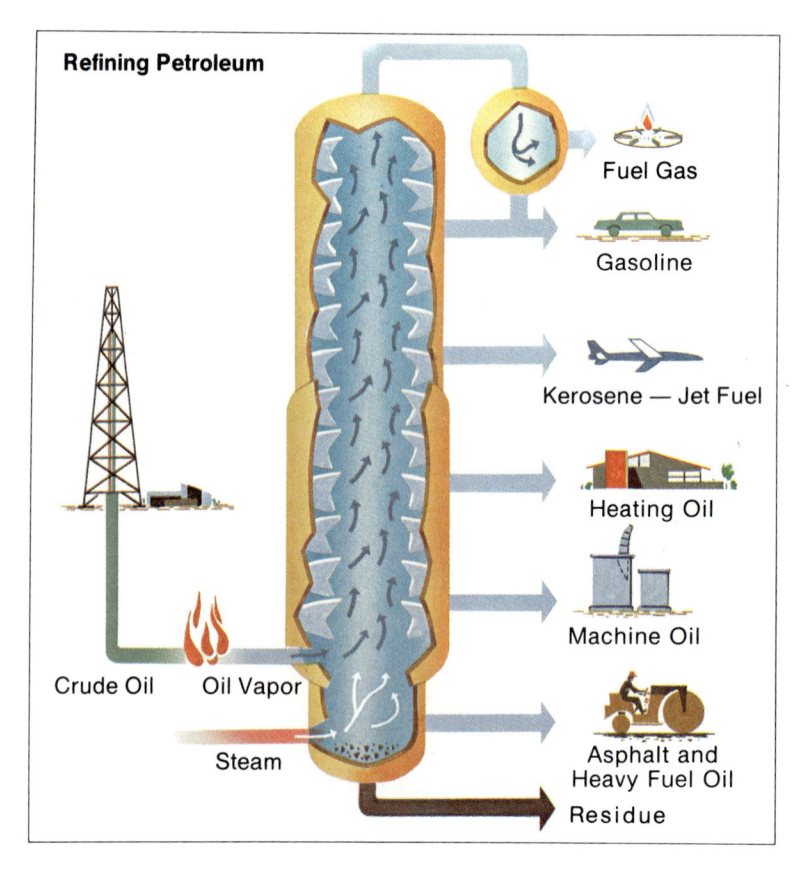

Figure 23.4 *above:* An oil refinery like this one turns crude oil into many useful hydrocarbons.

Figure 23.5 *right:* Through special heating and condensation processes, crude oil is separated into its different parts.

CHAPTER REVIEW

Main Ideas

- Petroleum is oil from oil-bearing rock. It is made up of a mixture of different hydrocarbons.
- Petroleum was formed over millions of years from buried plants and animals. It is thus called a fossil fuel.
- Petroleum is used as an energy source for transportation, heating, and generating electricity.
- Petroleum is a nonrenewable energy source. The United States supply may be used up between the years 2000 and 2050.
- Coal is a nonrenewable energy resource. It is a fossil fuel made up in varying amounts of the carbon, hydrocarbons, sulfur, and clay remains of former living things. The United States supply of coal may be used up within 2050 to 2200 years.
- The major kinds of coal are lignite, bituminous, and anthracite.
- When uranium 235 undergoes fission, it produces less massive atoms and more neutrons and it releases energy. The neutrons can cause other U 235 atoms to fission in a continuing reaction called a chain reaction.
- A nuclear reactor is a container in which a controlled chain reaction releases energy. This energy can be used to produce electricity.

Using Vocabulary

Make up a matching-column quiz. On a separate piece of paper, list the words below in one column and describe each word in another. Exchange quizzes with a classmate.

petroleum	coal	acid rain	nuclear reactor
hydrocarbon	peat	radioactive	containment building
fossil fuel	lignite	fission	control rod
oil field	bituminous coal	isotope	fusion
crude oil	anthracite	neutron	
refinery	fly ash	chain reaction	

23 / Nonrenewable Energy

Remembering Facts

On your paper, write the word or words that best complete each sentence.

1. Petroleum and coal are called _____ _____ , since they were formed from plants and animals that had died a long time ago.
2. A _____ _____ can keep going on and on by itself, releasing energy in the process.
3. The splitting of atoms with the release of energy is called _____ .
4. The youngest form of coal is _____ .
5. A _____ reaction requires very high temperatures.
6. The chain reaction within a nuclear reactor can be slowed down or stopped by the _____ _____ .
7. Rocks that give off invisible radiation are said to be _____ .
8. The black oil that comes from rocks is _____ .
9. The fine particles released into the air during the burning of ground coal is called _____ .
10. Petroleum pumped from wells that have been drilled in oil fields is called _____ _____ .
11. Another name for hard coal is _____ .
12. A _____ separates crude oil into groups of hydrocarbons that make up gasoline, kerosene, and other products.
13. Dead plants collect in a swamp and form thick layers of a brown material called _____ .
14. Petroleum that has collected in porous rock and can move no further has formed a(an) _____ _____ .
15. A thick steel vessel in which energy is released by the fission of uranium 235 is called a _____ _____ .
16. Sulfur dioxide combines with water in the atmosphere to form _____ _____ .

Understanding Ideas

On your paper, answer each question in complete sentences.

1. Compare the advantages and disadvantages of fueling an electric power plant using petroleum, coal, and uranium.
2. Why is most of the concern about acid rain focused in New England and eastern Canada?
3. Why does the burning of 1 km of coal release twice as much energy as the burning of 1 km of wood?

Applying What You Have Learned

1. What are the problems with petroleum, coal, and nuclear fuel supplies? How can these problems be resolved?
2. Compare the U.S. supplies of petroleum, coal, and uranium. Which of these will probably be used up first? Which will be last? What are the probable consequences?

Challenge

Transporting coal is expensive. A coal-slurry pipeline is one way to reduce the cost of transporting coal. The coal is prepared at a coal-slurry plant for shipment through the pipeline. First it is ground into sugar-sized grains, and then it is mixed with an equal amount of water. This slurry is pumped through a pipeline buried three or more feet underground. The pipeline is very economical. However, the disadvantage of such a pipeline is that large amounts of water are needed to make the coal-slurry mixture. More than 70 percent of U.S. coal reserve is found in the western states where fresh water is in short supply.

1. Look closely at the map on the right. Why is coal being transported in the first place?
2. What problems might arise if the pipeline were located aboveground?
3. What problems are caused by the movement of coal by trains and trucks?
4. What possible problems and benefits could the pipelines bring to producer and consumer states?

Research and Investigation

1. Some people feel that synthetic petroleum from coal will replace the dwindling petroleum supply. Research and prepare a report on how coal can be made into gas and liquid fuels. Is this being done now? What are the problems?
2. Investigate how the nuclear fuel supply can be increased. Prepare a report on how a breeder reactor works. Investigate how spent fuel rods can be recycled. Where are these things being done today?
3. A type of nuclear reactor called a breeder reactor is able to make more nuclear fuel than it uses. Find out why some people are skeptical of the use of breeder reactors.

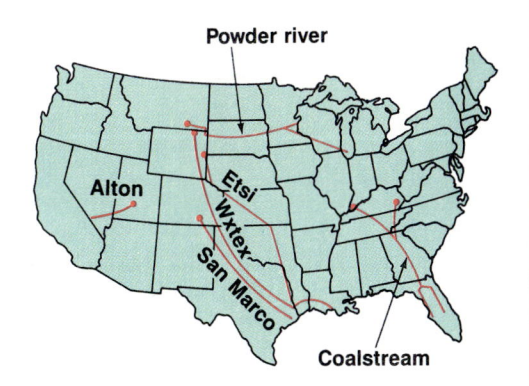

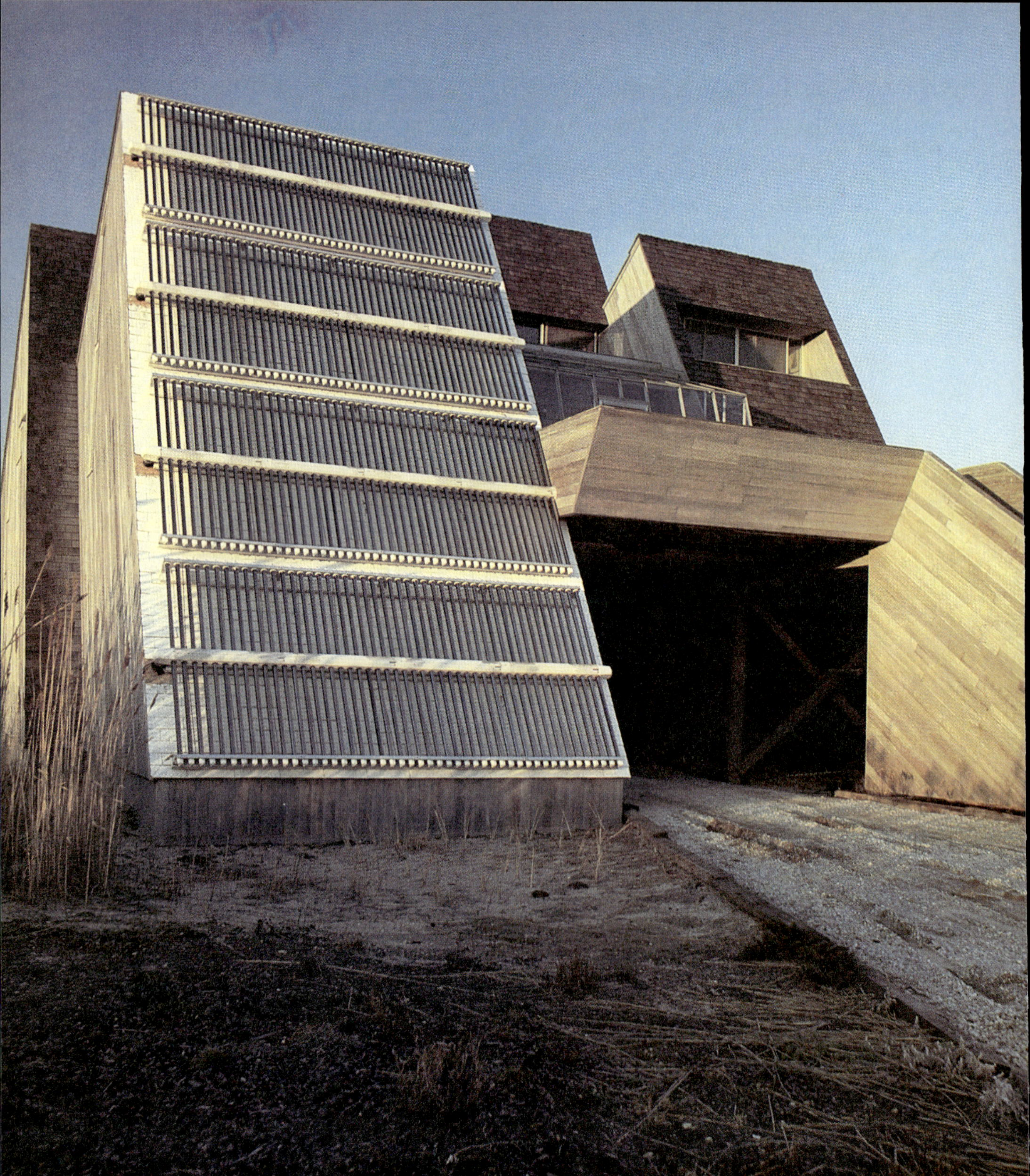

Chapter 24
Renewable Energy Resources

Lesson Titles
24.1 Solar Energy
24.2 Water, Wind, and Plants
24.3 Geothermal Energy

Most people around the world are aware that we are facing an energy crisis. Think of all the energy that is needed to run cars and trucks, heat and cool homes, and light our buildings at night. As you learned in Chapter 23, most of this energy comes from burning oil, coal, and natural gas. The problem is that the supply of these fossil fuels is limited. Therefore, people are developing ways to use alternative sources of energy.

One important energy source that people have turned to is the sun. They are constantly experimenting to find better ways to capture and store the sun's energy. They have used the sun's energy to warm greenhouses, heat water, and cook food. Scientists have even developed batteries that convert sunlight to electrical energy.

A more familiar use of the sun's energy is evident in the construction industry. Have you ever seen a house like the one in the picture? It was carefully designed to take full advantage of the sun's energy. Notice the solar panels, the slope of the roof, and the placement of windows. A great deal of scientific thought goes into the planning of these homes.

In this chapter you will learn more about the use of the sun's energy. You will also learn about other alternative sources of energy.

Figure 24.1 *opposite:* Whether in space or on Earth, people need a dependable source of energy.

24.1 Solar Energy

You will find out
- what a renewable energy source is;
- how a solar collector provides hot water;
- how to heat a house with solar energy;
- how heat from solar energy can be used to generate electricity;
- what a solar cell is;
- why more solar energy isn't used to generate electricity today.

As you pass through the 1990's and into the next century, you will be passing from one energy age to a new one. The old age was based on cheap and once-plentiful fossil fuels. The new age will be based on renewable energy sources. Renewable energy sources do not run out because they are constantly replaced.

You know how the sun warms you. Sunlight is an energy source called **solar energy.** Since the sun continues to send more solar energy each day, solar energy is called renewable. All you need to use solar energy is some way to collect it and put it to use.

Figure 24.2 *above:* The sun is the most abundant renewable energy source.

Figure 24.3 *right:* Sunlight provides energy for living things even under the ocean's surface.

24 / Renewable Energy Resources

One way to collect solar energy is to use a **solar collector.** One type of solar collector is like a small greenhouse. It is a box with a glass or plastic top. Inside the box are tubes that are painted black. Black is used because it absorbs more sunlight than colors do. Water moving through the tubes in the solar collector is heated by sunlight. In some solar collectors a pump moves the water from a storage tank, through the collector tubes, and back to the tank. The tank provides hot water for bathing, washing, or even heating a swimming pool.

New homes and apartment buildings are now designed and located to use solar water heaters. Roof lines are planned to provide the best angle for the solar collectors. The buildings can also be located so they face the direction that gets the most sunlight. Building sites are also carefully checked to be sure there are no high natural obstructions to cast shadows on the collectors.

Do You Know?
Of all the energy used in the United States in the early 1980's, 25 percent was consumed in warming or cooling buildings. The use of passive solar energy could reduce this to 10 percent.

Figure 24.4 *above:* A solar collector absorbs sunlight, which produces heated water.

Figure 24.5 *left:* Solar collectors are being used in more and more places to provide heat and hot water for people.

Solar energy can also be used to heat a house. A house can be built so the house itself collects solar energy. Sunlight enters the house through south-facing windows and is absorbed by materials in the house. The warmed materials then heat the living space during the day and night.

When a house is built to use solar energy and does not use electric pumps, fans, or heaters of any type, the house is called a **passive solar** house. You may think that a passive solar house would just have large windows to let sunlight in. This kind of design will not work because the house will become cold after sunset. A passive solar house has something to collect and store energy during the day. Sunlight warms some dense material such as concrete, brick, or stone. This dense material, or **storage mass,** then gives off the stored energy during the day and night. It warms people by giving off radiant energy. It also warms the nearby air. This sets up convection currents that can carry the warm air to the rest of the house.

Figure 24.6 During the daytime, sunlight coming through the windows heats the air inside and is absorbed by the storage mass. At night the storage mass radiates the stored energy into the house.

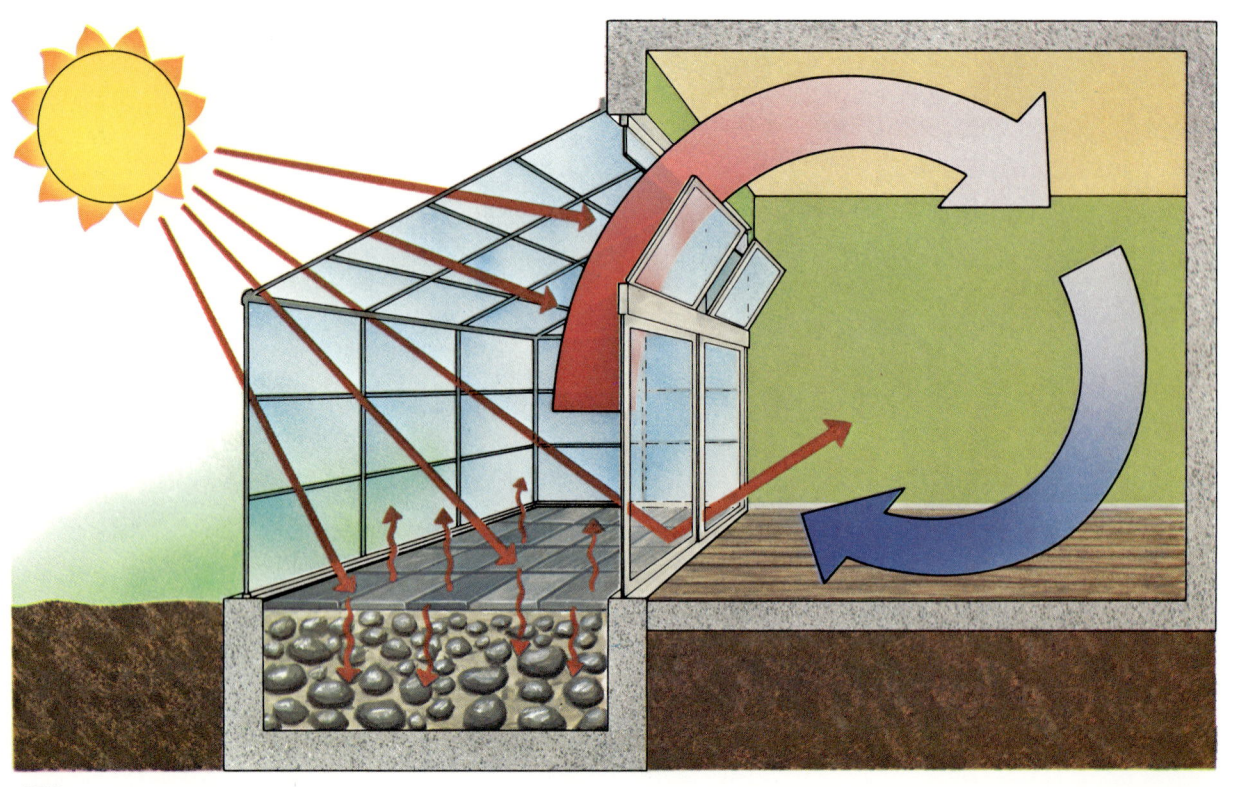

478

24 / Renewable Energy Resources

Activity

What Does a Storage Mass Do?

Materials

8 tin cans painted black
water
2 large cardboard boxes
2 thermometers
plastic wrap
tape
string
rubber bands

Procedure

1. Use two cardboard boxes to build two solar greenhouses like the one shown.

2. Fill each tin can with water and cover with plastic wrap and a rubber band.

3. Place all the cans in the back of one of the greenhouses as shown.

4. Hang a thermometer inside each greenhouse. Cover each greenhouse with plastic wrap and seal it tightly with tape.

5. Place both greenhouses side by side in sunlight so that the sunlight shines into each.

6. Make a record sheet as shown. Record the temperature every five minutes in each greenhouse for a half hour.

7. Now place the two greenhouses in the shade. Record the temperature every five minutes for another half hour.

8. Make a graph of the temperature changes in the two greenhouses.

Questions

1. What did you see happen to the temperature in the two greenhouses?

2. What was the purpose of the water-filled cans? How do your observations show this?

3. Which of the greenhouses is more comparable to a passive solar house?

Time in Minutes	Greenhouse with Storage Mass	Greenhouse
5	Sun ____ °C	Sun ____ °C
10	____	____
15	____	____
20	____	____
	Shade ____	Shade ____

24 / Renewable Energy Resources

Do You Know?
Solar power towers are expected to start replacing oil- and gas-fired electric power plants by 1990.

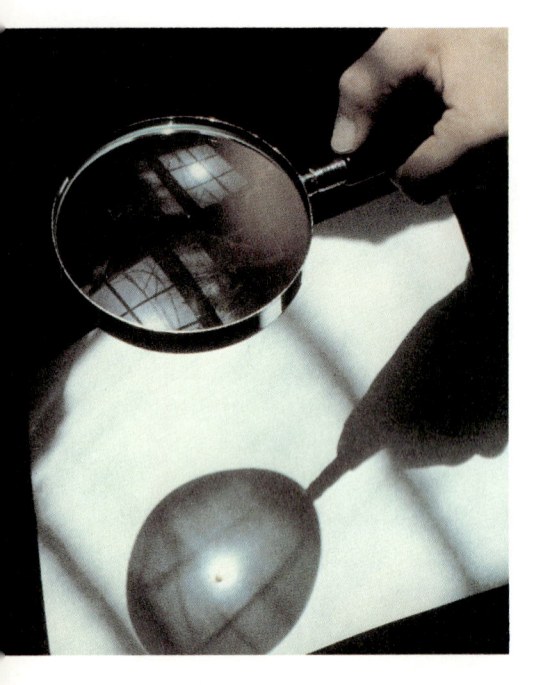

Figure 24.7 *above:* Heat coming from sunlight can be intensified by focusing the beams through a lens.

Figure 24.8 *right:* These mirrors act like hundreds of magnifying lenses and concentrate sunlight on the power tower.

Do You Know?
The first major use of solar cells was to provide energy for the *Vanguard* satellite in 1958.

Most electricity in the United States is generated by using steam. Fossil fuels or uranium is used to make the steam in a power plant. Why isn't solar energy used instead of fossil fuels or uranium in a power plant? Consider trying to boil a pan of water by placing it in sunlight. The water does not boil because not enough solar energy arrives at the pan to boil the water. The sunlight must be concentrated, or brought together, before it will boil water. You can concentrate sunlight, for example, by using a magnifying glass. It would take an enormous magnifying glass, however, to provide the energy needed by a power plant to make steam.

Mirrors, however, can be used to concentrate enough sunlight to produce steam for a power plant. Figure 24.8 shows one way this has been done. Mirrors have been designed that follow the sun and reflect sunlight to the top of a tall structure called a **power tower.** Sunlight from 2.5 square kilometers can thus be concentrated on an area of several square meters. Tubes in the top of this power tower are heated to over 500°C by the concentrated sunlight. Steam is produced from the heating in the power tower. This steam is used to turn a turbine to generate electricity just like in other power plants.

Figure 24.9 *left:* Solar cells.

Figure 24.10 *below:* Solar cells provide electricity in unusual situations.

Sunlight can also be converted directly into electricity in **solar cells.** A solar cell is made of silicon and tiny amounts of arsenic and boron and produces an electric current when sunlight falls on it. When rays of sunlight strike the top part of a solar cell, electrons are knocked loose. These electrons move to the bottom part. The top part now has an excess of positive charges, while the bottom layer is loaded with negative charges. The movement of charged particles produces an electric current.

You may wonder why solar energy isn't used more to generate electricity. The problem is the cost. Solar energy is free, but the devices necessary to convert it to your use are very expensive. A power tower, with its mirrors, for example, costs about one third more than a comparable nuclear power plant. You could use solar cells to produce all of your electric power. However, the cost of the solar cells would make electricity several times more expensive than it is today. Many people think the cost of solar cells will be less in the future.

Study Questions for 24.1

1. What are the characteristics of a renewable energy source?
2. Describe how a solar collector can be used to heat water.
3. Describe how a house can be heated with solar energy.
4. How does a power tower generate electricity?
5. Describe a solar cell.
6. Why isn't solar energy used more to generate electricity?

24.2 Water, Wind, and Plants

You will find out
- how energy is obtained from moving water;
- how the wind provides energy;
- why plants can be considered a source of energy.

Have you ever tried to swim or paddle a canoe in a fast-moving stream? Did you ever try to walk against a strong wind? Have you ever had to move back from a roaring campfire? Moving water, wind, and wood all contain energy. How are they used as energy sources?

Moving water provides energy by turning a waterwheel or turbine. Waterwheels have been used for many years to move a millstone to grind grains into flour and to run machines in factories. There was a problem, however. The waterwheels had to be located where there were waterfalls, and some streams where the waterfalls were located ran dry during part of the year. The building of dams and the development of electricity solved this problem.

Figure 24.11 *above:* The old-fashioned waterwheel is a reminder of a time when energy demands were small.

Figure 24.12 *right:* Dams control the flow of river water so that electric power can be generated on a regular basis.

Today moving water is used mostly to generate electricity. Water stored behind huge dams falls through large pipes in the dam to a powerhouse. Here the falling water turns turbines, which turn generators that make electric energy. Since electric energy moves through wires, energy can now be sent to homes and factories located elsewhere.

Do You Know?
The first waterwheel that generated electricity in the United States was used to provide electricity for a mine near Ouray, Colorado, in 1890. The equipment was built by George Westinghouse.

Wind power has been used for centuries to move ships, grind grain into flour, and pump water for crops and cattle. Wind was turning generators and producing electricity as early as 1910. The wind provides energy by moving blades of a wind machine or windmill. The moving blades turn a shaft that can run a water pump or do other work.

The wind seems stronger in some places than in others. Big wind machines for making electricity are usually located on mountains and near the seashore, which seem to have stronger and steadier winds.

The parts of plants or things made from plants can be used for energy. This source of energy is called **biomass** [BY-oh-mas]. Biomass includes wood, leaves, stems, and other plant parts as well as wood chips, trash, and even animal wastes.

Biomass can be burned for energy. It can be burned to heat houses, cook with, make hot water, and even generate steam. It can be used for just about anything that oil or coal can. It just isn't so convenient, and it does not give off as much energy for the same amount of material.

In addition to being burned directly, biomass can be converted into fuels. When biomass is rotted in a closed container without air, methane gas is made. This gas can be used for heating, cooking, or running engines.

Biomass that has sugar or starch in it can be changed to alcohol. When this kind of biomass is mixed with yeast and water, the yeast makes alcohol from the sugar. This alcohol can be separated and used as a fuel. When mixed with gasoline, the fuel is called gasohol. People use too much energy today to depend just on biomass. However, biomass is an important energy source that can be used to supplement other energy sources.

Figure 24.13 Wind is an old source of energy that is being used in new ways.

Do You Know?
Biomass provides about 2 percent of all United States energy needs.

Figure 24.14 Chemical changes occur in biomass-producing substances that can be burned for energy.

24 / Renewable Energy Resources

Where did moving water, wind, and plants get their energy? They got their energy from the sun as you will see. Using energy from moving water, wind, or wood is really an indirect use of solar energy. How is this so?

As part of the water cycle, the sun warms the ocean, evaporating water. The water vapor rises and moves in over the land and forms clouds. Then the water falls as precipitation from the clouds. The water that falls in higher elevations rushes downhill across the land and back to the sea, completing the cycle. Energy can be

Activity

Which Nut Has the Most Energy?

Materials
safety goggles
gloves
shelled peanut, walnut, and pecan
knife
wire coat hanger
test tube
aluminum foil
clay
straight pins
graduated cylinder
balance
thermometer
matches
water

Procedure

1. Unravel a wire coat hanger and form it as shown. The bottom should be 10 cm across. The loop at the top should hold a test tube.

2. Cover the wire with aluminum foil as shown. Carefully place the test tube in the top of the loop.

3. Trim a walnut and a pecan until they have the same mass as the peanut. CAUTION: Be careful when using the knife. Always point the blade away from you.

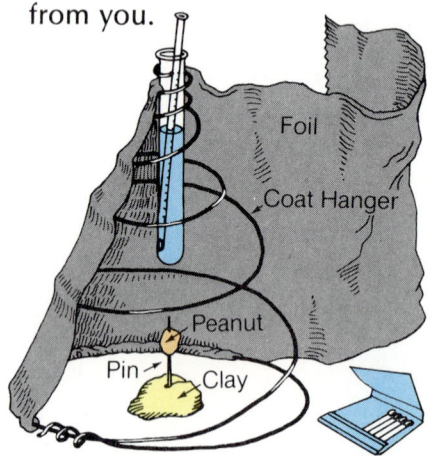

4. Push a pin into the peanut. Position the pin in a piece of clay as shown.

5. Pour 10 mL of water into the test tube. Measure and record the temperature of the water. Remove the thermometer.

6. CAUTION: Put on safety goggles. Light the peanut with a match. Place it under the test tube when it starts to burn.

7. When the peanut is through burning, measure and record the temperature of the water again. Pour out the water.

8. Pour 10 mL of new water into the test tube. Repeat steps 5–7 with the walnut and the pecan.

Questions

1. How much did the temperature increase from burning each nut?

2. What do your observations tell you about the energy in each nut?

484

24 / **Renewable Energy Resources**

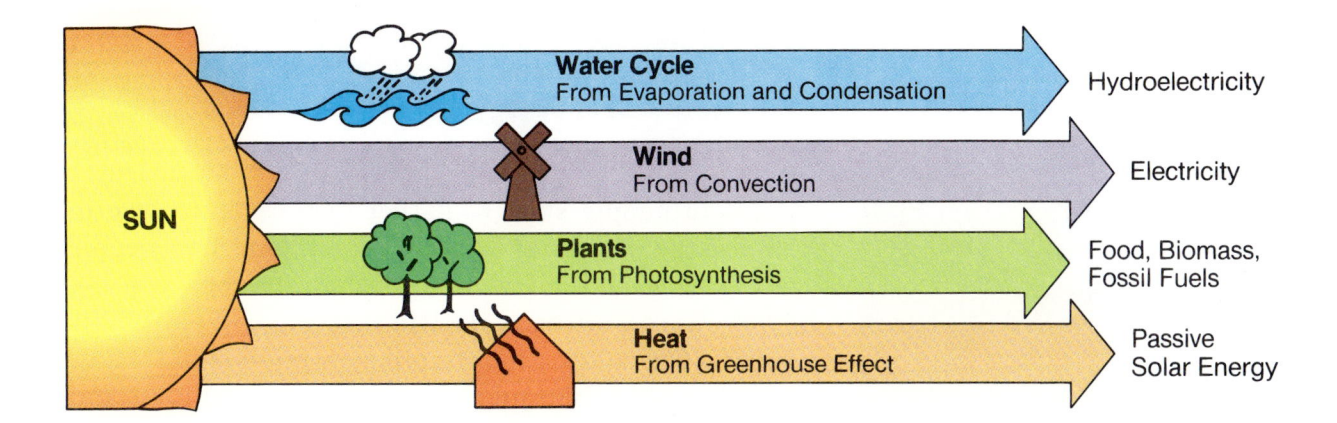

[Diagram: Sun energy flowing to: Water Cycle (From Evaporation and Condensation) → Hydroelectricity; Wind (From Convection) → Electricity; Plants (From Photosynthesis) → Food, Biomass, Fossil Fuels; Heat (From Greenhouse Effect) → Passive Solar Energy]

obtained from the moving water. Since the supply of moving water is continuously replaced, it is a renewable energy source. However, it is sunlight that is the original energy source that begins the water cycle. The energy in the moving water is indirect energy from sunlight.

The wind is another form of indirect solar energy. The wind blows because of energy the earth receives from the sun. Air is warmed because of energy from sunlight. The warm air rises and starts a convection current. This movement of the air produces wind. Energy can be obtained from the wind. Moving air, like moving water, is indirect energy from sunlight.

Now think about this a minute. All of your food, your clothes, and even the fossil fuels have been made possible by the sun. They can all be traced back to plants, and green plants use light from the sun. Green plants use sunlight to make the stems, leaves, roots, wood, and fruit of the plant. The sun's energy is stored in the plant. It is given off when the plant is burned. A plant, then, can be thought of as a living solar collector that stores the sun's energy. Using plants is another indirect use of solar energy.

Figure 24.15 *above:* In one way or another the sun supplies most of the energy used on Earth.

Figure 24.16 *below:* An orange is really a package of the sun's energy that has been stored as food by the tree.

Study Questions for 24.2

1. How is the energy from moving water used to generate electricity?
2. How does the wind provide energy?
3. Describe how energy from moving water, wind, and plants is indirectly solar energy.

24 / Renewable Energy Resources

24.3 Geothermal Energy

You will find out
- what geothermal energy is;
- how geothermal energy can be used.

Groups of people start to gather at a certain place in Yellowstone National Park in Wyoming. The people keep looking at their watches. What are they waiting for? They are waiting to see Old Faithful. Old Faithful is a **geyser** [GY-zuhr], a fountainlike eruption of hot water and steam. Old Faithful erupts for several minutes and is then still. Since the geyser erupts regularly about every hour, it was named Old Faithful.

Geysers and **hot springs** are found near old volcanoes. Surface water moves down through rocks to a place where the rocks are very hot. Convection then pushes the now hot water back to the surface, forming hot springs. In some rock formations steam is generated beneath the water. As the steam pressure builds up, it

Figure 24.17 *above:* The energy that heats water into steam and produces Old Faithful comes from within the earth.

Figure 24.18 *right:* The water in hot springs is heated by rocks below the surface of the earth.

24 / Renewable Energy Resources

periodically is released by forcing the water and steam to erupt through a surface vent, forming a geyser. All of this takes place near the surface. The rocks that heat this water are fewer than several kilometers below the surface.

Hot rocks can heat water and produce steam. How much energy can you get from this kind of source? Scientists think that it may have 30 times more energy than the United States uses each year. As you will see, however, not all of this energy can be used. Since this energy is from the land or earth's crust, it is called **geothermal** [jee-oh-THUHR-mel] **energy.**

Do You Know?
The worldwide use of geothermal energy for generating electricity is expected to be 17 percent greater each year until the year 2000.

Figure 24.19 Forms of geothermal energy shown here are being developed as new energy sources for people.

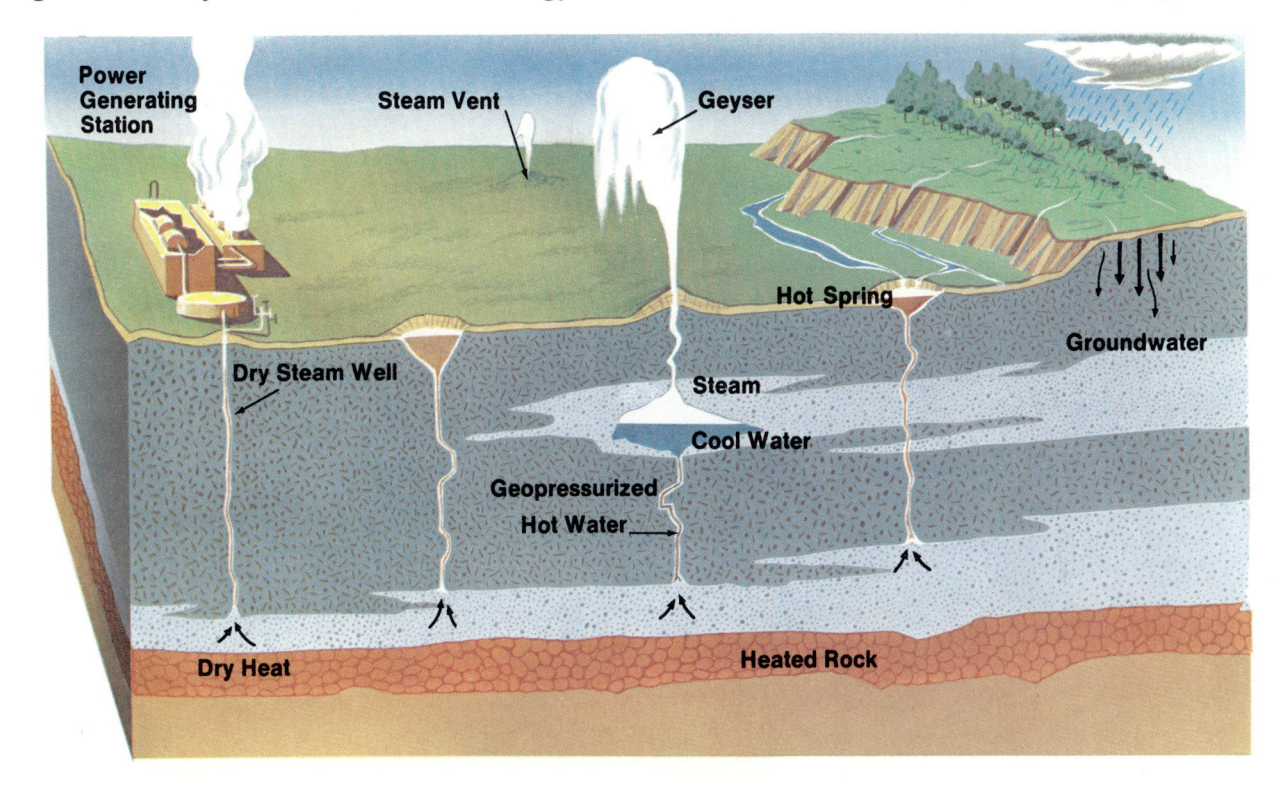

Each place where geothermal energy is found is different. There are differences in the rocks and in the size and temperature of the area. There are also differences in the amount of water present. These differences result in different forms of geothermal energy. Geothermal energy is generally found in one of four forms: (1) dry steam, (2) hot water, (3) geopressurized hot water, and (4) hot, dry rock.

24 / Renewable Energy Resources   487

Dry steam makes up only 0.5 percent of all geothermal energy in the United States. Steam is piped from wells to turbines. The turbines turn generators, producing electricity. Dry steam runs an electric power plant north of San Francisco, called The Geysers. More than half of San Francisco's electricity comes from this plant. Two more places are known to have dry steam. Both of these places are in national parks in California and Wyoming. Since they are located in parks, this steam cannot be used for power.

Figure 24.20 *right:* The Geysers dry-steam power plant

Figure 24.21 *below:* A geothermal hot water source in Iceland.

Hot water is heated by the hot, underground rocks. Many states have this geothermal resource. It is being used in California, Utah, New Mexico, Oregon, Idaho, and other states. Geothermal hot water, like geothermal dry steam, can be used to generate electricity. Geothermal hot water, however, requires a different type of power plant. The hot water is used to heat fluid with a low boiling point. Freon is often used, since it boils at about 30°C. The boiling Freon then turns a turbine which turns a generator, generating electricity.

Geothermal hot water can also be used any place heating is required. It is used for heating in Iceland, New Zealand, and Italy. It is also used in Klamath Falls, Oregon, and Boise, Idaho, to heat buildings.

Figure 24.22 *left:* Today's scientific research may lead to greater use of dry-rock geothermal energy in the future.

Figure 24.23 *below:* An electrically powered car

The two other forms of geothermal energy have yet to be developed. *Geopressurized hot water* occurs in deep reservoirs along the coast of Louisiana and Texas. This hot water is sealed off from the surface and is under pressure from the overlying rock. This water contains much dissolved natural gas. *Hot, dry rock* is the most common form of geothermal energy. There is much hot, dry rock in the western United States. Someday energy from hot, dry rock may be used by pumping water underground. After the water is heated underground, it can be pumped out and used as hot water.

Which of these renewable energy sources will you be likely to use in the future? The most likely answer is probably all of them. As fossil fuels are used up, other energy sources will be developed. It does not appear that any one of the new sources will be as abundant or as cheap as petroleum once was. It is likely that many different energy sources will be used instead. Costs, availability, and adaptability will largely determine which energy source is used. Maybe your future work will be in finding new energy sources and how to use them.

Study Questions for 24.3

1. What is geothermal energy? Describe four forms of it.
2. Describe two ways geothermal energy can be used to generate electricity.
3. Other than electric power, how is geothermal energy used?

Science and Technology

Dry-Rock Geothermal Energy

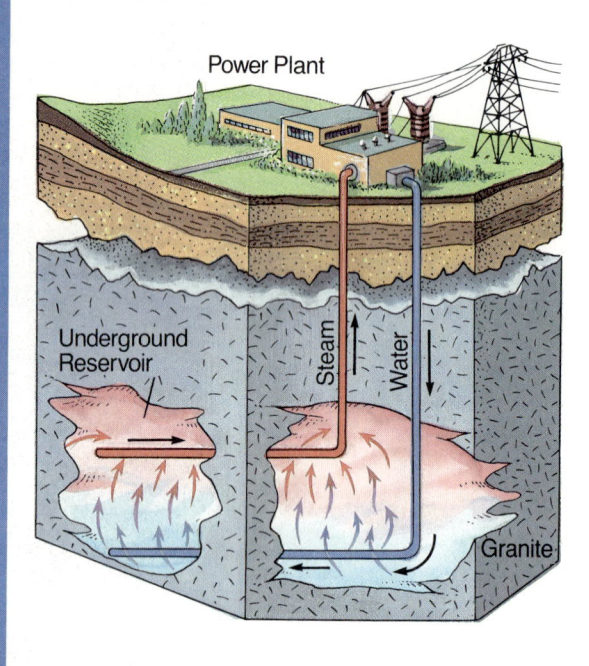

You learned in this chapter that hot, dry rocks underground may become an important source of geothermal energy in the future. At Fenton Hill, New Mexico, scientists have already begun to develop such a source. Fenton Hill is the location of the world's deepest and hottest dry-rock geothermal reservoir.

The underground rock at Fenton Hill is a granite. This granite is the core of a dormant volcano, that is, a volcano that has not erupted in modern times. Even though the volcano is not active, the rock underground is still very hot. Its temperature is about 250°C, much hotter than the temperature of boiling water.

The process of using this hot granite to heat water involves several steps. First a well was drilled to the granite. Then many gallons of cold water were pumped into the well under very high pressure. This caused the granite to crack. As the pressure continued, new cracks formed and old cracks became larger. These cracks are the reservoir in which the water is heated.

Once the reservoir was created, a second deep well was drilled to it. This well brings the water that has been heated in the reservoir back to the surface. There it can be used to heat other water or to do other work. Once the water is cooled, it is pumped back down to the granite for reheating.

The reservoir that was formed at Fenton Hill works as a heat exchanger. A heat exchanger is a system that contains a part that is hot and a part that is cold. The hot part gives up, or exchanges, its heat with the cold part. At Fenton Hill, the hot granite gives up its heat to the cold water to heat it.

Fenton Hill is important to geothermal energy development because the method used there can be used in any place where hot rocks can be found underground. For example, the eastern part of the United States has no natural geothermal areas. But the rocks deep underground are hot. Their heat could be used to heat water in the same way as that of the granite at Fenton Hill.

CHAPTER REVIEW

Main Ideas

- Solar energy is considered a renewable energy source because the earth receives solar energy each day.
- One type of solar collector is like a small greenhouse in which tubes of water are heated by the sun.
- Passive solar homes use a storage mass to absorb sunlight and release stored energy throughout the day and night.
- Solar energy can be converted to electricity in a structure called a power tower and in devices called solar cells.
- Energy from moving water is used to turn turbines, which turn generators, which produce electricity.
- Wind provides useful energy by turning the blades of a windmill or a wind machine.
- Growing plants capture and store the sun's energy in their biomass. Plant matter and things made from plants can serve as fuels.
- Geothermal energy results from the heating of rocks and water within the earth's crust.
- Dry steam is piped from underground wells to turbines that are used to generate electricity.
- Geothermal hot water is used in power plants and to heat buildings.
- Hot, dry rock is the most common form of geothermal energy.

Using Vocabulary

On a separate piece of paper, use the following words to make a crossword puzzle. Exchange puzzles with a classmate.

solar energy
solar collector
passive solar
storage mass
power tower

solar cell
biomass
geyser
hot spring
geothermal energy

24 / Renewable Energy Sources

Remembering Facts

Number your paper from 1 to 15. Match each term in column **A** with a phrase in column **B**.

A
1. solar energy
2. alcohol
3. hot, dry rocks
4. power tower
5. solar collector
6. geothermal energy
7. biomass
8. geyser
9. storage mass
10. hot spring
11. wind
12. dry steam
13. solar cell
14. renewable energy source
15. passive solar

B
a. hot water pushed to the earth's surface by convection
b. energy source that is constantly replaced
c. that which makes up 0.5 percent of geothermal energy
d. energy from within the earth's crust
e. the most common form of geothermal energy
f. something used to pump water and move ships
g. fountainlike eruption of hot water and steam
h. material that absorbs and stores solar energy
i. device that works like a small greenhouse
j. device that converts sunlight into electricity
k. describing a solar house without electric pumps or fans
l. source of energy stored in living things
m. sunlight
n. solar power plant with mirrors
o. what results from biomass that has sugar or starch in it

Understanding Ideas

On your paper, answer each question with complete sentences.
1. Describe at least two advantages and two disadvantages of using solar energy as a alternative energy source for a house.
2. What problems would you have to consider if you want to produce all of your own electricity from solar cells?
3. What problems might develop if everyone burned wood to heat his or her home?
4. What does the power tower have in common with other electric power plants?
5. What is the main thing that scientists could do to make the use of solar energy devices more widespread?
6. When are waterwheels not a reliable energy source?
7. Is energy of motion produced during the water cycle? Explain your answer.

Applying What You Have Learned

1. A passive solar house cannot have carpets or rugs on the floor. What is the reason for this?
2. Which renewable energy sources could be used where you live? Why do electric utilities continue to use petroleum, coal, and uranium rather than these sources to produce electricity?
3. What major disadvantage do wind power and water power have in common?

Challenge

Thousands of people in the United States cook and bake with solar energy. One type of solar cooker is simply a large cardboard box inside another cardboard box with insulation between them. Sunlight enters the smaller box through a tight-fitting glass lid. Sunlight directly enters the glass and is also reflected into the box by an adjustable reflector. The sunlight is absorbed and converted to infrared radiation by dark-colored cooking pots. The infrared radiation heats materials inside the cooker. The graph shows the temperatures of the outside air, the air inside the solar cooker, and a large container of water inside the cooker.

1. What is the source of energy for the solar cooker?
2. According to the graph, does solar energy cook the food directly? Explain your answer.
3. What are the advantages and disadvantages of using a solar cooker?

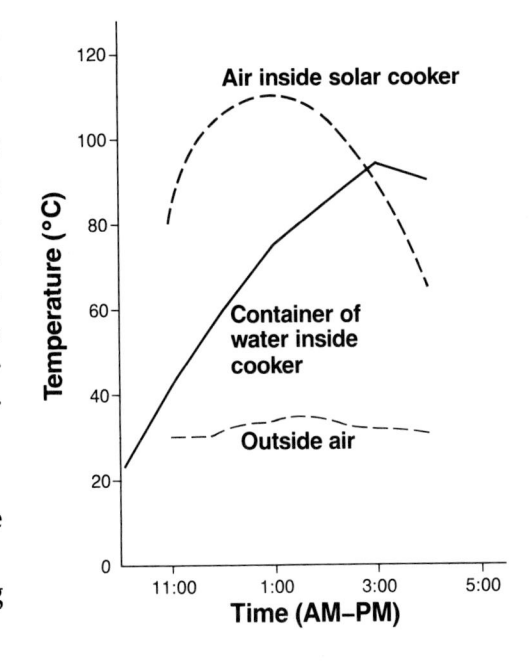

Research and Investigation

1. Talk to people who have passive solar homes or solar water heaters. Prepare a report on how people have to change their living habits when they use solar energy.
2. Interview someone from your local electric power company. Prepare a report on plans to use solar energy to generate electricity.
3. Discuss passive solar houses and solar water heaters with a city planner. Find out whether your city has building codes governing the placement of solar collectors. Report your findings to your class.
4. Prepare a written report on one of the world's successful geothermal energy plants.

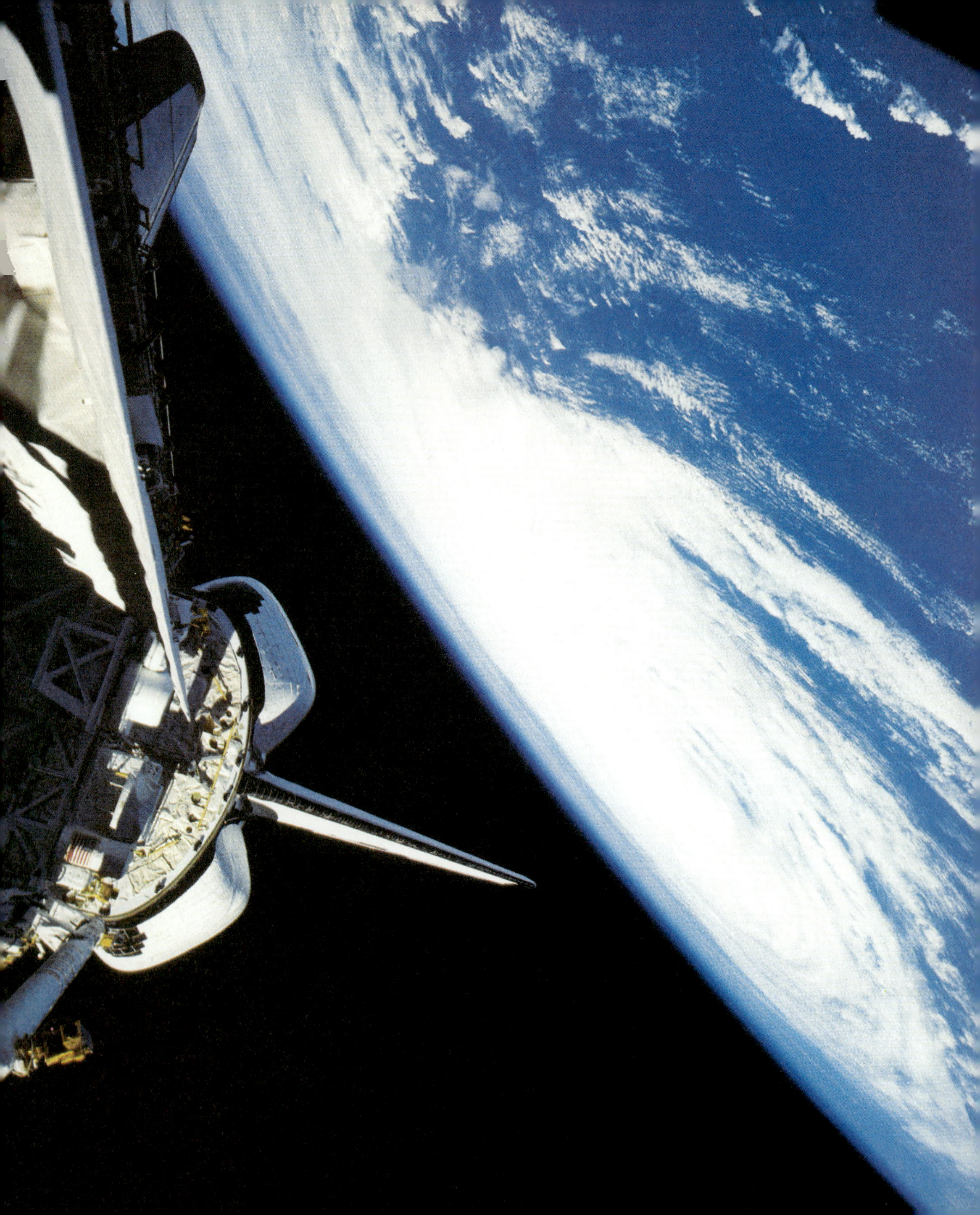

Chapter 25
Your Environment, Earth

Lesson Titles
25.1 Land
25.2 Air
25.3 Water
25.4 Making Choices

Astronauts looking back at Earth from their spacecraft often exclaim, "Oh, what a beautiful sight!" Among all the planets, Earth is the blue one because of its atmosphere and vast oceans. Earth, indeed, is a beautiful place to live.

Most people try to maintain the beauty of the earth. However, some people can do things to make the earth unsightly. Causing erosion of cropland and covering the land with buildings and pavement are ways people make the earth ugly. Failing to dispose of solid wastes properly and polluting the air, water, and land are some other ways.

In this chapter you will study how people and the things they do interact with the earth. You will learn that people have a choice. They can make the earth a more beautiful and healthy place to live if they want to do it.

Figure 25.1 *opposite:* With careful planning, people can improve the beauty of the earth.

25.1
Land

You will find out
- how land is used;
- what soil is and how it is made;
- what makes good growing soil;
- how farmers protect soil.

The surveyors in Figure 25.2 are working on a project that will make use of some land. What do you think they are helping to build? Perhaps a new housing development or a new university is planned. Maybe the project is a highway or a park. There are many possibilities, since land can be used in many different ways.

How do people use the land? Building is one way. People build homes, cities, factories, and schools. Land is also occupied by hospitals, offices, shopping centers, and athletic fields. Can you think of another use of land that you depend on every day?

Look at Figure 25.3. This is a farmer's field somewhere in Nebraska. There are no crops growing in the field now, but the farmer is getting ready to plant. The field will be planted, and the crop grown and harvested. Wheat is grown in fields like this. Wheat is used to make the bread you eat. In fact, most of the food you see on your table is grown on farms and then prepared for you to eat. Farms also produce dairy products and raise hogs, cattle, sheep, and poultry.

Figure 25.2 Land may be used in many ways, depending on the needs of the people who use it.

Figure 25.3 A field stands ready for planting.

Probably the most important use of the land all over the world is for crop production. You may eat the crop directly, as in the case of potatoes. You may also eat the crop indirectly if you eat meat. Some crops are used to feed the farm animals that eventually may become your food.

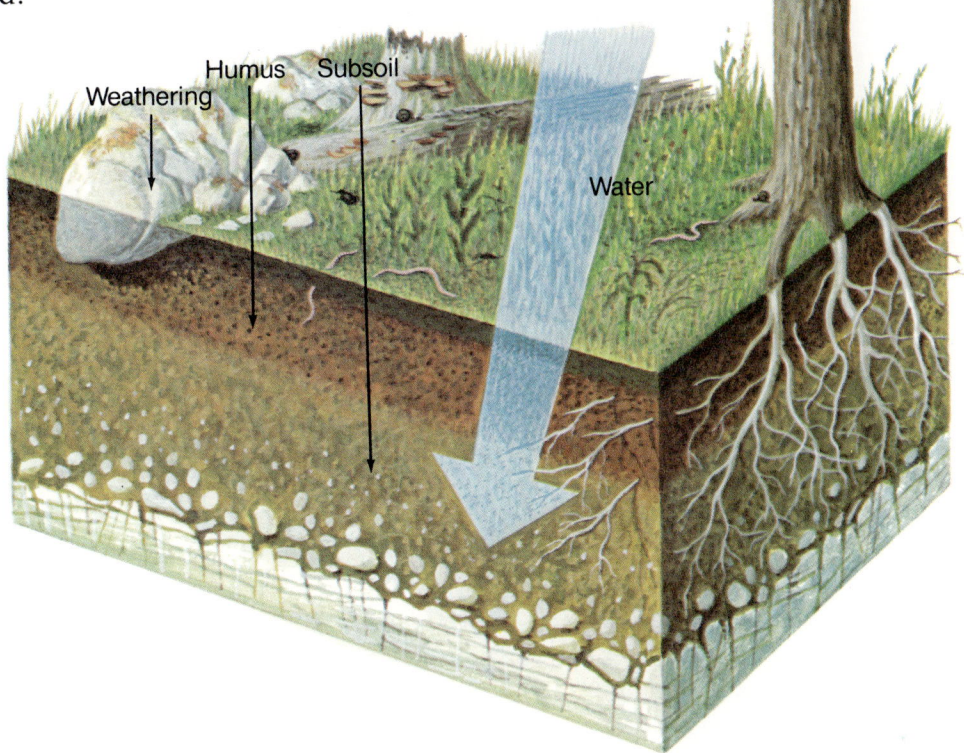

The farmer's crops grow in **soil**. Soil is the upper layer of the earth's crust in which plants grow. Three processes are important in making soils. Figure 25.4 shows how these processes work. First, weathering breaks up and changes the rock. Second, plants and animals growing and living in the weathered rock add **humus** [HYOO-muhs]. Humus is partially or completely decayed plant and animal matter. It adds the black color to soil. The third process is related to the movement of water through the soil. The water carries minerals and decayed plant material into the **subsoil**, the region beneath the layer containing humus. The soil you see on the next page, in Figure 25.5, was made that way.

Figure 25.4 Processes that produce soil from the earth's crust occur constantly.

Do You Know?
One person out of ten in the United States lives on a farm. The other nine out of ten people depend on the farmer for their food.

25 / Your Environment, Earth

Figure 25.5 Thickness and quality of the layers in a soil profile vary from one place to another.

Figure 25.6 *left:* This soil has the right texture for growing.

Figure 25.7 *right:* This soil has poor texture.

Look at Figure 25.5 carefully. Notice that the soil is layered. Geologists call this arrangement of soil layers a **soil profile.** The top layer containing humus is black. The middle layer is lighter in color. This layer includes minerals and decayed plant material that has been moved downward by water. The top of the lower layer often shows different larger-sized pieces of solid rock.

Soil profiles are different in different places. This is because the conditions that help produce soil can vary. The kind of rock from which soil is made is important. Climate, time, plant and animal influences, and the slope of the land all contribute to making different soils.

Good growing soils must be **fertile** [FUHR-tuhl]. A fertile soil is one that is capable of growing crops because of the materials it contains. It must contain nitrogen, potassium, and phosphorus. These three elements must be present in soluble form, which means dissolved in water, in order for plants to use them. To be a good growing soil, it must also have the right **texture** and **structure.** Soil texture is how the particles making up the soil are arranged. They must let water and air enter and leave the soil. The structure allows water to move through the soil layers.

498

25 / *Your Environment, Earth*

Why do farmers want to maintain good soil? Soil is a factory for farmers where they produce something that can be sold. Farmers can grow plants on the same land for hundreds or thousands of years if soil quality is maintained. In Egypt, some fields have grown a crop every year for more than 7,000 years.

Figure 25.8 Wheat is a major crop in the United States and must be grown in well-maintained soil.

Activity

Which Soil Holds More Water?

Materials
2 small containers the same size (Tuna-fish cans work fine.)
2 pieces of cloth
2 rubber bands
pencil
2 types of soil
water and container
graduated cylinder
2 pie tins

Procedure

1. Completely fill each container with a different type of soil.

2. Wet the cloths; then squeeze them to release excess water. Use a rubber band to secure a cloth over the top of each container.

3. Pour water into a graduated clinder and write down the volume. Add the water to container 1 until it is filled. Determine how much water you used.

4. Follow the same procedure for container 2.

5. Arrange each container upside down in a separate pie tin. Wedge a pencil under one edge of the can. Measure the water that drains into each tin.

Questions

1. How much water did you add to each can?

2. Calculate how much water remained in each can of soil by subtracting the amount of water that drained out of the can from the total amount of water that was added to it.

25 / Your Environment, Earth   499

Figure 25.9 *right:* Severe erosion from flooding

Figure 25.10 *below:* Overgrazing by animals removes plant cover. Soil may then be easily eroded.

What factors must farmers think about when planning how to maintain good soil quality? Erosion is the major threat to food soil. Figure 25.9 shows how water eroded a field. Wind also removes the soil. At present the United States is losing about four billion tons of soil annually by erosion. About 25 percent of the loss is caused by wind. The other losses are by water and by movements of the soil due to gravity. What is even more important about the loss of this soil is that three billion tons of it are lost from cropland.

Land that has a natural cover of trees or grass usually does not erode. All the roots of the plants help hold the soil together. When the forests are removed or when the land is overgrazed or left bare between crops, this natural protection does not exist. Farmers must carefully plan how they use the land. Animals are moved about to avoid overgrazing. Cover crops or new crops are planted to avoid leaving the land bare. Forest land is selectively harvested rather than cleared. Strip planting or contour planting is also used to prevent water erosion. If the rows went up and down the slopes, rain would create small streams and carry away the soil.

Irrigation can also cause a loss of soil quality. The water can change the soil texture and structure, making it harder for plants to grow. Water in the soil can provide a means for salts in the subsoil to move upward. The salts come to the surface and are deposited when the water evaporates. Irrigation water can also remove salts from the land. If such water is carried to other places where it is used again, the water may become too salty. Sometimes irrigation water can concentrate harmful chemicals from pesticides and insecticides in the soil. Farmers try to use good-quality water and follow good drainage practices.

Do You Know?
As much as 90 percent of the fertilizer put on fields in some areas is not used by plants but carried away with surface runoff and underground water movement.

Figure 25.11 Rows of contour planting cut across hillsides and make water erosion less likely.

Farms are the major source of food for the world's people and a major use of land. It is important to you and your family that good soil is available for growing food. Without this precious resource people could not exist.

Study Questions for 25.1

1. Name two major ways that land is used.
2. What is soil?
3. Describe the processes that produce soil.
4. What makes good growing soil?
5. Describe what farmers do to protect the soil.

25.2 Air

You will find out
- how air is used;
- what pollution is;
- what causes air pollution;
- how air can be kept clean.

Figure 25.12 Green plants use carbon dioxide during photosynthesis. They use oxygen for other life processes.

Earth, like several of the other planets in the solar system, has an atmosphere. Scientists often say that our atmosphere is special. Why would a mixture of invisible gases be special?

Think about the gases found in the air. You already know that most living things require oxygen to live, including humans. Can you think of another atmospheric gas that some organisms use? Carbon dioxide is important to green plants. They use carbon dioxide during **photosynthesis** [foh-toh-SIN-thuh-sis]. Photosynthesis is the process green plants follow to manufacture food, using sunlight, carbon dioxide, and water. While manufacturing food, the plants produce oxygen. Both plants and animals use air for life processes.

Another important function of the atmosphere is protection. Air forms a shield against damaging ultraviolet rays from the sun. Ultraviolet light can destroy simple life forms such as bacteria and harm other organisms too. **Ozone** [OH-zohn] is another gas present in the atmosphere that screens out harmful ultraviolet rays. You have already learned a third function of air. The atmosphere moves, and the shifting winds contribute to the climate and weather patterns on Earth.

Figure 25.13 *right:* Ozone gas, which is made from oxygen, stops most ultraviolet light from reaching the earth's surface.

Do You Know?
Some of the most dangerous air pollutants, such as sulfur dioxide and carbon monoxide, are invisible.

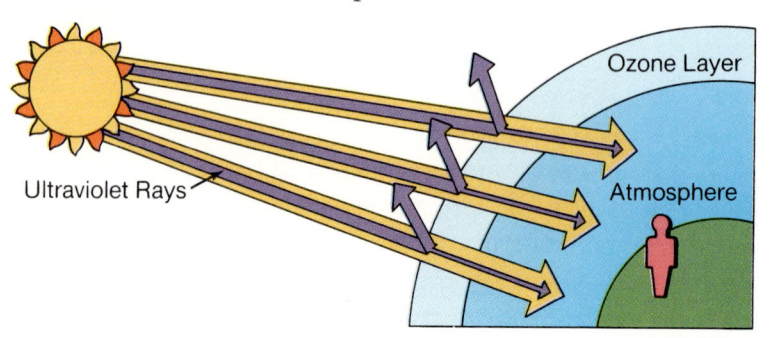

502

25 / Your Environment, Earth

It is obvious that air is an important resource. Is it possible to damage the air? Unfortunately, the answer is yes. The air can be damaged by **pollution** [puh-LOO-shuhn]. Pollution occurs when irritating or dirty substances accumulate in air. These irritants, or **pollutants,** might be chemical gases, dust and waste particles, and smoke. Figures 25.14 and 25.15 show some examples of air pollution. Another kind of pollution comes from aerosol cans. When sprayed, they release chemicals that destroy ozone. How might that affect life on Earth? Air pollutants also occur naturally as plant pollens or volcanic gases and dust.

Figure 25.14 *top:* Air pollution may come from people and their machines.

Figure 25.15 *bottom:* Air pollution may also come from nature.

How do you recognize pollution? Sometimes people can easily detect pollutants in their surroundings through their senses. For example, your eyes may sting and become watery after you have been in polluted air. Other times scientific instruments indicate if pollutants are accumulating. Pollution occurs when natural processes do not act fast enough to remove the irritants.

What can be done to reduce air pollution? People need automobiles and trucks. There have to be power plants, industries, and cities. If a way can be found to decrease pollutants, the air can become cleaner and healthier. One way is to pass laws regulating pollution. These laws limit the kinds of fuels which can be burned, where they can be burned, and when. Cars, trucks, and factories can also be made to use cleaner fuels. Manufacturers are changing processes and products to limit the release of harmful gases into the air. Of course, nothing can be done about erupting volcanoes. However, in places where people make a difference, air can be made cleaner.

Study Questions for 25.2
1. Name three uses of air on Earth.
2. What is pollution and how is it recognized?
3. What are two major pollutants of the air?
4. Describe some steps being taken to reduce air pollution.

25.4 Making Choices

You will find out
- what solid waste is;
- how solid waste is disposed of;
- why recycling is important;
- what must be considered when finding ways to protect the environment.

Figure 25.19 Is it junk or is it treasure?

You may have heard the remark that "One person's junk is another person's treasure." It is a very old saying. An old car that will not run is someone's junk. But to an auto hobbyist its parts and pieces are valuable. When you think of **solid waste,** that idea is true. Solid waste is anything that is considered to be useless, unused, unwanted, or discarded. It can be such things as paper, bottles, cans, rubber, plastics, and metals.

Activity

How Much Waste Does Your Earth Science Class Produce in a Week?

Materials
large box to collect waste
bathroom scale

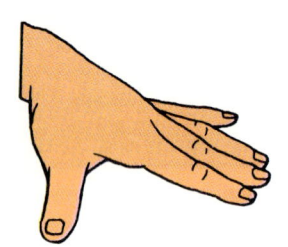

Procedure

1. On Monday morning, remove all old trash from the classroom.
2. During the week, place all trash produced by the class in a large box. CAUTION: Food waste should be placed in a separate container.
3. On Friday, separate the trash into categories of (1) paper or paper products, (2) metals, (3) glass, (4) plant materials, (5) plastics, and (6) miscellaneous. Weigh each kind of waste.

Questions

1. How much waste of each kind was produced?
2. What was the total amount of waste?
3. Calculate how much waste was produced per student per day.
4. Calculate how much waste per student would be produced per year.
5. Estimate the total amount of waste for your school.

In the United States enough solid waste is produced each day to cover almost 300 football fields to a depth of 3 m! Why is there so much? One reason is the way things are packaged. Packages make things easy to ship. They protect whatever is inside, but the wrappings are eventually thrown away as waste. Another reason is that people are accustomed to disposable consumer goods. It is easier and cheaper to replace things than to reuse or repair them. Of course, there are also more people now than there were years ago. More people produce more solid wastes.

What happens to the solid waste people produce? Most of it will end up in one of the following places: (1) a sanitary landfill, (2) incinerators, (3) a recycling plant, or (4) sometimes even in the ocean. Which method do you think is best? Sometimes people discard waste as trash onto streets or open land where it may remain for a long time.

Figure 25.20 *above:* Even the ocean suffers from the burden of solid waste pollution.

Figure 25.21 *left:* The accumulation of solid waste is a problem people must find new ways to solve.

Do You Know?
The average American produces nearly a ton of solid wastes each year.

25 / Your Environment, Earth

Many believe the current sites for waste disposal have reached a limit. Are there other ways to handle solid waste that might even be useful? One old method being tried in a new way is **incineration** [ihn-sihn-uh-RAY-shuhn]. Incineration is the burning of waste at high temperatures in furnaces. People are now using the heat that incinerators produce to warm buildings or produce electric power.

Recycling is another way to handle solid waste and make it useful. Recycling does not actually dispose of the waste. It provides a way to use the discarded materials again. For example, bottles are collected to be cleaned and refilled. Or they, along with cans, can be reprocessed, and the glass and metal used in other ways. Waste paper is recycled by many industries. Scrap metals can be melted down and cast into new, usable forms. Recycling may prove to be the best way people have to prevent themselves from being covered up by piles of solid waste. Recycling also conserves valuable resources. Do you know why? When paper, metal, and other wastes are recycled, there is less danger of using up our wood and mineral resources. Also, with a lower need for new materials, less energy and money are used for refining processes. With recycling, a waste is no longer a waste.

Figure 25.22 *above:* An incinerating plant burns solid wastes. It may also use the energy that is produced to supply other needs.

Figure 25.23 *right:* Wastes become useful when they are recycled. What things can you recycle?

Protecting the land, air, and water is a complicated challenge. How will everyone share resources while preserving them for the future? This is not an easy question to answer. The solution to the problem requires people to look at many facts and then make choices. In some cases the choices will be difficult.

Some of the factors to think about are cost, convenience, consequences, future needs, and fairness to people with different interests. For example, the amount of farmland needed to grow food for the world's growing population must double in the next 50 years. But the best farmland is also attractive to developers because it is often flat and well drained. Each year over 4,000,000,000 square meters of good farmland become new sites for building. People need to find ways to allow both the farmers and the developers to prosper.

People must consider how pollution affects them as well as how they can lessen those effects. Polluted land, air, and water are unpleasant and ugly. Pollutants endanger the natural balance of life on Earth because they may be poisonous or cause disease. Also, careless use of natural resources will waste them. People must remember that protecting natural resources may sometimes slow the growth of industries and cities. Recycling and regulation of fuels and waste treatment is costly. Will people accept the inconvenience of becoming better recyclers?

Not everyone agrees to the solutions of the pollution problems. Educating people about pollution will help them make decisions. The decisions they make for the future must benefit everyone and protect the earth too.

Figure 25.24 Careful choices for the future must be made about the best ways to use land.

Study Questions for 25.4

1. Define solid waste and give some examples of different types.
2. Describe ways in which solid waste can be disposed.
3. Why is recycling an important process?
4. What factors must people consider when making choices about environmental problems?

Biography
Dr. Bahe Billy

Dr. Bahe Billy was born on the Navaho Indian Reservation in Leupp, Arizona, in 1937. As a child he worked with his father helping with farm chores and with irrigation tasks. It was during this time that Dr. Billy became interested in soil and what happens when water enters and leaves the soil. At this early age he noticed the accumulation of salts in irrigated soil and wondered why this happened. Later he studied this very problem for his Master's thesis.

Dr. Billy studied agronomy at Utah State University in Logan, Utah. His Master's and Ph.D. degrees were earned at the University of Arizona at Tucson, Arizona. He is married and has seven children.

Currently Dr. Billy is teaching in Navaho Community College, Shiprock, New Mexico. During the summer months he serves as a consultant on soil problems. His work contributes to the solution of soil problems and irrigation problems in his part of the United States. For example, one project involved collecting soil samples to study the fertility of soils. Another project was determining the irrigation time for certain fields.

Dr. Billy recently received the Tanner Award, an Indian Alumni Award, from the University of Arizona in recognition of his soils work and teaching efforts on the Navaho Indian Reservation.

CHAPTER REVIEW

Main Ideas

- Land is used for new construction and for growing crops.
- Soil is the upper layer of the earth's crust in which plants grow. Soil contains weathered rock materials and decayed plant and animal matter called humus.
- Fertile soil is capable of growing crops because of the materials it contains.
- Soil is protected by using a variety of techniques.
- Air is a mixture of gases that plants and animals need to live.
- Air pollution is an accumulation of irritating or dirty substances in the air. It can be controlled by limiting the release of harmful matter into the air.
- Water is an important resource that is used for personal needs, industry, and agriculture.
- Water pollution is caused by human wastes, chemicals from cities and industries, hot water from industry and power plants, chemicals, and animal wastes from agriculture.
- Another kind of water pollution is acid rain.
- Water can be protected by careful treatment of waste water and by using fewer chemicals.
- Solid waste is solid matter that is thrown away or discarded. Some solid waste can be recycled.
- Cost, consequences, and future needs must be considered when protecting the environment.

Using Vocabulary

On a separate piece of paper, write a paragraph describing the environment. Use each of the words listed below.

soil	soil texture	pollutant
humus	soil structure	solid waste
subsoil	photosynthesis	incineration
soil profile	ozone	
fertile	pollution	

Remembering Facts

On your paper, write the word or words that best complete each sentence.
1. A soil that is good for growing crops is called (subsoil, humus, fertile).
2. (Nitrogen, Ozone, Carbon dioxide) stops harmful ultraviolet rays from entering the atmosphere.
3. Soil is made of weathered rock and (subsoil, humus, bedrock).
4. The gas (carbon dioxide, ozone, oxygen) is produced by plants through the process of photosynthesis.
5. Decayed plant and animal matter in soil is called (humus, texture, topsoil).
6. Any solid that is useless, unused, unwanted, or discarded is called (treasure, waste, fuel).
7. An arrangement of soil layers is called a soil (structure, texture, profile).
8. Smoke, chemical gases, and dust cause (water pollution, air pollution, solid wastes).
9. The soil (structure, texture, profile) allows water to move through soil layers.
10. Air pollution is caused by (gases, pollutants, dust).
11. The arrangement of particles is soil (texture, structure, profile).
12. The middle layer of a soil profile is the (black layer, subsoil, solid rock).
13. Incineration is one way to handle (air pollution, solid wastes, water pollution).
14. Another way to protect resources and handle solid wastes is (incineration, recycling, landfills).
15. One form of water pollution is (chemical gases, ozone, acid rain).

Understanding Ideas

On your paper, answer each question in complete sentences.
1. What pollutants can cause air pollution as well as water pollution?
2. Trace the use of petroleum in the steps taken for food to get from a farmer's field to your dinner table.
3. Explain why the best growing soils contain sand, clay, and humus rather than humus alone.
4. How is a forest fire a threat to the land resources of an area?

Applying What You Have Learned

1. What has to be done to soil to keep it producing a good crop for a long time?
2. Explain how fresh water can become too salty to be used in irrigation.
3. Why do people continue to incinerate and bury solid wastes when recycling would conserve the earth's resources?

Challenge

Farmers make the soils more fertile by adding chemical fertilizers. This means larger plants that grow in less time on the same land area. The overall result is more food grown on less land for an increasing world population. But much of the chemical fertilizer is dissolved and carried away in surface runoff. It ends up in lakes and bays, where it causes tiny plant life to grow rapidly. The water plants gradually use up oxygen and make it impossible for fish, oysters, and other plant life to survive.

1. According to the graphs, how does increased chemical fertilizer use per land area affect both food units produced and water pollution?
2. Does it make sense to sacrifice water resources for improved land use? Explain.
3. Propose a solution to this problem.

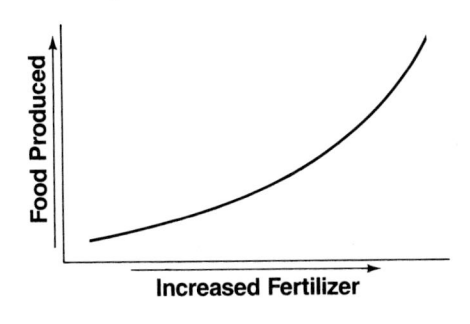

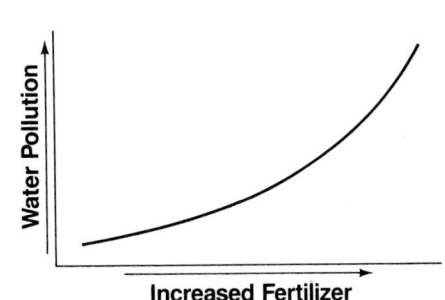

Research and Investigation

1. Find out what happens to the trash from your school. What kind of disposal site is used? How much does it cost per year to haul off the trash from your school? Is paper recycling possible?
2. Contact a TV weather station that broadcasts the weather in your area. Find out how the air in your city is checked for pollution. What time of year is your city most polluted? Has your city had a pollution alert? What causes most of the air pollution where you live?

APPENDICES

GUIDE TO THE METRIC SYSTEM

The International System of Measurement (SI) is used by scientists throughout the world. Each measurement unit in this system is based on 10 and may be multiplied by 10 to obtain the next larger unit or divided by 10 to obtain the next smaller unit. The basic unit of length is the meter; a kilogram is the basic unit of mass; and the basic unit of volume is the liter.

Metric System Prefixes

Greater than 1:
  kilo (k) = 1,000
  hecto (h) =   100
  deka (da) =   10
Less than 1:
  deci (d) = 0.1
  centi (c) = 0.01
  milli (m) = 0.001
  micro (μ) = 0.0000001

Commonly Used Metric Units

Length: The distance between two points
1 millimeter (mm) = 1,000 micrometers (μm)
1 centimeter (cm) = 10 millimeters (mm)
1 meter (m)   = 100 centimeters (cm)
1 kilometer (km) = 1,000 meters (m)
1 light-year   = 9,460,000,000,000 kilometers (km)

Area: A measure of the size of a two-dimensional surface
1 square centimeter (cm^2) = 100 square millimeters (mm^2)
1 square meter (m^2)   = 10,000 square centimeters (cm^2)
1 square kilometer (km^2) = 1,000,000 square meters (m^2)
1 hectare (ha)   = 10,000 square meters (m^2)

Volume: The amount of space an object takes up
1 milliliter (mL) = 1 cubic centimeter (cm^3)
1 liter (L)   = 1,000 milliliters (mL)

Mass: The quantity of matter in a body
1 gram (g)   = 1,000 milligrams (mg)
1 kilogram (kg)   = 1,000 grams (g)
1 metric ton   = 1,000 kilograms (kg)

Temperature: The relative measurement of hotness or coldness
0° Celsius (°C)   = freezing point of water
37° Celsius (°C) = human body temperature
100° Celsius (°C) = boiling point of water

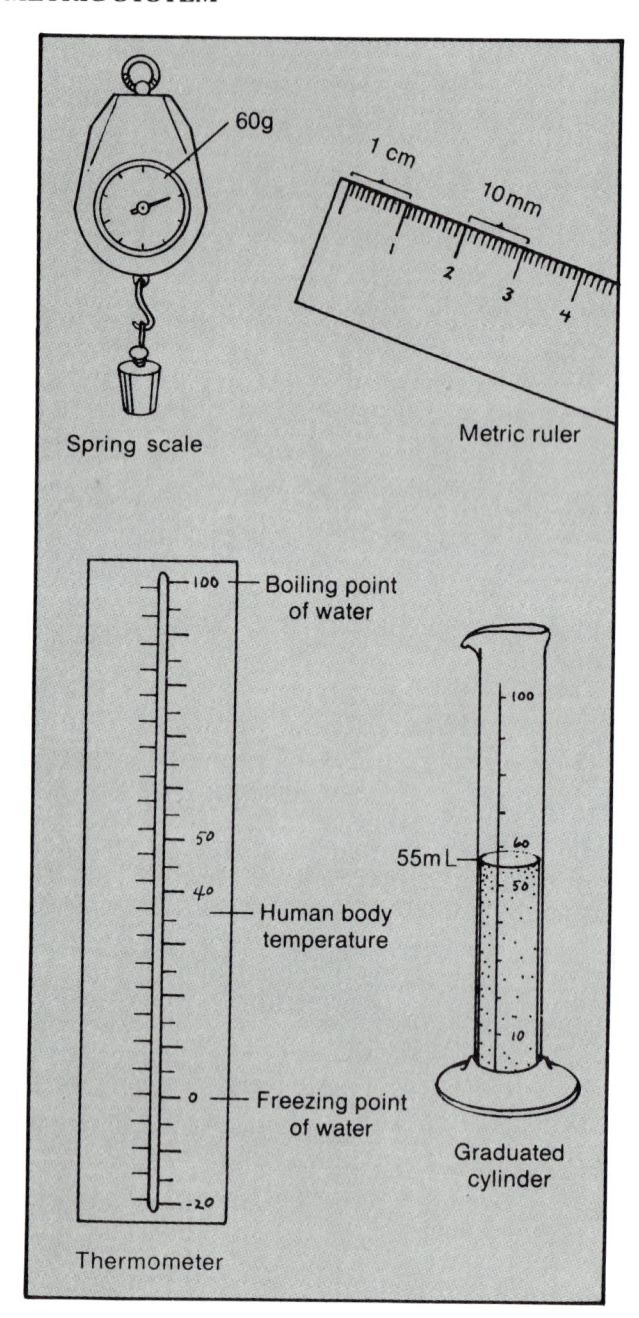

514

RELATIVE HUMIDITY (%)

Dry-bulb temperature (°C)	\multicolumn{20}{c}{Difference between wet-bulb and dry-bulb temperatures (°C)}
	1	2	3	4	5	6	7	8	9	10	11	12	13	14	15	16	17	18	19	20
0	81	64	46	29	13															
1	83	66	49	33	17															
2	84	68	52	37	22	7														
3	84	70	55	40	26	12														
4	85	71	57	43	29	16														
5	86	72	58	45	33	20	7													
6	86	73	60	48	35	24	11													
7	87	74	62	50	38	26	15													
8	87	75	63	51	40	29	19	8												
9	88	76	64	53	42	32	22	12												
10	88	77	66	55	44	34	24	15	6											
11	89	78	67	56	46	36	27	18	9											
12	89	78	68	58	48	39	29	21	12											
13	89	79	69	59	50	41	32	23	15	7										
14	90	79	70	60	51	42	34	26	18	10										
15	90	80	71	61	53	44	36	27	20	13	6									
16	90	81	71	63	54	46	38	30	23	15	8									
17	90	81	72	64	55	47	40	32	25	18	11									
18	91	82	73	65	57	49	41	34	27	20	14	7								
19	91	82	74	65	58	50	43	36	29	22	16	10								
20	91	83	74	66	59	51	44	37	31	24	18	12	6							
21	91	83	75	67	60	53	46	39	32	26	20	14	9							
22	92	83	76	68	61	54	47	40	34	28	22	17	11	6						
23	92	84	76	69	62	55	48	42	36	30	24	19	13	8						
24	92	84	77	69	62	56	49	43	37	31	26	20	15	10	5					
25	92	84	77	70	63	57	50	44	39	33	28	22	17	12	8					
26	92	85	78	71	64	58	51	46	40	34	29	24	19	14	10	5				
27	92	85	78	71	65	58	52	47	41	36	31	26	21	16	12	7				
28	93	85	78	72	65	59	53	48	42	37	32	27	22	18	13	9	5			
29	93	86	79	72	66	60	54	49	43	38	33	28	24	19	15	11	7			
30	93	86	79	73	67	61	55	50	44	39	35	30	25	21	17	13	9	5		
31	93	86	80	73	67	61	56	51	45	40	36	31	27	22	18	14	11	7		
32	93	86	80	74	68	62	57	51	46	41	37	32	28	24	20	16	12	9	5	
33	93	87	80	74	68	63	57	52	47	42	38	33	29	25	21	17	14	10	7	
34	93	87	81	75	69	63	58	53	48	43	39	35	30	28	23	19	15	12	8	5
35	94	87	81	75	69	64	59	54	49	44	40	36	32	28	24	20	17	13	10	7

PROPERTIES OF THE PLANETS

CHARACTERISTICS	Mercury	Venus	Earth	Mars	Jupiter	Saturn	Uranus	Neptune	Pluto
Radius (Earth = 1)	0.382	0.949	1.0	0.533	11.2	9.45	4.1	3.88	0.24
Volume (Earth = 1)	0.056	0.855	1.0	0.151	1,404.9	843.91	68.92	58.41	0.014
Mass (Earth = 1)	0.055	0.815	1.0	0.107	318	95.2	14.6	17.2	0.002
Surface Gravity (Earth = 1)	0.377	0.905	1.0	0.377	2.54	1.07	0.87	1.14	0.03
Orbital Period	88[d]	225[d]	365[d]	1.88[y]	11.9[y]	29.5[y]	84.0[y]	165[y]	248[y]
Spin Period	58.7[d]	243[d]	23.9[h]	24.6[h]	9.92[h]	10.7[h]	23.9[h]	18[h]44[m]	6.39[d]
Mean Distance from Sun (Astronomical Units)	0.39	0.72	1.0	1.52	5.2	9.54	19.2	30.1	39.4
Mean Density (gm/cm^3)	5.4	5.3	5.5	3.9	1.2	0.6	1.2	1.6	0.8
Number of Satellites	0	0	1	2	16	20★	15	2	17
Maximum Visual Magnitude	−1.9	−4.4	—	−2.8	−2.5	−0.4	+5.6	+7.9	+14.9
Mean Orbital Speed (km/s)	47.8	35.0	29.8	24.2	13.1	9.7	6.8	5.4	4.7

[d] = Earth Days, [y] = Earth Years, [h] = Hours, [m] = Minutes. ★Latest studies indicate number to be higher than 20.

GLOSSARY

PRONUNCIATION KEY

The glossary contains all the Key Terms in *Heath Earth Science* and their definitions. Some of these Key Terms are followed by their phonetic spelling, which shows you how to pronounce them. The words are divided into syllables and respelled according to the way each syllable sounds. The syllable that has the emphasis when the word is spoken appears in capital letters. The guide below is based on the Key to Pronunciation in *The World Book Encyclopedia*.

Sound	Respelling of Sound	Example	
hat, map	a	animal	AN-uh-muhl
age, face	ay	space	spays
care, air	ai	hair	hair
father, far	ah	charge	chahrj
child, much	ch	chocolate	CHAWK-luht
let, best	eh	energy	EHN-uhr-jee
equal, see, machine, city	ee	leaf	leef
		dream	dreem
term, learn, sir, work	ur	earthworms	URTH-wurmz
		turkey	TUR-kee
it, pin	ih	system	SIHS-tuhm
ice, five	eye, y	iodine	EYE-uh-dyn
coat, hook	k	cloud	klowd
hot, rock	ah	cotton	KAHT-n
open, go, grow	oh	program	PROH-gram
		row	roh
order, all	aw	corn	kawrn
		fall	fawl
oil, voice	oy	poison	POY-zn
house, out	ow	fountain	FOWN-tuhn
say, nice	s	soil	soyl
she	sh	motion	MOH-shuhn
cup, butter, flood	uh	bulb	buhlb
		blood	bluhd
full, put, wood	u	pulley	PUL-ee
		wool	wul
rule, move, food	oo	dew	doo
		shoe	shoo
pleasure	zh	treasure	TREHZH-uhr
		vision	VIHZH-uhn
about	uh	sofa	SOH-fuh
taken	uh	paper	PAY-puhr
pencil	uh	fossil	FAHS-uhl
lemon	uh	carbon	KAHR-buhn
circus	uh	syrup	SIHR-uhp
curtain	uh	mountain	MOWN-tuhn
section	uh	action	AK-shuhn

A

abrasion [un-BRAY-zhuhn]: process of erosion during which particles carried by the wind polish or break up things hit by the particles

acid rain: rain produced when sulfur dioxide from burning coal combines with water in the atmosphere

air mass: body of air over thousands of square kilometers, having uniform temperature and moisture

air-mass weather: weather that is about the same from day to day, with slow, gradual changes

alluvial [uh-LOO-vee-ahl] **fan:** large, fan-shaped deposit left by a stream

altostratus [al-toh-STRAT-uhs] **clouds:** stratus clouds that occur between 2 km and 7 km above the ground

amber [AM-buhr]: transparent yellow-orange fossil formed from hardened tree sap

analyze [AN-uh-lyz]: to separate things into parts for study

angular unconformity [uhn-kuhn-FOHR-mih-tee]: break in the rock record in which the older layers slope at a different angle from those of the younger layers

anthracite [AN-thrah-syt]: hard coal formed from bituminous coal by pressure and heat

anticlines [AN-tih-klynz]: layers of rock that have been bent upward into an arch

aquaculture [AH-kwa-KUL-chur]: process of farming the ocean

aquifers [AH-kwih-fuhrz]: permeable rocks with groundwater in them

arid: dry

artesian [ahr-TEE-zhuhn] **wells:** wells from which water flows without pumping

asteroid: small rocky object that moves around the sun between the orbits of Mars and Jupiter

astrogram [AS-troh-gram]: message sent into space by a radio telescope

astronomers [uh-STRAHN-uh-muhrz]: scientists who study objects in space

atmosphere: invisible sea of air around the earth

atmospheric pressure: pressure made by moving air molecules hitting a surface

atom: building block of all matter

axis: imaginary line around which the earth rotates

B

barometer [buh-RAHM-uh-tuhr]: device that measures atmospheric pressure

barrier bars: long sandbars usually parallel to a coast

barrier islands: islands formed from large barrier bars, usually parallel to a coast

batholith [BATH-uh-lith]: huge underground mass of rock formed by the cooling of a magma pocket

benthos: organisms that live in or on the ocean floor

biological weathering: process by which rocks are broken up by plant material and organisms

biomass [BY-oh-mas]: parts of plants or things made from plants that can be used for energy

bituminous [bi-TOO-mih-nuhs] **coal:** soft coal formed from lignite by pressure and heat

black holes: objects with intense gravitational fields, thought to exist in space

boundary: zone where plates come together

brachiopods [BRAY-kee-oh-podz]: ancient marine shellfish

breakers: wave tops that bend forward and break

bright-line spectrum: pattern made when light passing through a diffraction grating shows narrow, bright lines

C

cast: fossil formed when a mold is later filled with mud or mineral matter

celestial sphere [suh-LES-chuhl SFEER]: imaginary surface of the sky to which stars appear to be attached

cementation: process that occurs when the spaces between the sediment particles in clastic rocks are filled with chemical deposits

Cenozoic [see-nuh-ZOH-ihk] **Era:** geologic era of recent life

cephalopods [SEF-uh-luh-PODZ]: ancient, coil-shelled animals

Cepheid [SEE-fee-uhd] **variable stars:** stars that regularly change in brightness

chain reaction: continuous action that keeps going on by itself and releasing energy

chemical weathering: process by which substances in the atmosphere combine with materials on the earth and slowly change

chromosphere: lower part of the sun's atmosphere

cinder cone: volcano built of rock and ash

cirrostratus [STRAT-uhs] **clouds:** stratus clouds that occur more than 7 km above the ground and are made of ice crystals

cirrus [SIHR-uhs]: basic cloud shape that has a hairlike appearance and is made of ice crystals

clastic rocks: sedimentary rocks composed mainly of rock fragments

cleavage [KLEEV-uhj]: ability of some minerals to break along smooth parallel planes

climate: average weather over a long period of time

coal: black rock that burns

cold front: leading edge of a moving cold air mass

color: property of minerals

comets [KAHM-its]: small, icy, dusty bodies that orbit the sun

compaction [kuhm-PACK-shuhn]: pressing together of materials by the weight of layers above

composite volcano, or **stratovolcano:** volcano built up from combination of lava, solid rock, and ash

condensation nuclei [NOO-klee-eye]: particles present in the air onto which water droplets have been condensed

condensing [kahn-DENS-ihng]: more molecules returning to the liquid state than leaving as water vapor

constellations [kahn-stuh-LAY-shunz]: named groups of stars

containment building: large, heavy concrete structure that holds a nuclear reactor

continental: describing a climate influenced by air masses from large land areas

continental drift: movement of continents across the earth's surface

continental glaciers: glaciers that cover a large area of a continent

continental polar: describing an air mass having a polar land area as its source region

continental shelf: somewhat shallow area that surrounds a continent

continental slope: area beyond a continental shelf where depth increases rapidly

continental tropical: describing an air mass having a tropical land area as its source region

continuous spectrum: pattern made when light passes through a prism and is separated into its colors, as in a rainbow

contour [KAHN-toor] **line:** line that connects points of the same elevation on a map

control rods: rods made of material that absorbs neutrons; used to slow a chain reaction

convection: process of warmer air being pushed upward

convection cell: pattern of air movement created when warm air rises because of convection and then moves back down onto a cooler surface

convection zone: that portion of the sun that surrounds the radiation zone

converging [kuhn-VUHR-jing] **boundaries:** boundaries between plates that are coming together

core: center part of the sun or the earth

Coriolis [kawr-ee-OH-lihs] **effect:** tendency of all objects moving in the northern hemisphere to curve to the right and in the southern hemisphere to curve to the left because of the earth's rotation

corona [kuh-ROH-nuh]: uppermost part of the sun's atmosphere

correlation: comparison of the ages of rocks in different locations

crest: highest part of a wave

crude oil: petroleum pumped from wells

crust: outside layer of the earth

crystals [KRIS-tuhlz]: solids with repeating patterns of packed ions

cumulonimbus [kyoo-myuh-loh-NIHM-buhs] **cloud:** piled-up cloud that often produces stormy weather

cumulus [KYOOM-yuh-luhs]: basic cloud shape with piled-up appearance

currents: moving streams of water in a body of water

cycle [SY-kuhl]: series of events that keep happening over and over

D

dark-line spectrum: pattern made when light passing through a diffraction grating shows narrow dark lines

data [DAY-tuh]: information recorded from observations

deflation [dee-FLAY-shuhn]: process of erosion during which wind picks up material and moves it, often leaving shallow bowllike features on the surface

deltas [DEL-tuhs]: deposits at the opening of a stream into a lake or the ocean

density: comparison of how heavy something is to the space it occupies

desalinization [dee-SAL-uh-nuh-zay-shun]: taking salt out of seawater

dew: water vapor that has condensed on a surface as a liquid when the dew point is above 0°C

dew point: the temperature at which condensation occurs

diffraction grating [di-FRACK-shuhn GRAY-ting]: piece of glass or plastic with many narrow, parallel slits make a spectrum when light passes through them

dikes: magma that has cooled and hardened in vertical cracks

diverging [dy-VUHR-jing] **boundaries:** boundaries between plates that are separating

divide: boundary between regions that drain into one watershed and regions that drain into another

Doppler [DAHP-luhr] **effect:** change in pitch heard because of the change in distance from a sound source

Doppler shift: shift of spectral lines in the spectrum made by a moving object

drainage patterns: distinctive forms of streams and tributaries as viewed on a map

drought [drout]: period when there is not enough rain

E

earthquakes: sudden vibrations or waves in the earth

echo sounding: way to measure the depth of the ocean floor with a device that sends a sound signal through the water

electromagnetic radiation [ee-lek-troh-mag-NET-ik ray-dee-AY-shuhn]: energy in the form of waves from space

electron [ee-lek-trahn]: particle with a negative electric charge that flies around the nucleus of an atom

electron microscope [ee-LEK-trahn MY-kruh-skohp]: instrument for magnifying objects too small to be studied with the optical microscope

element: material made of only one kind of atom

ellipse [ee-LIPS]: oval shape

epicenter [EP-uh-sen-tuhr]: place on the surface of the earth directly above the focus of an earthquake

epochs [EP-uhks]: smallest dimensions of geologic time

eras [IHR-ruhs]: largest dimensions of geologic time, named for fossils

erosion [ee-ROH-zhuhn]: process of loosening and carrying away materials on the earth's surface by the action of water and wind

esker [ES-kuhr]: snakelike ridge of layered deposits left by glacial meltwater

evaporating [ee-VAP-uh-rayt-ihng]: more molecules going into the air as water vapor than returning to the liquid state

extrusive rock: rock that forms when lava cools quickly on the earth's surface

519

fault / half-life

F

fault: break or crack in part of the earth's crust; the plane along which rock breaks and slips

fault-block mountain: landmass noticeably higher than its surroundings and bounded by one or more faults

faulting: breaking of crustal rock into separate masses, as in mountain building

fertile: describing the quality of soil capable of growing crops because of the materials it contains

fetch: distance the wind blows over water

fission [FISH-uhn]: splitting of atoms with the release of energy

fly ash: fine ash that flies up the chimney into the air when ground-up coal is burned

focus [FOH-kuhs]: place along a fault where an earthquake begins

fog: cloud at or near the earth's surface

folded mountains, or **complex mountains:** mountains with zones of folded sedimentary rock alongside metamorphic and igneous rock

folding: bending of layered rocks

foliation: arrangement of mineral crystals in parallel layers, or bands

forecast: prediction about coming weather

fossil [FAHS-uhl] **fuel:** energy source formed from decomposed plants and animals

fossils [FAHS-uhlz]: traces of plants or animals preserved in rock

fracture: breaking of a mineral when it does not have cleavage

fresh water: water that is not salty

front: leading edge of a moving air mass

frontal weather: changes caused by a passing front

frost: water vapor condensed on a surface as a solid when the temperature is at or below 0°C

full moon: phase of the moon during which its sunlit side faces entirely toward the earth

fusion: process that occurs when nuclei of very light atoms are joined together to form a heavier nucleus

G

galaxies [GAL-uhk-seez]: large assemblies of stars

geologic column: sequence of rock layers placed in order of age

geologic cross section: view of the vertical arrangement of rock layers, as seen in a road cut

geologic cycle: cycle that describes gradual, continual changes in the earth's crust; builds and erodes mountains

geologic map: map that shows geologic features of the land

geologists [jee-AHL-uh-jists]: scientists who study the solid outer and liquid inner parts of the earth

geosynchronous [jee-oh-SIHN-kruh-nuhs] **satellite:** object that travels at the same speed as that of the earth and remains in a fixed position above the earth

geothermal [jee-oh-THUHR-mel] **energy:** energy in the form of heated water and steam from the land or the earth's crust

geyser [GY-zuhr]: fountainlike eruption of hot water and steam

giants: stars that lie just above the main sequence band on the Hertzsprung-Russell diagram

glacier [GLAY-shuhr]: large mass of ice above the snow line

globular clusters: close groupings of stars

Glossopteris [glahs-SAHP-tur-us]: plant whose fossils are found on five continents

graph: diagram or picture of organized data

gravitation: force of attraction between objects

greenhouse effect: warming of the atmosphere; happens when energy from sunlight is absorbed by earth's surface and released as infrared radiation

groundwater: water from an underground zone where all pore spaces are filled with water

H

half-life: time taken for half the atoms in a radioactive sample to change into simpler unchanging atoms

hardness: resistance of a mineral to being scratched

Hertzsprung-Russell [HUHRTZ-spruhng-rus-sehl] **diagram:** graph that compares brightness and temperature of stars

histogram [HIS-tuh-gram]: type of graph

horizontal fault: faulting that causes blocks to move sideways past each other

hot spots: columns of heated gases that expand and rise from the sun's convection zone

hot spring: water heated within the earth and pushed to the surface by convection

humid: moist

humidity [hyoo-MIHD-uh-tee]: amount of water vapor in the air

humus [HYOO-muhs]: partially or completely decayed plant and animal matter

hurricane: large, violent, circular storm that forms over tropical waters

hydrocarbons [HY-droh-kahr-buhns]: substances made of hydrogen and carbon

hydrologic cycle: never-ending movement of water between the atmosphere and the earth

hydrology [hy-DRAHL-uh-jee]: the study of water on or within the earth and in the atmosphere

I

igneous [IG-nee-uhs] **rocks:** rocks formed by the process of cooling liquid rock

image enhancing: technique that uses computers to strengthen certain portions of photographs

incineration [ihn-sihn-uh-RAY-shuhn]: burning of waste at high temperatures in furnaces

index fossils [FAHS-uhlz]: distinctive fossils used to determine the age of rocks

intrusive rock: rock that forms when magma forces its way into or between overlying rock layers

invertebrates [in-VUR-tuh-bruhts]: animals without backbones

ions [EYE-uhnz]: electrically charged atoms

isotopes [EYE-suh-tohps]: atoms of an element that occur in different forms

J

Jurassic [juh-RAS-ihk]: geologic period of the Mesozoic era

L

laboratory: place equipped for scientific study and testing

lake: standing body of fresh water so deep that sunlight cannot reach the bottom

landform regions: large areas that contain similar or related landforms, soils, rock types, and rock structures

landslide: mass movement of sliding rock materials

latitude: north-south distance of a point on the earth's surface

lava: magma that has reached the earth's surface

law of crosscutting relationships: fact that young features in rock cut across older features

law of superposition: fact that younger layers of sediment are always deposited on top of older layers

lignite [LIG-nyt]: brown coal made of compressed peat

loess [LOH-uhs]: fine dust deposited by winds over a large area

longitude: the east-west distance from the prime meridian

longshore current: current pushed along the shore by waves

lunar eclipse [ee-KLIPS]: blocking of the moon's light when the earth passes between the sun and the moon

luster [LUHS-tuhr]: glow of reflected light coming from a mineral's surface

Lystrosaurus [li-struh-SAWR-us]: reptile whose fossils are found on three continents

M

magma: liquid rock deep in the earth

magnetic reversal: change in direction of the magnetic field of the earth

main sequence stars: stars of the main sequence band on the Hertzsprung-Russell diagram

mammals: warm-blooded, hairy animals, the females of which nurse their young

map legend: symbols and colors on a map

map projection: technique used to show the earth's curved surface on a flat map

map scale: distance on a map compared to the actual distance on the earth's surface

mantle: layer of the earth below the crust

marias [MAHR-ee-ahs]: flat, dark, sealike areas of the moon made by ancient lava flows

marine: describing a climate influenced by air masses from ocean areas

maritime polar: describing an air mass having polar waters as its source region

maritime tropical: describing an air mass having tropical waters as its source region

marker layer: layer of rocks having a distinctive characteristic that identifies rocks of a similar age

mass movement: downward movement of weathered earth materials

matter: anything that takes up space and has mass

meanders [mee-AN-duhrs]: bends in level areas of streams that wind back and forth

mechanical weathering: process by which rocks are broken apart by the freezing of water in cracks

meridians: sets of lines running from pole to pole

Mesozoic [mez-uh-ZOH-ihk] **Era:** geologic era before recent life

metamorphic [meht-uh-MAWR-fihk] **rock:** rock that was once igneous or sedimentary rock but has been changed

meteor: small piece of dust or rock that enters the earth's atmosphere from space

meteorite: solid remains of a meteor that reaches the earth's surface

meteorologists [mee-tee-uh-RAHL-uh-jists]: scientists who study the atmosphere

microclimates: local patterns of climate

minerals: naturally occurring substances, generally having a crystalline structure, that have never been part of a living organism

Moho [Moh-hoh]: boundary between the crust and the mantle of the earth

moisture index: measure of the moisture gained by precipitation minus the moisture lost by evaporation and plant use

mold: fossil formed when water dissolves a shell or bone around which sand or mud has already hardened

molecules [MAHL-uh-kyools]: invisible particles of materials

mountain chain: mountain ranges and systems connected together

mountain range: series of mountains

mountain system: series of mountain ranges

mudflow: mass movement of fine materials

N

natural resources: supplies taken from the earth, including water, food, building materials, fiber for clothing, minerals, and energy

nebulae [NEB-yoo-lie]: thin, wispy clouds of glowing gas in outer space

nekton: animal that swims freely

neutron [NOO-tron]: particle with no electric charge; found in the nucleus of an atom

new moon: phase of the moon during which its dark side faces completely toward the earth

nodules [NAHJ-oolz]: small lumps of minerals on the ocean's floor

nonclastic rocks: sedimentary rocks formed from chemical deposits

nonrenewable resource: resource that is not available on the earth again once it is taken and used

normal fault: faulting that causes the earth's crust to be extended

nuclear reactor: thick steel vessel in which energy is released by fissioning uranium-235

nucleus [NOO-klee-uhs]: small inner sphere at the center of an atom

O

observation [ahb-zuhr-VAY-shuhn]: inspection of an object or event by using the senses

ocean basin: bottom of the ocean floor

oceanographers [oh-shuh-NAHG-ruh-ferz]: scientists who study the ocean

oil field: large oil pool collected in porous rock

open clusters: loose groupings of stars

optical microscope [AHP-ti-kuhl MY-kruh-skohp]: instrument for magnifying objects too small to be seen by the naked eye

ores: minerals from which metals can be taken at a reasonable cost

oxbow lakes: lakes formed when one bend in a stream meets another and cuts off a meander

oxidation [AHKS-uh-DAY-shuhn]: combination of a substance with oxygen

ozone [OH-zohn]: gas in the atmosphere that screens out harmful ultraviolet rays

P

Paleozoic [pay-lee-oh-ZOH-ihk] **Era:** geologic era of ancient life

Pangaea [pan-JEE-ah]: supercontinent that broke apart into separate continents

parallels: sets of lines that help identify the position of a place north or south of the equator

passive solar: descriptive of solar-energy use that relies on the collection and storage of solar energy

peat: thick layers of brown, rotted plant material

period of revolution: length of time it takes to complete one trip around the sun

periods: intermediate dimensions of geologic time

permeability: a measure of how well water flows through the pores and cracks in rock layers

petrified [PET-ruh-fyd] **wood:** fossil resulting when silica is substituted for wood cells that have decayed over time

petroleum [puh-TROH-lee-uhm]: thick, smelly, black, liquid fossil fuel

phases of the moon: changes in appearance of the moon during a month

photosphere: visible surface of the sun

photosynthesis [foh-toh-SIN-thuh-sis]: process by which green plants use sunlight, carbon dioxide, and water to manufacture food

plankton: small, floating organism that lives near the water's surface

plastic: solid material that can flow and change shape over a long period of time

plates: large pieces of the earth's crust

plate tectonics [tehk-TAHN-ihks]: theory and study of massive plates thought to move over Earth's surface

plume: localized hot spot of material rising from the earth's interior

polar: describing a climate near the poles with a cold average temperature

polar easterlies: surface winds generally blowing east to west in polar regions

pollutants: irritating or dirty substances that accumulate in air or water, such as chemical gases, dust and waste particles, and smoke

pollution [puh-LOO-shuhn]: accumulation of irritating or dirty substances in air or water

pond: standing body of fresh water shallow enough for sunlight to reach the bottom

pore space: space between soil particles

porosity: total amount of pore space in a volume of material

power tower: tall structure onto which sunlight is reflected by mirrors

Precambrian [pree-KAM-bree-uhn] **Era:** geologic era before ancient life

precipitation [pree-sihp-uh-TAY-shun]: water that falls to the earth's surface as solid or liquid; process that occurs when chemical reactions form a solid that settles out of solution

prevailing westerlies: surface winds generally blowing west to east near latitude 30 degrees north or south of the equator

primary waves: vibrations during an earthquake that cause material to move back and forth

prime meridian: a line that runs from pole to pole and passes through Greenwich, England

523

principle of uniformity: idea that the earth's features formed long ago were made by the same processes that operate today in the same way

prism: transparent body that bends light waves passing through it

prominences [PRAHM-ih-nehn-sez]: blasts of flaming gas that leap from the surface of the sun

proteins: substances that the body uses for the growth and repair of tissues

proton [PROH-tahn]: particle with a positive electric charge, in the nucleus of an atom

protoplanet [PROH-toh-plan-iht] **nebular model:** idea that explains the origin of the solar system

pulsars [PUHL-sahrz]: objects in space that emit radio signals in strong pulses

Q

quarter phase: phase of the moon during which half its lighted side is visible

quasars [KWAY-sahrz]: objects in space that emit strong radio signals

R

radiant energy: sunlight that has traveled from the sun to the earth

radiation zone: that portion of the sun that surrounds the core

radioactive [ray-dee-oh-AK-tihv]: giving off radiation

radioactive decay [ray-dee-oh-AK-tihv dee-KAY]: natural, regular process by which certain radioactive elements change into different elements

radiocarbon [ray-dee-oh-KAHR-buhn] **dating:** method for determining the age of material that was once part of a living organism

radiometric [ray-dee-oh-MET-rihk] **time:** method used when dating the age of rock with an atomic clock

refinery [ree-FYN-uhr-ee]: processing plant that separates crude oil into its many useful products

reflecting telescopes [ree-FLEK-ting TEL-uh-skohps]: instruments with lenses and mirrors used to study objects in space

refracting telescopes [ree-FRAK-ting TEL-uh-skohps]: instruments with lenses used to study objects in space

relative humidity [hyoo-MIHD-uh-tee]: amount of water vapor in the air compared to the total that could be in the air at a certain temperature

relative time: dating method that compares two events by asking which event came first

remote sensing: process used to identify or measure something distant through photographs

renewable resources: resources that become available on the earth again after they have been used up

reptiles [REP-tylz]: cold-blooded, air-breathing animals that lay eggs

reservoir: lake formed by building a dam on a stream or river

reverse fault: faulting that causes the earth's crust to be shortened

revolution: motion of the earth as it orbits the sun

ridges: underwater mountain ranges

rip current: unusually narrow, strong current that heads out to sea from a shore

rock cycle: endless changes of rock from one kind to another

rotation: turning of an object on its axis

S

salinity: measure of the amount of solid material dissolved in seawater

sandbar: pile of sand that is underwater near a shore

sand dunes: deposits of sand made by the wind

satellite: object that orbits another object

scientific model: idea or construction that shows the way something is

sea-floor spreading: movement of the ocean floor outward from a diverging boundary

seamount: submarine volcano that does not rise to the surface

secondary waves: vibrations during an earthquake that cause material to move from side to side

sedimentary [sehd-uh-MEHN-tuh-ree] **rocks:** rocks formed when sediments are pressed and cemented together

sedimentary structures: patterns formed in sediment before it becomes solid rock

sediments: solid materials that fall out of the water

seismic [SIZE-mihk] **waves:** vibrations that move outward from the focus of an earthquake

seismograph [SIZE-muh-graf]: instrument that measures seismic waves

semiarid: describing a climate with between 25 cm and 50 cm of precipitation a year

shield volcano: volcano built of lava flows

shore: area near land where waves are active

shoreline: place where land and water meet

sills: magma that has cooled and hardened in horizontal cracks

sink holes: funnel-shaped depressions caused by the collapse of underground caves

smog: fog combined with exhaust gases and smoke

snow line: edge of places where snow does not completely melt in summer

soil: upper layer of the earth's crust in which plants grow

soil creep: slow mass movement of soil

soil profile: arrangement of soil layers

solar cells: devices made of silicon, arsenic, and boron that produce an electric current when placed in sunlight

solar collector: device that uses sunlight to heat water moving within tubes

solar eclipse [ee-KLIPS]: blocking of the sun's light when the moon passes between the sun and the earth

solar energy: sunlight

solar system: all objects, including planets and moons, asteroids, and comets, that are in orbit around the sun

solar wind: stream of particles that flow out of the corona and away from the sun in all directions

solid waste: anything solid that is considered to be useless, unused, unwanted, or discarded

source region: birthplace of an air mass

space probes: objects designed to explore regions beyond the earth's atmosphere

space shuttle: spacecraft designed to take off like a rocket and land like an airplane

spectroscope [SPEK-troh-skohp]: instrument used to study light

spectrum [SPEK-truhm]: pattern made by light that has passed through a prism

spit: sandbar connected to the shoreline

stationary front: nonmoving zone or boundary between air masses

storage mass: dense material that absorbs sunlight and later gives off the energy as infrared radiation

storms: rapid and violent weather changes

strata: layers of rock distinguished by color variations or makeup of sediments

stratus [STRAT-uhs]: basic cloud shape with spread-out appearance

streak: colored mark left by a mineral when it is rubbed on a streak plate

stream: a moving body of water

structure: quality of soil that allows water to move through soil layers

subduction [suhb-DUHKT-shuhn] **zone:** converging boundary where one plate buckles downward into the earth

subsoil: region of the earth's crust beneath the layer containing humus

sunspots: dark, relatively cool markings on the surface of the sun

supergiants: stars found in the upper-right section on the Hertzsprung-Russell diagram

surf: zone where breakers occur

surface runoff: water that moves across the surface

surface waves: vibrations that cause the earth's surface to move up and down

swell: not very high, long, wide wave that can travel a great distance

synclines [SIN-klyns]: layers of rock that have been bent downward to form a trough

synthesize [SIN-thuh-syz]: to combine things into a whole

T

temperate: describing a climate between polar and tropical regions that is neither very cold nor very hot

temperature: measure of the average energy of motion of molecules

terminal moraine [TUHR-mi-nuhl muh-RAYN]: deposit of rock material at the farthest point reached by a glacier

test: experimentation or observation performed to prove whether or not a model is correct

texture of soil: quality of the arrangement of soil particles

thunderstorm: intense rainstorm with thunder, lightning, and often strong winds and hail

tidal marsh: broad, flat muddy area

tides: changes in water levels caused by changes in gravitation between the earth and the moon

till: rocks deposited in an unsorted way when a glacier melts

topographic maps: maps showing the contour and elevation of the land

tornado: storm with funnel- or rope-shaped clouds and violently swirling winds

trade winds: surface winds generally blowing east to west near latitude 30 degrees north or south of the equator

transform fault: boundary between plates that are sliding past each other

trenches: long, narrow, and deep submarine valleys

trilobites [TRY-luh-byts]: ancient shelled animals

tropical: describing a climate near the equator with a hot average temperature

trough [trawf]: lowest part of a wave

tsunami [tsoo-NAH-mee]: wave made by an undersea earthquake

turbidity current: movement of sand and mud along the ocean floor

U

unconformity [uhn-kuhn-FOHR-mih-tee]: break in the rock record

undertow: strong current that heads out to sea

V

valley glacier: glacial ice confined to a valley

volcanic neck: mass of igneous rock that remains after erosion has removed the volcanic cone

volcano: mountain formed from liquid rock

W

warm front: leading edge of a moving warm air mass

watershed: area of land drained by a river

water table: level below which the ground is full of groundwater

water vapor: water in the form of a gas

wave: rise and fall of the water's surface

wave height: vertical distance between the crest and the trough of a wave

wavelength: horizontal distance between two wave crests

weathering: process by which exposed rocks are broken down into smaller bits and pieces

white dwarfs: stars found below the main-sequence band on the Hertzsprung-Russell diagram

wind: horizontal movement of air

INDEX

NOTE: Page numbers in **boldfaced** type indicate a definition.

A
Abrasion, **364**
Abrasives, 438, 440
Acid rain, **462,** 505
Air masses, **144**–149; and fronts, 148–149; types of, 146–148
Air-mass weather, **148**
Alluvial fans, **348,** 363
Almathea, 90
Alps, 302, 303, 324
Altitude and climate, 168
Altostratus clouds, **135.** *See also* Clouds.
Aluminum, 436
Amber, **415**
Analysis, **7**
Andes, 302, 303
Andromeda Galaxy, 25
Angular unconformity, **378**–379
Anthracite coal, **461**
Anticlines, **314,** 378
Apollo missions, 61, 86
Appalachian Highlands region, 347
Appalachians, 302, 303, 324, 327, 347
Aquaculture, **445**
Aquifers, **194**–196
Area, 15
Arecibo (Puerto Rico), radio telescope at, 54
Arid climate, **173**
Artesian wells, **196**
Asbestos, 265
Asteroids, **72**
Astrogram, **54**
Astronomers, **2,** 93–94
Atmosphere, 50, **104**–107, 502–503; heating of, 108–111; water in, 126–137
Atmospheric pressure, **106**–107; and highs and lows, 150–152; temperature and, 114–115
Atoms, **234**–236, 398, 400–402, 465
Axis, **66**

B
Bacon-Bercey, June, **138**
Barometer, **107,** 151
Barrier bars, **217**
Barrier island, **217**
Basin and Range region, 348
Batholiths, **321**
Beaches, 214–216, 383; coral-sand, 215; quartz-sand, 215; volcanic-sand, 215
Becquerel, Antoine Henri, 464
Benthos, 225
Big-bang theory of universe, 36
Billy, Bahe, 510
Biological weathering, **356,** 357
Biomass, **483**
Bituminous coal, **461**
Black holes, **37**
Boundary, **294**–295, 326, 328
Brachipods, **423,** 426
Brahe, Tycho, 27
Breakers, **210**

Bright-line spectrum, **32**
Building materials, 438, 441

C
Calcite, 240
California Current, 213
Cambrian Period, 422
Cascades, 326
Cast, fossil, **417**
Caves, 356
Celestial sphere, **26**
Cementation, **261**
Cenozoic Era, **405,** 424
Central Plains region, 347
Cephalopods, **420**–421
Cepheid variable stars, **29,** 34
Chain reaction, **465,** 466
Chemical weather, **356**
Chromium, **257**
Chromosphere, **63**
Cinder cones, **319**
Cirrostratus clouds, **135.** *See also* Clouds.
Cirrus clouds, **134,** 135. *See also* Clouds.
Clastic, **260**
Cleavage, **240**–241
Climate, **164,** 358; and local factors, 168–170; precipitation and, 166–167; and temperature, 165–166; types of, 172–176
Climatologist, 179

527

Clouds, 132–135
Coal, 438, 448, **460**–463, 466, 469
Coastal Plain region, 347
Cold front, **148**–149
Color: of igneous rock, 257; of minerals, **239**
Colorado Plateau region, 348
Colorado River, 355, 396
Columbia Plateau region, 349
Comets, **28**, 72–73
Compaction, **261**
Complex mountains, **324**
Composite volcanoes, **319**
Concoidal fractures, **241**
Condensation, **127**, 130–133, 136, 137
Condensation nuclei, **132**, 133
Constellations, **26**
Containment building, **467**
Continental climate, **173**
Continental drift, **292**–293
Continental glaciers, **366**
Continental polar air mass, **146**
Continental shelf, **219**–220
Continental slope, **219**–220
Continental tropical air mass, **146**
Continuous spectrum, **32**
Contour lines, **342**–345, 388–389
Control rods, **467**
Convection, 112–**113**, 478, 485, 486
Convection cell, **113**, 116
Convection zone, **63**
Converging boundaries, **294**–295
Copper, 436
Core: earth, **275**, 277, 284–285; sun, **63**
Coriolis effect, **117**–118, 213
Corona, **63**
Correlation, **380**–381
Crest, **209**
Cretaceous Period, 425
Cross-bedding, 382
Crosscutting relationships, law of, **376**, 387
Crude oil, **457**–458
Crust, **274**, 282
Crystals, **236**, 256
Cumulonimbus clouds, **134**, 154–155. *See also* Clouds.
Cumulus clouds, **134**. *See also* Clouds.
Curie, Pierre and Marie, 464
Currents, **211**–213, 216; and climate, 170
Cycle, **136**

D

Dark-line spectrum, **32**
Data, **17**
Dating techniques, 400–403, 420–425
Deflation, **364**
Deltas, **363**
Democritus, 194, 195
Density, 15, **241**
Descartes, 74
Devil's Tower (Wyoming), 251
Devonian Period, 424
Dew, **130**, 131
Dew point, **130**–131, 133
Diamonds, 257
Diffraction grating, **31**
Dikes, **321**
Distance, 14
Diverging boundaries, **294**
Divides, **191**
Doppler effect, **35**
Doppler shift, **35**–36
Drainage patterns, **361**
Drought, **137**
Dry steam, geothermal, 487, 488

E

Earth, 75, 495; and moon, 67–69, 276; and plates, 291–307; structure of, 273–285
Earthquakes, 211, 221, **273**–281, 300–301, 307
Echo sounding, **218**–219
Electromagnetic radiation, **30**–31, 52–53
Electron microscope, **4**
Electrons, **235**–236
Elements, **234**, 398–402, 464–465
Ellipse, **70**
Energy: nonrenewable resources and, 456–469; renewable resources and, 476–489
Epicenter, **279**
Epochs, **405**
Eras, **405**
Erosion, 321, **359**–369, 387, 500
Esker, **369**
Evaporation, **127**, 136, 137, 188
Extrusive rock, **256**

F

Fault-block mountains, **322**–323, 327, 348
Faulting, **316**, 387
Faults, **279**, **316**–317, 376

Fertile, **498**
Fertilizers, minerals for, 438, 440
Fetch, **210**
Fibrous fracture, **241**
Findlay, Marsha, 350
Fission, **465**, 466–467
Fly ash, **462**
Focus, **279**
Fog, **133**, 135
Folded mountains, **324**
Folding, **314**–315
Foliation, **265**
Forecast, **150**–153
Fossil fuels, 438, 439, 448, **456**, 461, 480
Fossils, **296**–297, 375, 380–381, 414; dating of, 420–421; types of, 414–417
Fracture, **241**
Fresh water, **186**–187, 443. *See also* Water.
Fretwell, Judy D., 203
Frontal weather, **149**
Fronts, **148**–149, 151
Frost, **130**–131
Full moon, **68**
Fusion, **469**

G

Galaxies, **28**–29. *See also* Milky Way Galaxy.
Galileo, 27, 52
Gamma rays, 30, 31
Ganymede, 90
Garnet, 265
Gasohol, 483
Gasoline, 458
Gemini spacecraft, 86
Geochemists, 268
Geologic column, **404**
Geologic cross section, **386**, 388
Geologic cycle, **327**
Geologic maps, **388**–389
Geologic time, 395–399, 404–407
Geologists, **3**, 255, 318, 324, 377, 381, 388, 396, 444
Geomorphologist, 370
Geopressurized hot water, 489
Geosynchronous, 83
Geothermal energy, **487**–489, 490
Geyser, **486**, 487
Giants, **47**, 49
Glaciers, **305**, 366–369
Globular clusters, **28**
Glomar Challenger, 297
Glossopteris, **296**

Gold, 257, 436–437, 442
Graded bedding, 382
Grand Canyon, 355, 362, 396
Grand Tetons, 327
Granite, 257, 349
Graph, **17**
Graphite, 265
Gravitation, **64**–65, 69, 366, 368
Gray, Floyd, 450
Great Red Spot, 90
Greenhouse effect, **110**–111, 120
Groundwater, **192**–197
Gulf Stream, 213

H
Hahn, Otto, 465
Hail, 154
Half-life, **398**–399, 402
Halite, 240
Hardness, **240**
Hawaiian Islands, 221, 307, 319, 401
Hematite, 239, 435
Herodotus, 375
Hertzsprung-Russell (H-R) diagram, **46**–47
Himalayas, 302, 303, 324
Histogram, **17**
Horizontal fault, **316**
Hot dry rock, **489**
Hot spots, **63**
Hot springs, **486**–487
Hot water, geothermal, 488
Hubble, Edwin, 39
Humid climate, **173**
Humidity, **128**, 170
Humus, **497**–498
Hurricanes, **156**–157
Hydrocarbons, **456**, 457, 458, 462, 463
Hydrologic cycle, **136**–137, 186–187, 484–485, 504
Hydrologist, **203**
Hydrology, **126**

I
Ice, erosion by, 357, 366–369
Ice ages, 369
Igneous rocks, **252**–253, 256–259, 314, 324, 327, 348
Image spectrometry, 246

Incineration, **508**
Index fossils, **380**, 421
Infrared waves, 30, 31, 109
Intrusive rock, 256
Invertebrates, **423**
Io, 90
Ions, **236**
Iron ore, 257, 435
Irrigation, 501, 504
Isotopes, **465,** 466

J
Joly, John 397
Jupiter, 74, 90
Jurassic Period, **420**

K
Kant, Emmanuel, 74
Katsaros, Kristina, 178
Kelvin, Lord, 397
Kepler, Johannes, 70, 76
Kepler's laws, 70
Kerosene, 458

L
Laboratory, 10–11
Lakes, **191**
Landform regions, 346–349
Landslide, **359**
Laplace, 74
Latitude, **341**
Lava, **256**, 318–320, 349
Light, 30–31; speed of, 25
Lightning, 155
Light-year, 25
Lignite coal, **461**
Limestone, 261, 356, 383, 384, 388
Lind, Aulis, 96
Loess, **365**
Longitude, **341**
Longshore current, **212**, 216
Lopez, David, 390
Luna, 84
Lunar eclipse, **67**
Lunar Orbiters, 84
Luster, **239**
Lystrosaurus, **296**

M
Magma, **256,** 318, 321, 376
Magnetic reversal, **299**
Magnetite, 435
Main sequence stars, **47,** 49
Mammals, **424**
Mantle, **275,** 282–283
Map legend, **339**
Map projection, **340**
Map scale, **339**
Marble, 265
Mare's tails, 135
Marine climate, **173**
Mariner probes, 85
Maritime polar air mass, 146–**147**
Maritime tropical air mass, **146**
Market layer, **380**
Mars, 75, 89, 93
Mars probes, 85
Mass, 14
Mass movement, **359**
Matter, **234**–236
Maxwell Montes, 88
Meanders, **362**
Measurements, 14–16
Mechanical weathering, **356,** 357
Mercury, 74
Mercury spacecraft, 86
Meridian, **341**
Mesozoic Era, **405,** 424
Metals, 435–437
Metamorphic rocks, **254,** 264–267, 314, 324, 327, 348
Meteor, **73**
Meteorites, **73,** 277
Meteorologists, **2**–3, 138, 143, 150, 152–153
Methane gas, 483
Metric system, 14–15
Mica, 240
Microclimates, **176**–177
Mid-Atlantic ridge, 220–221, 295–298
Milky Way Galaxy, 44–53
Minerals, **238;** identification of, 242–243; properties of, 238–241; in soil, 497–498
Mississippian Period, 424
Moho, **282**
Mohorovicic, Andrija, 282
Moisture index, **175**
Mold, fossil, **415**
Molecules, **105;** in air, 105–106, 108, 110–111; of water vapor, 126–127, 132

Moon, 66–69; phases of, 68; tides, 69
Morisawa, Marie, 330
Mountain chains, **326**
Mountain ranges, **326**–329
Mountains, 314; and climate, 169; and plate movements, 294–295, 302–303, 313–329
Mountain system, **326**
Mount St. Helens, 318–319
Mud cracks, 382
Mudflow, **359**

N

National Weather Service, 152, 157
Natural gas, 438, 444, 457
Natural resources, **434**, 509; for energy, 456–469, 476–489; metallic, 434–437; nonmetallic, 438–441; from oceans, 442–445; renewable and nonrenewable, **434**, 459, 463; sources of, 446–449
Nebulae, **28**
Nekton, 224–225
Neptune, 91
Neutrons, **235**, 465, 467
New moon, **68**
Nickel, 257
Nodules, **444**
Nonclastic, **261**
Normal fault, **316**
Nova, 34, 49
Nuclear fuel, 464–469
Nuclear reactors, **467**–468, 470
Nucleus, **235**

O

Observations, 4, **7**
Ocean basin, **219**, 220–221
Oceanographers, 3
Oceans, 186, 207–225; resources from, 442–445
Ocean water, 186
Oil field, **457**
Old Faithful, 486
Olympus Mons, 89
Open clusters, **28**
Optical microscope, 4
Ores, **435**–437
Oxbow lakes, **362**
Oxidations, **356**
Ozone, **502**

P

Pacific Mountain region, 349
Paleozoic Era, **405**, 423
Palomar Mountain (California), telescope at, 50
Pangaea, **292**, 305–307
Parallels, **341**
Passive solar house, **478**
Peat, **461**
Pennsylvanian Period, 424
Period of revolution, **70**
Periods, **405**
Permeability, **189**
Petrified wood, **415**
Petroleum, 438, 444, 448, **456**–459, 460, 463, 466, 469
Phases of the moon, **68**
Photosphere, **63**
Photosynthesis, **502**
Pioneer X, 85
Pioneer Venus Orbiter, 88
Planets, 70–71, 74–75, 88–91
Plankton, **224**–225
Plastic, **283**
Plates, **294**; movement of, 300–305
Plate tectonics, **294**–307
Platinum, 257
Plume, **307**, 322
Pluto, 91
Polar climate zone, **166**
Polar easterlies, **118**
Polaris, 29
Pollutants, **503**
Pollution, 462, **503**, 509
Ponds, 191
Pore space, **189**–190
Porosity, **189**
Potassium-40–argon-40 dating, 401
Power tower, **480**, 481
Precambrian Era, **405**
Precipitation, **136**–137, 151–157, 185–193; and climate, 166–167, 169
Precipitation, chemical, **261**
Prevailing westerlies, **118**, 147
Primary waves (P waves), **280**, 283
Prime meridian, **341**
Prism, **31**
Prominences, **62**
Proteins, **445**
Protons, **235**
Protoplanet nebular model, **75**
Pulsars, **33**, 34–35
Pumice, **257**

Q

Quart, 215, 241
Quarter phase, **68**
Quasars, **33**

R

Radiant energy, **108**–109
Radiation zone, **63**
Radioactive decay, **398**–399
Radioactive rocks, **464**
Radiocarbon dating, **402**
Radiometric time, **401**–403
Radio telescopes, 33, 45, 54, 56
Radio waves, 30
Rain, 136
Ranger, 84
Recycling, 507, 508, 509
Refinery, **458**
Reflecting telescope, **28**
Refracting telescope, **27**–28
Relative humidity, **128**–129
Relative time, **403**
Remote sensing, 93
Remote-sensing scientists, 96
Reptiles, **424**
Reservoir, **191**
Reverse fault, **316**
Revolution, **66**
Richter scale, **281**
Ridges, **220**–221
Rip current, **212**
Ripple marks, 382
Rock cycle, **255**
Rock, 251; formation of, 252–255; igneous, **252**–253, 256–259; metamorphic, **254**, 264–267; sedimentary, **253**, 260–263
Rocky Mountains, 302, 303, 324, 326, 348
Rotation, **66**

S

Safety procedures, 11
Sagittarius, 44
Salinity, **222**–223
Salt, 438, 440, 442
Sandbar, **216**
Sand dunes, **364**
Sandstone, 261, 383, 384, 388
San Joaquin Valley, 349

Satellites, **82**–83
Saturn, 90–91
Scientific model, **8**
Sea-floor spreading, **294**, 299
Seamounts, **221**
Secondary waves (S waves), **280**, 281, 283
Sedimentary rocks, **253**, 260–263, 314, 324, 327, 347–348, 376, 378, 382–385
Sedimentary structures, **382**
Sediments, **253**, 260–261, 376, 378, 383, 397, 461
Seismic reflection profiling, 308
Seismic tomography, 286
Seismic waves, **279**–281, 283, 284–285
Seismograph, **280**
Semiarid climate, **173**
Shale, 383–384
Shield volcanoes, **319**
Ship Rock (New Mexico), 321
Shore, **214**–216, 383
Shorelines, **214**–217, 384
Sierra Nevada mountains, 326, 327, 349
Sills, **321**
Silver, 257
Sinkholes, **356**
Sleet, 136
Smith, William "Strata," 19, 404
Smog, **177**
Snow, **136**
Snow line, 366
Soapstone, 265
Soil, 188–189; **497**–501
Soil creep, **359**
Soil profile, **498**
Solar cells, **481**
Solar collector, **477**
Solar eclipse, **67**
Solar energy, **476**–481, 484–485
Solar system, **65**
Solar wind, **63**
Solid waste, **506**–508
Source region, **146**
Spacecraft, 61, 69, 86–87, 88–89, 90, 92, 93; and telescopes, 50–51, 433
Space probe, 83–86
Space shuttle missions, **86**
Spectroscope, **31**
Spectrum, 30, **31**, 52–53; bright-line, 32; continuous, 32; dark-line, 32; of stars, 46–47
Speed, 15
Sputnik I, 82

Spit, **216**
Stars: brightness, 46; Cephid variables, 29; clusters, 28; constellations, 26; galaxies, 28–29; life cycle, 49; motion, 35–36, 45; size, 34, 47; temperature, 46
Stationary front, **149**
Storage mass, **478**
Storms, **154**–157
Strassman, Fritz, 465
Strata, **253**
Stratovolcanoes, **319**
Stratus clouds, **134**, 135. *See also* Clouds.
Streak, **239**
Streams, 190, 360–362
Structure, soil, **498**
Subduction zone, **294**–295, 318, 319, 326
Submarine, *Alvin*, 226
Subsoil, **497**
Sulfur, 438, 440, 462
Sulfur dioxide, 462
Sun, 62–65; and radiant energy, **108**–109. *See also* Solar energy.
Sunspots, **62**
Supergiants, 47
Supernova, 34
Superposition, law of, **376**, 388, 403
Surf, **210**
Surface runoff, **190**
Surface waves (L waves), **280**, 282
Surveyor, 84
Swell, **210**
Synclines, **314**
Synthesis, **7**

T
Talc, 265
Temperate climate zone, **166**
Temperature, 15, **108**; and atmospheric pressue, 114–115; and climate, 165–166; and condensation, 127, 130–131; and energy of motion in molecules, 108, 126–127; and evaporation, 127; and humidity, 128–129
Terminal moraine, **369**
Test, **8**
Texture, soil, **498**

Thunder, 155
Thunderstorms, **154**–155
Tidal marsh, **214**
Tides, **69**, 211
Till, **368**
Time, 14
Topographic maps, **342**–345,
Tornado, **156**
Trade winds, **118**
Transform fault, **295**
Trenches, **221**, 295
Trilobites, **423**
Tropical climate zone, **166**
Trough, **209**
Tsunami, **211**
Turbidity current, **212**

U
Ultraviolet waves, 30, 31, 109, 502
Unconformity, **378**
Undertow, **212**
Uniformity, principle of, **377**, 378
Uranium, 448, 464–466, 469, 480
Uranium-238–lead-206 dating, 399–400
Uranus, 74, 91

V
Valley glacier, **366**
Varela, Alejandra Gloria, 408
Venera probes, 85
Venus, 74, 75, 88
Vidale, Rosemary, 268
Viking probes, 85, 89
Volcanic neck, **321**
Volcanoes, **318**–321; plate movements and, 300–301; in solar system, 89, 90
Volume, 15
Voyager I and *Voyager II*, 85, 86, 90, 91

W
Ward, A. Wesley, 370
Warm front, **148**–149

Water, 185–201; in atmosphere, 126–137, 462; climate and bodies of, 170; consumption, 504–505; below Earth's surface, 192–194, on Earth's surface, 188–191; energy of moving, 482; erosion by, 359, 360–363, 500; as limited resource, 198–201, 504; in oceans, 186
Watershed, **190**–191
Water table, **192**
Water vapor, **126**–127, 136; and humidity, 128–129, 130
Wave height, **209**
Wavelength, **209**
Waves, **208**–211, 215
Weather, 143–157, 163, 165
Weathering, **356**–359, 497
Weather radar, 158
White dwarfs, **47**, 49
Wind, **112**–118, 502; and air masses, 147; as energy source, 483, 485; erosion by, 359, 364–365, 500; and waves, 210–211

X
X rays, 30, 31, 37

Z
Zond, 84

ACKNOWLEDGEMENTS

Design Credits *Art Editing:* Julie B. Booth *Photo Research:* Nina Whitney, Carole Frohlich
Activity Art: Gail Burroughs
Challenge Art: ANCO/Boston

Illustration Credits **8:** Jeff Stock. **9, 12–13:** Gail Burroughs. **17:** Dave Hannum. **26:** Gary Torici. **27, 28:** Patrick Russell. **30–31, 32:** Jeff Stock. **33:** Patrick Russell. **35, 36:** Jeff Stock. **37:** Gary Torici. **44:** Michael Carroll. **45:** Gail Burroughs. **46, 47:** Dave Hannum/Jeff Stock. **49:** Gary Torici. **55:** Leo Abbett. **60, 62:** Michael Carroll. **64, 65:** Gary Torici. **66:** ANCO/Boston. **67:** Lloyd Birmingham. **68:** Gary Torici. **69:** Lloyd Birmingham. **70:** Dave Hannum. **71:** Michael Carroll. **72:** ANCO/Boston. **74:** Dave Hannum. **75, 77, 93:** Michael Carroll. **106, 107:** Gary Torici. **109:** Dave Hannum. **110, 111:** Jeff Stock. **113, 114, 116:** Gary Torici. **117:** Jeff Stock. **118, 119:** Gary Torici. **127:** Dave Hannum. **128:** Patrick Russell. **132:** Gary Torici. **134:** Kim Poor. **137:** Jeff Stock. **144, 147:** Gary Torici. **149:** James Teason. **150, 152:** Patrick Russell. **154, 155:** Kim Poor. **156:** Lloyd Birmingham. **166:** Patrick Russell. **167:** Lloyd Birmingham. **168:** Patrick Russell. **169:** James Teason. **170, 174, 175:** Patrick Russell. **178:** Robert Anderson. **186:** Gary Torici. **187:** James Teason. **188:** Lloyd Birmingham. **190:** James Teason. **192–193:** Lloyd Birmingham. **195:** James Teason. **196:** Lloyd Birmingham. **197:** James Teason. **198:** Gary Torici. **209:** Lloyd Birmingham. **210–211, 212, 213:** James Teason. **218:** Walter Hortens. **219, 220, 221:** James Teason. **222:** ANCO/Boston. **225:** James Teason. **234, 235, 236:** Leonard Morgan. **240:** James Teason. **244, 245:** Lily Yamamoto. **255:** Jeff Stock. **261:** ANCO/Boston. **264:** Jeff Stock. **265:** Gary Torici. **267:** Gail Burroughs. **274, 275, 277, 279, 280:** Walter Hortens. **281:** Dave Hannum. **282:** *t* Walter Hortens; *b* Lloyd Birmingham. **283, 285:** Walter Hortens. **292, 294–295:** James Teason. **294, 295:** Jeff Stock. **296:** James Teason. **297:** Dave Hannum. **298, 299, 300, 302, 303, 305, 306, 307:** James Teason. **314, 315, 316:** Jeff Stock. **318:** James Teason. **319:** Lloyd Birmingham. **320:** Jeff Stock. **321:** James Teason. **322, 323:** Jeff Stock. **325:** James Teason. **327:** Jeff Stock. **328–329:** James Teason. **339:** ANCO/Boston. **340, 341:** Bonnie Pauley McGrath. **342:** James Teason. **343:** Bonnie Pauley McGrath. **346, 358, 361, 362, 369, 378:** James Teason. **379:** *t* Jeff Stock; *b* Dave Hannum. **380, 383, 384:** Dave Hannum. **386:** Jeff Stock. **388, 389:** Dave Hannum. **398:** Lily Yamamoto. **399:** *l* Dave Hannum; *r* Gary Torici. **401:** James Teason. **402:** Gary Torici. **403, 404, 418, 420, 422–423, 439:** Dave Hannum. **444:** Walter Hortens. **446, 447, 448, 449:** Dave Hannum. **456, 458:** Walter Hortens. **460:** Dave Hannum. **461:** James Teason. **462:** Walter Hortens. **463:** Dave Hannum. **465:** Gary Torici. **466:** Leo Abbett. **468:** Walter Hortens. **469:** ANCO/Boston. **478, 483, 485:** Dave Hannum. **487:** Walter Hortens. **490:** Frank Schwarz (Lee Ames & Zak LTD.). **497:** James Teason. **502:** Dave Hannum.

Photo Credits **Front Matter and Chapter:** **iii:** NASA. **iv:** *t* Nasa; *b* Harbor Branch Foundation, Chris Chulamanis. **v:** Wedigo Ferchland (Bruce Coleman). **vi:** Robert Harding Picture Library. **vii:** Grant Heilman (Grant Heilman). **viii:** Bruce Molnia (Terraphotographics). **2:** *l* Dennis DiCiccio; *l insert* Jay Pasachoff (c. Pasachoff Educational Trust); *r* Dan McCoy (Rainbow); *r insert* Michal Heron. **3:** *l* Jeff Rotman; *l insert* Woods Hole Oceanographic Institution, Rod Catanach; *r* Michael Collier; *r insert* David Breed. **4:** *l* Bill Tillery; *r* Manfred Kage (Peter Arnold). **5:** BSCS. **6:** *l* Andrew Watt; *r* Talbot Lovering. **7:** Harold R. Hungerford. **8:** Harold R. Hungerford. **10:** Eric Anderson. **14:** Lee Gordon. **15:** Talbot Lovering. **16:** Paul E. Johnson. **18:** Lawrence Berkeley Lab. **19:** Sharon Gerig (Tom Stack & Associates).

Unit One: **22:** NASA. **24:** California Institute of Technology and Carnegie Institute of Washington. **27:** *t l* Culver Pictures; *t r* The Houghton Library, Harvard University; *r* Ken Launie; *b* Dennis Milon. **28:** Hale Observatories. **29:** *t* Hale Observatories; *b* Dennis Milon. **30:** Deidre Delano Stead. **31:** Dr. Ernest Hildner. **33:** Dan McCoy (Rainbow). **34:** Lick Observatory. **35:** Jay Pasachoff (c. Pasachoff Educational Trust). **38, 39:** California Institute of Technology and Carnegie Institute of Washington. **42:** Hale Observatories. **44:** Palomar Observatory. **45:** National Radio Astronomy Observatory. **48:** California Institute of Technology and Carnegie Institution of Washington. **50:** *l* Jay Pasachoff (c. Pasachoff Educational Trust); *r* NASA. **51:** Boeing Company. **52:** *t* NASA; *b l* Jay Pasachoff (c. Pasachoff Educational Trust); *b r* NASA. **53:** NASA. **54:** Arecibo Observatory, National Astronomy and Ionosphere Center. **56:** G. Galen Rowell (Peter Arnold). **57:** Hale Observatories. **63:** *t* Tom Pantages; *b* NASA. **68:** Tom Pantages. **69:** Robert T. Bradbury. **72:** Harvard College Observatory/Science Source (Photo Researchers). **73:** *t* Jay M. Pasachoff (Visuals Unlimited); *b* Grant

533

Heilman (Grant Heilman). **76:** La Foundation St. Thomas. **80:** Photri. **82:** *t* Jet Propulsion Lab; *b* NOAA. **83–88:** NASA. **89:** *t* NASA, Langley Research Center; *b* Larry Mulvehill (Photo Researchers). **90:** Jet Propulsion Laboratory. **91:** *l* NASA; *r* Jet Propulsion Laboratory. **92:** *l* NASA; *b* Photri. **93:** Boeing Company. **94:** NASA. **96:** Aulis Lind. **97:** Photri.

Unit Two: **100:** NASA. **102:** Daniel Forster. **104:** *t* Dan McCoy (Rainbow); *b* Will Tenney. **105:** FPG. **107:** *l* Maximum, Inc.; *r* Tom Magno. **108:** *t* Diedre Delano Stead; *b* Eric Anderson. **109:** *r* Diedre Delano Stead; *b* General Electric Corporation. **110:** Phil Degginger. **112:** Keith Gunnar (Bruce Coleman). **113:** Phil Degginger. **116:** Tom Bean (Tom Stack & Associates). **120:** Susan Anderson. **121:** NASA. **124:** Carlye Calvin. **126:** Jacques Jangoux (Peter Arnold). **127:** Tom Magno. **130:** *t* Clive Russ; *b* Stephen J. Krasemann (Peter Arnold). **131:** University of Florida Agricultural Station. **133:** *l* E.R. Degginger; *r* Gary Cregmile (Taurus Photos). **135:** *t* Keith Gunnar (Bruce Coleman); *b* William Sacco. **136:** Norm Clasen (After-Image). **137:** David Muench. **138:** Courtesy June Bacon-Bercey. **139:** Carlye Calvin. **142:** NCAR. **144:** Tom Magno. **151:** Imagery. **152:** Photri. **154:** John Shelton. **155:** Tom Ives. **156:** National Weather Service (Atoz Images). **157:** *t* Shostal Associates; *r* Hurricane Center, Florida. **158–159:** NCAR. **162:** Steve McCutcheon. **164:** *t l* Harry Engels (Bruce Coleman); *t c* Thomas Ives; *t r* Bill Borsheim (Tom Stack & Associates); *b l* Breck Kent; *b c* Carl Purcell; *b r* Breck Kent. **166:** *t* E.R. Degginger; *c* David Muench; *b* Antonio Mendoza (Stock, Boston). **169:** *t* Grant Heilman; *b* Dan McCoy (Rainbow). **170:** *t* Alan Pitcairn (Grant Heilman); Dallas Chamber of Commerce. **173:** *t r* William Ferguson; *r c* Tom Bean (Tom Stack & Associates); *b l* Grant Heilman; *b r* David Muench. **1177:** *t l & r* Grant Heilman; *b* Yoram Lehmann (Peter Arnold). **179:** Steve McCutcheon.

Unit Three: **182:** Chris Chulamanis, Harbor Branch Foundation. **184:** Hank Morgan (Rainbow). **188:** *t* Donald Dietz. **190:** E.R. Degginger. **191:** Breck Kent. **192:** Tom Magno. **193:** Bob and Zona Cetera, Mammoth Cave National Park. **194:** *t l* Grant Heilman; *t r* William Ferguson; *b l* Grant Heilman; *b r* Jack Dermid (Bruce Coleman). **196:** William Ferguson. **197:** David Brody (Stock, Boston). **198:** John Running (Stock, Boston). **199:** *r* Peter Menzel (Stock, Boston); *b l* Ted Spiegel (Black Star). **200:** *t* Grant Heilman; *b* Bechtel Power Corporation. **201:** *t* E.R. Degginger, *b* Erik Anderson. **202:** Judy Fretwell. **203:** Hank Morgan (Rainbow). **206:** Vic Cox (Peter Arnold). **208:** John Lopinot (Black Star). **209:** Louis Benoze, Raytheon Corp. **210:** *t* James Butler; *b* Clyde Smith (Peter Arnold). **212:** John Shelton. **214:** *t* John Serafin (Peter Arnold); *b l* Keith Murakami (Tom Stack & Associates); *b r* E.R. Degginger. **215:** *t l* Jerome Wyckoff; *b l* E.R. Degginger; *t r* Werner Stoy (Bruce Coleman); *b r* James N. Butler. **216:** Grant Heilman. **217:** *t* James Cribb; *b* Alex McClean (Landslides). **218:** Kenneth Garrett (Woodfin Camp, Inc.) **223:** Georg Gerster (Photo Researchers). **224:** *t* Roland Birke (Peter Arnold); *b* Carl Roessler (Animals, Animals). **225:** Grant Heilman. **226:** Woods Hole Oceanographic Institute (Visuals Unlimited). **227:** Vic Cox (Peter Arnold).

Unit Four: **230:** Wedigo Ferchland (Bruce Coleman). **232–238:** Breck Kent. **239:** *t* Breck Kent; *c* Lee Gordon; *b* Breck Kent. **240:** Lee Gordon. **241:** *t l & r* Breck Kent: *r c* Lee Gordon. **242:** Breck Kent. **246:** Jet Propulsion Laboratory. **247:** Breck Kent. **250:** Phil Degginger. **252:** *l* E.R. Degginger; *r* Wedigo Ferchland (Bruce Coleman). **253:** *l & r* Harold Hungerford. **254:** *l* Breck Kent; *r* Michael Collier. **256:** Breck Kent. **257:** *l* Breck Kent; *r* E. R. Degginger. **259–260:** Breck Kent. **261:** Wardene Weisser (Bruce Coleman). **263:** Breck Kent. **264:** John Shelton. **265:** Breck Kent. **267:** Breck Kent. **268:** Dr. Rosemary Vidale. **269:** Phil Degginger. **272:** Steve McCutcheon (Alaska Pictorial Service). **276:** NASA. **277:** *l* Michael Collier; *r* Breck Kent. **278:** *l* Lee Gordon; *r* Todd Harrington, Explosive Supply Company. **279:** John Shelton. **283:** Lee Gordon. **286:** American Petroleum Institute. **287:** Steve McCutcheon (Alaska Pictorial Service). **290:** Wolfgang Kaehler. **297–298:** Kenneth Garrett (Woodfin Camp, Inc.). **301:** *l* Randall Hyman; *r* NASA. **302:** Virginia Weinland (Photo Researchers). **303:** Bill O'Connor (Peter Arnold). **308:** American Petroleum Institute. **309:** Wolfgang Kaehler. **312:** Wayne Lankinen (DRK Photos). **314:** William Herbeck (After Image). **315:** *t* Jerome Wyckoff; *b l & r* John Shelton. **316:** *t l* Jerome Wyckoff; *t r* Harold Hungerford; *b* John Shelton. **317:** *l* John Shelton; *r* Jerome Wyckoff. **318:** Michael Collier. **319:** *t l* E. Segerstrom, USGS; *t r* Terry Domico (Earth Images); *b* Werner Stoy (Camera Hawaii). **320:** John Shelton. **321:** Harold Hungerford. **322:** John Shelton. **324:** J. Beckner (Shostal). **326:** John Shelton. **330:** Dr. Marie Marisawa. **331:** Wayne Lankinen (DRK Photos).

Unit Five: **334:** Carl Fischer (Shostal). **336:** USGS. **338:** C. Allen Morgan (Peter Arnold). **339:** Clive Russ. **340:** Susan Anderson. **344:** USGS. **347:** Grant Heilman. **348:** *t & b r* Michael Collier; *b l* John Shelton. **349:** *l* William Ferguson; *r* Harvey Lloyd (Peter Arnold). **350:** Michael Jones. **351:** USGS. **354:** David Muench. **356:** *t* Dan Budnick (Woodfin Camp); *b* Timothy O'Keefe (Bruce Coleman). **357:** *t* Susan Ray Field (Photo Researchers); *b* John Shelton. **358:** Audrey Tomara (Harold Hungerford). **359:** *t* Jim Sugar (Black Star); *b* John Lemker. **360:** Bill Henry (Photo Researchers). **361:** William Felger (Grant Heilman). **362:** Breck Kent. **363:** *l* John Shelton; *r* Grant Heilman. **364:** *t* Michael Collier; *b* John Shelton. **365:** *t l* Smithsonian Institution; *t r* Harold Hungerford; *b r* Lowell Georgia (Photo Researchers). **366:** *t* Jack M. Stephens (Bruce Coleman); *b* John Shelton. **367:** *l* E.R. Degginger; *r* Jack Fields (Photo Researchers). **368:** John Shelton. **370:** Dr. A. Wesley Ward. **371:** David Muench. **374:** Michael Collier. **376:** *t* Phil Degginger; *r* John Shelton. **377:** Harold Hungerford. **380:** Jack Fennell (Bruce Coleman). **382:** *t r* Jerome Wyckoff; *t l* Kenneth Fink (Bruce Coleman); *l c* Michael Collier; *l b* Breck Kent. **385:** Michael Collier. **386:** Jerome Wyckoff. **390:** Dr. David Lopez. **391:** Michael Collier. **394:** Adam Woolfitt (Susan Griggs). **396:** Michael Collier. **400:** Smithsonian Institution. **402:** Breck Kent. **404:** The Bettmann Archive. **406:** Field Museum of Natural History. **407:** WARDS Scientific. **408:** Alejandra Gloria Varela. **409:** Adam Woolfitt (Susan Griggs). **412:** John Reader c. National Geographic Society. **414:** Museum of Comparative Zoology, Harvard University. **415:** *t* Runk-Schoenberger (Grant Heilman); *b* Breck Kent. **416:** *t & b r* Michael Collier; *b l* Museum of Comparative Zoology, Harvard University. **420:** Breck Kent. **422:** Louise Broman (Photo Researchers). **423:** *t* Breck Kent; *b* W.H. Hodge (Peter Arnold). **424:** *t* Jane Burton (Bruce Coleman); *b l* American Museum of Natural History. **426:** A. D. Copley (Visuals Unlimited). **427:** John Reader c. National Geographic Society.

Unit Six: **430:** Grant Heilman. **432:** J. Zimmerman (FPG). **434:** Adolf F. Rohrer (Atoz Images). **435:** Jim Howard (Alpha). **436:** *t* Augusts Upitis (Shostal); *l* D'Avazien (Shostal). **438:** *l* Tom Carroll (FPG); *r* Michael Casino (Image Bank). **439:** Tom Magno. **440:** *t* Dan Guravich (Photo Researchers); *b* Tom Magno. **441:** Richard Hutchings (Photo Researchers). **442:** M.P. Kahl (Photo Researchers). **443:** Alain Mingam (Gamma-Liaison). **444:** Scripps Institute of Oceanography. **445:** *t* Karl Kummels (Shostal); *b* Lowell Georgia (Photo Researchers). **447:** Dennis Brack (Black Star). **448:** Dick Luria (Alpha). **450:** Floyd Gray. **451:** J. Zimmerman (FPG). **454:** Steve McCutcheon. **457:** Dennis Hogan (Tom Stack & Associates). **458:** Jim McNee (Tom Stack & Associates). **459:** Tom McHugh (Photo Researchers). **460:** Mark Antman (Image Works). **461:** *b l* Horst Schafes (Peter Arnold); *b r* W. Choroszewski (FPG). **462:** E.R. Degginger. **463:** L. Batterman (Alpha/FPG). **464:** Atomic Industrial Forum. **467:** *b l* J. Zimmerman (FPG); *r* Union Carbide, Nuclear Division. **469:** Richard Laird (Alpha). **470:** Russ Kinne (Photo Researchers). **471:** Steve McCutcheon. **474:** Greig Cranna. **476:** *l* Peter Schweitzer; *r* J. Rotman. **477:** *l* Werner Wolff (Black Star); *r* Bruce McAllister (Image Bank). **480:** *t* Mark Antman (Imgae Works); *b* Rockwell International. **481:** *t* Paul Johnson; *r* Norfolk Southern Corporation. **482:** *t* C. Meyer (Shostal); *r* Steve Krongard (Image Bank). **483:** Mark Antman (Image Works). **485:** Florida Department of Citrus. **486:** *l* Peter Arnold (Peter Arnold); *r* E.R. Degginger. **488:** *r* Pacific Gas and Electric Company; *b* E.R. Degginger. **489:** *t* Mark Antman; *r* Alon Reininger (DPI). **491:** Greig Cranna. **494:** NASA. **496:** *t* Larry Smith (DPI); *b* USDA. **498:** *t* Soil Conservation Service; *b l* Runk-Schoenberger (Grant Heilman); *b r* Joe Larson, Soil Conservation Service. **499:** Grant Heilman. **500:** J.C. Allen. **501:** Georg Gerster (Photo Researchers). **502:** Runk-Schoenberger (Grant Heilman). **503:** *t* Lou Jones; *b* Jacques Jangoux (Peter Arnold). **504:** Morten Beebe (Image Bank). **506:** Susan Anderson. **507:** *t* Norman Tomalin (Bruce Coleman); *b* Arthur Rochelle (Taurus). **508:** *l* Joe Azzara (Image Bank); *b* Photri. **509:** Thomas Horland (Grant Heilman). **510:** Dr. Bahe Billy. **511:** NASA.